C000025588

1 MONTH OF
FREE
READING

at

www.ForgottenBooks.com

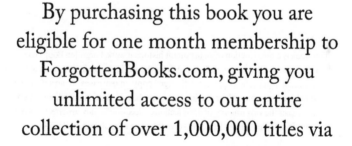

By purchasing this book you are
eligible for one month membership to
ForgottenBooks.com, giving you
unlimited access to our entire
collection of over 1,000,000 titles via
our web site and mobile apps.

To claim your free month visit:
www.forgottenbooks.com/free160160

* Offer is valid for 45 days from date of purchase. Terms and conditions apply.

ISBN 978-0-483-21659-4
PIBN 10160160

This book is a reproduction of an important historical work. Forgotten Books uses
state-of-the-art technology to digitally reconstruct the work, preserving the original format
whilst repairing imperfections present in the aged copy. In rare cases, an imperfection in
the original, such as a blemish or missing page, may be replicated in our edition. We do,
however, repair the vast majority of imperfections successfully; any imperfections that
remain are intentionally left to preserve the state of such historical works.

Forgotten Books is a registered trademark of FB &c Ltd.
Copyright © 2018 FB &c Ltd.
FB &c Ltd, Dalton House, 60 Windsor Avenue, London, SW19 2RR.
Company number 08720141. Registered in England and Wales.

For support please visit www.forgottenbooks.com

THE FORUM.

VOL. XXIII.

MARCH, 1897—AUGUST, 1897.

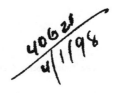

NEW YORK:

THE FORUM PUBLISHING CO.

Copyright, 1896,
By THE FORUM PUBLISHING CO.

AP
2
F8
v. 23

The Knickerbocker Press, New York

CONTENTS.

The Forum

MARCH, 1897.

TAXATION: ITS SUM, JUSTIFICATION, AND METHODS.

DISCUSSION over the sum, justification, and methods of taxation is increasing in volume and intensity.

We, in the United States, are always under the political dominion of two governments at once, one National, and one State; but in regard to taxation, each individual may, if his property is widely dispersed, be subject to many more than two governments. If he has property in each State of the Union, he is subject to the taxing powers of forty-five States, and also of the Government at Washington. There are, besides, territorial governments and minor divisions of States possessing the power of taxation in one form or another.

A great deal of deserved criticism of the rather antiquated "General Property Tax Law" of New York has grown out of the exceptions which the courts have imposed on the early rule that while realty must be taxed in the State in which it is situated, personalty follows the owner, and must be taxed where he has his domicile. A failure by New York farmers to fully appreciate how much of New York personalty is exempt from taxation, because in Federal or city bonds, or situated outside the State, underlies some of, but not all, their complaints that personalty escapes full taxation.

Exemptions from taxation need revision, and will before long receive attention; but plans for using such exemptions in order to inflict unequal and unjust taxation on a class will be scrutinized. A McKinley tariff which puts 60 per cent of imports on the free list in

Copyright, 1896, by The Forum Publishing Company.
Permission to re-publish articles is reserved.

order to furnish an excuse for higher protective taxes on the remainder, or an income tax beginning with a $4,000 exemption, will be
stripped of disguises.

The amount of annual Federal and State taxation is readily ascertained ; but there has been difficulty in the way of census compilers
who have endeavored to obtain accurate knowledge of the sum of all
taxes and assessments by counties, and by taxing-agencies inferior to
counties.   Assuming $365,000,000 to be now the average annual sum
raised by Federal taxes, that vast amount is far below the total sum
raised by other taxation and assessments in the United States.   In the
" Congressional Record " of July 18, 1894, there is a tabular statement,
by Mr. Wheeler of Alabama, showing expenditure for 1890 in the
several States to have been more than $569,000,000, and the total
disbursements for public purposes in that year by New York and its
minor divisions to have been nearly $91,250,000.

It is strange that it should be so ; but probably the voters and taxpayers of New York are more familiar with the sum, methods, and the
annual increase of Federal taxation than of taxation by their own
State, its counties, cities, and towns.

The total ordinary expenditures of the Federal Government in 1861
were only sixty-six and a half millions ; but twenty years later they had
risen to more than two hundred and fifty-nine and a half millions ; and
the recent average has been some three hundred and sixty-five millions.
For the government of the State of New York, omitting minor divisions
of the State, the aggregate appropriations at Albany were less than
ten millions in 1881, but more than twice that sum in 1896.   They
were only thirteen million dollars in 1890, but over twenty million
six years later.   What has happened at Washington and Albany in
regard to the increase of the yearly amount of expenditure and taxation has probably happened in the capital of each of our States and
Territories.

The causes of the great increase of the yearly exactions by governments from the rents, wages, profits, and savings of the country have
been many.   Some have been necessary, others unnecessary.   One
cause has been the recent tendency to enlarge the functions of the
State by placing in the hands of Government agencies the conduct of
certain classes of business, which was heretofore in the hands of individuals, partnerships, or private corporations.

This process of transferring to municipalities what was formerly
done by individuals, and of regulating by law the relation to wage-

earners of the owners of the instruments of production, seems to be going on rapidly in England. The same tendency in our own country is to be seen in the platform of doctrine erected July 24, 1896, by the People's party. Such an extension of the functions of the State, such a transit from individualism to socialism, are, of course, expensive for the State. The bills of socialism for State interference with enterprises heretofore regarded as individual enterprises, but now looked upon as "affected with a public use," must be paid. Only by taxes can the State now obtain the needed money.

If the socialistic State advocated by Populists shall (if ever) be established, will taxation be less? Office-holders may possibly then be found who will conduct telegraphs, railways, and banks more effectively, wisely, and with more commercial economy and commercial liberality, than do now their owners,—but that day has not yet come. If such occupations as farming, mining, transporting merchandise, transmitting news, exchanging products, and banking are to be taken out of the hands of those who own or can borrow the capital therein invested, they must fall into the hands of the State within whose jurisdiction they are conducted. Either organized capital, or organized political government, will manage those enterprises. Either banks, or the Federal Government, will receive deposits, make discounts, and issue circulating notes. As matters now stand there are: first, those who own or can obtain the capital for our industries; second, those who do mental and manual work therefor ; and finally, the consumers. Those three component elements have in this country been generally left to manage their own affairs in their own way, subject to the law that each person must so use what is his own as not to injure a right belonging to someone else. The Democracy, as distinct from the Populists, prefer, I think, that such condition of affairs shall continue, subject to such special legislation as may from time to time be found imperatively necessary to protect the rights of the State as well as the rights of each of the three elements to which I have referred.

Everyone will concede that our National and State Governments are not yet competent to successfully conduct those industrial enterprises of the country now in the hands of organized capital. Even the Comptroller of the State of New York will probably not contend that officials, of the class selected by the present Governor of New York, or those likely to be appointed by the next President of the United States, could superintend and conduct with advantage the farming, mining, transporting, exchanging, and banking of the country.

An increasing disposition to levy taxes for other purposes than revenue has created a tendency to consider the sum of taxation as secondary to the reasons which justify the infliction of taxes. Of course the advocacy of a protective tariff, either as an indemnification of manufacturers for prospective losses, or as an inducement to put capital in manufactures, is chronic. The taxpayers are never told what sum, *plus* the money required for Government expenditure, will be needed and exacted for such purposes. Importers and consumers of imported articles cannot read in the tariff law what rate of duty is laid for revenue and what additional rate is laid to enable capital invested in manufactures to secure exceptional profits which may or may not be used to increase the wages of workingmen already in the country. I do not need to enumerate the examples—more recent than the tariff,—of taxation for other purposes than revenue, as, for instance, the 10-per-cent bank tax.

The power of the majority to take away property from the minority by a tax is a tremendous manifestation of sovereignty. The American colonists went to war for the principle that the taxing-power must coincide with representation, and it is not credible when they formed a State that they put no restraints on the taxing-power either as to the yearly sum or as to the justice and equality of the levy. It must have been that the yearly sum required for the maintenance of the Government was to be the test of legislative power. In many of the States either the Bill of Rights, or the Constitution, proclaimed that each inhabitant should only be bound to contribute " his share," and the legislative power was limited to " proportional reasonable assessments, rates, and taxes." In Maryland, the phrase was " his proportion of public taxes for the support of the Government, according to his actual worth in real or personal property." Virginia said, " Taxation shall be equal and uniform . . . in proportion to its value." The courts of New Hampshire, Wisconsin, Minnesota, and other States have given most exhaustive judgments in regard to the limitations of the taxing-power in American jurisprudence. The total sum is to be limited to an amount that is reasonable in the opinion of the law-making power. If the New York legislature deems twenty millions necessary and reasonable, that sum must be raised ; but not for any other purpose than Government expenses.

Inhabitants of New York are not to have all their property swept into the possession of the State, under the taxing-power, if the State does not require the property to pay reasonable expenses. If it be not so, of what avail is the injunction in the Federal Constitution and that of New York also, that no person "shall be deprived of life, liberty, or property without due process of law"? which New York courts interpret as covering a deprivation by executive, or legislative, or judicial power, or all three combined, in derogation of the Constitution. And what of the injunction in the Fourteenth Amendment which declares that no State shall "deny to any person within its jurisdiction the equal protection of the laws"? Under the pretext of taxes there must not be that taking of private property "for public use without just compensation," which the Constitution forbids. The word "property" in the Constitutional phrase, "life, liberty, or property," may not have been interpreted by the courts as often as the word "liberty"; but the power assigned to the latter as used in the sentence is significant in many ways. Nearly ten years ago the late Prof. Dwight, of Columbia College Law School, published an elaborate paper on "The Legality of Trusts," in which he said of the word "liberty," as employed in association with the word "property":—

"The word 'liberty,' as here used, has been construed by the highest State authorities to include 'the right of a person to adopt such lawful industrial pursuits not injurious to the community as he may see fit.' It includes the right of one to use his faculties in all lawful ways, to live and work where he will, to earn his livelihood in any lawful calling, and to pursue any lawful trade or avocation. It is judicially declared (109 N. Y. Reports), that a liberty to adopt or to follow lawful industrial pursuits, in a manner not injurious to the community, is not to be infringed upon, limited, weakened, or destroyed by legislation."

That bears distinctly on associations formed by wage-earners to increase their wages. He adds:—

"The right of association is the child of freedom of trade. It is too late to banish it. As mercantile concerns under freedom of trade have tended to be more and more vast and comprehensive and have absorbed the smaller ones, so it is reasonable to suppose that the right of association will be made more and more available in manufacturing. In fact the two tendencies are, in substance, the same. If association is prevented by law, different manufactories may be moulded into one. The only way out of the difficulty, if there be one, is to invade the right of property, namely production by law, cut down the employment of large capitals, and perhaps, in the end, *hand over production to the State.*"

The Constitution of the State of New York offers to the legislative power a large discretion by unreservedly committing to its hands everything which the judicial power declares shall concern police or health, subject to the single qualification that no one's life, liberty, or property shall be interfered with unless by "due process of law," which phrase the courts are to limit and define. It is that existing constitutional qualification, and especially in regard to taxation, which socialism is endeavoring to invade.

New York law denounces as a crime every contract, arrangement, agreement, or conspiracy to prevent the exercise of a lawful calling, to injure the public health, morals, trade, or commerce, to prevent or restrain competition, in order to increase prices of articles in common use for purposes of life and health (wages are not included), but subject always to the power of the courts to decide whether or not, such laws and their interpretation are forbidden by the Constitution of the State. So long as our existing Constitution stands, liberty and property will be secure in New York, if prosecuting officers shall be faithful, and our magistrates shall be upright and fearless, as now.

A startling example of the tendency to employ the taxing-power for other objects than revenue, can be seen in the reasons recently assigned by the Comptroller of the State of New York for his advice to the legislature, that our Inheritance Tax Laws be so amended as to lay the tax as follows on estates of one million dollars and more:

"Five per cent on estates of one million, and less than two millions; 10 per cent on estates of two millions, and less than three millions; 15 per cent on estates of three millions and over." Comptroller Roberts has not explained why he stopped the progressive rate precisely at the point where the theory he urges on the legislature requires an application of the whole rigor of that theory in respect to the colossal estate he deals with.

Less than a year ago, an inhabitant of Suffolk County in New York State devised and bequeathed all his property to the United States Government. An inheritance tax of nearly four thousand dollars was levied upon it, and the levy was upheld by the New York Court of Appeals. But the United States, denying that the property which had been given to the Federal Government was liable to the tax, carried the question to the Supreme Court, which sustained the exaction. In its opinion that court is reported to have said:—

"The so-called 'Inheritance Tax' of the State of New York is, in reality, a limitation upon the power of a testator to bequeath his property to whom he pleases; a declaration that in the exercise of that power he shall contribute a certain percentage to the public use; in other words, that the right to dispose of his property by will shall remain, but subject to the conditions that the State has a right to impose. Certainly if it be true that the right of testamentary disposition is purely statutory, the State has a right to require a contribution to the public treasury before the bequest shall take effect. Thus, the tax is not upon 'property,' in the ordinary sense of the term, but upon the right to dispose of it; and it is not until it has yielded its contribution to the State that it becomes the property of the legatee. It is not a tax upon persons. *In re* Hoffman's Estate, 143 N. Y. 327, 38 N. E. 311; Schoolfeld's Ex'r *v.* Lynchburg, 78 Va. 366; Strode *v.* Com. 52 Pa. St. 181; *in re* Cullum's Will, 145 N. Y. 593, 40 N. E. 163.   In this last case, as well as in Wallach *v.* Miers, 38 Fed. 184, it was held that, although the property of the decedent included United States bonds, the tax might be assessed upon the basis of their value, because the tax was not imposed upon the bonds themselves, but upon the estate of the decedent, or the privilege of acquiring property by inheritance.   We think that it follows from this that the act in question is not one open to the objection that it is an attempt to tax the property of the United States, if the tax is imposed on the legatee before it reaches the hands of the Government. The legacy becomes the property of the United States only after it has suffered a diminution to the amount of the tax; and it is only upon this condition that the legislature assents to a bequest of it."

In another part of the opinion the court refers to the taxing-power as limited to the taxpayers' "share for public expenses," and also alludes to the right of a man or of a woman to dispose of his or her property after death. This is its language :—

" While the laws of all civilized states recognize in every citizen the absolute right to his own earnings, and to the enjoyment of his own property, and the increase thereon during his life, except so far as the state may require him to contribute his share for public expenses, the right to dispose of his property by will has always been considered purely a creature of statute, and within legislative control. . . .   Though the general consent of the most enlightened nations has from the earliest historical period recognized a natural right in children to inherit the property of their parents, we know of no legal principle to prevent the legislature from taking away or limiting the right of testamentary disposition or imposing such conditions upon its exercise as it may deem conducive to the public good."

I have introduced these extracts from the opinion of the court in order to exhibit the character of the New York inheritance law, and also its real relation to the right to make a last will and testament.

It will be seen that the tax is not on property, but on a privilege; that it is not upon a specific estate, as bonds or merchandise, but on the money realized, or to be realized, therefrom; that it is upon money in the hands of the court before distribution either to lineals or collaterals. It was not decided whether or not one rate of tax can be constitutionally levied on one part, and another rate on a different part of the same fund.

The existing New York inheritance law is not progressive in its rates. It does however make a difference in the rate between lineals and collaterals, and does exempt personalty bequeathed to a lineal, if under ten thousand dollars in value. Commenting on that, the Comptroller of the State of New York asked the legislature: "If an estate of less than $10,000 should be exempt, why should not one, millions greater, pay a higher rate than a $10,000 estate? A large estate would certainly be less burdened by the payment of a higher rate than a small estate would be by the payment of a lesser one."

A question presented by the chief financial officer of New York is, whether a sum of money can, under the Constitution, be divided into several parts, and a different tax-rate laid on the several parts. But there is another more serious question, which concerns the reason and justification of taxation. Of the latter, the Comptroller says :—

"It has been maintained by eminent authorities that it would be wiser and less demoralizing if Government should forego all attempts to tax personal property during the life of the owner, await a transfer following death, and then levy an assessment large enough to make up for the previous years of exemption. The tax, then, would be no hardship to anyone. The decedent would have been allowed the use and enjoyment of his fortune during life, and the beneficiary would simply pay a fee for the privilege of receiving an estate, in the creation of which he had little or no hand. Against the payment of such a fee or tax he would have no reason to complain, as his right to receive it comes from the State, is by the grace of the State. Another reason why large estates, particularly the personal property of such estates, should be made to pay liberally toward the support of Government in the way of an inheritance tax is, because many of them owe their very existence to favors conferred by Government in one form and another. The Government throws its strong arm around the capitalist in the shape of a protective tariff ; it gives the inventor exclusive rights in the way of a patent covering a long series of years ; it gives him and his friends special privileges in the shape of a corporation charter, whereby they combine large amounts of capital, and thus conduct a vastly more successful business than they could if acting individually ; it gives them the right of eminent domain, by which they overrun the interests of the individual, whether he likes it or not ; it grants them limited liability as members of a corporation ; it permits them to issue bonds and borrow money on them for long periods, something an individual cannot do ; it protects them in their corporate rights by the strong arm of the civil and military law ; it protects the lawyer, the doctor, and other professional men from uneducated and unskilled competition, by requiring a thorough course of study and a qualifying examination. In these special privileges conferred by Government lie the foundation of most of the great fortunes of the country to-day."

Fresh, novel, and unexpected as were those justifications of taxes under our American system of jurisprudence, they were not so surprising and innovating as the following, inspired, as it is to be inferred, by what happened in the case of the estate of the late Mr. Gould :—

"The estate that would have contributed a large part of this increased tax was rated upon the local assessors' rolls as being worth $500,000, and upon that amount a personal tax had been paid. But when the great equalizer—death—appeared upon the scene and forced a settlement, the estate was found to be worth $80,934,580, instead of $500,000, with only $6,553,520 debts charged up against it ; and upon these figures the inheritance tax was levied. If the above amendment had been in force at the time of decedent's death, and this estate had been required to pay its fair share of tax (in view of the evasion) into the treasury, it might have prevented a transfer to Europe of several millions of good American money. And who will say that any law that will divert to the people's treasury a part of the millions upon millions of American money now going to Europe to bolster up an effete and decaying nobility, is not a wise and judicious one ? "

If the local assessors found that only half a million had a *situs* in New York for taxation, under the law, then obviously the rate should have been levied only on that sum ; but this question is very unlike that raised by the new progressive rate.

The income tax enacted by the last Congress did not lay progressing rates ; but advancing rates were proposed in the House, on behalf of the Populists,—by Mr. Pence, and in the Senate by Mr. Peffer.

Mr. Henry George has a plan which is not intended to abolish private property in land, but to tax it up to its full rental value ; thereby relieving the community from all other taxation, and using the excess of revenue, not merely to pay reasonable and needed Government expenses, under our American plan, but—and this is the critical point—for the purposes of socialistic utility.[1]

It is undisputed that the legislature has authority to decide what sum of money is reasonable and necessary for public expenditure, and to compel each person to contribute his or her equal and proportionate share ; but the object of the tax must be solely to obtain the money to defray those expenditures, which is another way of saying that the tax shall be levied " for revenue only." When that line of taxation is passed the constitutional injunction against taking " private property for public use without just compensation " will be encountered.

All agree that the New York legislature has not the right, or power, to tax merely in order to prevent marriages of New York women to European men ; and if that be true, why or how has the legislature the power to tax merely in order to create a sort of escheat

[1] "A tax is called proportional when the relation between a man's property, and the amount which he pays is invariable for all contributors, so that the individual quotas increase in perfect correspondence with the increase of wealth. On the other hand, a tax is called progressive where its rate varies with the variation of the wealth itself ; so that the quotas increase more rapidly than the wealth itself. The adherents of progressive taxes . . . start from the idea that taxation should, above all other considerations, perform a social function." [" Taxation," etc., by Luigi Cossa, Professor in the University of Pavia, Italy, p. 85.]

of realty or personalty to the State, or to diffuse wealth, or to make the State a co-partner in the profits of one's business as well as a co-heir with one's children? Since the decision of the Supreme Court, to which I have referred, it is too late to contend that the legislature of New York has not the power, by taxing such privilege at the rate of 100 per cent, to destroy the existing right of making a last will and testament. But will the voters ever choose a legislature that shall exercise the power? A tax should not be discriminating and disproportionate, nor for other purposes than revenue to pay Government expenses. No purpose can be so good as to justify inequality in the rate and subject the taxpayers to exceptional and invidious exactions and to extortions in the name of taxation. It may be said that those who advocate an enlarged tax upon the right of the citizen to control the distribution of his property after his death, and an increasing rate of tax as the hundreds, or thousands, or millions increase, do not propose to take away altogether the right of bequest and inheritance, but to limit it in certain cases for wise reasons. The fact remains nevertheless that the right is to be limited, and limited for social reasons chiefly, and in the interest of a socialistic State. To place children in a better condition than that in which their fathers and mothers began life, is the most powerful motive which induces parents of every condition, in this country, to toil and save. No motive for industry and sobriety can be more powerful. That motive would be weakened if it should be felt or feared that the right of the citizen to bequeath his property to his children is to be taxed out of existence.

A few years ago the present Pope sent forth from St. Peter's an encyclical letter on " The Condition of Labor," full of sound doctrine and clear discernment from the point of view of economic facts collected in Rome by reports of ecclesiastical agents in every part of the world-wide jurisdiction of the Roman Catholic Church. It began with the following terse description of the conditions then existing,—conditions which exist to-day :—

" It is not surprising that the spirit of revolutionary change, which has so long been predominant in the nations of the world, should have passed beyond politics and made its influence felt in the cognate field of practical economy. The elements of a conflict are unmistakable : the growth of industry, and the surprising discoveries of science ; the changed relations of masters and workmen ; the enormous fortunes of individuals, and the poverty of the masses ; the increased self-reliance and the closer mutual combination of the working population ; and, finally, a general moral deterioration. The momentous seriousness of the present state of things just now fills every mind with painful apprehension : wise men discuss it; practical men propose schemes; popular meetings, legislatures, and sovereign princes, all are occupied with it—and there is nothing which has a deeper hold on the public attention."

It then made these comments on certain remedies proposed:—

"To remedy these evils the socialists, working on the poor man's envy of the rich, endeavor to destroy private property, and maintain that individual possessions should become the common property of all, to be administered by the state or by municipal bodies. They hold that, by thus transferring property from private persons to the community, the present evil state of things will be set to rights, because each citizen will then have his equal share of whatever there is to enjoy. But their proposals are so clearly futile for all practical purposes that if they were carried out the workingman himself would be among the first to suffer. Moreover, they are emphatically unjust, because they would rob the lawful possessor, bring the State into a sphere that is not its own, and cause complete confusion in the community.

"It is surely undeniable that when a man engages in remunerative labor, the very reason and motive of his work is to obtain property, and to hold it as his own private possession. If one man hires out to another his strength or his industry, he does this for the purpose of receiving in return what is necessary for food and living; he thereby expressly proposes to acquire a full and real right, not only to the remuneration, but also to the disposal of that remuneration as he pleases."

In the encyclical were these expressions alluding to private property, excessive taxation, and the right of bequest and inheritance:

"It is a most sacred law of nature that a father must provide food and all necessaries for those whom he has begotten; and, similarly, nature dictates that a man's children, who carry on, as it were, and continue his own personality, should be provided by him with all that is needful to enable them honorably to keep themselves from want and misery in the uncertainties of this mortal life. Now in no other way can a father effect this except by the ownership of profitable property, which he can transmit to his children by inheritance. . . . Since the domestic household is anterior both in idea and in fact to the gathering of men into a commonwealth, the former must necessarily have rights and duties which are prior to those of the latter, and which rest more immediately on nature. . . . Paternal authority can neither be abolished by the State nor absorbed; for it has the same source as human life itself. The child belongs to the father, and is, as it were, the continuation of the father's personality; and, to speak with strictness, the child takes his place in civil society not in its own right, but in its quality as a member of the family in which it is begotten. . . . The socialists, therefore, in setting aside the parent and introducing the providence of the State, act against natural justice, and threaten the very existence of family life. Our first and most fundamental principle, therefore, when we undertake to alleviate the condition of the masses must be the inviolability of private property. . . . This is the proper office of wise statesmanship and the work of the heads of the State. Now a State chiefly prospers and flourishes by morality, by well-regulated family life, by respect for religion and justice, by the moderation and equal distribution of public burdens, by the progress of the arts and of trade, by the abundant yield of the land—by everything which makes the citizens better and happier. . . . The

State is therefore unjust and cruel if, in the name of taxation, it deprives the private owner of more than is just."

It may be that such a change in taxation as will lay the highest rate on money invested or loaned, as those terms are usually employed, the next lower rate on other forms of personalty, the next lower on land, and the lowest of all on wage-earning, is not always advocated in the hope that the change will lead to placing in the hands of the State the management of production and distribution, the abolishment of contract, the fixing of the rate of wages by the State, the issuing of all paper currency by the nation, and that such a change will also lead up to all the other ideals of a socialistic State. Probably such a change in taxation can be so guarded as to be consistent with the security of private property, and not to interfere with the freedom of inheritance and alienation, provided a definite rule of taxation be made and enforced,—a rule prescribing that taxes shall be equal and uniform on each class of property, or its product, and shall never be laid except to obtain money for the needed current expenses of the State, or minor divisions of the State.

The earliest Constitutions of some of the original Thirteen States declared " that every member of society hath a right to be protected in the enjoyment of life, liberty, and property, and therefore is bound to contribute his *proportion* to the *expenses* of that protection." The rule was " proportion," and not progression. " Proportion " was based on ability, of which property, or its product, was the test; but in our day equality of ability, tested by property or income, has, by socialists and communists, been interpreted to mean equality of sacrifice, which means, they say, that taxes must be so adjusted that each taxpayer, the rich and the not rich, will feel equally the deprivation of the money paid to the tax-gatherer. Among the more modern State Constitutions, that of California makes arithmetical proportion and not arithmetical progression the rule, when it declares that " *all* property in the State, not exempt under the laws of the United States, shall be taxed in *proportion* to its value to be ascertained as provided by law."

Whether or not the Republican Comptroller of the State of New York was conscious of the socialistic and communistic tendency of the theories regarding the sum, justification, and methods of taxation which he has recently urged on the Legislature, the unfortunate effect may be to increase the fear which discerning men, here and there, are heard to express,—the fear that the economic State founded by the wisdom, patriotism, and courage of the statesmen of the Revolutionary epoch, cannot thus survive.   PERRY BELMONT.

THE ANGLO-AMERICAN ARBITRATION TREATY.

A TREATY of peace has heretofore been the postscript of a war. Nations fought their way to such a treaty through more or less sacri--fice of life and destruction of property. As a rule physical and financial exhaustion was a condition precedent to the establishment of friendly relations on a permanent basis. One nation had to be beaten into something like insensibility before the two could unite in the necessary declarations of good-will and the customary bonds to keep the peace. Tradition had ordained that a nation's honor required to be lubricated with blood in order to be kept in good working condition. Both of the conflicting nations usually assured the other nations that were looking on of the imperative necessity under which the honor of each was placed to do some fighting to keep it fresh and bright. When a sufficient number of men had been slaughtered, and a proper number of towns had been burned and plundered, and when the treasury of either or both was empty, Honor smiled once more with restored cheerfulness, made her graceful obeisance, and retired from the scene, leaving the victor to have his way. Honor, national honor, has been a priceless possession, but a very expensive one to keep; the more expensive because of its uncertain character, its vague definition, and its unreasonable demands. One thing is certain: that, when the leaders of a nation have concluded that the honor of the country is at stake, someone must be attacked and, if possible, destroyed. The salutary process of a bloody baptism can alone renovate and preserve this delicate and susceptible quality of a nation's constitution.

And now come before the world two quiet gentlemen, without any swords by their sides or revolvers in their belts, who venture to say that the old practice is really obsolete and perhaps a little foolish; that war is very expensive, very cruel, and quite unphilosophical; that perhaps it were better to make the peace before the war than after. They suggest that the experiment is worth trying, and may be tried without apparent danger; for, if it should fail, there would still be plenty of time to raise armies, to build fleets, to bombard ports, to blow up iron-clads, to make homes desolate, to break mothers' hearts, and to lay heavy burdens of debt upon generations to come. It may be that the instinct of destruction that lies so near the surface of human nature may break out in spite of all such efforts ; possibly atavism may be too strong, and the lion, the wolf, the hyena, and the jackal may still have their way ; but an inexpensive attempt to save much money, much human life, much property, and to avoid incalculable suffering is worth the effort. So the two gentlemen, who assured each other of their mutual consideration until they united in the proposed Treaty of Arbitration which is now before our Senate, deserve respect and the thanks of the world for their good intentions. It is barely possible that they are acting in advance of their generation, and that their efforts for the welfare of mankind may be premature ; but their credit will be none the less in the years to come. Their work is as certain to bring forth good fruit as the seed that falls on rich soil and receives the rains from heaven is sure to germinate and bud and flower. Reason must triumph in the end. Blind men in broad daylight may insist that all is darkness ; but that is the result of their infirmity. The light is there none the less.

It is no diminution of the merit of the chief actors in the Arbitration Treaty that all the conditions were in their favor. Arbitration was no novelty when they undertook their task of putting another brake on the savagery of men. The fashion of submitting international differences to the deliberate judgment of wise men had become so general as almost to create a practice. It is so cheap that it commends itself to the commercial instinct of the world; so humane that it strikes a responsive chord in the hearts of all those who love their kind. Its assimilation to the legal methods that serve men in their private disputes appeals to the reason of all who prefer to abide by law rather than resort to the shot-gun or the revolver. Nor can it be denied that the majority of those who do the fighting are quite willing to forego their chances of military preferment and renown, if the interests and honor of their country do not require their assumption of a soldier's duties. In brief, the moral forces of the day are in favor of a peaceful solution of international disputes, where such a solution is possible. Boys cannot go to the common schools without learning something about war—its uncertainties, its horrors, and its dangers. While their early instincts lead them to dream of martial renown as the *summum bonum* of life, they do not in their youthful dreams make much distinction between Alexander the Great and Captain Kidd. But they are content, as a rule, when they have donned the *toga virilis*, that is, outgrown knickerbockers, to become and remain quiet and hard-working citizens. All this without prejudice to a manly disposition to make a sacrifice of home and of comfort when the country calls; but then it *is* a sacrifice and not a choice.

Arbitration, in a word, has become one of the accepted dogmas of our national creed. Our nineteenth-century civilization is not content with such mitigations as a growing humanity claims to have introduced into the conduct of war. War is, at the best, cruel and brutal: it is the negation of law and the assertion of force in the place of law. Voltaire was not so far wrong when he said :

"The laws of peace I understand well enough,—they consist in keeping our word and leaving our neighbor to enjoy the rights which nature has given him. But as for the laws of war I do not know what they are. The code of homicide seems to me a strange inconsistency. I hope that we may soon be provided with the jurisprudence of highway robbery."

That Arbitration has satisfactorily stood the test of experiment, statistics demonstrate. The United States Government has entered into forty-seven agreements for international arbitration,—not to speak of the erection by it of thirteen Tribunals under its own laws to determine the validity of international claims. A simple explanation this of the fact that we have a small standing army of 25,000 men and do not know to-day what war taxation means. We pay one hundred and fifty millions a year, it is true, to old soldiers who have done their fighting well and in a good cause; but this is manifestly better than taking the same money to keep young men out of the workshop, the field, or the factory, to prevent war by making it easy.

In Europe, too, Arbitration has become a familiar visitor at the palaces of kings, and has become so popular a guest that her services are in constant and growing demand. What our example to-day may do, what splendid possibilities it opens to the world, what burdens it promises to remove from the overworked and overtaxed people, no imagination can describe. It may not,—cannot,—in a day or a century, lay at rest the spirit of violence and aggression; but it may teach a lesson that will make the world happier and better every day that it is studied.

The sole difference between the Olney-Salisbury Treaty and the half-hundred that we have already had, lies in the fact that in other cases specific instances of controversy were disposed of: to-day we are provided with machinery to adjudicate every dispute that may arise. Why the formulas and procedure should be renewed and readjusted fifty times or one hundred times to fit cases at intervals, rather than to cover all cases by a careful and intelligent scheme of practice, is not very clear. The only possible—I shall not say plausible—ground of objection must be that a controversy may arise of such a character as to make arbitration less desirable than blows. If our national honor were concerned, it is gravely alleged, no aspersion on that delicate organ could be treated otherwise than with bombs and guns. A great nation cannot talk, when her honor is assailed; action must be then prompt and energetic. Speech was not given to men to discuss questions where honor is concerned. Wholesale homicide is the only remedy for such an assault. Thus France twenty-six years ago refused Arbitration because her honor—her dignity she called it—was involved. Whereupon she sacrificed several hundred thousand of her bravest children, lost two of her finest provinces, and paid the assailant of her dignity eight hundred million dollars to go home. No doubt her honor (or her dignity) was worth being preserved at that price; but even those who love her and sympathize with her in her great tribulation so nobly borne, may wonder if she could not have preserved her unsullied fame even had she accepted a friendly power's mediation. It is not so clear that calm and temperate discussion may not co-exist with a jealous sense of self-respect: on the other hand, it is not certain that readiness to strike necessarily proves the possession of common sense or a reasonable knowledge of what is due by a nation to itself and to its citizens.

Those men, therefore, who oppose a general Arbitration treaty should be called upon to explain precisely what they understand by " a case involving the honor of the nation." It is evident that men will differ about the definition according to their education, temperament, or the necessities of their station, if they happen to occupy positions depending upon popular favor. Brave words are undoubtedly powerful agents of disturbance, and will effect what argument is powerless to accomplish. It is easier to inflame public resentment than to pour oil on the troubled waters of popular excitement. A dispute of any kind may be tortured by a demagogue into an insult that demands instant reparation. A denial of any claim by a foreign power may be argued into an assault upon a nation's dignity. But this readiness to magnify incidents that affect interests into events that affect honor has had its day; and we may be thankful that we have emerged from a condition of doubtful strength, which might increase our impatience of contradiction by leaving room for the suspicion of fear.

The advocates of Arbitration may, in considering this objection, derive much comfort from the reflection that during a century of existence, wherein we have arbitrated so many differences with foreign nations, we have not yet been confronted with a case which was not susceptible of amicable adjustment. We have never yet found that our national honor could not co-exist with legal processes. Irritating questions have undoubtedly arisen; the warlike element has sometimes asserted itself, as when it declared it was a question between "54° 40' or fight"; but our practical good sense overcame the ultra-patriotic men who were burning to immolate themselves on the altar of the country's honor. Boundary questions have been settled, money demands have been passed upon and liquidated, we have had the benefit of the judgments when in our favor, we have discharged our debt when the decree was against us, and in every case we have been infinitely the gainers.

No case in modern times has offered a better pretext for the avoidance of a submission to arbitration than the "Alabama" case. Here, if ever, it might be maintained that the honor of the two nations was concerned. Great Britain was charged with evading the rules of just international intercourse by allowing the "Alabama" to escape and to prey upon our commerce,—an imputation which might well throw the British chauvinist into a delirium of patriotic indignation. The United States might well, on its side, find in this hostile action the material for the war-producing insult which lies so close to the warrior's heart. But the two great nations quietly thrust aside these suggestions of the Evil One; they treated the question as one sounding in damages; a verdict was rendered for an enormous sum, which was promptly paid; and the two English-speaking nations gave to the world their first object-lesson in Common Sense and Reason and Justice. The present Treaty is merely the natural outgrowth of the "Alabama" case: it is its legitimate offspring and with it entitled to the admiration of civilized mankind.

The Lord Chief Justice of England, while professing that love for peace which so properly belongs to his cloth, asks, with an anxious solicitude, "Who will compel the contracting nation to arbitrate, if she should refuse? Who shall compel her to abide by the judgment, if she repudiates the award?"

It is of course within the bounds of possibility that, having solemnly agreed in the face of the world to arbitrate their disputes, either the United States or Great Britain may be false to its promises and recreant to its obligations. In such a case, it is manifest that there is no international *gendarme* to coerce the recalcitrant contractor to perform its

2

duty. But this is equally true of every national obligation. Every treaty between two great nations—whether for the settlement of a boundary or the payment of an indemnity—must rest on the good faith of the parties. The difficulty of coercing fulfilment is precisely one of the reasons that makes repudiation most difficult for a high-spirited nation. If the absence of physical power to enforce is to prevent the conclusion of Arbitration treaties, it is difficult to see why the argument will not apply in all other cases. We are encouraged by the history of the past to believe that the objection is without force. In no case that I can recall has a great nation dishonored her hand and seal by refusing to carry out the decrees of the tribunal to which she has submitted her claims or her arguments. Great nations *might* dishonor their signature, but as a rule they do not: hence the value of British Consols and United States Bonds.

But, granting that so unexpected an event should occur, in what respect would the situation be changed for the worse? The original claim would still exist, liquidated by a judgment and fortified by the approval of public opinion. This at least is a risk that either party may well run, even if this pessimistic view of what may be expected from a civilized nation should be more generally entertained than it has hitherto been.

A more specious objection is made by those who express and no doubt feel some solicitude lest the American doctrine, which dates back to the time of President Monroe, should be in some way endangered by a general agreement to submit disputes with Great Britain to arbitration.

The right to exclude Europe from fresh acquisitions on the American continent is one which our people will never surrender unless coerced by force. Not only do they cherish it as a sentiment based upon honorable tradition, but the instinct of self-preservation makes it just and reasonable. A nation is not bound to apologize for her insistence upon the right to live and to grow. Her natural expansion cannot, with her willing assent, be embarrassed by the creation of obstacles which it is in her power to prevent. The rival nations of Europe may fight for supremacy to their hearts' content on European soil, they may parcel out the Dark Continent among themselves, they may lop off slices of China, appropriate Egypt, or invade Japan,—we are disposed to abide by the rule of non-intervention with religious fidelity. So far as they, or any of them, have already acquired a foothold on American territory our good faith will not permit us in any way to intervene in their affairs. But, rightly or wrongly, we believe that our interests consist in checking aggression when it is directed against our weaker neighbors.

If, therefore, it be true that we should, by this Treaty, imperil rights of such vast importance, we might well hesitate to bind ourselves by its terms. It might be urged with great plausibility that such a sacrifice is not one that we should be called upon to make, even in so great a cause as that of International Peace. Prudence would require that, assuming such a danger to exist, we should in express terms except the Monroe doctrine from the operation of the Agreement, or, failing this, that we should continue as in the past to provide for each emergency as it arises. It will not be denied by the most earnest advocate of the Treaty that if, in terms, it provided that the Monroe doctrine and its applicability were subjects of proper submission to a Court of Arbitration, public opinion would almost unanimously condemn and most earnestly oppose its consummation.

Is there, in fact, any such grave peril? Is it to be assumed that a case may arise between the United States and Great Britain, the result of which, upon an arbitration, might be to eliminate from our unwritten code a theory of right which is deemed of such vast importance by the majority of our people?

There is nothing in the history of the past to make any such contingency a subject of legitimate apprehension. Any argument based on its existence may be ingenious, but it is purely academic. It should exercise no practical influence on the decision of the question.

The Monroe doctrine may be treated, in reasoning out this problem, as a part of our organic law. It is entitled to the same respectful consideration as though the Monroe Message had been made the subject of a Constitutional Amendment. The fact that it has not received the formal sanction of our people does not affect the matter: for the purposes of the argument it should be vested with the dignity of a constitutional provision.

No foreign power can properly complain that it has not had full notice of the jurisdiction that we claim over the concerns of the American continent.

If, under such circumstances, Great Britain may properly bring up the Monroe doctrine for review, she may also attack any other of the fundamental doctrines of American policy. She may, with equal propriety, ask the arbitrators to examine our Declaration of Independence. She may attack the commercial and police clause of our Constitution and insist upon a judgment that a Republican form of government, being far inferior to a constitutional monarchy, ought of right to be abolished, and the latter be permitted to take its place. This would naturally involve an equivalent right on the part of the United States to insist upon the abolition of the House of Lords as a useless encumbrance, and of royalty itself as an expensive anachronism. If Courts of Arbitration are formed for the purpose of amusing the world with Platonic discussions, any one of these topics might be appropriately considered; but no one would seriously contemplate the possibility of vesting a court, however eminent, with the right to pass upon questions which affect the fundamental principles of the respective governments. Concrete cases, not abstractions, are the proposed subjects of submission. The establishment of a boundary line, the payment of an indemnity, the restoration of a ship, the liberation of a prisoner,—all these are capable of investigation by a Tribunal and may reasonably be submitted; but a Court of Arbitration, no more than the Supreme Court itself, will not take cognizance of a contest which does not involve a personal or a property right.

It will no doubt be said that this *reductio ad absurdum* does not dispose of the difficulty, because the Monroe doctrine may be involved indirectly, although substantially, in a boundary question affecting Great Britain and the United States. We might then, it is argued, find the right of the United States challenged under such conditions as to compel us either to decline arbitration, notwithstanding our agreement, or to incur serious danger where fundamental rights are concerned.

The objection deserves examination.

The only contingency in which may arise a discussion involving, in any form, the nature, validity, or effect of the Monroe doctrine is one of boundary—where territory is or may hereafter be claimed by Great Britain on the one hand, and by a Southern American Republic on the other. Even then no dispute involving the interests or the dignity of the United States would arise unless (1) all efforts at settlement by diplomacy had failed between those countries; or (2) Arbitration was rejected by one of or both the parties in interest. The attempt of Great Britain to seize the tract in dispute by force of arms might, and probably would, arouse the susceptibility of the United States and call for the application of the doctrine which we are considering. This has already happened in the case of Venezuela and Great Britain: it may happen again. What would the course of action presumably be should a similar situation present itself in the future?

There is no misunderstanding between the United States and Great Britain as to the character and extent of the jurisdiction claimed by the former in cases of the character supposed. Great Britain has been informed that it is a cardinal principle of American policy—claimed to be reasonable and just—that the United States may, where its interests dictate, interfere to prevent the spoliation of a sister republic. Great Britain is as well informed of this as it is of the abolition of slavery in the South, or of our refusal to abolish privateering. The treaty is made *in view of this knowledge* and with the acceptance of that fact as fully as it is of the fact that we constitute a Union of Sovereign States. If Great Britain should attempt by force to take territory from Venezuela, Colombia, or Peru, the only question would be, *to whom does the territory belong?* This would be a proper subject of arbitration, and would regulate the extent to which this Republic might properly intervene. But there is no ground for supposing that Great Britain would ever claim, or that we should ever yield, a right on her part to bring into controversy a fundamental rule of which she had been duly notified before the Treaty had been made. The notice has repeatedly been given, and especially at so recent a date that she cannot plead that time has wrought a change in the views of our government. The terms of our most recent authoritative exposition were plain enough to leave nothing to interpretation, and were endorsed with such unanimity of approval that a pretence of ignorance would be as absurd as it must prove futile. We cannot suppose that the great nation that has ruled the seas for centuries and owns more real estate to-day than most of the others put together is laying traps for her junior in years; but if she is, so be it. We are not likely to suffer. The Monroe doctrine is safe, Treaty or no Treaty. It is quite as safe, if it is not mentioned by name, as if a timid reservation in terms should be inserted to show that the United States were not really quite sure that this repeated and solemn assertion of right had been heard and seriously considered by the world.

We should not forget that our Monroe doctrine is after all but the European doctrine of the balance of power transplanted to American soil. Great Britain might make a general Treaty of Arbitration with France or Germany. Will anyone seriously contend that she thereby waived, minimized, or imperilled her right to interfere, should Germany attack Holland, or France invade Belgium? Such scruples as these do not seem worthy of a great people who know their strength, and propose to deal in good faith with the other nations of the world. The purpose of the Treaty is peace : the aspiration, the interest, the prayer of the world is for Peace. Civilized mankind yearns for peace: the multitudes groan and suffer untold hardships because to-morrow may mean War and not Peace. Two of the great nations of the world, great enough to know that their honor does not consist in vague mut-terings about self-respect and dignity, are willing to abide by reason and to forego violence. The gain to the world if they succeed in their noble effort at systematic harmony is great beyond the power of pen or speech to define. The nineteenth century needs only this culmina-tion of its glories to stand out among the ages as blessed beyond all those that have gone before since the dawn of Christianity first rose upon mankind.

Above all, let us not be misled by high-sounding declamation about national honor. The only danger which our honor may run is in an exaggerated tendency to make readiness to strike the test of its deli-cacy and the proof of its existence. The day has come when we may smile at those who would urge us to prove our strength by the streams of blood that we can shed at short notice. A Republic with a united nation of seventy millions behind it may stop to discuss without being taxed with timidity, and will not care if the effervescent mob that clamors for blood on all available occasions shall feel outraged in *its* honor because of a generous forbearance to draw the nation's sword.

In 1870, the streets of Paris were filled with valiant men full of patriotism and absinthe, who were shouting eagerly, " À Berlin ! À Ber-lin ! " How many of those doughty champions of France's honor started on the journey to Prussia's capital? How many, alas! who said nothing, but did turn their faces toward Berlin, soon found their last resting-place before they had crossed the Rhine?

F. R. COUDERT.

SOME COMMENT UPON THE ARBITRATION TREATY.

REDUCED to its simplest terms, the Arbitration Treaty which has been signed by representatives of Great Britain and the United States provides as follows :

There shall be created three tribunals. To one or more of these tribunals three classes of questions shall be referred.

The make-up of the tribunals, their jurisdiction, and the classes of questions to be submitted, may be seen in the accompanying table.

QUESTIONS TO BE SUBMITTED.	TRIBUNAL A.	TRIBUNAL B.	TRIBUNAL C.
	Three members : one chosen by each state, with provision for choice of third.	Five members : two named by each state, with provision for choice of fifth.	Six members : three higher judges from each state. No provision for breaking a tie.
I. Pecuniary claims under £100,000 in value.	Original and final jurisdiction, award by majority vote.		
II. Pecuniary claims over £100,000 in value. Also claims growing out of rights "under treaty or otherwise," but not territorial.	Original jurisdiction, which is also final if by unanimous vote.	Jurisdiction upon appeal, if A. does not render unanimous award. Majority vote final.	
III. Territorial claims such as relate to servitudes, navigation, access, fisheries, boundaries, etc.			Original jurisdiction. Award final if by vote of 5–1, or if by majority vote, and no appeal is made within three months. If protested, mediation to be tried before hostilities.

The objections commonly urged against any general arbitration agreement between states, are of three sorts:

(1) Those based upon the weakening in efficiency of the diplomatic methods of settlement; (2) those springing from the impossibility of submitting *all* questions to arbitral settlement; (3) those inherent in the make-up and working of the tribunal as ordinarily devised.

Let us examine these objections, and see how the treaty now before the Senate for consideration succeeds in meeting them.

Diplomacy is the natural, friendly, effective, and quiet method of settling international disputes. Whatever tends to weaken its efficiency is to be deplored. The presumption should always be that a difference will be arranged by diplomacy; not submitted straightway to arbitration. Imagine the standing of a business house which made a practice of collecting its bills by legal process before their friendly presentation and adjustment through correspondence! Arbitration is sought after as a substitute for war; not as a substitute for diplomacy. It has been feared that the existence of a tribunal ready to settle international dif- ferences would greatly lessen the potency of the diplomatic method. Diplomatists would feel less responsibility for, and take less interest in, a matter which, in all likelihood, was soon to be transferred to other hands for settlement.

Thus the amount of international litigation would largely increase. Thus the efficiency of processes which now arrange nine tenths of the differences between states, without causing a ripple of excitement, would be seriously weakened. Arbitration, like all other litigation, arouses hard feeling. It is infinitely better than war; but it is much inferior to diplomacy, because less flexible and with no capability for compromise or adjustment.

In some measure, the Arbitration Treaty recognizes this, though not so fully as could be wished. In its first article, the contracting parties agree to submit to arbitration " all questions in difference between them which they may fail to adjust by diplomatic negotiation." Here the presumption is expressed that diplomacy will have been tried. That is right and wise. But there is an underlying presumption that diplomacy will fail. That is a fault inherent in the arbitration prin- ciple. Possibly it might be minimized by excluding the first class of differences, the minor claims, which neither country would fight over in any case. Or where individual, rather than national, claims are be- ing pressed, the cost of arbitration could be deducted from the amount recovered. Or a certain delay might be compulsory, before recourse was had to a treaty tribunal, during which the state departments must try to effect a settlement. Perhaps in some such way as this, the too free use of the international tribunal could be checked, and the methods now effectively employed could be preserved.

It has often been urged that no nation can afford to tie its hands in advance, by submitting to arbitration all possible questions, including those which involve its national policy, its national honor, its national life. To do so would be a surrender of national sovereignty in its highest expression, a waiver of that right of self-defence which is the first law of nations. This is fully recognized by the Treaty. It specifies the classes of questions which shall be submitted. These are: pecuniary claims; differences involving rights, under treaty or international law; territorial claims. By inference, all other questions are held to be incapable of submission; those involving national policy amongst them. So that we may direct the search-light of the Monroe doctrine at will upon this continent; we may declare British aggression upon Patagonia dangerous to our safety and free institutions, without the risk of being brought to book before a court of arbitration.

On the other hand the Treaty does require the submission of just those differences the like of which the two nations have already so often arbitrated. Fishery disputes, as at Halifax; pecuniary claims, as at Geneva; boundaries, as in the San Juan case—all such must be referred to the new tribunal, if not otherwise settled, and very properly. They are questions of law, or fact, or treaty interpretation, usually capable of this kind of settlement. A few cases perhaps remain where national policy and treaty obligations are so intermingled that they ought not to be, as they seem to be, included amongst the differences to be finally decided by Tribunal B. For example, under the Clayton-Bulwer treaty, the United States binds itself to abstain from exclusive control over an isthmian canal in Central America; nevertheless the prevalent national belief is that such exclusive control is our prerogative and our policy. Here a question of policy, under the guise of a right under treaty, might be referred for final decision. For myself, I am strongly inclined to the opinion that the proper status of any canal across Central America will be found to be its neutralization, guaranteed by the commercial powers. But its disposition is certainly a question of policy open to argument; and very likely the Senate may withdraw this particular case from the operation of the Treaty.

Turn now to the third class of objections to any permanent arbitration agreement—those relating to the framing and working of its machinery.

It is here that the Treaty deserves most praise and confidence. It is an ingenious, and should prove a successful, attempt to substitute the judgment of a court for the self-pronounced judgment of a people. It does this, not by promising an award, but by furnishing a trial. All pecuniary claims are, it is true, to be finally disposed of by it. The same is true of differences growing out of rights whether under treaty or the general law of nations. But a majority of the serious cases which may arise, which are called territorial claims by the Treaty, and include questions of access, navigation, fisheries, boundaries,—in fact most of those rights for which a nation would go to war,—must go to trial, but with no certainty of a final judgment.

Through this failure to ensure a binding verdict, paradoxically enough, the Treaty is strong where it seems to be weak. It is safe, because it does not attempt too much. It bids fair to be effective, because it does not promise efficiency. It is a hopeful attempt at arbitration, although technically speaking not arbitration at all; for the very essence of arbitration lies in the finality of its award. What it offers is a refuge from popular excitement,—the chance of a settlement, the certainty of a breathing spell. What it does *not* offer is a binding award on all the questions between its members, to fit like a strait-jacket upon the body politic and tempt it irresistibly sometimes to break the bonds. Notice the procedure in the third class of cases. If the award is unanimous or made by a vote of five to one, it is final. But if made by any less majority it may be protested, and is "of no validity." The next step is a recourse to mediation; which is the offer of good advice with no obligation to take it. Then diplomacy may try its hand again. Finally, the question may be put to the arbitrament of war.

In this chain of processes a final award is reached, if the matter in dispute is clear to an overwhelming majority of the Tribunal. But the certainty remains that if the question has elements of doubt in it, two out of the three judges who comprise each half of the court can and will prevent a verdict. For in matters essential yet uncertain they will retain their national bias and point of view. Nationality and human nature are stronger than the judicial temperament. It has always been so: it is even desirable that it should be so. We may safely conclude that the framers of the Treaty relied upon this fact in inserting this provision; and did so to prevent the infinite risk of a break-down of machinery, in case a beaten litigant refused to accept the award. They rested upon the presumption of peace which it contains; not upon the strength and completeness of its procedure.

Criticism there may be of this and that detail. No code of international law exists to guide the Tribunals. The judges who are to form Tribunal C. are already overburdened. The method of naming the umpires may prove clumsy or bad. Still, such objections as these are overshadowed and outbalanced by the strong probability that the plan would work. It would prevent war scares, because the popular mind,—always ready to take fright or to take fire,—would be conscious of various and lengthy processes which must precede war; and the popular interest soon tires. It would tend to prevent war, because it ensures a trial of most differences, gathers light upon them from several quarters, prevents action in hot blood, and presupposes peace. Being an experiment, to last for five years only unless proved satisfactory, it is a working basis upon which to build. It does not imperil the arbitration principle by attempting too much. It is a step—a considerable step —toward a better order of things.

When mountain-climbers reach ice they put on the rope, and, cutting step after step, slowly and carefully mount to their goal: they do not risk all by a hasty scramble up the incline.

Here are two nations, in speech, in laws, in blood, in institutions, in ideals, akin. Together they climb the slippery slopes of the Mount of Lasting Peace and Brotherhood. With this Treaty they rope themselves together. The step-cutting has begun. The ascent is slow; but if it be made sure, who can venture to set a limit to their upward progress.

THEODORE S. WOOLSEY.

RECENT TRIUMPHS IN MEDICINE AND SURGERY.

IF it be true that happiness is the negative result of freedom from pain and its incident condition, sickness, medicine has during the past decade or two added more to the substantial welfare of mankind than any of the sciences that have so lavishly ministered to human needs. Whatever may be the theory regarding the real means of bettering the condition of humanity, the records of alleviation of suffering and prolongation of life challenge the endorsement of every unprejudiced observer.

The history of the various improvements in the healing art made within the past few years reads like a fairy tale, and has so interested such as study passing events that it has become a part of the common knowledge of the people. For the obvious reason that the brilliant results of operative procedure are so easily demonstrated, they are the better understood and appreciated. All the recent possibilities of cure in this direction are in the main due to the principle of cleanliness in wound-treatment,—a doctrine entirely unknown previous to thirty years ago. The elaboration and establishment of this principle, due to Prof. Joseph Lister (formerly of Edinburgh, and now Lord Lister, of London), marked an era in surgery which was scarcely second in importance to that of the discovery of etherization. Both opened up new fields of successful endeavor which had before been impossible. Ether banished pain from the operating-table, and antisepsis prevented wound-infection. In olden times, before the advent of anæsthesia, many of what are now called simpler operations were followed by death from shock to the writhing patient, or by blood-poisoning from the infliction of comparatively trivial wounds. In former days abdominal operations were never attempted, because even accidental wounds of internal tissues were followed by poisonously destructful inflammations. Now the cavity is virtually a thoroughfare, every portion of which is invaded with impunity, and all operations upon which may be followed by recovery.

It cannot be said that the older surgeons were not earnest in their study of the apparent relation of cause and effect, and did not do their utmost to reconcile the presumable conditions of failure with the then prevalent theories of wound-treatment. It was generally admitted that some mysterious agency was at work, either in the surroundings, the state of the patient, the character and position of the wound, or possibly in the air itself,—one or other of which barred·all efforts at progress. Strange as it may seem in the light of recent events, the actual condition of the wound was scarcely considered in the mistaken effort to attend to everything else. Walls of hospital wards were scrubbed and repainted; supposed carriers of infection, either in the shape of nurses or medical attendants, were denied contact with patients; soiled wound-dressings were burned; and even instruments, proved by repeated trials to have been poisoned, were destroyed,—but all to no apparent purpose. Cleansing of the wound itself was almost a surgical heresy. According to the prevailing theories of the day, it was believed that interference with the discharges would prevent proper healing. Fouled bandages were therefore the rule; and the thicker and more abundant the discharges the more "laudable" they were considered to be. Hence in the older works on surgery the so-called "laudable" pus was as much a sign of safety as it is now of danger.

Cleanliness of instruments, now a prime consideration, was then entirely ignored. Oftentimes the same instruments would be used at different times upon the dead as well as upon the living body; and a celebrated operator of that day was accustomed to hold his knife between his teeth, when his hands were temporarily employed in the wound. If a cut healed rapidly it was a rarity sufficiently great to court comment. Now the exact opposite is the fact. The former result was rather an accident of cleanliness than the deliberate acknowledgment of what should have been the rule. Consequently the most careful surgeons—those who possessed instinctive habits of neatness and cleanliness — were the most successful. Valentine Mott, the Nestor of surgery in his day, was particularly exemplary in this respect. The care of his hands and instruments was a subject of jocular remark among his friends. He always washed his hands before and after handling a patient. An amusing anecdote of his laudable habit is related of him by a late assistant. Just before starting to make his calls, a patient presented himself having an abscess which required incision. The great surgeon saw at once what was necessary and asked his assistant to operate. Although he did not intend to touch the patient he rather absent-mindedly washed his hands. While the operation was in progress Dr. Mott stood at a safe distance from any possible contamination, with his hands behind him, and when all was over, carefully removing his snow-white cuffs, he yielded to his uncontrollable propensity for a final ablution, although to him the operation in question was an entirely imaginary one.

The very simplicity of the idea that mere cleanliness was the promise of success in the treatment of wounds was offset by its apparent absurdity. The theory that infection was due to poisonous microscopic organisms, directly or indirectly conveyed to the raw surfaces, was duly scouted by all such as were wedded to the then prevalent methods. The new-school men were derisively styled " bug-hunters " and were duly pitied on account of their strange delusion. Fortunately the leader of the new movement, having the idea fixed in his Scotch brain by the slow-and-sure corkscrew method, was more than willing to test the eradicating propensities of his numerous opponents. It was a question whether or not the conviction would loosen, or, holding its own, would bring his head with it. There is now but one answer to his valiantly persistent missionary work; and the name of Lister is gratefully associated with one of the grandest scientific advances of the nineteenth century.

The initiative efforts to reduce the theory to a rational working basis were necessarily crude and largely empirical; but the main considerations were kept constantly in view. The ultimate result has been that of simplification of procedure. While in earlier days every effort was made to destroy all poisonous organisms that might accidentally invade wounds, the principal aim now is to eliminate the possibility of any infection whatever. Thus what was called antiseptic surgery has now given place to aseptic surgery. By the latter method, which insures absolute cleanliness of the wound, of the instrument, of the operator, and of the dressings, both before, during, and after the operation, there is a guarantee of protection against infection which is well-nigh absolute. The general principles upon which such procedures are based are now so simple and so broad that they can be very successfully carried out by very ordinary means. Many of the germicides previously believed to be infallible are now replaced by the comparatively few proved to be trustworthy. The dressings are more carefully sterilized and more effectually sealed than formerly; while the preliminary washing of the hands, the careful ablution of the patient, and the thorough steaming of the instruments rightly elevate cleanliness to the position of a high art, and the surety of safe and rapid healing to a foregone conclusion. What, under other circumstances, would appear to be mere fussiness of scrubbing fingers, of immersing hands in aseptic fluids, of lathering and irrigating the operation-field, are now as much the essentials of a successful operation as are the manipulative skill, the anatomical accuracy, and the cool daring of the most skilful surgeon. In times gone by the essential qualities of the surgeon were supposed to be a lion's heart, an eagle's eye, and a lady's hand; but now we can attribute his best successes to that synonym of godliness which, better than all other qualifications, fits him for his higher ministrations.

With the advent of aseptic surgery, better opportunities were offered for more extensive and more radical operative ventures. The causes of previous failures being understood, the proper precautions against the possibility of their recurrence were more intelligently considered. It became with the surgeon more a question of conscience as to cleanliness than even skill with the knife. Hence new fields were opened to him. The abdominal cavity could now be opened with impunity; and the other formerly unexplored territories of the interior of the body paid willing and docile tribute to the daring and genius of brilliant work. It is almost impossible to calculate the number of lives saved in this field alone, which would otherwise have been sacrificed to previous incapacity. The possibilities of abdominal surgery have ceased to astonish the most casual observer. Every internal organ has paid its obedient allegiance to the knife, and has acknowledged the magic of its master-touch. Interrupted and obstructed intestinal channels have found new courses by the skilful union of adjacent coils; and the stomach itself has been compelled to maintain its functions, either through artificial external openings, or by neighborly understanding with attached intestinal loops. The gall-bladder has been opened and emptied externally, new currents have been made for the bile, and even the organ itself has been removed with the best results. The floating kidney has been successfully moored to its legitimate anchorage by stitching to the back; and, when so diseased as to be past redemption, it has been extirpated, resignedly shifting its functional responsibilities upon its obliging twin.

Even independently of the knife the hitherto hidden entrenchments of mortality have been revealed by the electric light, which has opened for intelligent inspection and successful invasion the interiors of all the hollow organs.

A still greater revelation was in store for workers in such fields, more especially for such as were in search of more marvellous methods. It is scarcely more than a twelvemonth since Röntgen of Wurz-burg cheated reason and tricked prophecy by demonstrating the mira-cle of the X-ray. With the first announcement of the discovery came the application of the new light to the needs of surgery. The skele-ton was laid bare in the warm and breathing body; and, for the first time, photographing the hitherto invisible was an overpowering fact. It is not necessary to speak of the world-wide astonishment with which this new discovery was received, nor of its probable benefit to the medicine and surgery of the future. In the enthusiasm of anticipation the possibilities of good appeared to be almost unbounded; but in the light of actually demonstrated results we must needs culti-vate patience and perfect methods. Thus far the bones in the living subject have been very clearly and beautifully shown through various thicknesses of super-imposed solids; but expectations in other direc-tions have not yet been realized. Opacity has lifted its veil and has approvingly blinked at the new light, but has not yet yielded absolute homage. Much more is yet to be accomplished. Although solid bodies of differing density have been duly located in the various tis-sues and cavities; though bullets, coins, and needles have by such means been discovered and removed, the outlines of the internal organs have not been so accurately rendered as was at first anticipated. This is in the main due to the want of distinctness in the demonstration of substance, and to the lack of sharpness of outline.¯

The best results so far from the X-ray have been obtained in cases of dislocated bones, of fractures, and in the discovery of imbedded bul-lets. In the present aspect of such accomplished facts there is a melancholy retrospect associated with the lost missile in the body of the lamented Garfield. All the devices known at that time were of no avail in locating the bullet. It was believed, and was thought to have been proven, that it had taken a downward course and lodged in the right groin; whereas, in reality it traversed the body in an entirely different direction, through the spinal column, and at the autopsy was discovered behind the region of the stomach on the left side. With the Röntgen ray the whereabouts of the truant could doubtless have been accurately determined, and a successful operation for its dislodge-ment might have been possible.

Although chloroform and ether—long the absolute safeguards against the most acute pains of major operations—fulfilled all special indications, there was always felt a pressing need for some pain-de-stroyer that should have merely a local action. Then came cocaine to claim her crown.   The discovery of its marvellous power to limit areas of anæsthesia without loss of consciousness settled all questions of pain in operations, great or small.   The credit of bringing this wonderful drug to the attention of the profession is properly tendered to Dr. Carl Koller.   Now the gap between the toleration of extreme agony and the endurance of lesser pains is so completely closed over by the dropping of cocaine on the eyeball, or by the direct injection of the solution under the skin, that the patient can witness the operation on himself in the surprise of entire absence of sensation, and can truthfully ask, " O pain, where is thy victory? O blade, where is thy sting?"

Many of the eye-operations which formerly required etherization are now performed with cocaine; obviating the discomforts and risks of general anæsthesia without adding to the shock of the patient.   Its efficacy in abolishing pain of mucous surfaces admits of no question.   In the earlier days of its use for that purpose it rose to world-wide fame when it touched the aching throat of General Grant and bade his pain be still.   It came in time for him as it has for thousands of similar sufferers since.

With the perfection of operative procedures comes the consideration of the advances made in the comparatively new department of brain-surgery.   As the result of long and careful observation of various nervous phenomena associated with head-injuries and as the outcome of much experimentation upon the lower animals, it has been finally demonstrated that the brain is merely a collection of nerve-centres, each one of which presides over a particular part of the body. Thus a tumor, a blood-clot, or other cause of pressure, can be located by the paralyzing effects produced upon the different supply-nerves connected with the affected centre; and many daring and successful operations can be performed for the relief of conditions which only a few years ago were considered as beyond hope.   Many of the brain-regions are now so accurately delineated by schematic charts that any trained observer can, by the attendant and reflected symptoms of localized cerebral derangement, as surely locate the source of trouble as one who receives a message directly from a storm-centre.   The signals are thrown out all along the line of nervous distribution throughout the body.   Each one is special in its kind, and distinct in its significance of danger; whether manifested in the dropped lid, dilated pupil, limp limb, staggering gait, numbed tongue, slowing breath-pant, or wild delirium.

In a general way, it may be said that medicine has advanced, as has surgery, by following the lead of bacteriological investigation, and

3

by applying the results of laboratory experimentation. The improvements of microscopical technique, made possible by the perfection of lenses and the use of stains for distinguishing differences of reaction in the diagnosis of micro-organisms, have opened up a wide field for future inquiry and promising progress. Especially can this much be said concerning the laudable endeavors made in many directions for ascertaining the real causes of disease, the successful efforts toward isolating them, and the hopeful prospect of eventually overcoming their destructive tendencies. In the previous attempts to reconcile the relations of cause and effect in the propagation of the communicable ailments, various theories were advanced concerning what was acknowledged as at best a mysterious agency; but of the poison itself nothing was definitely known until the microscope turned its searching eye upon the hitherto unseen horizon of the lesser world. It was then proved that many of the lowest micro-organisms held the balance of power with the highest creations in determining the life-limit. Thus we find in many of the commoner diseases that there is a special causative microbe for each. The familiar examples are those of typhoid and malarial fevers, diphtheria, cholera, and pulmonary consumption. It will not serve the particular purpose of this article to give a history of the ingenious experiments and the long and arduous labors of the different discoverers; but it is just and proper to group in the honor list the names of Pasteur, Roux, Strauss, Metchnikoff, and Bouchard of Paris; Koch, Fränkel, Behring, Klebs, and Loeffler of Germany, and Kitasato of Japan.

It was originally believed that the microbes were the direct active agents in poisoning the system, until it was demonstrated that the really morbific agency was due to the chemical product excreted by the micro-organisms themselves. Koch was at first led to suppose that his lymph, which represented the toxin of tuberculosis, would of itself destroy the tubercle bacillus in the living body. It was unfortunate for the future development of a more reasonable theory that the daily press so prematurely took the matter in hand, and placed what should have been a purely scientific question beyond the pale of possible explanation or reasonable argument. It, however, drew attention to new theories of cure which have since been practically demonstrated.

The next most natural step, after allowing the impossibility of killing the microbe, was to protect the body against its ravages by increasing the vital resistance of the patient. This was the inception of the serum treatment of infectious diseases, so strikingly exemplified nowadays by the use of antitoxin in diphtheria. The remedy, as its name implies, is intended to counteract the poison of the disease, and is the basis of a most plausible theory for the successful management of all similar affections. It may not be uninteresting in this connection to explain in a non-technical way how anti-toxins are obtained and how they are supposed to act. Taking the diphtheria product, for instance, the first step is to obtain the poison from the membrane by means of a sterilized platinum rod and to transfer it to what is known as a cultivating medium. In the latter the microbes propagate. Subsequently, by filtration, the real toxin is obtained and is then used for the inoculation of an animal,—the horse being in the present case the chosen one. Repeated inoculations are made at given intervals until the animal no longer reacts to the effects of a progressively increasing dose. Then the condition of so-called "immunity" is reached, which consists in the impossibility of making the subject of the experiment sick by any amount of similar poison that can be introduced into his circulation. The watery element of the blood of the animal is then used for the human patient, who, through its protective power, is in turn rendered "immune," or, in other words, is guaranteed against the poisonous influences of the disease. The horse does not suffer; and the human patient is in the end saved. The same may be said of many other experiments so absurdly combated by the anti-vivisectionists. In diphtheria the knowledge of its cause brings a promised means for its cure. Making every allowance for exaggeration of good results in the treatment of this dreadful disease, there is certainly enough of truth in the statements of enthusiastic advocates of the new method to warrant the hope that the same principle may be applied to other infectious diseases, and with like benefit.

It seems fair to conclude, from our present knowledge of the subject, that acute ailments are the only ones in which the serum treatment has a rational hold. Pulmonary consumption, which has now, rather prematurely, perhaps, assumed a position in the contagious class, is essentially of such a chronic nature and attended with such radical organic changes, that there does not appear to be much chance of altering the fundamental morbific condition by actively increasing any of the purely resisting tendencies of the blood itself. This is claimed to have been the mistake in the lymph treatment. Far from mitigating the disease, it appeared to favor the extension. It was a valuable though dangerous means for diagnosis, and has been very properly relegated to such use in cattle.

The more practical application of the microbic theory has been in the direction of preventing the spread of infection. From such a stand-point .science has had its greatest and most lasting triumphs. The reason for the spread of many of the common epidemics is no longer a mystery. It is now explained satisfactorily by a direct or indirect transfer of micro-organisms from one human body to another. A good illustration of the way in which this is done is that afforded by the spread of typhoid fever. In this disease there is of course a special germ, called the typhoid bacillus. Having been discovered in the dis-charges of the patient, and also in drinking water, it was not difficult to reconcile associated conditions. The contamination of the water supply by the sick patient was a theory easily substantiated. The origin of every epidemic was traced accordingly ; and there was no end of corroborative testimony. Now, when typhoid breaks out in any locality, the first thing done is the examination of the drinking water for bacilli. When the latter are discovered, the sources of typhoid are cut off and the epidemic is immediately checked. Certainly nothing could be more satisfactory in the whole category of prevention. Other and indirect methods by which the bacillus may enter the system are illustrated in the infection of the oyster from contaminated streams, and in the thousand and one ways in which milk and other foods may be fever-poisoned through the agencies of the utensils, hands, or clothing of the patient. The same may be said regarding the like causes of the invasion of cholera, and with a similar comforting assurance of the knowledge of the means for the prevention of epidemics of that dis-ease. Diphtheria is more liable to spread as the result of actual con-tact with the poison than most other infectious diseases. Thus, by unadvisedly kissing the sick one, using the same spoon, or by being exposed to the exhalation or expectoration of the patient during opera-tions upon the throat, many lives have been lost which by ordinary precautions might have been saved.

With pulmonary consumption the dust of the dried expectoration is believed to be the direct medium of infection. Considering the widespread dissemination of that material in crowded cities, and the thousands who breathe bacilli everywhere they go,—in street cars, sleeping-berths, hotels, parlors, and churches,—and taking into account the alarming bulletins of ambitiously active Health Boards, it would appear that the disease should be well-nigh universal. It is a satisfac-tion, however, to know that the chances of infection with a healthy person are so exceedingly small as not to merit mention, much less cause alarm. With every communicable disease it is a question of seed taking good root iñ the properly prepared soil. Especially is this the case with phthisis. The degree of vital resistance is the real element of protection. When there is no preparation of the soil by hereditary predisposition or lowered health standard, the individual is amply guarded against attack. Otherwise no one would be safe anywhere. The real good that may come from the agitation of the question of contagion in this disease is the opportunity afforded Health Boards of educating the victims to the necessary habits of cleanliness, which in individual cases will lessen the possibilities of disseminating the germs. If the ultimate result shall be nothing more than the abolition of the abominable habit of promiscuous spitting in public conveyances and assembly rooms, the present senseless scare may yet eventuate in the greatest benefit to the majority. The enforcement of regulations to such an end very properly belongs to the various Health Boards; but when the latter attempt to assume control of the patient, separate him from his family, forcibly confine him in a municipal sanitarium, and direct medical treatment by governmental authority, they exceed their legitimate functions and magnify the importance of so-called duties out of all proportion to the real necessity for their performance. It is proper, however, to say in this connection that Health Bureaus as such have very important relations to the public, and are very properly the legitimate agents for the enforcement of the general sanitary regulations of towns and cities. In fact, the establishment of these boards for such purposes is one of the most convincing evidences of the advance of medicine in the widest application of its benefits to the needs of the greatest number.

In noting in a general way the beneficial influences of progressive medicine, I may refer, in passing, to a few matters of detail which may not be uninteresting to the general reader.

There is a little history connected with the discovery of intubation, which carries with it a useful moral. Nearly half a century ago Bouchut, a distinguished French physician, startled the savants of that period by the announcement that it was much better to introduce a tube in the windpipe of a suffocating child than to trust to the chances of obtaining air for the sufferer by a cut in the throat. The prejudices of his colleagues were too strong for him to resist, and, being forced to abandon his idea, he lost the opportunity of putting it to the practical test. From that time until O'Dwyer of New York popularized the method, and became the means of saving hundreds of precious lives by what is now known as the intubation method, humanity was deprived of one of its greatest boons.

The belief at one time that extracts of different organs of animals could be used for the treatment of disease of corresponding organs in man, has not been confirmed by more recent experimentation. Brown-Séquard's so-styled " Elixir of Life " followed its inventor to a common grave ; and the disease of old age, to which all mankind is liable, is still considered incurable. A curious exception, however, to the efficacy of gland treatment has been shown in the cure of the newly-described disease, myxœdema, by the use of an extract of the thyroid. This was discovered by a somewhat novel yet strictly logical method of reasoning. It had long been known that, after complete extirpation of the thyroid gland for goitrous swelling, patients developed a peculiar condition of mal-nutrition which was manifested by a fleshy puffing of the face and hands, wasting of the nails, and a progressive physical and mental weakness. The absence of the gland being naturally associated with these phenomena, it was then advised that a portion of the goitrous swelling be left behind after an operation. The result was so satisfactory in preventing the occurrence of bad symptoms that a rule was established accordingly. In the cases in which the gland had been entirely removed, an attempt was made to supply the deficiency by feeding the patient with the raw or stewed thyroid of the sheep. The result was also very promising. Then another fact presented itself; viz., that myxœdema, a disease with essentially the same symptoms, was associated with marked deficiency of thyroid development. This gave the proper indication for a similar method of treatment, which, to say the least, has been surprisingly successful.

What promises to be a great service in enabling physicians to more surely recognize typhoid fever in its earliest stages, is the peculiar reaction of the blood of the suspected patient with a culture of the typhoid bacillus. This was first brought to the notice of the profession by Widal ; and the method rightly bears his name. If the case be one of typhoid fever, a drop of the patient's blood will kill the bacilli of a culture with which it is brought into contact; but if the bacilli are not affected, the patient has not the disease. The theory of the phenomenon is that the poison of typhoid in the blood of the patient is sufficiently strong and active to destroy even at that early period the typhoid bacilli from another source. Here, too, is a principle which may have a wide application to diagnosis under similar conditions with still other diseases.

The great improvement in the present as compared with the past methods of administering medicines deserves a passing comment. Scarcely a generation ago the threat of a dose of the nauseous drugs of the day was sufficient to suppress the worst of evil propensities in the most wicked boy. When actually in need of medication, he was held in the chair and gagged to exhaustion in the parental anxiety to measure the capacity of his unwilling stomach with the bulky contents of the justly hated bottle. Frequently the struggle had more to do with the perspiration than the medicine. Very often, for obvious reasons, the bottle broke before the fever. Castor oil was a punishment, rhubarb was a terror, and senna an abomination. The nauseous mixtures of our grandparents are now replaced by the elegant and almost tasty compounds of modern pharmacy. The essentials of the former medicines are now given in the forms of condensed extracts and alkaloids in proportionately reduced bulk, and in consistently concentrated form. Single remedies with special indications take the place of the old-fashioned shot-gun mixtures. Tablets, pellets, and pills no longer offend the palate ; and even quinine, the bitterest enemy of taste, now sues for favor in sugar-coated armor. The irritable stomach which denies the usual approach to the internal economy is now diplomatically checkmated by an injection under the skin, which, although a longer way round, is a surer way home.

In the adaptation of different climates to the cure of various chronic diseases, a new science of therapeutics has been created. The study of the temperature range, barometric pressure, and rainfall of different localities has been as faithfully carried on and with as careful reference to the needs of the invalid as the composition and strength of the various medicines composing his other prescriptions. Oftentimes change of air and scene is the only treatment indicated. It is the proper fitting of the patient to a new and necessary environment which makes the difference between an agreeable and helpful life in another country as compared with growing discontent and protracted suffering at home.

The vital resistance to disease, which must exist in every individual, has received new attention and study in consideration of the plausibility of the theory of Metchnikoff. This talented and indefatigable observer maintained that the white corpuscles of the blood had a peculiar power of destroying disease germs which so constantly found their way into the circulating fluid. In fact, with his microscope, he noted the manner in which the germs became devoured in the substance of the disks in question. Interesting and confirmatory experiments in the same direction were made in artificially produced areas of inflammation in the lower animals. Although the conclusions are not universally admitted, there is enough in the fundamental idea, and its adaptability to the present well-recognized conditions of general protection against disease, to warrant the further study which it is now receiving from other laboratory workers. Already we are learning that the watery portions of the blood have also a bactericidal property, and that the increase of the latter by anti-toxins may be an explanation of the good results of that class of remedies.

In attempting a general review of the progress of medicine in keeping with the purpose of this article, it is impossible to do more than refer in a casual way to some of the leading points of departure from the older methods to the newer and better ones. There are enough of these to give the best of assurances of good work already done and of promises for rapid advancement in the future. Medicine has kept its pace with the other sciences, slowly, perhaps, but surely. The days of supposed miracles have passed. Faith in the marvellous has given place to work in the actual. The greatest miracle of all is creation itself, upon which all science is founded. It is by the sweat of the brow that the best discoveries can be made. In these days of quackery and pretentious faith-cures it is a comfort for such as believe in honest effort to know that the pay for the same is in some solid good, some real advance, some lasting benefit. The history of medical discovery shows that nothing permanently useful was ever obtained by mere accident or by avowed inspiration. Belief in the faith-cure may be calculated for spiritual strength, but not for physical regeneration. The only miracle of the laying on of healing hands, of blessing handkerchiefs, and the like rests in the possibility of the ridiculous belief in such methods. As well might we expect that mere faith would set a broken limb, or start a silent clock. The same may be said of every other species of quackery. Scientific medicine is at least sincere, even if it cannot actually promise as much as it might wish. What it has, however, is truth and fact; consequently, her honest influences are felt in every direction in which the betterment of the race is possible. The lesson of the hour has its widest possible application in the preservation of health, the prevention of disease, and the cure of the sick. It is the faith, hope, and charity of the medical ideal.

The natural state of man should be that of health from the beginning to the end of the life-chapter. Disease is an incident of his want of adaptability to his environment. His real health needs are simple enough, and apply, to necessary clothing, sufficient food, and suitable shelter. All outside this is payment on the mortgage of luxury. Some one has said, " When men were made of oak they lived in houses of willow, and when the sacramental wine was drunk from chalices of wood, Christianity was golden ; but when the troth was pledged in cups of gold, the faith was wooden." It was the survival of the fittest in the race for the really good and essential in life. Now we have the struggle with the weak and unfit to match them with the much-coveted requirements of the unnecessary. Civilization, with all its benefits in the elevation of mankind to the higher sphere of its destined usefulness, has brought with it the penalties for abuses and excesses. Medical science strives to adjust the balance between the punishment and the crime. So far it has worked valiantly, consistently, and hopefully. The fundamental laws of health are now better understood than formerly ; the prevention of disease has become a law of necessity ; and the assuagement of human suffering has risen to the level of a high art. The dangers of excesses are appreciated and avoided; bad habits are condemned ; and the more helpful enforcement of sanitary laws is an accomplished fact. With the more extended application of the principles of hygiene large populations can live safely together; and even the vices of communities are counteracted by the indignant protests of educated public opinion. In forty-one States of the Union every young scholar educated by the public must learn that rum as a luxury is also a poison; that temperance in all things is nature's standard ; that all excesses are more than counterbalanced by consequent depression ; and that, most of all, the human body is the perfection of creation, the gift of a God with the ever-present responsibility of its safe and reverent keeping.

The history of the past is the best prediction for the future. In the light of recent events, we have no right to assume that there is any disease incurable to-day which may not in a near to-morrow be triumphantly vanquished by its remedy. Surely nothing should hinder the army of conscientious, arduous, and patient toilers whose greatest gratification is in the infatuation of the work itself, and whose higher aim is the saving of the lives of their fellow men.

GEORGE F. SHRADY.

THE TORREY BANKRUPT BILL.

THE Federal Constitution provides (Art. 1, Sec. 8, Clause 4) as follows: "The Congress shall have power . . . to establish . . . uniform laws on the subject of bankruptcies throughout the United States." It also provides (Art. 1, Sec. 10, Clause 1) that "No State shall . . . pass any . . . law impairing the obligation of contracts."

Under the power conferred as above upon Congress, laws were enacted in 1800, 1841, and 1867. The first two were of short duration; but the last was in force eleven years.

The law of 1867, for various reasons, was unsatisfactory to the people in all parts of the country. It contained provisions, not properly a part of a bankruptcy law, which brought it unnecessarily in conflict with State laws; and the fees exacted by it for the performance of official services were exorbitant, and were so paid that the officers receiving them were interested in delaying the administration of estates. An additional reason why the law became unpopular was that it did not apply alike to all our citizens; being limited in its operations to a class known under the general designation of "traders." The people do not like favoritism or caste of any kind: they desire that the laws shall apply equally to all. Prior to 1861, the bankruptcy law in England was limited to "traders"; but since then it has been applicable to all classes of citizens.

Shortly after the repeal in 1878 of the last law, it became apparent to the business men of the country that it should have been amended, and not repealed. They realized that the honest, unfortunate debtor who meets with financial misfortune should have a comprehensive discharge as contemplated by the Constitution; but this they knew he could not secure under any law which a State could pass. When the only recourse of creditors was to proceed individually against a common debtor,—as provided under State laws,—it frequently resulted in the debtor being financially ruined through undue selfish haste; and generally the result was the inequitable distribution of the estate, at a very large expense, between creditors of equal rights. They knew that under a wise bankruptcy law honest insolvent debtors would be discharged; that creditors would proceed collectively against a common debtor; and that, in the event of his being declared a bankrupt, the estate would be ratably divided between the creditors of equal rights, in accordance with the rules of equity.

This feeling of regret at the repeal of the old law, and the realization of the necessity for a new one, resulted in a national convention being held at Washington in 1881. A second convention was held in the same city in 1884; a third was held in St. Louis in the spring of 1889; and a fourth at Minneapolis in the fall of the same year. At the last three of these, I had the honor of presiding as permanent president.

The Lowell bill was approved by the first two of the conventions; and at the third convention a bill was drafted and presented by me, and was referred, together with the Lowell bill, to a committee composed of leading members of that body. The committee reported my bill favorably, and sent it broadcast over the country; inviting suggestions as to amendments. It was then considered at the Minneapolis convention for two days, and was finally approved unanimously. A resolution, introduced by Hon. John J. Hornor, a delegate from Fort Smith, Arkansas, providing that the bill should be named "The Torrey Bankrupt Bill," was also adopted.

It should be borne in mind that these conventions were not composed of representatives of great mercantile corporations,—as has been untruthfully alleged,—but of representatives of commercial, industrial, and professional bodies, the members of which were debtors and creditors in all parts of the country. Their object was not to secure the enactment of a purely voluntary or an involuntary law, but to formulate a law that should be at once voluntary and involuntary, equitable and comprehensive in its scope, and that should fully protect the rights of all classes. The bill solves the problem of bankruptcy legislation, it is confidently believed; for it has been very generally endorsed by business and industrial bodies in all parts of the country.

The Executive Committee of the convention at Minneapolis was authorized to amend the bill from time to time as I might recommend; and, pursuant to that authority, it has been amended as seemed best in the course of my studies upon the subject, or as has appeared desirable from suggestions of Members of Congress, from correspondence with insolvent debtors, members of the bench and bar, and debtors and creditors in all parts of the country. There have been successive editions of the bill, each rendered more perfect by amendment than the preceding one; but the framework, the objects, and the means of attaining them have never been changed.

In the Fifty-first, as also in the Fifty-fourth, Congress the bill was passed by the House; but in the Fifty-third Congress it was defeated in the House. The voluntary bill of Mr. Bailey was passed by that body, but was not voted upon in the Senate. There are also a number of bills pending in Congress in imitation of the voluntary measure introduced and championed by Hon. Joseph W. Bailey, a Member from Texas; but there has been no attempt on the part of any Member of Congress to draft a voluntary and involuntary measure; for the Torrey Bill, by the common consent of those who favor a complete law, meets all the requirements of the Constitution.

In countries where there is but one legislative body, a bankruptcy law would not be materially affected by its containing provisions which properly belonged to other laws; but in this country it is different. Here we have forty-five States, all having supreme legislative power, except to the extent to which it was surrendered to Congress by the Constitution. I remember that, in drafting the bill, I inserted in it provisions upon all subjects for which I found a precedent in other laws; and after completing it in that form, I spent two weeks in simply eliminating provisions which, in my judgment, were not properly a part of such a law. The scope then given to the bill has never been changed.

The bill is limited to such provisions as are necessary to make it comprehensively guard the rights of both debtors and creditors. Being national in character, it must, of course, be enforced in the national courts; it having been repeatedly decided that Congress has no right to require State courts to enforce national laws.

The essential features of the Torrey Bankrupt Bill are as follows:

Every person and firm owing debts may become a voluntary bankrupt. Corporations cannot go voluntarily into bankruptcy; but they may be adjudged bankrupts in proceedings against them by their creditors on the ground that they have committed an act of bankruptcy. In general terms an act of bankruptcy is an act for the commission of which by a debtor in most of the States an attachment would be justified; such as indicates insolvency and inability to prevent his property from being inequitably divided among his creditors while insolvent; or of protracted default in payments due while insolvent.

Since proceedings, when instituted, are for the benefit of all the creditors, it is provided that a petition cannot be filed except by three of them collectively holding unsecured claims of at least $500.

When a petition shall have been filed against a defendant alleging that he has committed an act of bankruptcy, he will be served with process as in ordinary suits ; and if he, or any of his creditors not joining in, the petition, deny the allegations of the petition, there will be a trial as in other cases. The defendant may, if he desires, have a trial by jury. An appeal may be taken from an adjudication of bankruptcy.

After the filing of the petition, and prior to the trial, the property rights of the defendant will not be interfered with in any respect unless the creditors shall file affidavits showing to the satisfaction of the court the commission of an act of bankruptcy by the defendant, as set forth in the petition, and shall apply for an order for taking possession of the property of the defendant. Before such order will be executed, the plaintiffs must give bond to the defendant to indemnify him in the event of such order proving to have been wrongfully obtained. Even then the defendant may give a forthcoming bond and retain the possession of the property. These provisions place the defendant in a bankruptcy suit upon the same footing as defendants in other suits. Such was not the case, however, under the old bankruptcy law ; and in consequence a great many hardships arose. For example, while the property might be left in the possession of the defendant, still, on his being adjudged a bankrupt, the title of the trustee dated back to the date of the filing of the petition and resulted in setting aside any conveyance of property which the bankrupt might have made during the proceedings.

After the adjudication that a defendant is a bankrupt, the rights and responsibilities of both the bankrupt and the creditors are the same, whether the case be a voluntary or involuntary one.

The bill encourages compositions between debtors and their creditors, and provides that they may be made after the filing of the petition and either before or after the adjudication. In order to prevent the debtor from imposing on his creditors, it is required that he shall be examined in open court, and shall file a list of his creditors and a schedule of his property. A compliance with these requirements will enable the creditors to judge of both the honesty of the debtor and the value of their claims. His proposed composition must be accepted by a majority in number of his creditors, who represent a majority in amount of the claims against his estate. He must also deposit in court, or subject to the order of the judge, whatever he proposes to pay or give to his creditors as a consideration for the composition ; so that, if the composition shall be confirmed by the judge, the amount of the consideration may be delivered direct to the creditors.   After, but not before, the foregoing provisions have been complied with, his offer may be filed in the bankruptcy court.   These provisions are inserted in order to preclude the possibility of creditors being trifled with by the debtor.   The creditors will all be notified of the hearing of the proposed composition ; and each creditor may favor or oppose it.   The judge will confirm only such compositions as are for the best interests of the creditors.   A composition which has been fraudulently obtained may be set aside.

Assistant judicial officers, called " referees," may be appointed by the bankruptcy courts in such numbers as shall prove necessary for the convenience of the people, and to enable the courts to dispose of bankruptcy business expeditiously.   It is contemplated that at least one such officer shall be appointed for each county ; and in larger counties a greater number.   These officers will receive a $10 filing fee for each case, 1 per cent on the amount paid in dividends by estates administered before them, and half that amount in cases in which there is a composition.   In every case both fee and commission will be withheld until the estate has been administered and closed.

Trustees will be appointed by and represent the creditors.   There may be one or three for each estate, as may be determined by the creditors.   They will receive a filing fee of $5 in each case, and 5 per cent on the first $5,000 paid to the creditors as dividends ; 2 per cent on the second $5,000 so paid ; and 1 per cent on amounts in excess of $10,000. Neither fee nor commission will be paid until the estate has been closed.

The fact that the commissions paid to the foregoing officers are upon net results will interest those officers financially in administering the estates as economically as possible.   The expenses of administering estates will be limited to those which are necessary and actual ; and they will not be paid until after being reported under oath and passed upon by the judge.   Moreover, since all compensation is withheld until the estates are closed, those officers will have a pecuniary interest in closing them as quickly as possible.

Litigation as to property rights will be conducted in the courts which would have had jurisdiction of such litigation if bankruptcy had not occurred.

Liens which may have been obtained by proceedings at law or in equity, commenced within four months prior to the filing of the petition, will be set aside. Liens which were given for a present consideration and in good faith, and not in contemplation of bankruptcy, will be upheld.

The transfer of property or the payment of money by a debtor to a creditor within four months prior to the filing of the petition in bankruptcy against such debtor, for the purpose of defeating the operation of the law, or of enabling such creditor to obtain a greater percentage of his claim than any other creditor of the same class, will be deemed a preference, and may be set aside at the instance of the trustee of the estate of such debtor if he shall become a bankrupt. Money paid or property transferred to a lawyer in excess of a reasonable amount for services may be recovered.

The bankrupt may apply for a discharge subsequent to the expiration of two months after the adjudication and within the next four months. If, for reasons over which he has no control, he should be prevented from making the application within that time, the judge may permit him to file it within the next six months; but not afterward. The discharge will not be granted if the defendant has been guilty of any of the offences enumerated in the act; e. g., of having given a preference within six months prior to the filing of the petition, which has not been surrendered; obtained upon credit, on a materially false statement in writing made by him to the person from whom the property was obtained, or to a mercantile agency, any property not paid for or restored at the time the petition was filed; made a transfer of his property which might be impeached by a creditor; or, with fraudulent intent, destroyed or neglected to keep books of account. The discharge, if fraudulently obtained, may be set aside upon application of creditors. The granting of a discharge will not release the defendant from debts which are due as taxes; which have been reduced to judgments in actions for frauds or wilful and malicious injury to the person or property of another; which have not been duly scheduled, unless the creditor had knowledge of the proceedings in bankruptcy; or were created by fraud, embezzlement, or defalcation while acting as an officer or serving in any fiduciary capacity.

Exemptions will be allowed as provided, at the time the petition was filed, by the laws of the State in which the bankrupt resides.

Suitable provisions are made for the punishment of bankrupts, creditors, and officers who have violated the provisions of the law.

Under the old law a number of the judges secured for their relatives desirable appointments. The Torrey Bill provides that no persons who are related by consanguinity or affinity within the third degree, as determined by the common law, to either of the judges of the United States courts in any district shall be appointed referees in such district.

The proof and allowance of claims will be a simple and inexpensive matter. If it be suspected that a claim is fraudulent, it may be suspended and examined.

All money belonging to estates must be deposited in a designated depository, and will not be paid out except upon the check or draft of the trustee.

The bill, in addition to the foregoing, contains such provisions as are necessary to make it comprehensive of the rights of unfortunate and dishonest debtors and their creditors.

The vote in the Fifty-fourth Congress in the House of Representatives, by which the bill was passed by the large majority of seventy-six,—after a five-day debate in which it was championed by Gen. D. B. Henderson of Iowa, Chairman of the Committee on the Judiciary,—may be summarized as follows:—

	Yea.	Nay.	Not Voting.
Eastern States....................	18	0	8
Middle "	49	4	27
Southern "	28	39	37
Western "	55	33	40
Pacific "	7	5	4
Totals......................	157	81	116

It will be noted that in the Eastern, Middle, Western, and Pacific States, the bill received a majority in its favor; while the majority against it in the Southern States was only eleven. Most of the one hundred and sixteen members not voting were paired; the presumption being that one-half of them were for and the other one-half against the bill. The Texas delegation in the House gave eight votes in favor of the bill, and only two against it; while three did not vote. In the Fifty-first Congress only one Member from that State, as I remember, voted with our friends. This change speaks volumes for the merits of the bill. Indeed it constitutes a great victory; considering the fact that Mr. Bailey, a Member from that State, greatly distinguished himself as leader of the opposition and in advocacy of his bill for purely voluntary bankruptcy.

The chief opposition to the enactment of the measure is by a few great houses in-different parts of the country, which have so perfected their credit and collection departments that, under present laws, they can legally take advantage of their unfortunate debtors and of all associate creditors not equally well equipped with themselves. These great houses do not want passed a bankruptcy law which will transfer from their private offices to the court-house the throne to which their unfortunate debtors must appeal for relief. They do not want their appropriation of the debtors' assets, to the full extent of their claims, in spite of the equal rights of other creditors, interfered with by a court of justice. To them the constitutional right of debtors and equity among creditors, when in derogation of their financial interests, are not to be encouraged; and hence they are violently opposed to the passage of the bill.

The fate of the bill in the Senate is problematical. The Committee on the Judiciary of the Senate acted upon the subject before the Torrey Bill was passed by the House. The majority reported a bill which had been introduced by Senator George of Mississippi, and amended by the Committee. A minority reported the Torrey Bill, and when it was referred by the Senate—as passed by the House—to its Committee on the Judiciary, all of it was stricken out after the enacting clause, and the bill of Senator George substituted in its stead. These bills are now upon the calendar of the Senate; and it is to be hoped that they will be considered and acted upon during the present session.

If, in the meantime, the friends of the Torrey Bill throughout the country shall make their wishes known to the members of the Senate, the result of the House will be more than duplicated in the Senate; and, as a result, the constitutional rights which are now dormant will be available to the people.

4   JAY L. TORREY.

The discoveries of the theatres of Assos, Thorikos, and Sicyon, as set forth in the preceding article, supplied valuable data for the elucidation of several unsolved questions relating to the theatre of the Greeks. And as the origin of the Greek drama is closely bound up with the worship of Dionysos, it was a judicious choice which determined the next venture of the American School. For Ikaria was reputed to have been the first abode in Attica of the god Dionysos, the birthplace of Thespis, and the original home of Greek drama.

As in the case of other ancient demes of Attica, the precise locality of Ikaria had long been the subject of controversy among geographers and travellers in Greece. These conjectures and arguments, quoted by the late Prof. Merriam at length, are typical of antiquarian controversies based upon mere theory and assumption; but they are usually disposed of in the end by demonstrations which are as simple as they are indisputable.

In the spring of 1887, Prof. Milchhöffer undertook an exploring journey through Attica, preparative of the text accompanying the monumental "Karten von Attika" of the German staff. In his search for inscriptions of topographical interest, he found rich materials imbedded in the walls of ruined chapels, built up of ancient fragments. He thus succeeded in determining with certainty the locality of several ancient demes. On May 9, returning from Marathon to Kephisia, he took the unusual route by the valley of Rapedosa along the northeastern declivity of Mount Pentelicus, and soon found himself in one of the most lovely and secluded spots in Attica. Here, in a thick wood, is a spot known to this day as "Dionysos"; and in a grove of pines and ivy, such as the service of the god would have demanded, are the ruins of a small, but remarkable, Byzantine church. Some fragments of beautifully ornamented Byzantine slabs show that a still earlier and probably larger church stood here. The tolerably well preserved walls of the ruin, about six feet high, are built almost entirely of large blocks of Pentelic marble, evidently taken from an ancient structure, and include the jambs and supports of doors. Other fragments are strewn about. To form the apse of the church a semicircular choragic monu-ment had been utilized, the architrave of which, apparently discarded in the process, and lying near, bore an inscription which has been published by Chandler. Among the ruins Milchhöffer now discovered another inscription, infinitely more important, since it recorded a dedi-cation to Dionysos by "Kephisos, son of Timarchos of Ikaria." This, coupled with the modern name of the place, left no doubt in his mind that he had hit upon the much-debated locality of Ikaria; and he announced his discovery in the "Berliner philologische Wochenschrift" of June 18, 1887.

A hundred and twenty years earlier, Chandler, while journeying from Athens to Marathon, had been attracted to this very spot by in-formation as to the existence of the above-mentioned inscription; and he then wrote:—

"We penetrated into a lonely recess and came to a small ruined church of St. Dionysius, standing on the marble heap of a trophy or monument, erected for some victory obtained by three persons named Ænias, Xanthippus, and Xan-thicles. The inscription is on a long stone lying near." ("Travels in Greece," p. 160.)

Chandler, nevertheless, did not suspect how narrowly he had missed the elucidation of one of the most contested points in Attic topography. Some eight years before Chandler, Stuart had drawn up, while in Athens, a list of "Modern names of towns, villages, monasteries, and farms, with their ancient names," which he prefixed to the third volume of his "Antiquities of Athens." In it he writes: "Dionys (modern) = Dio-nysia (ancient), between Stamati and Cephisia. A *metoche* [pendant] of Cyriani [*sic*, *i. e.*, Kæsariané] on the foot of Pentelicus near Stamati." He further quotes a passage from Suidas anent the Athenian festival of Dionysia, which Stuart evidently associated in his mind with the name of the place. But he also did not suspect its identity with ancient Ikaria; for the spot is not marked on his map. It figures for the first time on the map of Greece published by the French staff shortly after the establishment of the kingdom; and to this fact F. Lenormant refers ("Recherches archéol. à Eleusis," 1862, p. 243) when he goes on to say that, on the road from Rapedosa to Stamata,

"one meets the ruins of a small mediæval monastery to which the peasants of the mountain give to this day the name of 'Dionyso.' This monastery, which is mentioned by none of the learned who have treated of the geography of Attica, is shown only on the fine map of the French staff. The name it has preserved to the present time is undoubtedly connected with the ancient tradition which re-corded the sojourn of Bacchus in that district."

Lenormant, who also did not dream how near Ikaria he had been, does not mention the fact,—apparently known to few archæologists, although of great service in the identification of classic localities,— that in Greece churches erected on the sites of ancient temples were almost invariably dedicated to the saint whose attributes in Christian hagiography corresponded to the character of the divinity the worship of which Christianity had there supplanted, or whose name recalled that of the heathen god there formerly honored. In the present case, as Chandler clearly states, the small ruined church was dedicated to St. Dionysius, the Areopagite.

The summer resort of Kephisia, on the western extremity of Mount Pentelicus, is forty-five minutes by rail from Athens. Thence a stiff walk of an hour, through groves of pines and masses of arbutus and oleander, brings the traveller in view of the snow-clad Dirphys and the chain of mountains beyond—a continuous sweep of alpine grandeur that makes one forget all weariness of body in the exaltation of the moment. After a further walk of more than an hour one enters the "lonely recess," shaded by majestic plane-trees, which thrive on the perennial stream that flows in the glen close by. "The scenery," adds Prof. Merriam, "is in harmony with the twofold side of the worship of Dionysos, the gay and joyous, the sad and mournful, and is aptly fitted to inspire a Susarion and a Thespis. The spot is full of Theocritean dignity and simplicity." The region thus described is some twelve hundred feet above the sea; and, although the vine is not now cultivated there, the careful terracing of the ground below points to the existence in days gone by of a widespread viniculture, with which the cult of Dionysos and the legend of Ikarios are intimately connected.

Put in a few words, this legend personifies the heroic type of the Athenian farmer in Ikaria, who is visited by the god and is taught the culture of the vine and the art of wine-making. Ikarios then offers to Dionysos a goat that had injured the vine; and his inflated skin is tossed about in the sports and dances which the joys of wine-drinking provoke. Travelling through the country, Ikarios next proclaims the new cult, and offers far and wide the unmixed gift of the god. But the friends of the shepherds who had drunk themselves into a stupor, thinking Ikarios had poisoned them, kill him, only to lament the crime when the supposed victims begin to grow sober. Erigone, the daughter of Ikarios, overpowered with grief at her father's death, hangs herself by his tomb. Ikarios is now revered as the eponymous hero and mythical king of the township, the mournful dirge of the "Linos" being chanted in his honor; while the woes of Erigone are recited in a deeply plaintive song called "Aletis." Thus, the rural festival of the Dionysia, held yearly on the completion of the vintage, is instituted. The rough dances and mummeries gradually ripen into plays enacted by buffoons; and Ikaria becomes celebrated for her choruses and choreographic representations. Attracted here from Megara, Susarion upraised these rude performances by an infusion of the comic talent of the Megarians, and thus created comedy; while Thespis, a native of Ikaria, inspired by the mournful side of the legend, elaborated the tragic form of the drama. This origin of the two great branches of dramatic art is indicated in the words of Athenæus (ii. 40): "From strong-drinking came the invention of tragedy and comedy in the Attic Ikaria at the very time of vintage." Thenceforward Thespis was honored as the father of the Attic theatre; and dramatic art, the great invention of the Ikarians,—being the outgrowth of their worship of Dionysos,—became part of the service paid to the god throughout Greece. In Athens, especially, the great Dionysia were celebrated with much pomp; scenes from the Ikarian legend were represented in the reliefs of the Dionysiac theatre; and the priest of the god occupied there the seat of honor.

This short account makes manifest the interest attaching to the site of Ikaria, and also the importance of ascertaining all that the spot itself could reveal in connection with the early growth of the drama. It was an enviable task which thus fell to the lot of the American School; and it was prosecuted with zeal and signal success. Never has an exploration yielded more readily or more abundantly results of such importance, with so small an outlay of money or labor. "The work," we are told, "has been like the opening of a great chest of hidden and forgotten treasures." The site was the property of Mr. A. Heliopoulos, British Vice-Consul at Aivali, in Asia Minor; permission to excavate was readily granted; and on January 30, 1888, Mr. C. D. Buck, of Yale, taking a hammock and some provisions, established himself in an untenanted and the only house in the valley, and, with but half a dozen workmen at first, continued operations up to March 19. The exploration was resumed on November 13, and was brought to a close in the second week of the following January.

The first step was to take down the walls of the ruined church, which at once yielded a mass of fragments of reliefs, statues, inscriptions, architraves, and other architectural pieces. From among these were recovered the wall-blocks and flat roof-pieces belonging to the semicircular choragic monument, referred to by Chandler, of which only two courses were still standing. It was thus possible to arrive at an approximately accurate reconstruction of the whole, with the exception of the ornamentation of the roof, which possibly supported a tripod. The inscribed architrave, long known to exist, was found exactly where Chandler had seen it, the thick vegetation around having shielded it from harm; and the American explorers were now enabled to correct Chandler's inaccurate reading of "Ænias" instead of "Hagnias"—the name of one of the three choregi, the patrons of the chorus, who had erected the monument to commemorate their triumph in a tragic competition held in honor of Dionysos. In size the monument would be about two-thirds that of Lysikrates at Athens, if the circle were complete.

As the clearing of the site of the church and of its immediate proximity progressed, the most complete evidence, both artistic and epigraphic, accumulated; placing beyond all doubt the location of Ikaria, and proving it to have remained for many centuries the centre of an active cult of Dionysos. Among the earliest finds were two inscriptions with decrees of the township of Ikaria, the following being a translation of the more important of the two:—

"Callippos was the mover. Voted by the Ikarians to commend and to crown Nikon the town clerk (demarikos); and that the crier shall publicly proclaim that the Ikarians and the township of the Ikarians do crown Nikon with a crown of ivy, for that right well·and duly he hath ordered the festival of Dionysos and the competition. Voted also to commend the patrons of ·the chorus Epikrates and Praxias, and to crown them with a crown of ivy, and further that the crier shall make the same proclamation in regard to them that was ordered for the town clerk."

The orthography of this inscription indicates that the decree is not later than the third, and may be as early as the fourth, century B.C. Two other inscriptions, engraved on boundary stones, were found near the church: the one partaking of the character of a bill of sale; the other having reference to a dowry and to a mortgage involved in its payment. A third contains details of the production of plays. In one of the dedicatory inscriptions of the fourth century occurs the name of the poet whose play was victorious—Nikostratos, whom we know as the younger son of Aristophanes. Aristophanes himself refers, in the "Knights," v. 519, to the many victories of the comic poet Magnes, who had not then (424 B.C.) been long dead. He flourished about a century after Thespis, and was, next to him, the most renowned of

Ikarian dramatists. In all, some twenty inscriptions were here discovered; many of them choragic and of the first importance. Rarely,
if ever, has a site been identified so conclusively by means of inscriptions. Ikaria, when not treated as half mythical, was for centuries
driven from pillar to post through the length and breadth of Attica;
but it has now been located with greater certainty and distinctness
than any other of the Attic rural districts.

Besides the choragic monument, a large quantity of architectural
remains were found, including altars, pedestals, and bases,—many of
these in the course of trial trenches dug across the site. By this
means were unearthed, also, the foundations of several structures the
purpose of which is not clear. Among these, traces of a theatre, properly so called, were not met with; except indeed a rude wall, curved at
the extremities and facing a row of five massive marble seats, as if
intended to enclose an orchestra, or dancing-ground for theatrical representations. The slopes of the hill, rising behind the marble seats,
which were no doubt those of the priests and magistrates, would have
afforded excellent seating for the rural population, who thence would
have had a good view of the orchestra, with, perhaps, a wooden stage
erected for the occasion; and the prospect of the plain of Marathon and
the sea beyond supplied the sort of scenic arrangement the Greeks
loved so dearly. No temple of Dionysos was found; but the numerous votive offerings and inscriptions recovered, as well as the architectural fragments of which the Byzantine church was built, leave no
reasonable doubt that the latter replaced a demolished sanctuary of
the god. Two of the inscriptions found—both of the fifth century—
are of especial interest in regard to the rural worship of Dionysos.
They speak of the money of the god, state the amount in hand, and
make provision for the erection and repair of "the statue."

Portions of this statue are believed to have been traced among the
fragments of statuary found mostly within and around the church.
Beneath the wall, to the north, part of a colossal head or mask of the
bearded Dionysos, of the finest archaic art, was discovered; and, deeper
in the soil, a large fragment of the beard, as well as one of the large
curls, each an inch and a half across, in which the hair over the forehead is arranged. These curls are partly fashioned separately and
fitted into holes, and partly cut out of the block of marble. Similar
holes appear above the row of curls where a garland was attached; and
of this some bronze leaves were found. . The rest of the hair, as well as
the mustache and beard, is treated in a peculiar wavy fashion. Beneath

the floor of the church was next found a colossal archaic seated torso,
preserved from neck to thigh.   A socket in the neck marks the place
where the head, presumably the one just described, was fitted in.   The
sandaled feet were next met with, imbedded in the wall to the right;
and, in other parts of the ruin, the right hand, a portion of the right
leg, and a fragment of the left thigh were discovered.   Between the
thumb and first finger of the hand is a hole into which a cantharus, a
sort of drinking cup,—picked up close by,—fitted perfectly.   Curls
and long hair stream down the back of the torso; and four holes on
the left breast appear to have held some bronze ornament.   The type
bears resemblance to that followed, later, by Alkamenes in his celebrated statue of Dionysos.   Another torso, that of a satyr, of a good
period of art, a bust of a Pan or Silen, reliefs of a goat-sacrifice, a beautiful ivy wreath below a dedicatory inscription to Dionysos,—all found
here,—point to the prevalence of the cult of the god at Ikaria.

Prior to these latter finds, however, the torso of a naked male figure
of sixth-century style, and of the so-called Apollo type, was discovered.
It was followed by a bas-relief of a later period representing Apollo,
with long curls, seated on a round object, painted red, presumably the
omphalos, and holding a lyre, with Artemis and Leto standing behind.
Later, amid the remains of some walls, another relief appeared.   It
again represents a seated Apollo, holding in one hand a twig and in
the other a phiale.   Artemis stands behind; and a worshipper, heavily
draped, approaches the altar in front of the god.   The second relief
bears a dedicatory inscription; and both are notable by the fact that
they are decorated on both sides.   These finds indicated that, besides
the cult of Dionysos, the Ikarians must have practised also the worship
of Apollo Pythius, said to have been introduced to Athens from
Marathon.   This conjecture was presently confirmed by the discovery
of a marble threshold, which bore, in letters of the fourth century,
these words: "The Pythion of the Ikarians."   This inscription, the
more remarkable as being a unique instance of the "labelling" of a
Greek temple, gained greatly in importance when, shortly afterwards,
the scanty remains of the temple itself, to which it referred, were
laid bare.

The other sculptured remains yielded by these excavations number
some twenty-five pieces; including a very pretty female head and three
sepulchral bas-reliefs in excellent preservation.   But the most important of all is an archaic stele representing, in low relief of most
delicate and beautiful workmanship, a warrior holding a spear.   At

first sight it appears to be an exact replica of the famous Aristion stele, discovered in 1839 in another part of Attica, and now treasured in the Central Museum; but on closer inspection it reveals slight differences, indicative of a somewhat later style. It also shows but faint traces of coloring; whereas on the Aristion stele, which is assigned to the early part of the fifth century, the coloring is still vivid. It was found serving as a door-sill at the entrance of the church,—fortunately with the sculptured face downwards. Though broken into three parts, it is perfect, with the exception of the head.

As the work progressed, the field of operations extended, and a thorough exploration became a much greater undertaking than was originally expected. It cannot be said that the site has been exhausted. It still invites a closer and more systematic examination. Yet, within the space of three months, with but a few workmen, and at a total outlay of some $600, an important museum of antiquities was formed; and the monuments and inscriptions unearthed, dating from the sixth century B.C. to late Roman times, reveal to us the public and private life of an important centre in Attica, during a period of seven or eight centuries. Well might the late Prof. Curtius declare, at a meeting of the German Institute at Berlin, that these discoveries are "epoch-making." As the site excavated was private property, a portion of the objects found went to the state and a part to the owner; the latter refusing to sell them to the Government, but holding himself responsible for their safe keeping. They have been removed to Stamata, the residence of Mr. Heliopoulos.

At the very outset of the excavations at Ikaria, a third site was explored. The workmen led Mr. Buck two miles to the west of the valley on a ridge, where they said a stone existed "with flowers and letters on it." A grave, partially open, was found here, and near it the torso of a seated woman in high relief, the head of which had been broken off and sent to Germany! One of the sides of the grave was formed by a sepulchral stele which bore two rosettes and an inscription of the fourth century, recording the names of the two deceased: one an Ikarian, and the other an inhabitant of Plotheia. The proximity of the latter deme to that of Ikaria had been surmised, but was now rendered almost certain. Fortunately, fresh light was soon forthcoming on this point, as well as on the location of another deme,—that of Semachidæ.

A short distance from the point just spoken of, and a little beyond the ridge which shuts in on the north the valley leading to Ikaria, lies the village of Stamata, half-way between Kephisia and Marathon. In the vicinity of the older and now abandoned site of that village three ruined churches are to be seen. One of these, which Mr. Buck visited in November, 1888, promised to yield important information, built up, as it was, of débris collected indiscriminately from ancient structures. Mr. H. S. Washington, of Yale, who had accompanied Mr. Buck, took charge of this exploration on December 27, he generously providing the necessary funds. A couple of days' work sufficed to bring to light, besides various other pieces of sculpture, a very fine and well preserved female torso, larger than life, of archaic workmanship, as well as four inscriptions which satisfactorily established this to have been the chief centre of the hitherto doubtful deme of Plotheia. That of Semachidæ must therefore have been situated in the immediate vicinity.

Before proceeding farther afield, reference must here be made to an exploration which, though undertaken six years later than the Bœotian excavations dealt with at the conclusion of this article, is intimately connected, in point of topography and history, with the work just recorded. Prof. Merriam, under whose directorship of the School the excavations at Ikaria were carried out, encouraged by their brilliant results, had cherished the project of exploring another neighboring locality. He was urged by suggestions similar to those which had led him to St. Dionysius. Not far from that spot, about two and a half miles from the field of Marathon, and eighteen miles from Athens, a small valley, now known by the name of " Koukounari " (a pine-cone), is ensconced at the foot of Pentelicus. Plentiful tile fragments and the rich loam with which the place is covered—a rare feature in Attica—had attracted the attention of Dr. Milchhöffer, who surmised that this must have been the seat of an ancient deme of some importance. His conjecture was strengthened when, from the heap of stones surrounding a ruined church and cloister situated on a narrow and low foot-hill in the valley, he drew the fragments of two votive reliefs. He was now of opinion that the cloister was established on the site of an ancient sanctuary; and he thus wrote in his " Text zu Karten von Attika " (p. 58): " The spot, from its situation and the nature of the soil, promises to the excavator an easy and abundant reward."

Encouraged by this promise, Prof. Merriam, after an absence of six years, returned to Athens, eager to reap new triumphs in that world which he loved so much, and with which he was so intimately acquainted. Though ailing, he could not be deterred from ascending once more the rock of the Acropolis, as if bound on a pilgrimage to the shrine that centred his love and admiration. There he contracted a chill; and he died on the fourth day, leaving a void in American scholarship not to be easily filled, and a gap in the ranks of the best friends of Greece. He was a scholar of the ideal type, conscientious and accurate in research, reprobating superficiality, and delighting in that "infinite capacity for taking pains," which Carlyle considered identical with genius.

The appropriation of $200, which he had obtained from the American Institute of Archæology for the purpose of excavating Koukounari, was now entrusted to Prof. R. Richardson, with the request that he undertake the exploration as a memorial service. Under his intelligent superintendence, therefore, work was commenced on February 15, 1895, and was continued with a force of thirty men for four days, Messrs. W. A. Elliott and Th. W. Heermance sharing in the work, with all the hardships which the snow and winter cold in that high region entailed. The soil was soaked with the rains; and its handling became extremely difficult. Prof. Richardson was not sanguine as to the yield of the "old material" of which Milchhöffer speaks as being interspersed in the walls of the ruined buildings; but, in compliance with the wishes of Mr. Heliopoulos, the owner of the property, and in order to carry out the plan of Prof. Merriam, he took down the south and west walls, which were the most dilapidated. Only an anthemion, forming the apex of a sepulchral stele, was found imbedded in these walls. Some other blocks, of the coarse marble quarried from the adjoining hill, were found worked in a manner strikingly similar to the blocks of the same inferior Pentelic stone noticeable in the wall of Themistocles, by the Dipylon Gate at Athens. The door-posts of the church are more carefully wrought, and must have formed parts of some older and nobler building.

The search made outside the church proved more fruitful in evidence corroborative of Milchhöffer's belief that a temple had stood near. No foundations of such a structure were traced; but in the stone-heaps two more fragments of votive reliefs were found: the one, a horse's head,—which, however, does not agree with Milchhöffer's fragment representing a span of horses,—the other, a draped trunk of a male figure seated on an elaborate throne, of excellent workmanship. Eight trenches were next dug down to the virgin soil and bed-rock of the rising ground on which the cloister stood; and in these was discovered a third and important fragmentary relief. It contains the trunks of three persons,—two of majestic pose. The one to the left is nude: the other, draped, is apparently a female figure, with the right hand extended toward the lip of the nude figure. In the extreme end stands a smaller figure, probably a worshipper. From the joint hands of the two larger figures proceeds downward what seems to be a club. These details are essential, as bearing out Milchhöffer's theory that here lay the deme of Hekale. The relief appears to represent the meeting of Theseus and Hekale, as related by Plutarch ("Theseus," c. 14). A poor old woman, tradition said, befriended and entertained the young hero when he sallied forth to rid the country of the Marathonian bull; and she vowed to offer up sacrifices for his success. She died, however, before he returned; and Theseus therefore ordered the in-habitants of the Tetrapolis of Marathon regularly to offer up sacrifices to Zeus Hekaleius in honor of the good Hekale, after whom the deme, where her sanctuary stood, was also named.

In connection with this relief, Milchhöffer's conjecture that this deme lay here gained greatly in strength by the discovery, made during the very first half-hour of the exploration, of an inscription of exceptional importance. Between the church and the cloister a slab of Pentelic marble was found, originally inscribed on both sides; but as it had been reduced to serve as a door-sill, the exposed face had been trodden almost smooth. On the under-face, however, fifty-six lines, engraved in two columns, are still clearly legible. Though the beginning and the end of the inscription are broken off, the remaining text, which Prof. Richardson has published, accompanied with learned commentaries, shows it to be of the order of "sacrificial calendar" inscriptions, such as the Greeks set up in places where sacrifices were made very frequently. Lysias, in his oration (xxx. 17) against Nikom-achos, speaks of sacrifices offered according to the prescriptions of similar tablets, fragments of which had been recovered in the course of previous excavations; but this is by far the most complete and important specimen of the kind yet found. It enumerates, within its extant portion, no less than thirty-nine divinities, the names of several of which do not occur elsewhere; it prescribes the animals, etc. to be offered as sacrifices, and states the prices to be paid. This last feature alone is a valuable contribution to the history of prices of commodities in ancient Greece. With regard however to the identi-fication of the locality,—since the presumption is strong that so large a stele has remained where it was originally set up,—the inscription defines the sacrifice offered "by the inhabitants of the Tetrapolis" and repeatedly refers to the "hero" and the "heroine." So that, although the name of Hekale does not appear in the extant portion, it may, very probably, have been recorded in the missing preamble. The form of the letters and the style of orthography place the date of the inscription between 440 and 360 B.C. These not inconsiderable results—especially the importance of the inscription—had decided Prof. Richardson to resume and complete the exploration of Koukounari at some later season; particularly as only half the appropriation had been expended in the first attempt.

When the excavations of Ikaria and Stamata were brought to a close, the task of the American explorers was considered as ended in Attica; and their interest was centred in the adjoining province of Bœotia. The attention of archæologists had already been drawn to that quarter by a number of unusual objects—the outcome of surreptitious excavations—which dealers in antiquities had been offering for some time previously in the market of Athens. In the spring of 1888, the German School had undertaken some search near Thebes, in connection with the imperfectly known worship of the Kabeiroi, to which those objects related. And, consequently, with the recommendation of the Ephor-General of Antiquities, the American School applied, in the winter of 1888, and obtained permission of the Greek Government, to explore the sites of Anthedon and Thisbe.

The ancient geographer, Stephanus of Byzantium, explains the name of Anthedon by the abundance of flowers which remains to this day a distinguishing feature of the locality. Homer ("Iliad," ii. 508) first speaks of the town as the farthermost in Bœotia. Pausanias, Strabo, Theolytus,—the last-mentioned a poet quoted by Athenæus (vii. 296),—and the author of the description of Greece commonly attributed to Dikæarchos, refer to Anthedon as situated on the Euripus, the strait of Eubœa, at the foot of Mount Messapion, seventy stadia from Chalcis and a hundred and sixty from Thebes. These indications were sufficient to enable the most critical of modern travellers in Greece, Colonel Leake ("Trav. in N. Greece," 271–5), to identify the site by the remains of certain walls which he observed about a mile and a half to the north of the village of Loukisi; which latter he connects with the Nisa of Homer. Leake, whose inferences were confirmed by subsequent travellers, gives a sketch-plan of the site, which served as an initial guide to the American explorers.

The pseudo-Dikæarchos speaks of Anthedon as a small town with an *agora* surrounded by a double portico, and planted with trees. Pausanias refers to the sacred grove and sanctuary of the Kabeiroi "somewhere about the centre of the city"; close to it he places the temple of Demeter and Kora; outside the walls, that of Dionysos, with a statue in marble; and finally, near the sea, the so-called Leap of Glaucus, which, as Mr. Buck thinks, "was probably a natural cliff like the numerous Lovers' Leaps on our eastern coast";—most likely the abrupt declivity of the rock of the Acropolis facing the sea. Glaucus, Pausanius explains, was a fisherman of Anthedon, but was metamorphosed into a maritime deity, predicting the future, and delivering oracular responses which seafaring and other men believed. From him the Anthedonii derived their origin; and, like him, they led the lives of sailors, fishermen, and shipwrights. That they were of a different race than the rest of the Bœotians is certain; but the fact that they ultimately joined the Bœotian League has been established by one of the inscriptions recently unearthed.

Work on the site was begun on March 5, 1889, under Mr. J. C. Rolfe, of Harvard, son of the well-known Shakespearian scholar, and was continued, with some twenty-five workmen, for three weeks; Mr. C. D. Buck being also present. The entire area of the ancient town, which was soon ascertained to be more extensive from south to north than indicated in Leake's plan, was under cultivation as grain-fields. The exploration therefore was started at the "platform" by the sea; and fourteen trenches were dug in different directions from it inward. The foundations of a most extensive and intricate structure, connected with the platform, were thus unearthed; but nothing was found indicative of its character or purpose. It covers so large a stretch of ground that a visitor to the excavations thought it must be the town itself. Leake styled the remains, as he saw them, "a public building"; but the most reasonable surmise is that they were those of the *agora* and *stoa*. The foundations belong to a good Greek period; but some of the walls are of later and inferior workmanship. In the southern portion a beautiful Roman mosaic floor was laid bare.

As the area of the town contained no other visible remnant that could serve as guide to further search, a very long trench, with two lateral branches, was now dug across, from the southern slope of the Acropolis to the city walls, in the hope of coming upon the temple of the Kabeiroi. This work, as well as some trials made on the hill of the Acropolis, yielded no results; but an inspection of the city walls revealed more extensive remains than those indicated by Leake. A small hill, which rises immediately outside these walls, seemed a promising spot on which to seek for the temple of Dionysos; since the locality agreed with the language of Pausanias. Three trenches were consequently opened, in one of which certain foundations were met with; and these, having been followed up and cleared of earth, showed the substructure of a very small temple built of well cut blocks of the local porous stone. A Doric capital and the unfluted drum of a column, lying near, strengthened the belief that this must have been the site of the shrine of Dionysos. A further trial was made on a low hill, east of the town, on the road to Chalcis, where fragments of Doric architecture—one piece still retaining traces of color—and a number of inscriptions were unearthed. Two of these record dedications to Artemis Eilithyia, the goddess aiding women in child-bed; and these inscriptions, coupled with the architectural remains discovered, point to the existence of a temple of that divinity in this neighborhood.

In one of the trenches, which was carried a hundred feet beyond the temple of Dionysos, a collection of some twenty-five implements and small ornaments was found, together with sheet bronze and a quantity of bronze slag,—evidently remnants of a bronze-smith's factory. These objects, which are now exhibited in the Central Museum at Athens, include two-edged axes, chisels, drills, an awl, a sickle-like razor, and a large variety of knives. Some, similar to those recently discovered on the Acropolis of Athens are used; while others are apparently fresh from the hands of the maker. But the most considerable results of these excavations are the inscriptions. Hitherto only one inscription from Anthedon was known to exist. No less than sixty are now available for study; ranging from the fifth century B.C. to the second century of our era. Most of these are very short; but they are all of the highest importance, elucidating and supplementing, as they do, the local peculiarities of the Bœotian dialect.

The work at Anthedon, as it will have been seen, was rather promiscuous, and was considered as "merely experimental." While it was still in progress, Mr. Rolfe, entrusting the further superintendence to Mr. Buck, undertook, on March 27, at the head of fifteen men, the exploration of Thisbe, the site of which he had examined a week earlier. Leake ("Northern Greece," ii. 506) had identified the modern village of Kakosia with the ancient Thisbe. It stands at a small distance from the Gulf of Corinth, under the southern slope of Helicon,

"between two great summits of the mountain, which rise majestically above the vale, clothed with trees in the upper part and covered with snow at the top. . . The modern village lies in a little hollow surrounded on all sides by low cliffs. . . The walls of Thisbe were about a mile in circuit, following the crest of the cliffs, and are chiefly preserved at the southeast."

Leake further describes the masonry of these walls, the remains of a mole or causeway across the marshy plain to the south, as also the ruin of a Hellenic tower or station on a ridge looking down upon the port of Thisbe, now known as Vathỳ ("the deep"),—a beautiful little harbor encircled by rocks and wooded hills. These, as well as the islands beyond, are to this day peopled by flocks of the wild doves which, as Strabo and Stephanus of Byzantium state, earned for Thisbe the Homeric designation of *polytreron*, "abounding in doves" ("Iliad," ii. 502). Both Ovid ("Metam.," xi. 300) and Statius ("Thebaid," vii. 261) speak of the Thisbæan doves; and Leake found them to be equally plentiful in the woods around Kakosia. Pausanias refers to the temple of Herakles at Thisbe, and to the statue of the hero which it enshrined.

Though the modern settlement is a small one, it must have been a place of considerable importance—owing no doubt to its strong defensive position—in Byzantine times. No less than twenty churches of that epoch, most of them now in ruins, may be counted on the site. Around one of these, the church of St. Luke,—standing within the village, but outside the ancient walls,—Mr. Rolfe dug some trenches, which yielded only a pillar of very fine Byzantine workmanship and ornamentation. The walls of two other ruined churches were taken down; and here some inscribed tombstones were found. In all, fifteen inscriptions were recovered; and they are published by Messrs. Rolfe and Tarbell in the fifth volume of the "Papers." The earliest publication of a Thisbæan inscription is due to the Greek Meletius, who visited the spot a century before Leake. The original stone of this inscription, Leake was unable to find; but he transcribed four other engraved slabs. The abundant yield of inscriptions, even after so cursory and superficial a search, was full of promise. But the exploration of Thisbe also was confined to tentative operations only. It was explained that "as the modern village stands directly on the ancient site, extensive excavations must involve considerable expense." The explorers therefore decided to concentrate all their energies on the more attractive site of Plataia, which had been included in the concession made to them to excavate at Anthedon and Thisbe. And to Plataia I shall follow them in my next article.

J. GENNADIUS.

MR. CLEVELAND AND THE SENATE.

PRESIDENT CLEVELAND'S administration of eight interrupted years draws to its close. And eventful years they have been indeed; full of national difficulty and danger, of official trial, temptation, and discouragement, and yet, as the fair-minded of all political prepossessions must admit, stamped by an executive purpose, honorable, heroic, and conservative of the public interests.

Mr. Cleveland has long been a sturdy and striking figure in our politics. Whether, on the whole, successful or unsuccessful in his national policy, he must, at all events, be pronounced true and consistent to the grand principles which brought him twice into power, turning neither to the right nor to the left for adventitious favors. If ever open to censure as parcelling out some great offices to pacify unworthy feudatories, he has filled the best places for the most part with the best men, while in the lesser patronage that falls to a President he has done more than all his predecessors combined to place the civil service permanently above the reach of scrambling and scandalous jobbery. If, a year ago, he was execrated by many who had once praised him for outbidding, as they thought, the jingoism of Congress in menacing England with war, he has since conducted that Venezuelan issue to so happy an adjustment that the war clouds have cleared altogether and friendship with the mother country is reëstablished on surer foundations than ever before, under the auspices of an arbitration treaty which, if confirmed by the Senate, opens that new dawn of justice and humanity in the dealings of nations for which kings and prophets waited. For all the triumphs, external and internal, of his two administrations, Mr. Cleveland deserves the chief praise; in all the disappointments, and they are many, he has borne the chief obloquy. The wisest majority of our people, regardless of party ties, have learned to trust him for his steadfastness to principle, his prudence, his regard for the material needs of business, and his personal integrity. He has held the helm of state with a strong hand. He has saved us from many dangers, at his own seeming sacrifice. Unless we greatly mistake, his sure pilotage will be missed for many years to come. He is the only man of his party faith for nearly two generations who has been trusted with the guidance of this Union; and, unless the politicians of that party realize better their own need of leaders who are true Democrats and not levellers of prosperity, he is likely to prove the last of their candidates installed at the White House for a generation longer.

One source of Mr. Cleveland's strength and dignity in supreme office appears in the rare character and ability which he has brought into his cabinet under each administration. Democrats more deserving of the country's confidence could hardly be found than such as Bayard, Manning, Fairchild, and Whitney, during his first term; or Gresham, Olney, Carlisle, Wilson,—indeed one might name almost the whole list,—of his second. They were not only among the safest and best of representative democracy; they were statesmen besides, men of comprehensiveness in action by whose side the twaddlers and tricky managers of a political sect, never without lesser chiefs to blush for, must forever dwarf by comparison. The inability of such administration advisers to hold recent Congresses in smooth coöperation must be largely ascribed to adverse circumstances; perhaps in part to the stern attitude of the President himself, and still more to a policy which did not please the weather-wise of his party in the Senate. It is invidious to complain that some of these Presidential advisers were unused to Congressional ways; for Whitney, Manning, Lamont, and others of these Cleveland cabinets—who never sat in Congress in their lives—have worked the two Houses with a readier touch than Bayard or Carlisle, men whom, of all Democrats, one would have thought the most likely, just after leaving the Senate, to influence that body, and indeed both branches. President Cleveland's surviving associates of the past four years have shared loyally the fortunes and misfortunes of their chief; they now go together into political retirement, preferring firm and stable principle to mercurial popularity. Democracy as a responsible organism in the conduct of this Union is, for the present, overwhelmed.

With such leaders in exile among their opponents, Republicans may well rejoice. Their renewed opportunity for a long sway of the political sceptre is a bright one; and only the repetition of old follies, or an imbecile delay in restoring public and private credit and prosperity by wise legislation can harm the supremacy of that historical party for a long time. If overthrown four years hence under these new conditions of power, it will be by some essentially new party, to whose untried leaders a long-suffering and tossing community turns in despair. Never again will the plain people trust the delirium-tremens combination that, last summer, in the Chicago convention, profaned the sacred name of Democrat by refusing. to this truly democratic administration even a perfunctory tribute of valedictory praise for having striven to fulfil the party pledges given solemnly in convention four years earlier. Organized folly, if once invested with power, can, unquestionably, accomplish much toward impoverishing the rich and pauperizing the poor; but one might as well place a hammer and glass mirror in a young child's hands as expect such a coalition to manage finance or adjust those delicate relations of labor and capital which must always be mutual. We have enough public servants who will turn from the intricate problems of trade and finance, which their minds can never grasp, to the more congenial study of building up political capital and circulating the spoils of office; who are ready to tie up measures for the public welfare in order to gratify a personal spite or vanity; who show themselves either bosses or the minions of a boss; who, when revenue and economy are wanted, will increase wasteful expenditures and throw open the doors to hoggish protection; who rail at the sensitiveness of other nations to our interference in their domestic quarrels, forgetting the popular temper in America when France and England proposed to end the inhuman bloodshed of our own civil war; who, especially if dwellers far inland, are quite ready to plunge this country into a reckless war with Europe for an uncertain gain, before providing prudent coast defences on the Atlantic shore, and while the treasury staggers already under the incumbrance of our last war's pensions; and who, after the overblown bubbles of prosperity have collapsed, are ready to kick the bucket of common sense, hoping that somehow if things are only stirred up prosperity will come back. Of such miscalled statesmen we have enough and to spare at the present time; but of statesmen who comprehend what is needful for the people, and who stand up to their comprehension, the material is quite too scanty to be wasted.

Mr. Cleveland has stood for strong prerogatives as an Executive; and this again has been partly compelled by circumstances and by his frequent isolation from Congressional support. So in turn were those former great popular chieftains, Jefferson and Jackson, strong Executives, of whose honest sincerity in the democratic faith he partakes, while differing much in methods and character from either of them. Jefferson had the magnetism of recognized superiority and a plastic touch, such as moulded the Legislature implicitly to his will. Jackson forced and defied Congress, or rather the Senatorial branch of it, which

long possessed consummate leaders openly opposed to him; but, determined to have his own way, he used the whole force of his military
popularity and of the dispensation of patronage with bold, unsparing,
and even unscrupulous effect to exalt his personal friends in power and
displace all enemies.   Cleveland, on the other hand, has been faithful
and earnest for correct principles,—as posterity will some day acknowledge,—and the sympathy of the people has strengthened him against
his foes among the politicians; but in Jeffersonian tact he has been
greatly wanting; while to the rude Jacksonian push his self-restraint
and magnanimous nature prove a constant obstacle.   Principles more
than places have interested him; and, leaving his enemies to goad and
torment him without hindrance, he has used as his great compelling
force upon Congress, wherever he has used force at all, the pressure of
external public opinion.   On occasion, as in the repeal of the silver-
purchase act, he has used that force with telling effect; but latterly in so
exhausting an antagonism—for a man of his lofty endeavors and lofty
manner of putting things is sure to antagonize—he has been blocked
by his enemies and discomfited.   His fight with Congress, and an exasperating Senate more especially—that body which has so much to do
with approving or disapproving treaties and appointments—has been
almost incessant; during his first and more successful term it was with
a controlling majority of political opponents; but during his second
with a malignant faction rather of his own party.   How deep-set the
cause of opposition in this latter period we could only realize when the
Chicago convention showed the current that had set for socialism and
free silver at the South and West; and yet the schism was in some
sense that of personal resistance to a President who was autocratic for
law and order.   As a final consequence Mr. Cleveland has schooled
himself to a partial defeat.   Most of his grand achievements of the past
four years have been less by way of reform than in salutary constraint.
The bow of promise which spanned his first truly successful term and
reappeared at an interval has vanished in the terrible gloom of business
depression.   Yet these achievements, and the efforts to achieve, will be
gratefully remembered in coming years; and the only popular regret
will be that so great a statesman had not shown himself equally great
as a politician.

Among the public measures with which this second administration
is permanently identified are some which provoked criticism in various
quarters, as though the President had stretched arrogantly and illegally

his claim of constitutional authority. Most of those issues have ceased greatly to interest. There was first of all the Hawaiian conquest, aided artfully by an American minister for annexation to the Union, shortly before Mr. Cleveland came into office. We who sustained him heartily in his singular policy of sending out a commissioner paramount and blocking the whole game of national aggrandizement, and yet not without strong misgivings as to the feasibility of restoring the dethroned queen, have not ceased to rejoice over the final turn taken in getting rid of the whole troublesome business. If Hawaii comes up again as an incident, under Mr. Cleveland's successor, as perhaps it may, the real legal issue of interest will be, not whether commissioners paramount may be sent out; but whether, under our existing Federal Constitution, and without amendment of any kind, a President may at any time, by a secret negotiation confirmed in the Senate, with perhaps a quorum majority ready in the House to complete the transfer, annex to the United States and admit at discretion as a full State having coequal rights with our present mass of American citizens, Japan or any intermediate island of the Pacific archipelago, without popular appeal by intermediate election or ultimate reference of any sort, and with no change in the Federal organic law. Hitherto it has been supposed that sovereignty resided under our system in the American people, in those already of that description; and though, to be sure, as in the case of Texas, we have been dragged into unwilling war in times past, for the sake of adjacent annexation, we never were so compelled for distant conquest; and indeed, the widest scope of our "manifest destiny" ambition was bounded at farthest by the limits of this ample western continent, which appears to supply range enough for a single written instrument of organic law to unite, under a system which knows no permanent condition but that of co-equal and equally republican States.

Then came the Debs riot at the Central West, which but for the President's prompt intervention with Federal troops might soon have broadened into an organized rebellion against vested property. The constitutionality of that intervention—which so many deprecated—has been affirmed by the Supreme Court with an emphasis that rioters and dilatory State governors will do well to ponder over. Indeed, no constitutional issue is left over this courageous action on Mr. Cleveland's part, except for the late threat of the Altgeld Democracy at Chicago to pack that tribunal with more facile judges and get the decision reversed. The same resort has been threatened for reëstablishing a national income tax—that first grand error of legislation by the House

which came in with Mr. Cleveland, disclosing its socialistic leanings.
As to any permanent tax of the kind, it saddles in theory the cost
of Federal government upon the small fraction of citizens and of
States deemed wealthy, that the great majority of our people may go
exempt; while in practice it would discourage private prosperity,
already burdened with an annual State and municipal tax of the kind,
and so check accumulation as ultimately to drain off the common
resources of a livelihood.   Economy of expenditure is a far-better
public doctrine than increase of revenue for hard times like these.   At
this very day there are premature towns and cities near and beyond the
Rocky Mountains, the headquarters of present discontent, whose running expenses are largely met by oppressive assessments upon non-
residents of the East who invested a few years ago in their boastful
promises and then had to foreclose and take possession.

   Last and latterly we have that new constitutional issue between the
Executive and Senate, provoked by the Cuban Revolution, which involves the delicate decision of belligerent recognition and the risk of
European war.   That discussion is still open and has for our people
an immediate interest.   With all deference to the responsible claims
that have been advanced on either side of the question, it seems to the
present writer that neither the Executive nor Congress can monopolize
public authority, regardless of the other, so far as constitutional right
is concerned; but that their concurrence and coöperation are essential
to new action.   Neither, on the one hand, can Congress appropriately
initiate war or the recognition of a belligerent without the President; nor on the other can the President make war or admit a revolutionary community into the family of independent nations without
Congress.   The exercise of a veto power does not exhaust apparently the
opposing resources of the Executive; nor is Congress confined to passing or refusing to pass a joint resolution; but whenever Executive and
Congress honestly disagree in such foreign policy, negation becomes
the true constitutional result, unless public opinion or a spirit of concession can induce them to coöperate.
   Let us develop the argument somewhat in detail for the remainder
of this article.   During the American Revolution and while the old
Articles of Confederation lasted, all sovereign authority of this Union,
such as it was, vested in the Continental Congress,—a Congress, it will
be remembered, composed of only a single chamber, and, under a

system which ignored popular representation altogether, a body very much like our present Senate in being composed of delegates, chosen usually by a State legislature, who voted simply as the unit (not as now the duplicated units), of the co-equal State represented. To that Congress (which in these days we would consider rather a convention or grand committee) all the functions of war and foreign relations were given; and yet, without an Executive head, those functions were so hard to sustain properly, that a Secretary's bureau was created for a Congressional agency. When the Constitution of 1787 was promulgated for general adoption, with an independent Executive and Judiciary, the practice of European governments was closely imitated. A President headed a new and distinct department of government under the remodelled Union; nor were the framers of our Constitution the less inclined to strengthen the Executive, when Congress itself developed into a bi-cameral body, based in its House upon population, and when, too, it was understood that the first President of the United States to be chosen would equal in dignity and the capacity to rule any crowned head of the civilized world. To the new Congress, then, was left, as before, the fundamental power to declare war; coupled with authority to raise and support armies, to provide and maintain a navy, and to provide for calling forth the militia.[1] For had not the immortal Declaration of 1776 proceeded from a Congress? But as to foreign diplomatic relations and a republican court, the only specific and immediate grant of power was to the President of the United States; it was he alone who was vested with authority to appoint (with the advice and consent of the Senate) "ambassadors, other public ministers, and consuls," "to receive ambassadors and other public ministers"; and (with a two-thirds consent of the Senate) "make treaties."[2] This was no oversight; for the Articles of Confederation had pursued a different course.

Obviously then,—and the whole practice of government has hitherto conformed to that idea—the general management of foreign relations, which so often requires promptness of action and great secrecy in emergencies, besides the balancing of various foreign governments, belongs properly to the Executive branch alone; and, while communicating information to Congress on all such subjects, the President does so with a constant reserve of discretion, often in the strictest confidence, and sometimes for reasons of state refusing specific information altogether. It is the President's function to initiate public action in foreign rela-

[1] Constitution, Art. I, § 8.   [2] Constitution, Art. II, §§ 2, 3.

tions, which requires always the handling of many reins. And since any swerving from the line of strict neutrality in a particular instance is likely to embroil us in various quarters, the President of the United States, as responsible head and agent of the people in such concerns, as, with his cabinet, the best informed and most efficient department of government, as the only one in fact who can originate or negotiate a treaty, has, in every great case involving a national precedent, been relied upon, and usually by a message, to give the first immediate direction to war or to belligerent recognition, whenever Congress stands ready to sustain him. Thus was it with President John Adams in the short but indignant outbreak against the French Republic; with the reluctant Madison in our second declaration of war against Great Britain; with Monroe in recognizing the independence of the Spanish-American Republics; as also when denouncing the schemes of the Holy Alliance; with Jackson in taking the part of Texas revolutionists against Mexico; with Polk in leading up craftily to the Mexican war and then sending to Congress his war message; with Lincoln in dealing with the first civil commotions of 1861. During the Maximilian invasion of Mexico, in the course of our civil war, Secretary Seward applied at discretion the Monroe doctrine, as emergencies might permit; yet Congress was never at real variance with the Executive over that policy. True, Congress declares a war constitutionally and provides its sinews; but unless our Legislature is to take a leap in the dark the formulation of a war policy and its justification must rest upon Executive shoulders. And the vaporings of Congress while the Executive, knowing better the true situation, declines compliance, are never taken by our people very seriously. In older European practice, war and its declaration, as well as diplomacy, are vested in the monarch.

To suppose, for a moment, that Congress wishes active intervention and a war for the conquest of Cuba, while the President from his own point of view conscientiously disapproves the pursuit of such a policy. A joint resolution passes the two Houses, and, after an Executive veto, is sustained by a two-thirds vote. What follows? Our Constitution by its own express terms makes the President commander-in-chief of the army and navy of the United States and of the State militia whenever called into active service.[1] Not an order can lawfully issue for war operations save as he through his own Secretaries of War and the Navy may direct; not a high military officer can be detailed or ap-

[1] Constitution, Art. II, § 2.

pointed save upon his individual choice. If Congress has lawfully declared war, he can just as lawfully manifest his pacific disposition by making a treaty of peace; and if the Senate fails to confirm that treaty he may negotiate another. Or, supposing the immediate point is that of recognizing revolutionists of Spain as belligerents or as an independent republic, the President can, despite mandatory action by Congress, refuse to receive formally a public minister from the would-be nation, or to send a diplomatic functionary in return. It is often through the prudent concert of great powers that such delicate steps are taken at all; and all efforts for such concert lie within the breast of an Executive alone. Congress, to be sure, might impeach and remove summarily from office a President who thus disobeyed; but this would be a highly perilous and almost revolutionary proceeding in any grave crisis, unless the people heartily sympathized with that body, which would rarely happen if the President were believed honest in his convictions of pacific duty. And even if he were removed, the only effect would be to experiment with the constitutional discretion of the Vice-President or other person next in Executive succession, Congress remaining as much out of active control of the situation of the army and navy and of diplomacy as before.

But suppose, on the other hand, that the President, and not Congress, were obstinately bent upon such war or recognition. Though, of course, he might goad to desperation the foreign power he meant to humiliate, so as practically to force hostilities, a joint resolution by Congress, rebuking such a policy, might reconcile that power and smooth the situation; and unquestionably no Executive has the constitutional right to make active war until Congress at its own discretion has formally declared it. Any such Legislature, fitly representing the American sentiment, may rightfully announce its own views of a general foreign policy and strive by enlisting public opinion upon its side to compel the Executive to conform to them. It may, furthermore, under its powers to regulate commerce and raise a revenue, pass such laws over an Executive veto, as may discriminate, retaliate, or otherwise promote ends adverse to those of the Executive, and bind the President to enforce such laws. It may withhold appropriations for army or navy or appropriate under a proviso. It may refuse to aid an increase of the military establishment. And while the Senate may fail to confirm any Presidential nominations to office, or may reject treaties by the wholesale while such collision lasts, Congress in its two branches may hamper and embarrass an obstinate Executive in various ways by its enactments without transcending its constitutional powers at all. A fire of resolves making inquest may be kept up by the House; and then, as a last resort, comes impeachment once more; for it is a much easier matter to impeach and remove a President who is trying to plunge the people into a needless and unpopular war than to put out a President who tries honorably his best to prevent one that Congress is bent upon. These same considerations apply in only a lesser degree where the Executive effort which opposes Congress is to make a premature recognition of foreign independence that may compromise the good faith or jeopardize the peace of this Union. In this latter case, while a President may stand upon his constitutional privilege to receive or exchange public ministers, and to institute treaties and foreign relations with the world, Congress may quite as obstinately express its own dissent and refuse to appropriate money for maintaining any such diplomatic relations. Recognition may be with the President, as a formal act; but, where more than a mere recognition of belligerency abroad, it avails little against Congressional resistance.

It would seem, then, a fair conclusion, from the general scope and expression of our Federal organic law, that concurrence and coöperation are highly needful on the part of Executive and Congress, wherever a critical foreign situation is under discussion; and that neither department of government may rightfully or prudently ignore the other in shaping out results. I have of course assumed that on either side the disposition is, honestly and not recklessly or wantonly, to advance the permanent welfare of our people, and to conform to that standard of justice, forbearance, and considerateness toward other nations that we ask other nations to observe toward us in return.

JAMES SCHOULER.

KANSAS: ITS PRESENT AND ITS FUTURE.

TEN years ago, during the boom, when everything in Kansas was running on full time, and when "slam-bang" was the watchword, the head of a great railway system in the State, who had been suddenly called to New York, instructed his private secretary to select and appoint a president and a general manager for a branch road which the greater system had casually swallowed. When the chief returned, he noticed that the new men were not on duty. The private secretary explained that he had not made the appointments because he could not find the right kind of men. "The right kind of men!" cried the superior officer, indignantly. "The right kind of men! Well, in the name of Heaven, what kind of men were you looking for? Men with green ears, striped backs, and iridescent tail-feathers?"

That is the kind of men which the average citizen of the Republic expects to find in Kansas; and this is where the average citizen of the Republic is fooled. Anyone who cares to plod through the mazes of the census figures may learn that in intelligence the Kansas man is a grade or two above the average man; that the Kansas man buys a book or two more, owns a cabinet organ or two more, a watch or two more, reads a newspaper or two more, works a sulky-plow or two more, a reaper and a harvester or two more, rides on a railroad or two more, than the average man in the nation. He looks like a human being; on ordinary topics talks like a human being; loves with a human heart; and fights with human valor. Yet of late, when the Kansas man has flitted down the election-tables, there has been the mystifying apparition of the gentleman with green ears, striped back, and iridescent tail-feathers. The spectacle is startling enough to merit the attention which it attracts. Yet the phenomenon has its natural causes; and when these are understood it is no longer alarming, though it may be interesting.

It may be useful to describe these causes, and to thereby make it clear to our Eastern friends, that Kansas is an American community passing through a process of American civilization in a thoroughly American manner,—kicking as she goes.

Kansas was marked out on the desert about a generation ago. The word "aid" appeared on the first page of her history, in connection with the "Emigrant Aid Society." The people of the State have received aid ever since. For a while it came in boxes, during the early battles with grasshoppers and drouths: later it arrived in the shape of loan companies, mortgage companies, trust companies. Growth has been forced in the State. A great commonwealth—and it is indeed truly marvellous—has been builded on these prairies by the Kansas people with other people's money. The trouble with Kansas is not that she has forgotten what a great community she has established, but that it has been established with other people's money. Hence the popularity of the slogan, "the rights of the user are paramount to the rights of the owner." That, by the way, is no new theory. It is as old as debt; and the proposition has appealed to the man in debt ever since the first borrower. Seldom, however, has the theorem found an entire community in debt, as it found Kansas. The wonder is not that Kansas was won by the guileful paradox,—for weakness is a very human attribute,—but that so many people should have been found in one community, whose condition was such that the philosophy of the dishonest debtor would move them all alike. In other communities there were debtors. They voted just as the Kansas debtor voted. But Kansas is a young State. She has found little time to pay her debts. She has been busily engaged in making them. The difference between Ohio and Kansas, for instance, does not lie in the kinds of men that inhabit each State, but in the fact that Ohio has had fifty years' start of Kansas in increasing the number of creditors,—the savers, the men on the right side of the ledger. Ohio had as many gentlemen who voted for the rights of the user as Kansas had. When Kansas thrift has been working and saving as many years as Ohio thrift, Kansas may have as virtuous a point of view as Ohio has to-day.

However, there is neither sense nor charity in palliating the transgression of the debtor who refuses to pay his debt by pointing out the fact that the offence is common. It may benefit the Kansas Populist to remember that the guillotine was established in France by people who desired a release from the eternal payment of moneys for which they received no return; while the Kansas man—who flaunted the legend "Hang the Plutocrats!"—was seeking a release from the payment of money which he had received, which he had enjoyed, and which he had spent. The Kansas man is not unique. A considerable minority of the people of every State in the Union voted with the majority in Kansas. And because that minority is still rather uncomfortably in evidence .all through the States it may be worth while to try to get a glimpse of the world from the standpoint of—to denominate him plainly—the American socialist.

And nowhere else is the American socialist so earnest, so outspoken, and so unhampered by scruples as in Kansas. That is because the Kansas man is an American, with no guiding motive, save his desire to kick. When the American does get off the track, he goes farther than anyone. His good sense, however, always brings him back; but while he is away from the reservation, he is a very bad Indian. There are indications that the ghost-dancing in Kansas is done; yet the State remains an excellent field wherein to study existing conditions of American socialism. For in this State men—average men, plain everyday Americans—are living in a social and economic atmosphere rarely to be met with.

'Kansas was settled by men who went there for two reasons: First, to maintain a principle. This indicated that they were men of ideals. Second, to make their everlasting fortunes. The people of this generation who live in the Middle, Eastern, and Southern States were born where they live. They were satisfied to let well enough alone. But the men and women who went West, who now populate Kansas and the Western States, were men and women of marked force of character. They had ambition and will-power enough to pick up and leave their former environments. Now it is impossible in any community that everyone can be rich. Some must fall by the way-side ; and when many are debtors, as the Kansas people, by force of circumstances, were, the percentage that fail must necessarily be large. In Kansas, and in the West, the man whose life's ambition was thwarted, who, by the edict of nature, was doomed to failure, still had force enough left to complain; to seek some way out of the inevitable misfortune that had overtaken him. A child of the tenement, an hereditary coward, a beggar by association, a menial by education, may be ground lower and lower by the great machine of commerce; but here was a man who had grit and ambition and character enough to cross a continent, who had sufficient intelligence to appreciate the comforts and to long for the luxuries that American civilization uses as rewards of merit. When this man gets tangled up in the machine, the inexorable play of its cogs maddens him. In his anger he has not tried so seriously to get out of the grinding burrs as to break the machine.

The Kansan, in this struggle, has attracted general attention. The world, knowing that the nature of things will not be changed for the Kansas man, any more than for the man who wraps his talent in a napkin, has marvelled at the fantastic fight, and has said, "What a very peculiar man!" He is not a peculiar man. He has merely lost his temper; and he is strong. He is an American off on the wrong tack. Wherever this American is found battling against the natural order,—the order which makes every man responsible for his own success and blamable for his own failure; wherever a man is found seeking aid, other than that of his own two hands and the devices of his own brain, to escape destruction in the industrial mill; wherever a man is found asking his fellow-men to make him, by legislation, the mental or the financial equal of another man,—there is the exponent of the new socialism. The contention with the new socialism is the chief political affair before the American people to-day. And it is a question as vital in Massachusetts as it is in Kansas.

The term "new socialism" may be misleading; for it is the old socialism,—old as the envy of Cain, whose gift was not acceptable. But it is the old socialism under new conditions—conditions exemplified with unusual brilliancy in Kansas. There the average man is the product of the school-house and the printing-press. Indeed it is the very universality of education and enlightenment—which we in Kansas brag of—that brings all this picturesque discontent. For generations the socialist dreamers have said the race would be entirely happy, if men only had equality of opportunity; if every man started out in the world with the same mental equipment that another man enjoyed. In Kansas this condition virtually exists. Yet the mental habit of a considerable number of the people is but a garment of sackcloth. Viewed casually this seems to be a hopeless situation. To the outsider Kansas seems to be a great commonwealth, peopled with strong, ambitious, intelligent men and women, a majority of whom are sitting among the potsherds, and throwing ashes into the air, that is vibrant with lamentations because there are no truffles for dinner. When this description appears as a fairly truthful picture of Kansas, it is natural that the home-seeker and the investor should avoid the State.

The most unfortunate phase of the situation is that the average Eastern observer does not see how conditions in Kansas may be changed. Nevertheless, they may be changed, and are changing.

In extreme Western Kansas, crops are uncertain, and the man on the farm, like *Uncle Remus's* rabbit, is "done bleedged to climb." There the farmer must work ten days in the week and sleep only on holidays.

Life is a serious business with the farmer on the highlands; and, because he has a hard, rough time of it, the casual observer in the East thinks the Western Kansas man is a Populist. The truth is that Western Kansas is more surely a Republican stronghold than any other portion of the State. That is Jerry Simpson's district. Mr. Simpson's vote in the Far-Western counties was smaller this time than it had ever been before. He was elected through Republican defection in the fertile valley of the Arkansas, and in the city of Wichita—the second city in population in the State. Take the Populist vote of this city from Mr. Simpson, and he would still be marshal of Medicine Lodge. And hereby hangs a moral. People who are seriously at work have not time to dawdle away in dreams of Utopia. Put Kansas to work, —at reasonably profitable work,—and the Populist statesmen will be in search of an employment bureau.

It is one of the remarkable facts of the election-table that, with all the noise and hullabaloo of free silver in the late campaign, the Kansas Republicans held their own and increased their vote in the farming districts,—among people honestly at work,—and lost the State by reason of a changed vote in the cities and towns. There the collapsed boom of eight years ago left a considerable number of people with a surplus of leisure on hand, in which to brood over what they called their wrongs. The agricultural statistics indicate that the honest, energetic farmers of Kansas raised one of the largest crops of corn in the world. Other advices seem to furnish conclusive proof that the town-lot agriculturists harrowed the feelings of their fellow-men, and raised a somewhat larger crop of a Kansas staple not to be mentioned "in the presence of *Mrs. Boffin.*" These gentlemen called themselves free-silver Republicans. What a motley crew it was! A galvanized reminiscence; the tail-end of a long and once triumphant procession of demagogues, that had been tramping through Kansas since the days of that prince of demagogues, General Jim Lane. In the beginning this crowd took for its watch-word, "The Smooth Thing"; and never, since the first election was held in Kansas, has it been at a loss to find a gold-brick to trade for an office. Under the guise of Republicanism, every fad, every ism, every fake, every form of "soft soap and molasses," known to politics, has been hawked about the State of Kansas by these charlatans. They never dared to educate a constituent, or advocate a principle because it was right. They have been the curse of Kansas. They were the forerunners of Simpson and Peffer. These mountebanks played upon the emotions of the people until the drivel of the Populists fell upon the ears of the dazed and disheartened voters as the wisdom of seers. The successive defeats of the Republicans in Kansas for the past seven years had decimated the ranks of these Don Quixotes. Some of them had been crucified and buried; others had chased their own folly to the political mad-house; while others were in temporary exile for their greed. But free silver was a trumpet-blast that resurrected them all. The free-silver Republicans, —the tail-end of the procession,—under the banner of. Buncombe that had led them to many a victory, wheeled out of the Republican line into the ranks of the Populists. It was an affecting spectacle; and it was a great thing for Kansas. For, as a result, the friends of sound money and good government cast the largest vote ever known in the State,—when the decreased population is taken into consideration.

The combined opposition to the Republican party defeated good government in Kansas last fall by a narrow vote; but Election Day left the Republican party in the State stronger than it had ever been before. For the first time in the history of the Republican organization, it made an honest fight on an issue. The gentlemen who have appeared before conventions in the past, advising a " straddle,"—the "smooth thing,"—are either dead or in the " sure-thing " party. For the first time since the war, honest patriotism is doing business in Kansas politics. Young Republicanism—as opposed to old demagoguery—is in the saddle. This party made a manly fight for truth, and increased the party vote of two years ago several per cent.

So much for what, until the next election, must be called "the minority party" in Kansas. As for the majority party,—the party now in power in the State,—there is every reason to believe that it is badly frightened at its own shadow, and that the war-whoop of the campaign will not be carried into the Leedy administration. Leedy seems to desire to cease blowing blood into the ears of capital; and, if he be left to his own counsel, he will probably make a reasonably good Governor. The danger that now threatens is, that the free-silver demagogues who left the Republican party for cause will get around the Governor and persuade him to be a demagogue. If a man may be judged by the first days of his administration, one would say, that Leedy will have backbone enough to cast out the whole nefarious, designing *junta*, and to give Kansas an ordinary administration.

Just now there is much talk of conservatism among the Populists; and if this bear fruit, Kansas will indeed have cause to be happy. This apparent change of heart has been the direct result of a salutary drubbing which the Republican papers of Kansas and the editors and public men of the East gave the Kansas Populists after the election. It made them wince; and it tamed them. They had a great deal to say about the defamers of Kansas at the time. The gentlemen who have really defamed Kansas are they whose official careers in the State have made the truth about Kansas highly objectionable reading. The defamers of Kansas are the gentlemen and others who are trying to make the darkest chapter in Kansas history repeat itself.

To-day, Kansas offers the best field for conservative investments in certain lines to be found in the United States. The demagogues having been driven out of the party that stands for honest money and good government, that organization is to-day stronger—morally as well as numerically—than it has ever been. The cranks among the Populists having been frightened into silence, that party, although in power, is less dangerous than it has ever been. Kansas has been cleansed by fire; and the cleansing seems to be thorough.

Kansas has been in a ferment; and the explosion has come. Every new community passes through something of this sort,—the settling of the first mortgage, either by foreclosure or by partial payment and renewal. In the Middle States the war came with its rising prices and averted bankruptcy. Kansas had no civil war; but the mortgage came due on a falling market. The hardships incidental to settlement made many otherwise sane and honest men forget reason and honor. They have been taught a lesson. The gas of the ferment has escaped. Kansas is steadily decreasing her public debt; and her citizens are paying off the principal and keeping track of the interest coupons. There are, however, boom debts that never will be paid. These debts were made by crazy men on both sides of the bargain; and such debts are made and cancelled by time in every community in the world. They should not be laid at the door of the thrifty people of Kansas.

For three hundred miles west of the Missouri River there lies the most fertile territory on the globe. The rainfall is bounteous and regular. There has not been a total crop-failure within the memory of man. The men and women who settled here in the 'sixties and the 'seventies have been following the course pursued by settlers of other new countries. They have been laying out section lines, surveying, taking directions, and speculating in land. They found it so easy to get rich in making out deeds, that they did not establish industries. They did not take an inventory of their resources. Trading was followed by

6

speculation; speculation, by gambling; gambling, by collapse, depression, and stagnation. That has been the usual history of pioneering; and it has been the history of Kansas. For the past six years business in the State has been stagnant. But these years have been a season of debt-paying and saving. No Kansas banks of importance have failed during that time. Populism has not affected the people who have been actively engaged in reclaiming the credit of the State,—the people at work. When one considers what a narrow majority the combined opposition to good government had last fall, one may realize what a determined army of sane, hard-working people there is redeeming Kansas from the discredit which the idle dreamers have put upon her. And herein lies the hope of Kansas. Put every one in the State to work. Then there will be no more "new socialism" in Kansas; no more airy persiflage about the rights of the user.

Already encouraging signs may be seen. Nearly every Kansas newspaper contains references to the establishment of small industries, by local capital, all over the State. It is the old story. Kansas is finding herself,—just as the Middle States found themselves a generation ago. The people now in Kansas are finding out what there is to do business on; and they are beginning to do business.

This natural development of the resources of the State should not be confused in the minds of the investor with the mad waste of money that occurred in Kansas ten years ago. Looking backward to that time, it seems strange that people should have put money into the schemes that then flourished,—a car-wheel foundry, for instance, a thousand miles from iron; a freight-car factory hundreds of miles from lumber, with nothing but corn to haul in the cars; a bridge foundry a hundred miles from any stream that might not be cleared by an agile steer at a single jump; a watch factory in a country where people were borrowing money to pay their interest coupons; a woollen-mill a day's journey by rail from fuel or power; a carriage factory, where people could not pay cash for wagons. These economic air-castles, and hundreds like them, arose, absorbed Eastern money, and fell,—leaving Kansas with nothing but a bad name. Then, the syndicate flourished. Now, the man with a few thousands in the bank is the *entrepreneur*. During the boom, printing-presses were clicking off stocks and bonds day and night. Now, one man—a thrifty foreman from some Eastern shop, or a practical business man with growing boys—is "the captain and crew of the Nancy brig." There is no display of double leads and startling heads in the newspapers in these days; no "Dirt Will Begin To Fly" announcements; no clamors to "Vote The Bonds." The growth is slow, easy, and unpretentious.

By this sign, the sign of the village smoke-stack, shall Kansas conquer. An idle man is emotional, often erratic. There is logic in work. Work is the order of things. A man at work may be trusted with any charge. And as Kansas gets more and more deeply interested in business she will drop politics. Kansas politics has always been "a bad lot" because the people have taken it so seriously. They have expected to find in the wares of the fakirs the magic stone that would transform the prairie into a paradise. They have been sold time and again. It is still the hard old prairie. From now on, the friends of Kansas—and what a host of true friends Kansas has in the East; friends who feel a warm and tender sentiment for her—will not talk politics. They will talk business. She is a little queer on politics, is Kansas; but careful, considerate treatment for a year or two will stop the local irritation altogether. It will not be wise to send pamphlets and speakers to Kansas for some time. The best way to lend a hand in Kansas to-day is to make two small smoke-stacks breathe blackly where but one has breathed before. Small industrial investments, wisely and conservatively made and closely managed, will yield fair returns. The State is eaten up with freight rates. All raw materials are shipped a thousand miles and shipped back again for consumption. The smoke-house, with its hickory chips and its corn-cobs, is unknown. The rock that once held down the pickled pork in the barrel under the cellar stairs has been cut into a corner-stone for some empty building, —a monument to the folly of the boom. Industrially Kansas is little in advance of the Indians. The Kansas farmer swaps off everything he has for something to eat and something to wear. He manufactures nothing. He pays freight on his raw material to the mill, as well as on the finished product back to the farm.

All this must change. The second generation proposes to change it. The transformation will perforce change Kansas. And in the future, the apparition of the gentleman with the green ears, the striped back, and the iridescent tail-feathers may cease to hover over the Kansas election-tables. The State may become humdrum, like Indiana perhaps. She may lose her place, "top of column next to pure reading-matter," in the newspapers. For thirty-six years, Kansas has been always interesting, and seldom right. Let us hope that when she becomes less interesting she will be more frequently right.

WILLIAM ALLEN WHITE.

NEW LETTERS OF EDWARD GIBBON.

THE two volumes of Gibbon's "Letters" now first published with his "Memoirs" are most pleasant reading; they throw new light on the character of the historian and his age; and they are thoroughly well edited and annotated. The so-called "Letters" that the first Lord Sheffield gave to the world just a hundred years ago were merely scraps, cuttings, and occasional specimens culled from the great mass which the third Earl now gives to the curious public. Most of the personal history, all the scandal, and many of the piquant epigrams were withheld by the prudence of the noble executor and the prudery of his daughter. Those who wish to look into the inner life of one of the greatest of English men of letters, and into British society at home and abroad in the first half of the reign of George III, may now study both in the exact transcript of Gibbon's "Familiar Letters."

The "fierce light that beats upon" a great name now reveals to us the historian as one of the most genial, affectionate, sane, and contented natures in literary history—with a genius for friendship, indulgent almost to a fault toward all failings, gently fond of all pleasant things and people, and willing to put up with much for the sake of an easy life. Never was any man less heroic, who less pretended to the heroic, with more perfectly worldly ideals, and a more instinctive repugnance to any enthusiasm. A cosmopolitan *philosophe* of the eighteenth century to the bone, with all the optimism, the cool brain, the *apolausticism*, the insensibility to the moral and spiritual reformation to come, which mark the literary aristocrat of the time. We are not likely now to over-rate the good sense and good nature of such men. We see all their blindness, their grossness, their egoism. But their culture and their balance of mind still interest us. The life they led fascinates us in a way, as does the life of Horace and of Pliny. Peace to their ashes! Let us utter a half-pagan sigh over the classical urn, sacred to the *Dîs Manibus* of the historian of Rome.

His friend judiciously expunged from the published remains nearly all that records the troubles and embarrassments which weighed on him through life. We now see well enough why the historian gave up

Parliament, public life, London society, and at last his native country. His father kept Gibbon until middle life strictly his dependant under his own will and rule; and at his own death left his only child, then aged thirty-three, a man practically ruined, with several estates hopelessly incumbered. The son, then a grown man of reputation and ambition, struggled manfully for some years to maintain his stepmother, to clear the wreck of their fortunes, and to keep the position into which he had been bred. At last, without repining, he quietly withdrew to the foreign land where so large a part of his life was passed, and devoted himself entirely to his gigantic task. The father, an insatiable man of pleasure, was one of those popular men of the world whose charm and *bonhomie* disguise the real selfishness and cruelty of their domestic lives.

At the age of nine the poor child who became Edward Gibbon was sent from his father's home, which he saw very little again until the age of twenty-one. From sixteen to twenty-one, he was kept at Lausanne, in spite of his entreaties that he might leave it, and he was forced to give up the admirable woman to whom he had engaged himself. At twenty-one, he was brought home and called on to cut off the entail of his settled estate and to join in raising a heavy mortgage. A year later he was dragged into the militia by his father, and served as a soldier in camp for two years and a half. His foreign journey, from which such great things resulted, was cut short by the extravagance and commands of the father. And when, after a few more troubled years, the father died, the young student found himself involved in difficult family embarrassments which were not finally disentangled at his death at fifty-six. It is plain from this entire correspondence, and especially from the dignified remonstrance to his step-mother in 1771 (Letter 113), that the son was in no way to blame, but had acted, as he proudly says, with filial duty and personal economy. His good sense enabled him to see all the weaknesses and follies of his father; but he uniformly speaks of these with affectionate reserve. Nor is there in this mass of letters any trace of ignoble complaint.

Another remarkable feature of these Letters is the complete absence of those controversies, jealousies, and heartburnings which so often distress the lives of literary men. Gibbon never seems to have had an enemy—except the gout; and he never grumbles at any one but the lawyers and the money-dealers, and that in a tone which is half burlesque. The cruel sarcasms of the history melt in his letters into playful banter; as a correspondent at least, if not as an author, he is perfectly clean, good-natured, and natural. There is an amazing silence as to all that is spiritual and profound—but nothing cynical, nothing profane. He is shrewd, sensible, self-possessed to a fault, but he never has to resort "to the obscurity of a learned language" to cover his indecorum. He has nothing of the devil and rattle of Byron, nor the inimitable babble of Horace Walpole. He has not the pathetic charm of Cowper, nor the burly passion of Johnson. But the imperturbable good sense and the vast erudition and experience of this typical cosmopolitan *virtuoso* throw a vivid light—it may be a somewhat lurid and melancholy light—upon the highest stratum of culture on the eve of the great Revolution.

His first letter, at sixteen, is all that the good boy ought to say to his papa who had banished him abroad. His books were seized at Calais, in order to be examined by the censor (this was in 1753). In a month he understood French, and in a year or so he had almost forgotten how to write English. He talks of his "*evasion*," "what *party* can he take?", a "plain *recite*," and he hears of a thing "by the *canal* of a certain Mr. Hugonin." At nineteen he cannot exist at Lausanne without his d'Herbelot's "Bibliothèque Orientale." Though he had never seen his new step-mother, he writes to his father in French—"assurez ma chère mère (c'est avec bien du plaisir que je lui donne ce titre) de tous les sentimens que ce nom sacré emporte avec lui." Arrived in England, he is commissioned to buy tickets in the public lottery. They all come up blanks. And the young philosopher of twenty-one thus consoles his father who was evidently a hardened gambler,—"All our visionary plans of grandeur are disappointed, the dream of those who had the ten thousand pounds will last a little, but perhaps not much, longer." Meeting the son—"a little odd cur" of a Doctor Maty, whom Johnson called "a little black dog"; a man whom Gibbon despised—he tells his father that he "tipped the boy with a crown, and the father with a coal of fire."

At twenty-one, the young gentleman begins to be a man about town in the best society of London. He is introduced to the famous Lady Harvey's Assembly, "where ('t is true though wonderful) there is no card-playing, but very good company and very good conversation." There he is to meet "the great David Hume." Here is a portentously solid apophthegm for a youth of fashion:—"My unfashionable politics are that a war can hardly be a good one, and a peace hardly a bad one." What a curious folly was the mania for saving the postage of letters by the begging of Franks. "I have got four dozen of Franks for you

from Sir G. Napier, which I shall send you by the waggon." It had
come to be a sign of gentility, never to pay for a letter, but to worry
your acquaintances in Parliament in order to evade the tax, which fell
upon the common people. At twenty-six he goes again to Paris where
he is delighted, and much prefers to London society. "Much less
play, more conversation, and instead of our immense routs, agreable
[*sic*] societies where you know and are known by almost everybody
you meet." He is struck with the French respect for the English
character. "The name of Englishman inspires as great an idea at
Paris as that of Roman could at Carthage, after the defeat of Hannibal." . . . —"We are now looked on as a nation of philosophers and
patriots."

At the age of twenty-six, we seem to catch the first germ of his
life-long work. He writes from Lausanne in May, 1763 (thirteen years
before the appearance of his first volume),—"I am busy upon the
ancient Geography of Italy *and the reviewing my Roman history and
antiquities.*" A little later he is engaged upon "a considerable work"
—"a description of the ancient Geography of Italy taken from the
original authors." He sees Voltaire, at seventy, "act a Tartar Conqueror with a hollow, broken voice, and making love to a very ugly
niece of about fifty." But he is amazed at the veteran's energy. ."Show
me, in history or fable, a famous poet of Seventy who has acted in his
own plays, and has closed the scene with a supper and ball for a hundred people." A year passes and he still has his great task in view—
"I have never lost sight of the undertaking I laid the foundations of
at Lausanne, and I do not despair of being able *one day to produce something by way of a description of ancient Italy, which may be of some use to
the publick,* and of some credit to myself." (Letter 37. June, 1764.)

But if the historian of ancient Rome was already a great scholar, he
had a curiously wrong judgment as to Mediæval things. " Of all the
towns in Italy, I am the least satisfied with Venice; objects which are
only singular without being pleasing produce a momentary surprize
which soon gives way to satiety and disgust. Old and in general ill
built houses, ruined pictures, and stinking ditches dignified with the
pompous denomination of canals, a fine bridge spoilt by two Rows of
houses upon it, and a large square decorated with the worst Architecture I ever yet saw." And this is Venice! Shades of Byron, Rogers,
Shelley, and George Sand! It needed a hundred years before Ruskin
could proclaim the glory of these "ill built houses," "ruined pictures,"
and the "worst Architecture" ever seen. Well! they did n't know

everything down in the eighteenth century. We learn that the "grand
tour" of a young gentleman who frequented courts, embassies, and the
best society abroad, cost him about £700 per annum in the middle of
the last century; and the young Gibbon who was careful and did not
gamble, but travelled rather *en seigneur* with a valet, plumes himself on
spending only £150 in ten weeks.

Gibbon's remarks on public affairs, though never profound or serious, are worthy of note. The Royal Marriage Act (12 Geo: iii, c. 11)
—"this most odious law will be forced on Parliament. I do not remember ever to have seen so general a concurrence of all ranks, parties,
and professions of men. Administration themselves are the reluctant
executioners, but the King will be obeyed, and the bill is universally
considered as his, reduced into legal or rather illegal form by Lord
Mansfield and the Chancellor." In 1772, before the American Independence, George III was really a king, not unlike his descendant
Wilhelm of Prussia to-day. All Gibbon tells us of the partition of
Poland in 1772 is, that he will "back Austria against the aged Horse"
—(*i. e.* Frederick the Great). Ah! short-sighted historian of Rome,
how little did you understand the greatest of your contemporaries!

As is well known, Gibbon was steadily against the independence of
the United States, until his good sense convinced him of the folly of
continuing the struggle. At first he is sure "that with firmness, all
may go well." "Returned this moment from an American debate.
A Remonstrance and Representation from the Assembly of New York,
presented and feebly introduced by Burke, but most forcibly supported
by Fox . . . . The House tired and languid. In this season and on
America, the Archangel Gabriel would not be heard. On Thursday
an attempt to repeal the Quebec Bill [for the free exercise of the Roman Catholic religion], and then to the right about, and for myself,
having supported the British, I must destroy the Roman Empire." To
Edward Gibbon what were George Washington or George III compared with Belisarius and Justinian? In May, 1775,—"this looks
serious, and is indeed so. . . . unless the *Insurgents* are determined to
hasten a famine, they must have returned to their own habitations!"
Oh! profound historian, these "insurgents" were not Sicilians or Syri-
ans but Anglo-Saxons of the old blood! June, 1775,—"I have not
courage to write about America. We talk familiarly of Civil War,
Dissolutions of Parliament, Impeachments, and Lord Chatham. The
boldest tremble, the most vigorous talk of peace." (31, Oct: 1775.)
"The conquest of America is a *great* work: every part of that Continent

is either lost or useless." "What a wretched piece of work do we seem to be making of it in America!" "They have almost lost the appellation of *Rebels*." How drolly this sounds after a hundred and twenty years! "Unless Howe has success we shall be less unanimous for the design of conquering America!" At last Gibbon gives in (Dec : 16, 1777)—"What will be the resolution of our Governors I know not, but I shall scarcely give my consent to exhaust still further the finest country in the World in the prosecution of a war from whence *no reasonable man entertains any hopes of success*. It is better to be humbled than ruined." Sensible—but not heroic. The historian who could so well describe a hero, had little of the hero in himself—"Half my acquaintance," he says, "are running down to Bath for the holydays." Nero fiddled whilst Rome was burning : Gibbon concocted epigrams and friendly letters whilst a British army of 10,000 men was surrendering to "*rebels*"! It was all over by Feb., 1778. "Lord N. [orth] does not deserve pardon for the past, applause for the present, or confidence for the future." To his friend Holroyd he writes—"You will see that America is not *yet* conquered . . . . there seems to be a universal desire of peace even on the most humble conditions. Are you still fierce?" And Gibbon voted with Fox against the Government on his motion to refuse more troops to go to America in Feb., 1778. Fox, Burke, and Chatham honestly condemned Lord North and the American war on just and patriotic grounds. Gibbon supported and approved of the war, till he lost heart, and thought he had better get on with the sack of Rome by the barbarians. Never was able man less of a hero, less of a patriot, less of a statesman.

As to the French Revolution Gibbon, as we always knew, was uniformly hostile and wrong-headed. "Burke's book is a most admirable medicine against the French disease." "The strange Revolution which has humbled all that was high, and exalted all that was low, in France." "Burke is a most eloquent and rational madman." Lord Sheffield says, "every one asks—is Fox mad?" We now learn that the king fell into Homeric laughter over a pleasantry of Gibbon's that the French Revolution reminded him of a childish caricature in which a hog was shown roasting a cook! But Lord Sheffield, who, with his daughter, outdid Gibbon in violent abuse of the "Gallic wolves on the prowl," the "Gallic dogs," and the "French disease infecting other countries," himself published most of the historian's tirades against a movement which he wholly misconceived ; and thus we have little new to learn on this head from Gibbon's own letters, though much that is significant from the unpublished letters of Lord Sheffield himself and of his brilliant daughter, Maria Holroyd. They show how the great movement in France, even before the Terror and the Guillotine, had roused the British aristocracy to real passion.

In small things and in great the familiar notes of the historian are curious reading, now strangely blind, now remarkably sagacious and detached. "Blessings on the man (his name is now buried in oblivion) who first invented the loud trumpet of Advertisements." The trumpet is now of stunning volume, and too often brays us deaf; and opinions to-day are divided whether they are a blessing or a nuisance. We are taken into the library in Bentinck Street where the early part of the great history was composed—"the paper of the Room will be a fine shag flock paper, light blue with a gold border, the Book-cases painted white, ornamented with a light frize [*sic*]; neither Doric nor Dentulated (that was yours) Adamic." It is "my own new clean comfortable dear house"—"I now live, which I never did before, *and if it would but rain*, should enjoy that unity of study and society, in which I have always placed my prospect of happiness." "I have never formed any great schemes of avarice, ambition, or vanity: and all the notions I ever formed of a London life in my own house, and surrounded by my books, with a due mixture of study and society, are fully realised." An omnivorous reader—an unwearied student—but no recluse—no puritan !

From this lettered ease, Gibbon was torn by the unexpected offer of a seat in Parliament, and ultimately by the office of a Lord of Trade —"an event which changes the whole colour of my future life." He was elected M.P. for Liskard in his absence. He was but thirty-eight, but he thought himself too old to become an orator. "I have remained silent, and notwithstanding all my efforts chained down to my place by some invisible—unknown invisible power. *Now America and almost Parliament are at an end* [April, 1775] I have *resumed my History* with vigour and adjourned Politicks to next Winter." Gibbon was a scandalously indifferent Senator, and a *fainéant* official: but at least he knew his own weaknesses and impotence as a man of affairs. He came to hate Parliament, which he calls *Pandemonium*. "I am heartily tired of the place"—"this Parliamentary prattle."—"I again descend into the noise and nonsense of the Pandemonium." He fears that his friend may regret being "excluded from that Pandemonium which we have so often cursed so long as you were obliged to attend it." When retired permanently to Lausanne, he still expects to *sell* his seat and talks of "the little but precious stock *which I had so foolishly embarked in the Parliamentary bottom.*" So that a seat in Parliament was a mere investment, which he proposed to sell to the highest bidder! And his Lordship of Trade, or any other minor office which he could fill without trouble, was a mere convenient escape from pecuniary embarrassment. Naturally such a man "shuddered at Grey's motion" [for Parliamentary Reform], and thought that "such men as Grey, Sheridan, Erskine, have talents for mischief." We cannot wonder at the origin and issue of the struggle with America when we see that men like Edward Gibbon were the Members and Ministers whom Lord North could select. And yet Edward Gibbon was a man of learning, sagacity, and honour, not a whit worse than his colleagues, who all clung to the principles of Pitt and Burke.

Amongst the smaller points in the Letters may be noted the startling prevalence of disease. People in full health and youth are continually dying of measles, fevers, small-pox, and apoplexy. Small-pox is as common as influenza to-day, and is treated as one of the familiar nuisances of life, so that patients who recover are congratulated on being safe from a second attack—at any rate for many years. As to the gout, it comes and goes like a common catarrh. Gibbon himself is crippled by it every half year or so; and he talks of paying up his "gout-tax" with a solemn and somewhat awkward humour. How he lived at all with such a constitution is a mystery. It is even a greater mystery how he worked so voraciously to the age of fifty-six. Gibbon did not drink, and he was not a glutton—in days when all Englishmen ate and drank like brutes, when Pitt could not speak without a bottle or two of port, and Sheridan was picked up from the gutter by the watchman, whom he told he was Wilberforce. But it is plain that Gibbon liked a good vintage and an elegant dinner. His plaintive appeals to his friend to send him out to Lausanne some old Madeira— "he trembles for his Madeira"—his despair when he runs short of the generous fluid—are droll enough to us: there was nothing to laugh at in his own day. An English gentleman of that age regarded "the laying down" of a cellar of old wine as a duty that he owed to his country and his order. Some of the historic Madeira still remains: and the present Lord Sheffield delights to give a friend a glass of that most precious ambrosia which sent the blood coursing in the veins of the historian of Elagabalus and Attila.

The great scholar led a pleasant life in London—in August "a delicious solitude"—"I lead the true life of a Philosopher, which consists in doing what I really like, without any regard to the world or to fashion." "A few friends and a great many books may entertain me, but I think fifteen hundred people the worst company in the world." His friend's cook was taken with religious mania—which they then called "fanaticism"—"That furious principle which has sometimes overturned Nations has in this instance been contented with unsettling the reason of a Cook." Religious enthusiasm seems to be almost the only thing which really rouses the philosopher's indignation. He has no high opinion of Trial by Jury—"Out of twelve jurymen, I suppose six to be incapable of understanding the question, three afraid of giving offence, and two more who will not take the trouble of thinking. Remains one who has sense, courage, and application." His step-mother and his friends proposed marriage to him, and he allowed them to play about the idea. As to one suggested alliance, he feels scruples about the *religion* of the lady. He will not submit to sermons and family prayers—"I would not marry an Empress on those conditions." He does not believe in marriage. "Sir Stanier and Lady Porter exhibit a very pretty picture of conjugal fondness and felicity, and yet they have been married very near three weeks."

The "grand style" of the "Decline and Fall" was evidently part of Gibbon's nature. His most hasty and familiar confidences are continually dropping into it unconsciously. At times he amuses himself by openly burlesquing it himself. "I think that, through the dark and doubtful mist of futurity [this sonorous exordium has nothing to do with the fall of Empires, or the rise of new religions] I can discern some faint probability that the Gibbon and his Aunt will arrive at Sheffield Place, before the Sun, or rather the Earth, has accomplished eight diurnal Revolutions." To Lady Sheffield he writes—"Inconstant pusillanimous Woman! Is it possible that you should so soon have forgot your solemn vows and engagements, and that you should *pretend* to prefer the dirt and darkness of the Weald of Sussex to the splendid and social life of London?"—One thinks he went to bed in ruffles, and rose to a march performed by the band of the Guards. "The supplies for the journey [a trip to Paris] will be paid by the Roman Empire." The Roman Empire could well bear the strain even of the pomp of its historian. "After decking myself out with silks and silver, the ordinary establishment of Coach, Lodgeing [*sic.*], Servants, eating, and pocket expences does not exceed sixty pounds pr. month. Yet I have two footmen in handsome liveries behind my Coach, and my apartment is hung with damask."

Here is his day in Paris. " I am just now going (nine o'clock) to
the King's Library, where I shall stay till twelve. As soon as I am
dressed I set out to dine with the Duke de Nivernois, shall go from
thence to the French Comedy into the Princess de Beauvan's *loge
grillée*, and am not quite determined whether I shall sup at Madame du
Deffand's, Madame Necker's, or the Sardinian Embassadress's. Do not
be fond of shewing my letter; the playful effusions of friendship would
be construed by strangers as gross vanity." The brilliant society of
France danced and supped on the crater of the volcano. And the
courtly historian, whom it welcomed with open arms, could obviously
unbend from his philosophic " solitude " when the humour seized him.
He has even more famous society in London. " This moment Beau-
clerck, Lord Ossory, Sheridan, Garrick, Burke, Charles Fox, and Lord
Cambden (no bad set you will perhaps say) have left me." Gibbon
knew almost all the famous men and women of his age—but with one
notable exception. Samuel Johnson disliked Gibbon as an infidel and
a prig. Gibbon disliked Johnson as a fanatic and a bear. Both were
right as well as wrong. No two men could be more unlike, or less
indulgent to each other's failings.

In practical affairs of life Gibbon is eminently sensible, cool, and
just. Here is a capital letter to his fiery friend, Lord Sheffield, who
apparently wanted to measure swords with a gallant officer.—" I have
seen the General. You are both wrong: he first in lending you papers
without *special* leave; you in the serious anger you expressed on so
trifling a business. Unless you wish that this slight scratch should
inflame into an incurable sore, embrace the lucky opportunity of his
illness and confinement, which will excuse your dignity and shall
assuage your resentment. Call on him this evening, give and receive
between jest and earnest, a volley of *damns*, and then let the whole
affair be no more remembered than it deserves. *Dixi et liberavi ani-
mam meam.*" His advice to Lord Sheffield as to his parliamentary
election is thoroughly wise and practical. He had the *mens sana in
corpore insano!* " Next Wednesday I conclude my forty-fifth year,
and in spite of the changes of Kings and Ministers [he might have
added of the Royal visitations of King-Gout] I am very glad that
I was born." " I am now seated in my library before a good fire, and
among three or four thousand of my old acquaintance." Lausanne, to
which he retreats, is " in the most beautiful situation in the world. I
shall exchange the most unwholesome air (that of the house of Commons) for the purest and most salubrious, the heat and hurry of party

for a cool lit*t*erary repose." Yet this "step is dictated by the hard law of œconomy or rather of necessity." He had been ruined by his father's extravagance; his embarrassments were incessant; he had lost his seat in Parliament, his office, his public career, and at last he had been driven by pecuniary difficulties to abandon the brilliant society he loved. Yet Lausanne seems to him a Paradise. Never was there such an optimist. He can even write kindly "of the decline and fall of his old Enemy—not the Devil—but the Gout."

His enormous erudition—his passion for books, his historic imagination—these things were the real Gibbon—his airs of a dandy, of a *bon vivant*, of an *esprit fort*, were merely the accidents into which he was born. Now and then he had toyed with the idea of marriage. He had seen a young lady "with very tolerable eyes," good sense, and good humour. But he was himself *indifferent*, and she was *poor*. Another was religious, and he "abhors a devotee, though a friend to decency and toleration." He sought and admired many women; but they never could stir him to surrender his liberty. "The habits of female conversation have sometimes tempted me to acquire the piece of furniture, a wife; and could I unite in a single Woman, the virtues and accomplishments of half a dozen of my acquaintance, I would instantly pay my addresses to the Constellation. [A man only perceives "the bright particular star" when he is already in love: before love the very thought of the stars drives out love.] In the meantime I must content myself with my other wife, the decline and fall of the Roman Empire, which I prosecute with pleasant and constant industry."

But though Edward Gibbon was as insensible as ever man was to the love which leads to marriage, he had two fine passions in his nature —the love of his books and the love of his friends. His intimacy with Deyverdun, the Severys, the Neckers, was a type of romantic attachment between persons of different nations; his affection for Reynolds, Garrick, and Fox does him honour. But the brotherly terms on which he lived with the Holroyds rises to the height of one of those historic friendships which will one day adorn a new treatise "De Amicitia." One cannot read these intimate outpourings of confidence between Gibbon and the first Lord Sheffield—a correspondence maintained unbroken for thirty years—without being struck with this fine example of friendship between two men so curiously unlike, and yet so perfectly sympathetic. It was the union, Gibbon wrote, of "the lion and the lamb, the eagle and the worm." Holroyd is all fire, energy, business capacity, ambition, governing power. Gibbon is placid, indolent, unpractical, and unaspiring. Holroyd does everything for his friend: is his agent, banker, his host, his patron, and his counsellor. Never had helpless student a more vigorous and devoted man of the world to extricate him from all his troubles. Never did an ambitious statesman, with a thousand cares on his shoulders, fling himself more assiduously to rescue and comfort an embarrassed philosopher. One is struck as much with the self-devotion of the peer to his friend as by his many-sided capacity and his indomitable energy. As Gibbon declares in his grand way, "Alexander may sleep, if Parmenio is awake."

Nor is Gibbon's beautiful confidence in his friend, his affection for him, for his wife, and his daughters, less memorable in the record of literary friendships. To him Lady Sheffield is "my dearest My Lady, whom I have now loved as a sister for something better or worse than twenty years" . . . "he has a memory, a conscience, a heart, and that heart is sincerely devoted to Lady S." The fine letters that he wrote to the husband on the death of the wife have been already published. It was on receipt of the sad news of his friend's loss that the historian set out from Lausanne to console him. And the long and difficult journey undoubtedly increased the fatal complaint from which he had long been suffering. For the eldest daughter of the Sheffields, Gibbon had the highest admiration and affection—"that fine diamond," "indeed a most extraordinary young woman," who united "the strong sense of a man with the easy elegance of a female." She was indeed an extraordinary woman, and justified the historian's deep interest in her education. And now at last, by the wise decision of this lady's nephew, the present Earl of Sheffield, the world is permitted to know how much the reputation of Gibbon has owed her, and how closely the memory of her own family is entwined with that of the illustrious historian of Rome.

FREDERIC HARRISON.

WHAT ARE NORMAL TIMES?

In all parts of the country people are talking about the restoration of normal times in the business world. There is general discontent with existing conditions, a general belief that these conditions are unnatural and therefore temporary, and that something is going to happen that will bring about a speedy change. It may be well to inquire what the normal times are for which people are longing, and whether there is any reasonable prospect that we shall see such times again.

The popular conception of wholesome and natural conditions in the domain of industry, commerce, and finance must be based upon some standard of comparison in the past. People must be looking back to some epoch within their own recollections when times were good; and it must be because the present times fall far short of that standard that there is such widespread dissatisfaction and such a longing for change. Now is it not true that the comparison in almost every man's mind is made between the present times and the era of prodigious national development which followed the resumption of specie payments in 1879? From 1861 to 1879 the prevalent conditions in the United States could not be regarded as normal and permanent. We were then engaged in making war, or in repairing the enormous waste of the war in life and property; and we were working under an inflated and irredeemable paper currency which imparted fictitious values to many forms of property and to most kinds of labor.

Few memories are long enough to go back to the conditions of business which prevailed from 1850 to 1860; and those who can recollect thus far will certainly not be able to recall a state of affairs which they would desire to see restored. At that time we had an abominable currency system, composed of State-bank issues of fluctuating value and often of no value at all, which entailed great losses upon the producing classes. The transportation system of the country was in a rudimentary state; and the exchange of products was burdened with very heavy charges. It cost then about four times as much as it costs now to get a bushel of wheat from the Mississippi Valley to the seaboard. We shall not, therefore, find a just standard of comparison in the decade before the war, or in any decade in the earlier history of the Republic. Unfortunately there seems to be no way for the public mind to institute a comparison and to judge of the condition of general business at the present time, except to go back to that wonderful period of rapid progress and general expansion which lasted until about 1890 and came to a dead stop in the panic of 1893.

Would it not be wise to inquire whether those years constituted normal times, and whether we have any reason for expecting that the conditions then prevailing will be restored, either by legislation on the tariff or the currency, or through the country, under the action of world-wide economic laws, gradually lifting itself out of the rut of depression? During the eleven years between 1879 and 1890 this country ran an almost breathless race of eager and rapid development. We constructed more than 88,000 miles of railroad. We transferred more than 2,000,000 people from the densely settled portions of the country to the Mississippi Valley, to the plains beyond, and to the Pacific Coast. This displacement of population opened improved opportunities to the laboring classes remaining in the East. At the same time we brought from Europe about 1,000,000 emigrants; planting them mainly in the old and new West. We built up new cities, and added greatly to the population of the old ones. We created thousands of new villages and towns. We opened hundreds of thousands of new farms on the Western prairies. We established a multitude of new manufacturing concerns, to supply the enormous demand for railway and building material, for machinery and implements of all kinds, and for the innumerable articles of comfort and luxury required in the hundreds of thousands of new homes and new places of business. To do all this we borrowed vast sums of money. We drew upon the accumulations of our Eastern communities, and obtained from Europe, in the aggregate, probably not less than $2,000,000,000. We created six new States in the Far West, and made immense additions to the population of the older, but still young, States in that region.

Certainly those were not normal times. On the contrary, they were very abnormal times. They were based upon conditions that will never be seen again upon the American continent. To long for their restoration is to indulge in the fascinating but profitless occupation of chasing rainbows. We have no longer any vast areas of fertile land, with sufficient rainfall for agriculture, upon which we can build up great farming communities, with towns and cities and thousands of miles of new railroads. I have shown in previous articles in THE FORUM that settle-

7

ment during the boom period went out on the great plains beyond
the line of sufficient rainfall and was obliged to draw back; leaving
abandoned homes and shrivelled towns behind it. I have shown that
further development of agriculture in the Far West must depend
largely upon irrigation works, which require large capital, engineering
skill, and years of time to bring into operation. I by no means maintain that the progress of the West has ceased; but I insist that future
advance in that region must be a matter of the steady filling up of the
good lands in States already fairly well settled, and of irrigation enterprises which can be carried on successfully only when money is obtainable at low rates of interest.

The primary condition of our great epoch of national growth was
the rapid peopling of the new West. This it was that made such an
active demand for a great variety of raw materials and manufactured
products. It was this, too, which gave to the whole nation a buoyant,
enterprising, and speculative tone. The farmer or mechanic who was
plodding along in the older communities of the country was almost
sure of improving his condition if he went West. The small store-
keeper in the East became a large merchant in the new Western city.
The lawyer without clients and the doctor without patients went West,
to find an encouraging field for their talents. There was not only an
enormous farming development, but there was an immense development of mining resources in gold, silver, copper, lead, and iron. The
transportation service of the new West opened a career to tens of
thousands of energetic young men. Money-making was rather an easy
matter to anyone possessed of shrewdness and the acquisitive spirit.
Fortunes were quickly made in converting prairie acres into town lots,
in the opening of gold- and silver- iron- and coal-mines, in exploiting
the pine- and fir-forests, in establishing new factories, and in the promotion of railway building. To that Golden Age we might well apply
Shakespeare's words,

"And should I live a thousand years I never could forget it."

Now what is there in our present condition or in our future pros-
pects to justify the hope that those times will return? Our new West
is already fairly well peopled; and its business conditions have conformed themselves to those of the rest of the country. Except in a
few mining districts, it no longer offers a field for adventure or speculation. Our great transcontinental railway systems are already constructed; and not one of them can earn interest on the money it cost.

Our new towns and cities went rather beyond the capacity of the tributary country to support them, under the stimulus of inflated real-estate values and with the temporary opportunities they offered for employment of labor. We shall not again have a flood of foreign money pouring in, to loan upon anything or everything having the semblance of property. The foreigner has had his experience; and he now wants to be doubly sure that he is going to get his capital back and his regular interest payments, before an American investment has any-attraction for him. Is it not on the whole probable that we shall . have to make up our minds to plod along in the slow-going way of older nations, and to be satisfied with moderate profits and a slow accumulation of wealth? If these be our reasonable expectations, would it not be sane and wholesome for people to cease dreaming of a Golden Age which is gone forever?

There are other circumstances which tend to sickly o'er the rosy dreams of easy money-making and of a feverish activity in all departments of business, in which so many people are indulging. We have been steadily, but inevitably, forced out of our old conditions of exceptional well-being, which came from our possession of a virgin continent, and have been brought into the competitive struggle in which all other civilized nations are engaged. We have our special advantages, and must make the most of them; but we are no longer a country exceptional and apart, easily maintaining higher standards of living than those which prevail elsewhere, supplying largely our own needs, and selling the excess of our natural products in markets practically controlled by ourselves. Our great staples of wheat, cotton, and petroleum meet with sharp competition from the products of fields and wells in other lands. In a word, we are in the great world-struggle for existence. We must adopt the close economies practised by other nations, and must depend upon our superior energy and skill, and our genius for inventing and running machinery, to hold our own in the struggle.

I think that we shall unquestionably witness a steady improvement in business conditions in the immediate future. We have just escaped a great danger. So long as the menace of lowering the money standard was hanging over us it was impossible for business to get into anything like a normal condition. People do not put out their money willingly when there is any uncertainty as to the kind of money they are going to get back. Some lines of business will no doubt be aided by new tariff measures; but it will be a mistake to expect too much from that quarter. Nothing magical is going to result from a new tariff bill.

The danger ahead, which thoughtful men now see, is that there will be widespread disappointment at the failure of the old boom times to come back again, and that this disappointment will show itself again in political agitation. Unfortunately we still have some millions of voters who imagine that the Government can and ought to put money in their pockets; that by some contrivance of law-making it can make farm products higher, wages better, and labor more fully employed. Times may be a great deal better than they are now and yet the prevalent discontent may continue; and undoubtedly in that case either we shall see a revival of the irrational and injurious free-silver agitation or there will come up out of the depths of ignorance and unrest a new paper-money craze. It will be wisdom on the part of men who can reach public opinion through the press and from the platform to take up and discuss the question of what normal times really are, and thus, perhaps, prevent another wild rush toward ruin like that from which we have just safely emerged,—almost by the skin of our teeth.

If the McKinley Administration succeeds in getting its tariff and currency policy adopted by the new Congress, the new measures will hardly have time to demonstrate their wisdom before the Congressional election of 1898. We know that the present expectations, entertained by a multitude of voters, of the possibility of good times growing out of a change in the Government are not likely to be realized, because the times for which they long can never be restored. We may be doing fairly well in all our main lines of business activity, in farming, in manufacturing, and in transportation, but the prevailing discontent may not be cured. If it shall not be greatly modified by educational influences, a House of Representatives hostile to the sound financial policy of the Administration will be elected; and we shall then find ourselves on the flood-tide of another cheap-money agitation,—to culminate in another sharp struggle at the Presidential election in 1900, with renewed disturbance of business, the unsettlement of all values, and the peril of a great catastrophe. There is no better way of averting these threatened misfortunes than to continue, through the conservative press of the country,—the newspapers, the magazines, and the reviews,—the excellent educational work on financial questions which saved the country from disaster in the recent campaign.

EUGENE V. SMALLEY.

IS ENGLAND'S INDUSTRIAL SUPREMACY A MYTH?

In June last the Cobden Club celebrated the fiftieth anniversary of the repeal of the corn laws by a jubilee banquet and the presentation of a congratulatory address to the Right Hon. Charles Villiers, M. P.,—sole survivor of the great quadrumvirate who led the remarkable agitation that finally triumphed in 1846. The anniversary milestoned an event which has exerted a more profound influence upon the world's economic development than any other series of fiscal laws. The principle of free trade, as applied by Great Britain under the circumstances which then existed in that country and in her international trade, has been abundantly vindicated by events. It has consequently followed that the notion has since dominated the English mind, that necessarily, in all conditions, in all countries, at all stages of industrial development, free trade is the only logical, tenable, and defensible economic policy of the state. The teachings of the Manchester school have enormously influenced the economic thinking and writing of the scholastic world. Nevertheless they have not influenced in the slightest degree the fiscal legislation of other nations. The rest of the world remains more rigidly protective in policy than at any time during these fifty years, and shows no sign either of wavering in allegiance or of suffering in consequence. The Cobden Club has affected to marvel at this world-blindness, and to deplore its consequences to the nations which are its victims. Never, until this jubilee meeting, has it occurred to its members that the lapse of time, whatever it may have established in the case of England for the doctrines of Adam Smith and Richard Cobden, has not less triumphantly vindicated the economic teachings of the well-nigh forgotten Friedrich List. It is opportune, therefore, to compare the results of fifty years of List's economic principles, as illustrated in the industrial development of Germany, with the fruits of fifty years of Cobdenism in England.

Singularly enough this comparison is unconsciously suggested by the remarkable speech of Mr. Leonard Courtney, M. P., who occupied the chair at the Cobden Club jubilee. The burden of that speech was the coming decline of England's commercial prestige; and its key-note is contained in his remark, "If the catastrophe comes, it will be in spite of the free-trade principle; it could not be the result of it. . . . The office of free trade will be to mitigate that which it is not within its power to avert." Thus the exuberance of this jubilee occasion was tempered by the presence of the skeleton at the feast. For, when the Cobden Club admits that the decline of England's industrial and commercial supremacy is at hand, we need no longer hesitate to accept at their full significance the declarations, demonstrations, and lamentations to the same effect which have so persistently obtruded themselves into all recent discussions of this question in Great Britain. We may discount the Cassandrine utterances of the "fair-trade" propaganda, but we cannot blink the recent declaration of Lord Rosebery, that Great Britain is no longer the undisputed mistress of the world of commerce, and that the decline in her export trade is due to the alarming increase in that of her Continental rivals. The ex-premier fortified his statement by the skilful analysis of the Board-of-Trade returns made in Mr. Williams's book,[1]—one of the most notable publications of the year. "The industrial supremacy of England has long been an axiomatic commonplace," says Mr. Williams, in his opening sentence; "it is fast turning into a myth." When the former premier joins the presiding officer of the Cobden Club in certifying to the general correctness of Mr. Williams's diagnosis, further argument is superfluous.

But the statistical aspects of the question have recently been grouped so tersely and graphically by Lord Masham, the great worsted manufacturer of Bradford (better known in this country as Samuel Cunliffe-Lister, the founder of the Manningham mills), that we can here reproduce his summary without overdosing the reader with figures.

ENGLAND'S BALANCE SHEET FOR TWENTY YEARS.

	1874.	1884.	1894.	1894 over 1874.
Agricultural Imports....	£41,117,187	£59,357,167	£77,438,130	Increase 88.3%
Manufactured Imports..	70,897,391	81,490,963	104,489,699	Increase 47.3%
Manufactured Exports...	202,254,531	186,800,386	157,744,241	Decrease 22%
Coal, Machinery, etc....	19,382,321	21,809,235	30,945,199	Increase 59.6%
Population	32,501,517	35,724,231	38,786,053	Increase 19.5%
Imports retained for Home Manufacture...	89,143,995	79,421,719	64,369,715	Decrease 27.8%
Export Trade to British Possessions, 1890–4 over 1870–4				Increase 29.9%
Export Trade to Foreign Countries, do. do.				Decrease 10.6%

---

[1] "Made in Germany." By ERNEST EDWIN WILLIAMS.

Lord Masham holds this table to embody conclusive evidence of England's industrial dry-rot. He makes it the basis of a passionate appeal in behalf of Mr. Chamberlain's scheme for an imperial trade federation or zollverein. The English export trade to foreign countries has decreased from an average value of 175 million pounds sterling for the five-year period ending 1874 to an average value of 155 million pounds sterling for the five-year period ending 1894,—a loss of over 11 per cent; while the exports to the British colonial possessions have risen from an average of 60 millions to an average of 78 millions, —an increase of 30 per cent; the net result being an actual loss, though a small one, in the total export trade, during the twenty-year period.

Lord Masham would conserve and increase the colonial trade by differential duties; but Mr. Courtney castigates Mr. Chamberlain for daring to suggest the reproduction, within the empire, of the salient features of the policy that prevailed within the kingdom prior to 1846. So that, while the doctrinaires are agreed in the diagnosis of the disease, they remain at loggerheads as to the remedy. The "fair-traders" have at least this advantage over their opponents: they have a specific remedy to suggest. The latter are hopelessly without any.

The significance of Lord Masham's figures can be grasped only by a study of the minute analysis made in Mr. Williams's book. To take some of the more striking items: English exports of iron and steel have declined from £31,190,256 in 1874 to £18,688,763 in 1894; of hardware and cutlery, from £4,403,399 to £1,834,481; of linen, from £8,832,533 to £5,443,860; of woollens, from £28,359,512 to £18,728,-946; of cottons, from £74,247,625 to £66,554,529. The effect of the last reduction is seen to-day in the wide-spread paralysis of the manufacturing districts of Lancashire, where the mills of the joint-stock companies stand idle by the score.

It is true that some considerable measure of the decline in the value of these exports is represented by the falling prices of recent years; but the returns by quantity tell much the same story; and the fact remains that in every branch of manufactures where the English exports show a decline, those of Germany exhibit an increase, and generally a large increase. What is true of Germany in this respect is true of all the manufacturing nations of western Europe.

Side by side with this decrease in English exports has come a large increase in the imports of manufactured articles into England; as, for instance, in woollens, where the imports have grown from £5,600,194 in 1874 to £11,464,015 in 1894. The total increase in manufactured imports is from £70,897,391 in 1874 to £104,489,699 in 1894; and this is confined almost exclusively to articles which England made better and cheaper than any of her competitors could make them in the years immediately following the repeal of the corn laws. It will be noticed that the total value of manufactured articles imported into England is greater than the value of similar imports into the United States.

Mr. Swire Smith, a distinguished Yorkshire manufacturer who remains true to the doctrine of free trade, draws, in one of his recent addresses, an almost pathetic picture of the effects of Continental competition. He says:—

> " On every shop counter where our goods are sold, we have to overcome the low wages and long hours of all our competitors, and also the high tariffs which even our own colonies have erected against us. There are none who can really appreciate the severity of the struggle but those who are in it. It grows keener every year ; and old firms who, in prosperous times, built up great establishments, and enriched the country by their energies, have dropped out of the race, their capital exhausted, while their workpeople have been compelled to suffer with them. These are some of the incidents which show how merciless is the warfare of commerce ; and, unfortunately, the painful confession has to be made, that in many industries we are losing ground, and not gaining."

Machinery is the single item of manufactures in which English exports show an increase during these twenty years. The ominous portent of this increase is brought out by Mr. Smith. He was one of the members of the Royal Commission on Technical Education, appointed in 1880; and he declares, in the address already quoted, that it seemed to the members of that Commission, as they travelled from factory to factory on the Continent, "as if half our people at home are engaged in making weapons to be used abroad against the other half." Even in machinery the Germans have latterly discovered that they can make a better article than the English ; while, in the iron and steel industries generally, the English no longer dispute German supremacy. In 1894, the English Iron Trade Association sent a deputation to Germany and Belgium to discover, on the spot, the reasons why those countries were extending their export trade in iron and steel so much more rapidly than England. The report of this deputation emphasized the superior character of the machinery and labor-saving appliances found in the German and Belgian foundries; showing a remarkable advance as compared with the best-appointed works in the Midlands. It attributed this advance and others to the great attention paid to technical education during the last half-century ; and concluded with the announcement that German superiority rests upon its merits, rather than upon any adventitious circumstances. The London "Times," commenting upon this report, remarked that it was fairly to be inferred that "the days of the South Staffordshire iron trade, with the exception perhaps of the sheet-iron branch, are numbered."

Four years prior to this report, the United States had succeeded in wresting from England the place of honor in the iron industry, by producing a larger quantity of pig-iron. On the basis of the statistics of the last ten years, it will not take more than four years longer for Germany to drive England from the second place—into which the United States has forced her—into the third position.

Iron is called the barometer of industry; and it is not necessary to follow the exports of England into other lines to establish the point that her foreign trade is declining,—not rapidly, but none the less surely,— while that of Germany is advancing, and advancing at a more rapid rate than the decline in England. It is an elementary mathematical proposition that, if these processes continue, the time is not far distant when German trade will exceed English trade. Shipping returns are a pretty safe test of commercial prosperity: it is, therefore, significant that in 1893 the total tonnage of the sea-going ships which touched at Hamburg for the first time left Liverpool behind; and in 1894 Hamburg surpassed her record of the previous year.[1]

These facts are the comment of half a century upon the respective economic theories of Cobden and List.

Following faithfully and doggedly in the pathway blazed by Cobden, England, after fifty years of manifest and augmenting advantage, has at length reached a point where the advantage and the disadvantage of that economic policy so nearly balance each other that a partial restoration of the protective policy has come to be regarded as an imperative necessity by one of the leading members of the British government, and perhaps by others, including the present premier; for that is the accusation brought in Mr. Courtney's jubilee address. "Lord Salisbury!" he exclaimed, "you want other nations to believe in free trade: begin by believing in it yourself!" It is not for outsiders to attempt to measure the real sentiment of the English people; but we can at least venture the prediction that the time is coming when the battle which Peel and Cobden fought to a finish in 1846 must be fought over again.

On the other hand, Germany, adopting Friedrich List's economic theory at about the same time that England assented to that of Cob-

[1] "Made in Germany," p. 13.

den, has seen her consolidated empire emerge, as with seven-league boots, from a position of purely agrarian industry into an industrial development so perfect, so homogeneous, so aggressive, that she can meet and beat her English competitors in any market of the world, not excepting England itself.

Here is an industrial paradox; on its face irreconcilable with economic theory, yet upon analysis perfectly simple and self-explanatory. The contrast presented by the practical operation of the two antagonistic economic theories in these two widely different fields covers the most important and significant chapter in the world's industrial history. It shows that in 1846 Cobden was right for England, and that List was right for Germany. By parity of reasoning, it shows that there is no hard and fast rule, no iron-clad economic law, in the present condition of human development, which predetermines what fiscal policy is necessarily best for every nation at any given time. It will afford curious commentary on the acres of eulogy that have been written about the Manchester doctrine, if, sometime in the future, we shall find England enforcing differential duties within an imperial zollverein, and Germany throwing open her ports to all the world. Yet this is not the least probable of the many strange things which the future may have in store.

Generations of drastic protection had made England, on the advent of Peel, the workshop of the world. A number of causes, some natural, others artificial, had aided in making her the imperial mistress of commerce and industry. Her isolated position exempted her from invasion and home wars, and favored the maritime and commercial instincts of her people. The genius of that people made her the home of modern methods of mechanical manufacturing. She developed the steam-engine and all its indescribable possibilities in the way of cheapening and increasing production. The Arkwright spinning-machinery, the power-loom, the worsted-comb, with their accoutrements, were not only all her own, but had been successfully kept her own, until early in the present century, by laws which forbade and punished the export of either parts or patterns. That Goliath of modern industry, the factory system, was a product of English institutions, enormously stimulated by exhaustless stores of iron and coal.

Never had Providence so favored a nation as England was favored in the last half of the eighteenth and the first half of the nineteenth centuries. Industrially, she was a half-century in advance of the rest of the world.

The problem which occupied her statesmen was how to keep the advantage thus secured. There were certain hindrances which threatened to offset it. Never had there been a nation in so artificial a position. She was living on imported food, and earning it by manufacturing imported raw materials. The tax upon corn and other food products necessarily increased the cost of living, and thus, indirectly, the cost of manufacturing. Her tariff taxes were chiefly imposed upon food supplies, and upon raw materials, nearly all of which, save iron, coal, and wool, it was necessary to import. At the same time she was manufacturing many times in excess of the needs of her own people, with a surplus constantly growing larger. For this surplus new markets must be found and held; which meant that the cost of production must be kept at the lowest possible point.

As we look back through the vista of this half-century, and sense in retrospect the situation as it existed in the days of Cobden and Bright, the marvel is, not that they saw things as they did, but that they should have found it so herculean a task to convince the English people that free trade was the only possible way out for them. We marvel that the landed and agricultural interests should have been strong enough to so long delay it; for the limit of agricultural development had long since been reached, and was pitiably inadequate to the daily wants of the people. On the other hand, no imagination was bold enough to attempt to measure the possibilities of development which lay before the manufacturing interests. Agriculture suffered the full measure of the blow which the repeal of the corn laws inflicted, and suffers from it to-day more keenly than at any earlier epoch; but the nation as a whole gained from that repeal immeasurably more than the farmers and landed interests lost.

The two things necessary to preserve to England what she had gained were obvious. First,—Food and materials must be as cheap with her as with any other nation. Second,—If England was to hold her own outside England, where her markets lay, she must at the same time discipline and equip herself for that struggle by meeting and matching any and every competition on her own soil. Absolute free trade was necessary, not only to permit, but to *compel* England's manufacturers to produce as cheaply as her possible competitors. With a wisdom born of profound selfishness, with that enlightened national spirit which regards home interests before those of any and all other nations, she accepted these conditions.

The results, as Mr. Courtney says, magnificently vindicate the policy of 1846. The export of British and Irish produce increased from £97,000,000 in 1854 (the earliest date supplied by the statistical abstracts of the Board of Trade) to £248,000,000 in 1889, which is the largest year in the series; but one subsequent year (1891) approximating that total. Here is an increase of 150 per cent in thirty-five years of free trade. Other nations, notably the United States, have shown a larger percentage of growth during corresponding years; but the English ratio is substantial enough to justify any encomium that may be lavished upon the economic policy that stands behind it.

No other nation has ever found itself in like circumstances, nor ever will. Therefore, Mr. Courtney has no occasion to marvel that England has not succeeded in luring any other nation along the same primrose path. On the contrary, the challenge of England—for it was nothing else—supplied the strongest of reasons why no nation which hoped to share in her industrial development should accept her guidance. The legislation of 1846 was notice to the rest of the world that England, deeming herself industrially invincible, proposed to reap the rewards of that invincibility. It inevitably drove every would-be competitor to seek refuge, in self-defence, in protection ; and thus, in the end, it has proved to be a two-edged sword.

Contemporaneously with English statesmen and economists, Friedrich List had sensed this situation, and thought out its bearing upon the industrial future of Germany. Accepting the abstract theories of international trade announced by Adam Smith, and admitting the economic advantages of free trade as a cosmopolitan policy, he detected and exposed its weakness when applied to the case of an individual nation situated as his own country was. In the cosmopolitan status, where all nations were completely developed industrially, international freedom of trade was the natural and best status for all. But without that equality of conditions, international free trade inevitably meant the further aggrandizement of the nation industrially superior, at the expense of every country that remained incompetent to hold its own against the superior nation. He applied this test to his own country. He saw no permanent gain from German free trade to anyone but England, so long as Germany remained inferior at every point save agriculture; and he announced the great theory of nationalism, *i. e.*, that it is the purpose of a national fiscal policy not simply or chiefly to gain mere matter by exchanging goods for goods, but rather *to gain in productive and political power.*

List was educated to this philosophy by his residence in the

United States (1825-1830), during which he studied the workings of the protective policy in this country.   He saw how rapidly the United States was gaining upon his own country, by reason of a policy which tended directly to the development of industrial independence. To List's efforts chiefly Germany owed her zollverein, the customs association of the German states, which was the cradle of the empire. Internal free trade among the German states led naturally into the correlative policy of protection against the trade encroachments of outside states.   English manufactures were everywhere; and industrial headway was uncertain and spasmodic.   Thus, during the years that England was agitating for free trade, all the internal conditions favored List's propaganda for protection in Germany; and, during the last half-century, the two fiscal theories have practically paralleled each other in the two countries.

The record of German progress during this half-century is certainly not less impressive than that of England,—from certain points of view it is far more significant.   Applying the test already employed for England,—the value of the manufactured exports,—we find that German commerce has increased from £36,000,000 in 1850 to £163,-000,000 in 1889; the percentage of increase being 350, as compared with 150 per cent of increase in British commerce.   Admitting that these percentages are not a fair test, it must nevertheless be agreed that German progress has been much the faster of the two; and very much faster, when we consider the relative disadvantages under which Germany started in the race.   In twenty years Germany had doubled her exports, and lifted herself to a point of vantage equal to that at which England started in 1846.   In twenty years more she has attained an industrial development on a par with that of England, in practically every line of manufacturing; in many lines surpassing it. German ambition sets no limit on the progress of the future; for it looks upon the development of the half-century as merely preliminary and preparatory.

If Germany had accepted England's dictum instead of following the teachings of List, she must have remained industrially dependent upon England.   As it is, she has become her rival.   Some sacrifices she has undoubtedly made to reach that end; some burdens she has borne, of which the advocates of free trade are apt to make very much when arguing the abstract question.   Notwithstanding them all, and accepting the utmost dimensions that may be placed upon them, the increase in the wealth and resources of the German nation has been prodigious. List recognized these losses and burdens; but he predicted that they would be recuperated with interest, in the shape of productive force,—a force pregnant with future wealth and prosperity. And his prediction has been overwhelmingly fulfilled.

To this development Great Britain has unwittingly contributed more than all other nations combined. The Germans are apt pupils; and they have improved upon their schoolmaster. England has contributed nothing new to labor-saving machinery that Germany has not promptly adopted. She imported no machines from England, except with the purpose of learning to make them herself. She sent her young men into English factories and counting-rooms; and whatever there was to learn there she appropriated or improved upon. She did not merely imitate. Very early she saw that the hereditary superiority of English workmanship was a prime factor in reducing the cost and increasing the excellence of production. Thereupon she established the most comprehensive system of industrial and technological education to be found anywhere in the world. In the course of time her artisan class has grown conspicuously superior in skill and intelligence to the English workman. Her best brains have been drafted into the work of improving and cheapening the processes of manufacture, through the aid of scientific investigation. In school and college, in factory and laboratory, they have set in motion a system of industrial forces which is working out results with the precision to which years of the most patient preparation have logically led. It is not too much to say that German contributions to the development of the chemical side of manufacturing have been as important as the English contributions to the mechanical side. During all these years that the Cobden Club has been reiterating the glories of the *laisser faire*, and pointing to the wonderful expansion of English trade and manufactures, the Germans have been gaining steadily upon Great Britain; following her first into the world's neutral markets, then into her own colonies, and finally into her own island. Whatever the government itself could do to strengthen and foster this industrial competition, it has done without stint, and with aggressive diplomacy. It has established its commercial agencies on every continent; it has negotiated differential treaties of vast advantage to German manufacturers; it has subsidized transportation routes and industrial schools with equal generosity; it has encouraged new enterprises by every agency which a paternal government can invent. And it has its reward, in this fiftieth year of Cobdenism, in the nearly general admission of British statesmen and manufacturers, that the German can undersell the Englishman to-day, in his own markets, in all great lines of manufacture. It has had its reward too in the·fact that while the declared value of English exports (produce and manufactures) to Germany fell from £19,293,636 in 1890 to £17,698,457 in 1893, the value of the exports of Germany to Great Britain has steadily advanced from year to year until in 1893 it reached £21,632,614. An examination of the detailed tables shows that Germany has for many years been selling a much larger quantity of manufactured articles in England than England has sold in Germany. These are, in nearly every instance, articles which England makes at home and exports to other countries. The Germans are underselling the English in England; while the German tariff prevents England from underselling the Germans in Germany.

Undoubtedly the Germans have had other advantages besides their tariff, their energy, industry, ingenuity, and system in this great industrial advance. German manufacturers have thus far escaped many of the impediments which have hampered those of England. Notably they have been exempt from the minute and perplexing restrictions of English factory legislation; and notably also, the relations between employer and employed have been far less troublesome. Trades-unionism exists in Germany; but it is neither so rampant nor so pigheaded as trades-unionism in England. Strikes and wage disputes are comparatively infrequent there, notwithstanding the fact that the hours of labor remain long, while those of England are the shortest of any nation in the world; notwithstanding the fact, also, that German wages are as a rule considerably lower than those of England. Longer hours and lower wages are very material aids in reducing productive costs, and have been of tremendous value to Germany in bringing her abreast of England in the field of international competition. ·But these are advantages which, in the nature of things, cannot last. Indeed the steady rise of German wages is apparent in all recent investigations. The deputation of the British Iron Trade Association, already alluded to, reported that, contrary to the general belief, German wages in the iron industry were slightly higher in 1895 than those prevailing in Staffordshire and the north of England. It has long been a favorite argument with Englishmen that the shorter hours and higher wages of their country tended to greater efficiency and larger production. We find it difficult to reconcile this contention with the admission, now quite general in England, that the German workman, by reason of his superior technical education, is a better workman than the Englishman. Side by side with this admission is the universal declaration of British manufacturers that the eight-hour day, for which the Trades Union Congress has just reiterated its demand, is the one step now necessary to drive the final nail in the coffin of English industry.

This analysis of two contemporaneous industrial developments establishes the economic fact, admitted by Mr. Courtney,—for the first time in any utterance of the Cobden Club,—that nations may flourish under a protective system and may decline under free trade. Thus is swept away a mass of superfluous and beclouding dogma the partisan and passionate reiteration of which has shut from view the only sound basis from which to approach the consideration of the question. The fiscal policy which is one nation's meat, may be another nation's poison. It is purely a question of national expediency; to be determined, by each nation for itself, in favor of the one policy or the other, or of a combination of some features of both, according to the exigencies of the situation of that nation at a given period. It is not impossible, nor is it altogether improbable, that, before the close of the first half of the twentieth century, we shall see Germany flourishing under free trade, and England renewing her youth under some form of limited protection,—perhaps the industrial zollverein for which Lord Masham pleads and Mr. Chamberlain appears to be ready.

S. N. D. NORTH.

MODERN GREECE.[1]

THE Greece of to-day, forming, as it does, the only living bridge between the past and the present of European history during a period of nearly three thousand years, from Homer down to Rangabé and Bikellas, certainly does not always receive the recognition from intelligent Englishmen which it so eminently deserves. For this there are various causes. First, there may be some persons, brought up in the school of the politicians of the third decade of the present century, who are accustomed to look at Greece only from the side of Turkey, and who, in this regard, consider every loss of territory in that quarter as dangerous to the balance of power in Europe, an incentive to Russian aggression, and perilous to England's commercial movements in the Mediterranean and to her imperial influence in the East. Let Greece perish; but let Turkey stand and hold the keys of Constantinople against the ever-watchful burglars of the North!

This view of the Hellenic question was perhaps pardonable enough at the outbreak of the Greek Liberation war in 1821; and the Emperor Alexander, as a member of the Holy Alliance, was, personally, so far as his motives were concerned, worthy of praise rather than of blame in regarding the revolt against the Turkish yoke as an act of lawless insurrection, which should receive no encouragement from any well-constituted government. But times have changed since then: we know now what the Greeks were who fought that noble battle; and our fathers have seen that merciless sweep of blood and butchery by which the Turks, had they been allowed free scope by the European Powers, would have exterminated the noble people to whom we owe the most valuable part of our spiritual and intellectual heritage. For, though Christianity was born in Judea, it grew up to manhood with the sway of the Greek tongue; and as for intellect, there is not a science of the most recent birth in modern Europe that does not bear the stamp of Greek thought and Greek expression on its forehead. It was not, therefore, a common but a nobly exceptional case which

[1] This article, written toward the end of 1894, was the last from Professor BLACKIE'S pen.—Ed. THE FORUM.

8

induced the European Powers,—especially England, France, and Russia,—though with a slow and cautious advance, ultimately to proceed to an intervention in favor of the revolted subjects of the Porte in the Morea and adjacent districts of the ancient Hellas. It was the voice of humanity prevailing over the negations of a heartless policy. The wholesale atrocities of the Turks had put them, to use Archibald Alison's words, "beyond the pale of international civilization"; and the laws that regulate the warlike intercourse of nation with nation, and of man with man, were wholly inapplicable to the cry of a noble people, bleeding under the oppression of a Power that could not maintain the right of the stronger without revelling, with the ferocity of the tiger, in the butchery of human shambles. There is, we may say with confidence, at the present moment [1894] not a single human-hearted person in the British dominions who could wish the independence of Greece, established by the interference of the three Allied Powers in 1827, undone for the sake of keeping up a strong Turkey; on the contrary, every person who has studied the details of the patriotic struggle which ended victoriously at Navarino will agree with Alison in describing the "untoward event" or, as the friends of Greece call it, "that happy blunder," as "one of the most glorious events in the annals of Christendom."[1]

Another and a more efficient cause for the scanty acknowledgment of living Greece by British travellers is, that though no man can compare the attractive power of Switzerland, for instance, to that of Greece, the country of *William Tell* is in every way more accessible and more open to the perambulation of strangers than the scene of the exploits of Colokotronis, Canaris, and other prime actors in the drama of the Greek Liberation war. John Bull is a comfortable animal; and even Scotch Sandy, in these days of swift and easy travel, is not so ready to buckle himself to the treading of thorny glens, or the scaling of rocky braes, as he was half a century ago, before the appearance of railways. Travelling nowadays, in the old style known to Ulysses,—where a certain amount of personal skill and daring was necessary to the successful achievement of a tour,—may be said to be extinct: we do not travel; but, as Mr. Ruskin has it, we are *sent*. But even in respect of steam locomotion by railways, Greece is following fast in the track of more favored countries. When the new line shooting northward to Larissa is finished, there will be eight hundred and seventy-five miles—more than twice the distance from Edinburgh to London—in

[1] "History of Europe," by ARCHIBALD ALISON, chap. xiv, p. 159.

efficient action. Add to this the railway to Patras, which has brought Greece into closer connection with its natural commercial ally, the West of Europe, and the most dainty tourist will understand how easy it is to jump into the train at Patras, and, after an hour or two's rattle, land at Olympia, the great centre of Greek gymnastics and of Greek art.

So much for present facilities of communication; though I must say that, to fix the features of a country permanently in the mind's eye, the old style of travelling—by pedestrian tramp, or quiet jolt on the back of a lazy mule—is the best. But there is another hindrance in the way of a tourist in Greece, which, if it does not check his advance through the most picturesque and the most interesting of all European countries, certainly makes a large deduction from his pleasure. A human-hearted traveller is eager, not only to set foot on the ground which was once the seat of fateful oracles, and the stage of early Christian apostleship, but to speak with the people who, through a thousand years of mediæval struggle, and four hundred years of Turkish oppression, have preserved, in unbroken continuity, the language of Aristotle, of the Apostle Paul, and of Clemens of Alexandria. It was Jean Paul Richter who made the remark, that, as the way to a mother's heart is through her children, so the way to a people's heart is through their mother tongue. This is most true. One kindly "la math dhuit" will do more to win a Sassenach tourist an entrance into a warm Highland heart, than a hundred good-day-to-yous in the best English style. And, though our English travellers are by no means celebrated for their colloquial mastery of European tongues, a modicum of French or German will enable them without much trouble to shake hands and hearts with the "honest men and bonnie lassies" that people the winding glens or the sloping braes of the German and Swiss Alps. But with Greece it is otherwise. German and French, when taught in our schools, are taught as they are understood and used familiarly in the daily intercourse of the people who speak them; but Greek and Latin are taught as dead languages, for the purpose of reading only, wherein the eye usurps the province of the ear; and when the voice asserts its place in the business, as it must do, it is the English orthoepy that is allowed freely to give vocal law to the manly majesty of a Ciceronian sentence, or the rich note of a Platonic period. The absurdity of this insular peculiarity of our English classical teaching, with regard to Latin, was shown some years ago by a well-known Cambridge scholar—Munro; but the pedagogues besouth the Tweed, like the Pope on the banks of the Tiber, still stand on their own Anglified Latin, and mouth it in a fashion that no inheritor of the old language of the Western Church in Italy, France, or Ireland can understand. But if this Anglified trick is bad in Latin, it is doubly bad in Greek; for, if Latin under the influences of the last two centuries may be said to be now a half-dead language, or a language with only an artificially prolonged academical life, Greek is a living language as much now as in the days when Demosthenes rolled his thunder against the Macedonian in the *agora*, or when, four hundred years later, the Apostle Paul on the hill of Mars used the same weapons more effectively against the sneers of the Stoic and Epicurean babblers of his time.

To talk of Greek as a dead language is to show an ignorance of the historical fates of western Asia and southeastern Europe, of which men pretending to culture should be ashamed.   How could Greek ever die during the thousand years of the Byzantine Empire, when, from Constantine downward, it had driven Latin from its throne, and asserted its existence, not only in a continuous stream of literary authority in church and state, but in the daily intercourse of all educated persons from Cyprus to Crete, and from Crete to. Corfu? Then, from the taking of Constantinople by the Turks in 1453, classical Greek stood yet more firmly against the Osmanli dominance than it did against the Latinizing influence of Justinian and the earlier emperors of the eastern Rome.   The Normans, when they conquered England, found it an easy matter to encroach largely on the Saxon speech of the people, and to form a mixed language—the modern English—out of Anglo-Saxon and Frenchified Latin; but to any occupation of the linguistic ground of literary Greece by the language of the Turks, the Greek mind was as much opposed as its Christian conscience was to the creed of Mohammed; so that, from the time of the Council of Florence in the fifteenth century down to Coray at the date of the French Revolution, through Tricoupis, Paparegopoulos, and Rangabé to Bikellas and Polylas and Roides in our own times, we have an uninterrupted flow of living Greek.

These being the facts that stare even the superficial observer in the face, what possible reason, I ask, can there be for throwing an artificial hindrance in the way of our converse with this noble, self-sustaining people, by treating their language in a purely bookish fashion, as if it were Syriac or Aramaic? Assuredly it is high time for our influential men at Oxford and Cambridge to put an end to such a gross violation of the laws of philological science and international comity. Porson, the greatest perhaps among English Hellenists, and Jelf, one of the most accredited of Greek grammarians, insist in the most indubitable terms that Greek should be spoken with exact observance of the accents put on the words by the Alexandrian grammarians two hundred and fifty years before Christ, and handed down to us through the Church service and the living speech of the people for a period of more than two thousand years ; and yet we persist in treating Greek as we treat no other language. Italian, French, German, and Spanish get fair play; while Greek must be content to have its orthoepy expounded in abstract rules, so neglected and inverted in practice as to make it, in the mouth of an Englishman, utterly unintelligible to the noble people from whom we are proud to have borrowed it.

So much for the hindrances in the way of fact or imagination that prevent Greece from being so largely betravelled by English tourists as many less interesting countries. Let us now plant ourselves on the ground, and first, naturally, at Athens, at once the centre of the national life and the most convenient starting-point for the tourist. And what do we find here ? In 1836, Dr. Christopher Wordsworth, then head-master of Harrow School, wrote of the great city, the world-famous stage of Periclean statesmanship and Phidian art, as follows :—

"The town of Athens is now lying in ruins. The streets are almost deserted; nearly all the houses are without roofs. The churches are reduced to bare walls and heaps of stones and mortar. There is but one church in which the service is performed. A few new wooden houses, one or two of more solid structure, and the two lines of planked sheds which form the bazar are all the inhabited dwellings that Athens can now boast. So slowly does it recover from the effects of the late war. . . . In this state of modern desolation, the grandeur of the ancient buildings which still survive here is more striking, their preservation is more wonderful. There is now scarcely any building at Athens in so perfect a state as the temple of Theseus. The least ruined objects here are some of the Ruins themselves."

Five years later, in MacCulloch's " Geographical Dictionary," we find it stated that this nest of ruins was a flourishing small town of 17,000 inhabitants. And what is it now ? According to the most recent authoritative tables, published by Mr. R. A. H. Bickford-Smith, its population in the year 1889 was 114,355, having, in round numbers, sextupled in the space of fifty years. Nor does this increase stand alone. Volo, a seaport town in the east of Thessaly, in ten years, from 1879 to 1889, nearly trebled its population, and Tricala—the classical Tricca—increased in the same proportion. The small ruined village has thus

grown before our eyes to a large city ; a city not so large certainly as
Liverpool, or Birmingham, or even Newcastle,—great English centres
of commerce and manufactures,—but as large as the metropolis of the
northeast of Scotland, the city [Aberdeen] that draws its granite length
so gracefully between the Dee and the Don.

The growth of population in Manchester, Liverpool, and other English towns, from the beginning of the eighteenth century downward,
is notable enough ; but this upstarting of a ruined village into a
mighty city before the eyes of a single generation deserves special
attention. To understand it we must bear in mind that, though the
Greeks had been miserably down-trodden by the Turks for four hundred years ; the best hope of the people borne by an unholy tribute
far away from their mothers' homes, and trained into the tools of an
inhuman tyranny ; and though, had it not been for the " untoward
event " at Navarino, the whole population of the Morea would have
been exterminated beneath the merciless tramp of Turkish hoofs ; there
nevertheless lived, behind the outward show of slavish debasement,
a heart of sturdy independence, that cherished the patriotic memories of ages, and seized eagerly on every chance that might enable
it to stand before the world in the attitude and character that had
given it the most prominent place in the history of the human race.
The two years' struggle that gave to Greece the right to look Europe
in the face, as a noble people determined to die rather than live the
slaves of a hateful tyranny, at the same time gave to Europe the assurance that Greece was living Greece again ; and Christian conscience
and classic memories combined, when once the yoke was broken, to
enable the Greeks to show to the world that, in spite of the bombshells of
Venice and the sabres of Turkey, not only should a Greek mother bear
sons to grow up free from the rapine of Turkish hands, but desolate
Athens should rise to her old position, and, along with Edinburgh,
Glasgow, and Aberdeen, assert its place among famous European
cities that combine commercial enterprise with cultivated intelligence.
It was this noble patriotic pride that, in the short space of half a century, turned the little ruined village into an imposing city.

Nor is it difficult to see by what steps of sure ascent this noble ambition to be their own best selves again has been so splendidly gratified.
The Greeks, though extinguished politically by the Osmanli irruption in
1453, were never conquered intellectually and morally : they were bound,
but they were not paralyzed. The Turk could rule by the sabre, as
the violent blast rules the ship in storm ; but when quiet came, and not

rude force, but active intelligence was required, he was glad to employ, as useful ministers in the sphere of public business, the very men whom, in the lower sphere of political submission, he had treated as slaves. In this way the Greeks of the Fanar in Constantinople often became the most influential and effective governors of the half-conquered provinces of the Turk; and so, while externally doing duty for him, were silently and effectively preparing the way for the happy hour when a favorable chance might enable them to throw off their gilded chains, and stand before their Eastern oppressors in the same attitude of manly independence that Leonidas and his Spartans assumed at Thermopylæ.

But not only in the capital of the Turkish rule was there a special sort of expectant Greek nationality, under the outward recognition of the Turk, but all over Europe, in Asia Minor, and in Africa, there were colonies of expatriated Greeks, waiting and working for the hour of national regeneration. The Greeks in modern as in ancient times had never been slow to use the advantages, commercial and naval, which their varied coast and richly islanded seas presented; and, while in classical times Salamis and Eurymedon taught the Persians to confine themselves within the natural cincture of the Tigris and Euphrates, in recent times the names of Canaris and Miaulis and the Hydriotes taught a similar lesson to the Turks, who were destined to lay the corner-stone of Greek independence by the "happy blunder" of Navarino. Not at Hydra only, at Scio, at Psara and Parga, were colonies of patriotic and high-spirited Greeks, ever ready to take up arms and lay down life when the call of Providence should blow a blast of liberation in their ears; but in all the centres of commercial activity in the Mediterranean and the Adriatic,—in Smyrna, in Alexandria, at Livorno, at Venice, and Trieste,—a strength of Greek nationality was being nursed, ready to start into efficient manhood, the moment a vulnerable point was opened in the mail of their hereditary oppressors. Of this expectant patriotism the Greek churches in England—in London, Liverpool, and Manchester—remain to the present hour speaking witnesses. Such and so numerous was the class of Greeks,—outside of Greece bodily, but intensely beating with the warm pulses of patriotism,—who, from the moment of the publicly recognized independence of the fatherland, looked to the ruins of Athens as the natural soil into which their liberal patriotism was to cast the seed of a swift resurrection. Forthwith funds were supplied with which schools and colleges, museums, and benevolent associations of all kinds were set in motion; and when to this were added the palatial display of the young kingdom beneath the Acropolis, and the commercial opportunities of the adjacent Piræus, the charm worked so potently that in the course of half a century a rotten old Turkish village rose into a position of honorable rivalry with the fairest cities of western Europe.

And now let the human-hearted student of social fates take his station for a minute on this ground so miraculously recovered from barbarism; and look around. All the world is loud in praise of the beauty of "the modern Athens," commonly called Edinburgh; and though this epithet was given to our Scottish capital more from a notion of intellectual relationship, than of topographical coincidence, there can be no doubt that the latter element in the comparison exists. The great advantage of Edinburgh consists in its preserving the natural lines of the elevated situation on which lie its main streets, open, not only freely and grandly to east and west, but, with recurrent openings to the north, commanding a fair and far view of the high ground on both sides of the Forth. With this wonderful combination of rural and urban charm, the Greek Athens may not dare to compete. Still, there are in both cities striking points of similarity, which may serve to give a preference to the topographical source of the popular designation, so currently given to the Dunedin of the old Celtic stronghold. Let the traveller in Athens take his stand before the beautiful temple of Theseus, and, looking southward, he will, point after point, command the same view of the Hellenic city as that of Edinburgh presented to the eye of one of its citizens looking in a similar direction from Fettes College. Directly in front of the Attic traveller rises the hill of Mars, with the adjacent Acropolis crowned with the Doric strength of the Parthenon and the Doric grace of the pillars still bearing the name of the most ancient Attic king, Erechtheus, who stands in the same relation to Pericles as Abraham did to David and the flourishing Jewish monarchy under his wise son. To this, in the Scottish Athens, the Castle rock, with its military towers, the Armoury Hall, and other lofty buildings sloping down to the Scottish Bank, and the cathedralic crown of St. Giles, correspond. Then to the left, for Lycabettus in the classical picture, we have Arthur's Seat; for the Ilissus, the Water of Leith rushing grandly beneath Douglas Crescent, with an environment of palatial hospitals unequalled in the three kingdoms. Beyond the city bounds, southward and southwestward, we have in Edinburgh, corresponding to the honeyed Hymettus of classical

Greece, the Pentland Hills, sacred to the memory of the defenders of freedom of conscience in the days of the Stuarts; and, turning round in an opposite direction, we have in Greece Pentelicus and, beyond that westward, the mountain ranges of Thebes and Megara, corresponding to the East and West Lomonds and the Ochil range in Fife. Then, of course, in the comparison we must not forget that the Piræus stands in the same relation to the classic Athens that Leith does to Edinburgh; the distance of four miles from the city being compensated by the steam transit of the railway, which, wherever it appears, turns miles into minutes, and physical distances into social identities.

In this topographical planting of the Scottish beside the Hellenic Athens, while there can be little doubt that, if only by virtue of Princes Street and its outlooks, the palm in respect of pictorial effect must be given to the northern competitor, on the other hand, in wealth of historical retrospect, the relation of the ancient to the modern Athens is that of a giant to a dwarf. From Margaret, the sainted spouse of Malcolm Canmore, to Kirkcaldy of Grange, and the stout presentation of our great Reformer, John Knox, to the seductive grace of the fair Queen Mary at Holyrood, the parallel line of the old Edinburgh, facing the architectural splendor of Princes Street, carries with it, to a purely Scottish eye, memories of the past as rich and as precious as the circle of heroic traditions which holds the mind captive when contemplating the Acropolis and the hill of Mars from the vestibule of the temple of Theseus; but in world-wide significance and in the record of the Clio of all times and places, the names of Theseus and Miltiades, of Themistocles and Pericles and Phidias, outweigh all that the rich story of Scottish manhood can number from Bannockburn to Drumclog and Prestonpans.

Nor is it only within the precincts of the city walls that the ground of the classical Athens teems at every step with a significance with which no other European city, not even colossal Rome, can vie; but all around, in every direction, mighty monuments, whether in the form of white marble columns or in the more eloquent form of shattered ruins, tell a tale that can perish only with the world to which they belong. Fronting the eye as it looks southward from any lofty position in the city is the island of Salamis, corresponding in situation to Inchkeith, or the Isle of May, in our Scottish Athens; and jutting out with a sharp projection into the sea, corresponding pretty much to St. Abb's Head in the landscape of the Lothians and Berwickshire, is Sunium, with the pillared shrine of the patron goddess of Athens,

Pallas Athene, supreme in celestial wisdom, as Jove was in power. Turning this far-viewed promontory and tramping northward some thirty or forty miles, we plant our feet on the plain of Marathon, a name which stands in the same relation to the political fates of Europe that Jerusalem does to its religious story ; for had it not been for Marathon, five hundred years before Christ, Persia might have strangled Greek freedom in the cradle, and Rome might have had to fight her ground with an Asiatic, as she did later on with an African, Hannibal. Then, shooting southwestward under the shade of Pentelicus and Parnassus, the traveller can return to Athens by Eleusis, a name as sacred to the ancient world as Papal Rome was to the Catholic Europe of the Middle Ages, and of which the great Roman orator says, that it taught a doctrine which was the mother of all higher civilization, and enabled those who were initiated in its mysteries to live with a purer joy and to die with a brighter hope.[1]

Let us now cast a glance at the social and political state of this most interesting of reconstituted kingdoms. And first, of agriculture. In Greece, as in every well-constituted country, the cultivation of the ground by an industrious and intelligent peasantry is the primary condition of a healthy nationality. It does not make the most show, but is, nevertheless, the base of the pillars that support the cornice and the pediment. In this important department, though Greece stands by no means so high as most of the older and more firmly rooted European states, it exhibits on the whole, since the accession of King George, satisfactory marks of progress. In the four most important fields of agriculture,—corn, currants, vines, and olives,—Mr. Bickford-Smith reports the following increase of cultivated ground during a period of twenty-seven years; viz, 1860, 2,322,524 stremmata[2]; 1887, 6,863,666 stremmata. This is good; nevertheless, all our travellers agree in depicting the working-power and the rural style of operations in Greece as far from model. This was indeed only what was to be expected in a country groaning for centuries under the domination of a foreign despotism, and deprived of the fatherly superintendence of a native proprietorship.

So much for the land. But the element on which the strength and glory of the Greek people, from Themistocles and Cimon down to Canaris and Miaulis, has been displayed, is the sea; not only, as these names indicate, in significant epochs of national struggle, but in the adventurous and gainful march of commerce in times of peace.

[1] Cicero ; De Legibus, ii, 14.   [2] A stremma is equivalent to .219 of an acre.

This, of course, was just what was to be anticipated from the combined action of circling waters on all sides of the country and of intelligent and enterprising Greek settlers in all the principal commercial
centres of Asia, Africa, Italy, Russia, and England. On this subject
Mr. Bickford-Smith waxes eloquent, and spreads forth the whole
flattering summary of Hellenic commercial strength in the fifth
chapter of his valuable book; but my limits permit me only to state
the general result of his naval tabulation in a single sentence. "Before the revolution," he says, "Greece had about 60,000 tons of shipping, but was left in 1833 with very few ships; Galaxidi, for instance,
being reduced from two hundred and fifty ships to ninety. In 1891,
she had reached a total of ninety-three steamboats, of 46,688 tons, and
4,772 sailing vessels, of 228,976 tons." On this head, therefore, there
is no doubtful balance-sheet. Whether at the Piræus or Galaxidi, at
Smyrna or Trieste, Greece will know to rule the waters with which
nature has so liberally encompassed her shores.

But a more difficult matter than commerce for new Greece, and,
so far as compact nationality is concerned, a more important matter, is
government; government and the growth of years, the rudder without
the sure management of which the good ship may in one gusty moment
be driven on a rock and wrecked. On this, therefore, every lover of
revived Hellas must fix his most serious regard. The detailed account
of the sad story of recurring misgovernment and revolt in Greece,
during the thirty-five years that elapsed from the Presidency of Capo
d'Istria in 1828 to the accession of the present King of Greece in 1863,
will be found in Finlay, Sergeant, and other writers on the social position and fortunes of the Greeks of to-day. The character of the whole
of that unhappy period may be summed up in a few sentences. In the
first place, it must be borne in mind that Greece being, both by its geographical formation and historical traditions, a democratic country, and
at the era of the great Liberation war owing its independence to the
self-assertion of individual patriots incapable of combination for common action, presented a political problem of unusual difficulty when
unity of action was the demand of the hour. Greece was Greece again
by the "happy blunder" of Navarino,—a recognized, distinct factor in
the complex body of European states. But the body must have a
head; and for a head,—having among themselves no man of pure Greek
blood, who could represent Hellas as grandly as Garibaldi did Italy,
—the National Assembly elected Count Capo d'Istria, a Russianizing
Corfiote, to be the President of the associated states of liberated Greece.

Of course, no more difficult political position can be imagined.
A strong arm and a kindly hand—a rare combination in rulers—were
equally necessary for success in the management of a people proud of
their national history and hot with the spur of recent successful revolt
against hereditary tyranny.   Capo d'Istria did not recognize this : he
would wield the mace of his Presidency like the sceptre of an absolute
monarch : and, after a wild year or two of fret and violence, paid for
the abuse of power by the penalty of death.   On October 9, 1831,
he was assassinated as he went to hear mass in the church of St. Spi-
ridion at Nauplia.   An ugly business; but political government in
troubled times deals in blood, just as gusty skies and rainy spouts deal
in mud : a most ill-omened start for the march of free Greece into the
arena of European politics; but the bloody omen of the first step was
more than matched by the flagrant folly of the next.   The Greeks had
sense enough to know that, as a people, they were essentially democratic; yet, partly from the necessity of the case, and partly from a
desire to gain the confidence of the great European Powers, they determined to change their Presidency into a Kingship, and gave the
Powers authority to choose a monarch for the Kingdom of revived
Greece.   And whom did the Powers choose?   A young German
bursch just escaped from school, a green Bavarian boy of seventeen.   He arrived at Nauplia on February 6, 1833, in an English
frigate.   Of course such an unpractised stripling could not play the
full-grown man anywhere, much less enact the part of a wise king in a
troubled country ; so a brigade of Bavarian notables, headed by Count
Armansperg, was sent with him, who succeeded in misgoverning that
unfortunate country on the principles of German officialism and centralization for nine years, when, in 1843, they were dismissed with
general satisfaction and without assassination.   The boy-king then
accepted the limitation of a constitutional government, of which his
dismissed ministry had known nothing.   From that period onward,
the Bavarian princeling made a trial of governing for himself, but
proved unequal to so slippery a business.   His German ideas of
ruling did not suit Greeks; so he too, in 1862, received notice to
quit, and the following year, the present monarch, King George of
Denmark, walked in.

After this, to the present date [1894], we have over thirty years of
comparatively fair sailing, during which the good ship of the Hellenic
state, if not altogether without danger, has managed to steer clear of the
rocks which ruined the Capo-d'Istrian and the Bavarian governments.

And, in spite of many disadvantages, the government of King George presents itself to Europe in an attitude of stability that gives good hope for the future. Personally the monarch has known to maintain his authority firmly in the *via media*, without either asserting his kingly prerogative too stoutly on the one hand, or shrinking timidly before the gusts of political factions on the other. This, under the most favorable conditions, is no small praise; but is especially praiseworthy under the conditions of political life as they exist in the Hellenic traditions, and under the action of the Constitution of 1863, sworn to by the monarch on his acceptance of the throne. These conditions and this Constitution imply three things: universal manhood suffrage; legislation by a single chamber, untempered by the salutary check of an Upper House; and, worst of all perhaps, an army of professional politicians far outnumbering the public need, and living on the pay and place which it is the privilege of the party in power to distribute. Under such a system, the natural nurse of faction, the throne of a king is, of course, no easy seat; and that King George has sat upon it now for more than thirty years without any recurrence of the social earthquakes that shook his predecessors, must be attributed to his own good sense, in the first place, but partly also to his good luck in having united himself to a Russian princess. Greek in her ecclesiastical kinship, womanly and kind in her social relations, and—better even than these qualifications — having presented her royal lord with young princes and a princess, the growth of Greek soil, thus guaranteeing the proud young nation against the degradation and the danger of having to beg from door to door of haughty European courts for a king,—the Greeks have reason to be gratified with their monarch's choice.

But at the present moment, as already stated, the grand difficulty with which revived Greece has to struggle is not so much democracy, or other one-sidedness in the Constitution, but simply the national debt and the finance. This is a matter which outweighs all others, both in embarrassment for the present and in apprehension for the future of this brave little kingdom; and it is extremely difficult at a distance to form a reliable judgment on the state of affairs. Through this atmosphere of painful doubt, however, there is a bright ray of hope cast from the report of two of the best informed specialists on the subject of Greek finance: the one is M. Joseph D. Beckmann, in his "Les Finances de la Grèce: étude composée sur la base de documents authentiques," published at Athens, in November, 1892, and of which the substance is given in three detailed chapters by Mr. Bickford-

Smith ; and the other is Mr. Law, in his important "Report on the present economical and financial position of Greece," presented to both Houses of Parliament, April, 1893. From Beckmann, Bickford-Smith tabulates the following reassuring points :—

"(1) Though Greece has borrowed a large amount of money, she has something to show for it : Thessaly, many miles of roads, many miles of railways, a respectable little navy, and a very rapidly developed commerce.

(2) Her budgets have been gradually improving, and are now nearly in stable equilibrium."

And Mr. Law sums up the general heads of his report in even more hopeful terms.

The remaining points that call for notice in a summary view of the social state of revived Greece are : religion, education, literature, and language. Fortunately the facts in these departments are so certain and so prominent that a very few words will amply satisfy the impartial enquirer. First, in regard to the Church, there is reason to fear that, though Hellas is happily free from the sacerdotal conceit and the unreasonable dogmatism of the Roman Pope, neither in point of intelligence, nor in the moral influence that belongs to a healthy Christian Church, does she realize the ideal which, from the past history of her Church, and the positive danger of a godless contagion from France, she might reasonably be expected to cherish. On the urgent necessity of reform from within, Mr. Bickford-Smith is very emphatic.

On education and culture, there is but one voice ; a voice calling aloud to all intelligent hearers, that it is both the ambition and the practice of modern Greeks to present themselves to the world in an intellectual garb not unworthy of their classical descent. They have a just pride in the memory that, whatever may have been their position in the political world at various critical periods of their history, intellectually through their wisdom, and morally through Christianity, they have always conquered their conquerors, have even commanded the respect of the sanguinary Turk. One of the first things, perhaps the one good thing, that the Bavarian boy-king did, when seated on the throne, was to establish a complete array of free national schools, in four degrees,—after the model of Germany,—from the humblest infant-school to the proud platform of the National University. Since the date of the Bavarian regency great changes in the schools have taken place, more after the French than the German example ; but, whether French or German, all agree that the popular education in the Greece of to-day is, as regards character and completeness, in no respect inferior to that of the most highly cultivated countries of Europe. So little, indeed, have foreign critics discovered in it to find fault with, that they have paraded excess as its main defect, and no doubt with a certain amount of justice. It is not only in Greece, but in this country [Scotland] and elsewhere, that young persons are sometimes educated above the level to which their social destiny points; but this is a danger perhaps inseparable at the first start from a general elevation of the intellectual platform of a whole people; and especially in a people with such intellectual precedents as the Greeks.

It remains to wind up this rapid outline of the wonderful history of revived and regenerate Greece by a single word on the relation of modern Greece to the world of books,—a world which the most intellectual of all peoples have gloried to claim as peculiarly their own. Greek, with an altogether unique vitality, is, in fact, as I started with saying, the only living bridge that connects the memories of the great Past of the human race with the promise of the great Present. The names of Zosimus and Zonaras, of Acominates, Nicander, Nucius, and Phranzes, to all who are even superficially acquainted with the authorities on which our most interesting mediæval history is based, indicate clearly enough the line of literary continuity which binds into a historical whole the intellectual life of the Greek people, from Diodorus, Polybius, and the early Church fathers downward to the ill-omened capture of Constantinople by the Turks in the middle of the fifteenth century. But this baleful overthrow of their political independence did in no wise cause the enslavement of their souls. The chains which bound the body could not reach the soul. A single glance into a volume of Greek history will show how little the eagle of the soaring Greek intellect had been taught to droop its wings when the political Jove, whom it had served, was dethroned by the Turk. Then, as for the living power of Greek literature in the century which commenced with Coray, thirty years before the epoch of national resurrection in 1821, the least that can be said is, that the spokesmen of Greek thought during that period were in every way worthy of their great ancestors. The names of the distinguished Greek writers mentioned above, and a host of others, point to the pages of a great living drama, as rich in human interest and in social significance as the most valued chapter of Herodotus or Xenophon, of Polybius or Diodorus.

In conclusion, as to the type and character of the language in which the modern Greek intellect has so richly expressed itself, it would re-

quire a separate article of a purely philological character to deal with
it fully.   Meanwhile it may be sufficient to warn the general reader
against lending his ear to the vulgar assertion that Greek, if not a
dead language, is at least so corrupt that the study of it would tend
rather to injure than to promote the study of the Greek of the great
classical period.   This notion proceeds either from gross ignorance or
more gross conceit, or perhaps, on a more charitable interpretation,
from a confounding of the Greek of the local ballads with the Greek
of educated men,—a comparison just as misleading as it would be in
a student of English to confound the local dialect of Lancashire, or the
phraseology of Scottish song, with the style of Tennyson or the London
" Times."   Then as to corruption : That is a vague word ; but how it
can be, with any propriety, applied to a language which is characterized
by an almost superstitious horror of any strange word of Turkish, or
Italian, or French extraction, it is difficult to understand.   The few
slight changes which differentiate the Greek of living Greek writers
from the so-called classical Greek of the ancients, are merely as the
lopping off of a few superfluous branches from a tree of exuberant
growth,—a loss amply compensated by the daily addition of fresh
branches from its own native root, a procedure diametrically opposed to the sewing together, in a crude style, of borrowed scraps
and patches so characteristic of our mixed English tongue.   Lastly,
let the young Hellenist who wishes to shake hands and hearts in a
kindly human and a nobly Christian style with the living Greeks of
to-day, know by practice, that living speech, and not dead grammar, is
the oracle from whom he must learn.   The living alliance of mind and
ear and speech, acting on interesting objects in the immediate surroundings of the learner, with daily practice, will produce a more intimate familiarity with any foreign tongue in five months than will a
purely bookish regimen in as many years.   " Vixere fortes ante Agamemnon "—" Brave men lived before Agamemnon " ; and with great
results men spoke eloquently before books or printed paper were
known.   Books, though extremely useful in a subsidiary way to
supply the deficiencies of direct personal observation and experience,
when substituted for these are unnatural and pernicious ; and their
direct action, as Plato taught long ago in the " Phædrus," is to weaken
the memory, to dull the ear, and to change the music of a sounding
voice into the mute service of a peeping eye.

JOHN STUART BLACKIE.

The Forum

APRIL, 1897.

HAS THE SENATE DEGENERATED?

It cannot be doubted that there is a widespread and growing impatience with the condition of things in the Senate. Indeed, it is becoming something more than impatience. It has already become distrust; and I am afraid we shall soon be compelled to say—condemnation. This feeling seems to be growing among the men who, if the Senate be what the framers of the Constitution meant and hoped, should be its strongest support.

It will not do to say that the most passionate utterances of this feeling come from what we should term the populace, were we speaking of other countries. Fortunate in so many other things, our country, if it have a populace at all,—and a populace is a very different thing from a people,—is especially fortunate in the character and quality of this usually undesirable element of a state. Elsewhere this eager, frantic, excitable, headstrong element of society burns dwellings and warehouses, collects in mobs, hangs from lamp-posts those who are obnoxious to it. It is made up of what are called the lower classes,— the poor and ignorant, half-starved women, workmen out of employ, ruffians and criminals. Here, with some very few exceptions in the large cities, there is little disposition to revolution or to turbulence. Our poorer and illiterate classes are orderly, quiet, and submissive. They have pretty decided political opinions; and they are constant to their political objects. The few mobs we have had of late years have grown out of the contests between organized labor and organized capital, and have been conducted under circumstances which in other

Copyright, 1896, by The Forum Publishing Company.
Permission to re-publish articles is reserved.

countries would have meant revolution, or a large destruction of property and the overthrow of social order.   Our populace does not come from the poor or ignorant classes.   It is made of very different material. It has white and clean hands.   It parts its hair in the middle.   It often understands foreign languages, sometimes Latin and Greek.   It has a cultivated taste in matters of art.   It has sometimes a professor of art among its numbers, although it has never done much to stimulate a virile sentiment as to painting, sculpture, or architecture.   It is polished by foreign travel.   It lives on its income.   It expresses its indignation in excellent English in magazine articles, in orations before literary societies, or at the Commencements of schools for young ladies.   It takes the facts of current history, on which it bases its judgments, without original investigation, from the hasty reports of careless correspondents, or the columns of some favorite newspaper.   It prates and chatters a good deal about the sentiment of honor and political purity; but it is never found doing any strenuous work on the honest side when these things are in peril.   It never helps us by an argument; although it has settled for itself, and would like to settle for us without either study or experience, the subtle questions of free trade, of protection, of · fiscal mechanism, and of political economy.   It contributes to public discussions nothing but sneers, or expressions of contempt or pessimistic despair.   It is found quite as commonly on the wicked side as on the honest side.   It is never troubled by election frauds, nor by the corruption of the elective franchise, if only thereby its purposes may be accomplished, or the men to whom it takes a fancy may be elevated to power.   It has harassed and hampered the bravest champions of righteousness when they were engaged in their death struggles.   It judges everything that is excellent by its defects, and accepts nearly everything that is base at its pretences.   It has concluded that this country of ours is not worth living in; and its highest ambition is to cultivate foreign friendships and to spend abroad as much of its time as possible.

This cultivated and lettered populace of ours is not to be taken too seriously.   Still less is it to be for an instant confounded with the company of admirable, simple-hearted, great-hearted, wise, and faithful scholars and teachers—the Mark Hopkinses, the Woolseys, the Peabodys, the Thatchers, the Whitneys, the James Walkers, the Parks, the Francis Walkers, the Julius Seeleys, who have adorned our great universities and colleges, and to whom thousands and thousands of our leading· men in public life have owed what is best in their training and character. All honor and praise and gratitude to the great teachers who have turned many to righteousness and who shine as the brightness of the firmament and as the stars forever and ever!

But, as I have said, let us not take our cultured and lettered populace too seriously. Above all let us not fail to take to ourselves whatever lesson it can teach us. While its reflections are not very profound or original, yet for that very reason it may be the more likely to repeat what other and wiser men are thinking.

It is best to look this thing squarely in the face. Let us see what the Senate itself can do and what the people can do to amend what is matter for just complaint, and to defend and explain matters of which there is unjust complaint. How much that we suffer or think we suffer is incident to all government? How much is incident to all popular government? How much is the necessary and cheap price which we pay for the peerless blessings of Union and Liberty? How much of the evil we have seen within the last few years has been cured, and how much is in the process of cure? What proposals of reform seem wise, and what seem unwise? Above all, what of the matters complained of are from mistakes, faults, or evil qualities for which the Senate is responsible, and what from mistakes, faults, or evil qualities for which the people are responsible, and which would as surely exist if the will and purpose of the people had found expression in the way most direct and prompt consistent with constitutional freedom?

We must admit that in recent years there have been important cases in which the Senate, through obstructions to the will of the majority, which are possible under its rules, has failed in its duty to enact measures which the people desired, and which a majority of its own membership favored. What is called filibustering, that is, making dilatory motions and occupying by them the time which ought to be given to business, has been occasionally, though not frequently, resorted to. Probably this has not happened once in the Senate where it has happened twenty times in the House of Representatives, or in some of our State legislatures. But it is still possible; and it is a great evil. It is likewise true that the desire of the people and the will of the Senate itself have been frequently baffled by using the power of lawful and constitutional debate, not for the purpose of discussing practical questions which are expected to be brought to an issue, but for consuming time so as to prevent action. Senators who have great measures in their charge are compelled to sit in vexed and angry impatience while other Senators pour out an endless stream of inane and empty chatter,

chatter, chatter, about matters which have no present practical importance whatever.   I use the plural—Senators.   I am somewhat
doubtful whether I should do that.   Certainly the men who have ever
done so can be counted on the fingers of one hand.   We are often compelled, also, to refrain from even defending or advocating important
and valuable measures, and to leave them to make their way, without
explanation, against attack and objection.   Important salutary bills
have often been beaten by able and sensible speeches in their favor,
because so much time has been consumed, even in brief and needful
debate, that the vote has not been reached.

Now, in answer to these complaints, it is not enough to say what I
shall presently say, that it is essential to have in at least one of our
legislative bodies opportunity for free speech, for full debate, and for
unlimited amendment.   It is certainly essential that full discussion and
consultation should exist in the Supreme Court.   Yet, if four judges
out of nine undertook to prevent the entry of judgment in a case
involving a great constitutional question, by endless discussion, by
reading extracts from law treatises or from the Revised Statutes, by
eternal talking about little cases so that great ones could not be reached,
—if such a supposition may be made in regard to that august tribunal,—I think we could find some way to put an end to the nuisance,
and perhaps the official head of the offender would be very quickly
detached by the salutary process of impeachment.

The Senate has the powers of free speech and free amendment.
Important as they are to the Senate, they are only important to promote and secure the best exercise of its power and duty to enact
wholesome and necessary laws.   The mechanism to accomplish the
object ought not to be used to defeat the object itself.   This evil
is but the manifestation in the Senate of a pestilent and prevalent evil which is showing itself elsewhere in many parts of the
country.   It is the attempt by minorities to prevent the constitutional action of majorities whenever the minority happen not to like
it.   The worst form of it is the election frauds which have prevailed
over a great part of the country, and which are viewed with indifference, and even with satisfaction, by some persons who are most
earnest in their condemnation of filibustering in the Senate.   They look
with great complacency on processes like those by which the constitutional right of suffrage of the colored man was extinguished in Alabama,
and, afterward, the constitutional right of the white was extinguished
in the same State.   This is not disagreeable to them, so long as the

senatorial power acquired by the process is used to defeat a protective tariff. But when it happens to be used to defeat an arbitration treaty, or a bankruptcy bill, or to promote the free coinage of silver, they discover their mistake. But I agree that it makes no difference whether they have been mistaken or to blame. It is our duty to recognize the evil and to cure it, whoever may have been to blame for it.

This is but a manifestation in the Senate of the same treasonable spirit which has led men to interfere with the organization of State legislatures for the mere purpose of defeating the election of Senators with whom the men who are guilty do not agree in political opinion, or of men who stand in the way of the personal ambitions of aspirants for the place. This has happened in some recent most humiliating instances,—notably in the State of Oregon.

I think a practical cure can be found for both these evils, if only we can have the support of an aroused, wise, well-instructed public sentiment. The cure will not be found in intemperate reviling of the Senate, nor in passionate expressions of despair for the Republic.

First. We ought to have laws upon the statute-book, both national and State, punishing by sufficient penalties every Senator or Representative who absents himself from the body to which he belongs, for the purpose of preventing the exercise of its constitutional functions, and declaring that such absences shall operate as a resignation of the seat. The failure of a Senator or Representative-elect to qualify, should be punished in the same way ; such failure being declared a refusal to accept the office. This can be done without any amendment of either national or State Constitution.

Second. I believe a rule can be, indeed it has been, devised which will secure reasonable opportunity to vote in the Senate and at the same time secure reasonable debate and reasonable amendment.

When these two things are accomplished, we shall have done everything we can to cure the evil until we shall elevate and purify the character of the people itself. The stream will not rise higher than its source. Our great legislative bodies will represent always what is evil and what is good in the popular character. Wherever universal suffrage exists, the tares and the wheat will be gathered into the same bundle. Other generations will have their faults; and those faults will be manifested in the two Houses of Congress. But we have virtue and intelligence enough to cure ourselves, if we will but keep sober and not yield to either unreasoning anger or weak despair.

Now, having admitted the truth of so much that is said in condemnation of the Senate, let me state some things that ought to be said in its favor.

The Senate, when Washington delivered his first Inaugural, had twenty-two members. It will begin the twentieth century with ninety. It is likely that before many years five more States, formed from our present territory, will bring up the number to a hundred. If—which Heaven avert!—there shall be additions from the continent on the South, or from the islands of the sea, they must come in and take their equal share in our self-government, and the number will be still further increased. Neither our institutions nor the temper of our people are adapted to the government of dependencies. We wish for no vassal states, nor subject citizens.

This increase of its numbers, if there were no other reason, makes it interesting to examine anew the original constitution of the Senate, and to see how far it has met the expectations of the Fathers, and whether any changes may profitably be made.

It is proposed to take the appointment of Senators from the legislatures and have them elected by the people. This is the first change in the structure of the Constitution that has been seriously proposed. The other amendments have been either to secure personal rights, to limit national or State legislation, or (in a single instance) to provide a better method of action by the electoral colleges in choosing the President.

Such a method of election would essentially change the character of the Senate as conceived by the Convention that framed the Constitution and the people who adopted it.

Practically it would transfer the selection of the members of this body from the legislatures, which are entrusted with all the legislative powers of the States, to conventions,—bodies having no other duties, whose election cannot be regulated by law, whose members act by proxy, whose tenure of office is for a single day, whose votes and proceedings are not recorded, who act under no personal responsibility, whose mistakes, ordinarily, can be corrected only by bolting and choosing Senators who do not represent the opinions concerning public measures and policies of the men who choose them.

It requires the substitution of pluralities for majorities in the election.

It will create new temptations to fraud, corruption, and other illegal practices, and in close cases will give rise to numerous election contests which must tend seriously to weaken confidence in the Senate.

It will absolve the larger States from the constitutional obligation which secures the equal representation of all the States in the Senate by providing that no State shall be deprived of that equality without its consent.

It implies, what the whole current of our history shows to be untrue, that during the past century the Senate has failed to meet the just expectations of the people, and that the State legislatures have proved themselves unfit to be the depositaries of the power of electing Senators.

The reasons which require this change, if acted upon and carried to their logical result, will lead to the election by the direct popular vote, and by popular majorities, of the President and of the Judiciary, and will compel the placing of these elections under complete national control. It will result in the overthrow of the whole scheme of the Senate and, in the end, of the whole scheme of the national Constitution as designed and established by its framers and the people who adopted it.

We are not to answer just complaints of the behavior of the Senate by simply saying that it was intended by the Constitution to resist popular passion, and caprice, and impatience. It was intended also to enact into law the just and considerate desires of the people. We cannot answer complaints of modern degeneracy by appealing to ancient glory. The Senate must be justified by the behavior of the men who compose it now, and not by the behavior of the men who composed it in the time of our fathers. We must find a cure for existing evil. We must show that with added years our great legislative body is improving and not degenerating, or we must record not alone the shame of the people, but our own. We must look the grievance in the face. We have a right, when we do it, to show in what we have improved. We have a right to say that the evil influences of the lobby in legislation for private and not public ends, which, like the ointment of the hand, bewrayed themselves in the atmosphere of the Senate Chamber and in its corridors, are all gone to-day. We have a right to say that drunkenness, which existed when I first entered public life, is not known there to-day, and that Senators no longer bring whiskey-soaked brains to meet the high demands of the public service. We have a right to say that the use of executive patronage for personal advancement—so that each Senator who supported the Administration had a little army of followers devoted to his personal interests, supported at the public cost—has gone by. We have a right to say, also, that if important legislation, demanded for the public welfare, is often defeated by obstructive measures or prolonged and needless debate now, for the eighty years while slavery ruled, and while the strict State-rights construction prevailed, such legislation was not even introduced and its chances were not worth considering. We have a right to say that the work the Senators now give to the public service, day and night, is a constant, hard work which was unknown in either House of Congress, save to a very few persons, fifty years ago. Men who belonged to the minority were not permitted to share even in the ordinary routine business of legislation. It was considered almost an audacity in former times for one of them to move to adjourn. Levi Lincoln told me that his time, when he was a Whig member of Congress, hung heavily on his hands, and that neither he nor any of his Whig colleagues was permitted to take the slightest share in the duties of legislation.

Talk about the degeneracy of the Senate! I am writing these lines upon the desk, I am seated in the chair, by whose side Charles Sumner was stricken down in the Senate Chamber for defending liberty,—his comely and beautiful head the target for a ruffian's bludgeon. There were Senators standing by and looking on and approving. There were others standing by without interfering. The Senate neither dared to punish nor to censure the action; and the offender was fined $300 in a police court. This was forty years ago. Read Oliphant's account of the passage of the reciprocity treaty of 1854,—a treaty which, as Lord Elgin described it, floated through on waves of champagne! Lawrence Oliphant, the British Secretary, tells the story to his mother,—a story, if it be true, as disgraceful to him and to his superior as to us. But he excuses himself with the comment, "If you have got to deal with hogs, what are you to do?"

Talk of the degeneracy of the Senate to men who remember the time when a Vice-President was inaugurated in a state of maudlin intoxication; or the earlier day when Foote uttered in debate his threat to Hale, that he should be hung on the tallest tree in the forest if he should come to Mississippi; when the same man drew his pistol on Benton in the Senate Chamber; when Butler poured out his loose expectoration, and Mason gave exhibitions of his arrogant plantation manners; or when Sumner likened Douglas to the noisome, squat, and nameless animal, who switched his tongue and filled the Senate with an offensive odor,—therein quoting an epithet once applied to Lord North in the House of Commons!

In 1876 it became my duty, in an important State trial, to point out to the Senate, then sitting as a court of impeachment, the corruption which had grown up in the country during and after the war. I did not exaggerate it in the least. But the evil which I then pointed out has been almost cured, so far as national politics is concerned, by an aroused and intelligent public sentiment. A day or two after my speech in the Belknap trial, I was sitting at lunch with General Garfield, talking over the subject. I told him that although all I had said was true, at the same time I believed that the amount of this evil was greater, not only in proportion but actually, during the first sixteen years of the Constitution—including the Administrations of Washington and John Adams and Jefferson's first term—than it was at the time we were speaking. He asked me to put together the facts, and to state them in a public speech. This I undertook to do, and in part did, in a speech made in the House of Representatives on August 9, 1876. But as I ransacked histories and old documents, I felt like a ghoul in reviving the evil stories of an age which we were accustomed to think so pure.

There has been great complaint of the recent policy of admitting new States. It is claimed that they were admitted solely to accomplish partisan objects ; that the number of their people did not warrant bringing them into the Union ; and that the conduct of their Senators, —especially in the matter of currency and finance—has been unpatriotic and highly injurious to the public interest.

Let us see how much truth there is in this complaint. The seven States to which this complaint applies are South Dakota, North Dakota, Montana, Washington, Wyoming,—all admitted between November 2, 1889, and July 10, 1890,—and Utah, admitted January 4, 1896. Nevada was admitted during the war, as a part of the Republican policy of Abraham Lincoln, it is said—I suppose truly—to secure the adoption of the Thirteenth Amendment. She had then a population of six thousand. She has now a population of forty-five thousand. Whatever injury the admission of Nevada caused, and whatever benefit came from the abolition of slavery, must be charged to profit and loss of the policies which saved the Union. In the seven States I have just mentioned, the aggregate population, in 1890, just after their admission, was 1,344,071—an average population slightly less than 192,000. Of the other thirty-eight States, there were but thirteen which had at the time of their admission a population equal to this average. There were only five which had a population equal to the three largest of these States ; only three equal to the two largest. Eight at the time of their admission were smaller than the smallest of these new States ; seventeen were smaller than the second smallest ; and twenty were smaller than the third smallest.

Now when we consider the great evil of governing these States in a Territorial condition—a very eminent statesman of large experience in the Cabinet and in the Senate told me the other day that a Territory was not much better than a bundle of snakes—and consider the fact of the rapid future growth to be expected from nearly all of them, I do not think so great a mistake was made in their admission as is some-times supposed. Without accepting the above statement, I think it must be admitted that the government of Territories by our methods is very bad for governors and governed.

Great complaint has been made of the vote of these new States upon some questions which have arisen of late. It is said that their power has been exerted in favor of wild and dishonorable schemes which en-danger the prosperity and honor of the country. But they have done no harm. When the purchasing clauses of the act of 1890 were re-pealed, their votes were evenly divided. Between McKinley and Bryan, they certainly did as well as the solid South. All the States that went into the rebellion voted for Bryan ; and they were reinforced by Mis-souri. If we make a comparison of the large States and the small States, the States that have four Representatives, or less, did pretty well. They gave forty votes for McKinley to thirty-one for Bryan. The States that have two Representatives, or less, gave twenty-two votes for McKinley to thirty-one for Bryan.

Passionate complaints are made in some quarters of the personal quality of the Senators representing the new States. I think these complaints are in most instances the result of political prejudice, and that the gentlemen concerning whom they are made are industrious, honest, and faithful public servants. But the men who make them cer-tainly express quite as much impatience with the Senators, past and present, from the largest States in the Union. I am not expressing or suggesting any judgment of my own. But these complainants certainly will be slow to admit that the great States have done better in this regard than the small ones.

There is a great deal which affects the character and happiness of a free people, which is not effected by its legislation, and with which neither statesmen nor politicians have to do. But it is likewise true that a good history of any civilized people can be written from its statutes. To this statement the United States is no exception. I think it would be easy from the history of the action of Congress to write the history of the intelligent opinions of the people. It would likewise be easy to show, if there were time and place for an enumeration, that by far the larger part of the great and humane statutes by which the people have expressed their will have originated in the Senate. This is true, notwithstanding the fact that by the Constitution all money bills, including appropriation bills, must begin in the House, and that a great deal of such legislation has been placed upon appropriation bills.

At the session of Congress which has just closed, the Sundry Civil Appropriation Bill passed the House under a suspension of the rules. No member had an opportunity to discuss an item, or to move an amendment in an expenditure involving fifty-two million dollars. That bill was considered in the Senate. Large additions were made. They passed the House without opportunity for amendment or discussion. This was because that body did not dare trust itself to exercise its great responsibility freely and deliberately. The great statesman who is its leader is supported by a majority in the House in his iron rule, although there is much muttering and individual discontent. The majority of the House agree with him in thinking that it is not safe or practicable to trust the Representatives of the people to deal with the items of expenditure one by one after full discussion. There is no time for the discussion necessary to expose improper claims; and, in any such discussion and amendment as could be had, the good would be as likely to fail as the evil.

It is true that the House of Representatives has sometimes prevented the enactment of mischievous legislation which had passed the Senate, or would have passed the Senate if it had had an opportunity. But it is equally true that the House is a changeable body, and that nearly every alternate Congress is ready for what a large and most conservative portion of the people deem infinite mischief.

There were in the House elected in 1890, 167 Democratic majority. In the House elected in 1892 there were but 84 Democratic majority. This majority changed to a Republican majority of 137 at the next election. The House elected in 1892 contained 84 new members. The House elected in 1894, contained 168 new members. The present House, elected in 1896, although the same party remains in power there, contains 156 new members. In spite of the previous-question and the hour rule, the House at its best is an infinitely more obstructive body than the Senate. The obstructions in the Senate can be caused only by large minorities. Great measures are delayed and defeated by the power of 20 or 25 men out of 90. But the same thing is constantly done in the House by one man alone.

You go to Mr. Speaker Reed and tell him you are poor, that you have an honest claim against the United States ; that it has taken your entire property without compensation ; that your claim has been found to be due by the Government's own court, appointed for that very purpose ; that it has passed the Senate unanimously ten times ; that ten committees of the House have reported in its favor; and you pray him to let your Representative tell the story to the House and ask them to pass it—a motion which, to be successful, requires a vote of two to one.   He will answer you, that he has no doubt all you say is true ; but that there are thronging at the gate millions of unjust, corrupt, or extravagant demands against the Treasury, which the House is eager to pass if it can get at them; and that he does not open the door to one honest claimant because, if he should, a hundred dishonest ones would pass in.

There are two reasons why we provide so carefully for paying the bonds : One—a good one—is, that this is required by honor and good faith.   The other is a bad one; viz., that there are numerous powerful and wealthy persons interested in their payment.   If, in cases like that I have described, we are not moved by the first reason, we must admit that we are only impelled by the last to keep faith with the bondholder. For myself, I have little respect for the man who keeps his credit good at his bank and cheats his washerwoman and his grocer; and I have as little respect for the statesmanship that deals with public obligations on the same principle.   If ten men can defeat, and oftentimes do defeat, righteous legislation by too much debate in the Senate, one man can defeat it in the House by preventing all debate.   Repudiation is repudiation, and dishonesty is dishonesty; whether the foreign bondholder or the humble citizen be the victim.

The promptness with which the House of Representatives deals with some important questions is a good thing; but its capacity for prompt action is purchased at the price of the repudiation of public debts, and the suppression of the constitutional rights, personal dignity, and official authority of the great mass of its members.   Gentlemen occupy seats there who, from the beginning to the end of their term of service, are not permitted to make a motion or to utter a word to the assembly of which they are members.   Perhaps wise legislation may be secured while one House is conducted on that principle; but I am afraid free government would not long endure if it were applied to both Houses.

The Senate contributes as large a part to the legislation of the country to-day as it has done at any period of our history. This legislation I believe is better done than ever before. As many good and wholesome laws are enacted to-day as have been at any other period of our history. This is true, although we must now legislate for seventy millions instead of for three millions; although the doctrines of State rights and strict construction are overthrown; although the subtleties of the question of currency and finance present themselves for solution as never before; although we have been brought so much nearer to foreign countries by steam and electricity, and our domestic commerce has multiplied many thousandfold. I believe the people, as a whole, are better, happier, more prosperous, than they ever were before; and I believe the two Houses of Congress represent what is best in the character of the people now as much as they ever did.

We must put a stop in some way to the obstruction by minorities of the will of the people and of the will of majorities. It must be done, if it can be done, without sacrificing the right of reasonable debate and of unlimited amendment. We have also to devise some way for securing the honest election of Representatives and Senators. If these two things can be accomplished, the legislation of the country will reflect the will and the character of the people. If it be bad, if it be unwise, if it be hasty, it will be because we have a bad, foolish, or rash people; and the people can be elevated only by the elevation of the personal character of the individuals who make up the state.

The Senate, as I have said, was created that the deliberate will, the sober second thought of the people might find expression. It was intended that it should resist the hasty, intemperate, passionate desire of the people. This hasty passion and intemperance is frequently found in the best men as in the worst. But so long as the political management of the country excites eager interest, so long these feelings will be excited; and when they are excited the body whose function it is to resist them will be, for the time being, an object of dislike and of attack. It has, therefore, always been true, is true now, and always will be true, that the Senate is an object of bitter denunciation by those persons whose purposes are thwarted or delayed. That will be especially true when the House and Executive, the popular majority, are of one way of thinking and the Senate, representing the will of the majority of the States, is of another way. It is fair, therefore, that the Senate should be judged not by considering its conduct or its composition at the time when the judgment is to be expressed, but by a review of a whole century of its history.

Delay, needless discussion, wrangle, public reproach of the Senate, postponement of much needed and desired legislation, disappointment of good men, are the price we pay for three things. They are to be remedied. If possible, they are to be amended. But the blessings they buy for us, even at their worst, outweigh ten thousand times the evil which attends them.

The things they buy for us are these: First. The possibility of a Union of forty-five States—soon to be fifty States—covering a continent larger than Europe, with greater interests and more precious hopes. But for the constitution of the Senate as it exists, these States would be separate nations, each with its standing army; each seaboard State with its navy; a line of custom-houses along every frontier; and a history made up of eternal wrangle, strife, and war. This condition of things would last until, one by one, the smaller States became the prey of the larger States, to repeat again the Old World's story of disappointment.

Not only are we saved from the necessity of maintaining standing armies and costly navies. We are saved from a war of tariffs. Here are forty-five sovereignties without a fortress or a custom-house on their frontiers toward each other, and with but one soldier to every three thousand people. We are saved from the contests which must grow up between different countries dwelling on the banks of great navigable rivers. We are saved from the strife which must be engendered by a great trade carried by rail through populous States. All this would have been impossible, but for the constitutional compromise from which came the Senate.

Second. The constitutional arrangement of the Senate protects the American people from government by a pure Democracy representing and enacting the immediate passion and desire of the passing hour. The President represents the majority of the whole people; the House of Representatives, the present and immediate popular desire of the constituencies. But the Senate stands also for the will of the American people. It stands for its deliberate, permanent, settled desire,—its sober, second thought.

Third. The present constitution of the Senate, though in this respect it might be altered by a change of rule, secures one place in our Government where debate is unfettered, and the power of amendment —perhaps more important even than free debate—is preserved to the fullest extent.

In the natural growth of the country—a growth fruitful of benefit to mankind—the Senate feels the strain to which all other parts of our constitutional mechanism are subjected. We must adapt to the new conditions so much of our proceeding as may be within our own control. We must strive to secure action. The rest must depend on the intelligence and virtue of the people. A seat in the Senate is still the highest object of ambition which any State can confer on its children, and, with a single exception, the highest object of ambition within the gift of the country.

Suppose it turn out that the body, created that it might give effect to the sober and deliberate judgment of the people, and withstand excitement, folly, and haste, compelling deliberation and wisdom to prevail, should be itself under evil influences and be found only withstanding the best and never resisting the worst popular emotions. What must become of us then? The cure is to be not by changing our present mechanism, which is the best that could be devised, but only by those means that elevate and educate the people themselves. If the people themselves will learn to avoid those tempests of excitement which belong to what, in speaking of other countries, we call a populace, and utter only well-considered and deliberate judgments when dealing with great matters which concern their own welfare, every department of their Government will respond.

Certainly in no generation has there been such a powerful Drummond light turned upon the lives of public men as now. The desire of Mr. Sumner's old Roman to dwell in a glass house is almost literally realized. Not only is every word uttered by a Senator in public taken down in shorthand, but his footsteps are dogged. He is watched at every street corner. He is the object of caricature—sometimes good-natured, sometimes malicious. The press of each of the great parties attacks the leaders of the party to which it is opposed. The so-called "independent" press attacks the leaders of both indiscriminately, and with far less scruple. For one, I do not complain. I am willing to take my chances of the good opinion of my countrymen, even in going through this ordeal. The process is not an unhealthy one, so far as it affects the men who are subjected to it. I know well that the lessons from which I can derive most improvement come to me from my enemies and not from my friends; from critics, not from admirers. I often wonder at the generally sure instinct by which the people form accurate judgment of the characters of good and wise men of whom they read nothing but derision and calumny.

We should consider also how much of the disparagement of the

Senate comes from men who judge quite as harshly of all other American institutions, of all American history and of the great characters of that history, both past and present. To men of this temper, so numerous nowadays, nothing seems to be worthy of respect. The fault is with the critic and not with the institution or the history. No man is a hero to his valet. The reason is not that the quality of the hero will not bear close inspection, but that the valet is of such quality himself as not to recognize greatness. The history of no people is heroical to its Mugwumps.

We must, so far as possible, limit national legislation to matters of first-rate importance. It must be marked by the greatest possible simplicity. The laws must be plain and few, such as are clearly required, and such as meet obvious wants. I agree with Dr. Channing that a refined and subtle policy of complicated legislation which cannot be understood but by laborious research and reasoning is hostile to the genius of Republican institutions.

Our people are as intelligent a people as live or as ever lived. But a people of seventy millions is an inconvenient tribunal to deal with complicated legislative mechanisms. The claim that the National Government was but an agency of the States, to be revoked by any one at its will, is departed never to return. But the constitutional principle which requires the most careful preservation of State authority, and the most zealous limitation in the exercise of national power, is sound and salutary and must not be forgotten.

Let us not think or speak of these, the best days of the American Republic as if they were the worst. Let us trust the Republic, and the ideas which are its strength and safety. Renown and grace are not dead. The patriotism which builded the Union, and the patriotism that saved it, burns brightly and purely as ever in the bosoms of the people. The youth who are pressing forward to take their share in our citizenship are not a whit behind their sires either in love of their country or in their capacity to govern it. Let us not forever be fixing our gaze upon warts and blotches. To the wisdom of experience let us add, as our great Teacher told us, the wisdom of hope; and let hope and trust and instinct claim a share in the guidance of affairs.

This Republic has weathered too many storms to go down in sunny weather, in calm seas, and in prosperous gales. The God who was with our fathers, if we will but trust in Him, will also be with us, their children.

GEO. F. HOAR.

RETRENCHMENT,—OR RUIN?

An efficient republican form of government is the organization of an intelligent people into a political corporation by which *all* are pledged to maintain and protect the natural rights of *each*. And the natural rights of a person are: life, liberty, and the privilege of owning and controlling his lawful accumulations. In a state of savagery, each had to defend himself against all; but in civilization, Law—evolved out of the recognition of individual rights—compels all to protect each. It is logical therefore to state that, whenever a statute takes from the citizen, or abridges for the citizen, any part of his natural rights, civilization is retrograding and inviting a return, by revolution, to that barbaric condition in which each must defend himself.

The power to levy duties and collect taxes was vested in this democratic form of government for the sole purpose of raising revenues to protect the life, liberty, and property of each of its citizens. It never was intended that the legislative branch of the Government should impose taxation upon *all* to enrich a *few*. It never was suspected that the Government would use the power to tax for the purpose of increasing private incomes instead of public revenues. But, insidiously and designedly, the legislation of the United States has, at times, been manipulated so as to prescribe in many ways privileges for the few, and taxes and burdens for the multitude.

This is really a Government of committees. Each new Congress and Administration are merely committees raised from the entire body of the American people; and to them are committed certain duties and functions of government which the people themselves, in their primary capacity as a committee of the whole, cannot discharge or perform. And the mass of citizenship never did commit and never intended to commit to any legislative, judicial, or executive committee the power to abridge, to invade, or to destroy any inherent rights of individual citizens. The multitude of voting men in the United States never intentionally cast ballots in favor of taxing all of themselves, either directly or indirectly, for the purpose of putting money into the pockets of a few of themselves. Nor did they ever by vote declare in favor of taking the public domain away from the people for the purpose of donating it to corporations or bestowing it as a gratuity in single tracts upon individuals. Nor has the American ballot ever approved the raising of money from the people of all the States to improve alleged rivers and harbors—of a purely local utility—for the benefit of a relatively few citizens in single States.

The day of retrenchment, or the day of ruin, for this Government is awaiting the people of the United States in the not remote future. We shall very soon step from the nineteenth into the twentieth century. We shall carry with us either the germs of dissolution and decay or of life and conserved energy. To avoid the former and secure the latter the American people should begin at once in the household, in the factory, in the counting-room, in the management of great lines of transportation, and in all other incorporations of capital, to practise something of the economy and frugality which character- ized our New England ancestors. The cost of local governments must be lessened. Administration of county and city and village affairs must be made more and more businesslike and economical. In short, the fixed charges of American citizenship must be cut down. To-day in many cities the rates of taxation reach from 3 to 6 per cent upon the assessed valuation. This is altogether unendurable. This creates dis- content. This makes popular unrest. This came to us, in many in- stances, however, by levying taxes and issuing bonds as subsidies to railroads, or to construct unneeded sewers and pavements, or to erect city and county buildings of extravagant proportions and ostentatious styles. And not a few of those public debts for which we now suffer terrible taxes were conceived and suggested by promoters and specu- lators for their own profit. But the reasons for them, which were served steaming hot to the voters, were the " general welfare," and the delight of benevolently furnishing the poor and unemployed with re- munerative work. But it never was surmised in the earlier days of this Republic that those who, by sobriety, industry, and frugality, had acquired property, must at last suffer a penalty, in the taxation of that property, to create artificial means of employing and compensating those who had been indolent, improvident, and intemperate. The founders never anywhere indicate that it is a duty of the state to provide remunerative occupation for the citizen. That vagary found expression in the statutes of France ; and experimentation with it brought on revolution and a new Empire. It cannot be tried in this country without similar results.

Americans, if they sincerely wish to perpetuate the Republic, must return to the ancient faith, that the sole business of the Government is to protect life, liberty, and property. They must spurn the doctrines of communism, which would have the Government do everything for everybody. They must maintain their individuality by refusing to be pooled,—as to abilities, character, and earning capacities,—into guilds, trade-unions, or any other associations which tend to de-individualization and a return to tribal relations, under which a few head-men and braves think and act for the whole tribe.

- The tendency to depend upon Government for favors—from the distribution of prize-package gratuities in the form of printed books and cent-a-packet garden seeds to the disbursement of millions of dollars upon harbors and rivers, the waters of which are never shadowed by a sail, nor vexed by a paddle-wheel—has been growing enormously in recent years. The annexed table has been specially prepared to show how in sixty years the cost of administering the Federal Government has been so augmented that in 1890, with a population of more than sixty-two millions, it was $4.75 *per capita ;* whereas in 1840, with a population of less than eighteen millions, the *per capita* expense was only $1.41.

COST OF ADMINISTERING THE FEDERAL GOVERNMENT.

(This table deals exclusively with single years, not with averages.)

Year.	Population on June 1.	Net ordinary expenditures in fiscal year.	Amount per capita.	Gross expenditures in fiscal year.	Amount per capita.
1840	17,069,453	$24,139,920	$1.41	$28,226,534	$1.65
1850	23,191,876	40,948,383	1.77	44,604,718	1.92
1860	31,443,321	63,200,876	2.01	77,055,126	2.45
1870	38,558,371	309,653,561	8.03	702,907,843	18.23
1880	50,155,783	267,642,958	5.34	700,233,238	13.96
1890	62,622,250	297,736,487[1]	4.75[1]	630,247,078	10.06

In the face of these figures, can any intelligent citizen fail to observe that, in proportion to cost, there can hardly be found a local government which makes so small a return to the citizen as that made by the Federal Government? Sound economists hold that, under ordinary conditions, the cost of administration should decline *per capita* as population increases. And no authority will contend that with a popula-

[1] If premiums were included, as was done in 1870 and 1880, the net expenditure would be $318,040,711, and the amount *per capita,* $5.08.

tion of sixty-two millions the cost *per capita* should aggregate three times as much as it was in 1840, when the census showed less than eighteen millions of people.

But, coming a decade nearer to the present, the following is a table showing the total expenditures of the United States from 1850 to 1890, in four periods of ten years each:—

TOTAL EXPENDITURES OF THE UNITED STATES FROM 1850 TO 1890,
IN FOUR PERIODS OF TEN YEARS EACH.

(The amounts given are the totals for ten years, not the yearly averages.)

Period.	Net ordinary expenditures, *not* including premiums or interest.	Premiums.	Interest.	Paid toward extinguishment of public debt.	Gross expenditures.
July 1, 1850, to June 30, 1860	$568,363,368	$5,733,530	$27,729,197	$76,374,511	$678,200,606
July 1, 1860, to June 30, 1870	4,415,723,822	37,262,113	850,327,718	4,039,621,128	9,342,844,781
July 1, 1870, to June 30, 1880	1,631,164,380	25,271,375	1,058,852,635	4,126,676,615	6,841,965,005
July 1, 1880, to June 30, 1890	2,098,348,562	46,928,678	538,848,213	2,857,080,577	5,541,206,030

From 1870 to 1880, the total disbursements for *pensions* were $326,088,179, or 19.99 per cent of the net ordinary expenditures, not including premiums or interest.

From 1880 to 1890, the total disbursements for *pensions* were $702,232,652, or 33.47 per cent of the net ordinary expenditures, not including premiums or interest.

From July 1, 1890, to June 30, 1896 (a period of six years), the net ordinary expenditures, not including interest, were $1,977,379,887. At this rate of increase the net ordinary expenditures for the decade ending June 30, 1900, would aggregate $3,295,633,145,—nearly as much as for the *twenty* years ending June 30, 1890!

From July 1, 1890, to June 30, 1896, the interest on the public debt amounted to $182,394,108; making a total of $2,159,773,995.

During this period the total disbursements for *pensions* were $840,-363,077, or 42.50 per cent of the net ordinary expenditures, not including interest.

Why should there be billions appropriated now, when five hundred millions to eight hundred millions would be sufficient for legitimate governmental disbursements? Does the appropriation of nearly eleven hundred millions of dollars by the Fifty-fourth Congress afford citizens more security for life, liberty, and property? Is it patriotism, or party policy and personal ambition, that, without particular regard to services rendered the Republic, constantly talk and vote in the American Senate and House of Representatives for an enlargement of the number of military pensioners? Why should the decade from 1880 to 1890 show more than seven hundred millions paid for pensions, when that from 1870 to 1880 shows less than four hundred millions? Have pension laws sometimes been made the means of converting rolls of honor into lists of mere beneficiaries, regardless of services or disabilities, merely to gain or to perpetuate party power? How shall revenues be devised that can automatically adjust themselves to the ever-expanding extravagance of pension laws which add annually to the rolls more than time and death remove? No good citizen objects to pensions for those real soldiers who incurred genuine disabilities in the service or consequent upon the service. But the thousands of men who draw pensions from the Government of the United States, because by sworn testimony they have proved themselves victims of chronic diseases, and at the same time have policies in life-insurance companies to which they have solemnly declared themselves free from all chronic maladies, aggregate a stupendous swindle upon citizens who pay taxes or upon those who carry life insurance. Why should not investigation be made and such cases eliminated from the pension rolls? How can any man, without perjuring himself, have a pension because he *has* a chronic disorder and a life-insurance policy because he *has not* such an affliction? And how many thousands of such cases now stain the pension rolls can only be ascertained by an investigation—which can be carried on easily and inexpensively—in which the Government and the life-insurance companies shall coöperate. Why not petition Congress to order such an inquiry? Who can be injured by it? Can honorable, truthful, and meritorious veterans suffer from such a cleansing of the pension rolls?

Next, let us take up the public-building mania, which has crazed Congressmen in so many districts, and caused the erection of custom-houses, court-houses, and post-offices of extravagant proportions and cost at inconsequential villages and little cities, all over the United States; needlessly disbursing millions upon millions of dollars. These buildings are appropriated for by every Congress. In nine cases out of ten they are not required; and when the public business does require the erection of an edifice it is generally made bigger and more costly than it ought to be made. During the last nine years the appropriations for public buildings have aggregated more than forty millions of dollars.

The interest on half the money invested in the Public Building at my own town—Nebraska City, Otoe County, Nebraska—would rent quarters commodious enough and good enough for the post-office. And that is the only use the Government of the United States has for a building in that place; for it has less than fifteen thousand people. And what is true of the outlay of public money in that town for a Government building is true of scores of similar cities. But the most significant, unbusinesslike feature in this fallacy of furnishing elegant and expensive post-offices to certain towns in certain districts that are represented by those patriotic and rustling statesmen whose lives are fervidly spent in seeing how much they can get *out of* the people and the Government, rather than in seeing how much they can do or save *for* them, is the fact that, as soon as the post-office is finished, free delivery is instituted in the same community. Thus a fairly decent income from box-rents in the new building is cut off, and the utility of the edifice minimized to housing and assorting the mails. That was the case in Nebraska City. The history of the new building there, and of its extravagance in construction, heating, and manning with engineers, janitors, and watchmen, is the history of scores of post-offices scattered throughout the Union, which have been de-utilized to a great extent by being supplemented by an expensive, unnecessary, and farcical free-delivery system which never ought to have been established, and should not now be continued in any town of less than forty thousand population.

A tax, whether indirect or direct, is the payment which the citizen makes to the Government for the service which the Government renders him in the protection of his life, liberty, and property. A little money taken from each, and committed, for public purposes only, to those representing and acting for all, makes the revenue. And it is collected from each of the people to be legitimately expended only for conserving the rights of all the people. And as the population of the United States increases, the *per capita* cost of administration ought to diminish; provided good judgment, honesty, and a reasonable economy direct disbursements. But what do the figures from 1867 to 1896 teach as to this? The following table of net ordinary expenditures from 1867 to 1896 gives the answer:—

NET ORDINARY EXPENDITURES PER CAPITA OF POPULATION, 1867 TO 1896.
(From the Statistical Abstract of the Treasury Department.)

1867	$ 9.87	1873	$6.97	1879	$5.46	1885	$4.64	1891	$5.55
1868	10.21	1874	7.07	1880	5.34	1886	4.15	1892	5.28
1869	8.55	1875	6.25	1881	5.07	1887	4.47	1893	5.73
1870	8.03	1876	5.87	1882	4.89	1888	4.33	1894	5.39
1871	7.39	1877	5.21	1883	4.90	1889	4.38	1895	5.11
1872	6.84	1878	4.98	1884	4.39	1890	4.75	1896	4.94

Perhaps no other system of making appropriations has been so prolific of extravagant disbursements as that which sets apart gigantic
sums of money in a sort of omnibus bill and terms it an appropriation
for Sundry Civil Expenses. Under this masquerading legislation the
Congress of the United States has deftly despoiled the National Treasury during the last twenty years of $510,988,245 ; and during the
period from 1878 to 1887 this omnibus hauled out of the public Treasury more than $226,000,000. And all that almost incomprehensible
and bewildering number of dollars had first been collected from the
people.

This Government, like all others, is penniless and a pauper, except
for the power to tax its citizens. It was born without money. It can
create no money. It handles only tax-raised money. And it has no
constitutional or other right to levy taxes, except for the purpose of
getting money into its Treasury with which to pay the public debt, to
provide for the common defence, and to promote the general welfare.
All other taxes, some of them falsely called " protective," ought to
be speedily and utterly abolished. The gigantic sums smuggled out
of the Treasury, disguised as necessary for sundry civil expenses, are
increasing from year to year. This is shown by the fact that during
the years from 1888 to 1897 there was taken by this method $284,-
602,604. This startling sum is an increase of more than fifty-eight
millions of dollars over the amount appropriated by the same system
of false pretence in legislation in the preceding decade. Thus ten
years developed an increase of 25 per cent in appropriations for " Sundry Civil Expenses." As a further comparison, the appropriations by
Congress under this heading for the fiscal years 1878, 1879, and 1880,
amounted to $61,772,715 ; while for the fiscal years of 1895, 1896, and
1897, the amount was $90,764,590,—an increase of more than 47 per
cent.

Following closely upon the heels of the " Sundry Civil Expenses "
method of burglarizing the United States Treasury, comes the annual

appropriation for Rivers and Harbors.   This bill is a masked looter of the public funds; and its successes are often applauded by those deluded constituencies who follow predatory politicians because the swag is to be scattered in their immediate neighborhood.   From 1878 to 1887, the money taken out of the Treasury for Rivers and Harbors aggregated only $86,730,070; but between the years 1888 and 1897 the same system of legislative piracy has taken from the public funds $134,158,925.   Thus the total amount appropriated was about 55 per cent greater than during the preceding ten years.   And how much more security to the life, liberty, and property of the American citizen was guaranteed by this expenditure of more than two hundred and twenty millions of tax-gathered dollars for harbors and rivers during the last twenty years?   How much of that sum was absorbed in profits by political contractors?   How much was needlessly expended? How much was intended and used for the promotion of personal, pecuniary, and political betterment?

But all sorts of schemes for tapping the public till are concealed in legislation simulating patriotic desire to advance and exalt the " plain people," about whom the ubiquitous and voluble office-hunter is ever discoursing with pathos and bathos.   Among a multitude of those methods for getting money out of the United States Treasury for personal purposes which have succeeded best in recent years, none has been more adroitly worked than the " Exposition."   It was inaugurated at Philadelphia to celebrate the Centennial Anniversary of this Republic in 1876.   This first exposition appropriated for from the public Treasury was the beginning of a series of shows to be viewed and enjoyed by a few taxpayers at the expense of all the taxpayers of the United States.   The annexed tabulated statement tells how much success in a financial way the " show business " as a function of Government has achieved.   In the beginning of its career even the Philadelphians and other personally interested patriots dared to propose only a loan from the general Government; and no man declared for an out-and-out donation.   The idea of a continuous line of " Mrs. Jarley's wax figgers " at governmental cost did not then exist, any more than the idea of stopping appropriations for such purposes exists now.

Where will promotion, establishment, and maintenance of exhibitions and expositions by the Government cease?   Where is the line to be drawn?   What rights to run shows at the Federal expense inhere at Philadelphia, New Orleans, Chicago, Atlanta, Nashville, or Omaha, that do not belong equally to Pittsburg, New York, Chicopee,

Atlantic City, Louisville, Kalamazoo, Oshkosh, Niagara Falls, or any other American town?

APPROPRIATIONS BY CONGRESS IN CONNECTION WITH THE PRINCIPAL EXPOSITIONS IN THE UNITED STATES, BEGINNING WITH THE CENTENNIAL, 1876.

Exposition.	Donations.	Appropriations for Government buildings and exhibits.	Total.
Philadelphia, 1876....................	[1]	$505,000	$505,000
New Orleans, 1884–85..............	$1,350,000 [2]	300,000	1,650,000
Chicago, 1893.....................	2,500,000	2,668,354 [3]	5,168,354
Atlanta, 1896......................		200,000	200,000
Nashville, 1897....................		130,000	130,000
Omaha, 1898.......................		200,000	200,000
Total.........................	$3,850,000	$4,003,354	$7,853,354

The above table does not include the sum of $250,000 appropriated by Congress for the Paris Exposition of 1889, nor various small amounts expended in connection with other expositions at home and abroad.

The educational argument, and the assumption that such governmental expenditures inspire patriotism, and the assertion that they exalt, refine, and sublimate humanity in general, by taxing everybody to enable relatively nobody to have salaries and profits, see pleasant things and enjoy life intensely at the expense of the great majority who are not in attendance, are constantly reiterated by those voluble promoters of personal enterprises that are always masked as the "general welfare."

But it is unnecessary to elaborate or enumerate the evils of the Government show-business. It is only one of many modern methods of buncoing our common Uncle Sam out of the taxes which he has harvested from his full and applauding field of nephews. The Government waxwork business, menagerie and general show-business can only be destroyed by sending men to the National Legislature for the purpose of doing something *for* the people, instead of trying to get everything possible *out of* and *away from* the people. Statesmanship

[1] Congress loaned the Centennial Exposition $1,500,000, which was repaid.

[2] $1,000,000 of this amount was a loan; it was not repaid; and Congress had to appropriate a further sum of $350,000 to extricate the Exposition from its embarrassments.

[3] Actual disbursements by Treasury Department.

needs a new definition in the United States. It now seems to many men, "the art of living profitably in office, and getting offices and appropriations for personal and political friends."

Formerly the youth of the United States came to adult age inspired with the patriotic idea that every American citizen should support the Government in war, in peace, and always. But to-day multitudes really hold that it is the duty of the Government to support its citizens—in office, with contracts, or by special legislation.

This article is hastily written merely as a suggester of serious thought among tax-paying and patriotic citizens upon the need of economy in the administration of Government, and it cannot be better quickly ended than by quoting the last annual report of John G. Carlisle, than whom there has never been an abler, more diligent and conscientious Secretary of the Treasury :—

"The great increase in the ordinary expenditures of the Government during the last seven years has been without precedent in our history, in time of peace, and presents a subject which imperatively demands the most serious consideration of Congress. In 1870, for the first time after the close of the War, our public expenditures, excluding premiums on loans and purchases of bonds, but including interest and pensions, fell below the sum of $300,000,000 ; and they continued to decrease, with some fluctuations, until 1886, when they reached their lowest point, amounting to $242,483,138.50. During the four fiscal years beginning July 1, 1885, and ending June 30, 1889, the annual average expenditure, excluding premiums on loans and purchases of bonds, but including all the other items mentioned above, was $263,016,473.18 ; but during the next four fiscal years, beginning July 1, 1889, and ending June 30, 1893, the annual average was $345,405,-163.60,—an increase of $82,338,690.42 for each year. The average annual ordinary expenditure of the Government during the three fiscal years beginning July 1, 1893, and ending June 30, 1896, was $358,633,341.40,—an annual increase of $13,-228,177.80 over the next preceding four years. The ordinary receipts of the Government during the last fiscal year—$326,976,200.38—would have paid the average annual expenditure during the four years from July 1, 1885, to June 30, 1889, and left a surplus of $63,959,727.20 at the end of each year, or of $255,838,908.80 at the close of the period. The expenditures for the year 1896, although $31,298,-508.41 less than in 1893, were nearly 25 per cent higher than in 1889."

J. STERLING MORTON.

THE UNITED STATES AND CUBA.

THE Cuban problem, among all the problems which agitate our epoch, is certainly one of the most exciting; for, while full of deep reverberations both in the United States and in Europe, it is linked with an epic of other ages.

The sociologist, the philosopher, the statesman, agree that republicanism, so difficult to acclimatize on our old continent, is irresistibly destined to triumph among the nations of the New World; that the political changes in the Greater Antilles tend toward an industrial and commercial upheaval from which shall result moral transformations; and that the definitive victory of the revolution in Havana may possibly bring about the proclamation of a republic in Madrid. But the masses, always more impressed with facts than with abstract reasoning, see quite another thing.

They see two armies seeking each other, spying upon each other, pressing upon each other, and, for two years, mercilessly renewing the same struggle. The one, formidable in numbers and armament, led by generals starred with decorations, and marching with terror—if not with victory—amid the noise of fusillades, of women, and of prisoners; the other, six times less numerous, without pay, without uniform, with insufficient military equipment, but marching to battle with the cry of "Cuba libre!" shouted alike by beardless youths and old men whose bodies are riddled with bullets like a flag.

This latter army has with it the soul of the entire Cuban people. This it is, above all, that in France (and doubtless it is the same in America) strikes the masses,—at least that part of the masses wherein imagination, enthusiasm, and generous sentiments reside.

The Cuban revolution,—what a factor in the future transformation of the world; but then, also, what a prodigious epic! An epic in our prosaically sceptical society, when the old Republicans had declared the heroic age ended! Well, no! It has not ended,—at least, not everywhere; and it is just because the people do not live for the gratification of their material wants alone, but also for the ideal and in aspirations for the future, that they followed Barbès to the barricades, applauded Garibaldi, saluted John Brown, and to-day unite in imagination in glorifying the imposing figure of Maceo. Not a day passes that men of all ages do not present themselves at the office of the "Intransigeant" and ask to be enlisted to fight for Cuba; and they grow disconsolate when told that our third Republic, more retrograde than the old monarchy of divine right, does not countenance Lafayettes and Rochambeaux.

For nearly a century and a half France has felt its heart throb within the bosom of all oppressed nationalities. Its geographical situation and the origin of its ethnical elements have made of it in the past a field of battle: some day they will make of it a ground of union between the Celtic, Latin, and Saxon races. It is not, therefore, surprising that the French have, in thought, communed with other nations; that their patriotic spirit—sometimes clamorous, but far from confining itself to a selfish particularism—should have always been imbued with a profound humanitarian sentiment. The same country that, since the last century, has enlightened the world by its philosophers, has often, too, shed its blood for the enslaved; compelling even monarchs, such as Charles X and Napoleon III, to come to the aid of insurgent Greece and of Italy.

How then, without ignoring all the traditions of republican France, without declaring the moral rôle of our country forever at an end, could our countrymen declare themselves indifferent in presence of the titanic struggle undertaken by the Cuban people to obtain their independence?

Scepticism, joined to an unbridled desire for pleasure, which is the characteristic of our times, is followed, like all other excess, by a reaction. It is exactly for this reason that, while, amid the general debasement of character, the men of to-day appear for the most part vulgar, covetous, and contemptible, enthusiasm and sympathy are enlisted in behalf of those whom the smallness of their contemporaries makes appear all the more great.

Such are the psychological and ethical causes which in our country draw to the insurgents of the Antilles all hearts responsive to a lofty thought, a generous sentiment. How much more actively ought these sympathies to manifest themselves in the great American republic, which, by its proximity, as well as by economic interests, is bound to Cuba, and which certainly has not forgotten in a century the history of its struggles for its own independence.

Reflection for a single moment in men of good faith would suffice to definitely answer the question, "Who is the adversary that endeavors to retain Cuba under its yoke?" This adversary is the most retrograde and the most savagely ecclesiastical monarchy in Europe; the one which, at the present moment, under a varnish of constitutional government, exerts an intolerable oppression over free thought, reëstablishes in its prisons the tortures of the Middle Ages, and sullies itself by atrocities similar to those perpetrated by the worst of despots,—the Bourbons of Naples, the Stambouloffs, and the Abdul-Hamids. It is the power, at once imbecile and tyrannous, that disseminates everywhere anger and revolt,—in the Philippine Islands, as well as in Cuba,—after having caused the whole of Latin America to rise up against it.

Between republican Cuba and monarchical Spain, can those hesitate who believe in the meaning of the words "progress," "liberty," "humanity"?

To take the side of the executioners against their victims, on the ground that there are in the Greater Antilles negro inhabitants (albeit inferior in number to the white population), would be a simple monstrosity for those who proclaim the Rights of Man and the principles of Equality of the French Revolution, as well as for those whose fathers have fought for the abolition of slavery. On the other hand, ignoring the ethnical traits created more by environment and social conditions than by the color of the skin, have we not seen by a number of events, most of them recent, how erroneous was the theory of "the superior races"?

Which, then, is the greater figure, the Ethiopian Menelik, or the European Baratière? And would it not be infinitely more glorious to be a mulatto like Maceo than a Castilian like Canovas?

The modern Latin nations, whatever may have been their literary, artistic, or even military, glories, have never, it must be confessed, known how to colonize. In their hands, the countries beyond the seas have become the prey of all those favorites upon whom the mother country has bestowed office; of cantankerous bureaucrats; of administrative officials swelled with their own importance. The church and the barracks were the two sacrosanct institutions; and government by the sword and the *goupillon* has very naturally extended across the seas from the conquering country to the conquered.

While England, profiting by the lessons of history, endowed Canada, Australia, New Zealand, and the Cape with autonomous institutions, and allowed initiative action to freely take its course sheltered from official interference, giving over the country not to functionaries, to soldiers, and to priests, but to the civil and laboring population,—the producers of all wealth,—Spain persevered in the errors of the past. She had lost Mexico, Peru, Chile, Argentina, and Guatemala in less than fifteen years by the revolt of their exasperated inhabitants. But this lesson did not suffice. On the contrary, the colonies which still remained to it, notably Cuba, were ground down more cruelly than ever, and were obliged to pay for themselves and for those that had shaken off the yoke.

Robbed, gagged, having no influence where their interests were concerned,—for all their rulers (one might say their convict-keepers) were sent them from the mother country, which chose by preference the ruined gamblers of the court,—enjoying in reality, despite a seeming semi-liberty of the press, no constitutional guarantees whatever,—for the Captain-General assumed all power, as he does to-day,—the Cubans, after patient endeavors to obtain pacifically the most indispensable reforms, realized that their only effective course was a resort to arms ; and, on October 10, 1868, the first insurrectional movement broke out at Yara.

I will not review this epic, which endured for ten years,—one year longer than the struggle of the Gauls against Cæsar. Half-naked, almost without arms, led by chiefs that no peril daunted, no obstacle, however great, repelled, and who to-day meet again as old men in the new revolution, the Cubans inflicted upon their enemies a loss of one hundred thousand men and of nearly one thousand millions. And these, finally incapable to crush the rebellion, were forced to treat with it. The pact of Zanjon, concluded between Martinez Campos and the Cuban chiefs, stipulated a number of reforms : administrative decentralization, admission to public office by competitive examination, establishment of new customs laws, creation of boards of works, representation in the Cortes on the basis of copyhold tenure ; finally and above all, cessation of a shameless system of malversation.

Of these clauses, some were flagrantly violated, others were put in force under conditions that worked to the disadvantage of the Cubans. Thus it was that a *law of mercantile relations* was enacted, which, instead of reforming the customs system in a liberal sense, strengthened existing protection, compelling the island, without any kind of reciprocity, to supply itself with the costly and indifferent products of Spain. The presence of Cuban representatives in the Chamber and Senate of Madrid served only to demonstrate the complete futility of this measure, as the voices of these few men were drowned by ministerial majorities. In short, thefts and peculation became worse.

The Cubans could thus by experience convince themselves that the Liberals were no better than the Conservatives. The only rôle the one or the other assigned to them was in fact that of taxpayers.

Deceived, robbed, subjected to incessant arbitrary acts, eaten up by militarism and bureaucracy, hindered in the free cultivation of the most fertile soil in the world,—for it was above all necessary to favor Spanish importation, which had lost all its other outlets,—the Cubans felt their misery all the more, from having before their very eyes the picture of the great American republic, so free, so prosperous.

They realized anew that force alone could insure the success of their claims. It was at this moment that José Martí appeared.

The American continent is acquainted with the life and death of this man, as great as he was modest, whose every effort was devoted to the realization of that grand idea,—"Cuba libre." An organizer of the first order, writer, counsellor, indefatigable conspirator,—the Antillian Mazzini prepared during ten years the elements and resources of the second revolution. It broke out on February 24, 1895, and has continued ever since.

Two years of desperate conflicts—ruinous for Spain, which is to-day on the verge of bankruptcy—have not weakened the efforts of the insurgent patriots. In the United States, better than anywhere else, one could follow day by day the varying fortune of this titanic duel: the landing of the two Maceo brothers, survivors of a family of heroes, both of whom were to find, a few months apart, the most glorious of deaths; the advent in the campaign of Maximo Gomez, the veteran of the ten years' insurrection; the death of Martí, fallen in ambuscade before seeing the triumph of his labor; the revolt deepening, spreading from the eastern to the western department, toward Pinar del Rio, and threatening Havana; the recall of Martinez Campos, powerless to conquer; his replacement by General Weyler, a wild beast with a human countenance; and finally, the dissolution, greater each day, of the prestige and credit of monarchical Spain.

This is the state of things at present: The entire people of the United States have espoused the cause of those who are struggling with so much valor and abnegation to break so odious a yoke. Will the Federal Government show itself less generous than the great nation in the name of which it speaks? Will the American eagle allow the Spanish vulture to settle upon its prey?

Certainly, international policy is not determined by sentiment alone. But reason and interest in no wise conflict with the sympathy which the cause of free Cuba can awaken in America and even among the democratic nations of Europe.

The greed of those who have kept the island in subjection has prevented it from developing. But it is evident that the advent of a new era of political liberty will cause the fall of the old economic barriers so jealously created and maintained. Commercial transactions,—chiefly with the United States,—imports and exports, will cease to be subjected to crushing duties. Cuba, without passing through ruinous intermediaries, will be able to enrich the international markets with its sugar, its coffee, its tobacco, and in return will receive manufactured products which it still lacks. Americans and Europeans will be able to establish themselves and work in peace in an island that requires but brawn and muscle to see its wealth increased tenfold.

Societies have their laws of evolution, against which the will of a few despots or exploiters cannot prevail. Having reached a certain degree of development, and being governed against their interests by a blind metropolis, colonies must either end in emancipating themselves or in perishing.

If, by extraordinary circumstances, Cuba should not emerge victoriously from the present struggle, the question will not be settled for all that. Peace would become but a brief truce, a preparation for a renewed resort to arms ; a new Martí, a new Gomez, a new Maceo would arise; one would see other Calixto Garcias marching to battle as old men bearing upon their brows—engraven by a bullet—the lone star of Cuba.

Rather than await further struggles,—floods of blood and accumulation of ruins to end in the inevitable,—is it not better to settle the matter now ? The great American republic holds in its hands the destiny of an oppressed people, whose heroism and patriotic sacrifices have rendered it a hundred times worthy of liberty. Will the United States decline to speed the hour of justice?

" What will become of Cuba, once it is separated from Spain ? " we are asked, with a feigned anxiety, by those who are so interested in the welfare of the island that they prefer to see Order reign there in the fashion of Weyler, rather than confront the possible risks of a stormy liberty at the outset. " Will peace be reëstablished as by enchantment ? " " Will not the island be destined to come under the rule of the United States, increasing still more their great power ? "

I do not pretend to forecast the future at long range; for an unknown factor may arise at any moment to overthrow the most plausible hypotheses. We can only adduce our knowledge from the past, and state conditions in the present. Once their liberty acquired, the Cubans will do what they deem most necessary to their interests, and will conclude with other nations such economical or political agreements as they may approve.

The United States have too often shown their abstinence from any policy of conquest for them to be accused of endeavoring to do with Cuba what they declined to do with the Sandwich Islands when a powerful and the ruling party of that power offered to them the possession of that archipelago.

That particularly intimate relations will be established between Americans and Cubans is likely and very desirable.

We are now at an era when the old barriers, between which the despotic governments fenced in the nations, are more and more destined to fall. The increasing needs of civilization and the development of natural affinities conspire to merge and fuse human groups far more surely than conquest. Reconciliations based upon entire liberty and respect of mutual rights,—should these cause us any uneasiness, when we earnestly wish for the termination of international conflicts and the advent of a grand federation of nations?

Meanwhile, until progress shall, sooner or later, realize this ideal, as it has realized the suppression of prehistoric anthropophagy and ancestral barbarities, we shout, "Cuba libre!"

Revolutions can never be defined; and it is possible that, after a long rule of pitiless suppression, the exuberance of the newly emancipated may be great at the beginning. And afterward? Have not nations their periods of youth and maturity the same as individuals? Is it necessary to remind our Republicans of the motto of the Palatine Posnanie: "Better a stormy liberty than a calm of servitude"?

The cause of the Cuban insurgents is that of Humanity. We see, too, even among the Spaniards themselves—whom it would be profoundly unjust to class as a mass with the Canovas and Weylers—the most respected men of the democracy, such as Pi y Margall, the former president of the republic, declare their sympathy for the brave patriotic fighters, their abhorrence for the butcher general who maintains order by means of ambuscade, torture, the shooting of prisoners, and the violation and massacre of women. It would need volumes to recount the transgressions of this monster whom, since the first

11

insurrection, the Cubans had named "the Hyena," as they had called his superior officer, Balmaceda, "the Tiger." The American continent has been aroused from one ocean to the other. From Hudson's Bay to Tierra del Fuego, there has been but a cry of horror against this miserable torturer and perjurer, who, always defeated by the heroic Maceo and threatened by him even in the capital itself, has only been able to come to an end with his formidable adversary by having him murdered!

What a contrast to the conduct of the Cuban general, causing wounded Spaniards to be nursed, and setting prisoners at liberty! If walls, which it is said have ears, had also a voice, those of Morro Castle could tell a tale of numberless atrocities, the knowledge of which, by fragments, has reached even to us: the accumulation of suspects of all ages in underground places without air and without light; tortures, similar to those of Montjuich,—crushing of the organs, deprivations of food and drink,—inflicted upon prisoners to force them to betray their friends and parents; secret executions; and drownings.

All this is done in the name of Order, as it was also in the name of Civilization that the Spaniards imported into Cuba the garrote; while the Americans, on the other hand, built railroads there.

Of this "Order," which may be described as spoliation in time of peace, and assassination in time of war, the Cubans will have no more at any price. It would be difficult to say they are wrong.

Alone or not alone, they will continue to struggle until the monster who holds them relinquishes his prey. But America—Saxon and Latin America,—the America of Washington and Bolivar will not leave them without assistance. It would lie to itself, its principles, its destiny, its still recent but already great history, if in this combat to the death between republican liberty and monarchical despotism, between the Future and the Past, it should allow the latter to strangle the former.

HENRI ROCHEFORT.

THE FUTILITY OF THE SPELLING GRIND.

IN the opening articles of the present series, I endeavored to prove that the first step toward placing elementary education on a scientific basis must necessarily lie in determining what results may reasonably be expected at the end of a given period of instruction. If we have no definite notions in regard to what our teachers ought to accomplish, our ideas must be doubly vague as to how much time need be devoted to each branch. And, as long as this remains unanswered, no well-founded opinion can be given concerning the possibility of broadening the course of study without detriment to the formal branches,—the point around which the entire question of educational reform revolves.

Believing that the most rational method of determining what our teachers might be expected to accomplish would lie in discovering what results the more successful ones had been able to obtain, I ventured to undertake a series of researches which I hoped might serve as an initial step toward bringing this problem to a solution. And it is upon the data thus collected that this and the remaining articles of my series will be based.

The material to be submitted in the present article is intended to show what our teachers have accomplished in spelling, and what, therefore, may be reasonably demanded of our schools in this subject. The traditional standard in spelling is perfection ; but this standard is unreasonable, and cannot be too soon abandoned. In view of the fact that in many cases the spelling faculty is weak, perfection could not be attained even if the number of words taught in an eight-year course should not exceed a thousand. And when we consider that the number of words in ordinary use is certainly not less than 15,000, including derivatives,—and the derivatives are frequently difficult to spell,—the absurdity of our standard becomes evident. Moreover, as some of our most scholarly people are deficient in spelling, and as, in this subject, some of the brightest pupils cannot keep pace with the dullest, our high-pitched sensibilities on the spelling question may be regarded as one of the mysteries of civilization. If these facts were more fully considered, we should undoubtedly feel more inclined to pardon an occasional mistake in spelling, and to refrain from abusing the schools for a weakness which, whatever might be done by our teachers, could not be overcome.

My researches in spelling were begun in February, 1895, and extended over a period of sixteen months. During this time three different tests were made; the number of children examined reaching nearly 33,000. In the present paper, space will permit me to state only the results of these tests, with certain conclusions that I have drawn from them; while I shall be obliged to defer to the next article the details concerning the methods of teaching, and the influences of certain modifying conditions, such as age, nationality, and environment, which were studied as closely as possible in order that the comparisons might be fairly drawn. · The results of the various tests, which are shown side by side in the accompanying tables, will be fully explained.

My first test consisted of the following fifty words: furniture, chandelier, curtain, bureau, bedstead, ceiling, cellar, entrance, building, tailor, doctor, physician, musician, beggar, plumber, superintendent, engine, conductor, brakeman, baggage, machinery, Tuesday, Wednesday, Saturday, February, autumn, breakfast, chocolate, cabbage, dough, biscuit, celery, vegetable, scholar, geography, strait, Chicago, Mississippi, Missouri, Alleghanies, independent, confectionery, different, addition, division, arithmetic, decimal, lead, steel, pigeon. These words, together with a set of questions concerning the methods employed by the teachers, as well as particulars in regard to the pupils, were sent to school superintendents in various sections of the United States. Of these superintendents, some twenty responded; sending me, in total, the work of more than 16,000 children. Of the two tables presented with this article, the first shows the general average obtained in individual cities by grades, every class-room examined being represented in the figures; while the second shows the results in individual schools,—the most characteristic among those examined having been selected for publication in this form. In the first table the results of only two tests are shown; while the second includes the results of the three. As it was thought inadvisable to publish the names of the localities from which the papers were received, the various cities have been represented by numbers, and the individual schools by letters. All the papers received are still in my possession.

On directing our attention to the results of the first test we are startled by the enormous variations, when the extremes are considered,—particularly in the fourth-year classes, where the averages range from 33 to 95.3 per cent. Such brilliant results as the latter might lead one to believe that the spelling problem had already been solved, and that nothing was needed to put all our teachers on the right path beyond a careful study of the methods employed where the highest standards had been secured, and carrying the message to those whose results had been less favorable.

As the replies to my questions concerning the methods used by different teachers were not sufficiently clear to enable me to penetrate to the root of the matter, I decided to undertake a special tour for the purpose of obtaining more definite information from the teachers who had taken part in the test. During this tour, which extended over a period of two months, more than two hundred teachers were visited. Long before I had reached the end of my journey my fondest hopes had fled; for I had learned from many sources that the unusually favorable results in certain class-rooms did not represent the natural conditions, but were due to the peculiar manner in which the examinations had been conducted. As the tests had not been made under my personal supervision, I could not, of course, vouch for the figures; and, having found that under these circumstances experienced school people were unwilling to accept them, I was obliged to become resigned to the idea that most of my trouble had been for nothing.

An unfortunate feature of the first test was the fact that in many of the words careful enunciation would give the clue to the spelling. In such words, for example, as *tailor, doctor, different, independent,* the difficulty is entirely obviated by placing the accent on the last syllable. Under these circumstances, even the most conscientious teachers could not fail, unwittingly, to give their pupils some assistance, if their enunciation were habitually slow and distinct; while in those instances in which my test had been looked upon as an opportunity for an educational display—in which the imperfections of childhood were not to be shown,—the teachers had been afforded the means of giving their pupils sufficient help, through exaggerated enunciation alone, to raise the class average very materially. I am confident, however, that, if any irregularities were practised, they were committed without the knowledge of the superintendents, who as a class are well known to discountenance such acts and do all in their power to stamp them out. That, moreover, in the vast majority of instances, the teachers were conscientious, is proved by the numerous papers sent to me in which the results were unfavorable.

If I could safely have done so, I should have discarded the first test entirely rather than express these doubts. But to ignore this test might have submitted me to the charge of hiding results which did not substantiate my pedagogical theories; whereas, in truth, I had fully determined, in advance, to base my theories on the facts, whatever their nature might be. As the results of the second and third tests are placed side by side with those of the first, no danger can arise by presenting figures which, if shown by themselves, might be misleading.

In view of my doubts concerning the first test, I decided to undertake another, and to personally supervise the examinations. Moreover, by giving a second test I believed that I might be able to discover whether or not my fears had been well founded. In the latter the words were written in sentences; fifty test-words being employed in the fourth- and fifth-year classes, and seventy-five in the sixth-, seventh-, and eighth-.[1] In preparing this test special care was exercised to omit words whose pronunciation would tell the secret.

In the second test more than 13,000 children were examined under my personal direction; and the papers, although temporarily marked by the pupils, were finally corrected by my assistants. Although I could not be present in every room during the entire course of the examination, and although children cannot be prevented from copying,

---

[1] While *running* he *slipped*. I *listened* to his *queer speech*, but I did not *believe* any of it. The *weather* is *changeable*. His loud *whistling frightened* me. He is *always changing* his mind. His *chain* was *loose*. She was *baking* cake. I have a *piece* of it. Did you *receive* my letter? I *heard* the *laughter* in the *distance*. Why did you *choose* that *strange picture* ? * *Because* I *thought* I liked it. It is my *purpose* to *learn*. Did you *lose* your *almanac* ? I gave it to my *neighbor*. * I was *writing* in my *language* book. Some children are not *careful enough*. Was it *necessary* to keep me *waiting* so long? Do not *disappoint* me so *often*. I have *covered* the *mixture*. He is *getting better*. * A *feather* is *light*. Do not *deceive* me. I am *driving* a new horse. * Is the *surface* of your desk *rough* or *smooth* ? The children were *hopping*. This is *certainly* true. I was very *grateful* for my *elegant present*. If we have *patience* we shall *succeed*. He met with a *severe accident*. *Sometimes* children are not *sensible*. You had no *business* to *answer* him. You are not *sweeping properly*. Your reading shows *improvement*. The ride was very *fatiguing*. I am very *anxious* to hear the news. I *appreciate* your kindness, I *assure* you. I cannot *imagine* a more *peculiar character*. I *guarantee* the book will meet with your *approval*. *Intelligent* persons learn by *experience*. The peach is *delicious*. I *realize* the *importance* of the *occasion*. Every rule has *exceptions*. He is *thoroughly conscientious; therefore* I do trust him. The *elevator* is *ascending*. Too much *praise* is not *wholesome*.

The fourth- and fifth-year test ends with " This is *certainly* true." The higher test includes all the sentences except the four marked with an asterisk. The test-words are italicized.

especially where the rooms are furnished with double seats and where the teachers have no control over their classes, I nevertheless believe that, for all practical purposes, the results of the second test demonstrate quite fairly what the children were able to do. In addition to those already mentioned, an indirect test in spelling was made in the form of compositions. The compositions represented the reproduction of a story specially prepared for the purpose. This story, which was accompanied by a picture, was read to the pupils by the teacher. The compositions also, in a large number of schools, were prepared under my personal supervision, and in many others under the special supervision of persons whose conscientiousness could not be doubted. In those cases in which the papers were marked for spelling, I feel morally certain that the true results were shown.

The marks for the language spelling which may be found in table No. 2, are based on the actual number of words written by the child, and represent the number of correctly spelled words per hundred. When the same word was misspelled more than once in an individual composition, only one error was counted. The average ages were computed from the returns of the first test. The details concerning this question, as well as the time devoted to spelling, will be more fully considered in my next article.

Of the three examinations, the first has been generally regarded as the least efficient in demonstrating the child's ability to spell, as such a test does not represent what he is able to do in ordinary writing. That this argument is worthy of some consideration, particularly in the case of the more immature children, is indicated by the fact that some of the fourth-year averages which on the first test were in the thirties, on the second advanced to the seventies. The second test appeared to meet with general approval, although a few teachers believed it too difficult for the sixth-year classes. As the test was purely comparative, however, this objection could not affect its validity. As to the comparative merits of the sentence- and the composition-tests, most teachers favor the latter, on the ground that the most rational test of the child's ability is one that shows his power to apply what he has learned. On the other hand, some have argued in favor of the sentence-test, believing that compositions do not include a sufficiently broad range of words to show the pupil's strength in all directions. If, however, an agreement might be secured to judge the spelling by the general written work, at least a temporary standard would be indicated by the results of my composition-test, which lead to certain definite conclusions.

4th Grade	First Test			Second Test	
	Average Age.	No. Papers Ex.	Average %.	No. Papers Ex.	Average %.
	11.4	205	70.8	114	66.7
	10.9	183	70.7	…	…
	12.2	147	51.9	…	…
	12.7	171	56.1	…	…
	10.7	94	50	…	…
	11.6	132	62.9	304	63.9
	11.1	479	61.8	345	67.9
	11.6	166	41.3	191	65.4
	11.4	132	46.7	…	…
	11.1	146	79.6	466	57.7
	11.2	213	45.4	…	…
			53.6	…	…
	12	280	56.5	389	69.3
	11.2	236	57.5	173	64.7
	11	120	54.1	…	…
	11.6	142	47.6	146	59.1
	11.6	129	50.2	…	…
	11.8	194	56.5	…	…
	11.1	227	55.3	…	…
		264	48.7	…	…
		157	51.5	…	…
	…	3820	53.5	2128	64.2

5th Grade	First Test			Second Test	
	Average Age.	No. Papers Ex.	Average %.	No. Papers Ex.	Average %.
	12.4	171	78.1	120	78.1
	11.6	194	67.6	…	…
	12.3	78	66.9	…	…
	12.4	190	64.3	…	…
	11.8	145	69.5	…	…
	12.9	140	70	…	…
	11.9	436	58.6	319	75.3
	12.2	137	59.4	…	…
	12.6	239	83	312	76
	12.4	165	65	200	73.8
	12.5	132	66.6	…	…
				362	73.4
	13.1	296	66	…	…
	12	240	65.3	525	77
	12.2	87	68.2	189	75.1
	12.4	150	62.2	…	…
	12.7	138	64	…	…
	12.7	172	71.9	209	71.2
	12.7	326	67.3	…	…
	12.7	286	68.4	…	…
	12.2	97	59.5	…	…
	…	3819	64.3	2236	75.1

6th Grade	First Test			Second Test	
	Average Age.	No. Papers Ex.	Average %.	No. Papers Ex.	Average %.
	13.2	131	86.9	91	74.9
	12.9	218	75.4	…	…
	13.8	58	76.6	…	…
	13.8	123	71.3	…	…
	13.7	172	79.8	…	…
	13	104	81.5	…	…
	12.9	553	67.9	432	69.4
	13.2	120	81.3	…	…
	13.7	382	86.5	251	73.2
	13.6	91	69.8	194	67.4
	13.1	197	79	…	…
				237	75.9
	14	137	75	…	…
	12.7	179	71.3	401	70
		64	73.7	107	63.8
	13.2	150	68.7	…	…
	12.6	121	76.1	…	…
	13.5	162	81.9	164	67.7
	13.8	327	73.8	…	…
	13.2	269	72	…	…
	12.9	104	73.3	…	…
	…	3662	75.6	1877	70.4

7th Grade	First Test			Second Test	
	Average Age.	No. Papers Ex.	Average %.	No. Papers Ex.	Average %.
	14.3	123	88	74	77.6
	13.8	187	84.3	…	…
	14.8	40	81	…	…
	14	120	82.7	…	…
	13.5	147	84	…	…
	14.5	91	79.5	…	…
	13.7	574	78	283	76.5
	14.6	123	79.6	…	…
	14.8	232	89.6	229	82.8
	14.2	87	74.9	86	81
	14.5	140	88.7	…	…
				89	84.6
	14.6	165	79.8	…	…
	14.3	206	77	262	79.8
	14	78	85.6	175	72.7
	14	110	76.4	…	…
	14.4	100	78.2	…	…
	14.6	36	87	172	78.3
	14.3	298	79	…	…
	14	254	82.8	…	…
		73	79.6	…	…
	…	3184	81	1370	78.8

8th Grade	First Test			Second Test	
	Average Age.	No. Papers Ex.	Average %.	No. Papers Ex.	Average %.
	15	86	93.6	87	84.6
	14.6	187	89	…	…
	16	23	82	…	…
	14.9	153	85.5	…	…
	14.3	81	85.7	…	…
	15.4	66	81	…	…
	14.8	376	82.1	409	82.8
	15	86	86	…	…
	15.2	98	78.5	100	83.3
	15	50	90.9	…	…
				154	90.6
	15.9	59	85.1	…	…
	14.5	188	82.2	…	…
	15.3	73	89.6	211	86.1
	15.3	123	77.7	127	81.8
		81	84.9	…	…
	15.7	231	86.1	133	83.5
	15.6	144	86	…	…
	14.9	57	82.3	…	…
	…	2162	84.2	1221	84.4

City	School	4th Year Column-Test	4th Sentence-Test	4th Composition-Test	4th Average Age	4th Minutes Daily	5th Column-Test	5th Sentence-Test	5th Composition-Test	5th Average Age	5th Minutes Daily	6th Column-Test	6th Sentence-Test	6th Composition-Test	6th Average Age	6th Minutes Daily	7th Column-Test	7th Sentence-Test	7th Composition-Test	7th Average Age	7th Minutes Daily	8th Column-Test	8th Sentence-Test	8th Composition-Test	8th Average Age	8th Minutes Daily	School Av., Column-Test	School Av., Sentence-Test
19	B	63	57.4 / 68.4		11.8	40	67	73.2		12.8	40	76	61.3 / 69.5		14.7	30	83	69.5 / 84		15.9	30	87.6	85 / 86.8		15.8		74.7 / 74.3	74.7 / 73.3
19	A	61	61.8	97.9	10.9	30	67	76.6	95.2	11.9	30	74	73	94.1	13.7	35	84	84	98.3	14.5	30	81	84.3	99.3	15.5	5	73.4 / 73.8	73.4 / 73.8
16	B	36	65.4		11.5	30	63	70.6 / 74.4	96.1	12.7	15	69	61.9 / 69.8	97.6	13	15	78	71.1 / 73.8	98.5	13.5	10	79	81.2 / 80.2	99.2	13.8	5	65.6 / 72.0	65.6 / 72.0
16	A	48	66.4 / 59.2	97.4 / 97.9	10.6	30	68.2	76.2 / 79.1	98.3	13.7	30	70	69.6	96.7 / 98.7	13.7	30	75	71.8 / 73.8	98.3 / 99.3	14.7	30	88	80.9 / 89.9	99.2	14.1	6	67.6 / 72.7	67.6 / 72.7
15	H		62.6 / 69.1	97			68.6	73.6 / 79.4	98.1 / 98.3			71.8		98.1		15	85	73.8 / 81.4	98.7		25	90.6	84 / 89.6	99.4	15.1	95	79.5 / 77.9	79.5 / 77.9
15	E	53.6 / 39.6	66.2 / 70.8	96.6		15	70.4	74.4 / 81.6	97.8		30	72.2	69.8 / 72.7	98.5		30	80.4	80.6	98.7		30	87.6	89.6 / 86.6	99.9		90	73.2 / 77.3	73.2 / 77.3
15	D					30		73 / 73.4	96.8 / 97.4		30	78.8	57 / 71.5	97.7 / 98.1		30	90	74.7 / 84.7			30	89.6	86.2 / 88.6	99.2		90		
13	B		74.8				81.6					72.7	73.4				80.4	76.7 / 83.3	98.3			87.6	86.2 / 88.6				78.8	78.8
13	B		33.2 / 63.1			18	73	66.4 / 73	96.6		18	57	73.7	97.1 / 98.1		9	78.9				19	83.9 / 94.6	87.2 / 88.6	99.4		19	78.4	78.4
11	A		33.2 / 63.1					73.4	97.4		10	73.1	75.1 / 73.7										90.3 / 94.6	99 / 99.4				79.0	79.0
11	B	53	76.4 / 70.8	96.3	11.5	35	69	76.6 / 81.8	98.6 / 98.9	12.9	35	80	74	98.5	13.8	30	81	80	98.8	14.9	40	90.5	90.3 / 98.7	99.1	14.8	40	74.7 / 73.4	74.7 / 73.4
11	A	63	63.6 / 65.6	98.3	10.5	25	75	70.4 / 70.6	97.9 / 98.9	13.1	30	87	65.5 / 79.6	99.2	13	30	82	76		14.8	30	91	88.7 / 90.4	99.1	13.1	40	76.9 / 73.9	76.9 / 73.9
10	A	50	61.2 / 68.6	96.6 / 98.3	11.5	35	70	76.8 / 77.2	98.5 / 98.9	13.9	30	71	72.7	99.2	14.1	20	83		18.7 / 18.8	14.9 / 14.8	30				15.6			
10	B		61.4 / 75.9															78 / 79.5	98.8	15.4	30	80	83.5 / 83.5	99.1		30	70.2 / 76.3	70.2 / 76.3
9	C	85	66.4		11.5	40	88.5	83.9	97.6 / 97.9	12.3	45	98	76.4 / 78.4	98.7	13.8 / 13.4	35	78	80 / 79.5	98.6	15.3	30	83.5	83.5	99.1	15.6	30	87.6 / 77.9	87.6 / 77.9
9	B	95.3	66.4 / 65.4	96.1 / 96.8			97	74.8 / 76.8	97.6 / 97.9		15	97	73.2 / 76.8	98.7	14.3	45	97	84.7 / 86.5	99.2	15.8	60							85.7 / 77.7	85.7 / 77.7
9	A	86	70.8 / 66.6		11.1	40	57	71.8 / 78	97.6 / 97.9	12.4	15	85.5	66.5	99.1	13.6 / 13.4	30	88	66.6 / 86.6	99.4	14.8	30	89	99.4		14.6	15	65.6	65.6
7	C	39	73.8 / 63.6	97 / 97.5	11.2	30	73	73.6 / 72.1	98.6 / 98.1	13.8 / 13.6	40	66	64.3 / 73.4	97.8 / 98.2	13.9 / 13.4	45	78	72.9 / 72.1	99.3 / 99.3	13.6 / 13.6	30	82	87.9 / 87.9	99.4	14.9	15	68.4 / 77.9	68.4 / 77.9
7	A	33	77 / 68.6	95.9 / 97.5	11.2	40	49	72.6 / 68.9	98.4 / 98.2	11.4 / 11.4	30	67	64.9 / 98.4	97.3 / 98.2	13.1 / 13.4	30	74	72.1	99.4	14.1 / 14.1	30	84	87.2 / 84.9	99.4	14.3 / 14.2	30	64.5 / 73.5	64.5 / 73.5
1	C	71	73.4 / 68.3	96.7 / 97.5	11	30	55	75 / 81.1	96.9 / 98.3	11.9	30	66	80 / 81.1	99.1	13	45	79	78.1	98.7	13.8	50	83	98.1	99.6	15.2	35	83.4 / 73.3	83.4 / 73.3
1	B	67	61.8	96.8	11.9	50	73	72.6	97.4	13.9	50	90	77.7	98.3	13	50	87	78	98.7	13.7	40	93	86.8	99.6	15.3	30	83.5 / 75	83.5 / 75
1	A	66	67.6		12	50	81	79.6	97.4	12.8	45	79	77.2	98.3	13.9	30	90	76.7		14.8	35	94	86.8	99.6	15.3	30	80	77.1

In regard to the first test, I shall do no more here than direct attention to a few facts substantiating my statements concerning its validity. In the first place, it will be seen, by glancing over the averages in the last two columns of the second table, that the schools which towered above the others on the first test showed no marked superiority on the second. This is strikingly apparent in the case of School A, No. 9, which, on the first test, stood head and shoulders above the others, and, on the second, secured only eleventh place among the twenty-one on my list. The condition becomes doubly interesting when these marks are compared with those secured on both tests by School A, No. 7.

In order to allay my fear of harboring unwarranted suspicions in the case of the remarkable class average of 95.3, secured in the fourth grade of School A, No. 9, I compared the papers of the individual pupils who had taken part in the first test with those presented by the same pupils on the second. Most of these pupils, in the meantime, had been promoted to the fifth grade. Of course if their papers had again shown the same degree of perfection, it would have been but fair to conclude that the figures at first secured were reliable, and that we had simply discovered a remarkable group of children. The second examination proved, however, that these children had not been born in Wonderland, but that they were of the very same stamp as other children had proved to be. In fact the average made on the second test by those who had received 95.3 on the first was only 73, or exactly the same as that made by the pupils of School A, No. 7, who on the first test obtained not more than 41.

In Schools E and H, No. 15, the figures are reliable, as the words were dictated by myself. Again, in City 18, the examinations were made in my presence, the words being dictated by the teachers. In no instance in which the tests were made under my supervision—the words being pronounced by either the teacher or myself—was the class average for the fourth year, in boys' or mixed schools, higher than 59 per cent. I desire to say, in passing, that the results in the girls' schools were higher than those in the boys' and mixed schools. In the accompanying tables the girls' schools have been omitted; otherwise the comparison would have been misleading. They will be considered separately.

Leaving the first test and directing our attention to the others, we are confronted by a number of interesting phenomena, almost equally manifest in both. The most striking of these are: First, that in the vast majority of instances the results are very close when the averages for entire buildings are compared. In fifteen of the twenty-one schools on my list, the averages on the second test, as the table shows, run from 73.3 to 77.9. Second, while the results in the lower grades of different schools show considerable variation, those in the eighth-year classes, which represent the end of the school course, are remarkably even. In twelve of the seventeen eighth-year grades, the averages are from 84 to 88, the A and B classes being taken together. And in fifteen of a total of twenty sets of eighth-grade compositions examined for spelling, the variations were only three-tenths of 1 per cent, the results lying between 99.1 and 99.4, the A's and B's being taken as one. These facts are doubly remarkable when we consider that the twenty-one schools not only represent institutions in many sections of the country, but that they are samples of schools conducted under all conceivable conditions. For example, No. 7 is a Western city of moderate size; while No. 15 is a large city in the East. Again, most of the children attending School A, No. 7 are of American parentage, and their home surroundings are particularly favorable; while the children attending School B, No. 7 represent the foreign laboring element. Further, from a pedagogical standpoint, all varieties of schools are included; some of them belonging to the most mechanical, while others are among the most progressive in our country.

If the best results had been secured in the mechanical and the poorest in the progressive schools, the question would arise, whether the small additional return would warrant the latter in placing additional pressure on spelling at the expense of other subjects. But even this question does not arise; for it did not happen that the results in most cases were best in mechanical schools. Indeed, in both the mechanical and the progressive schools, the results were variable; so that while, in some instances, the higher figures were secured by the former, in others they were obtained by the latter; and the same is true of the lower figures. For example, School B, No. 11, in which the best average (79.4) was obtained, belongs to a very progressive system; while School A, No. 12, which made only 73.9, belongs to one of our most mechanical systems. And it is a peculiar incident that, in both these cities, the results in the only other school examined are exactly reversed, although the environment is about the same.

Further, just as it is impossible by the results to distinguish the mechanical from the progressive schools, so it is impossible to distinguish the schools attended by the children of cultured parents from those representing the foreign laboring element; the results from this stand-point also varying equally.   Consequently, so far as spelling is concerned, the influence of environment, appears to be insignificant.

The second point to which I have referred; namely, the small variation in the eighth-year results,—regardless of how much time had been devoted to spelling, or what methods had been employed, or under what home influences the children had been reared,—is also well worthy of consideration.   And it is no less striking that the same level was reached in the end, regardless of what had been accomplished in the lower grades,—a fact which becomes obvious on comparing the results in the eighth-year classes with the average obtained by the entire school.   In the composition-test, where the results in fifteen of the twenty sets of eighth-year papers were within three-tenths of each other, this fact is still more clearly demonstrated.   To make a further study of eighth-year results a few variations in the tests were tried; and no modifications were found.   For example, in a special test of twenty-five very simple words, I examined four eighth-year classes representing three different cities.   The extremes did not vary more than two points; the results being respectively 92.0, 93.2, 93.6, and 94.4.   In one school, the compositions were written from the picture alone; so that the pupils were absolutely free in the selection of the story and the choice of words.   The average was 99.3.

Do not these results indicate that, in learning to spell, maturity is the leading factor, while method plays only a subordinate part?   And, if the superiority of the old-fashioned spelling grind cannot be demonstrated, is it not our duty to save the child from this grind?   Moreover, as the results prove that, beyond a certain minimum, the compensation for time devoted to spelling is scarcely, if at all, appreciable, have we not here discovered an element of waste, which, if eliminated, would open the way to an equal enrichment of the course of study without detriment to the formal branches?

It might still be argued that while pressure could be omitted in the case of pupils who are likely to complete the grammar-school course, it would nevertheless be needed for those who cannot attend school longer than four or five years.   But, in view of my results, this argument is equally controvertible.   For, in the first place, while the fourth and fifth grades, individually considered, show considerable variation, we find many instances in which a low fourth-year average is followed by a high fifth-, and *vice versa;* so that when the two grades are averaged together, the results for the different schools are very close.

Again, while the differences in the fourth year are marked, the results do not speak in favor of mechanical primary schools. On the contrary, the poorest fourth-grade results—Schools A and B, No. 12—were obtained by the products of primary departments as mechanical as any to be found; while, on the other hand, among those who did best were the products of some of our most delightful primary schools, such as School A, No. 7, and School B, No. 11. That no dogmatic statements on this point can be made on either side, however, is proved by the fact that a contrary statement would be equally true; for in some of the mechanical schools the fourth-grade averages were high, while in some of the progressive schools they were comparatively low.

In the majority of instances, the results of the first test, also, were confined within narrow limits; for, in twelve out of eighteen cities— Nos. 1 and 9 being excluded—the averages ranged from 70.6 to 74.8, the number of correctly spelled words thus lying between 35 and 37. On the second test, the general averages in seven cities out of nine ranged from 73.5 to 76.8. The smallest variations, however, were found in the results of the composition-test, where, in spite of the great variation in the character of the institutions, the extreme difference in ten schools out of eleven was only five tenths of 1 per cent—98.2 to 98.7.

Finally, as in most localities the general results were nearly equal —those secured under the same system of instruction varying as much as those obtained under different systems—it is clear that the remedy does not lie in a change of method, nor in an increase of time. And this conclusion accords with the fact that the dissatisfaction with spelling is as great in communities where this subject constitutes a special feature as in those where spelling plays only a subordinate part in the schools.

Whether or not the spelling in a particular locality is actually below the average can be learned only by comparing the results of an examination conducted on the same basis in many localities. By examining children in any one city, on a set of arbitrarily selected words, the question cannot be solved, because the results in other places, on the same list of words, would remain an unknown quantity. A common standard is offered, however, by a composition-test such as I have undertaken. And when a test of this nature shows results similar to those presented in this article, interested citizens may rest assured that the spelling in their own schools is no worse than it is in those of most other localities.

J. M. RICE.

REMARKABLE SUCCESS OF WOMAN'S ENFRANCHISEMENT IN NEW ZEALAND.

THE agitation in favor of what are familiarly known as "Women's Rights" has now been going on for more than a quarter of a century with varying success in different parts of the world, but chiefly in the countries occupied by the English-speaking race. No movement has been advocated with more enthusiasm by those who have embraced its principles: few, if any, have been met with a more unsympathetic and dogged opposition by those who have rejected them. This was perhaps to have been expected to some extent, owing to the nature of the questions involved; but it may be worth while to inquire whether it has not been due, at least in part, to the methods generally adopted by its most earnest and energetic advocates. Should it appear that these are faulty, it is not yet too late to amend them. Should it be possible to produce evidence that other methods than those generally employed have proved more effective in any instance, it may at any rate be worthy of inquiry what these methods have been, and why they have been crowned with a success which, it must be admitted, has not hitherto been very general in civilized communities.

The history of social development in all ages presents a picture of gradual, frequently of almost unnoticed, concessions by the strong to the weak—by those possessed of the good things of existence to those who have sought to share them—rather than of great victories won, and great advantages forcibly wrested by the one class from the other. It would be an endless task to trace the steps by which nearly every far-reaching and beneficent reform in social life has been attained; indeed, generally it would be impossible, owing to the fact that formal demands were not made, nor a formal programme blazoned on the banner of the party of progress. It may be granted that in many respects times have altered, and that the present, more than any former time, is a period of programmes and blazonry; but it by no means follows that it is on that account necessarily superior to the times that have preceded it, even in the effectiveness of its methods. In spite of all the changes that have come about during the century now drawing to its close, it has yet to be proved that human nature has undergone any material alteration ; and one of the best ascertained and most widespread characteristics of human nature has always been its reluctance to accede to demands even where it could easily be approached and managed by less ostentatious methods.   It may well be so in the case of the great social and political revolution of our own day ; and it is far from unlikely that the progress of the movement for securing what are known as "Women's Rights" in matters political would be greatly accelerated if many of its advocates could be contented to ask rather than to demand, to persuade rather than to denounce those who as yet remain unconvinced.

Men may listen much and do little ; and it would seem that that is very much the position at which the "Women's Rights" movement has halted in most parts of the civilized world to-day.   Where the point at issue is a great and practical one, it is not enough to get men to listen to arguments, either from the platform or the press.   It is not enough to organize companies of enthusiastic women to carry— perhaps even to flaunt—the banner of their political creed in the face of unbelieving mankind.   Two things, it may be asserted, are necessary to render victory widely possible: (1) the practical instincts of men must be satisfied by having it demonstrated that the proposed changes will work well in practice ; and (2) the great mass of women must be taught to interest themselves in the movement as one which is to be of practical and not merely of theoretical value to themselves.

It is a fact which can hardly be too strongly insisted on, that only a very small minority of human beings—whether male or female—is greatly interested in pure theories.   The few indeed, can grow enthusiastic upon abstract questions of right, and indignant about abstract wrongs ; but, although it may be contended that they are the salt of the earth and of society, they are not, it must be admitted, a very influential or popular condiment.   The vast majority want to know what is to be gained by practically recognizing the right demanded, or by remedying the wrong complained of.   For them, things as they are have at any rate the authority of experience in their favor.   If the world seems on the whole to be a pretty good world,—as it undoubtedly is,—in spite of a few drawbacks, most men, and a large majority of women also, want something more than an argument upon abstract principles and the eternal fitness of things to render them willing to accept what looks like a sweeping innovation.   It may be feared that this fact has been too little considered by the advocates of women's rights,

They have confined themselves generally to arguments founded on the equality in intellect which exists—or at least is said to exist—between the sexes, and to the superiority which is claimed for women in all that pertains to the finer sentiments and moral convictions of human nature; and having, as they consider, triumphantly demonstrated these things, they are too apt to pause for the assent of men to their conclusions that, consequently, women should vote at elections, sit as Senators, and occupy the Presidential chair. They are astonished that this assent is so slow in coming, and are only too ready to attribute the delay to selfishness and the tyranny of the strong over the weak, blended with a little uneasiness at the prospect of losing that position of preëminence which men have usurped so long.

Men, on the other hand, so far as they have taken an interest in the matter at all, have generally troubled themselves little about questions of abstract right. The problem has presented itself to them usually as a practical one; and its commonest form may be taken to be, "How will this proposed overturn of existing arrangements affect my family? Will my home-life be as safe and as harmonious when my wife talks and lives politics as it is now? Will my daughters be as safe from undesirable associations and situations as I am able to keep them at present? And furthermore, will it do any good? Will politics really become purer because a new half of the population has suddenly been taken into active partnership in their management,—the half which up to this time has taken no interest worth mentioning in the matter?"

These will no doubt appear trivial objections to the enthusiasts in the cause. They are at all times prepared with the high-sounding motto, "Fiat justitia, ruat cœlum"; and, having fully convinced themselves that theirs is the cause of justice, they are more than ready to ignore the questionings of doubt and the hesitations of prudence. It is probably not wholly unfortunate that the matter does not rest with them. They, however, have to face the situation and acknowledge that, as things stand, the task before them is not to convince themselves, but the men of the community. To do this they must condescend to ordinary methods. They must convince men that the proposed change will be for the better; they must remove from men's minds the idea that it is a mere fad, the creature of a handful of enthusiastic and not very wise nor well-balanced women; they must furnish men with some practical grounds for believing that to give the women of the community votes and admission to public life will result in positive benefit to politics, and will not tend to destroy the life of the home and the happiness of the family.   Until this is done there is every prospect that the progress of the great proposed reform will be slow ;—indeed, in many countries there is even a risk that a reaction may set in and that the movement may collapse altogether.

As a single object-lesson is often worth a dozen lectures, it is fortunate for the cause of woman's political enfranchisement that it is now possible to study in several parts of the world the operation of a system by which both sexes are placed on something like an equality in political privileges, and—which is perhaps even more likely to be of practical use to the cause—to trace the steps by which this change has been brought about, and the results which appear to have followed its introduction.   I propose to state here, as a contribution to the fuller understanding of this important question, the history and results of woman's franchise legislation in the self-governing colony of New Zealand.   In doing so I may call attention to the fact that the country referred to has special claims to attention owing to the fact that it is a comparatively small and compact country, inhabited by a community of almost unmixed British, and particularly English, origin, widely separated from any other community, and generally possessed of a high standard of culture and education.   As a consequence, it may be, of these peculiarities, the colonists of New Zealand have been remarkable among the communities of Australasia for the number of their new departures both in their legislation and institutions.   Thus it was in New Zealand that the system now known as the Australian ballot had its origin ; and it is there that it is found to-day in its most complete form.   It was there that a system of perpetually leasing instead of selling state lands was introduced ; and the system is now in practical working.   There, also, a complete system of local option in the sale of intoxicating drinks has for many years been in operation.

It is now four years since the electoral franchise was granted by act of the local parliament to all women twenty-one years of age ; and, as the parliaments in New Zealand last for three years, there have been two general elections in which the women's vote has been a most important factor.   It is only just to note that there are no symptoms of public regret at the step thus taken, nor are there, so far, any indications of the change having altered in other respects the ordinary usages of society.   On the other hand it is important to observe that the change was no new idea in New Zealand.   It was not the result of female agitation, either through the press or on the platform. There were no "Women's Rights" leagues organized; nor was any public attempt made to denounce the selfishness of men, or to magnify the virtues and intellectual powers of women. To the persons who have put themselves forward in positions of prominence in the "Women's Rights" movements in America and Great Britain the attitude of the women of New Zealand would undoubtedly have seemed slow and supine to an extraordinary degree. They held no meetings; they sent no petitions; they published no letters or pamphlets—either to denounce men or to praise women. What they did was to take advantage of every opportunity that was given them of taking part in the management of public affairs, and of showing an active and intelligent interest in public questions.

It was in the year 1877 that the first step was taken by the legislature, which has found its natural result in the full enfranchisement of the women of the colony. In that year the Parliament enacted the first general education law for the country; and by that act the women—or rather, to speak more correctly, a small section of the women of the country—were granted their first share in the management of public affairs. By that act the country was divided, for educational purposes, into six provinces, and the entire control of the schools—subject only to the provisions of the law—was vested in an elective Education Board for each province. These Boards had the spending of all the money voted by Parliament for educational purposes, divided among the provinces on the basis of population; they had the appointment of all officers and teachers within their own districts, and the erection and maintenance of all school buildings; so that their powers and patronage were large. The members were elected annually by the votes of the committees of the school districts throughout their provinces; and these school committees were in turn elected every year by the resident heads of families in each school district. Thus a school district might contain two or three schools in a country district, where the population was scattered, and half a dozen, or even more, in a town, where it was more concentrated; and it was the duty of the resident heads of families living within it to elect seven of their number each year to exercise a local oversight of the schools, in accordance with the regulations laid down by the Board of the province.

It was found that no class of the inhabitants took a more active and intelligent interest in the proper management of the schools than

12

the women who chanced, either from widowhood, or the absence of their husbands from home, to be in the position to vote for members of the school committees. At first they confined themselves to attend-ing the meetings and there taking part in the election of the committees; but within a year or two the interest which they took in the subject led to their being gradually elected as members of the committees themselves. Until within a very few years, it was the exception rather than the rule to find a school committee on which there was not at least one female member. It is worthy of note that the tribute was entirely a voluntary one on the part of the male householders; and, so far as is recorded, there was no attempt made to agitate for the election of committee-women. Women are equally eligible for election on the provincial Boards of Education; but I am not aware that any woman has been elected to the position. This is probably owing to the fact that the constituency, embracing as it does all the school committees of a province, is more easily approached by well-known men than by any member of the other sex.

Five years after the establishment of the national system of educa-tion a complete revision of the licensing law of the colony took place; and it was determined to place the issue of licenses entirely under popular control within each electoral district of the country. A local board was provided for, the members of which were to be elected once in two years by the votes of all the ratepayers in each district, with whom it should rest whether any, and, if any, how many, licenses to sell intoxicating liquors should be granted in each year. The original proposal was that the right of electing members of Licensing Boards should vest in the male ratepayers only; but, after discussion, the prin-ciple which had already been found to work so successfully in the case of the Education Boards was extended to that of Licensing Boards throughout the colony. Since the year 1883, therefore, all female rate-payers have been in a position to exercise the franchise with respect to the liquor traffic as fully as the other sex. It was feared at the time that the result would be to strengthen the hands of the total abstainers, by the election of men wedded to the idea of closing all licensed houses; but experience failed to justify the expectation. From the first the Licensing Boards have been remarkable for their moderation; sternly repressing all inferior or doubtfully conducted houses,—there are no saloons, or mere liquor shops, recognized by the New Zealand law,—but in no single instance attempting to deprive any populous district of hotel accommodation altogether. These elections, being conducted

in all respects like elections for members of the legislature, enabled the
public to judge how far the fears of those who dreaded unpleasantness
as the result of male and female voters attending the same polling-
booths were well founded.   It was shown that all such fears were
groundless, and that the result appeared rather to be a marked improvement in the orderliness of the proceedings.

  · Encouraged by the excellent results following the gradual extension
of the right of voting to women, the next step was to admit all female
ratepayers to an equal voice with the men in municipal elections
throughout the colony.   So complete had been the success attending
the female franchise as applied to Licensing Boards, that the new proposal was adopted with scarcely a show of opposition; and the grant
of the privilege was followed not only by its general exercise by all
female ratepayers, but by a very decided improvement both in the
class of men elected and in the general orderliness and quietness of
the proceedings.   In this way public opinion in New Zealand advanced step by step, uninfluenced by declamation, or arguments based
upon theories which must, in their very nature, be open to question,
but moulded gradually by the results of experience, and feeling its
way by practical methods to a practical result.   From first to last it
may be said to have been the doing of the women of the colony themselves, who quietly accepted the power placed in their hands and used
it so intelligently as to impress the other sex with the conviction that
its possession did the women no injury, while it had a decidedly beneficial effect upon the conduct of public affairs.

  It was under these circumstances that the proposal was finally
made to confer the full electoral franchise upon all persons of full age,
without regard to sex.   It was really a foregone conclusion, because
every one of the natural objections to the change had been gradually
undermined in advance.   It had become useless to allege that women
knew nothing of such matters, and would not take any interest in
learning, in a community where for sixteen years the women had
been showing an ever-increasing interest of the most intelligent
kind in each question that was successively placed within their
control.   It was felt that if the wives and daughters of the colonists
could without injury or annoyance vote at municipal elections, and
elect men in whose hands should vest discretionary power on such
questions as the granting of licenses to retail liquor, they could certainly take part in a parliamentary election, where local feeling was
likely to be less acute.   Finally, no real attempt was made to exhibit

the cherished bogey of those opposed to female suffrage which draws its terrors from pictures of homes divided by differences of political opinion and of husbands and wives quarrelling over the ballot-box. There was really no weapon left in the armory of the opponents of a revolution which had been preparing during sixteen years.

By the same statute which granted the franchise to women it was provided that the registrars should expunge from the electoral rolls after every election the names of all persons who, according to the certified copy of the electoral roll of their districts supplied by the returning officer at each election, had failed to register their votes. It was thus cast upon each elector either to appear and excuse, to the satisfaction of the court of revision, his failure to perform the duty of giving his vote or to suffer the loss of his franchise at the succeeding election. It may be in consequence of this provision, that the proportion of votes recorded to the number of qualified electors on the roll is an unusually high one; and the results of the two general elections which have taken place since the franchise was extended to women show that the female voters of New Zealand have exercised their newly acquired right in as nearly as possible the same proportion as the men. At no time have more important questions been agitated in the colony, and at none does there seem to have been a more general interest taken in the result of the elections; yet it is reported that there has been a marked and increasing improvement in the proceedings of all kinds, from the public meetings and platform speeches to the quiet and orderly conduct of the voters on election day. There have been a few women's political clubs started and organized; but as a rule the idea of separate action has met with little favor; and the female voters of New Zealand have been content to take an intelligent but unostentatious share in the ordinary political movements of the party to which they have been attached. Political meetings in New Zealand are no longer assemblies of men alone, but are largely attended by women also; and it is said that the change has led to a great improvement both in the character of the proceedings and in the oratory. As yet, female speakers on public platforms would seem to be rare; and at the late elections they appear in almost every case to have belonged to the extreme temperance or anti-liquor-traffic party. The innovation does not indeed seem to be a popular one in the colony; and its strongest opponents are said to be the mass of the female voters themselves; but it is not reported that women have ever been refused a fair hearing, especially by the male part of their audience.

Something remains to be said as to the results of the change on the personnel of the parliamentary candidates elected, and on the policy which has received the popular support. It is to be noted that the alteration in the law added, within 3 per cent, a number of new voters equal to those already upon the electoral rolls; and had it been the case, as was expected by many, that on political questions women would take an essentially different view from that held by men, the result could hardly have failed to be as startling as alarmists had prophesied. As a matter of fact no such results have followed at either of the elections, which have taken place with an interval of three years between them. At both elections—and markedly so at the last, which took place a few months ago—candidates were favored whose personal character stood high and whose political record was irreproachable. Ability, even where it was well known and had long been publicly recognized, failed in many cases to secure election where personal character was questionable; men new to politics, but credited by the public with honesty and good character, were again and again victorious over others who were not only better known, but presumably far more able; finally, party distinctions seem, to a considerable extent, to have lost their hold upon the voters, who, in not a few cases, appear to have preferred to trust a candidate ranged on the less popular side rather than vote for a partisan in whose character they had no confidence. Such would seem to be the results, so far as candidates in New Zealand are concerned; and they are universally attributed to the influence of the female vote. This experience has been summed up in the statement that, in New Zealand at any rate, female electors think more of men and less of questions than male voters do.

It cannot be denied that the results, so far, have been a great surprise and disappointment to some extreme classes of politicians in New Zealand. It was confidently expected that the first consequence of granting the franchise to women would be an overwhelming strengthening of the anti-liquor party. At the first elections held after the new law took effect there was an increase in the temperance vote large enough to encourage the party to believe that it only needed sufficient breathing-space, during which the female voter might grow accustomed to her new powers and have an opportunity of considering the arguments of the party, to lead to an overwhelming vote in favor of prohibition,—or at least of a law leading directly to prohibition. Such a law was proposed and rejected by the last parliament, although it had a majority in the House of Representatives, as the more popular chamber is called in New Zealand; and the question became a leading one at the elections just completed. The result has been a blow to the anti-liquor cause. Throughout the country the extreme measure has been discredited; and in a great many cases its advocates were rejected in favor of candidates who maintained that the power of local control, by which any district could practically prevent licenses being granted within its own boundaries, was sufficient. On the whole it would seem that the introduction of the female vote in the colony has had very little effect upon general politics. The party in power when the change was made continue in power still, but with a considerably smaller majority. Extreme change of every sort appears to be objected to; and yet no alteration is manifested in the general trend of political feeling throughout the country. The parliament has lost some well-known figures, but scarcely any who were not open to suspicion on grounds of character; and parties appear to be more evenly balanced to-day than at any previous period during the last ten years.

The example of New Zealand should be of advantage to the cause in many ways, but in none so much as this: that it teaches not only how men can be induced to consent to women taking an equal share in the government and law-making which is to affect themselves and their children, but also how women may fit themselves to discharge well the new powers thus acquired. The case of New Zealand is no example of the advantages that might flow from granting the franchise, merely on grounds of natural right, to a female population unprepared by education and practical training to use the privilege and exercise their new duties well. To tell the truth, that was an argument which might have been sought in vain in the records of the New Zealand parliament at any one of the stages of the political emancipation of women in that country. It was, in the first place, because women were sure to take an interest in the state of the schools to which they sent their children that they were allowed a voice in the election of the school committees. It was because they had shown themselves capable of doing this work well, and even more anxious than men to give it their intelligent attention, that it was thought wise to let them exercise a vote in the regulation of the liquor traffic. It was only when experience had shown that they were second to none in their efficient and moderate performance of this duty that they were admitted freely to take a full share, as voters, councillors, and even as chief executive officers, in the management of municipal affairs. Finally, it was the fact that experience had proved women capable not merely of taking part in, but of improving the management of, local affairs which led to the grant to them of the full electoral franchise in New Zealand.

It may be said that, after all, the case of the women of New Zealand only proves the arguments true which the advocates of "Women's Rights" have so long been using. It may be maintained that, if all the women of America were granted the franchise, the results would vindicate the policy. It may be so; but the case of the political emancipation of women in New Zealand affords no proof that such would be the case. There her emancipation was founded not on theory, but on experience. It was not taken for granted that she was in all respects the equal of man, and that, therefore, she must be able to do efficiently at once all that man had taken centuries to learn to do. Above all it was not supposed that interest in, and a reasonably sufficient knowledge of, political affairs came to women any more than it did to men, by the gift of nature. There may be other methods of arriving at the results attained by the women of New Zealand which may be safely tried in other countries; but the experience of that colony is certainly no argument in their favor.

One step remains which has not yet been taken in New Zealand, and there is as yet no sign of its being demanded in that country. While women enjoy the full electoral franchise, they are not yet capable, according to law, of being themselves elected to seats in Parliament. No doubt there is something of a want of logic in this lingering disability of the sex; and yet it may be said to be characteristic of the methods hitherto pursued in that colony with so much success. That the right to sit in Parliament, as well as to vote for men to do so, will ere long be extended to women in New Zealand, there is no room to doubt: indeed it must come as soon as the female voters of the country desire it. As yet they have shown no wish to possess this privilege, but have contented themselves with the exercise of the powers they already possess. In this moderation they are probably as wise as they have shown themselves from the first; and it may be confidently predicted that in New Zealand the proposal to remove the last political distinction between the sexes will come from the men,—convinced that by such a reform they will add to the dignity of their parliament and the purity and wisdom of their executive.

HUGH H. LUSK.

SOME OPENED TOMBS AND THEIR OCCUPANTS.

WERE I to attempt any full enumeration of the tombs of the illustrious dead which have been opened, and even rifled, by the irreverent and reprehensible, yet not wholly unnatural, curiosity of later generations, I should require the space of a volume rather than of an article. Yet it may not, I think, be uninteresting to the readers of THE FORUM to refer to a few memorable instances in which the peace of the grave . has been thus invaded.

Of the three greatest poets of the Christian world—Dante, Shakespeare, and Milton—Shakespeare alone has escaped the indignity of disinterment. This is due, beyond all doubt, to the energetic warning and curse which, with prophetic insight, he recorded on his tombstone :—

> " Good frend, for Jesus sake, forbeare
> To digg the dust encloased here :
> Blest be ye man that spares these stones,
> And curst be he that moves my bones."

The temptation to try and look once more on the dead lineaments of that immortal countenance has, I believe, been at times very strong. It has been resisted only because no one cared to incur the anathema which the poet pronounced against anyone who should dare to violate his earthly rest by tampering with his mortal remains.

But Dante has not escaped. He was buried at San Francesco in Ravenna; but, on the expulsion from Ravenna of his patron, Guido Novello da Polenta, his remains "were with difficulty protected from the persecution of the Florentines and the excommunication of the Pope." The Cardinal Legate of Pope John XXII ordered Dante's bones to be burnt, together with his treatise "De Monarchia." In 1483, the Podestà of Ravenna built a mausoleum for them, which was rebuilt by Cardinal Valenti Gonzaga in 1780. But in 1865, on the sexcentenary of Dante's birth, the suspicion was verified that the body of the poet was no longer in the mausoleum; and in repairing an old chapel in the Church of San Francesco a wooden box was discovered, containing a perfect skeleton of a man of Dante's age and stature, with an inscription on it, in which Fra Antonio de Santi says that he had removed the body thither in 1677. Only a few small bones were found in the mausoleum. The skeleton was transferred to Lombardo's urn in the mausoleum; and Fra Antonio's object in removing it may have been to prevent the depredation of such sacred relics.

And Milton has not escaped. In his early Latin poem he had anticipated that he would one day wear the Parnassian laurel; and added: "Ast ego . . . secura pace quiescam." The first part of his youthful prophecy was amply fulfilled; not, alas! the second. Dr. Garth complained that "E'en churches are no sanctuaries now"; and the complaint is emphasized by what befell the remains of the great Puritan. He was buried in St. Giles's, Cripplegate, on November 12, 1674; and for one hundred and nineteen years,—until 1793—no monument was raised over his grave, and the exact spot of his interment was forgotten.

But in 1790, search was made; and on August 3 it was announced that his coffin had been found. The church authorities rightly "disdained to disturb the sacred ashes." But that night a publican, a pawnbroker, a surgeon, and a coffin-maker got into the church and opened the leaden shell. The publican "pulled hard at the teeth" and at last got one knocked out by a stone! These body-snatchers felt strongly inclined to steal the whole lower jaw; and, after pawing and handling the hallowed remains, these sacrilegious wretches tore out some of the hair and stole some of the bones. As recently as 1852, a writer in "Notes and Queries" says: "I have handled one of Milton's ribs." Well might the poet Cowper protest against these grewsome and indecent familiarities committed by ignorant and graceless boors!

The relic-hunting superstition, which came on the Church like a flood in the fourth century, caused the violation of the tombs of multitudes of saints and great ecclesiastics, and from the first opened the way for boundless imposture. That, however, is a branch of the subject on which I shall not here touch. I will confine myself to England, and will allude only to English kings; though, if space permitted, I should have some interesting tales to tell about the resting-places of English primates.

The "strange stories of the deaths of kings," and the desire to find some historic verification or confutation of them, are partly accountable for the opening of some of our royal coffins. But mere stark antiquarianism and blind love of relics have something to answer for.

In a cantata by Dr. Burney, three antiquaries appear in character and sing:

1st Antiquary:
   " But where so long did linger
    These relics rare and rum?"

2d Antiquary:
   " I filched the monarch's finger."

3d Antiquary:
   " I stole the monarch's thumb."

The body of Edward the Confessor has twice been seen since his interment on January 6, 1066. His coffin was opened in the reign of Henry II, after the king had, at Becket's instigation, procured his canonization by Pope Alexander III. On that occasion, on October 13, 1163, Becket and the mitred Abbot Lawrence saw the face and long white down-curling beard of the king. They took out his splendid robes and made three capes of them. Once more, on October 13, 1269, the saint's body was removed by Henry III from its original grave under the lantern of Westminster Abbey, before the high altar, to the once-gorgeous shrine which they now occupy. On this occasion the king took out of the coffin the famous ring which the Confessor is said to have given to a beggar who turned out to be St. John the Evangelist in disguise. According to one account Henry II was the depredator of the ring. This ring (says the legend) St. John, *in propria persona*, returned to two Ludlow pilgrims in Palestine, bidding them take it back to the royal saint with an injunction to hasten the completion of the Abbey, because his death was near at hand. These three scenes— the bestowal of the ring upon the apparent beggar, his appearance to the pilgrims, and their return to the king—are all carved, with much vivid expression, over the interesting screen in the Confessor's Chapel. In the second scene, St. John is a colossal figure. In the third scene, the two pilgrims, with their staves, are kneeling before the banquet-table, at which the king is seated in his crown, with Archbishop Stigand at his right. The palace in Essex, where this is supposed to have occurred, received the name of Havering atte Bower.

The coffin was once more rifled by King James II; but the disturbance of the saintly relics on this occasion was accidental. In the preparations for James's consecration the Confessor's Chapel had been boarded over, in order that seats might be placed at its summit for the Members of the House of Commons. In removing this temporary structure a plank fell down and broke open the coffin of St. Edward.

The antiquary Harding, who happened to be present, put in his hand and took out a large gilt cross which lay on the saint's breast. This cross was given to James II, and has finally disappeared. No one knows what has become of it; but it has been conjectured that, when James attempted his escape from Faversham, and was stopped and roughly handled by the fishermen, the cross may have been torn from him. At any rate, since his days it has been heard of no more, though now and then some old gilt cross turns up which purports to be the lost relic—but fails to gain the sanction of professional archæologists.

The bones of William the Conqueror lie undisturbed at Caen, in St. Stephen's Abbey. William Rufus, when he had been fatally wounded by the arrow of Wat Tyrrell in the New Forest, fell dead from his horse. His body was carried in a common cart by two rustics to Winchester; and the fall of the Cathedral tower soon afterward was regarded as a judgment on the building which enshrined the wicked "Red King." His coffin was opened in 1868, and even then it became clear that the bones had been previously disturbed; for they lay in a promiscuous heap. The corpse had been clad in a red cloak embroidered with gold; and with it lay the fragment of an arrow and a massive uncut turquoise. It is said that the Puritans had previously rifled the tomb and taken from it a gold ring and a chalice. This is, however, very doubtful; for chalices were buried only with great ecclesiastics.

Henry II was buried at Fontevrault; and his son, Richard I, was laid at his feet. Their remains, like those of other royal personages buried there, are said to have been scattered to the winds by anarchic mobs during the French Revolution. The tombs, though much injured, are still beautiful.

When Edward I died, he left instructions that his bones were to be *boiled*, and yearly to be carried by his army to the invasion of Scotland. These instructions were probably ignored; for, when his tomb was opened by the Society of Antiquaries in 1771, those present gazed for a moment on the features of the great victor before they sank into dust. The gold cloth was still folded round the colossal corpse; and the cast in the eyes was distinctly noticeable. The snow-white hair still remained. The coffin was then filled with pitch. So far as I know, the tomb of Edward III at Westminster has never been opened, nor that of his famous son, the Black Prince, at Canterbury. But the remains of Richard II underwent various vicissitudes. As there were dark rumors on the one hand about his murder, on the other about his supposed escape from prison, and as these rumors disturbed the House of Lancaster, Henry IV had Richard's body dug up from its resting-place in Pomfret Castle, and carried, with the face exposed, to Langley, to prove to the people that their former king was really dead. In the days of Henry V, the remains were again disinterred and carried to the royal tomb in Westminster, where the unhappy monarch—if indeed it be he—lies by the side of his first wife, Anne of Bohemia. His tomb was accidentally opened in the last century, and the bones and skulls were seen and examined; but the doubts which existed were not thereby set at rest. The universal rumor about the murder of Richard II— a rumor which found a place in history—said that his skull had been broken by a blow of the battle-axe of Sir Piers Exton, who, while the king was bravely defending himself against those who assailed him in front, got upon a bench and brained him from behind. If that story be true, the skeleton in the royal tomb is not that of Richard II, for the skull of it was found to be entirely uninjured. There were, however, two legends about the deposed Richard,—one, that the body which was carried on a bier to London, with the face uncovered in order that all men might recognize it, was after all *not* the body of the king at all, but that of his chaplain Maudlin, or Maudsley, who closely resembled him; the other, that the story of his murder was a pure invention, that he had been suffered to make his escape to Scotland, and that there he died in peaceful obscurity at Perth, where legends still speak of him as "the Mammet King."

King Henry IV was buried, in 1413, by his own direction, in Canterbury Cathedral, though he died in the Jerusalem Chamber in Westminster Abbey. The tomb was opened in 1832, to set at rest a historic doubt. The Yorkists, who hated the Lancastrian usurper, asserted that his body did not rest in the tomb at all; but that when he died his body had been thrown into the Thames, between Barking and Gravesend, during a terrific storm which instantly ceased when the coffin was thrown out of the boat. Strangely circumstantial as the story is, it is an absolute fiction. When the coffin in the chantry of Henry IV in Canterbury Cathedral was opened, there the king's body lay; and, for the few seconds before the prominent features collapsed, the few who were present saw "the cankered Bolingbroke" as he looked in life,—or rather as he looked in death after that memorable scene in the Jerusalem Chamber, which Shakespeare has so pathetically described. The face was in complete preservation; and all the teeth but one were perfect.

His warrior-son, the hero of Agincourt, perhaps the most popular of all English sovereigns before the present reign, rests at peace in the stately tomb erected for him by his wife, Katherine of Valois. It is true that the silver head of his effigy and the silver plates which covered its heart of oak were stolen from the great Abbey as far back as the reign of Queen Elizabeth ; but the tomb itself has never been disturbed. It has been far otherwise with his consort, the daughter of Charles VI of France, whom, on her arrival in England, the chroniclers describe as having been as "beautiful as an angel of God." Either in repentance for her wilful disobedience to her husband, in going to Windsor for the birth of her son, Henry VI, in spite of the prophecy—which turned out to be true—that "Henry of Windsor should lose what Harry of Monmouth had won," or else in remorse for the monstrous *mésalliance* of which she was guilty when she married the Welsh yeoman of the guard, Owen Tudor, she ordered that her coffin should be "meanly apparelled" and placed in the Lady Chapel. Her grandson, Henry VII, laid it beside that of her first royal and victorious husband. The coffin, therefore, was a poor and common one. In the course of years it had more or less mouldered away ; and her skull was visible, covered with skin which looked like a thin yellow parchment. Samuel Pepys tells us that he went into the Abbey on his birthday (February 24, 1668) in the reign of Charles II, and kissed the skull ; and he glories in the fact that, on that occasion, "he had kissed a queen." This state of things became more and more scandalous ; and at last the dean and chapter, some century ago, ordered that a new coffin should be made and that the queen's body should be removed. It was most incongruously thrust into the vault of Sir George Villiers, the Buckinghamshire knight whose ghost appeared to his son, the Duke of Buckingham, in the reign of Charles I to warn him of his approaching murder. Not many years ago, when Dr. Stanley was Dean of Westminster, the Percy vault, which communicates with the Villiers vault, was opened for a funeral ; and Dean Stanley thought this a good opportunity to see if the Queen's coffin was secure. Mr. Wright, the clerk of the works, went through the aperture, found the coffin with Katherine's name on it, and, by the Dean's order, it was brought out to us. It had long been in a damp place ; and it had no sooner been lifted out of the dark vault into the chapel above, than it fell to pieces, and the body of the queen of Henry V lay before us. I say "the body," for there were still some skin and some tendons on parts of it ; but it was mainly a skeleton, and its enfolding cerements had crumbled into dust. Nothing else was in

the coffin except some fragments of cere-cloth and remains of the silk
cushion on which the head had rested.   A small piece of this was cut
off as a relic for one who had a right to ask for it; otherwise, nothing
whatever was touched or disturbed.   No one but myself was permitted
to see the remains, except the late Sir George Scharf, and, I think, one
of the canons.   The clerk of the works was ordered immediately to make
a solid oak coffin; the body was reverently deposited within it, and was
then reinterred under what had been the altar of the chantry which she
herself had caused to be erected above the tomb of her husband, and
immediately beneath his helmet, shield, and saddlebow, which are
fastened to a beam between the two great columns.   The Dean wrote
an appropriate Latin inscription; and so, for the first time after some
two hundred years, the mortal spoils of the daughter, wife, and mother
of French and English kings—who with her husband had been crowned
at Paris—found there a fitting resting-place, perhaps for ages to come.

There is a dim tradition that, much more than a century ago, the
tomb under which the two sister-queens—Mary, the Roman Catholic,
and Elizabeth, the Protestant, *regno consortes et urna*—lie side by side
had fallen into disrepair, and that a bold Westminster boy crept into
the hollow vault, and, through an aperture in the coffin, laid his hand
on the heart of the mighty Tudor queen.   Passing over this incident,
I will only mention the discovery of the body of Charles I, when
George IV was Prince Regent.   It has been asserted, and is I believe
true, that the nation wished the body of him whom they always called
"the saint and martyr" to be removed from Windsor and buried in
Westminster Abbey; and that a sum of no less than £70,000 was entrusted by Parliament to Charles II to erect a tomb over the remains of
his father.   If the story be true, the entire sum disappeared and was not
put to the intended purpose.   It was however supposed that the "White
King's" *coffin*, at any rate, had been transferred to the Abbey.   It was
in order to settle a doubt on this point that George IV, then Prince
Regent, went down into the vaults of Windsor with the famous physician, Sir Henry Halford.   There they found the coffins of Henry VIII
and of his wife, Lady Jane Seymour; and between them lay a coffin
on which were rudely scratched the letters " C. I." In order to be
sure that this was indeed the coffin of the executed king, they opened
it—and there lay before them the handsome face, just as Vandyke depicted it; though (as always happens in such cases) the nose fell in immediately that the corpse was exposed to the open air.   Then—I
simply tell the tale as it was told to me; for, though there must be some

printed accounts of the event, I have never seen them—Sir Henry Halford took up by the hair the decapitated head, and placed it on the palm of his hand, which was covered by his silk handkerchief. When he replaced the head in the coffin the vertebra of the neck, which had been smoothly severed by the axe of the executioner, was lying on his handkerchief; and the Prince Regent remarked to Sir Henry that this would be an interesting relic for him. He took it; and had it set in gold with the inscription, " Os Caroli Primi, heu intercisum." I believe that, by the wish and right-feeling of H.R.H. the Prince of Wales, this relic of the hapless king has been replaced in the coffin. Everyone will recall the sanguinary epigram of Lord Byron upon the incident which I have narrated.

It must not be supposed from the instances which I have given that royal tombs in Westminster Abbey and other cathedrals are peculiarly liable to be disturbed by irreverent curiosity. For one coffin that has thus been opened there are hundreds which have not been touched.

Vaults may be opened for some important end; but the actual disturbance of the relics of the dead, and the stealing of these relics, has on the whole been the exception. During the restoration of my church, St. Margaret's, Westminster, I could have had a splendid opportunity of opening the coffins of William Caxton, the first English printer, and of Sir Walter Raleigh, "the father of the United States," as during the repairs, the vault containing their mortal remains was exposed to view; but even the chance of deciding the uncertainty about Sir Walter's decapitated head—which, some say, his son buried in St. Margaret's—did not tempt. Of all the dead, I say : " Let reverence triumph over curiosity. *Requiescant in pace !* "

F. W. FARRAR.

THE FUR SEAL AS AN ANIMAL.

THE regulations adopted by the Paris Tribunal of Arbitration in 1893 for "the protection and preservation of the fur seal" have signally failed of their object. This failure is chiefly due to the treatment of the creature as an object of international litigation, not as an animal having habits and prejudices to which international statutes must conform if they are to serve any purpose. In the compromise adopted by the Tribunal were embodied certain propositions, apparently fair from the legal side of the case, but wholly repugnant to the animal. As the only possible basis for a final arrangement for the protection and preservation of the fur seal must conform perfectly to its habits, we may profitably consider the habits of the animal in some detail. That such a settlement must finally be made admits of no doubt. It is not to be supposed for a moment that England, Russia, and the United States will fail to settle so simple a problem, or that these great nations are so weak or so barbarous as to allow this wonderful animal to be wasted without mercy, when the conditions of its preservation are fully understood. To balance land killing against sea killing, to kill with guns in one sea and with spears in another, to kill on land in July and at sea in April and August, to have a closed zone of sixty miles and an open zone of two hundred,—all these compromises are ingenious on paper, and find their precedent in the checks and balances of constitutional law, but not in the facts of natural history. How such regulations affect the animal is not to be settled by compromise. It is a question of fact; and any system of regulations must be judged from the standpoint of the animal itself. The whole Bering Sea dispute belongs primarily to natural history, not to international law. If existing forms of international law fail to protect a noble and valuable animal in its migrations or its feeding excursions at sea, then more international law must be written; and the actual habits of the animal must determine the nature of such law.

The "fur seal" or "sea-bear," known to science as *Callorhinus ursinus*, inhabits certain islands in Bering and Okhotsk Seas, unknown to aboriginal man, and, so far as we are aware, never visited by man before the discovery of Bering and Medni Islands by Vitus Bering in 1741, and of St. George Island by Gerassim Pribilof in 1786. The species form three distinct herds, which must be recognized as three distinct species, each type being distinguishable from the others by several characters of importance. The most important of the three herds is the American or Pribilof herd, living on the two islands of the Pribilof group—St. George and St. Paul. Next in importance comes the Russian herd of the Komandorski or Commander Islands, Bering and Medni. The third herd is that of the Okhotsk Sea, inhabiting Robben Island, where a remnant of a few hundred still remains, and formerly also having rookeries on four islands of the Kuril group —Musir, Raikoke, Srednoi, and Broughton.

The American herd is present at its home on the Pribilof Islands from May until December, the seals going out at intervals to feed over a radius of about two hundred miles. In November and December they are driven away from the Islands by the winter storms, going southward in the open sea as far as the latitude of San Francisco, returning northward near the coast of the United States, British Columbia, and Alaska. They are not known to come on land anywhere except on the Pribilof Islands. In like manner the Commander Islands herd moves southward in winter, along the east coast of Japan; and the herd from Robben Island passes from the Okhotsk Sea along the west coast in the inland Sea of Japan.

The fur seals of the different herds do not intermingle on their migrations, and probably not on their summer feeding-grounds. The fables of the colonization of the Commander Islands by fur seals from the Pribilofs at some comparatively recent date have no basis in knowledge. Each adult seal returns year after year, not merely to the same island, but as nearly as may be to the same spot. With the younger seals this return as to exact place is doubtless less certain. But it is more than likely that the young of both sexes return to their home rookery; the one- and two-year-old females coming to the breeding-grounds late in the season, and the males taking up their places among the older bachelors on the adjoining " hauling-grounds."

The eccentricities of the nomenclature of the fur seal have been frequently noted. It seems, for example, incongruous that a " bull " and a " cow " should occupy a " harem " on a " rookery " and bear a " pup," which, if a male, is a " bachelor " for the first four years of his life, and that the business of killing and skinning these animals,

13

though legitimately carried on wholly on land, should be known as a "fishery." But these names when understood have a distinct justification in the peculiarities of the animal, and create no confusion. Moreover, the term "seal" in connection with these animals is itself a misnomer. The original name of "sea-bear," given them by their first discoverer, George Wilhelm Steller (1741), is in every way preferable. The fur seal is not a "seal," nor has it any close affinity with the sub-order of *Pinnipedia*, to which the true or earless seals belong. Beyond the fact that both the fur seal and the hair seal are carnivorous mammals, feeding on fish and adapted for life in the water, the two types have little in common. In structure, appearance, habits, disposition, and method of locomotion, they are entirely distinct; and their evolution as pelagic animals has been along separate lines. The fur seals, with their associates, the walrus and sea-lions, are obviously related to the bears. The hair seals, whatever their origin, must have come along other lines from a different parent stock; and their relation to land *Carnivora* is more remote.

The male fur seal, or "beachmaster," reaches full maturity at the age of seven years. At that time his weight is about four hundred to five hundred pounds; being considerably heavier when first in from the sea in the spring, or after feeding in the fall, than in the intervening period, when he fasts on land and grows gradually lean and weak. The males vary considerably in color, the general shade being black or dark brown, with longer hair or bristles of yellowish white. These are especially long and numerous on the thickened back of the neck; forming the so-called "wig." The wigged males have a rough, coarse coat; and their skins are without market value. The animal makes its home on the rocky shores of the islands in large, closely-massed bands, forming what are called "rookeries." It is extremely gregarious; individuals seldom venturing far from the main body while on land, though wandering about singly in the sea.

The female fur seal is much smaller than the male, and has soft, smooth hair of varying shades of brown, under which is the dense, short, brown fur. The majority of the younger females are silvery white underneath the throat; but some are simply lighter brown. The female bears her first offspring at the age of three years; but her full growth is not attained till two or three years later. The average weight of the grown female is about eighty pounds. The young of the fur seal, called a "pup," is born soon after the arrival of the female. Its weight at birth is about ten pounds.

The fur seal is polygamous, each male capable of holding a place on the breeding-grounds having from one to one hundred females in his charge, constituting what is known as a "harem"; the average number being about thirty. But the size of each family is subject to variation; depending not chiefly on the strength of the male, but on the prefer- ence of the female for a location, and on the topography of the ground.

The young male is very similar to the female in color and appear- ance. He is not permitted to enter the rookeries in the breeding- season. The old males are very particular in this regard; and the "bachelors," as they are called, are forced to herd by themselves on what are known as the "hauling-grounds," located near the breeding- grounds, but distinct from them. While the males and females on the islands are more or less definitely fixed to the spot selected by them on the breeding-rookery, it is not so with these young males; and their movements are very irregular. For this reason the hauling-grounds are much more variable than the breeding-grounds; their occupancy changing from day to day. From these hauling-grounds, in the sea- son when their fur is at its best, the bachelors are driven and killed.

Mixed with the bachelors are found the so-called "half-bulls." These animals have the size and appearance of grown males, but lack their strength and courage, and cannot maintain themselves on the rookeries. Later in the season they leave the hauling-grounds and place themselves around, behind, or above the rookeries, or on rocks awash on the sea-front, where for weeks they watch the operations of their seniors. When the older bulls go out to sea to feed in August, these younger ones come down and take their places with every expression of satisfaction.

The Pribilof group, which constitutes the home of the fur seal, consists of volcanic islands composed entirely of lava and cinders. Two only of these islands, St. Paul and St. George, are important. The smaller islands, each of but a few acres in extent, are known as Otter Island and Walrus Island; and in addition there is the little islet of Sivutch Rock. These islands are in Bering Sea, about two hundred miles to the northwest of Unalaska—the principal harbor of the Aleutian chain of islands—and about forty-five miles apart. St. Paul lies to the northwest of St. George, and is the more important island. It is very irregular in form; its greatest length—about thir- teen miles—being from northeast to southwest. Its greatest width is about six miles. St. George Island is about ten miles east and west, by five north and south. It is more elevated than St. Paul;

its central peak, Aluckeyak, being nine hundred and thirty feet high. Its shore outline is scarcely broken by bays or indentations; and most of its coast is formed by walls of basaltic rock. Neither island has a harbor of any sort.

The elevated parts of both islands are covered in summer with mosses and grasses, in which, in July, are surprising numbers of showy wild flowers. The islands are almost constantly enveloped in mist and fog throughout June and July; and the sun is seldom seen. Many stormy days occur; but the storms in summer are not violent, although approach to the islands in rough weather is dangerous on account of the dense fogs. In August there are more clear days; and in bright weather the islands are very picturesque. With the fairer weather the occasional storms become more violent; and by the middle of September all vessels which can get away find it well to leave Bering Sea. With the winter come many clear days alternating with days of tempestuous storm. The snow piles high between the hills; and the floe-ice gathers about the islands, filling the bights and inlets until April or May.

Wherever there is a rocky beach of some breadth, or a sloping, rocky hill on the Pribilof Islands, the fur seals have established their rookeries. The best type of a rookery-ground is a moderate slope, covered with coarse rocks and descending to a beach of shingle or rounded bowlders. On these rookeries the gregarious habits of the fur seals cause them to crowd together as closely as may be,—often to their own disadvantage, as on crowded areas many pups are trampled under foot by the fighting males.

The hauling-grounds of the bachelors are usually sandy beaches adjoining the rookeries, or ascending to the heights above them. Here and there are neutral strips in the long rookeries which have been abandoned to the bachelors, and along which they go back and forth to their hauling-grounds or parade-grounds in the rear. On certain rookeries the bachelors attempt to cross the breeding-grounds by runways which are not recognized as neutral by the adult males. Along these strips, which may be said to be not officially recognized as hauling-grounds, there is constant disputation between the beachmasters and the bachelors.

There are at present twelve breeding-rookeries on St. Paul Island and five on St. George. The largest continuous breeding-area is on St. Paul Island. This great breeding-ground contains fully one-fourth of all the seals on the island. From the summit of Hutchinson Hill, up the seaward slope of which the harems extend, one can get a magnificent view of this rookery. The sight is most impressive; a greater number of fur seals being visible there than from any other point in the world.

The rookeries of St. George Island are five in number. They contain only about one-sixth of the total number of the fur seals on the two islands. Four of these rookeries, East, Little East, North, and Staraya Artil (old camp), extend along the southern face of the island; while the fifth, Zapadni, lies isolated in the southwestern bay.

So far as is known, every individual fur seal visits the islands in the course of the summer. The youngest come latest; and in general all categories remain until driven away by the winter storms in November and December. The adult males arrive as soon as the ice leaves in the spring (in April or early May). They take up their positions on the rookery-grounds and await the arrival of the females, which event is preceded and accompanied by constant fighting among the males. The earliest cows appear the first week in June. Until the pups are born, and for a few days after, the females are held in rigid control by the bulls; after which time they go to sea to feed, returning at intervals to nurse their young. The cows do not come in all at once; the period of their arrival extending from early June until the middle of August.

The height of the season when there is greatest activity in love and war on the rookeries is from the fifth to the twentieth of July. At this time the harems are ruled with absolute sway by the bulls, which are constantly "rounding up" the cows and crowding them close together. But even then many of the adult cows are absent at sea, feeding, and none of the two-year-olds has arrived. These young cows arrive for the most part during the last week in July, and gather around the young bulls outside the rookery proper. The cows are constantly coming and going; and at no time are much more than half of them present on any rookery.

One pup is born each year, and the sexes at birth are equal in number. For a few days after the pups are born the cows show a maternal interest in them. They nurse them frequently and a cow will lift her newly born pup, as a cat would a kitten, out of the way of the bull. While it is still helpless the cow cannot easily be made to desert her young; but when the pup gets old enough to toddle about she pays little attention to it beyond feeding it. She will run away from her pup without scruple, leaving it to its fate. The pups seem to accept the situation, and get off in pods by themselves;

playing and sleeping together like a lot of little Newfoundland dogs. When the pups are about a month old they begin to play in sheltered pools of water, and gradually learn to swim. When they have fully learned they go boldly out into the sea in all kinds of weather, and spend much of their time in the water.

Any intrusion upon the breeding-grounds, whether by man or by one of their own number, causes great confusion. If the intruder be a luckless bachelor attempting to make a short cut to the sea, he finds himself "collared" by the first bull into whose domain he comes, and thrown out. The master of the next harem seizes him and treats him in like manner. By the time the unfortunate bachelor has run the gauntlet of bulls and been finally thrown over the cliff into the sea, with torn hide and spent breath, he probably resolves to take next time the farthest way around. If the intruder were a man and fell into the clutches of the bulls, doubtless the result would be practically the same. The old bull is quick to detect the approach of man. He will plunge at him, and, for a few yards, will give him a lively chase. But he rarely goes beyond his square rod of territory; and one can depend on his turning to see what his cows are doing. Experience has taught him that if he leaves his harem the cows will desert, or some of them will be stolen, or even his whole claim may be jumped by another bull. After he has once turned about he will not renew the attack, unless he is forced to do so: malice and revenge are unknown to these ferocious creatures.

When the rookery is thrown into confusion in this way the individual bulls succeed in quieting their harems and restoring order in a surprisingly short time. The bull's method is to rush about the cows, rounding them up, snorting, growling, and blowing his musky breath at them. He often seizes an unruly cow by the neck and pins her to the ground; occasionally he will even catch one by the back and toss her over his head back into the harem. These peremptory measures soon restore order. The cows are always more afraid of the bull than of any intruder. They seem to accept the rough treatment as a matter of course, and to admire the bull's masterful way of doing things. Later on in the season, however, when the harem system has relaxed, the cow loses her fear of the bull and becomes more independent. When she wants to go from the harem and the bull interposes, she bites him in the neck; sometimes tearing away the fur with her sharp teeth. The bull takes it patiently enough; and ultimately, when his back is turned or when he is asleep, the cow gets away.

The bachelor seals have a wholesome and well-grounded fear of the bulls, and keep away from them and the rookeries in the breeding-season. This leads, as already stated, to the institution of separate hauling-grounds on which they wander, play, or sleep at will. The sea in front of the rookeries is also a play-place for them. When the old bulls leave the rookeries in August the bachelors scatter themselves over the breeding-grounds with their brothers the half-bulls; the latter endeavoring to round up harems and play the part of the older bulls. The cows pay very little attention to them,—a fact which in no wise diminishes their pride in their new relations. From these older bachelors the harem masters are recruited year by year, and at the beginning of each season a certain number of these young fellows appear on the rookery-grounds to fight for places. Most of them are whipped and thrown out at their first attempts; but gradually they gain the strength and the experience which ultimately enable them to win and maintain harems of their own.

On the islands for the last half-century only the young males have been killed. As these herd by themselves they can be driven up without disturbing the breeding seals, and they can be handled much as a flock of sheep are handled. The regular killing season begins about the first of June and closes about the first of August. After the tenth of August the skins become "stagy" from the change of fur, and are not in prime condition again until after the middle of October.

From the hauling-grounds the bachelors of all ages are driven up in bands to the killing-grounds, located at convenient distances from the rookeries, and near ponds of fresh water in which the seals can be cooled off after their exertions. To prevent, as far as possible, over-heating, the drives are made at night, usually beginning at two A.M. As the severity of the drives has been the subject of considerable discussion, and as many impossible results have been attributed to them, the following detailed account of a drive on St. Paul Island, witnessed by the writers, may be of interest:

"We left the village at two o'clock in the morning to make the drive of seals from Reef and Gorbatch rookeries. It was then light enough to make our way without difficulty. After a few minutes we reached Zolotoi sands, a beach about one-fourth of a mile from the village, at the angle of which the bachelors from Gorbatch rookery haul out to reach the rocky slope above. The drivers ran in quickly between the seals and the water and soon had the animals rounded up in a large pod. From a similar hauling-ground on the shore, just across the neck of the peninsula, another pod was in like manner rounded up. The two pods combined were left in charge of three men to be driven across the sands to the village killing-ground a few hundred yards beyond.

We then proceeded to the extreme point of Reef peninsula. The hauling-ground of Reef rookery lies in the rear of the breeding-ground and has four well-marked runways connecting it with the sea, on which no harems are located. A line of idle bulls keeps clear a considerable space between the hauling-ground and the harems. From the head of the various runways and in the intervening space pods of sleeping bachelors were rounded up; the Aleuts passing between the idle bulls and the bachelors and turning the latter up the bank to the flat parade-ground back of the hauling-ground. Here the pods were all united in one large group; and the drive started on its way at half past three o'clock.

After passing over a short space of ground, scattered at wide intervals with irregular bowlders and having a gentle downward slope, the drive came to the level plain of the parade-ground. Here the herd, which numbered about 1,500 bachelors, was separated into two parts, for greater ease and safety in driving. While one pod was allowed to rest, the other was driven slowly forward in the direction of the village. Three men were now assigned to each pod, and the rest of the drivers allowed to return to the village to make ready for the killing.

Over the green turf of the parade-ground the drive moved quietly and without difficulty. The drivers took their positions, one on each flank to repress any lateral movements; and a third brought up the rear. There was no noise or confusion. In general the seals were allowed to take their own time and to go at their own pace. Those in advance acted as leaders and the rest of the herd followed naturally after them. At the beginning the seals showed some reluctance in leaving their hauling-grounds, and made ineffectual attempts to break away. But after the drive got under way they moved forward as a matter of course. When the leaders showed any inclination to turn aside, the man on the flank simply stood up and raised a hand, which was sufficient to turn them back into the course. For the most part the man kept out of the sight of the seals.

There was a tendency on the part of the younger seals to go faster than the older ones, of which a number were included. By a gradual shifting process the old fellows fell to the rear; and on several occasions pods of from a dozen to twenty were cut off and allowed to return to the sea.

All the seals, and especially the larger ones, showed signs of fatigue. They became hot and excited; and a cloud of steam having a strong musky smell arose constantly from the moving animals. When the herd stopped, individual seals would often sprawl out on the ground, raising their hind flippers and waving them fan-like; evidently in an effort to cool off. After resting a moment the seals were ready to move on again refreshed. Continuous exertion is evidently hard on them; but they quickly recover from exhaustion. As soon as the flock comes to rest for a few moments' breathing, they begin to bite one another and push each other about in an unconcerned fashion until they are reminded by the movements of their companions that they too must keep moving. When the herd has been brought to rest for a few minutes, to start it again the rear man has only to clap his hands or rattle his stick on a rock.

A short distance brought us to the end of the grassy plain and into an area of ground filled with embedded bowlders. These were for the most part flat and worn smooth. It looked like hard ground for the seals; but they really seemed to get over it better than the flat ground, on which there was constant crowding, while the rocks kept the seals apart.

After passing over a slight ridge where the passage-way became narrowed by projecting cliffs and where there was a good deal of crowding and scrambling, the drive left the bowlder-strewn path and passed into a valley overgrown with tall rye-grass and lying between sand-dunes also grass-grown. The seals seemed to be refreshed by the moisture of the grass, which was wet with dew and rain.

This grassy plain led into the top of the bowlder-set slope above Zolotoi sands, from which the earlier seals were driven. Down this slope the herd moved without difficulty and came into the level sand-flat. Here the first really hard work of the drive began. The seals seemed to find their greatest difficulty in walking on the yielding sand. Their flippers take hold of the rocks like rubber, but slip back on the sand. They stepped on each other's flippers, became much excited, and seemed generally worried.

But in a few minutes the sands were passed and the herd emerged into the grass-grown killing-ground. As soon as they came to a standstill all seemed at once to forget their troubles. They began biting, snarling, and blowing at one another as though nothing had happened. They were turned into the little lake beside the killing-ground to cool off, and were then herded up on the bank to rest before their turn came to be killed.

It was five minutes after five when the first herd reached the killing-ground. The second arrived three-quarters of an hour later, having taken more time on the way."

This drive is the hardest one made on the Pribilof Islands. It is, however, less than a mile in length, and has no hills. One or two other drives are longer; but the ground covered is grass-grown and easier for the seals to get over.

After the seals have cooled off and rested the killing is begun. The larger droves are separated into small pods of twenty to thirty, which in succession are driven up within reach of men armed with stout clubs. These "cull" out the killable seals by striking them on the head, allowing those not suitable for killing to escape and go back to the sea. The blow of the club renders the animal unconscious. It is then bled by sticking to the heart with a knife, and is immediately afterward skinned. Only three-year-olds and very small four-year-olds or large two-year-olds are taken. No females are ever killed on the Islands. The methods of killing and skinning seals are the results of many years of experience, and though simple, are effective and well adapted to the animals with which they deal. Occasionally accidents occur. On warm mornings a seal may be overcome by heat on the drive, or it may be smothered by the crowding of a pod, or clubbed by mistake; but deaths from such causes are rare, not over a dozen having been known to occur during the past season out of a total of 30,000 seals killed, besides many driven up but rejected on the killing-ground.

There is no evidence that the race of fur seals as a whole has been in any way affected by the arbitrary selection of males for killing, or by the methods of handling them. Only strong, vigorous males can maintain themselves on the rookeries in any case, and those allowed to live to replenish the stock are not more nor less vigorous than the others would have been. A strong selective influence is exercised by the migrations in the sea. No decrepit individuals have been known to come back in the spring. The rough sea of the North tells no tales ; and we know very little of the severity of the sorting process which every year sends back to the Islands only those fit to survive. From the ruthless natural destruction of all seals, in which the geographical instinct or the instincts of feeding and reproduction are defective, re-sults the extreme perfection of those few instincts which the animal possesses. The life-processes of the fur seal are as perfect as clock-work ; but its grade of intelligence is low. Its range of choice in action is very slight. It is a wonderful automaton ; and the stress of its migrations will always keep it so. A fur seal will do to perfection what its ancestors have had to do ; but if it is forced to do anything else it becomes dazed and stupid.

Owing to the polygamous habit of the fur seal, a limited num-ber of males suffices for the needs of the herd. The land killing of males, therefore, is not only possible without injury, but becomes a positive necessity to the growth of the herd. For the 143,071 females in the Islands during the past season there were 8,005 adult males, and 2,996 of these were superfluous, as they could not get possession of cows until the height of the season was past. They spent their time in fighting among themselves or attacking the more successful bulls. The evil effects of an overstock of males have never hitherto been fully understood or estimated. The chief natural cause of death on the rookeries among females and young pups is found in the wrangling of the bulls and the struggles of the reserve of idle bulls to steal cows from the harems. In 1896, 11,045 pups were thus trampled to death on the Pribilof Islands ; and about 130 cows were killed by the rough seizure of the bulls in their struggle for possession. As the fur seal herd has year by year grown less crowded, this mortality has probably never reached so low a percentage before. In the original or wild state of the herd, when the number of adult bulls was nearly equal to that of the cows, this destruction must have been enormous, perhaps approaching 200,000 each year. It was undoubtedly the chief check to the indefinite increase of the herd, the death of these thousands being adequate to compensate for the natural increase.

During the breeding-season the adult males do not eat or drink or leave their places on the rookeries. During the killing-season the stomachs of the bachelors are found to be empty. It has been supposed on this account that they fasted or ate very little during the summer. This is not necessarily the case; for examination of the stomachs of a number of cows on land also disclosed no food. The fur seals simply do not come on land until the food in their stomachs is digested. A mass of seals is to be seen throughout the entire season sleeping or swimming about in an aimless fashion before the rookeries and hauling-grounds; and from this fringe of idle seals off shore—never directly from the sea—the landing cows and bachelors are seen to come. These are seals that have arrived before their food was fully digested.

The seals feed at great and various distances from the Islands. They are found from June to November between 165° and 175°, west longitude, in a broad tract stretching northwesterly from the vicinity of Unimak Pass to latitude 61°, which is their great feeding-ground.

The food of the fur seal consists mainly of surface-swimming fishes and of squid. As to the species of fish, the animal has probably little choice. It does not dive deeply; and its food naturally comprises the shallow-water or surface fishes on its feeding-grounds. In Bering Sea, in August and September, a still undescribed species of deep water smelt is by far the most important fish. Next to this comes the Alaskan pollock. Salmon are eaten when found, and occasionally species of smaller fishes. No cod has yet been found in the stomach of a seal.

The size of the Pribilof Islands herd, according to the traditions of the Aleuts, reached its lowest possible point some fifty or more years ago at the time of the great ice-jam, in which many thousand seals, males and females, were drowned while attempting to climb the inaccessible bergs and floes. Of the condition of the herd in Russian times we have no very clear record, but when it passed into American control in 1868 it was in good condition and rapidly increasing. Until 1872, and perhaps a few years after, the herd continued to increase. During the ten years following it doubtless remained practically in a state of equilibrium under the various checks acting upon it, of which the trampling of pups was the chief. This loss can be checked in future, or almost entirely prevented, by covering the level and open parts of the rookeries with large rocks, under which the pups can hide, and which check the movement of the bulls. The "death-traps" on Zapadni have been already thus treated. In 1883 the herd began to decline—slowly at first, then more rapidly.

In the days of its maximum prosperity—1872 to 1882—there were doubtless about 2,500,000 seals of all classes on the Islands. To-day there are about 450,000 seals of all classes, the herd having declined to about one-fifth its greatest size. The sole cause of this decline is pelagic sealing,—the killing of fur seals in the open sea with fire-arms or with the spear and club. After feeding, the seals lie and sleep on the surface of the water while digesting their food. Taking advantage of this habit, the hunter steals up in his boat, and shoots or spears the sleeping animal.

Other things being equal, the maintenance or increase of a herd of animals depends upon the birth-rate; that is, on the number of breeding females. On shore the life of the female fur seal is sacred: she is like a domestic animal of high value. Even in those days when there ran "no law of God or man to the north of fifty-three" severe penalties were visited on men taken in the act of killing female fur seals on St. George Island. It was well known that if there were to be seals in the future the lives of the females must be preserved. On the seas, however, the female is treated as a wild beast, to be killed on sight. The sealers cannot distinguish the sex of the animal in the water, and so kill every one they can get. Pelagic sealing is, therefore, indiscriminate killing, or killing without reference to sex, age, or condition.

On the Pribilof Islands the number of female fur seals, exclusive of the young of the year, is about double the number of males. The smaller number of the males is due to land killing, the quota of skins taken by the lessees of the Islands being made up wholly of young males. On the feeding-grounds the same disproportion of the sexes holds true, heightened by the fact that the cow must feed regularly and constantly because of the necessity for nursing her offspring. It follows, therefore, that the greater part of the animals taken at sea are females; and the records of pelagic sealing bear this out, showing that upwards of 75 per cent of the catch are cows.

Each adult female fur seal found on the feeding-grounds in Bering Sea has a pup on the Island dependent upon her for nourishment. It has been clearly demonstrated the past summer that the pup fur seal does not feed on other food than its mother's milk while it remains on the islands. It necessarily follows that whenever the mother seal dies or is killed before weaning, the pup, however large or vigorous, must starve to death. In 1896, 16,019 pups dead from starvation were found on St. Paul and St. George. These deaths resulted from the killing of the mothers at sea. And not only does the death of the mother involve the death of her nursing offspring, but, since the cows are never permitted by the bulls to leave the harems in the short interval between the birth of the pup and re-impregnation it also involves the death of the unborn pup. The death of a nursing female fur seal, therefore, involves the loss of three lives, and is wasteful and ruinous in the extreme. Since pelagic sealing began, upward of 400,000 adult female fur seals have been killed at sea, 300,000 pups have been starved to death on land, and 400,000 unborn pups destroyed.

The pelagic sealing fleet attacks the herd in January off San Francisco, where its return migration begins. It follows the animals northward along the coast of British Columbia and Alaska to the passes of the Aleutian Islands. The females are then heavy with young. Being more sluggish in their movements and sleeping more soundly than the males, they form here also the greater majority of the seals taken. In May, June, and July, pelagic sealing is forbidden off the American shores, and the predatory fleet crosses to Japan and attacks the herd of the Commander Islands. With the first of August the fleet returns from Japan, enters Bering Sea, and continues its work until driven out in September by the winter storms.

The returns from the American schooners engaged in pelagic sealing for the past season show the percentage of females in the Northwest or coast-wise catch to have been 92, in the Bering Sea catch, 72.

To understand the relation of pelagic sealing to the decline of the herd, we have only to consider the history of the decline in the light of the history of the catch. During the greater part of the period of maximum prosperity of the herd (1872–1882), pelagic sealing was carried on off the Northwest coast chiefly by Indians in open canoes, the annual catch averaging about 5,000,—a scarcely appreciable drain on the herd. In 1878 this catch increased to 8,000; in 1881 to 10,000; the following year to 15,000; and in 1883 to 16,000. Under this increased catch the equilibrium was broken and the decline began. With this year the pelagic sealers entered Bering Sea. In 1885 the Northwest catch numbered 21,000, and the following year the Bering Sea catch amounted to 14,000. Up to 1887 the loss had been so gradual as to excite but little notice. In that year it manifested itself in a difficulty in getting the quota. Since that time, with an interruption of two years (1892–3), during the *modus vivendi*, pelagic sealing has rapidly increased and the herd has correspondingly declined.

Since the establishment of the closed season for Bering Sea in May, June, and July, the sealers have crossed over and spent these months preying on the herds of the Commander and Robben Islands off the coast of Japan, returning to enter Bering Sea in August. Pelagic sealing began in 1891 on the Asiatic side but it was then already a full-grown industry; and the result has been that these Asiatic herds have suffered even more heavily than the Pribilof herd in a much shorter time. The Commander Islands' herd—at its best but half the size of the Pribilof herd—is now barely one-third the latter.

The conditions of the fur seal question are very simple. A race of animals having their breeding-home on certain islands in Bering Sea, and going out from these islands long distances for food, are attacked on their feeding-grounds and indiscriminately killed; the females being the chief sufferers, and their dependent as well as unborn offspring dying with them. Driven by the stress of climate to migrate to the south in winter, these animals are again attacked on their return in the spring, and again indiscriminately slaughtered.

No one considering these facts, none of which is now open to dispute, can fail to see that this indiscriminate killing—in other words, pelagic sealing—is an adequate cause for the decline of the fur seal herd. There being no other cause discernible, it must be accepted as the sole cause. It is equally plain that if the fur seals are to be preserved and protected the one and only way is through the absolute prohibition of pelagic sealing. There is no way to distinguish and exempt the females in the water; therefore no form of regulated sealing will answer. No regulation giving a closed season to Bering Sea but allowing an open season off the Northwest coast will answer. For it makes no difference to the herd whether the cow is killed with her unborn pup within her, or whether she is killed after its birth and the pup left to starve to death.

Land killing, properly managed, does not affect the herd except in a beneficial way. The natural mortality due to overcrowding can be greatly lessened by the still closer killing of the males, and can be practically removed by proper care of the breeding-grounds. With proper protection to the females, the herd may be restored to its greatest prosperity: it may even be largely increased. But there is no hope for the herd unless and until such protection is accorded.

The regulations "for the protection and preservation' of the fur seal adopted by the Paris Tribunal have failed of their object. All familiar with the facts knew that they must fail. But the mistake is not fatal, and the rectification is not difficult. The ultimate end in view in any future negotiation must be an international arrangement whereby all skins of female fur seals shall be seized and destroyed by the customs authorities of civilized nations, whether taken on land or sea, from the Pribilof herd, the Asiatic herds, or in the lawless raiding of the Antarctic rookeries. In the destruction of the fur seal rookeries of the Antarctic, as well as those of the Kuril Islands and Bering Sea, "American enterprise" has taken a leading part. It would be well for us to lead the way in stopping pelagic sealing by restraining our own citizens, without waiting for the action of other nations. We can ask for protection with better grace when we have accorded unasked protection to others. The moral strength of the American contention has been lost through the fact that we have shamelessly allowed American vessels to prey on our own herd and that of friendly Russia. To-day off San Francisco our vessels are destroying female fur seals worth to us under protection $40 each for breeding purposes, in order to get their skins, which are worth in the London market about $9 each.

The monstrous proposition to destroy the fur seal herd because it has been injured by pelagic sealing ought not to be considered for a moment. It would be a confession of impotence unworthy of a great and civilized nation. If a mere "bluff," the proposition is ineffective: if taken seriously, it is abominable. Its results would be to transfer to ourselves any odium which has deservedly fallen upon those who would recklessly destroy a most useful and interesting race of animals.

Nor are we driven to this extremity. If we fail to secure a remedy through mutual agreement with Great Britain we can ourselves destroy pelagic sealing by branding the females and herding the males during August. Experiments carried on by us show that the female pups can be branded so as to destroy the value of the skin, without injury to the animal. This is a safe and effective method, and should be tried if it should be impossible to secure fair play. But now that the conditions are clearly understood, there is no good reason why the matter cannot be honorably and amicably adjusted, to the satisfaction of all the nations concerned. The McKinley Administration has few duties more important than to bring about this adjustment.

DAVID STARR JORDAN,
Chief of the Bering Sea Commission for 1896.

GEORGE ARCHIBALD CLARK,
Secretary to the Commission.

ARBITRATION THE ONLY SOLUTION OF THE FINANCIAL PROBLEM.

THE Presidential campaign of 1896 did not result in the decisive settlement—so essential to an era of substantial prosperity—of the question, *What shall be the coinage, currency, and banking system of the United States?* Twenty years of political agitation of this problem have failed to bring its solution. All that has been gained is time in which to consider and bring the question to a direct issue before the people, during which time existing conditions should stand unchanged. Is it therefore necessary that the welfare of the people should suffer from a confidence-destroying agitation of the currency question for two or four years more? I answer—No. In the light of experience it is just and right for the people to demand that the disputants shall now submit their cause to some tribunal competent to decide it in the interests of the general welfare.

The Greenback-Silver coinage and currency demands originated in the Greenback agitation of 1874–6, which resulted in the prohibition of any further cancellation of United States treasury notes. Agitation was resumed in 1878 by the Greenback-Silver demand for a larger use of silver; their opponents contending simply for the maintenance of existing conditions. This agitation resulted in the enactment of the Bland Law, under authority of which 378,166,793 silver dollars were coined.

The coinage and currency question again became acute in 1890. Greenback-Silver advocates demanded the free coinage of silver. Their opponents contested that demand, and finally agreed, as a compromise, to the purchase of 4,500,000 ounces of silver per month and a monthly issue of treasury notes to the amount of the silver purchase. Under authority of the Silver Purchase Act of 1890, $155,931,002 in greenbacks (treasury notes) were issued.

The legislation of 1874–6, 1878, and 1890 terminated in the monetary panic of 1893, at which time a general demand was made for the repeal of the mandatory purchase of silver contained in the act of 1890. The repeal measure became a law November 1, 1893, since which time no coinage or currency legislation has been enacted.

In 1896, the agitation for currency reform again became acute. Greenback-Silver advocates demanded the free and unlimited coinage of silver at the ratio of 16 to 1. Their opponents, although conscious that some measure of currency reform was a vital necessity, formulated no proposal looking to that end; again contenting themselves with contending for the maintenance of existing conditions. The 7,100,000 voters who supported the successful ticket were in agreement in desiring the maintenance of the existing gold standard. For this cause alone persons differing widely on questions of tariff or currency reform voted the same ticket. A clear-cut, well-defined scheme of currency reform was not before them. The 6,500,000 voters who supported the unsuccessful ticket, which demanded the free and unlimited coinage of silver at the ratio of 16 to 1, and the prohibition of all banks of issue under State or national charters, included those who believed in the policy advocated, and those who believed in party regularity regardless of the principles affirmed in the national platform. It cannot be said that a ruling majority was in agreement regarding a single measure requiring legislative action necessary to establish such conditions.

In October, 1893, I read a paper before the American Bankers' Association, under the title of "A Plea for a Sound Currency and Banking System," * for the purpose of creating which I urged the appointment of a non-political national commission. This demand was immediately repeated by influential newspapers, boards of trade, and chambers of commerce throughout the country, and was recommended by the Comptroller of the Currency in his Annual Report for 1894.

In his remarks addressed to the Association, immediately following the reading of my paper, Mr. George S. Coe said :—

"Is there not in the natural exchanges of property passing through the hands of producers and consumers the real and fundamental currency most required for all sound banking?

Aside from the great subject of coined money, which will doubtless be deemed of prime importance, the question of currency, by which the exchanges of the whole community are chiefly made, must demand the most serious consideration. . . . The attempt must now be most diligently made to create a system that will take the place of all others, and, if possible, one that will eminently deserve the national preference."

In a paper read before the New York Board of Trade and Transportation, December, 1893,* I said :—

* Published in full in " A Sound Currency and Banking System ; How it may be Secured." G. P. Putnam's Sons, New York.

14

" The mistakes of 1874–6, 1878, 1890 must not be repeated. Those who favor sound money are fully as responsible for these mistakes as are those charged with advocating monetary fallacies. When the demand first came from the South and West for still further issues of United States legal-tender notes, and, this failing, for the suspension of the redemption and cancellation of such notes, it should have been treated as a signal of distress. Sound-money advocates from every section of the country should have met this call by examining promptly the needs of the sections from which it emanated, and, after sufficient investigation, they should have proposed sound-money measures which would have brought the desired relief. Had this been done then, the monetary fallacies from which we are now (1893) suffering would be powerless for evil."

These appeals were not heeded. After the struggle to secure the repeal of the silver-purchase measure in 1893 the ruling majority of the people made no effort to follow up that result with a determined movement to secure an intelligent and comprehensive revision of coinage, currency, and banking laws, and thus to remove all cause of want of confidence in, or dissatisfaction with, our monetary system. As a result, the prosperity they fondly expected to see follow the repeal of the silver-purchase measure never came.

The compromises of 1874–6, 1878, 1890, resulted, as all settlements based on unsound economic principles must result, in retaining or injecting poison into our monetary system. So long as this poison remains, it will render a condition of perfect health impossible.

Having cast their votes in accordance with their judgment as to the best policy for the promotion of prosperity, the people now earnestly desire a cessation of confidence-destroying currency agitation, in order that they may again devote themselves with energy to money-making vocations, to produce the prosperity they had eagerly hoped to see follow the close of the Presidential campaign. It will be a sad day for the people of this country if they repeat in 1897 the mistakes of 1874–6, 1878, 1890, and 1893, cherish the delusive idea that prosperity will follow the results of this election, and fail at once to set themselves earnestly to provide for a complete revision of coinage, currency, and banking laws, with the view of permanently settling the question. If this is not done, and our monetary system is not brought into accord with the requirements of correct economic principles, the evils resulting from the errors of the past will be perpetuated. Twenty years' experience should be sufficient to teach the people that this conclusion is true. Every intelligent observer who has closely studied the course of events since 1873 is now ready to admit that, if a season of satisfying prosperity is not realized before the Congressional campaign of 1898 and the Presidential campaign of 1900, the Greenback-Silver advocates may be victorious at the first, and will surely be successful at the later, election.

One evil resulting from the political agitation of the past lies in the fact that much has been taught to the uninformed that is not true, and much that is true has been rejected by the people because it was urged upon their attention by professional political orators and in the publications of campaign committees. The lesson that should have been taught to those who cried out for "more money," in the years from 1873 to 1897, must now be taught to the people of all sections of the country. It is this: An intelligent use of the resources possessed by any community will supply all the currency that can be required to promptly effect the legitimate exchanges of its industry and commerce. Prosperity is dependent upon an intelligent use of resources and opportunities, regulated by correct laws, and should not be the victim of changeable State or Congressional legislation. Assisted by a correct coinage, currency, and banking system, the people of every section can so use their own resources as to secure all the monetary relief for which they have ever asked. They will then realize the truth, that self-help is the countersign of economic freedom. Then prosperity will come.

It may be well at this point to examine briefly some fundamental economic conditions.

Natural economic laws are true standards. By complying with their requirements man may govern natural forces; but he cannot by his edicts suspend their action. They are unaffected by his ignorance, unchanged by his importunity, uninfluenced by his necessities. If, by understanding and conforming to the requirements of natural laws, man cannot satisfy all the needs of his being, some of his needs must remain unsatisfied. There is no source of supply except the resources of nature, prepared and distributed by human industry for the use of man. If legislation which controls production and distribution is not properly aligned in every detail with correct economic principles, it cannot operate with equal justice for all men: it will make the labor of production unnecessarily burdensome for some; and it will create a deficiency in some places, a surplus in others.

Applying these observations to the subject under consideration, as an answer to those who demand "more money," the following, from a recently published book,[1] is pertinent:—

[1] "The Natural Law of Money," by WILLIAM BROUGH. G. P. Putnam's Sons, New York.

"Money is a product of man's labor—a commodity. It is not any one specific thing, but may be almost anything, and is money only by reason of its fitness, at the time, for the service to be performed. In any given community there is a limit to the number of articles produced, and, in earlier times, this limit was very much narrower than now; but, however limited the number of commodities may be, there are always one or two that supply the money-want more efficiently than others. Now, as almost any commodity may be used as money, such a thing as a lack of it is not possible so long as man continues to be a producer of commodities; although he may, by false legislation, corrupt his money or throw restrictions around it, and thus lessen its efficiency. All over the world there have been examples of such false legislation wherever governments conceived it to be their function to regulate the value of money."

Coined money is a natural development from a primitive system of effecting exchanges by barter. It is itself a commodity, the product of man's labor, and is a refinement in the processes and instruments of distribution. As a means for effecting exchanges its services are of high value, but not of the highest.

With a growth of the knowledge of the science and art of commerce there came not only a knowledge of the utility of coined money, but also a knowledge of money arithmetic, which developed a new form of money known as "the money of account." Its service is to cause all commodities to lose their identity as commodities and to become factors of *value*. In making a bill of merchandise each commodity is listed by name: its quality, quantity, and value are given. Value is expressed in terms of the money of account. By this process all commodities are reduced to a common denominator, and are thereafter treated as items of value expressed as dollars. Being dollars, they can be dealt with by the rules of arithmetic, added, subtracted, multiplied, divided, or broken into fractions, as the case may require.

A bill of merchandise must represent commodities delivered at an agreed price, before it can become a legal claim. It is therefore a medium of exchange, as it is a means by which the ownership of commodities is shown to have passed from seller to buyer. Whoever sells a commodity, whether it be his labor or the product of his labor, by that act creates dollars. There must always be as many dollars in the money of account as are required to represent the full value of all exchanges of labor, or the products of labor. A lack of dollars cannot exist unless there is a lack of commodities, or where no buyer can be found who will purchase the commodities offered for sale. The dollar of the money of account is not created by the fiat of law, of the seller, or of the buyer alone. The seller expresses his idea of value in *price asked*. The buyer expresses his idea of value in *price offered*. When an agreement is effected, *value is determined by the agreed price*. At its value so determined, the commodity is represented as dollars in the money of account.

Following the development of the money of account, by means of which all commodities are transformed into dollars, the next and highest refinement in the monetary processes and instruments of exchange was made by devising written or printed instruments to represent the latent value and ownership of commodities. A promise to pay, expressed in dollars, is an order given by the maker upon himself for the delivery of commodities on demand, or at maturity if it has a time limit, to the value expressed in the order. The credit involved in such an order may be based on any exchangeable commodity. It may be predicated on but one commodity, as is the case with gold or silver certificates, or it may practically include the value of all commodities "passing through the hands of producers and consumers," as is the case with clearing-house certificates or bank-note currency secured by "quick assets."

An important and far-reaching step in facilitating exchanges was taken when bank-note currency was devised, by means of which any and every commodity, at its value in the money of account, can be made current in the channels of commerce. The cause of suffering experienced from lack of currency with which promptly to effect all desired exchanges of commodities at an *agreed price-value*, originates in legislation which deprives the people of the right to use the current value of their commodities as a basis for the currency they require. Instead of issuing currency on the broad foundation of the values of *all* commodities, the basis has been narrowed by false legislation to but two commodities — gold and silver — which are produced by a few people. In this way the people have been deprived of the facilities and benefits derivable from the free use of the most effective form of monetary instruments of exchange, — bank-note currency based on "quick assets."

When this evil has been remedied, and not until then, will sound currency conditions be created that will induce prosperity to the full extent to which it can be induced by a comprehensive and correct revision of coinage, currency, and banking laws. There will then be established a sound "American financial policy for the American people."

The first effort in every controversy should be to find all points of agreement and use them as a common basis upon which to construct the final and complete agreement sought. If this be not the object of a controversy, it is objectless, and should not be permitted to engage the thought and time of earnest men.

All advocates of currency reform, regardless of their party affiliations, claim that they desire "honest money," "sound currency," the faithful discharge of all public and private obligations in strict accord with the requirements of national and personal honor and integrity, and that the policy they advocate receives their endorsement solely because they believe it to be best for the welfare of the people and of the nation. No party has a monopoly of wisdom, practical common sense, or personal honor. Each can concede to opponents all they claim in these respects, and use this as a common basis of agreement. The present is an opportune time to call a halt on partisan discussion, and to raise the issue of currency reform to the higher level of patriotic emulation, where party advantage and party regularity will give way to a united endeavor to promote the general welfare.

All parties declare their earnest wish to see the people of the United States in the full enjoyment of a continuous era of satisfying prosperity. Every truly loyal citizen will be glad to see prosperity come, even though its coming is induced by a policy or methods differing, no matter how radically, from those he has advocated.

Mr. Cleveland in his Annual Message to Congress, December 7, 1896, said:—

" Our business interests and all good citizens long for rest from feverish agitation, and the inauguration by the Government of a reformed financial policy which shall encourage enterprise and make certain the rewards of industry."

Senator Teller, speaking in the United States Senate, December 16, 1896, remarked :—

" I want prosperity in the United States. I believe it can be brought to the people by a decent financial system. I do not believe it can be brought in any other way. I am not so wedded to the silver question, however, as not to welcome prosperity from any source that it may come."

Twenty years of partisan discussion and strife is sufficient. All honest-minded, patriotic men can now afford to submit to arbitration for final settlement their differences of opinion on monetary questions.

Tariff- and currency-reform issues are issues wholly unrelated, and should be separated for consideration and action. Partisans favoring certain measures pertaining to one issue should be prevented from demanding concessions for their proposals as the price of their support of measures pertaining to the other issue. The vital importance of these issues is acknowledged by the prominence given them in the discussions and creeds of all political parties; but there is a wide difference in opinion as to which of the two is paramount. Upon this point opinions may be condensed into three groups :

1. That prosperity can be most effectually secured by a thorough revision of tariff laws to give adequate protection to all American interests, and to increase the revenues; existing currency conditions remaining substantially unchanged, and the agitation for currency reform to cease.

2. That tariff revision to give adequate protection to American interests and to increase the revenues is necessary; that such measures are not of themselves sufficient to induce an era of substantial prosperity; but a comprehensive reform of our monetary system must be effected and the agitation for changes in our currency system by this means be stopped.

3. Agitation for currency reform must result in a comprehensive revision of all coinage, currency, and banking laws; and, until this result is gained, efforts for its accomplishment must continue without abatement. Tariff reform cannot of itself improve conditions or stop currency agitation.

From this grouping the deduction may be made that the objective point of all parties is prosperity, and that a settled condition of the tariff, whether for protection or revenue only, and of the currency, whether under existing conditions or those proposed by the advocates of Greenback-Silver measures, or such other basis as may be agreed upon, is a fundamental prerequisite to prosperity. In this deduction one fact is prominent: For both the tariff and the currency systems stability of conditions must be established, so that those engaged in industrial and commercial vocations may be relieved from the uncertainty, the strain, and the disasters resulting from every Congressional or Presidential election.

By making the tariff the special issue for consideration by the Fifty-fifth Congress, and the currency the special issue for consideration by the Fifty-sixth Congress, the tariff and currency issues may be isolated for consideration and action. To facilitate the work for currency reform, without continuing the confidence-destroying effects of a feverish public agitation, and without permitting it to be interposed as an element of obstruction or compromise in the settlement of the tariff issue, a scientific, practical, non-partisan currency commission, to report in March, 1898, should at once be authorized and provided for.

The consideration of currency-reform measures having been provided for by the creation of a special commission for that purpose, and all proposals pertaining to that subject being referred to the commission, the Fifty-fifth Congress and the Administration will have a clear field for a comprehensive discussion and revision of tariff legislation, the improvement of the revenues, and for all other subjects pertaining to the domestic and foreign policies of the nation. If, by these efforts, prosperity for the whole people is induced, who will be so unjust, so unpatriotic, as to wish to overturn that result? On the other hand, if those who oppose such an adjustment of the tariff as may be made by the advocates of legislative protection for American industries are right, the failure of the effort so to induce prosperity will be a source of never-failing strength to them when the issue of currency reform is before the people for final settlement. By this arrangement the advocates of both issues will have an opportunity to assume the responsibility of their convictions and to formulate proposals for carrying them into effect, each without hindrance from the other in securing consideration or action; for both will obtain consideration simultaneously, the one before Congress, the other before the commission; and each will be brought to final action in a separate Congress,—the advocates of currency reform having the advantage of bringing their proposals for final action before a Congress elected with special reference to that issue.

Another reason for constituting a currency commission, as proposed, is found in the fact that the advocates of the gold standard, of bimetallism, and of Greenback-Silver measures have become so intensely earnest in their convictions that they can see nothing but dire calamity in store for the people, if their peculiar views are not expressed in practical legislation.

William J. Bryan, in his lecture at Atlanta, Georgia, December 23, 1896, said :—

"If I should tell you what system will establish that [least changeable unit] you might believe me wrong. If you told me what system you thought would give me the best dollar, the dollar most nearly honest, I might not agree with you. But when I tell you that the aim of both of us should be to come to the nearest approach to absolute stability and absolute justice between man and man, you must agree with me in the purpose, however you differ from me in the means of arriving at it."

This statement shows clearly that the period for general discussion should be closed, that the time for arbitration has come. When unyielding disputants holding opposing views of methods are in agreement as to their objective point,—and every intelligent, honest-minded person in this country can unreservedly agree with Mr. Bryan in his final proposal,—the only rational course the contestants can pursue is to submit their opposing views to the arbitration of a jury of their peers for adjustment, and agree to abide by the decision rendered.

It is assumed that the personnel of the commission will command the confidence and respect of the people; that it will be composed of men whose intelligence, honor, sagacity, ability, and judicial fairness, considered individually or collectively, will be questioned by no intelligent, honest-minded person. The people can accept the judgment of such a commission as being the opinion of capable men who have deliberately listened to all arguments, examined all evidence, considered the condition and requirements of every section and vocation, and made its recommendations solely for the highest good of the nation. Recommendations so made, and acted upon after having been submitted to the people for approval, will eliminate from future discussions all such base insinuations and derogatory charges as those which followed the revision of coinage laws in 1873, and the subsequent demands for the free coinage of silver. In devising an "American financial policy for the American people" it is not only necessary that the policy shall be right in itself: it is of equal importance that it is believed to be right by the ruling majority of the people.

The recommendations and report of the commission, if made during the month of March, 1898, would be before the people in sufficient time to become the paramount issue in the Congressional campaign of that year. This would bring the proposals of the majority and the minority to a direct issue before the people on their respective merits. The Congress then elected would have no doubt as to what course it should pursue in enacting measures for currency reform, and would not be retarded in its action by other issues of overshadowing importance. Every man who places national welfare and the prosperity of the whole people above party advantage will approve this course. Any man can afford to be proved wrong, if thereby prosperity comes.

An American financial policy formulated by a commission approved by a popular vote of the people, and then enacted into law by their representatives, can be made the soundest, most stable, and most helpful system ever devised for the welfare of any nation or people. It will be as unchanging a cause of prosperity, as beneficent and far-reaching in its power for good, as the Declaration of American Independence and the Constitution of the Republic.

ALLEN RIPLEY FOOTE.

THOREAU AND EMERSON.

EVERY year testifies more and more to the increasing fame of Henry Thoreau,—careless of popularity as he was, and much looked down upon by many of the critics who noticed him when he began to publish his original writings. The recent essays on him by various writers are quite unlike in tone much that passed for criticism thirty years ago,—notably the ill-disguised pique and prejudice of Lowell.

There is now a call for the completion of his diaries of the seasons —which still lack four months of filling out the round year—in the manner of editing chosen by his editor. After that has been done, still much of the journals will remain unprinted; something also of other manuscripts, and a few letters that have escaped the collectors.

One almost fancies Miss Amelia Watson's pretty colored sketches to illustrate Thoreau's " Cape Cod " are too dainty and bright for the sober hues of that cape, and the cool atmosphere of Thoreau's prose; but the varied mysteries and glittering beauties of that region are in this mode of illustration well brought out. The next book to be illustrated should be " Walden," and the lovely tameness of Concord scenery might be reproduced by engravings as it has never yet been. An English edition of poems selected from the "Dial" of 1840–44, containing some of Thoreau's verses, is announced by W. R. Nicoll, with short biographical sketches of the writers. Thoreau hardly needs a biographer; already six books of biography, besides a dozen sketches, have appeared since his death in 1862. The most original of these is Ellery Channing's; the most recent, the shorter "Life" by Henry Salt, Thoreau's English disciple.

Maria Mitchell, visiting Dr. Whewell at Cambridge, England, in 1857, reports him as complaining that Emerson wrote bad English, and imitated Carlyle,—a remark that showed how little the omniscient Master of Trinity knew about the style of either. Lowell could see the contrast between the dialect of these two friends, and pointed it out in a memorable passage in his " Fable for Critics "; but Lowell made the kindred mistake of thinking that Thoreau imitated Emerson. He said much the same about Ellery Channing, between whom and Emer-

son, in style, there was hardly a shade of resemblance.   This passage
is worth citing, with the blanks filled up:—

> "There comes Channing, for instance ; to see him 's rare sport,
> Tread in Emerson's tracks with legs painfully short ;
> How he jumps, how he strains, and gets red in the face,
> To keep step with the mystagogue's natural pace !
> He follows as close as a stick to a rocket,
> His fingers exploring the prophet's each pocket.
> Fie, for shame, brother bard ! with good fruit of your own,
> Can't you let Neighbor Emerson's orchards alone?
> Besides, 't is no use,—you 'll not find e'en a core,—
> Thoreau has picked up all the windfalls before.
> They might strip every tree, and E. never would catch 'em;
> His Hesperides have no rude dragon to watch 'em :
> When they send him a dishful, and ask him to try 'em,
> He never suspects how the sly rogues came by 'em ;
> He wonders how 't is there are none such *his* trees on,
> And thinks 'em the best he has tasted this season."

This is good drollery, and illustrates well enough the generosity of
Emerson; but it is ludicrously untrue.   Channing the poet, and Thoreau the poet-naturalist, being some fifteen years younger than Emerson, naturally came under his influence; both were too original to
borrow.

There were traits of manner and of speech in which Thoreau, like
so many of his younger friends, unconsciously imitated Emerson; and
this made so much impression on the superficial observer—on myself,
for instance, when I first came into daily relations with the two men—
that all sorts of remarks were in vogue about it.   "Look at Thoreau,"
said a Boston wit, in 1849, glancing at the Concord recluse, across the
street, "he is getting up a nose like Emerson's."   In truth, he could
as easily have altered the aquiline form of his nose, as have changed in
any essential respect his sturdily original character.

With Channing this was still more true; and I doubt if anyone
who really knew him ever charged that he imitated Emerson in nose,
manner, or anything else.   I once fancied the form of Channing's verse
had been influenced by Emerson's frequent use of the octosyllable,
as in " Woodnotes," or " The Humble-Bee," and my choice example of
this influence was a poem of Channing's to " The Spider," commencing,

> "Habitant of castle gray,
> Creeping thing in sober way,
> Visible sage mechanician,
> Skilfullest arithmetician,
> Aged animal at birth,

> Wanting joy and idle mirth;
> Clothed in famous tunic old,
> Vestments black, of many a fold,
> Spotted mightily with gold."

Now would you not call that an imitation of Emerson?—especially if indoctrinated with Lowell's scoffing critique. But,—as I found out many years after reading it,—"The Spider" was first published in 1835, before Emerson had published any verse.

Nobody ever charged, I think, that Thoreau's verse was modelled on that of Emerson: it had a quality of its own so peculiar that no such imitation was supposable. In the substance of what they wrote, whether verse or prose, there was a certain resemblance, due to the fact that they were born in the same atmosphere of New England's thought and morals; looked upon the same phenomena of nature and man; read the same books, to a great extent; and associated much with each other. We have often laughed at the story of Thoreau's mother, proud of her son's genius, and accounting for this similarity of thought between him and Emerson by saying,—"O yes! Mr. Emerson has been a good deal with David Henry"; but, in fact, it will be found that the direct influence of the younger friend on the thought of the elder was quite as great as the reverse. And this because, with all his originality, Emerson was more sensitive than Thoreau to literary influence.

It is not easy to trace the parentage of Emerson's thoughts; but it is very easy, oftentimes, to see whence came their rhetorical expression in that particular form which he chose to give them. In Thoreau's case, as in Channing's, the form is quite as original as the sentiment or thought. Thoreau said of Channing, "He is naturally whimsical, as a cow is brindled"; and never was a remark more true of both the sayer and its object.

But beneath this whimsicality (much less marked in Emerson's case, though he glorified Whim, as we know) there burned a steady, pure flame of poetic thought and moral purpose. This was a trait of all the Concord authors, not excepting Hawthorne, whose mode of expression was so much his own. In what, then, does the difference between Emerson and Thoreau consist? And is it fundamental, like their resemblance on intellectual and moral grounds, or only casual, from slight dissimilarity in temperament and training? Closely connected with this question is that other one, which some of the younger readers of Thoreau are raising,—whether the fame of Emerson in literature and philosophy will be so permanent as that of his younger and more scientific contemporary; whether, indeed, the style of Thoreau is not better suited to literary immortality than that of Emerson.

I take it that the striking characteristic of both these men was their wisdom,—their distinct superiority to most contemporaries in those things for which men ought to care, and which they ought to know. They were both philosophers, in the ancient sense; that is, men who followed truth wherever it led them, and who valued intellectual and spiritual truth more than the transient rewards of human labor, or the shining premiums of mental distinction. Both were, obviously, persons of unusual endowment, who, had they so chosen, might have won many prizes in the contest for honor and wealth, which so engages the effort of most men. Instead of this struggle, they declined the competition, and, in comparative seclusion, devoted themselves to the observation of nature, the pursuit of wisdom, and the instruction of their fellow-men in the nobler ways of human occupation. Both were of a poetic turn of mind, incapable of looking at life in the literal, prosaic way habitual to most of us; both were of a hardy moral constitution, so that self-denial and retirement were not difficult for them. They were even inclined to be stoïcal, and perhaps undervalued the prizes of life. But with all this, they were full of sentiment, quick to love that which appeals to the affections, and with all the aspirations and generosities which a movement for the uplifting of the social condition of mankind requires. They were reformers, rather than conservatives; yet with a great infusion of that which constitutes true conservatism, —a devotion to the primary objects of human existence. To preserve any given institution did not seem to them so important as to hold sacred that out of which all worthy institutions have grown,—the fundamental principles of moral and political action. In all this, Emerson and Thoreau were alike; but they differed widely in the inherited traits which distinguish one soul from another, and which seem to acquire greater force the longer our race continues.

Heredity has had at different times a very different consideration among men; but we must regard it as always a potent influence on individual character. If arts and gifts and tendencies are inherited (as we know they are), so are faults and contradictions and maladies, whether mental or physical. Education may correct these tendencies, or increase them; restrain these faults or inflame them; cure these maladies or induce them; but in our cup of life there lies, after all, a strong sediment of hereditary influence, more and more perceptible as

the draught grows shallower and the bottom is almost in sight. As
an old Englishman observed, in another connection,

> " Clouds of affection from our younger eyes
> Conceal that emptiness which age descries."

Now the inheritance of Emerson was from a long line of clerical
and gentlemanly ancestors, to whom the conventionalities of life had a
value which they never could have acquired among the trading, seafaring, joking, and nonchalant forebears of Henry Thoreau. To this inheritance Emerson owed that matchless propriety and decorum which
was as manifest in him as in George Washington,—a sense of what was
fitting on all the occasions of life, and a consideration for the tastes and
feelings of others, which makes him almost unique among reformers.
There was also in him that inborn leadership which gives its charm to
ancient aristocracies, no less than to new potencies like those of Napoleon and Cromwell: the princely quality was most evident in his
nature, and finds expression in his pages more than in those of any other
modern author. With Thoreau, these traits were replaced by a sturdy
and trenchant individualism, somewhat scanty of respect for what is
merely conventional, especially if a little outgrown; and he was little
disposed to make those concessions in minor matters which the daily
intercourse of life requires for its smooth movement. He was at heart
profoundly unselfish and courteous; but on the surface rather brusque
and pugnacious; and, at times, with all his distinction, a little plebeian
in his bearing. Such qualities provoked opposition, and did not pass
unnoticed even by Emerson.

As time slipped by with these chosen friends, and the young en-
thusiast of 1837 became the settled and audacious questioner of 1857,
the unavoidable collision of such opposite traits took place. We find
in the published journals of Thoreau—and doubtless should find in the
unpublished diaries of Emerson—evidences of this collision, some of
which may be quoted.

It was in the diaries of Thoreau, as we know, that those lofty utterances on Friendship, which appeared in his "Week," were first entered;
and, after 1849, he had the habit of continuing that topic from year to
year, in his Journal, in which the "Week" was published. Thus, in
December, 1851, he says:—

" Last night I treated my dearest friend ill. Though I could find some excuse for myself, it is not such excuse as under the circumstances could be pleaded
in so many words. Instantly I blamed myself, and sought an opportunity to
make atonement; but the friend avoided me, and, with kinder feelings than be-

fore, even, I was obliged to depart. And now, this morning I feel that it is too late to speak of the trifle ; and besides, I doubt now, in the cool morning, if I have a right to suppose such intimate and serious relations as afford a basis for the apology I had conceived ; for even magnanimity must ask this poor earth for a field. The virtues even wait for invitation. Yet I am resolved to know that one centrally, through thick and thin ; and though we should be cold to one another,—though we should never speak to one another,—I well know that inward and essential love may exist under a superficial coldness, and that the laws of attraction speak louder than words. Methinks our estrangement is only like the divergence of the branches which unite in the stem."

Only two persons could have answered in 1851 to this description of "my dearest friend,"—Emerson and Ellery Channing ; and I suppose the first-named to have been the one meant.

But five years later a more serious estrangement occurred ; after the return of Emerson from a lecturing tour in the West, begun in December, 1856. What was its occasion, there is nothing in print to show ; but that Thoreau believed it (incorrectly) to be final, is evident from the sad tone he adopts, in contrast to that just cited :—

(February 8, 1857.) "And now another friendship is ended. I do not know what has made my friend doubt me ; but I know that in love there is no mistake, and that any estrangement is well founded. But my destiny is not narrowed,—rather, if possible, the broader for it. The heavens withdraw and arch themselves higher. I am sensible not only of a moral, but even of a grand physical pain, such as gods may feel, about my head and breast,—a certain ache and fulness. This rending of a tie, it is not my work, nor thine. It is no accident that we may avoid : it is only the award of fate that is affecting us. I know of no æons or periods, no life and death, but these meetings and separations. My life is like a stream that is suddenly dammed, and has no outlet. But it rises higher up the hills that shut it in, and will become a deep and silent lake.

Certainly there is no event comparable for grandeur with the eternal separation, if we may conceive it so, from a being that we have known. I become in a degree sensible of the meaning of ' finite,' and ' infinite.' What a grand significance the word ' never ' acquires ! With one with whom we have walked on high ground, we cannot deal on any lower ground ever after. We have tried so many years to put each other to this immortal use,—and have failed. Undoubtedly our good genii have found (mutually) the material unsuitable. We have hitherto paid each other the highest possible compliment ; we have recognized each other constantly as divine ; have afforded each other that opportunity to live that no other wealth or kindness can afford. And now, for some reason inappreciable by us, it has become necessary for us to withhold this mutual aid. Perchance there is none beside who knows us for a god, and none whom we know for such. Each man and woman is a veritable god or goddess, but to the mass of their fellows disguised. There is only one in each case who sees through the disguise. That one who does not stand so near to any man as to see the divinity in him is truly alone.

I am perfectly sad at parting from you. I could better have the earth taken from under my feet than the thought of you from my mind. One while I think

that some great wrong has been done, with which you are implicated ; again, that
you are no party to it. I fear that there may be incessant tragedies ; that one may
treat his fellow as a god, but receive somewhat less regard from him. I now,
almost for the first time, fear this. Yet I believe that in the long run there is no
such inequality."

A few days later, Thoreau returns to this painful theme, and almost
implies one of the reasons for the estrangement :—

(February 16, 1857.) " I perceive that some persons are enveloped and confined
by a certain crust of manners, which, though it may sometimes be a fair and
transparent enamel, yet only repels and saddens the beholder ; since by its rigid-
ity it seems to repress all further expansion. They are viewed at a distance,
like an insect under a tumbler. They have, as it were, prematurely hardened
both seed and shell, and this has severely taxed, if not put a period to, the life of
the plant. This is to stand upon your dignity. Manners get to be human parchment, in which sensible books are often bound, and honorable titles engrossed,—
though they may be very stiff and dry."

(February 19.) " A man cannot be said to succeed in this life who does not
satisfy one friend." (February 23.) " I say in my thought to my neighbor who
was once my friend, ' It is no use to speak the truth to you. You will not hear
it. What then shall I say to you? You cheat me, you keep me at a distance
with your manners. I know of no other dishonesty, no other devil. Why this
doubleness, these compliments? They are the worst of lies : a lie is not worse
between traders than a compliment between friends. Lying, on lower levels, is
but a trivial offence compared with civility and compliment on the level of Friendship.' "

These sayings identify Emerson as the friend whose manners keep
others at a distance,—since Thoreau had no other intimate of whom
this could be said ; while it was true of Emerson, as Alcott and others
have left on record. What the primary occasion of the estrangement
was, we cannot know : that it was exaggerated by Thoreau in these
passages is quite evident, since a part of his rhetoric consisted in exaggeration. But it was a real and profound grief to him, as the following
entries in his Journal show :—

(February 23, 1857.) " At the instant that I seem to be saying farewell forever to one who has been my friend, I find myself unexpectedly near to him ;
and it is our very nearness and dearness to each other that gives depth and significance to that 'forever.' Thus I am a helpless prisoner,—and these chains I
have no skill to break. While I think I have broken one link, I have been forging
another.

I have not yet known a friendship to cease, I think. I fear I have experienced its decaying. Morning, noon, and night I suffer a physical pain, an
aching of the breast which unfits me for my tasks. It is perhaps most intense at
evening. With respect to Friendship I feel like a wreck that is driving before
the gale, with a crew suffering from hunger and thirst, not knowing what shore
they may reach,—so long have I breasted the conflicting waves of this sentiment,

my seams open and my timbers laid bare. I float on Friendship's sea, simply because my specific gravity is less than its,—but no longer that stanch and graceful vessel that careered so buoyantly over it. My planks and timbers are scattered ; at most I hope to make a sort of raft of Friendship, on which, with a few of our treasures we may float to some land. . . That aching of the breast,—the grandest pain that man endures,—which no other can assuage !

If the teeth ache, they can be pulled. If the heart aches, what then ? Shall we pluck it out ? Must friends then expect the fate of those Oriental twins,—that one shall at last bear about the corpse of the other by that same ligature which bound him to a living companion ? "

 This is immensely sad ; but it seems to have been a passing cloud over one of the longest and fairest friendships. In an earlier diary we find this quatrain addressed to the sun coming out in the afternoon :—

" Methinks all things have travelled since you shined,—
  But only Time and clouds, Time's team, have moved ;
Again, foul weather shall not change my mind,
  But in the shade I will believe what in the sun I loved."

Thoreau was wise enough to allow for both sun and shade ; or if a parting with friends must come, he could address them in a more cheerful strain, as in the Journal for March 28, 1856 :—

" Farewell, my friends ! My path inclines to this side the mountains,—yours to that. For a long time you have appeared farther and farther off to me. I see that you will at length disappear altogether. For a season my path seems lonely without you. The meadows are like barren ground. The memory of me is steadily passing away from you. My path grows narrower and steeper, and the night is approaching. Yet I have faith that in the infinite future new suns will rise and new plains expand before me ; and I trust I shall therein encounter pilgrims who bear the same virtue that I recognized in you,—who will be that very virtue that was you. I accept that everlasting and salutary law, which was promulgated as much that spring when I first knew you, as this, when I seem to leave you."

I have compared these passages, as they stand in the printed pages which Mr. Blake has edited, with the original Journals in his possession,—and he seems to have given all that is essential in the manuscript. No name appears, to identify the person mentioned ; but there can be no doubt who he was. The final passage reminds me, in its imagery, of a mystical poem of Thoreau's which remained in Emerson's possession long after its author's death, and came to me from Emerson, inscribed in his handwriting, " H. D. Thoreau, June, 1843." It was probably intended for the " Dial," but withheld, and is now printed for the first time, so far as I know. Thoreau entitled it, " The Just Made Perfect " :—

15

" A stately music rises on my ear,
Borne by the breeze from some adjacent vale;
A host of knights, my own true ancestors,
March to the lofty strains and pass away.

In long procession, to this music's sound,
The Just move onward in deep serried ranks,
With looks serene of hope, and gleaming brows,
As if they were the temples of the day,
Gilt by some unseen sun's resplendent beam.
They firmly move, sure as the lapse of Time,
Departed worth, leaving these trivial fields
Where no aim worthy sedate valor finds,
And still the noblest cause of all is Fame.

Forward they press and with exalted eye,
As if their road, which seems a level plain,
Did yet ascend, and were again subdued
'Neath their proud feet.   Forward they move, and leave
The sun and moon and stars alone behind :
And now by the still fainter strains I know
They surely pass ; and soon their quivering harp
And faintly-clashing cymbal will have ceased
To feed my ear.

It is the steadiest motion eye hath seen ;
A Godlike progress,—e'en the hills and rocks
Do forward come, as to congratulate
Their feet ; the rivers eddy backward, and
The waves recurl to accompany their march.
Onward they move, like to the life of man,
Which cannot rest, but goes without delay
Right to the gates of Death,—not losing time
In its majestic tread to Eternity.

As if Man's blood, a river, flowed right on
Far as the eye could reach, to the heart of hearts,
Nor eddied round about these complex limbs,
'T is the slow march of life,—I feel the feet
Of tiny drops go pattering through *my* veins.
Their arteries flow with an Assyrian pace,
And empires rise and fall beneath their stride ;
Still as they move flees the horizon wall,
The low-roofed sky o'erarching their true path ;
For they have caught at last the pace of Heaven,
Their great commander's true and timely tread.

Lo ! now the sky before them is cast up
Into an arched road, like the gallery
Of the small mouse that bores the meadow-turf :
Chapels of ease swift open o'er their road,
And domes continuous span the lengthening way."

Is there not something Dantesque in this interchange of lofty and humble imagery? The thought is a familiar one with Thoreau and Emerson,—the moving of life to music. Thoreau's "Rumors from an Æolian Harp" has the same image, which we meet elsewhere in both writers. Their souls were attuned to each other,—as Persius said of himself and the Stoic Cornutus, "Nescio quod certe est quod te mihi temperat astrum."

Still there were wide differences; and this temporary separation may serve to point out another distinction between them. With all his seclusion and stoicism, Thoreau was less impersonal than Emerson: nay, his very retirement and his paucity of friends made him cling the more firmly to the few he had. Emerson's range was wider; his horizon was more ample; but he did not attach himself so closely to those things and thoughts in which he took an interest. Hence we find more form in the thought of Emerson, more color in that of Thoreau; and, so far as literary style is concerned, the page of Thoreau often excels that of Emerson. Both are epigrammatic; but the epigrams of Thoreau are the more keen and searching, if not so elegant. Emerson dealt more with principles, Thoreau with facts. He had the homely wisdom of Socrates, while Emerson rejoiced in the lofty sweep of Plato. In their learning, which was great,—as Americans reckon the scope of learning,—Thoreau was the more exact, Emerson the more comprehensive and suggestive. Both were masters of English; but in Emerson was more mannerism, in Thoreau more rhetorical art in his best pages, more simplicity in his ordinary writing. Both will endure as authors; and will continue to attract and to instruct, by their deep, cheerful wisdom, and their high moral purpose.

A few years after the date of the sorrowful diaries cited, Thoreau fell ill and was cared for in many ways by Emerson, as by his other friends; but they had come together long before that, in their mutual regard for John Brown, the Kansas hero, whom Emerson first met, in 1857, at Thoreau's house. At Brown's funeral service in Concord, December 2, 1859, they joined in praising his valor; and at Thoreau's own funeral, less than three years later, Emerson closed his eulogium of his friend by saying: "His soul was made for the noblest society; he had in a short life exhausted the capabilities of this world; wherever there is knowledge, wherever there is virtue, wherever there is beauty, he will find a home."

F. B. SANBORN.

SHALL NEVADA BE DEPRIVED OF STATEHOOD?

In the course of a spirited editorial article entitled, "How to Deal with Nevada," the Chicago "Tribune" remarked:—

"Congress is perfectly able to deal with the unprecedented condition of affairs which exists in Nevada. The silver-mines which made her all she was have been exhausted. She has no other mineral wealth. She has no agricultural resources. She has nothing to attract people ; and, as a consequence, she is flickering out."

The "Tribune" urges that the thing to do is to deprive Nevada of her statehood, or at least to exclude her Senators from Congress, as was done with the seceding Southern States during the war and reconstruction periods. The same newspaper serves timely notice upon Wyoming that, failing to show a satisfactory growth in population when the census of 1900 shall be returned, that State also may be invited to march out of the Union with her unfortunate neighbor. These suggestions have been quoted with approval by many newspapers ; and the feasibility of merging Nevada into the more populous State of Utah has also been widely discussed during the past few years.

To degrade loyal States by depriving them of important attributes of their sovereignty would be radical, if not revolutionary. If it were suspected that the real motive for their unprecedented humiliation was the fact that they disagreed politically with a view strenuously held by about 52 per cent of the voters in the nation, and persistently acted with the minority of 48 per cent, it is possible that the proposed proceeding would be worse than radical,—perilous indeed, and fraught with new evils more dangerous than those which it is sought to remove. But happily the time has not come when it is necessary to appeal to the deeper and graver arguments which might be urged against the dissolution of the Union on the instalment plan.

There are four simple and lucid reasons why the Chicago newspaper's prescription, "How to Deal with Nevada," should not be thoughtlessly taken. The first is that it is not true that "the silver-mines which made her all she was have been exhausted." The second is that it is not true that "she has no other mineral wealth." The third is that it is not true that "she has no agricultural resources." And the fourth is that it is not true that "she is flickering out," in consequence of the fact that "she has nothing to attract people." If I may be permitted the pleasure of introducing the State of Nevada to the American people, through these pages, I think it may be proved that the eminent Chicago physician entirely misunderstood the symptoms of the disease, utterly failed in his diagnosis, and, as a matter of course, erred in his suggestion of remedies. As the so-called "sage-brush States" (sage-brush is unerring evidence of kindly soil and abundant sunshine) have been the objects of ardent abuse, which serves no other purpose than to feed the hateful passion of sectional distrust, such an introduction seems well worth while.

Nevada, then, is potentially one of the great States of the Union. Her natural resources are more varied, more valuable, and more extensive than those pertaining to most of the States east of the Mississippi, and even some of the States west of the river. The statement that her silver-mines are "exhausted" is a palpable absurdity. The humor of it is so broad that all readers of gold-standard newspapers should instantly appreciate it, since they have repeatedly been told that Nevada asks for free coinage in the purely selfish hope that that policy would re-open her silver-mines and thereby restore her former extraordinary prosperity. If the mines were really "exhausted," an unlimited demand for silver at $1.29 an ounce would benefit Nevada no more than Vermont. Nevadans believe, of course, that the entire public would be benefited by the higher prices and enlarged circulation which they confidently expect would follow free coinage; but they make no pretence of denying their further expectation that their own State would receive a peculiar benefit in consequence of the revival of her leading local industry. The hand that would rob Nevada of her reputation as a silver-producer should at least make haste to restore her reputation for disinterested patriotism. She cannot logically be deprived of both at the same time.

The silver-mines which made the State "all she was" were principally those of the famous Comstock lode, which produced more than $500,000,000 in precious metals; of Eureka, $125,000,000; of Austin, $36,000,000; of Lincoln County, $30,000,000; of Esmeralda County, $20,000,000; of Elko County, $10,000,000. There were many other camps of lesser moment. Now, it is perfectly true that the extraction of such vast amounts wrought material changes in the character of some of these mines,—notably the Comstock. It by no means follows, however, that the deposits of ore have been "exhausted." The richer ores were utilized at a time when silver commanded a high price, and when economy in milling was not important. But it may be asserted upon the best authority that even the mines of the Comstock, some of which have been worked to a depth of 3,000 feet, possess well-nigh unlimited quantities of ore running from $6 to $15 per ton, and that under more favorable conditions for silver-mining the famous lode would perhaps duplicate its peerless record of the past. It is not likely that fabulous profits will ever again be realized. It is certainly not to be desired that the old romance of life in Virginia City, with its hot fever of speculation, its glittering successes, and its tragic disappointments, should be reënacted. But, though bonanza days are of the past, better days of sober industrial development are in the future.

This statement applies yet more forcibly to other old camps. With few exceptions, deep mining has not been pursued. Only the richer ores near the surface have been utilized, and these by expensive processes and at high cost of transportation. Eureka, Austin, and Tuscarora, and the districts in Lincoln and Esmeralda Counties—all great producers in the past—are yet rich in silver ore averaging $8 to $20 per ton. Not only are the old camps far from "exhausted," but the undeveloped resources in this direction are far from explored. It is not denied by anyone that admittedly great silver camps in Utah, in Colorado, in Idaho, and in Montana have been compelled to cease operations, partially or completely, as a result of the depression of prices. The same is true of Nevada; but she also labors under peculiar disadvantages in the lack of transportation facilities. In the extreme southern counties mines have to ship ore to the reduction works at Salt Lake City at a cost of $15 per ton. There are other localities where the transportation charge ranges from $20 to $100 per ton, and where great ore-bodies, carrying $30 to $60 per ton in precious metals, lie unworked in consequence. The prostration of the silver industry in Nevada is due to a number of causes; but the fact that the "silver-mines which made her all she was have been exhausted" is not one of them.

The statement that Nevada "has no other mineral wealth" is equally wide of the truth. The actual extent and value of such resources in any country cannot be known in advance of thorough development; but the amazing variety of Nevada's natural endowments is a fact which no well-informed person ventures to dispute. Calling the roll of the fourteen counties, nearly all answer to the truth of this claim.

Elko, in the extreme northeastern corner of the State, yielded placer gold to the earliest prospectors of the Great Basin, and has gold-ledges of promising extent and value which are now being carefully explored. Humboldt, central on the northern boundary, presents as great a variety of resources as any district in the United States. Besides silver, it possesses gold, copper, lead, tin, iron, antimony, nickel, cobalt, bismuth, nitre, sulphur, gypsum, borax, soda, and salt. Coarse gold, to the value of several millions, has been taken from its placer and gravel mines. Gypsum is shipped to San Francisco for fertilizer. Near Lovelock, in this county, are great hills of fine bessemer-iron ore, yielding 86 per cent of iron and 12 per cent of aluminum, with no trace of impurities. Eureka County, in the central part of the State, has many mines in which gold predominates, besides large deposits of magnetic-iron ore, of lead, of granite and other building stones. Lander, adjoining Eureka on the west, has valuable undeveloped gold deposits, and the richest mines of antimony in the world. Of the western counties, Washoe reports recent discoveries of gold, copper, and iron; Douglas, quartz and placer gold; Lyon, mines which run high in gold, with but little silver; Churchill, gold, copper, and other minerals; while Storey contains the Comstock. Esmeralda, bordering California on the extreme southwest, is very rich in gold-bearing quartz, and is being actively developed. Lincoln and Nye, the two great counties of the south, have gold, copper, lead, antimony, zinc, quicksilver, fire-clay, chalk, soapstone, borax, and alum. In Lincoln there is a deposit of zinc, estimated to be worth several millions, which cannot be worked for lack of transportation facilities. There are hills of salt the product of which commands locally but $1 per ton, owing to its inaccessibility, though other localities in the State pay $20 to $40 per ton for a similar product. White Pine County, along the eastern boundary, has extensive gold-placers. Finally there is a large deposit in Elko County of something which is said never to have been discovered elsewhere; viz., mineral soap, superior in cleansing virtues to any of the manufactured varieties known to the students of modern advertising. As the country was principally occupied by Piute Indians the deposit remained undisturbed for nameless centuries; but it was exhibited at the World's Fair where, it is feared, it added nothing to Nevada's fame. The thing was so palpably and unmistakably the perfection of toilet articles that it overtaxed Eastern credulity, and was quietly set down as a larger piece of mendacity than of soap.

It is further charged that Nevada "has no agricultural resources."

Of all arraignments, this is the most mistaken and unjust; yet it is the one which will find readiest credence by those who know the State only through the experience of a restless day's travel by railroad across its waste of sage-brush, of sunshine, and of dust. The more need, then, for its emphatic refutation; for there are millions of Nevada acres which might answer the cry of thousands of homeless men.

The territorial grandeur of the Battle-born commonwealth is not a matter of dispute. In the East it would fill a space from central Pennsylvania to Georgia, and from Delaware Bay to Ohio. But as Nevada is very arid, having but ten inches of rainfall and but little of that in the growing season, the measure of its capacity to support population is the extent of the water-supply. Upon the all-important subject of the water-supply of an arid and half-explored country authorities seldom agree. They cannot do so in advance of thorough scientific investigation; especially where the dependence is largely upon flood-waters, springs, and artesian wells. But the most painstaking and systematic inquiry ever made into this branch of Nevada's resources resulted in the conclusion that at least 6,000,000 acres of rich soil could be irrigated. Such was the report of the State Commission, appointed under the auspices of the Irrigation Congress in 1893, of which the late Governor John E. Jones was chairman. The material for the report was gathered with the assistance of sub-committees in every county; and the conclusions undoubtedly represent the best judgment of practical men intimately acquainted with the subject in its local details. The Commission reported twenty lakes and sixteen rivers of importance. Of the utility of the latter, it said that the Carson, Walker, and Truckee, flowing eastward from the Sierras, would irrigate in Nevada 1,000,000 acres; the Humboldt, another 1,000,000; the Salmon, Bruneau, and Owyhee, in the extreme northeast, 400,000; the Quinn, which descends from its Oregon sources into Nevada, 175,000; the Virgin, on the extreme southeast, 100,000. Minor rivers and a multitude of springs were counted available for the reclamation of 2,400,000 acres; while the artesian supplies would bring the total for the State to at least 6,000,000 acres.

The authors of these conclusions—among the most responsible men in the State—declare them to be well within the bounds of conservatism. For the present purpose, however, the figures may be reduced two-thirds, and still leave an ample foundation for population in Nevada. Two States which no one dreams of expelling from the Union are Colorado and Utah. The splendid agricultural prosperity of those arid commonwealths is based on a cultivated area of only about 2,000,000 acres. There is no excuse for assuming that with a reasonable development of her resources, mineral and manufacturing as well as agricultural, Nevada could not sustain at least as many people as do Utah and Colorado in their present condition of partial development. Neither of those States has begun to approach the full realization of her possibilities, though even now they maintain a combined population of about three-quarters of a million. This figure is a low estimate of Nevada's capacity in that direction.

The products of the irrigated lands of Nevada are the fruits, vegetables, cereals, and grasses of the temperate zone, and, in the extreme southern portions, the more delicate fruits of the semi-tropics. Average crops are thirty-five bushels of wheat per acre, sixty bushels of barley, seventy-five bushels of oats, three hundred bushels of potatoes, and four to eight tons of alfalfa, which is the leading forage grass. In the extreme southern counties, where the altitude is but 400 feet above sea-level, and where the warm breath of the Gulf of California is received through the cañons of the Colorado River, figs, olives, pomegranates, almonds, English walnuts, and, in sheltered places, even oranges, may be produced. The climate of Nevada, as these products indicate, covers a wide range. Like all parts of the arid region, it is distinguished by pure, dry air, an extraordinary amount of sunshine, and, consequently, a very high degree of healthfulness. It is a climate fit to breed a robust and vigorous race.

These are not the popular impressions of Nevada; but the traveller who has left his hot and dusty car to breathe the cool fragrance of the little oasis at Humboldt, to walk for a few moments within the shade of its trees, and to hear the music of its waters, should not hesitate to accept them as true. The little patch of green which a hillside spring has spoken into being here is a sample of what millions of desert acres will become. Farther on, the traveller catches a twilight glimpse of the thriving farms of Lovelock, or of the green Truckee meadows. But the larger examples of irrigation lie off the beaten path. Such an instance is the Carson Valley, hidden between the sheltering shoulders of the Sierras. To appreciate the possibilities of this derided State, the critic should visit that valley in the perfect Nevada springtime, and look upon its farms, homes, and villages. There he would behold a memorable picture of thrift, of beauty, and of peace,—from the white blossoms in the dooryards to the white summits of the mountains. And there he might read the true prophecy of Nevada's future.

If, then, this State is "flickering out," it is emphatically not due to the fact that "she has nothing to. attract people." Resembling Utah and, less closely, Colorado in climate and resources, there are reasons which account for her poverty of population and backwardness of development. It is perhaps worth while briefly to review them.

The men made rich by the mines of Colorado had the gratitude and patriotism to spend their money where they made it. Tabor gave Denver her first important impulse by erecting splendid buildings as monuments to his faith in the city's future. Hagerman planted the Midland Railway on the continental divide, and invested millions in reclaiming arid lands tributary to Colorado commerce. General Palmer, the railroad pioneer, founded Colorado Springs, encouraged improvements in every direction, and built his home in the State which had rewarded his daring enterprise. Such was the spirit of most of the successful Coloradans toward the country which gave them their opportunities. The wealth taken from the mines and railroads of Nevada, on the other hand, contributed nothing to the embellishment of her cities or the conquest of her waste places. It went to build palaces in San Francisco, New York, and London, and to increase the social gayety of Newport and Paris. It would not be just to infer that the difference in the attitude of the two sets of millionaires was wholly due to their individual characteristics. Circumstances had much to do with it,—notably the fact that in Nevada the mining industry was mostly concentrated in a single great camp, which enhanced its speculative character, and the other fact that the superlative attractions of California lay within a few hours' ride of Virginia City. But the difference, nevertheless, wrought momentous results in the fortunes of the States.

The railroad situation is another important factor in the backwardness of Nevada. Whenever a single railroad controls the inlet and outlet of a State, the industrial and commercial destinies of that State are, to a large extent, committed to the keeping of that railroad. These facts are further emphasized when it happens that the railroad runs through agricultural territory and possesses a land grant covering every other section for a distance of twenty miles on both sides of the track. Development necessarily hinges on the policy of the railroad, both as to rates and as to the encouragement of enterprise. The only alternative is to build a competing line; and this is extremely difficult if the construction of the first has not resulted in the development of the country and in the growth of its population. Nevada in a flourishing condition would invite competition not merely for her own business, but also for the rich spoil of California's traffic. Nevada as a stretch of hopeless desert, on the other hand, constitutes a perfect insurance against competition for the larger prize on the farther side of the Sierras. It has not been the policy of the Central Pacific to make this "risk" extra-hazardous, or to increase its cost, by developing the territory between Utah and California. It is sometimes charged that the Central Pacific is distinctly hostile to Nevada. The probable truth is that, having the interest of their whole great system to consider, the managers arrange their policies according to the dictates of shrewd business sense, and that Nevada has merely the ill-fortune to be pinched in the process. If it would have paid the Central Pacific better to develop the State than to let it remain a wilderness, it would have been developed. Just criticism should be directed to the system which permits the private ownership of public highways and not against individuals; since human nature is everywhere much alike.

Utah was developed without the aid of railroads or millionaires; but Utah has always had a colonization policy. If Brigham Young had not recalled his colonists from the valleys of the Carson, the Walker, and the Truckee during the 'fifties no one would now complain of a decreasing population,—a sin never charged against the Mormons. The difference between the sister States of the Great Basin is not an affair of raw materials. It is the difference between the results of speculative mining, on one hand, and of the patient development of agricultural resources by methods of sober industry on the other.

Nevada is the victim of circumstances. Rich in the potentialities of material greatness, and therefore strong in the capacity to support a social structure, she presents the baffling paradox of a declining population in a Western State. If she were located in South Africa, the nations of Europe would plot and struggle for possession of her minerals, lands, and waters; if in New South Wales, the colonial government would employ the public capital to reclaim her deserts, and to enable the surplus population of Adelaide to make homes upon her soil; if in Germany, the Imperial government would charter "rent banks" to operate under a commission in preparing the land for settlement and building humble houses, to be purchased by home-seekers on generous terms; if in Holland, the servants of the little Queen would extend the admirable colonies which have flourished for seventy-five years, graduating thousands of needy men from beggary to tenantry, from tenantry to proprietorship. But Nevada is in the United States; and the remedy for her misfortune is—to deprive her of her Senators!

If anything is to be done for Nevada, the impulse must come from without. Ninety-five per cent of her great area is public land and the property of the nation. The present land laws were made in ignorance of the conditions imposed by aridity, and are practically unsuited for any honest and intelligent purpose of home-making. The citizenship of the State is composed of miners, who care nothing for agricultural expansion; of farmers, who are not anxious to foster competition; of stockmen, who want undisturbed possession of water-privileges for their herds; and of merchants and professional men who are helpless to turn the wheel of progress. Congressman Newlands made an elaborate effort to awaken interest in irrigation development a few years ago, offering to back it with his large means; but it came to nothing because of public indifference and subtle opposition. The same conditions prevented the strong effort of the late Governor Jones—a man who had the progress of his State deeply at heart—from reforming the water-laws and providing an irrigation administrative system. It would not be difficult to suggest palliative methods which would help to turn the tide in the right direction. For instance, certain favored districts might be withdrawn from settlement under present laws, and granted, with special inducements, to organizations like the Salvation Army, or Commander Booth's Volunteers, who might reclaim and colonize them in coöperation with philanthropic persons. But the truth is that Nevada's decadence is due to economic evils common to the arid region,—to evils which call for deeper and broader measures than can be applied to any single locality.

If the proposition to alter the political status of Nevada shall become a live issue, it must result in a full discussion of the anomalous and harmful conditions which exist throughout the West. In that case the public conscience will be aroused, and new ideals of national greatness will take possession of the popular imagination. Such a process will lead inevitably to a better understanding between the sections. It will inaugurate a new era of settlement and development; binding together the Far East and the Far West with new ties of blood and new commercial interests. In that case the decline of Nevada will have served a noble end.

WILLIAM E. SMYTHE.

THE DRAMATIC CRITIC: HIS WORK AND ITS INFLUENCE.

ABOUT thirty newspapers, daily and weekly, printed in New York city, employ dramatic critics to express their opinions of the artistic value of plays and acting, and, incidentally, to utter prophecies as to the fate, commercially speaking, of new theatrical productions. Primarily the object of such newspaper criticism must be to inform the public about the plays and the actors, and to advise people who have money to spend for theatrical diversion where best to invest it. Judged from that point of view, no individual expression of opinion can be of much value, except to persons of precisely the same tastes and temperamental peculiarities as the writer. But the higher aim of art criticism—which some distinguished critics are fond of saying is "only the narration of the adventures of one's soul among masterworks," while many cling to the old-fashioned idea that it ought to be the dogmatic expression of final, incontrovertible judgment—is surely not often missed in the contemporary "press notices" of theatrical proceedings. There are always discontented or malicious persons too ready to assert that newspaper dramatic criticism has yet other objects in view; such as the overpraise of one actor or manager to the detriment of others, or the subjection of æsthetic purpose to commercial expediency. The fable is ever cherished by some unsuccessful actors and the disreputable hangers-on in the theatrical calling and journalism,—the thirsty and venomous horde of camp-followers,—that the business offices of the various journals exert an undue influence upon the critic in favor of theatres that advertise well. This may have been and may be still true of certain newspapers; and it is a fact that the "press agent" of theatres is permitted to wield too much influence in the field of journalism. But the "advance notices" and dubious yarns circulated by this too zealous officer, whose persistency and ingenuity are remarkable, cannot fairly be charged to the critic, who often has no responsibility at all beyond the writing of his own reviews in time for the press. As a matter of fact, the most striking faults of current theatrical criticism are, probably, undue severity of judgment, on the one hand, and a too flippant view of serious effort on the other; and these are frequently attributable to a young writer's zeal and his ebullient spirits. Perhaps the publisher may be held accountable for the too generous supply of free announcements of theatrical plans which some of the "live" newspapers give to their readers. But every experienced journalist knows that the public appetite for stage gossip at the present day is insatiable; and the commercial spirit now seems to have conquered all fields, and to rule in the fine arts as well as in the theatre and in journalism. Personally I can testify that, in many years of experience as a reviewer of plays and acting, no publisher or editor has tried to influence in any way my individual expression of opinion; and I am convinced that jealousy and sheer malice prompt most of the charges against critics that relate to overpraise.

Similarly, the charges of bribery, of the evil influence of friendships between critics and actors, are most unlikely, and generally originate with men who have not a shred of reputation for honesty. The idea that some writers for the press largely increase their incomes by accepting payment for "puffing" various enterprises, artistic or otherwise, is occasionally fixed in the public mind by the revelation of the dishonesty of some fellow who calls himself a journalist and is popularly believed to be powerful in his calling, but who could not get employment to sweep the offices of a well-conducted newspaper. There are in New York and some other American cities, as in London and Paris, coteries of so-called journalists, to which not one gentleman of good standing in the editorial rooms of Printing House Square belongs, but who, nevertheless, have some power for evil. Stuff emanating from such sources frequently finds its way into print; but it bears no closer resemblance to the work of decent journalists than the cheap tricks of the shysters bear to honest and dignified legal practice.

A newspaper man must suffer always from his profession's lack of well-defined boundaries. Who can describe the qualifications of the modern journalist? A practical knowledge of bicycling, prize-fighting, or mountain-climbing, coupled with a supreme ignorance of the English language, may nowadays secure to a man lucrative employment on a newspaper. "Specialism" has been forced to its limit in that calling; and there is no longer a community of interests among journalists. And, even more than other writers for the press, the dramatic critic must keenly feel the lack of a clear understanding of the essentials of personal fitness in his particular branch. The professional critic of music is supposed to possess a sound technical knowledge of the art he writes of; to be able to score a composition for the orchestra, for instance, and to analyze a musical work in the manuscript. He frequently possesses, also, if unusually well-equipped for his task, good executive ability in music, and may be a pianist, a violinist, a singer, or all three. The critic of the fine arts who holds a recognized position in his field of duty must have important qualifications for his task other than mere sympathy with art. He is likely to be a fair draughtsman, at least, and to have a knowledge of the mixing of colors and the knack of modelling in clay. He is often a dabster at etching. Sometimes he has been a painter or sculptor; indeed, he may pursue both vocations—the artist's and the critic's—at once, although such a feat of double riding has its dangers and disadvantages. Still, there is no reason why a man should not pursue an art successfully as a craftsman and be at the same time a wise and just critic of the works of other followers of that art,—no reason, except that the combination in one mind of the judicial and creative faculties is not common.

But the qualifications of the dramatic critic are less easily defined. Actual experience on the stage is surely not required of him. He is not expected to know all the ins and outs of theatre management; while there is a standing complaint against a critic who is also a playwright, notwithstanding the fact that some of the ablest and fairest critics in France, England, and this country have been dramatists of distinction. That most of them who write plays are still enrolled in the great army of the unacted is due partly to the fact that the dramatist's task demands undivided attention; but perhaps more largely to the other fact, just noted, that inventive and analytical skill do not often go hand in hand. Some well-directed practice in the art of modern play-making will measurably improve a dramatic critic's understanding of other men's plays; and the spirit that would prevent him from nourishing his ambition to become a dramatist would also prevent any person who had written a book from serving as a literary reviewer.

The theatrical art of to-day partakes somewhat of the characteristics of all the sister arts; and it is undoubtedly desirable for a critic of the stage to have some sound knowledge of music and painting. But, while it is not uncommon to find among men of ordinary intelligence one who does not claim to be an authority on music or the fine arts, or even in certain branches of literature, one rarely meets a man who goes to the theatre at all who does not hold himself quite competent to pass final judgment on actors and dramatists who have devoted years of labor to their work. The ideal dramatic critic would be a man of the keenest sensibility, the clearest and broadest comprehension, and the most catholic taste; thoroughly trained for his task by the study of the literature and history of the stage; familiar enough with its mechanical limitations not to demand the impossible; a student of painting, sculpture, anatomy, dancing, boxing, and fencing, as well as of elocution and rhetoric; and, above all, capable of honestly appreciating the best in all forms of the drama and all varieties of acting,—free, that is to say, from settled prejudices and strong personal bias. But that ideal would be possible only in an ideal world. Sarcey, in Paris, and Archer, in London, with all their aptness and learning, would scarcely serve as leaders of thought in their calling, if so much were expected of the reviewers of plays and acting. That any large part of the dramatic criticism which now occupies so much space in the public prints, is written by men so well equipped, is doubtful: that much of it is composed in the spirit of the casual theatre-goer, who may pause before he commits himself to an opinion on a picture, or a book of poems, but is quick to praise or blame the actor or the play, is very likely.

It is commonly thought that the output of criticism is largely in excess of the visible supply of drama worthy of criticism; but this seems to be true now in all departments of literary and artistic endeavor, and, indeed, of our life in general. This is preëminently the age of criticism—constructive, destructive, dogmatic, and impressionist. The seeds from the old Quarterly Reviewers' gardens were scattered broadcast by the winds; and where one critic flourished in the good old days of trenchant analyses and hard and fast judgments, thousands have sprung up. All in all the press produces more criticism than anything else,—even tales of crime. Fiction in this era is no longer storytelling, but "a criticism of life"; and here, too, the supply exceeds the material on which it feeds; namely, manners. The increase of dramatic criticism is due, of course, to the large increase of daily newspapers; which is to be attributed to the growth of education (by which I mean merely the multiplication of people who know how to read), the cheapening of white paper, and the replacement of the old-fashioned editors with convictions by speculators in the purchase and sale of news and sensational equivalents for it. The number of theatres in this country has quadrupled in a quarter-century; and the theatre-goer of the antique world, who too had convictions, is almost as rare a bird as the conservative editor.

The typical playgoer of to-day cherishes no traditions, has no well-established ideals, and is not, I fancy, easily susceptible to a dramatic illusion. We know that a large proportion of the playgoers in the era of few theatres and the concentration of dramatic art in large capitals were people who had inherited the taste for playgoing and imbibed a love for the stage, if not an understanding of its principles, in early youth. They might not have been, on the whole, more intelligent than the people who seem to predominate in theatrical audiences to-day; a large proportion of whom are descendants of men and women who never set foot in a playhouse, and who themselves had reached maturity long before the acquisition of sufficient money and leisure made them actually aware of the stage as a source of entertainment. It is curious to find these very persons most violently possessed of a critical or pseudo-critical spirit; to find them rarely willing to believe, when in the theatre, that they are listening to the talk and watching the actions of personages in a castle at Elsinore, the Forest of Arden, or a Virginia mansion used for army headquarters in the civil war. Before the drop has fairly fallen on an act one can hear them whispering-loudly to each other their premature and ill-formed judgments of the play and the actors. This unsusceptibility to the illusion of a play must be peculiar to the bustling and confused age of transition in which we live; for I can trace nothing like it in those chapters of standard fiction relating to the drama, or even in the personal reminiscences of aged writers and artists. In these, to be sure, there are often passages of amiable criticism; but the fact is strongly impressed upon one that in the time of Kemble and Kean the finest and most thoughtful people felt the illusion of the acted play. They surely did so in later epochs; and in this country, until the social revolution after the civil war developed many thousands of new and unsophisticated supporters of the theatre, disorganized that ancient institution, and multiplied the number of daily newspapers. Now, perhaps, the influence of dramatic criticism causes so many persons to assume the critical attitude so destructive to the real enjoyment of the play. If that be true, there is one very serious evil to be charged to the dramatic critic's account.

In the old days, to speak only of New York city, the body of dramatic critics on the daily press was very small, and was made up of individuals who were supposed to possess superior artistic attainments, and especially to be rich in the personal qualities which make a man prominent within the mystic boundaries of Bohemia. Some of them were gentlemen of ripe cultivation and poetic feeling, gifted with eloquence, and pursuing their not very onerous tasks with rare enthusi-

16

asm; others were doubtless dissolute, dirty, and morally corrupt. Now, however, there is no Bohemia. New York has now no body of dramatic critics the members of which are even aware of one another's identity; while there are half a dozen daily newspapers where one formerly existed, each giving more space to theatrical incidents than used to be allowed, and each publishing weekly many columns of criticism of which it may be fairly said that if the best of it scarcely equals in literary nicety, exalted tone, and clearness of standards the best of the past age, the average of quality is certainly very good: much of it is sensible and interesting. It must be borne in mind that theatrical standards of taste have greatly changed. With a theatre which still esteems Shakespeare, but rejects all his contemporaries and nearly all his seventeenth- and eighteenth-century successors, as well as most of the playwrights of the first three-quarters of our own century; in which are contending side by side, Ibsen, the German realists and pessimists, the young English writers of social drama and intellectual farce, the unabashed manufacturers of machine-made melodrama and horse-play burletta, and the dramatist of newspaper jokes, it is not possible for either actor or critic to adhere to one unchanging point of view. The best the reviewer of plays can do is to record clearly the impression made by any performance upon his own mind; and this in itself is a hard task which requires good training and the possession of a mind as sensitive to quick impressions as the film of the camera. That, under the circumstances, the general quality of newspaper criticism of the stage is so fair and interesting, seems to me to be remarkable. In all newspapers of repute the "regulation notice," which used to be merely a fulsome, heavy, and ill-expressed puff of a sort now fallen into disuse except in very small cities, has been replaced by a vivacious and graphic account of the performance. Still, a doubt may fairly be entertained as to whether the immense mass of well-intentioned dramatic criticism is altogether beneficial either to the theatre or to the public. I am convinced, however, that nearly every newspaper, according to its kind, aims to provide for its readers the best reviews of plays it can obtain.

A dozen or more years ago, when the New Journalism was first planted in New York city, a young managing editor declared in my hearing that if he owned a newspaper he would employ no acknowledged critics at all. To the theatre, he said, he would assign men from the various editorial departments, according to the character of the entertainment, and would instruct them to record plainly their personal opinions. To the music-halls, for example, he would send the office-boys. The young managing editor never owned a newspaper; and he is no longer a managing editor. His plan would not have worked well. When you have found a person who can receive a clear mental impression from any event or series of events, and can honestly record it in perspicuous English, you have found a critic of so great promise that it would be folly to employ him thereafter in menial duty. It is difficult enough to find men of decent education who can thus receive impressions and intelligently record them. The ordinary young reporter, no matter how quick he may be to accumulate facts and how handy in arranging them for print, will go to the theatre so overweighted by a sense of responsibility that he cannot enjoy the play at all; and he brings away from it only a determination to prove his wisdom by severity. The present aim of most newspaper editors in the appointment of dramatic critics seems to be to secure, above all things else, strong individuality. Still, these critics write with the tastes and understanding of their readers in view. One must not be invidious and use names; but can we imagine Jules Lemaître writing his subtle feuilletons for "Le Petit Journal," or Arthur Walkeley and Bernard Shaw contributing their weekly reviews of London plays to that solace of the cockney "sport," known familiarly as "The Pink 'un"? To say, therefore, as some folks do, that the aim and tone of current dramatic criticism should be higher and more serious, that it should exhibit a deeper perspective of learning, and sound a clearer, sweeter note of artistic sympathy, is simply equivalent to saying that the general public ought to be more serious, more refined, and fonder of art for art's sake. With the theatrical reviewers of perhaps half a dozen New York journals striving to preserve a high standard of judgment, and cherishing lofty ideals, it seems to me that the supply of serious dramatic criticism is rather more than enough to meet the public demands; and to ask newspaper owners to do more than that is to expect of them supernatural virtues and an abandonment of commercial sense.

Many of the incidents of any theatrical season to which the professional reviewer is obliged to give his attention, and out of which he has to make interesting "copy," have small claims to serious artistic consideration. The stage is largely occupied by frivolity; and most of the utterances that proceed from it are merely chatter. Yet, with all this nonsense and rubbish, which, to say the truth, counts for as much labor in the critic's routine as the noblest endeavors of fine actors, we still have the best the modern stage offers. No European actor of distinction fails to visit us early and often. We get all the worthy, and most of the unworthy, plays of all countries,—all that we want, all that the multitude would not be sure to reject. Probably the foreign artists find that their efforts receive here a fair share of critical consideration as thoughtful and able as they have been accustomed to at home ; yet they must be keenly aware that the humorist is ever present when they act, and always ready to subject them to ridicule. It is not the custom in this country to view any subject seriously for a long time ; and the greater the praise an actor receives the greater will be the ridicule he must eventually submit to. With the actors, after all, it is notoriety that counts. Praise is always welcome ; but without publicity they cannot live. Moreover, dramatic criticism is not written for the actors ; and few of them heed the best of it, though they may recognize the good intention of the critic. After all, the best criticism is only one man's opinion of another man's work ; and an actor who has developed his powers of observation and expression by patient labor is not often inclined to change any detail of his work because some other man objects to it. So, also, with the attitude of one honest critic toward all his fellows. He lends all his mind and all his strength to his task ; and if his conclusions do not agree with those of some of the others, it is not wise for him, perhaps, to hold that the others are wrong, though it would be human for him to do so.

The discrepancies of opinion frequently noticed in the mass of criticism are not more striking than the contradictions the reader of newspapers will find if he glances over the several editorial pages every day. Yet one of the gravest charges against dramatic criticism is that the writers do not agree ; as if it were likely that men of so widely differing tastes, convictions, and training could be unanimous on any subject. Newspaper critics being such an inharmonious body, it is surprising, rather, how often there is an approach to general agreement. Perhaps in the twentieth century we shall have an ideal theatre and an ideal press, and with them the advent of a new race of ideal critics, each of whom shall combine the eloquence of Shakespeare's self with the virtues of a saint and the infallibility of the Pope.

Meanwhile, the dramatic critic is little more than human ; and his lot is not so desirable that I should advise young men to aspire to his calling, or rather to his particular branch of a calling which contains no sinecures and offers few prizes. His hours are long and irregular ; his work is hard ; and he is continually at war with his own moods, which must not be permitted to obscure his judgment. Necessarily a man of some strength of individuality, he must night after night subject his will to that of others and keep his mind in a perfectly plastic condition; and, if he gains any sort of distinction in his labors, he will find that the theatre pursues him wherever he may go in his rare hours of leisure. He soon learns the common desire of his fellow creatures to talk about actors, to the exclusion of every other topic. His authority, of which he makes no boast at all, is both proclaimed and denied; for, though he is likely to be transformed into a sort of minor and inferior lion,—a cub perhaps,—yet he never by any chance meets a human being who does not feel perfectly competent to speak the last word of judgment on any play or actor.

Still, if he have enough philosophy, he may console himself with the thought that he labors in a good cause, and that even if, in his efforts to make better understood a form of art that can never die, he has somewhat overstepped himself and helped to develop a race of imitation critics rather than a multitude of frankly receptive and highly appreciative spectators, that evil will in time be remedied. The theatre will grow in strength, in seriousness and in influence; and more good will come out of it in the future than ever came in the past. Now it is too much of a toy,—just as the phonograph and kinetoscope are toys,—because it has not been perfected. Modern development has affected it, thus far, only to the extent of bringing it nearer to the public. It is at the mercy of half-educated and tolerably well-to-do people, who are no longer satisfied with the few simple diversions of their fathers, who have found the cheap newspaper a substitute for the lecture, and who have been bred above dog-fighting, and yet are not capable of appreciating the best the drama affords.

The dramatic critic's work is more useful than ever; and no modest craftsman can ask for better encouragement than the knowledge that he is needed. As a medium for the expression of his views of life in general, he finds theatrical reviewing an especially congenial exercise. The drama is comprehensive and ever expanding; and to write about it day by day ought to be inspiring work for a man burdened with a "message."

EDWARD A. DITHMAR.

THE IMPERIALIZATION OF GERMANY.

THE Holy Roman empire, of which, from the coronation of Charles the Great by Pope Leo III, in A.D. 800, the princes of Germany claimed the sovereignty, and which hence was frequently called the German empire, came to a formal end in 1806. Sixty-four years later arose the new German empire. Though the two institutions are historically connected, in the sense that, but for the one, the other would not have been, and though they have some elements in common, they, nevertheless, rest upon different foundations and—ostensibly at least—aim at different objects.

The old empire, claiming to be at once the heir to Roman imperialism and the bearer of divinely derived authority, communicated through God's earthly vicegerent, occupied a unique position. Though it confined its action to man's earthly life, yet, since it regarded this as a mere preparation for his eternal life, it allowed itself to be guided by the exigencies of the latter. In other words, it became a means to an end lying beyond itself; and, as the realization of this end was the special function of the Church, it naturally assumed a position of subordination to that institution, becoming its "advocate," and the executor of its mandates. As such, it claimed the right not only to regulate men's outward conduct, but also, since eternal salvation was conceived to depend upon the beliefs and thoughts of the heart, to determine and control those by its own special weapons—law and force. Though this theory of the empire was seldom lived up to, yet such *was* the theory accepted by both Pope and Emperor. As a matter of fact, the Emperor was far oftener the foe of the Pope than his agent; and, since his claim to universal jurisdiction was due to the authority communicated to him by the latter, it was natural enough that, when this was withdrawn, he should become in reality what he was often called, German Emperor, or Emperor of Germany. The last Emperor crowned in Rome was Frederick III (A.D. 1440). But, however circumscribed the Emperor's jurisdiction might become, and however incapable he might be of making his authority felt, the German people never forgot that to them had once been conceded the civil government of the world.

Nay, even when the great body of them broke loose from the Roman Church, by which that concession had been made, they still delighted to think that, when Frederick Redbeard should issue from the Kyff-häuser, disrupted, suffering Germany would again become united and strong under the eagles of the empire. *Das heilige deutsche Reich* inspired many a poet and many a statesman who did not care to think of the source or meaning of the *Heiligkeit.* Thus it came to pass that, when the new empire came into existence, it was almost universally recognized and celebrated as the fulfilment of an ancient prophecy, a long-deferred hope.

And yet the new empire is in no sense a restoration of the old. It is not " holy " or " Roman "; it is not the agent of the Church, deriving its authority from the Pope or from God; it makes no claim to universality; it has nó regard to any life beyond the present. On the contrary, it is secular, German, and anti-Roman; deriving its authority from the states composing it. It is, in fact, simply that form of national unity-which, after the failure of several attempts at federation, recommended itself to the political leaders of Germany as most feasible under the circumstances, and as best suited to its grade of political culture. Under analogous circumstances the United States became a republic; the states of Italy, a kingdom.

But, though this is the declared theory of the new empire, as understood by its framers, whether princes or subjects, we need not be surprised if we find that, among a romantic people like the Germans, highly cultivated intellectually, but untrained in the use of political freedom, certain features of the old empire should cast their shadow over the new. As a matter of fact, the present unity of Germany is due not so much to a desire for liberty on the part of her people as to the dreams of her poets and the theories of her philosophers; the former inspired by the romance of the old empire, the latter by the course of history generally. Schiller, Arndt, and Uhland; Kant, Fichte, and Hegel are its true fathers. Under these circumstances, it is but natural that there should be a tendency, almost unconscious, to assimilate the new empire to the old; to substitute for the modern ideal of democratic self-government the mediæval one of government by the grace of God. And such, indeed, is the case, in a marked degree.

This tendency is favored by a large number of circumstances of different sorts. The most obvious of these may be thus enumerated:—

First,—The great body of the German people have no aspiration after political liberty, no desire for self-government. The very patriotic rector of one of the chief German universities said to me not long ago, "Die Deutschen wollen regiert sein" (The Germans want to be governed), and added that they were longing to feel again the strong hand of Bismarck over them.   The truth is, the ordinary German cares as little for politics as the ordinary Anglo-Saxon, English or American, cares for art.   His family, his business, his beer, his music—these are the things that occupy him; and he resents being called away from his easy-going devotion to them by any interests of a higher order, whether political or religious.   While admitting the existence of these, he is glad to be relieved of the burden of them, even at the expense of a considerable amount of liberty.   Instead of the Frenchman's fiery, spasmodic enthusiasm for freedom, or the Anglo-Saxon's calmer devotion to it, he has a fervent loyalty toward his political superiors, which, in large degree, prevents him from feeling his unfreedom.   The notion that he should take any initiative in political matters, draw other people over to his opinions, and form a party for political reform, hardly ever dawns upon him.   If parties of this sort exist in Germany, they are all, or nearly all, due to the Jews.   The present socialistic movement, in so far as it is more than a mere theory, is altogether of Jewish origin.

Second,—The princes of Germany, accustomed during the long dissolution of the empire and afterward to irresponsible dealing with their subjects, have retained a certain brutal instinct of despotism, which makes them eager to relieve the mass of the people of the burden of self-government, and leave them to the easy, narrow life which they so much covet.   This instinct has always been strong in the Hohenzollern family, and was particularly and obtrusively so in Frederick II, the founder of the greatness of Prussia, under whose auspices the new empire came into existence.   That it should be tolerated in his successors, and especially in those in whom the long-desired unity of Germany is personified, is not surprising.   Germany can never forget, and, indeed, ought not to forget, that she owes her present existence as a nation to the ruthless despotism of Frederick II.   Thus the natural tendencies of people and princes play into each other's hands.

Third,—Germany at present needs a strong, united government; and this seems to be best realized in an Emperor of the mediæval type, of which the three Fredericks were memorable examples.   The fact is, she is in a most perilous position, and has no salvation save in unity and strength.   She is beset with foes within and foes without.   She is divided against herself (a) politically, (b) religiously, (c) socially.   Her external enemies, (α) Austria, (β) France, (γ) Russia, are powerful and watchful. It will be well to dwell for a moment on each of these elements of weakness.

(a) The political tie which, in an hour of patriotic enthusiasm over a great victory, bound the numerous states of Germany into the unity of the empire, is in many parts very feeble; and it holds together many mutually repellent elements. Between the North and South Germans there exists that natural antipathy which always holds asunder peoples of widely different temperaments, ideals, and modes of life. In the case of Prussia this is aggravated by the fact that her parent, eponymous stock is not German at all, but Lithuanian. Then some of the larger states—Baden, Bavaria, Württemberg—hold an almost independent position, having their own armies, and could not be prevented from detaching themselves at any time, if they were so minded; while other states, like Schleswig-Holstein and Saxony, having been forced into closer union against their wills, can hardly be over-loyal. Altogether the empire is a congeries of loosely connected, largely heterogeneous, and unsympathetic elements.

(b) Germany acknowledges three religious professions: Protestant, Catholic, Jewish; and every child born in the country must be enrolled in one of these,[1] notwithstanding which regulation, a large portion of the German people, and these the most intelligent, belong to no profession at all. Between the different professions there is much jealousy and suspicion; while the Freethinkers despise them all. The Catholics are practically subjects of a foreign potentate, and accept orders from him even in political matters; while the Jews, almost universally unpopular, are persecuted in a thousand ways. Thus in Germany, religion, instead of binding men together and making them strong for good, divides them into mutually hostile classes, unbrothers and enfeebles them.

(c) That the interests of the different social classes in Germany—the land-owning, the capitalist, and the laboring—are at variance, is a matter of course; but, apart from this, there exists a social antagonism which has no parallel elsewhere,—an open warfare between economic individualism and socialism. Socialism, as a practical programme, is, as we have seen, of Hebrew origin: the theory of it, however, has a different source, which must now be considered.

---

[1] This absurd regulation is the cause of much ill feeling. The ablest and freest thinker in Germany to-day told me that he would be obliged to have his son confirmed; else every civil and military career would practically be closed against him!

When the monarchic socialism, or feudalism, of the Middle Ages, with its supernatural sanctions, fell to pieces, it was succeeded by a crude individualism, which, being unconscious of its own implications, proved at first merely destructive. Toward the end of last century, its long pent-up forces found an outlet in the French Revolution, which began a new era in human history. But the dislocations and horrors which were its immediate consequences so frightened the ordinary, unintelligent world at the very name of individualism that, in the early part of this century, a great reaction took place in favor of strong institutions,—especially in France and Germany, which had suffered most. In France, among the more conservative classes, there arose a sentimental neo-Catholicism, which sought to call back the picturesque romance of the Middle Ages, without its stern piety, and to reinstate kings by the grace of God; while among those who had sat at the feet of Rousseau, Voltaire, and the Encyclopædists, and for whom the supernatural had no meaning, there sprang up various schemes of economic communism, all tending to bind the individual in the chains of a social order. In Protestant Germany the problem of reaction was more difficult. She could not well return to Catholicism, though some of her romantic sons did; and she was in no mood to barter her supernatural faith for dreams of communistic Utopias. Since Protestantism itself was the outcome of individualism, the problem took this form : How shall Protestantism be freed from its individualistic virus, and made to seem the highest expression of human reason—in other words, the absolute religion? Obviously, if this could be solved, a scheme, and one already in operation, would have been found for rendering individualism innocuous, by subordinating it to institutions unimpeachable, because absolutely rational. This solution was undertaken, on the basis of the then popular German idealism, by Hegel, who, after being an ardent individualist, became, as professor in Berlin, an equally ardent socialist (using the word in its original sense) or institutionalist. Assuming thought to be the absolute, and identifying that with his own thought, as well as with the process of the world, he first analyzed it into its simplest elements, and then proceeded to recombine these in such arbitrary fashion as to obtain the desired result. By a truly wonderful, because simple, process of thought-prestidigitation, by distortion of history, and by misinterpretation of dogma, he, of course, succeeded; proving not only Christianity to be the absolute religion, but, what was equally important, the Prussian military state to be the absolute form of civil government.[1] So great, indeed, was his success that his philosophy became almost official in Germany, haughtily extruding every other; and over his coffin a distinguished Berlin divine pronounced him the promised paraclete, and his philosophy the teaching of the Holy Ghost. In this way, Prussia settled down into a military despotism by the grace of a god, now identified with the reason or idea immanent in the process of history. Then, when she assumed the hegemony of the new empire, and her kings became emperors, the principles of the Prussian kingdom passed over to the German empire, which thus found itself in a condition in many ways forcibly recalling that of the old empire, with this difference: that the Emperor, instead of being the political agent of the Pope, now combined both offices in himself. But, when everything seemed most promising, the reaction came. It soon turned out that Hegel's game was one that other people could play at. Certain very able Jews, who had no reason to feel kindly toward either Christianity or Prussian rule, learnt it, and then played with counters of their own make. If Hegel had, as he said, adopted all the principles of the materialist Heraclitus into his own logic, Lassalle, the founder of German socialism, turned the tables by reading the whole process of Hegel's logic back into Heraclitus's materialism.[2] Thereupon two other Hebrews, Marx and Engels, taking the hint, substituted Matter for Thought in Hegel's process, and produced a system of materialism which found no place for either Christianity or military despotism. Assuming, as the mainspring of the historic process, the form of economic production, they showed, with a cogency quite equal to Hegel's, that the true and necessary outcome of this process was state socialism, their own political ideal.[3] Though Hegel, having maintained that every system of thought necessarily calls up its own negation, or opposite, could not logically have objected to this result, yet it was a very unwelcome one to both his school and the German government. The school, indeed, has completely vanished from Germany; but the government is left facing the trying dilemma, whether it shall continue to rest its claims on the grace of Hegel's obsolete god, or, embracing the materialistic reaction of the socialists, pose as the necessary outcome of the process of economic production—in other words, identify

---

[1] In all this, and in his attempt to decry the free institutions of England, there is no need to suppose that Hegel was more insincere than is any man who allows himself to be wafted along by the breeze of official popularity on the currents of his time. Not every man can be a martyr.

[2] See his "Die Philosophie Herakleitos des Dunklen von Ephesos," 1858.

[3] See ALESSANDRO CHAPPELLI, "Le Premesse filosofiche del Socialismo," 1897.

itself with socialism. Bismarck even, for a time, apparently wavered between the two alternatives, and sought to take Lassalle into his confidence; but, later on, miscalculating the strength of the socialistic movement, resolved to persecute it. His persecution was worse than unavailing; and to-day, socialism, stronger than it ever was, faces the empire as a colossal danger that cannot be conjured away, compelling it to live armed to the teeth. Every one who knows Germany must feel that among the possibilities of her future is the capture of the empire by the socialists, and the consequent restoration of feudalism in a modern form. There are not wanting signs and concessions to show that, while the powers that be are opposing socialism with one hand, with the other they are making preparations for its peaceful triumph. Meanwhile socialism is a cause of division and weakness. If the internal relations of Germany—political, religious, and social—are such as to render necessary an almost despotic government, her external relations are no less so. Lying, without natural boundaries, in the heart of Europe, she is beset by enemies on every side. (α) Austria, however apparently friendly, can never forget her sudden defeat in 1866, or the remoter treachery of Frederick II; while (β) France, still smarting from her humiliation in 1870, is watching impatiently for her opportunity to take vengeance, crush the empire, and break it up into its component fragments; and (γ) Russia is ready to make common cause with her, as soon as she sees that such a course would be to her advantage.

All these circumstances,—the character of .the people and the princes of Germany, her geographical position, her relations, internal and external,—and others might be added,—contribute to transform what was intended to be a confederation of free states under the hegemony of Prussia, *prima inter pares*, into something closely resembling the old empire, the memory of which has never ceased to exercise a strong fascination over the German people. The present Emperor is reported to have said publicly on one occasion, "Des Kaisers Wille ist das Gesetz" (The Emperor's will is law); and, if one may judge of his principles from his actions, there is every reason to believe that such is his conviction. When, moreover, we realize the position of his country, we can easily see why, desiring, as he certainly does, its highest good, he should wish to add to his power by surrounding himself with all the prestige and sacrosanctity of that which belonged to the mediæval emperors. At the same time, there is no reason why we should not admit that, in doing this, he resorts to methods which would be utterly intolerable to a free-spirited people. Among these may be mentioned: (1) his system of espionage; (2) his endeavor to control the Church and to gain political ends through it; (3) his attempt to interfere with the free expression of truth; (4) his exaltation of the military above the civil status. We may dwell on these for a moment, as facts incident to the imperialization of Germany.

(1) There is something specially degrading about espionage, especially when practised by a national government, as it is in Germany. This was brought very vividly before me by the following incident: One day there dined with me, in a public restaurant in Berlin, an aged clergyman and his wife. The former had occupied the same pulpit for over forty years, had proved a father to his parish, had been a leader in many liberal movements, and in all ways had served his country nobly; while the latter had for the same length of time been a very great blessing to her neighborhood for many leagues around. In the course of conversation I asked him how he felt about the Emperor's policy. Before replying to me, he turned and looked anxiously about him in all directions, and then said: "If Fritz had lived ten years longer, things would have been different." When I asked, "Were you looking about for anything?" he said, "No; but one never knows who may be listening; and it would go hard with me if it were known that I expressed such opinions." To my surprise, I then learned that Berlin was full of spies of all sorts, ready to catch, and report to the authorities, the slightest word reflecting unfavorably upon the Emperor, his family, or his actions; and that on such reports many persons, especially young men, had been seized by the police and kept in prison for months—one, because, in the heat of discussion, he had said the Emperor was a *Schafskopf!* When I asked my guests what they thought of such a system, they looked mysterious and declined to reply. I afterward spoke of the matter to several persons, who, whether from fear or conviction I cannot tell, informed me that they thought it quite right that the Emperor, his family, and actions should be above criticism, and that he should enforce this rule. I learned also afterwards that the president of the Berlin Ethical Society, a man of eminent scientific attainments, had been imprisoned for three months for venturing, in a public address, to express views on socialism different from those of the Emperor, although he did so without naming him. I could not help feeling that the Germans were paying dearly for their empire.

(2) Theoretically, the King of Prussia is head of the *Landeskirche;*

and the Hohenzollerns have generally taken this office quite seriously, one of them having even compiled a prayer-book. No one, however, ever assumed the attitude of the present King, who, as Emperor, logically wishes also to be Pope. He has not only built churches and made church-going fashionable (it is four times as great in Berlin now as it was before his accession), but is erecting a national cathedral, as his own St. Peter's; and he undertakes to guide the councils, and regulate the creed, of the Church. When I was in Berlin in 1894, a church synod was in session. At a previous meeting, a committee had been appointed to draw up a new prayer-book, the old one having been found meagre and, in parts, antiquated. This committee had reported; and the discussion of their report was the chief business of the later meeting. I was present in a club when a leading member of the synod, a professor of divinity, gave a most lucid account of this discussion. The committee, he said, had presented a new prayer-book far richer than the old, and taking full account of the recent "Higher Criticism." It even omitted from the confirmation and ordination services the Apostles' Creed, as containing articles no longer believable. "No one," said the speaker, "can now believe in the virgin-birth of Jesus; and there are in the New Testament traces of an older belief. No one can believe in the descent into hell; while, as to the communion of saints, no one knows what it means." An overwhelming majority of the synod had, accordingly, declared in favor of the omission, and it was about to be carried, when a message was received from the Emperor saying that he desired complete unanimity. This was sufficient; but, as neither party would give way, nothing remained but to patch up a compromise satisfactory to neither. It was, accordingly, agreed that the Creed should be retained, but that it should be prefaced by a note, saying that only its general spirit was to be insisted on, not belief in its separate articles. Hereupon the Emperor telegraphed to the synod a message of congratulation. "His desire," said the speaker, "was to show the Catholics that Protestants could reach uniformity of dogma, as well as they." The audience received this explanation with strong marks of disapproval.

A few days afterward I asked one of the profoundest thinkers in Germany what he thought the result of this compromise would be. He answered, "A boundless and bottomless hypocrisy"; adding that the Emperor, unable to bring about agreement among political parties, and rule through them, was trying to bring the Church to unity of faith and to rule through it.

(3) That, in his capacity of Pope, the Emperor should seek to control thought and the expression of truth, is but natural. Indeed, through his system of espionage, he has already taken the first steps toward the establishment of an Inquisition. We have already alluded to the punishment of Dr. Förster for political heterodoxy. A Berlin professor of divinity, a man of vast learning, liberal views, and noble character, told me that even the old Emperor, if he had not dreaded public opinion, would gladly have deprived him of his chair, and that, if he were to deliver one of his university lectures before a mixed audience in Berlin to-day, he would be denounced to-morrow and deposed next day. "The present Emperor," he added, "would gladly depose Prof. Harnack, were it not for his great popularity." [1] Harnack's offence is that he has shown the true nature and historic origin of the Apostles' Creed. These examples are typical and need no comment.

(4) Along with the Church, the Emperor has taken the army under his special protection, and has done everything in his power to exalt its officers. The lowest of these, he says, takes precedence of the highest civil official,—such, at least, is the report. Be this as it may, it is certain that German army officers find it possible to treat civilians with a contempt and a brutality which show them to be a favored class. Examples of this could easily be cited, if space permitted.

Surveying the above facts, it is difficult to resist the conclusion that the present ruler of Germany is seeking to restore the old empire, —with this difference, that he tries to combine in himself the offices of Emperor and Pope. His desire seems to be to govern his subjects as absolute sovereign,—their bodies through the army, their souls through the Church. If he should succeed in dominating, directing, and universalizing the socialistic movement, he might even restore feudalism in an aggravated form. The outlook is not a pleasant one; and yet it does not follow that the Emperor is either an unwise man or a bad sovereign. It may well be questioned whether, with any other policy than his, it would be possible to harmonize the discordant elements of Germany, and make her strong against foreign foes. "To be, or not to be, that is the question" for her; and she may well find it more advisable to bear those ills she has—including loss of liberty—than, by revolution, to fly to others that she knows not of. From this point of view,

[1] Two years ago, a government organ published a violent attack upon him. The day after its appearance, when the Professor entered his class-room, his whole class, which was a large one, rose to their feet in dead but ominous silence. He almost broke down.

it is perhaps well that the Germans, being a learned rather than a cultured people (and learning is always confined to a small, select class), are willing to be ruled, and do not keenly feel the want of liberty. This is conclusively shown by their tendency toward socialism, which could be realized only under the form of an economic despotism.

No one can prophesy the future of Germany; but so much, at least, seems clear, that it will largely depend on the course pursued by the socialists. Three alternatives seem open to them: They may indefinitely continue their present opposition to the government, and then they can only be a source of weakness; or they may absorb the empire, transforming it into a feudal state, fatal to liberty and, therefore, unstable; or they may, in return for certain timely concessions, place their powerful organization at the service of the empire, and be its chief pillar of strength. This is the consummation that every friend of Germany and of humanity must devoutly wish. It would bring advantage to both sides and put an end to autocracy. The empire would have to abandon its attempt to return to mediæval military despotism, and allow its subjects large liberty of thought, speech, and action; while the socialists would have to abandon their notion of the state as a mere economic beehive, and accept it as the great institution for raising man above slavery to physical needs into spiritual freedom and culture. In this way Germany might be strong without being enslaved; and the present condition of things, against which all thoughtful men rebel, might come to an end.

THOMAS DAVIDSON.

The Forum

MAY, 1897.

THE PROGRESSIVE INHERITANCE TAX.

IT has become the fashion in certain quarters to speak of any person who proposes a change in our present inequitable tax system as one who advocates communism, populism, or at least socialism,—hoping thereby to bury a great issue beneath a weight of popular prejudice. I disclaim any connection or sympathy with these "isms"; but, as a result of my experience as Comptroller of the State of New York, I have become more and more impressed—I had almost said oppressed—with the growing inequality of taxation. In view of this fact, it will not be out of place to submit briefly to fair-minded criticism some of the reasons that have led me to believe that a change in the taxing system is necessary, and that a graduated progressive inheritance tax on personal property, which may be imposed upon the devolution of property, is in accord with (a) economic science; (b) enlightened and advanced national policy; and (c) the principles of justice.

(a) The earliest science of taxation justified the imposition of a property tax, upon the theory of benefit received or service rendered; in other words, the theory held that each person should be taxed according to the benefit received from the government, or that he should pay to the government the cost of the service rendered by the government for him. Adam Smith regarded the "benefit" or "service" theory as logically leading to proportionality in taxation, and that under such theory each person would be taxed according to the value of his property. Many other economists have arrived at the same conclusion. Proportionality of taxation, based upon the "benefit" or "ser-

Copyright, 1896, by The Forum Publishing Company.
Permission to re-publish articles is reserved.

vice" theory, therefore, became at one time the ideal to be sought in taxation; and the influence of that school is felt to-day. It is true that if this ideal were even approximated to in actual practice, far less cause for complaint would exist; and it is equally true that to-day the highest purpose of the practical man in dealing with the question of taxation is generally to attain to something like proportionality. But from the beginning many eminent economic writers disputed the assertion that the "benefit" or "service" theory led to proportionality; and, as modern society developed and wealth increased, it became more and more evident that they were right. The rich largely protect their own property by their hired servants; they educate their children; and in their independence and exclusiveness do many other things for themselves which the public does for the less fortunate. In these later times, however, the benefits conferred upon the average citizen by the government have been greatly increased. Free schools have been established and extended; charities designed to help almost every human misfortune are open to all; and in many other ways gratuitous aid is given to the poorest citizen. Thus the benefits which the government confers upon the rich man, or the service which it renders him, clearly do not increase proportionally with his wealth. To justify taxation, therefore, some new theory was necessary; and modern economic science says that we should pay taxes because we are a part of the government, and, in strengthening and supporting that which is so important a part of ourselves, we contribute to our own security, advantage, and happiness. Reasonable consideration should consequently be given to that which will best serve the entire state. Taxation is a necessity of government; but that necessity should be met by an equitable distribution of the burden. And the burden should be so adjusted as to be the least onerous; the weight being placed, within reasonable limitations, where it can be most easily borne.

The "faculty" or "ability" theory follows logically from this idea, —that taxes should be distributed somewhat according to men's ability to pay them. The propriety of the application of this theory, and the injustice of a proportional tax have been often illustrated. A tax of 10 per cent taken from an income of $500 may deprive a man and his family of some of the necessaries of life; while a tax of 10 per cent taken from an income of $100,000 would deprive no one of anything except expensive luxuries, or an addition to wealth. It is not to the highest interest of the state that the physical comforts of the family whose income is only $500 should be thus limited, nor is it to the interest of any constituent part of the state; and every person who can do so should assist in preventing it.   Higher civilization is marked by a greater diversity of wants; and the best policy of the state is not to make the rich richer, but to help the man of small or moderate means, in order that he may enjoy more of the comforts and advantages of civilization : hence some of the burden which proportional taxation would place on the man whose income is only $500 should be placed on the "ability" of the $100,000 man to pay.   It has been said that there should be something like an equality of sacrifice between them.   Lincoln's homely expression, "It is easier to pay a large sum when you have it than a small sum when you have n't it," has a vein of modern political economy in it.   This idea did not originate with the socialist: it was the thought of the political economist and the humanitarian.

It does not follow from this that the whole tax should be borne by the rich.   Every person should contribute something to the support of the government under which he lives: his appreciation of its favors and value is increased by reasonable sacrifices which he is compelled to make for it.   Again, no taxation should be so burdensome as to weaken the desire to acquire wealth.   That desire, held within proper limits, must always be recognized as a great factor in national prosperity; nor should such taxes be so burdensome as to encourage wholesale evasion or transfer of property.   These and many other economic laws form a safeguard against any radical or confiscatory tax.   John Stuart Mill, in his "Political Economy," says:—

"I conceive that inheritances and legacies exceeding a certain amount are highly proper subjects for taxation, and that the revenue from them should be as great as can be made without giving rise to evasions by donations during life, or concealment of property, such as it would be impossible adequately to check. The principle of graduation (as it is called), that is, levying a larger percentage on a larger sum, though its application to general taxation would be, in my opinion, objectionable, seems to me both just and expedient as applied to inheritance and legacy duties."

Prof. Seligman, of Columbia University, whose writings on questions of taxation are most logical, exhaustive, and clear, and of which I have made use says, in his "Progressive Taxation" (p. 215):—

"From the standpoint both of production and consumption true equality of taxable faculty means progressive taxation of inheritances.   Moreover, scarcely any of the objections which attach to the progressive rate in our general property tax applies here.   The third argument is what we have termed a special compensatory argument.   This alone would suffice, even if the other arguments were inadequate; for, even granting that proportion is the ideal to be kept in view, it may be said, with some measure of truth, that our existing taxes fall with less severity on the wealthy class. Not only are many of our indirect taxes regressive in their nature, but the general property tax in its practical application is scarcely less objectionable in this respect. A progressive rate in the succession duties, especially where personalty is concerned, would simply tend to reëstablish the desired proportionality. . . . It is the function of progressive taxation not so much to obtain increased revenue as to apportion the burden more equally among the taxpayers."

Quotations might be multiplied indefinitely. Among others who regard a progressive inheritance tax as wise and just may be mentioned such eminent economists and statesmen as Prof. Ely, of Johns Hopkins University; Prof. West, of Columbia College; Sir William Vernon Harcourt; Pierson, the distinguished Dutch professor and minister of finance; Cohen-Stuart, Buckingham, Neumann, Meyer, and many others. These gentlemen are not socialists; indeed nearly all of them have taken strong ground against socialism and communism.

It may perhaps have escaped the memory of the American of the present day that the United States income tax of the Civil War was progressive, varying at last from 5 to 10 per cent; and no less a person than Secretary Fessenden defended the principle and recommended its extension on the ground that "the ability to pay increased in more than arithmetical proportion." Thus it will be seen that, while the student has produced the theory, such practical and eminent statesmen as Fessenden, Harcourt, and Pierson have endorsed it. The principle of progression seems justified in theory, and is demanded in practice to obtain even proportionality.

(b) The general property tax—a tax levied alike upon all property, real and personal—embodies the most primitive idea of taxation. As the nations of Europe advanced beyond the ideas of securing revenue by predatory war, by the king's right to take any property because it was his own, by voluntary or forced loans, or by the grant of exclusive rights or privileges, they recognized that some principle of regularity and justice must be introduced in taxation; and they successively, almost without exception, adopted the general property tax. Probably in the early stages of a nation's development this may be as fair a tax as can be imposed. Property then consists almost entirely of real estate and tangible effects, which cannot elude the assessor's vigilance. But, as the nation progresses, an ever-increasing proportion of its wealth is represented by intangible property, which can and does elude the most stringent laws and the most active officials. A general property tax then becomes practically a single tax on real estate, and more and more regressive; that is, in general, the larger the estate, the smaller in proportion the tax it pays. That New York is no exception to this rule will be shown hereafter. Nation after nation, recognizing the impossibility of doing justice in taxation by a general property tax, has abandoned the attempt to tax personalty directly, and is seeking to accomplish the purpose by other means,—particularly by an inheritance tax. The only civilized countries in the world to-day that still retain a direct tax on personal property are the United States, Switzerland, and a part of Australia.

Apart from every other consideration, a progressive inheritance tax is amply justified as a means of reaching proportionality in taxation. As a rule, the larger the estate, the larger the proportion of it invested in personalty, and the larger the proportion which escapes taxation. Laws can only be enacted to do justice in a great majority of cases. Human wisdom cannot devise a law which will do justice in every case. A reasonably progressive inheritance tax might give inequality of taxation in some cases; but in the great majority of cases it would simply reach a fair approximation of proportional taxation. The essentials of a system of taxation are conceded to be the collection of the necessary revenue for the state at the smallest possible expense consistent with the equal and fair distribution of the burden. Governor Hoffman, in a Message to the Legislature in 1871, said:—

"The interests of the people require a method of taxation at once equitable, effective, and free from unnecessary oppression; one which will yield the requisite revenue, while subjecting them as little as possible to inquisitorial vexation, and which shall be attended with the least expense for official service, and afford the fewest temptations to fraud, concealment, or evasion."

It may be said of the inheritance tax in general that it has the great advantages which are, or should be, sought by governments in every tax system; to wit, difficulty of evasion, impossibility of shifting, and ease and cheapness of collection; and, in addition, as Prof. West says, "as to the time of payment, it is the most convenient of all direct taxes." Certainly the person who has died can be put to no inconvenience by it; and the person who is receiving a fortune for which he has not labored or sacrificed can afford to pay it. An inheritance tax of 10 per cent has been claimed by political economists to furnish an additional encouragement to industry and thrift, for the reason that the person knows that his estate is to be diminished by that amount; and the reduction is not large enough to cause discouragement.

A graduated inheritance tax, progressive according to degree of relationship, has for many years been a feature of the tax system of nearly every country in Europe. This system seems to have had its origin in Holland, and to have spread thence to almost the whole Western world. An inheritance tax, progressive as the estate increases, is to us a feature of more recent growth, although it was a form of Roman taxation. In modern times, this latter principle seems to have been first adopted practically and successfully in Switzerland; and it is now employed in taxation in nearly all the Swiss cantons. In 1892, Holland adopted a new tax system, a notable feature of it being progressive property and income taxes; and these were advocated and sustained by the government upon the "faculty" or "ability to pay" theory. In 1894, England adopted the progressive principle in her inheritance tax; the rate varying, according to the value of the estate, from 1 to 8 per cent. These rates were in addition to a tax varying from 1 to 10 per cent, according to the degree of relationship. The English tax, therefore, runs from 2 to 18 per cent.

If one were to select the two countries of the world least influenced by communistic or socialistic ideas, he would certainly select Holland and England; and, while the fact that they have not been affected by these "isms" is due mostly to the character of their people, their freedom from them is also due to the promptness with which they adopt principles of government which are demonstrated to be just and politic.

Nearly all the dependencies of England have adopted the progressive inheritance tax. In Victoria the rates are progressive as the estate increases, running from 1 to 10 per cent; in Queensland, the same; in New South Wales, 1 to 5 per cent; in New Zealand, 2½ to 10 per cent; in Tasmania, 2 to 3 per cent; in the Province of Ontario, 2½ to 10 per cent; in Nova Scotia, 2½ to 10 per cent.

The United States is practically the only English-speaking nation in the world that has not adopted the progressive principle. There is now pending in the *Corps Legislatif* in France, with probability of passage, a bill for a progressive inheritance tax varying from 1 to 10 per cent.

Nearly all these progressive-inheritance-tax acts have been adopted within the last ten years.

A quotation from Prof. Seligman's "Essays in Taxation" (p. 339) seems not inappropriate here:—

"After this survey it is needless to point out the lessons applicable to the United States. The economic conditions of the civilized world are everywhere fast becoming the same ; and upon the changes in economic condition depend the changes in financial systems. In old Europe, as well as in young Australia, the same tendency is unmistakable—the trend to greater justice in taxation. When four widely distant countries reform their systems almost simultaneously, and upon the same general lines, the inference is irresistible that the causes of the movement are of far more than mere local significance. To shut our eyes to this world-wide movement would be supreme folly : to profit by its lessons and to bring our own system into line with the demands of modern science and to modern conditions will be no less wise than it is inevitable."

(c) Every person who has dealt either practically or theoretically with taxation must have been impressed with the fact that men, honorable in all other dealings, and who would under no circumstances take a dollar which did not rightfully belong to them, will shirk, without scruple, the burden of taxation which the law has imposed upon them; and thus their generally less fortunate neighbors must pay more than their fair share. Because this practice is so common, it seems almost to have acquired moral sanction.

Let us consider how the idea of proportionality, which the opponents of a progressive inheritance tax so loudly approve, is in practice realized. It does not require argument to prove that nine out of ten men, worth from one to twenty thousand dollars, have their property in tangible form. It is in a home, a farm, a shop, or some other form easily reached by the assessor. On the contrary, that which is owned by a man worth more than a quarter of a million dollars, will be, in three out of four cases, in intangible form, so that the assessor never learns of its existence until after the owner's death. There has hardly been a report of a State financial or assessing officer in the United States in the past twenty-five years that has not discussed, in a tone almost of despair, the wholesale escape of personal property from taxation. Hundreds of legislative committees and commissions whose duty it was to revise tax laws have joined in this chorus. The same complaint comes from States that have adopted a listing system or other more stringent methods ; and the difference in results in these States hardly seems to warrant the moral hazard involved.

I think it will be readily conceded that in personal property New York is proportionately the richest of all the States. And yet, in the percentage of its assessed personalty to its assessed realty, it is the lowest among the wealthier States. The assessed value of real estate in New York is \$3,952,451,417, and of personal property, \$539,863,305, or $12\frac{6}{10}$ per cent that of the realty. The following table shows that the same difference exists elsewhere, though not in so marked a degree.

State.	Real Property.	Personal.	Per cent.
New Jersey...................	$640,188,332	$134,210,000	$17\frac{4}{10}$
Ohio........................	1,215,540,454	528,977,260	30
Illinois	687,510,306	143,800,000	17
Indiana	813,820,000	286,000,000	26
Massachusetts	1,964,834,106	577,614,889	$22\frac{7}{10}$
Pennsylvania.................	2,471,000,000	647,000,000	$20\frac{8}{10}$

Some interesting facts may be gathered from a comparison by counties of New York's table of valuations. The proportion which the personalty bears to the realty in the various counties ranges from six-tenths of 1 per cent in Richmond County, to $22\frac{1}{2}$ per cent in New York. The counties which show the largest percentage of personalty in the rural districts are Washington County, with nearly 20 per cent, Livingston, with nearly 14 per cent, and Jefferson and Genesee, with 13 per cent. Kings County, containing the city of Brooklyn, has but $4\frac{1}{2}$ per cent; Monroe County, with the city of Rochester, has but $5\frac{6}{10}$ per cent; Erie County, with the city of Buffalo, has but $6\frac{4}{10}$ per cent; Onondaga County, with the city of Syracuse, has but $6\frac{7}{10}$ per cent. The counties in the first group are largely devoted to farming. Does anyone for a moment suppose that these farming counties have a larger percentage of personal property than the counties in which are located the flourishing cities named ?

The amount of equalized personalty paying taxes to the State of New York in 1896 was $459,859,526; and, by the report of the Superintendent of the Banking Department, it appears that the capital, surplus, and undivided profits of the banks, trust companies, and safe-deposit companies of the State was $311,386,372. Under the law these institutions could not escape taxation. They are required to pay on the value of their capital stock; and that includes the surplus and undivided profits. There was then only $148,473,154 of personal property over and above the banking and trust-company capital which paid taxes in 1896. In 1857, Sanford E. Church, then Comptroller, felt called upon in his annual report to direct the attention of the Legislature to the way in which personal property was escaping taxation. He reported the amount of personalty then paying taxes to the State to be $319,897,155, of which $110,000,000 was banking capital, leaving $209,897,155 of other personal property then paying taxes; that is to say, in round numbers, there was $61,000,000 more of such personal property paying taxes in 1857 than in 1896. Yet everybody knows that personal property in the State of New York has increased enormously in the last forty years.

One hundred and seven estates were selected at random in the Comptroller's office, with the amount of appraised personal property found after death; and the amount of personal property, on which the decedent in each case was assessed the year before death, was ascertained. The estates were selected from various portions of the State. Of the one hundred and seven estates, thirty-four, ranging from $54,559 to $3,319,500, were assessed the year before decedent's death *absolutely nothing whatever*. The following table gives the figures in the remaining 73 cases :—

Amount of Appraised Personal Property after death.	Amount Assessed to Decedent year before death.	Amount of Appraised Personal Property after death.	Amount Assessed to Decedent year before death.
$3,544,343	$15,000	$247,358	$10,000
2,544,008	10,000	221,353	5,000
1,400,000	15,000	3,592,846	20,000
2,756,323	20,000	2,188,710	5,000
10,252,857	500,000	319,986	10,000
1,222,116	10,000	107,233	5,000
1,000,000	10,000	2,876,387	18,000
1,167,015	5,000	645,147	15,000
1,303,057	15,000	2,327,075	55,000
3,458,408	80,000	121,858	18,000
1,083,928	12,000	102,432	6,412
1,146,101	5,000	166,290	51,000
3,800,000	100,000	160,960	30,000
4,703,424	220,000	1,016,227	28,000
3,060,238	75,000	1,649,018	10,000
1,100,000	12,000	2,125,577	400,000
1,500,000	100,000	1,374,039	12,000
1,077,357	100,000	3,284,819	25,000
1,484,265	87,000	1,056,809	10,000
934,164	50,000	2,770,570	200,000
1,160,629	10,000	342,672	3,000
1,063,406	75,000	411,212	5,000
1,000,000	100,000	6,685,785	100,000
1,600,000	50,000	217,844	10,000
1,500,000	50,000	388,429	20,000
6,500,000	160,000	410,058	30,000
800,000	40,000	1,435,816	10,000
800,000	50,000	1,160,656	20,000
3,500,000	20,000	1,117,908	5,000
1,296,516	34,000	361,678	5,000
80,000,000	500,000	943,979	30,000
170,655	10,000	947,504	10,000
260,214	5,000	441,543	3,000
526,585	25,000	2,015,852	5,000
312,894	35,000	677,644	3,000
263,266	20,000	306,183	2,000
539,552	10,000		

No names have been given in this table, because these ·cases are neither singular nor exceptional. The decedents were not sinners above all the men that dwelt in New York; but they simply did that which everybody in the community was doing. These one hundred and seven estates disclosed personalty to the appraiser aggregating $215,132,366; and yet the decedents, the year before their respective deaths, had been assessed in the aggregate on personal property to the amount of $3,819,412,—or on $1\frac{77}{100}$ per cent of the actual value of the property. This table is both interesting and instructive. It shows not only wholesale evasion of taxation, but ridiculous disparity in assessing even the $1\frac{77}{100}$ per cent. It shows also that thirty-four, or almost one-third, of the estates absolutely escaped the tax, and that, in the estates which did pay, the tax varied from two-tenths of 1 per cent to nearly 19 per cent. All these facts furnish cumulative evidence that, in its practical operation, the present system is defective, unfair, unjust, and monstrous; and the inquiry is pertinent, "Why longer continue it?" Why not, instead, levy an inheritance tax which shall be approximately a payment of back taxes evaded or not imposed during life—a tax paid in a lump sum once in a lifetime? The estates above given were impartially selected without previous knowledge of the amounts at which they had been assessed; and I believe they may be taken as fairly indicative of the proportion of personal property in New York which is actually paying taxes.

It would seem, therefore, that it would be a conservative estimate to say that the $148,473,154 of non-banking personalty that paid tax, as shown above, bore the same relation to the whole amount of personalty in the State that the $1\frac{77}{100}$ of the above estates which paid tax before death bore to the appraised value after death. It is conservative because there was undoubtedly included in the $1\frac{77}{100}$ per cent a considerable amount of bank stock.

If this were so, then 100 per cent, or the whole non-banking personalty of the State, would be $8,388,313,779. Add to this the banking capital and we have, as the total personalty of the State, $8,699,700,151.

Nearly all this enormous amount of personal property is subject to tax in the same manner as real estate. There are a few exceptions; the most important being government bonds and the refunding bonds of our cities. The total bonded debt of the United States is $1,598,758,-100. Admitting for the moment that one-fourth of these bonds are held in the State of New York (and everyone will concede this to be an over-estimate), and we have $399,689,525 of government bonds exempt from taxation. The amount of municipal indebtedness cannot exceed 10 per centum of assessed valuation, except for water purposes. The water debt will not exceed 5 per cent of the assessed valuation of our cities. The assessed valuation of the real estate of our cities is, in round numbers, $2,875,000,000. Fifteen per centum of this amount is $431,250,000,—which certainly would form the limit of the bonded debt of our cities. New York City's total bonded debt is $188,153,-107; and of this, $34,936,900, or a little over 18½ per cent, is refunding bonds. The amount of refunding bonds would thus not exceed $80,000,000 in the whole State. Deducting these two amounts from our estimate of personal property for the State, and there is left $8,220,-010,625 of personalty taxable under the law. But we are told that much of this property, if taxed, would be unjustly taxed, because it is in the form of mortgages on real estate already subjected to its full burden of taxation, or in stocks of corporations the property of which is largely real estate, and that taxation of personalty in such cases amounts to double taxation. A careful calculation of the amount of real estate assessed to corporations in the city of Buffalo disclosed $41,-095,030: the total assessed value of the city's real estate is $225,485,-795. Thus 18½ per cent of the real estate is assessed to corporations. In that city unusually large tracts of land are held by land companies, and the railroad holdings of real estate are very large ; so that the percentage of corporate holdings of real estate in the city of Buffalo would surely be as great as in the State at large. The equalized assessed value of the real estate of the State of New York for the year 1896 was $3,908,853,377; and 18½ per cent of that amount, or $711,-411,314, may be taken as fairly representing the value of the corporate real estate of the State. The total of the mortgages on New York's real estate, as reported in the last United States census, was $2,276,-932,371. Deducting these two amounts, there is still left $5,231,666,-940 of untaxed personal property (or considerably more than the entire assessed value of all New York's real and personal property) which, according to every principle of justice and fairness, ought to be taxed. The burden of taxation on real estate is, therefore, at least double what it should be ; and a large portion of this burden falls upon our farmers, our mechanics who own their own homes, and our men of moderate means. Is this right, or is it good public policy ?

There can be no doubt that private ownership of property is one of the great civilizing forces; that the man who has acquired a home is made thereby a better citizen; that the government is more necessary to him; and that he is more fixed in his loyalty, more reliable in his principles, and less liable to be a communist or an anarchist. For this reason, if for no other, men should be encouraged to acquire property, and not punished for it by being made to pay double the amount of taxes which proportionately belongs to them to pay. Roscher, in his interesting work on political economy, speaking of the tendency to a conflict between the rich and the poor, says in substance, that such a conflict would be inevitable were it not for that great class who are neither rich nor poor, and who shade up gradually in their property holdings from the poor to the rich, and who stand as a wall of defence for the rich against the intensity of life and desperation of the poor. A moment's reflection will convince anyone that this is so. Should this great class be punished for the protection they thus afford the rich? It is upon them, as I have already said, that a greater burden of taxation falls than, according to any proportional, equitable, or politic principle, they should be compelled to bear.

In every exciting political contest, such as that of 1896, the great question which agitates the mind of a man interested in the result is, "How will the farmer and the industrious and intelligent mechanic act?" There was no doubt in 1896 where the rich man would stand; but there was grave doubt as to what the farmer and mechanic might conclude to do, because everyone realized that the condition of these men was particularly hard. Unless some effort is made to lighten their burden, their attitude may become still more doubtful. The comparatively few dollars of tax which the farmer or the mechanic has to pay seem such a paltry sum to the multi-millionaire that he cannot realize how hard their acquisition has been, nor that necessaries or comforts of life have been sacrificed in saving them. But such is the case; and no one need congratulate himself that these men do not fully realize that they are paying more than they should pay.

As to the cry that property would be driven from the State by the progressive inheritance tax, I may say that this cry is not new. It was raised in the State of New York when the proposition was made to levy a general property tax in 1842; it again arose in 1880, when the proposition was made to tax corporations; and it was heard yet more loudly in 1885 when the act to tax inheritances was passed. Yet New York has increased her corporations and wealth at least proportionately with other States since these acts became law. Consideration certainly is due to the question of what is just and right. No nation or State can lose, in the long run, by pursuing a course of justice.

Charles Sumner said that "Nothing is settled which is not right"; and on this principle our system of taxation cannot be regarded as settled. I, for one, do not believe that any patriotic man of wealth will expatriate himself, or remove from the State whose protection and opportunities enabled him or his ancestor to accumulate a great fortune, simply because his estate will be called upon to pay its fair proportion of taxes when it passes to heirs who had little or nothing to do with its accumulation.

- The average rate of State tax in New York for the past thirty-two years has been not far from 4.2223 mills on the dollar per annum. Multiply this by thirty-two, the average of human life, and you have a tax of $13\frac{5}{10}$ per cent, which the farmer and the owner of real estate have paid to the State of New York in that period. What hardship is it to the man whose personal property has escaped taxation all through his life, or to his heir, that his estate must pay a tax of 10 per cent after his death? As has been shown, the removal of personal property from the State would affect very little the amount of annual tax which is now collected. So little of it is taxed that practically it would be almost as well, and in point of honesty far better, to abandon the attempt to tax it in a general tax. There is abundant testimony that such a tax has not tended to drive capital away from countries in which it has been adopted; and in some of these—notably the Swiss cantons and some of the British colonies—the conditions are very similar to our own. A person might move from one canton or colony to another without leaving his country in the same way that he might move from one State to another and still be a citizen of the United States; but no perceptible transfer of estates is reported.

The inheritance tax has been held by the courts to be not a tax on property, but rather a tax on its devolution; but, while I do not propose to discuss the constitutionality of progression in such a tax, I believe a fair interpretation of the decisions shows that it is not a violation of the Constitution of the United States. The language of the United States Supreme Court, in Kentucky Railroad Tax cases, 115 U. S., 321, seems strongly in point :—

"A State law for the valuation of property and the assessment of taxes thereon, which provides for the classification of property subject to its provisions into different classes; which makes for one class one set of provisions as to modes and methods of ascertaining the value, and as to the right of appeal, and different provisions for another class of those subjects, *but which provides for the impartial application of the same means and method to all constituents of each*

*class, so that the law shall operate equally and uniformly on all persons in simi-
lar circumstances, denies to no person affected by it ' equal protection of the laws'
within the meaning of the Fourteenth Amendment to the United States Constitution.*"

I think I have answered Mr. Belmont's suggestion, in the March
FORUM, that I had forgotten the teachings of our forefathers in my
proposal for progressive inheritance taxation. I have said that, in
the earlier stages of a nation's development, a general property tax is
probably as fair as any, because property is then nearly all in tangible
form. So I approve of the wisdom of our fathers in adopting that
system of taxation at the time of its adoption. But, in the century
that has intervened, economic conditions have undergone marvellous
changes ; and no one who has examined the question at all can for a
moment claim that the general property tax is now a proportional tax.
It is highly regressive, favoring the rich, and is as repugnant to a just
recognition of our present economic conditions, as is slavery (which our
forefathers also established) to our present moral convictions.

JAMES A. ROBERTS.

HAS THE SENATE DEGENERATED?

WHEN George F. Hoar first took his seat in the United States Senate, bringing up from the House the fruits of eight years' experience as a Representative and that serious interest in the public business that for more than a quarter of a century has made him a conspicuous figure at Washington, he gazed about him upon a body of men of whom nearly one-half were already distinguished for their ability and influence, while several of them were destined to still higher honors and larger responsibilities in the service of the nation.

It was on March 5, 1877, at the first meeting of the Senate of the Forty-fifth Congress, called in extraordinary session by President Hayes for the confirmation of executive appointments. There sat Anthony, whom Rhode Island obeyed and the country respected, and Allison, then as now one of the most just-minded men of his party. Thomas F. Bayard was there, a man of gifts and true democracy, whom a Democratic President was to call to his aid as Secretary of State and, later on, to the first ambassadorship. The lamented Beck sat there for Kentucky, and Newton Booth, the finest mind ever placed at the service of the State of California in either House of Congress. Mr. Blaine, whom Mr. Hoar did not like, and Roscoe Conkling, who did not like Mr. Hoar, were the two most powerful partisan chieftains in the Chamber. David Davis, a very able man, was equally noted for his independence of party. Edmunds and Thurman, good friends in private, fair foes in politics, expounded the Constitution with a breadth and soundness of learning unknown to the Senate since they retired leaving no successors. Windom, Lamar, Howe, and Kirkwood were later on to be called to Cabinet places, and Stanley Matthews to the bench of the Supreme Court. Other men of real strength were Oliver P. Morton, the eloquent Benjamin H. Hill, of Georgia, Justin S. Morrill, Angus Cameron, Hannibal Hamlin, Francis Kernan, and Plumb, of Kansas.

Here were twenty-two men every one of whom was a moving force in the work of the Senate. Every one made his influence felt in committee or in debate, and imposed himself upon the public attention as a distinct and energetic personality.

As the eye of Mr. Hoar roams about the Chamber in quest of the notables who take part in the proceedings of the more numerous Senate of to-day, it rests upon no figure so great and striking as the greatest of these, nor marks out more than a score who are in any way distinguishable from the mute herd whose senatorial activities are limited to the hunting of patronage and the care of private pension bills. As I study the list, I see no names but these that, under the most liberal interpretation of the term, could be called distinguished: Morgan, Allison, Hale, Frye, Gorman, Hawley, Lodge, Hoar, C. K. Davis, Chandler, Platt, Hanna, Foraker, Quay, Aldrich, Elkins, Tillman, Mills, Gray, and Stewart—twenty in all.

There are no great names here. What Senator among them can pretend to a tithe of Blaine's power to stir the hearts of the people? How unpersuasive in leadership would the ablest of these men be if he should set his heart on the Presidency and sally forth among the masses to build up a following. There would be no inspiration in the appeal of any of them. They would be impotent, ineffective, absurd. What constitutional lawyer is there here to match Edmunds or Thurman? Platt may be the equal of Conkling in political leadership, and Quay may offset Oliver P. Morton as the boss of a State: but the moral weight of Bayard, Beck, Booth, David Davis, Windom, and Lamar, or of Edmunds and Thurman already mentioned, has no counterpoise; and the Senate of to-day must kick the beam.

Let us broaden the comparison. If, as Mr. Hoar so strenuously contends in THE FORUM for April, the Senate has not degenerated, it must now be of such high distinction that we may, without fear, set it over against the Senate of a time, now remote, when the roll bore names so illustrious that our children know what they stand for in the nation's history. I trust Senator Hoar will not accuse me of taking an unfair advantage if I go back half a century to a decade when the slavery question roused the patriotism and kindled the passions of the country, and centred its attention upon the giants contending in the Senate Chamber for the settlement of sectional differences that only later and sterner disputants could adjust. I will select the most conspicuous names that stood on the rolls of the Senate during the ten years from 1843 to 1853, the Twenty-eighth to the Thirty-second Congress, inclusive, and, for comparison and contrast, the most shining names among those elected to the Senate from 1889 to the term ending with 1899, — the ten years including the Fifty-first Congress and the Fifty-fifth.

From 1843 to 1853: Senators Thomas H. Benton, James Buchanan,

Rufus Choate, Daniel S. Dickinson, John A. Dix, Levi Woodbury, Silas Wright, John C. Calhoun, Lewis Cass, Simon Cameron, Sam Houston, Reverdy Johnson, Daniel Webster, Thomas Corwin, Jefferson Davis, Stephen A. Douglas, R. M. T. Hunter, Salmon P. Chase, Henry Clay, Thomas Ewing, John C. Frémont, John P. Hale, Robert C. Winthrop, William H. Seward, James A. Bayard, Solomon Foot, Henry S. Foote, Hamilton Fish, Hannibal Hamlin, Charles Sumner, and Benjamin F. Wade.

From 1889 to 1899: Senators Morgan, Allison, Hale, Frye, Gorman, Lodge, Hoar, Sherman, Foraker, Hanna, Aldrich, Justin S. Morrill, Pugh, Teller, Palmer, Voorhees, Vest, W. E. Chandler, David B. Hill, Brice, Quay, Don Cameron, Mills, Elkins, Hawley, Cullom, Peffer, Vilas, Evarts, Stewart, Vance, and John P. Jones.

I do not expect Senator Hoar to throw up his brief after an inspection of these lists. No doubt he does intellectual homage to Webster and Clay and Calhoun and the men who were grouped about them in the 'forties. He reveres them as he reveres the second aorist, something majestic and pervading, but shadowy and far off; while the Senators with whom he now every day sits or strives look big to him and dwarf the figures farther down the gallery. Besides, I am afraid the Massachusetts Senator is not imbued with the scientific spirit. To a candid world, the comparison I have made will be convincing, I think. In the laboratory of social and political science, these exhibits will suffice for a demonstration that the Senate *has* degenerated. To employ the lingo of the neo-scientific charlatanry, the stigmata of degeneration are visible upon the body and in the behavior of the Senate. I prefer the reasoning and the terminology of the older and sounder men of science, the Darwins and Spencers and Tyndalls who have traced for us the laws of change in the organic world. Accordingly, I should say with them that the Senate has undergone a variation from the type. The upper House of Congress is an organic structure : it is one of the organs of the Republic. Its present form and functions are the result of evolution, up or down, from the original type. If we would measure the possible changes it has undergone, we must examine the early structure in comparison with the structure of to-day, and note the divergences.

The Senator admits that "the Senate must be justified by the behavior of the men who compose it now, and not by the behavior of the men who composed it in the time of our fathers"; and he finds it "interesting to examine anew the original constitution of the Senate, and to see how far it has met the expectations of the Fathers."

18

We know what were the "expectations of the Fathers." In the Federal Convention of 1787, Edmund Randolph, of Virginia, in giving his views as to the constitution of the "second branch" of the Congress, declared that "it ought to be made much smaller than the first, so small as to be exempt from the passionate proceedings to which numerous assemblies are liable"; since, in tracing to their origin the evils under which the Federation labored, "every man found it to be in the turbulence and follies of democracy," and a good Senate seemed most likely to answer the purpose of a check against "this tendency of our governments." No part of the creative work of the Convention was the subject of more anxious consideration, or was more carefully matured. In order to insure a measure of experience and soberness of judgment, no person was to be elected Senator until he had attained the age of thirty years. As the Senate was, with the President, to exercise control over foreign relations, it was prescribed that Senators must have been for nine years citizens of the United States; while a citizenship of five years, with a minimum age limit of twenty-five, sufficed to qualify for election to the House. In those days the possession of wealth brought no reproach upon any man; and General Pinckney seriously proposed, and Dr. Franklin seconded the motion, that Senators should have no salary, since that body ought to be composed of men of wealth and position. The authors of the "Federalist" essays, writing in support of the Constitution and with the purpose of procuring its adoption by the States, dwelt with expository fulness and visible pride upon the constitution of the Senate. Historic precedents of Greece and Rome and all nations that had set up a second house of legislature were marshalled to show that the Convention had profited by the wisdom of the ancients, and had improved upon it. Hamilton wrote:—

"Through the medium of the State Legislatures—which are select bodies of men, and which are to appoint the members of the national Senate—there is reason to expect that this branch will generally be composed with peculiar care and judgment; that these circumstances promise greater knowledge and more extensive information in the national councils, and that they will be less apt to be tainted by the spirit of faction and more out of reach of those occasional ill humors or temporary prejudices and propensities which, in smaller societies, frequently contaminate the public councils."

What a picture of the Senate as it appeared in February last when Senator Cameron was pressing a resolution that would have brought on a war with Spain, and Senator Morgan was stamping on the Arbitration Treaty to relieve a spirit overburdened with hatred of Grover Cleveland and Richard Olney! Was Jay any nearer the mark when he prophesied that in the choice of Senators the votes of the State Legislatures "will be directed to those men only who have become the most distinguished by their virtue and in whom the people have perceived just grounds for confidence."

Was it in this spirit that the New York Legislature chose Edward Murphy, Jr. ? Was it after a prayerful search for men of virtue and ability among the available male population of the State that the choice of the Albany Solons fell on Mr. Platt? And did the Pennsylvania legislators send Quay to the Senate because they discovered in him "just grounds for confidence "?

Here is the original type of the Senate as clearly present in the minds and pictured forth in the language of the framers of the Constitution; and along witlf that delineation I have presented some individual deviations that show how it has failed to meet "the expectations of the Fathers." It is not in individual variations, however, that we can best trace degenerative changes, but by a study from time to time of the behavior of the entire body when engaged in the performance of its functions.

The Senate is now fighting for its place, and angrily protesting that it ought to have the respect and confidence of the country.

In the old days, Presidents were fain to consult at every step the wise, experienced, and eminent men of the upper branch. The people reverenced them and, by their greatness, proudly affirmed the greatness of America.

In comparison with the heroic age when Webster and Calhoun and Clay and Douglas and the fiery tribunes of the "peculiar institution " compelled the attention of every intelligent man and woman in the country and quite overshadowed the Executive by their dominating contentions, the Senate nowadays is a parvenu family, struggling for social place and recognition, sure neither of its clothes nor its manners, ignored by the great, rebuffed at every door, and ridiculed by the whole community. You can find fairly intelligent men who would be unable to name more than two or three Senators of the United States. It could not have been so in Webster's time.

> " We are selfish men.
> Oh ! raise us up, return to us again ;
> And give us manners, virtue, freedom, power."

Not long ago Senator Hoar personally listened to most conclusive evidence of the degeneracy of the Senate. During the discussion of the resolutions providing for the recognition of the sovereignty of the "Republic of Cuba," when Senators were mad with jingo frenzy and sober-minded people were apprehensive, Secretary Olney contemptuously remarked that the recognition of sovereignty was none of the Senate's business. It was exclusively a Presidential prerogative; and he very plainly intimated that the President would pay no attention to any resolutions relating to Cuban recognition which the Senate might be pleased to pass. Immediately there was a great ruffling of feathers among the Senators. The declaration of the Secretary of State was denounced as an affront, an outrage upon the Senate's dignity, and an attempt to abridge its constitutional powers. I do not know why Secretary Olney chose the unusual medium of a newspaper interview for this important utterance; but it is probable that there was at the moment no official channel through which he could communicate to the jingo Senators the salutary and needed information. The form and manner, no less than the matter, of the communication roused his and the President's enemies in the Senate to a pitch of rage, in which they freely exhibited themselves in full possession of the passions and the factious spirit from which the Fathers fondly imagined they would be free.

This very question of the respective powers of the legislative and the executive departments in the recognition of the sovereignty of newly created governments came up in the first Administration of Monroe, and again, in 1836, in the Administration of Jackson. Clay, while still a member of the House, in 1817, began to urge a prompt recognition of the revolted colonies of Spain in South America; and nearly twenty years later it fell to him, as chairman of the Senate Committee on Foreign Relations, to press for a speedy greeting to the Republic of Texas as a nation. In each case the Executive took its time: but in the courteous exchange of views each branch behaved with the dignity of conscious power; and in the case of the Spanish Republics it was not the Senate at all, but the House, that attempted to force the President's hand. President Tyler's plans for the annexation of Texas were checked by the Senate, which defeated his treaty. He could not control so strong a body: he could do nothing without it. He canvassed the strength of the opposition at every step, and sought to win over its members. Finally he was obliged to abandon the treaty, which required a two-thirds vote, and to ask that Texas be admitted by a joint resolution, for which a majority was sufficient. The weakness of Tyler, and the power of the Senators, both those who were for and those who were against annexation, were apparent throughout the contest. Polk could despatch Gen. Taylor to the Rio Grande, with instructions that meant war; but the moment Mexico prepared to accept the challenge he hastened to put the responsibility on Congress. To be sure, the Constitution required him to invoke the help of Congress if war was to be declared; but the support of Congress was necessary to make his war policy acceptable to the people. "Polk's war," they called it; but he was fortified behind the Senate's vote of 40 to 2 for money and troops. Both these Presidents intrigued and manoeuvred to win the coöperation of a body that was strong enough to have destroyed them, had they been rash enough to defy it. They were wise; and they consulted the Senate, as the Executive will always do when the Senate is also wise.

When Seward, annoyed by House resolutions declaring that the United States could not longer tolerate the presence of the French troops of Napoleon III in Mexico, wrote to Minister Dayton in Paris that "the question of recognition of foreign revolutionary or reactionary governments is one exclusively for the Executive and cannot be determined internationally by congressional action," the Senate did not shriek out that President Lincoln was a usurper and Seward his willing tool. On the contrary, Charles Sumner, as chairman of the Committee on Foreign Relations, rendered valuable assistance in carrying out the policy of the Secretary of State by discreetly pocketing every resolution about Mexico that was referred to his committee. Both the President and the Senate being inspired by the highest patriotic purposes, relations of confidence and coöperation naturally existed between them, by which the national welfare was promoted.

It has thus far been shown that the Senate has now no party leaders or constitutional expounders of such power as those whom Senator Hoar found in that Chamber when he entered it twenty years ago; that while some of the greatest names that have adorned the pages of American history were upon the roll of the Senate half a century ago, there is now no Senator, and in the last decade there has been none, who has impressed the world by his abilities or made the age illustrious by his achievements; that the Executive, instead of seeking the aid and counsel of the Senate, as was the earlier custom, is obliged to rebuke it for its officious and offensive meddling, and must resort to extraordinary means to thwart its mischievous intentions; that, in place of spontaneous tributes to its greatness, it constantly receives popular testimonials of want of confidence and respect, which provoke its members to undignified exhibitions of resentment; and that, by its obstructive and fractious behavior, the Senate has become a body totally unlike the type planned and created by the Fathers.   These changes constitute degeneracy.   The organism has undergone a marked modification of form and function.

But it is not alone by obstinate ill-doing that the Senate has forfeited the public respect.   In what it refuses to do, or does grudgingly under the lash of compulsion, it is unbearably exasperating.   The mulish stubbornness with which it has resisted the will of the people in respect to the Treaty of Arbitration is a flagrant example of degenerate practices.   That treaty was conceived in the spirit of higher civilization, of advancing humanity.   It was of that indisputable expediency that is an inherent quality of truth and honesty and justice. No right-minded man sufficiently advanced to have laid aside skins, and discarded the stone hatchet and the club, could have refrained from acclaiming the principle of arbitration as a happy means of escaping the barbarism of war.   The instrument had been perfected by the diligent labors of men incomparably abler and broader than any that now sit in the Senate.   It was such a pact as an enlightened branch of the treaty-making power would have ratified after a delay sufficient only to allow its chief statesmen to express worthily their pleasure at joining in a work of such beneficence.

Yet, from the moment it received the Treaty from the hands of the President, the United States Senate has railed at it and rent it savagely, as though it were a league with death.   Senators of twenty years' service have shown themselves not ashamed to plead the general issue against it; openly avowing a hostility to arbitration and to England, which it was their judgment the country also ought to feel.   Others have opposed ratification as a means of revenge upon Mr. Cleveland and Mr. Olney, and have been unable to conceal their detestable motive.   Still others, and I grieve to say that Senator Hoar is one of these, have put upon the Treaty unsightly and perverting patches of amendment that well-nigh extinguish its usefulness, and endanger its acceptance by England.

These are the characteristic procedures of a degenerate Legislature. It is impossible that in any Senate where sat a Webster or a Sumner the meaner and uncivilized half would, in so grave a business, achieve an almost unresisted triumph.   The savages would slink away before the majesty of their countenances, or be persuaded by the eloquence of their lips.

I suppose that when Senator Hoar invented the new social stratum which he describes as the American "populace"—a rank neologism as he employs the term—he had in mind the thousand or more bishops, clergymen, college presidents and professors, philanthropists, authors, jurists, and prominent men of affairs, who recently sent to the Senate their fervent prayer that the Arbitration Treaty might soon be ratified. This "cultivated and lettered populace" of ours is described with circumstance in Senator Hoar's FORUM article:—

"Our populace does not come from the poor or ignorant classes. It is made of very different material. It has white and clean hands. It parts its hair in the middle. . . . . It prates and chatters a good deal about the sentiment of honor and political purity; but it is never found doing any strenuous work on the honest side when these things are in peril. . . . . It contributes to public discussions nothing but sneers, or expressions of contempt or pessimistic despair. It is found quite as commonly on the wicked side as on the honest side."

On the heads of these learned blatherskites the Senator pours out his wrath with sacerdotal austerity as though he were the high-priest pronouncing upon the people the penalties of their impious conduct. Is not the Senate, by constitutional designation and the mode of its election, set far above the people to protect them from their own gusts of passion? May it be importuned by petition like a dirty little board of aldermen? Must it listen to lectures as to its duty from the turbulent milksops of the colleges and the pulpits? Shall its precious freedom of debate be abridged or its sage deliberations be hurried by the irresponsible clamor of bishops and judges? Every feeling heart will sympathize with the evident sense of injury under which the Massachusetts Senator declaims his arraignment of the white-handed and lettered mob. His position is deplorable, his task difficult. Nothing is so injurious to a man's dignity as to have it questioned. And when the dignity with which the Senators solemnly invest themselves is stripped off with irreverence and jeers they must be pardoned if they show some irritation.

Upon two other occasions within the last four years the Senate has stood out in stiff-necked opposition to the sentiment of the country. If its attitude toward the Arbitration Treaty was barbarous, its prolonged haggling over the repeal of the Sherman Silver-Purchase Act in 1893 was wicked. The nation was in the throes of a financial convulsion. Upon the urgent recommendation of the President, the House of Representatives passed a repeal bill promptly. The Senate held it under pointless and inane debate for two months, while confidence fled the country and business went to rack and ruin. Even when this immeasurable harm had been done, it was only in obedience to extraordinary outside pressure and by a narrow majority that the Senate finally assented to the repeal. In its treatment of the Wilson Tariff Bill of 1894 it showed the same unreasoning disregard of the public wish and interest. Considerations of low tariff and high tariff do not enter at all into my condemnation of its behavior. The Bill was held in the Senate not for amendment along the lines of either policy, but for individual and disconnected assaults upon its schedules of such strange persistency that men grew suspicious, and at length became convinced that no honorable motive could actuate certain of the Senators in their highwayman-like attitude toward it.

If a comparative study of the personnel and efficiency of the Senate at different periods and the record of its malfeasance and non-feasance afford insufficient proof of its degeneracy, some light may be thrown upon the problem by observation of its manners. Here Senator Hoar feels himself upon solid ground. "Talk about the degeneracy of the Senate!" he exclaims, to a man who is writing at the very desk beside which Charles Sumner was struck down by the ruffian's bludgeon, who remembers that Foote—the same Foote who drew a pistol upon the indispensable Benton—in debate warned Hale that he would be hanged upon the tallest tree in the forest, if he should visit Mississippi, and who recalls the days when honorable but convivial Senators came into the Chamber "with whiskey-soaked brains."

Alas! men had their failings even in the heroic age. It is true that the passions of the Southern Senators were sometimes violent and ungovernable. It is true that Brooks was a coward and a ruffian; and it is true that at various periods in the history of this nation United States Senators have been too much given to the indefensible practice of alcoholic stimulation. We hope Senator Hoar is right in his assumption that no Senator now ever drinks more than is good for him. But, deplorable as were the exhibitions to which he refers, they were perfectly compatible with the concentration in the Senate Chamber of more brains and force and greatness and general efficiency than can be assembled there from forty-five States in these days of decorum and degeneracy. The politest little man in the world may be a less interesting example of a nation's virility than the swaggering fellow who can "clean out" a caucus. *Tom Jones* was a sad dog and got into no end of scrapes; but we can put up with his frank irregularities better than with the meaner vices of the sanctimonious *Blifil.*

Daniel Webster, in that seventh of March speech in which he made the " grand renunciation " of his former views against the extension of slavery, gave more convincing proof of the greatness of the Senate than a dozen statesmen of the present senatorial calibre could do by years of perfectly consistent and irreproachable public conduct. The prostrate trunk of some centennial oak speaks more eloquently of the majesty of the forest than the scrubby exuberance of the living underbrush. Webster's fall awakened echoes that have not yet died away from our historical discussions. Of the present Senate, the perversities of one day are forgotten the next.

> " All else is gone ; from those great eyes
> The soul has fled ;
> When faith is lost, when honor dies,
> The man is dead."

No muse is stirred to such a glow of indignation by our modern Ichabods. We impale them with a paragraph, and let them squirm while we turn to weightier things.

To sum it up,—the Senate lacks moral authority and holds no leadership of opinion. Once it had both.

Senator Hoar, admitting some of the defects in the body he so skilfully defends, casts about rather helplessly and hopelessly for a remedy. It is not to be found in a change of the rules or in the manner of electing Senators. The evil lies deeper,—in the social conditions and tendencies of the time. The Senate was once the goal of every bright young man's aspirations. It no longer attracts them; and public life in all its stations has lost much of its old allurement. For one thing, the great questions that stirred the popular heart and roused those emotional fervors so dear and so necessary to the platform orator have mostly been settled by the growth of the country. During the slavery agitation strong men entered public life as devout young men enter the ministry,—in obedience to an inward call. But, with our tremendous industrial development, invocations more numerous and compelling come from other directions. To the young man casting about for the choice of a calling in life, the rewards which brains and ability can command in business or the professions séem far more generous and substantial than any degree of public fame tó be won in discussing the sordid questions of tariff and free coinage. Great lawyers no longer go to the Senate. They cannot afford to give up corporation practice.

If Webster were alive to-day he would be neither in the Senate nor in debt.   C. R. MILLER.

THE IGNOMINY OF EUROPE.

"To one small people, covering in its original seat no more than a hand's-breadth of territory, it was given to create the principle of Progress, of movement onwards and not backwards or downwards, of destruction tending to construction. That people was the Greek. Except the blind forces of Nature, nothing moves in this world which is not Greek in its origin. A ferment spreading from that source has vitalized all the progressive races of mankind, penetrating from one to another, and producing results accordant with its hidden and latent genius, and results of course often far greater than any exhibited in Greece itself."—SIR HENRY SUMNER MAINE, "Village Communities," p. 238.

THE Cretan insurrection and the part which Greece is playing in it are generally so little understood in their true bearing and significance that it is easy for the "Powers of Europe"—now banded together against both Greece and Crete—and their agents, paid and unpaid, to delude the general public with meaningless phrases and misleading pretences, and thus to stifle that natural sympathy which all rightly constituted men feel for heroism and a long-sustained struggle for freedom. Under these circumstances, it does not seem inopportune that one who has devoted much study to the history of Greece, ancient and modern, who has spent considerable time, at different dates, in Greece, has travelled over the length and breadth of it on foot, and who has done his best to make himself acquainted with the character, aspirations, and difficulties of the Greek people should endeavor to make a brief statement of the sober facts of the case. With a view to this, we must cast a rapid glance at the history of Greece from the day of her greatness onward.

In the fifth century B.C., "plucky little Greece," having developed, through right living, a consciousness of inner freedom, was able, by a series of heroisms to which the story of the nations affords no parallel, to hurl back the huge billows of Oriental despotism that threatened to engulf her, found free institutions, and lay the basis of political and individual liberty. This achievement was hardly completed when the man was born who discovered the formula of rational liberty and dignity, brought it into consciousness, and thus made a permanent return to despotism forever impossible. This was Socrates, who placed the source of moral authority in the individual soul, recognized as an embodiment of universal reason. From the death of Socrates Greece pursued a downward course. Through internal dissensions, and the consequent victories of Macedonia, she lost her political liberty; while her philosophers, Plato and Aristotle, pretending to expound Socrates, produced theories which threw men back once more into the arms of external authority. The despotism of Macedonia, which had spread a somewhat degraded, Platonized form of Greek civilization over the whole Eastern world, thereby contributed to degrade that civilization still further, by introducing into it sensual and irrational elements. The process begun by Macedonia was continued by Rome. Under her, especially after the removal of the seat of power to Constantinople, the Greeks were imperialized,—which means that they were reduced to slavery. Finding this intolerable and yet unavoidable, they sought refuge in the dreamy other-world opened up to them by certain corrupt, fantastic, and mystic forms of Christianity, and so lost all hold upon the life of this world. The result was, as always, fanaticism, weakness, and barbarism. There are few sadder chapters in human history than that which describes the gradual, certain, thousand-year-long decay of the Greek Empire. At last the "Sick Man's" hour came. In 1453, the mummified carcass of the Greek nation was ground to powder by the unspeakable Turk, and flung to the winds of heaven. From that time forward the Greeks were homeless vagabonds.

But, notwithstanding the long and slow corruption of the Greek Empire, the spirit of liberty and culture inherent in it never entirely died out. There never was a time when a faithful "remnant" of the old Hellenism did not exist. Under the Turk, this spirit, so long held in sleep by the opiates of decay, returned to consciousness and began to look about. Those in whom it awoke, finding no place amid the coarse barbarism of the Turks, betook themselves to the deserts and the mountains, and lived the life of freebooters or, as they were called, "Klephts."

> " In the forest, the glen, and the wild lonely darkness,
> Where never the sword of the tyrant can come "[1]

they lived a life of freedom and excitement, defying the Turk, so that the term " Klepht " came to be a title of honor. This lasted for more than three hundred years, during which the Turk sank more and more into sluggish abasement, and the Greek rose in courage and sense of

[1] So begins one of the Klephtic ballads, still dear to the heart of the Greeks.

freedom. Aware of this, the Turks seized Greek boys and trained them as soldiers. Such is the origin of the Janissaries. When we study the life and history of the Klephts, we may fairly say that Greece was never conquered. Her people, for a time overpowered by force, only waited for the moment when, made strong by heroic discipline, they should be able to claim their own. And that moment at last came. In the early decades of this century, when the teaching of the wilds had restored the race of Marathon, they suddenly emerged from the darkness and burst like a thunder-cloud upon their oppressors. After a heroic struggle of ten years, in which deeds were done worthy to rank beside the best of old, and with the sympathy of Christian Europe,—not yet dead to all sense of nobility and manliness,—a portion of them, the inhabitants of Greece proper, were able to escape from Turkish brutality and declare themselves free. The people that invented liberty had once more a local habitation and a name.

But alas! the Greeks, having gained their freedom, knew not what to do with it. In their long ages of Klephtic rebellion against accursed slavery, they had developed an individualism that made harmonious coöperation almost impossible. How, indeed, could it be otherwise? Moreover, their country, once the garden of the world, had, under Turkish misrule, become a desert, treeless and houseless. Poor, homeless, suffering from over three hundred years of proximity to the Turks, the Greeks began their political life. Surely no people ever started with greater odds against them. They had, in fact, nothing but themselves, their high hopes,—sometimes romantic enough,—hopes nourished by Klephtic ballads, and the memories, never lost, of the glorious days of yore. But, in spite of poverty, misery, and dissension, they struggled bravely on. Europe looked on and applauded; and some of its peoples even so far forgot their caution as to lend them money at exorbitant interest, the first instalment of which was deducted from the principal before it was paid over. Nay, more: Those countries which had helped Greece to vindicate her liberty felt so vain of their achievement, and so anxious that their coöperation should find due and lasting recognition, that they insisted upon treating her as a baby, and giving her a nurse in the person of a pompous Bavarian prince. This wooden figure-head, after wasting the nation's borrowed money in building himself a hideous barn of a marble palace, and drilling a useless army in fustanella and fez, was finally expelled by the outraged people in 1862. But, though Greece had rebelled against one nurse, her guardians, whose money was now invested in her, insisted that she must have another; and, while the Greeks demanded a tried and honest statesman, like Mr. Gladstone, who would devote himself to their interests, the guardians said no, and forced her to accept a young Danish prince of untried ability, who should be a tool in their hands and further their interests. Russia, moreover, insisted that he should take a Russian wife, and that she should have a Russian private secretary, whose duty it should be to keep the Czar acquainted with everything that went on in the court—a duty which he faithfully performed.

Fortunately for Greece, King George has proved to be a good and loyal if not a very showy man. During his reign of more than thirty years, he has more and more withdrawn himself from the influence of his guardians, and has identified himself with the life and aspirations of his people. His queen, in defiance of the Czar, has done the same; while their children, born and bred in Greece, are Greek to the core. Of course, this action of his has been the cause of great fear and suspicion to his would-be guardians—especially Russia and Great Britain. These two nations, as soon as they find that they cannot control Greece, show themselves to be her bitterest enemies. For them she must be an obedient child or nothing; and the more babyish and feeble she is, the better. It is an open secret that, from the very hour of Greece's declaration of independence, Russia has done everything she could to thwart her and to prevent her from rising above absolute helplessness. Every effort to improve and open up the country has been frustrated for half a century by the underhand influence of Russia. Her purposes are clear enough. She wishes to keep both Turkey and Greece in a moribund state, until some European complication shall arise enabling her to seize the territory of both, erect her throne at Constantinople, restore the Eastern Empire, and proceed to extend it, with its Asiatic despotism, to the whole of Asia. England would fain prevent this; but she too has her selfish projects, and is strongly averse to allowing the territory of the Turk, which forms the bridge of trade between Europe and Asia, to fall into the hands of a capable, eminently commercial people like the Greeks. ` Thus, Russia and England, though with different motives, conspire to keep Greece in a state of childish imbecility; and herein they are seconded, from still other motives, by Austria, who wishes to appropriate the Balkan provinces and extend her dominion to the Ægean Sea. The reasons which induce Germany to make common cause with these reveal the existence of deeper and sadder motives,—of a combined effort on the part of the three empires, Russia, Austria, and Germany, to stem the whole modern movement toward democracy and rational freedom, and to restore the dehumanizing despotism of the Middle Ages in Church and State. Of the first and third, Mr. Gladstone well says :—

> " In the one case, the government is a pure and perfect despotism, and in the other, equivalent to it in matters of foreign policy. . ... These Powers, so far as their sentiments are known, have been using their power in the concert to fight steadily against freedom."

And the same is true of Austria. Now these facts are pitiful enough and disheartening enough ; but there is something far more so, and that is, that the Powers of Europe which stand for freedom—England, France, and Italy—are so cowed by the impudent bullying of the three despots, as to allow themselves to be chained to their chariot-wheels, as these roll ruthlessly over the most sacred rights and instincts of humanity. The aristocratic element in England, represented by Lord Salisbury, who now steers her ship of state, sympathizes with the despots ; and to this fact are due both the Armenian massacres and the coercion of Crete and Greece. Had Mr. Gladstone and his party been at the helm, neither of these things would have happened. France, the only really unselfish and chivalrous friend that Greece ever had, desires to remain friends with Russia, in the hope that that despotic power will some day help her to free Alsace and Lorraine from German despotism. Poor, deluded, misguided France ! That will happen only when the lion lies down with the lamb. Finally, Italy, amid her chaos, fears to break with the Triple Alliance, although its other members snub her on every occasion. Thus all the Powers of Europe, led on by her despots, are combined against the progress of Greece, the freedom of Crete, in fact,—let us recognize it frankly !—against freedom altogether. Their present bearing toward Crete is but one manifestation of their general spirit : another was their bearing toward the Armenian massacres. It is perfectly fair to conclude that, had the poor, oppressed Armenians shown any likelihood of success against their oppressors, the European Powers would have sent an army to shell them into submission. It has come to this, at the close of the nineteenth Christian century !

And what excuses do the Powers put forward for their action ? They are mainly three ; and these are paltry and mendacious enough. They wish, they say, (1) to preserve the peace of Europe ; (2) to maintain the integrity of the Turkish Empire ; and (3) to insure to Greece the conditions of safe development. As to the first, could anything be more untrue? Are they not, by refusing to Crete and Greece their just demands, endangering the peace of Europe? Let Crete unite herself to Greece, as she ought to have been allowed to do seventy years ago, and the present danger will be at an end. Turkey and Greece are willing to settle their difficulties between themselves and to restore peace; but the Powers, instead of helping them, step in to prevent them, so bent are they on war. As to the integrity of Turkey, there is no such thing to preserve. As Mr. Botassi says, in a recent article:—

"The dismemberment of Turkey began over a hundred years ago. In 1783, Turkey lost the Crimea. In 1830, she lost Greece. In 1857, Moldavia and Wallachia . . . were united, and finally became the present flourishing kingdom of Roumania in 1881. In 1862, the Turkish garrison evacuated Belgrade; and in 1878, Servia became an independent kingdom . . . and Turkey quickly acquiesced in the absorption of Eastern Roumelia in 1887. Kars and Batum were snatched by Russia in 1878. England seized Cyprus in the same year; and Austria was comfortably installed in Bosnia and Herzegovina. Where is the alleged integrity of the Turkish Empire, in the face of the above historical facts?"

Where, indeed? And there is a deeper sense in which Turkey must be denied all claim to integrity—a moral and political sense. Turkey has always been a dissolute barbarous nation, a mere band of robbers and ravishers occupying the seats of ancient civilization, bringing ruin wherever they came. It has no more claim to a place among civilized peoples than a nest of assassins, a brothel, or a gambling-hell. No government has any claim, as such, to existence, except in so far as it fulfils the function of government in promoting justice, culture, and well-being; and herein Turkey has absolutely failed, being a mere organ of injustice, savagery, and misery. It ought incontinently to be swept from the face of the earth, as a moral nuisance and horror, and its place given to the Greeks, who, though not without faults, everywhere represent freedom, education, culture, energy. Lastly, as to the desire on the part of the Powers to ensure to Greece the conditions of safe development, no more mendacious pretence was ever put forward. The truth is, the Powers, with the exception of France and, perhaps, Italy, are utterly opposed to the development of Greece, and would abolish her to-morrow if they felt strong enough to defy public opinion. Thus one and all the pleas put forward by the Powers for their dastardly behavior to Crete and Greece are mere pieces of falsehood and impudence, such as the foes of freedom are forced to screen themselves with to avoid public scorn.

With regard to Crete, in particular, the Powers tell us that they are willing to grant her autonomy under the suzerainty of the Turk!

"Autonomy" is a fine, vague, oracular word, a word to conjure with: unfortunately it has, thus far, only started devils, as the Cretans, whom the Powers are trying to dupe with it, know to their cost. All that the Powers want is to keep Crete from joining Greece and entering on the path of civilization until such time as some one of them is in a position to grab it with impunity. And so, in defiance of all political and human rights, they are protecting, arming, and aiding the Turks,—aye, even the savage Bashi-bazouks,—and shelling the Christians, who are risking their lives for liberty. Is it any wonder that the Cretans have lost all faith in the Powers?

There is one more very insidious plea often put forward by the Powers in defence of their conduct to Greece. They tell us that the Greeks, being excitable, headstrong, and new to political life, are not fit to govern a large territory; still less to take the place of the Turk, and govern a mass of peoples of different races and religions and hostile to each other; and that, since all their efforts at aggrandizement tend in this direction, the people must be frowned down, thwarted, and enfeebled. This conclusion is, indeed, made a rule of action; but the premise, I believe, is utterly false and calumnious. Since my first visit to Greece, twenty years ago, I have watched the life and progress of her people; and I know few things that are more encouraging. Despite all the vexations to which their guardians have subjected them, and all the obstacles they have thrown in their way, despite also their own natural shortcomings, they have shown, in both material and spiritual things, all the virtues of a progressive and civilized people. Their country, left them a desert by the Turks, has become, to a large extent, productive and beautiful. The population, now 2,600,000, has doubled in the last twenty years. In 1877, there were hardly a hundred miles of carriage-roads, and only five miles of railway in the whole country. To-day, there are roads everywhere, and hundreds of miles of railway. In 1877, it was hardly possible for the traveller to find a bed outside Athens: to-day, there are numerous hotels, with all European conveniences, in all the principal cities and towns. But the true test and proof of Greece's indomitable spirit of culture is her educational system. By that she stands or falls. I have visited Greek schools throughout the length and breadth of the land, from the infant-school kept by the peasant in the open air, against a sunny hovel-wall, to the Arsakeion, or girls' academy, and the noble university, with 2,200 students, which now grace and honor the city of Athene. Anyone who will do the same, and listen to the records of the sacrifices made by rich and poor for the sake of education and culture, will not doubt for a moment that Greece is amply able to govern and civilize the lands now marred and wasted by Turkish misrule. The sums of money given by rich Greeks for schools, and the hardships undergone by the children of the poor in remote districts to avail themselves of these have no parallel anywhere, save in the United States and Scotland. Who dares assert of such a people that it is not capable of ruling its ancient patrimony—the first home of liberty—better than the barbarous Turk or the despotic Russian? There is but one just, beneficent, and effective solution of the Eastern Question, and that is the restoration of the Greek Empire to Greece, and the placing of a great civilizing Power, such as neither Turkey nor Russia can ever be, as guardian of the bridge between Europe and Asia. It is the disgrace of Europe that this was not done long ago.

But the question remains : What can we, citizens of the United States, do in the matter ? We can do a great deal, both in our private and in our public capacity. We can do what our people did at the time of the Greek Revolution : we can give Greece our moral and material support. We can rouse the free spirit that animates our people and let it find expression through the press, through public resolutions, through motions in the national Senate and House of Representatives, and, finally, in formal encouragement and protest expressed through the Chief of the Executive and his foreign ministers. But we must not stop here. We must find another Dr. Howe, and send him with shiploads of food and clothing, not only to those Cretans who, in dread of butchery or worse, have fled from their native land and are starving in Athens, but to those who cannot get away, and whose food the soldiers of Great Britain have burned. Then, if the Powers refuse permission to our ships to land, on their errand of humanity and mercy, we must enter such a protest as President Cleveland entered against English encroachment upon Venezuela, backed by the same drastic sanction. *That* protest will be listened to, as the other was ; for there is one country that the bullies of Europe dare not bully, and that is the United States. If we follow this course, which is our simple duty to humanity, we shall find a warm response from the great popular heart of the elder continent, and rouse a healthy public opinion that will cow tyrants, paralyze bullies, and wipe out the ignominy of Europe ere she have to blush in the light of a new century.

THOMAS DAVIDSON.

19

OUR EXPORT TRADE.

AMERICAN commerce was first colonial, is now national, and must become international. In the earlier period of our industrial life, it was natural that the energies of our people should be applied mainly to the discovery and development of our vast and varied resources, to the construction of post-roads, canals, and great systems of railways, to the establishment and extension of inland navigation, to the building of towns and cities, and to the founding of manufacturing industries. One development stimulated another, and thus produced finally an era of unexampled prosperity. A period of depression followed, owing largely to the fact that "we were our own best customers"; our power of production and our output of manufactures far exceeded the demand for home consumption; and one-half of our industrial energy had to lie unemployed. Such is our situation to-day. The present, therefore, seems a most fitting time to discuss the influence of our export trade upon our national prosperity.

In this latest period of contraction, particularly during the past year, the importance of our exports has been brought home to our people. Financiers have appreciated it because the large balance of trade in our favor ($325,322,184) the last year has not only enabled us to buy back our securities at low prices from foreign holders, but has assisted in the accumulation of large gold reserves. Our farmers have found, as before, markets abroad for their surplus products. But, above all, the export trade proved a special blessing to our manufac-turers, who, under the impulse of an abnormal home demand, had de-veloped a productive capacity double the requirements of our domestic trade. During the past four years, if it had not been for the sustain-ing power of foreign orders, many factories would have been forced to close; thus breaking up organizations which it had required years to perfect, and throwing laborers out of work at a time when they would have been unable to obtain other employment. How foreign orders came to the rescue of many of our manufacturers is seen from the Treasury reports, which show that our exports of manufactured goods increased during the three months preceding the last election 72 per cent over the corresponding months of 1892, while our bank clearings for the same period—the only statistics we have for measuring interstate commerce—decreased 20 per cent. Hitherto our trade in manufactured goods has been almost exclusively among ourselves; but during the recent years of depression the feeling has grown that the only way out of our straits is through commerce with all the world. Thus will be brought about an industrial revival that will end the present popular discontent.

Mr. E. V. Smalley, in the March number of THE FORUM, states that the conditions which made possible the abnormally prosperous times in this country from 1879 to 1892 no longer exist. "Our new West," he says, "is already fairly well peopled. . . . Our great transcontinental railway systems are already constructed. . . . Our new towns and cities went rather beyond the capacity of the tributary country to support them. . . ." While it is desirable that discontent should be replaced by the contentment of industry, it would not be wise to wish for a return of "boom times." We can and should build on a broader, and therefore safer, foundation. We cannot remain wholly dependent for our active industrial life upon the home demand; and the markets of the world are open to us, ready to absorb the surplus products of our utmost manufacturing capacity. Economists recognize that the industrial greatness of a nation depends on the possession of the main sources of mechanical energy—coal and water-power—and of abundant deposits of iron ore. That nation which has the cheaper fuel and cheaper iron has a steady advantage in the contest for supremacy in the world's trade. Besides being singularly endowed with these inestimable gifts of nature, the United States has also every variety of soil and climate, great forests, and the best natural facilities for inland transportation. Our people are gifted in a marked degree with inventive genius and untiring energy; and all their forces, mental, moral, and physical, are disposable for civil and economic ends, being free from the enormous drain of men and money demanded by standing armies. Wages are higher in the United States than in the more densely populated countries: but we have met that condition in many industries by utilizing the best labor-saving machinery and methods; thus effecting economies through centralization of manufacture.

Every dollar's worth of merchandise exported represents just so much wealth given by the foreigner in exchange for our own people's industry. It is, therefore, natural that we should supplement our great interstate commerce—the greatest commercial intercourse in the world conducted under the conditions of absolute free trade—by securing markets abroad. A comparatively small additional demand often turns bad times into good times. The total wealth of the United States is about $80,000,000,000; the total amount of money is about $2,300,000,-000; yet at times, if the bank reserves of New York decline ten millions, anxiety is created in financial circles, and money required for the legitimate wants of trade is unobtainable. But if the reserves advance ten millions, money becomes a drug in the market. So it is with our industries. A moderate increase in the sale of our products abroad would give an impulse to some of our industries, which would stimulate others and thus bring about a wholesome industrial activity.

In widening our field of distribution, there are several reasons why it is most important to create markets for our *manufactured* goods, including flour, canned foods, and other manufactures of farm products, as distinguished from " raw materials."

(1) The percentage of profit on manufactured goods is much larger than on raw material. The French best appreciate this. Importing the crude products of other countries, they add to them features that please the eye and gratify the taste, and thus make a vastly greater profit than the producers of the raw materials.

(2) There is a greater necessity to widen our market for manufactured goods. Raw materials are readily marketed; and though it requires much time and expense to build up a trade in manufactured goods, yet, when once developed, it is not only more profitable than that in raw materials, but is less vulnerable to competition.

During recent periods of depression, the manufacturers who had had the foresight to introduce their goods into foreign countries secured most of the orders for export, and were making substantial profits while their neighbors were forced to close their factories or run at great loss.

(3) The United States is becoming yearly more of a manufacturing nation. The value of our exports of manufactured products in 1870 was $68,279,764; in 1890, $151,102,376; and in 1896, $228,489,-893. While these figures show a large increase, the largest shipment of manufactured goods in any one year ($228,489,893) is small as compared with our capacity and opportunities, and with the exports of manufactures by our competitors of Western Europe. The latter reach an annual value of $3,500,000,000. Our export trade is less than one-fifteenth of this.

The vital question arises, How can this export trade be developed? The answer is: (1) By the establishment of international banking facilities based upon a currency of undoubted stability; (2) by controlling means of transportation; (3) by manufacturing what is most suitable for the needs of foreign markets; (4) by proper legislation, commercial treaties, and intelligent representation abroad; and (5) by manufacturing products of good quality at low cost.

One of the first steps to take toward the extension of our export trade in the neutral markets should be the establishment of our own banking facilities. In London alone there are no less than sixty incorporated banks, having for their sole function the conduct of international finance as related to commerce; and these have branches and agencies in all foreign ports. Similar banking institutions exist in France and Germany for coöperation with the exporters of each of those countries; but there is not an American bank, or branch of an American bank, in South America, Africa, or Asia. Our merchants and manufacturers are dependent for banking accommodations—which would be largely withdrawn in case of war or rumors of war—upon institutions principally under the control and influence of their competitors abroad. By act of Congress, an invitation was extended to the representatives of eighteen American republics to assemble in Washington for the purpose of providing means for the extension of inter-American trade. That conference recommended the establishment of an international American bank, with branches in all the American republics; thus committing the South American governments to its support. No charter has yet been granted, although the bill introduced into Congress provided that the bank, while subject to governmental supervision, should not receive governmental assistance nor have the right of issue.

There are grave objections to the Government directly assisting private enterprises; but it is nevertheless true that the export trade is greatly increased by improved facilities of communication. Every vessel flying the American flag "is a commercial traveller for the American farmer and manufacturer." By possessing superior means of communication, Europe, though more distant, is nearer to South America in point of time than the United States. Lines of steamships to South America could be established, if aided with liberal mail contracts by our own and other interested governments. The ships should fly the flags of the United States and of the republics of South America. Our Southern neighbors are looking forward with interest to the time when we shall be joined together by a system of intercontinental railways; thus establishing close commercial union. Awaiting that consummation, they are to-day prepared to respond to a movement on the

part of this country to facilitate steamship communication. They believe it would be an additional source of national strength, as well as of
commercial advantage.

In order to develop trade with foreign countries, it is necessary that
we should manufacture what they want, and as they want it, instead of
insisting upon their taking what we are producing for home consumption. With a comparatively small export trade, the manufacturer often
finds it inconvenient to supply the special wants of foreign markets;
but, as his export trade increases, this difficulty decreases. When a
foreign trade is once secured it should be held. Owing to the rapidity
with which American demand sometimes springs up, manufacturers,
who rely naturally and properly upon the home market as their principal support, forget the advantage to be had from an export trade in
times of depression, and advance their prices too rapidly as against the
foreign buyer and refuse to meet his special requirements. He becomes
disgusted, and reverts to his former sources of supply in Europe; and
it is much harder to regain a foreign customer once lost than it is to
secure a new one.

The question of legislation as affecting our export trade, is too complex to be discussed comprehensively within the limits of this article.
Substantial advantages would have been secured from reciprocity arrangements had they been continued. It is natural and proper that we
should ask countries from whom we are buying four times as much as
they are taking from us, to facilitate the interchange of products. We
bought last year from Brazil, La Plata, and the Spanish West Indies,
$126,000,000, and we sold them only $30,000,000,—the balance against
us being $96,000,000, which we had to remit in gold to Europe to pay
for manufactured goods which those countries bought from Europe instead of from us. While reciprocal arrangements are of undoubted
benefit, the field of opportunity under reciprocity is small, as compared
with the greater opportunities obtainable through economic manufacture.

It is important that we should be represented in our diplomatic and
consular service by men of experience and industry, speaking the languages of the countries to which they are accredited. The present
Administration can lead reform in this respect by reappointing capable men who have become familiar with the countries in which they
have served. Such representatives—particularly those accredited to
our Southern neighbors—would be of valuable assistance, in bringing
about a simplification and unification of customs regulations and
generally in assisting to develop inter-American trade.

The most important element in securing foreign trade is price. The average wages of Western Europe are less than half those of the United States; and the serious question is, How can we compete with countries paying much lower wages? Many advocate the reduction of wages; arguing that the reduced prices which would follow would largely increase the demand for products, thus stimulating the demand for labor. The reduction in prices, being equal to the reduction in the rate of wages, would enable the wage-earner to buy then as much as he can now; and, instead of working half-time, as at present, he would have continuous employment and thus earn a larger annual income.

In considering the question of wages, however, we should look at it from a higher point of view than that of cost. Undoubtedly a reduction of wages would enormously increase demand at home and abroad. But is not the general distribution of wealth in this country through the payment of high wages an element of national benefit? Is it not a guarantee of national unity and strength that so many of our wage-earners own their homes, and that our savings-bank deposits are rapidly increasing, now amounting to more than $1,800,000,000? There are instances where the workman would undoubtedly be benefited by a reduction of wages; and in several recent cases the leaders of labor combinations have favored a reduction of wages in order to increase employment in their localities. A radical reduction in wages, such as would have taken place had we gone upon a silver basis,— "cutting money in two and cutting wages in two,"—would undoubtedly have increased our exports; but the same benefits can be secured without putting our laborers on the European plane. The cost of production can be reduced by utilizing the advantages of consolidation; by the adoption of whatever is best in methods, machinery, styles, and materials;—points generally ascertainable only through comparison of the processes of different establishments brought together by combination;—by closing obsolete, badly located plants, and perfecting the best; by the reduction (by centralization) of the percentage of general expenses of factory superintendence, buying, selling, accounting, and advertising; by running full time because of added orders for export; by eliminating litigation through a common ownership of conflicting patents; by discarding needless· brands and styles; by stimulating interest and effort through distribution of ownership in centralized manufacture; by supplanting with sound, honest goods the inferior, and often counterfeit, goods produced by obsolete machinery and poor organization. With these advantages—and without cutting wages—

we can maintain and extend our position in the markets of the world. We are shipping steel billets to England, where the laborer in steel plants gets far lower wages than are paid at Pittsburgh. We are supplying refined oil to China and Japan, where the laborer gets 12c. per day as against $1.50 paid in our refineries. We ship straight cotton goods to the neutral markets, agricultural implements even to the nations of Europe, machinery and tools to every part of the globe.

European manufacturers, even with their low wages, have been recently agitated by the industrial activity which has manifested itself in Japan. The people of whom Mulhall, the British statistician, was able to say, two years ago, "If we take a survey of mankind in ancient or modern times, as regards the physical, mechanical, and intellectual force of nations, we find nothing to compare with the United States," may view without alarm the threatened competition of the Japanese and Chinese in manufacture. The productive capacity of our labor-saving implements and machinery is greater than that of the entire population of China. We have no stronger guarantee for the future prosperity of the country than the maintenance of the high standard of intelligence of the American artisan; and we require that superior intelligence to use highly organized machinery and labor-saving implements which take the place of the "pauper labor" of other countries.

That we hold our position in the world's markets through such superior organization is shown by the fact that of our exports of manufactured goods 85% are produced by the organizations representing centralized manufactures; while those articles the manufacture of which cannot be centralized to advantage are being supplied to the neutral markets by the countries that have low-priced labor. With our high wages we cannot compete with Europe in paying close attention to individual wants; but by centralization we can manufacture in great quantities for the masses goods of uniform and better quality for the price.

The most serious obstacle to our continued advance in the exportation of manufactured goods is indicated in the recent opinion delivered by Judge Peckham, of the Supreme Court. He admits that,

"In business or trading combinations they may even temporarily, or perhaps permanently, reduce the price of the article traded in or manufactured, by reducing the expense inseparable from the running of many different companies for the same purpose. Trade or commerce under those circumstances may nevertheless be badly and unfortunately restrained by driving out of business the small dealers. . . . Mere reduction in the price of the commodity dealt in might be dearly paid for by the ruin of such a class."

It is impossible to protect that class. The law of the "survival of the fittest" is inexorable; and attempts by Government to favor the few result in loss to the many. No human law can ever be devised to take the place of that higher law which gives a monopoly to superior intelligence.

If the evolution in economic manufacturing is to be interfered with and legislative enactments are to be substituted for natural laws, if world competition is to be prohibited by preventing combination, on which low prices depend, the result will be less employment, low wages, and consequent pauperization of American labor. The wars of to-day are industrial wars; and the essential element of success is low cost of production. That can be best secured through centralized production. At the present time an attempt is being made by demagogues in journalism and politics to gain popular favor by appealing to popular discontent. Bad times are largely due to the attempt to "hold up" capital and enterprise; and the march of progress is thus retarded. But our struggle for a share in the markets of the world goes on. The consumer fighting for low cost of living, the workman to maintain the American standard of wages, the Captains of Industry fighting for low cost of production through centralization, upon which the maintenance of wages depends,

"in mutual, well-beseeming ranks, march all one way."

The existence of a great export trade in the United States would have an educative influence on our people. It would cause them to look at great economic questions from a higher point of view. Contrasting their wages with those of other countries would tend to make our laborers satisfied with their more favored condition. The farmer would realize his dependence on facilities for transportation by land and sea; and granger agitation would gradually cease. Our manufacturers would be stimulated to renewed efforts to occupy this wider field; and the Legislature would be forced to study—closely and intelligently—national finances and trade not from the standpoint of narrow partisanship or local conditions, but from the higher ground of the rights of all and the general good, and in view of the ultimate domination of the universal law of supply and demand.

CHARLES R. FLINT.

INDUSTRIAL COMBINATIONS.

WITH the exception of the problems relating to the currency, the question of industrial combinations is probably the most absorbing one before the American people to-day. It is worthy of the careful study of every patriotic citizen, of the earnest, vigorous efforts of our wisest statesmen. It seems likely, on the contrary, to become rather the plaything of empirics, or the tool of political charlatans. In many States legislation on this subject is pending,—crude, undigested, and revolutionary,—which, if enacted and enforced, will retard the industrial development of the country and increase the evil it is intended to eradicate.

These combinations of capital assume many forms; but in general they may be divided into two classes—*permanent* and *transitory*. The first of these may be subdivided into consolidations and trusts; which, however, are simply different means of reaching the same end—the merging of two or more competitive establishments into one concern under one management. In a consolidation this is done openly. There is one central or general office; and the different plants are operated as branches. In a trust, on the other hand, certain individuals hold, as trustees for the actual owners, all the capital stock of different corporations engaged in the same line of manufacture. These subsidiary companies continue to operate their respective plants,—apparently independently of each other, but in reality guided in all their movements by the trustees. This form of combination has of late years been severely handled by the courts; and most of the industries which were once operated under trust agreements have reorganized as corporations.

Permanent consolidation of interests, whether arrived at by an open merger or the more subtle form of a trust, is the only perfect combination. All others are mere makeshifts for the purpose of temporary profit at the expense of the consumer. This is a means whereby permanent and substantial benefits can be secured, always for the combination itself, and occasionally for the public. It is at once impregnable and remorseless. Unless it openly and persistently flies in the face of public opinion, it is absolutely beyond the reach of the law; for it is hard to conceive how any law can be enacted and enforced which, without infringing on private rights or interfering with industrial development, can prevent a corporation, or a private firm, or an individual from owning and operating plants in different parts of the country, even if such ownership does involve the control or monopoly of any given commodity.

If one of these aggregations is safely launched, thoroughly organized, and ably managed, it can go a long way toward making its position impregnable and holding it in perpetuity. It can shut down a sufficient number of its plants to prevent over-production of the commodity it manufactures, and thereby make sure of a profit the extent of which is measured only by the moderation or rapacity of its management. Able, conservative, and far-sighted managers will dictate a policy of low prices, which will disarm public criticism as well as discourage private competition. If a daring competitor refuses to capitulate, or a new competitor appears, one or more of the plants of the consolidation can be detailed to follow his salesman into every market, and undersell him at every point, no matter what the loss may be, until at last he sees before him the alternative of bankruptcy or surrender. If the new competitor is backed by such ample capital, or his affairs are so well-managed, that the loss involved in the crushing-out process would be too great, another and simpler means is employed. Able negotiators are set to work; and the new competitor is either bought outright, or a new consolidation is effected, or an understanding is arrived at under which the two apparent competitors will, for the future, work in harmony. These efforts are nearly always successful: for commerce knows no sentiment; and in business it is true, almost without qualification, that "every man has his price."

But the ablest and strongest efforts of the combinations are directed not toward the stifling of competition, but at forestalling it. In other words, when once intrenched in a commanding position, they aim to reduce the cost of manufacture so that they can undersell old competitors and discourage new ones. All that science can devise or human ingenuity invent in the way of labor-saving machinery is taken advantage of; and the records of the United States Patent Office show that most of the great inventions (and, indeed, many of the great inventors) of recent years are owned by corporations who use them to maintain and, as far as possible, perpetuate their various monopolies. Their establishments being located at different points, they can ship to each locality from the plant most convenient ; effecting a large saving in freight as against a competitor who ships from one point only. While the general expenses, or what are known to the trade as "fixed charges," of such concerns are necessarily large, their output is so great that when these charges are divided by the unit of product they are invariably less than those of smaller producers.   Being purchasers of the largest class, and generally of undoubted credit, they can in most cases secure their raw material and supplies of various kinds at the lowest possible cost.   By comparing the record of one plant with another, they are able to introduce into the entire system small economies, each meaning little in itself, but amounting in the aggregate to enough to insure a fair profit on the whole investment.   In short, they are able in the highest degree to exemplify the saying, " In union there is strength "; and, with the strength born of a common and united purpose, they attack fearlessly and destroy relentlessly all who stand in the way of their onward march.

But in many branches of trade where over-competition exists it is found impracticable to consolidate all interests.   In fact it is the exception that this can be done.   In such cases, resort is had to a "pool"; which means that, as there is not enough business for all, what there is shall be divided among the different members in proportion to their capacity,—or that some members shall take the entire business, paying the others a certain proportion of the profits in compensation for their enforced idleness.   To raise this money each member taking any of the business is compelled to pay into the pool all, or a certain proportion of his profits; and these profits, after paying expenses, are divided back among the members in proportion to their respective percentages—the percentages being fixed at the time of organization, and generally based on capacity.   In this way, the man who stands idle makes approximately as much money as the one who operates his plant and continues in active business.   If a manufacturer is obdurate, and refuses to join the pool, an effort is made to subsidize him, either by paying him a stipulated sum per month for shutting down, or by agreeing to purchase his product at a price which will yield him a large profit.   To provide for such payments and other like "contingent expenses," a certain percentage of the pool payments is set aside from time to time.   Some of these organizations even go so far as to subsidize the manufacturers of machinery adapted for the turning out of the product which is "pooled," in order to discourage new competition.

Such is a brief outline of the operations of the organizations called "pools."   They vary in details; but the general form is the same.   They all involve a contribution by those who run, for the benefit of those who do not. A brief study of this plan will easily demonstrate that these associations bear in themselves, from their very inception, the seeds of their own destruction. They are vulnerable both from without and within. Even if the original or basic percentages are adjusted in a manner satisfactory to all parties (which seldom happens), it is not long before some member convinces himself that he is entitled to a larger share, and demands a readjustment. This invariably causes trouble, and often leads to a shipwreck before the bark has been fairly launched. Being composed of men whose natural attitude toward each other is one of intense competition, there is of necessity no cohesion amongst them, except, perhaps, "the cohesive power of plunder"; and their meetings generally resemble a council of war composed of allies hastily gathered together to oppose a common enemy, but whose traditions and anticipations alike point to a long line of conflicts with each other. Formed of such discordant elements, looking backward to a competitive past and forward to a time when that competition will be intensified by the very reason of their present truce, it can be easily seen that profits—immediate, continuous, and enormous—are a necessity to their existence; and the moment the profits cease (even temporarily), the structure falls.

The excessive prices demanded for their goods by the members of the pool naturally attract the attention of the outside world; and it is not long before a new crop of competitors appears. These competitors must be bought off if the pool is to continue, or they will gradually attract the business to themselves. To do this, prices must be still further advanced, and a continually increasing proportion of the pool profits must be set aside for "contingencies." As a result, the short life of the pool is one of continual warfare, with certain defeat at the end. I can now recall but a single instance where one of these organizations continued in successful operation over a number of years; and this it was enabled to do only by reason of the fact that the business controlled by it involved so enormous a capital as to deter outsiders from entering the lists against it. But even this combination, seemingly irresistible, has at last succumbed to the natural laws of business; and its downfall has just been chronicled. It has but few mourners; and these are not inconsolable.

In considering the question of the good or evil effect of these combinations, the above division of them into two classes—permanent and transitory—should always be kept in view. These two classes bear to each other about the same relation that a barn-stormer bears to a Booth or an Irving, or a penny-a-liner to one of the masters of literature. Of the transitory combinations but little that is good can be said, even by their strongest advocates. The most plausible argument in their favor lies in the fact that they allow the profits of a business to be divided among all who are engaged in it; whereas by unrestricted competition the entire business would be gradually absorbed by those who are best equipped, and the weaker ones would be driven to the wall. There is no doubt that the doctrine of "the survival of the fittest," when put into practical operation, is an extremely hard one, for the survivors as well as for the vanquished; but that is no justification for the unscrupulous rapacity which characterizes the operation of most pools, when for a brief period they gain control of the output of any article of general consumption. When everything possible is said in their favor, the conclusion is irresistible that, both in their effect on the public and their ultimate influence on the participants themselves, their result is absolutely and unqualifiedly bad. The evil that results from them, however, is neither far-reaching nor permanent in its nature; for their lives are necessarily short ones, and, when they die, an era of low prices invariably follows their funeral. It is questionable, therefore, whether, on the whole, the public is much the worse for these fitful attempts at combination.

The question of the merits and demerits of combinations, when they take the form of a complete consolidation of interests, is a far more difficult one to solve. I will present as briefly as possible some of the arguments advanced by the advocates of these organizations to prove that their existence is a benefit and not an injury to the public.

In the first place, a very large proportion of the general expenses of a manufacturer are caused, directly or indirectly, by competition; and, if competition be eliminated, many of these expenses can be cut off. If a dozen concerns are engaged in selling the same article in competition with each other, all of them must have salesmen patrolling the country, or agents representing them in each district. Each concern must also spend large sums in calling the attention of the public, through the newspapers or by other methods of advertising, to the merits of its goods. All these expenses, which in the aggregate are enormous, can be divided almost exactly by twelve if the plants are combined under one management. Each one of the twelve must also maintain a general office with a large salary list; and, while expenses of this kind are not wiped out by consolidation, they can be largely reduced. Another item of saving lies in the purchase of the various raw materials and supplies used in their different plants. On account of the great volume of their purchases and, generally, their ample capital and ready payments, their trade is eagerly sought after; and they are usually able to buy everything they need at much lower prices than could be obtained by even the best of their constituent members when operating separately. When we consider that, as a rule, the cost of raw material amounts to about 60 per cent of the value of the manufactured article (I allude to staple articles, not to specialties), it will be seen what an advantage is gained by this ability to purchase everything at the lowest price.

But the chief advantage possessed by these combinations, and one which overshadows all others, lies in the ability to cheapen the cost of manufacturing by the introduction of careful and intelligent management into their various operating departments. When once a merger is effected, and the managers are able to compare the past records of the various plants, it is invariably found that, owing to abler management or better facilities, some plants were turning out their product at a much lower cost than others. Under the new régime all this is at once changed. Incompetent managers are discharged; and the methods which before prevailed in the most favored and best equipped plants are introduced into all. If it is found that there is a greater aggregate capacity than the legitimate consumption demands, some plants—usually those in which the cost of operating is greatest—are closed down, and the remainder operated to their full capacity. In this way each plant is enabled to turn out the maximum of product at the minimum of cost,—which is the perfection of manufacturing. This may seem hard for the workmen in the idle plants, who are thrown out of employment; and so it is. But it must be remembered that the aggregate of labor employed is as great in the one instance as in the other. It is simply shifted from one place to another; and a smaller number of men are employed on full time, instead of a greater number working short hours only. From my own observation, extending over many years, and including all branches of manufacture, I am satisfied that combinations of this kind are not inimical to the interests of the workingman. On the contrary, the men employed by them receive steadier employment, and generally at better wages, than the same class of labor under open competition. In fact, reductions in wages are oftener brought about by excessive competition than by any other cause. If one competitor reduces wages, the others are of necessity compelled to follow; and the laborer, who is least able to help himself, is ground between the upper and nether millstones. When there is a virtual monopoly of the trade, this necessity does not exist; and instances are very rare in which manufacturers have compelled their employees to accept reduced wages, unless driven thereto by sheer necessity. It is the least grateful task that is laid on the manager, and the one that is last resorted to.

Having stated, and I believe fairly, the main arguments advanced in favor of these artificial combinations, let us look at those presented on the other side. The chief of these are, the watering of their stock, and the consequent necessity of extorting high prices for their products in order to pay dividends on the inflated values; their unscrupulous course in maintaining a monopoly of trade and in dealing with their competitors; and the fact that in many of them the guiding motive in the conduct of their business is not the good of the business itself, but the effect it will have on values in Wall Street.

If all the firms and companies engaged in a certain line of manufacture would unite,—making the capital of the united company equal to the fair aggregate value of the several plants, with the addition of sufficient cash to provide working capital,—and would avail themselves of all the advantages I have outlined, it is beyond question that they could defy competition, sell their wares at prices lower than ever before known, and still reap for themselves a liberal return on their legitimate investment. This, however, is not the course usually followed. In an investigation into this subject, lately conducted by a committee of the New York Legislature, it was developed that, in the organization of one of these companies, stock to the amount of about $5,000,000 was issued for live assets and about $20,000,000 for "goodwill"; and there are many other instances of a like nature. In other words, the stock was watered to the extent of five times its legitimate value. In order to pay dividends on this inflated value, it is of course necessary to advance the price of goods far beyond what is fair and right, and to extort from the public money which without question comes under the head of "ill-gotten gains." This, it must be confessed, is the course pursued by most of the so-called trusts. There are, however, honorable exceptions: but the exceptions are few; and the rule applies to the many. One of the notable exceptions is the oldest and ablest concern of them all, which for a quarter of a century has held almost undisputed sway over one of our greatest industries. To-day it has the power to fix, and actually does fix from day to day, the prices at which it will buy its raw material and sell its product. The sellers of the one and the buyers of the other are compelled perforce to bow to its dictates; but this absolute power is wielded with a far-seeing liberality that, considering its opportunities, is amazing. Its securities are not used as a football to be kicked from side to side on the Stock Exchange; and the time, energy, and brains of its managers are devoted exclusively to the conduct of its legitimate business. It is noticeable that this company has, to a certain extent, escaped the universal criticism which has been heaped upon organizations of a like character during the past few years. Yet, even in this instance, the upward path to power is strewn with the wrecks of competitors; and, though the company in question has laid the foundations of colossal fortunes, it has made many men poor.

As to the remedy: It is now nearly seven years since Congress placed on the statute-books of the nation a law making it a misdemeanor for any individual, corporation, or association to monopolize, or attempt to monopolize, any part of the trade or commerce among the several States, and providing for the punishment of the same by fine, or imprisonment, or both. This law emanated from the pen of the present distinguished Secretary of State; and, so far as its motive goes, it is a tribute to the patriotism of that wise and experienced statesman. The legislatures of several States have also enacted laws looking to the same end. That of Illinois has attracted especial attention by reason of the drastic nature of its provisions, and the vigorous efforts of the Attorney General to enforce it. Yet in no period of our history have artificial organizations in restraint of trade run riot to such an extent as during the years that these laws have been in force; and in no place, with the possible exception of the city of New York, have their operations been more conspicuous than in Chicago. The explanation is not hard to find. No law can be continuously enforced which makes a crime out of that which the average, every-day common sense of the people does not recognize as criminal. The man who violates the Sherman Law is no more a criminal than a fraudulent bankrupt is an honest man because the law has discharged him from the payment of his debts. If this law were rigorously enforced, and every man guilty of its infraction were punished according to its provisions, many of our great lines of commerce would soon have to be entrusted to mediocre hands; for our ablest and brightest men of affairs would be denizens of the penitentiary.

20

It has been freely charged that a protective tariff is the parent of combinations; and it is proposed that Congress shall empower the President to place upon the free list any article which, after investigation, he finds to be controlled by a monopoly or a trust. This is good so far as it goes; but I prophesy that it will afford but scant relief. Many of the great industries are not now dependent on the tariff for their existence. They are no longer infants: they are able to stand alone. The withdrawal of protection will, therefore, do them no harm. But, in my opinion, the contention itself is altogether erroneous, and the facts will by no means bear it out. It is well known to all users of the commodity affected that the most successful pool carried on during the last year was among the manufacturers of an article which is, and for years has been, free of duty, and the demand for which has been supplied, in a large measure, from abroad. This pool was worked by the simple but very effectual method of distributing the business in agreed proportions between the foreign and home manufacturers. The whole thing was carried out very quietly. The price of the commodity was nearly doubled; the consumers had to pay; and the "combiners" smiled with a smile that extended across the ocean. In this one case at least, the revocation of the tariff would have accomplished no good.

I contend that combination in trade is not an evil *per se*, but only by reason of its abuse. The tendency of the times is toward consolidation and coöperation. The people have a right to demand that articles of general use shall be made at the lowest possible cost, and sold at the lowest possible price consistent with a fair return to the producer. To do this they must be produced on a large scale, with little waste, and under the best management. The evil results spring from the abuse by monopolies, or partial monopolies, of the privileges they enjoy, and from the fact that these privileges are often used as instruments of injustice and extortion. It is to this abuse of power that the attention of our law-makers should be directed. In short, the effort to *abolish* combinations having failed, let an effort be made to *regulate* them. Let us avail ourselves of what is good in them and, as far as possible, extirpate what is evil.

Ten years ago Congress undertook, with marked success, to regulate the methods of the great corporations engaged in transporting freight and passengers from State to State. It seems to me that it is just as feasible to control the operations of the great industrial corporations,—especially those engaged in the production of staple articles necessary to the daily life and well-being of the citizen. These corporations all depend upon legislation, either State or national, for their existence. They are in the daily enjoyment of franchises granted by the public. They are, without exception, engaged in commerce between the States, and are consequently legitimate subjects for congressional action. I would propose, therefore, either to enlarge the duties of the Interstate Commerce Commission, or to create a new tribunal with ample powers to investigate the methods of corporations, associations, or individuals engaged in the manufacture or supply of articles of general or public use. Upon the complaint or relation of any citizen, setting forth that such corporation had obtained a substantial monopoly of any industry, and by reason thereof was oppressing the public by extortionate charges or unjust regulations as to trade, it should be the duty of this tribunal to summon the parties and, after a full hearing, to award damages to the party injured, to punish the delinquent by a heavy fine, and to certify its decision to the Governor of the State in which it was incorporated, with a recommendation of the withdrawal of its charter privileges. This, of course, would involve legislation by the various States as well as by Congress; but I feel certain that if Congress would take up the matter in earnest the States would not be slow to follow. I would also provide that the fine should be increased with each succeeding offence, so that industrial corporations would soon find from experience that it is better to be satisfied with a fair profit than to extort unearned money from a helpless public. I would likewise make it a misdemeanor, punishable by fine, for any manufacturer, corporate or otherwise, to attempt to fix the price at which his customer should sell his goods after he had once purchased them, or in any other way to interfere with the free movement of his products after they were out of his possession.

I am aware that this plan will meet with strong opposition,—and none will oppose it more vigorously than those in control of monopolies, who are perfectly willing to work under the ban of a prohibitory law which they know to be impossible of enforcement, but will protest against a reasonable proposition to limit their exorbitant gains. I am also aware that many strong and cogent arguments can be brought against it; but I believe those in its favor will far outweigh them, and that if the plan be once tried it will, to a certain extent at least, solve the problem of industrial combinations, and lift many heavy burdens from the shoulders of the people.

GEORGE T. OLIVER.

NEW-ENGLAND INFLUENCES IN FRENCH CANADA.

THE causes of the exodus from the Province of Quebec are not political, but economic. Quebec is larger than France, or any State of the Union except Texas; but the cultivable portion consists of a mere fringe on the north shore of the St. Lawrence, with a some-what wider strip between the St. Lawrence and the United States frontier. All else belongs to the subarctic desert of rock, muskeg, and jack-pine. The settlements of New France lay to the north of the river and on the south shore from the Etchemin eastward to Gaspé; and when, forty or fifty years ago, they became overcrowded, population flowed into the southern forests, known as the Bois-Francs,—now a well-settled country traversed by the Grand Trunk,—and into the Eastern townships, which were peopled in the early part of the century by stragglers from the United States and emigrants from Great Britain. It also crossed the Ottawa on the west into Upper Canada, and is still moving slowly along the line of the Canadian Pacific and the water-stretches between the Ottawa and Lake Huron.

The French Canadian is of a roaming disposition, and, as every-one knows, bore a conspicuous part in the exploration of the Western and Northwestern States; while in the Canadian Northwest, where he served the fur companies, he became the progenitor of a race of half-breeds. After the political troubles of 1837, and during the Anti-Slavery War,—when they got bounties for soldiering,—a good many French Canadians migrated to the neighboring States; but the rush did not begin till the depression of agriculture set in, about 1880.

Like the New-England States, Quebec has long ceased to grow wheat for export. The soil, except in favored spots, is thin; the whole region, geologists say, having been planed by the same ice-cap that passed over New England. Much of the arable land has been ex-hausted by overcropping. Under the seignorial tenure,—a modified feudalism based on the Custom of Paris, that was not abolished till 1854,—the *habitant* carried on a ruinous system of tillage; first cutting down the bush, then scraping the surface of the ground with his Nor-man plough,—a clumsy wooden affair hung between a pair of wheels,

—and then sowing wheat year after year till the soil gave out, when he moved to another holding and repeated the process. Of rotation of crops, manuring, growing grass and turnips, he knew nothing till Scotch farmers came in after the British conquest.

The early colonists brought flower-seeds and apple-trees from France; and an apple known as the *Reinette du Canada* was produced: but, owing probably to climatic drawbacks, the taste for orchards and gardens has to some extent been lost. Dairy farming is handicapped by the long winter. On most farms, hay and potatoes are the staples; and the people complain of American duties on these as well as on their poultry, cattle, and peas. New England is the nearest, and, if it were free, would be the best, market for all their wares. As it is, they have to be content with Boston prices less duty, middleman's profit, and cost of transport, which in these days leaves little for their labor. The export of square timber has diminished, and the building of wooden ships—once an important industry—ceased; whilst the minerals and sea-fisheries cannot be turned to much account owing to taxation of the products at the United States frontier. It is safe to say that the richest State of the Union would suffer if, like Quebec, it were severed from the continental market by a double set of tariffs.

At one time the clergy endeavored to divert the stream of migration toward Manitoba. But it costs less to go to Lowell or Nashua; and factory work, at which the *habitant* and his large family make good wages, is preferred to raising forty-cent wheat in such high latitudes. The Dominion Parliament and Quebec Legislature have built a considerable railroad mileage in order to open up the Province;—perhaps also to bribe the people to stay at home;—but these local roads have, in fact, done something to swell the exodus, by supplying a ready means of getting across the frontier, as well as by bringing the *habitant* in contact with visitors from the United States.

In winter, committees are formed to prepare a list of those intending to emigrate, so that a special rate may be obtained from the railroads. When spring comes the trains are crowded with young and old bound for the land of promise. Others go in the fall, after the crops have been gathered, and return in the spring: these are known as the *hirondelles.* The village band accompanies the party to the railroad: the *curé* gets some to sign the pledge, and gives his blessing to all. *La fièvre des États-Unis* is so general that, as Father Lacasse, a distinguished Oblate, observes, " We are all asking in a whisper, ' What is going to become of the race ? What is going to become of Canada ? ' "

In some parts churches have been closed because of the flight of so many people. Every parish contains abandoned farms. The *hiron-delles*, on returning for the summer, describe in glowing terms what they have seen; telling in particular of "those of ours" who have won distinction in the professions or are making money in business.

The French-Canadian newspapers printed in New England circulate in Quebec; and Quebec papers devote space to New-England news. The Saint-Jean-Baptiste societies in both countries hold an annual convention,—sometimes in Canada, at other times in the United States,—at which topics affecting the welfare of the race are discussed. Aside from formal reunions of this sort, there is a constant ebb and flow of population across the frontier. The New-England French organize pilgrimages to the shrine of Saint Anne at Beaupré, and visit their old homes on returning: of late they have been getting up bicycle parties.

At rural postoffices most of the letters and newspapers are for or from New England. The letters from New England usually contain money; for, like the Irish emigrant, the French Canadian is deeply attached to his kindred, and counts no sacrifice on his part too great if only he can induce them to join him. When work is scarce in the States there is a backwash: but so soon as business revives the migration revives also; and it carries off the most active of both sexes. Lecky, writing of the emigration from Ireland in the eighteenth century, says:

"The removal from a nation of tens of thousands of the ablest and most energetic of its citizens must inevitably, by a mere physical law, result in the degradation of the race."

It is perhaps too soon to look for the effect of the migration upon the character of the French-Canadian race; but the injury to the material interests of the Province caused by the annual flight of the best is painfully apparent. The French-speaking population of Quebec numbers 1,200,000. According to the abstract of the census of 1890, the number of French Canadians and of persons of French-Canadian extraction in the United States is 840,000. Mr. Mercier predicts that in twenty years there would be more French Canadians by birth and descent in the United States than in Canada.

The French Canadian is remarkably prolific; marrying young, and having a patriarchal family. The difference in physique between the French of French Canada and the French of France has received some attention from a resident at Saint-Pierre-Miquelon, where five or six thousand fishermen from the Channel ports of France gather every spring to fish on the Banks of Newfoundland. The French-Canadian fisherman is slightly taller than his Old-World kinsman, but not so fleshy. Measurements of fishermen from Saint Malo and of French-Canadian *Malouins* by descent give an average weight of 155 pounds to the former and 148 to the latter. The average height of the French Canadians is 5 feet 5¾ inches; of the Frenchmen, 5 feet 5¼ inches. The French Canadian has lost the ruddy complexion of the French *Malouin;* his feet are longer and narrower, his arms and legs longer, his features sharper; and the color of his hair and eyes is more uniformly dark. The physical variation, in short, is somewhat similar to that which distinguishes the people of New England from the people of Old England.

According to the Canadian census, the average number of persons in a family in purely French-speaking counties exceeds 6; *viz.,* in Bonaventure 6.2, Temiscouàta 6.4, Gaspé 6.4, Charlevoix 6.7. This is the average found by the census-taker. The actual average is higher, however: for there is scarcely a farmhouse from the Ottawa River to the Gulf of St. Lawrence that has not sent children to the United States; and when they have been gone a year or more they are not included in the official count. The average in France is about 5. Various causes, such as the law of equal inheritance, are blamed for the falling off in France. In French Canada wild land can be had for nothing, and there is freedom of bequest. In the seventeenth century, Jean Poitras, a carpenter of Quebec, was the Priam of the colony with 25 children. Mr. Gédéon Ouimet, a recent superintendent of public instruction, was one of 26 children by the same father and mother. When the French Chamber appropriated a million francs to pay for the education of the seventh child of indigent parents, the Legislature of Quebec offered free land to parents with 12 or more living children; and a surprising number forwarded attested claims.

The fecundity may be due in part to the selection, in a Darwinian sense, of the original settlers. The voyage across the Atlantic in the small sailing vessels of the seventeenth century, usually with ship-fever as a fellow-passenger, together with the hardships incidental to pioneering in the forest amid the alarums and incursions of the Iroquois, weeded out the weak and sickly, for whom smallpox and *mal de terre*— a wasting scurvy supposed to be caused by exhalations from the virgin soil—also lay in wait. " Our survivors," wrote an official in 1650, " are to a man robust fellows and true *gens de cœur.*" On top of this natural selection Colbert introduced artificial selection by shipping girls chosen not for beauty so much as for vigor of body, who were met at the wharf at Quebec by settlers and married out of hand. The cargo of one vessel comprised one hundred and fifty girls, twelve mares, two stallions, and one hundred and fifty sheep, "all destined," wrote the minister, a master of detail, "to put stamina into the colony." Several hundred settlers obtained wives thus; including the men of the Carignan regiment which, fresh from fighting the Turks in Hungary, was sent out and disbanded in 1670–72. It is easy to believe with Colbert that the product of these marriages was, physically speaking, *une marchandise choisie.*

Emigration from France to Canada practically ceased about 1700. When the Intendant Talon begged him to send more settlers, Colbert answered that the King could not think of depopulating France to build up a colony; to which an ecclesiastic retorted, below his breath, that His Most Christian Majesty sacrificed more men in a single campaign than would suffice for half a dozen New Frances. At the census of 1695, the population was 14,000; and from this handful, selected in the manner described, the French-Canadian people have sprung. When England took possession in 1763, there were 65,000 souls between Gaspé and Detroit. Very few emigrants have come from France since. The *habitant* himself has multiplied till the race now numbers 1,300,000 in all Canada (exclusive of 100,000 Acadians in the seaboard provinces), and, counting American-born children of French-Canadian parents, more than 800,000 in the United States. Clerical writers used to maintain that this rapid increase was a miracle, of which the object was the firm planting of the Catholic religion in North America. Yet the increase has not been any more rapid, relatively, than that which took place in the Thirteen Colonies, where the religion was not Catholic. The same class of writers now affirm that the migration to New England is a special providence designed to bring Puritan New England to the Catholic faith. The Jesuit Hamon, whose book, "Les Canadiens-Français dans la Nouvelle-Angleterre" (Quebec, 1891), is well worth reading, is of this opinion. I have no means of knowing what effect the exodus is likely to have in that respect; but anyone acquainted with French Canada can see that intercourse with New England is changing the ideas and conceptions of the French-Canadian people in regard to many things. A Montreal newspaper scarcely exaggerates in saying that the change "already amounts to a revolution."

First and foremost, the clergy no longer dread American institutions.

At the War of Independence Monsignor Briand issued a fierce *mande-ment* against Americans. He pointed out that *la religion Bostonienne* was the form of Protestantism most inimical to the Catholic Church, her priests, altars, and saints; that its professors had reviled King George for passing the Quebec Act because of its generous treatment of the Church, and now, taking the French Canadians for dolts, were represent-ing the Act to be a tyrannical measure and promising to abolish seigno-rial dues and even tithes.   The aim of these Puritans and Independents being, in short, to overthrow human and divine order, it followed that the *habitant* who sympathized with them was bound to land in monstrous heresies and to incur the wrath of God and his lawful sovereign.   The Bishop had just received a pension from the Crown, over which the ballad-mongers made merry: but his detestation of republicanism was no doubt perfectly sincere; for, like all the bishops down to that time, he was a Frenchman from France, an aristocrat and believer in the divine right of kings,—British as well as Bourbon.   The French Revo-lution, with its atheism, served to confirm the clergy in their hostility to the United States; and their loyalty to Britain waxed all the stronger when, in return for their services in 1776 and 1812, Britain granted the Church more extensive privileges than she had enjoyed under French rule.   A *Te Deum* was sung for Trafalgar; the Sulpicians helped to erect a monument to Nelson in Montreal; in the Papineau insurrection of 1837 the last rites were refused to rebels in the field.

When the exodus began the bishops spoke bitterly of the United States; Americans being usually described as a nation of money-getters without respect for religion or authority. ·But the old prejudice has now wholly disappeared.   According to Father Hamon, the French Canadians in New England and New York have built in twenty years one hundred and twenty churches and fifty convents, many of which are served by priests and nuns from Quebec, who get on better with their compatriots than Irish or German priests.   The Sulpicians have built colleges at Baltimore, and elsewhere; the bishops attend confer-ences in the United States; French-Canadian priests collect money there for the erection of churches in Quebec; and American students of theology frequent the Montreal seminary and Laval.

The clergy are the natural leaders of the French-Canadian people. The first settlers came from what Colbert called the 'more religious provinces" of France;—Normandy, Brittany, Perche, Anjou, Poitou, and Saintonge;—and the colony was founded not to extend the French empire so much as the empire of Christianity.   Nature herself, as a

Jesuit wrote, conspired to promote devotion,—"the savage Indians, the dark forests, the mighty lakes and rivers, the sense of complete isolation from home and kindred." Even the earthquakes which shook the valley of the St. Lawrence for weeks in 1663, though "bad for chimneys," were "un grand bien pour les âmes," the churches being crowded.

Popular government did not exist; there was no such institution as the town-meeting; there were few books and few able to read them. The people were thrown back, in a believing age, upon religion. The regular offices on the numerous days of obligation; processions for rain or against distemper; celebrations in honor of the parish saint; the "white mass" or prayer-meeting, when a priest was not on hand; entertaining the Récollets or begging friars; preparing for the confessional; baking the *pain bénit* [1]; pilgrimages to Saint Anne at Beaupré; and various special services—sometimes in churches so poorly constructed that in winter, notwithstanding pans of burning charcoal in the aisle, the altar wine froze—occupied much of the time they had to spare from the drudgery of the bush. If the clergy of France in those days were lax, the clergy of Canada were, and have always been, distinguished for purity of life, zeal, and self-sacrifice. While not free from the weaknesses of their caste, they are, as a body, men of exemplary bearing.

When England came on the scene it was natural that the people, no longer able to make a shadowy fetich of their king,—now of a different race and creed, and a conqueror to boot,—should bestow the whole of their affection upon the Catholic Church and its ministers, who had stood by them through dark days. The influence of the clergy is not so great as it was, but is still very considerable; and the fact that they are now reconciled to the exodus to the United States, and like to go there themselves, is doing a good deal to promote it.

The impression carried away by the summer tourist, that the French Canadian speaks a *patois*, is not well founded. He employs words and phrases not recognized by the Academy; but that is not altogether his fault. The first settlers had to invent a terminology for their new surroundings. They accepted the Indian names for some of

[1] The *pain bénit* was bread prepared by each family in turn, taken to the church, blessed by the cur é, distributed among the congregation, and carried home. On receiving it from the priest they used to pray :—

> " Pain-bénit, je te prends—
> Si je meurs subitement,
> Sers moi de sacrament."

This pious custom is dying out.

the strange birds, fishes, and fruits. In other cases there was nothing for it but to coin words; for what did the French of France know of sleighing, canoeing, snow-shoeing, portaging, clearing land, barn-raising, driving logs, or making maple sugar? In the Lower parishes the *habitant* gets married "at the herring," baptizes his child "at the capelan," does something else at the "squid"; the seasons when the fish "run," *i. e.*, strike the shore to spawn, being as important in his reckoning as are the *vendanges* to the peasant of France. Some of his phrases date from his struggles with the Iroquois; thus he speaks of going to the "fort" when he means the village,—the first villages having been provided with stockades,—and, to frighten a naughty child, he threatens to call in *les sauvages*. He has preserved a number of words that were good French in the seventeenth century, but have since changed their meaning or gone out of use in France. He also employs sailor phrases in an odd way,—as when he "moors" his horse to his sleigh, and "disembarks" from that vehicle with his "dunnage." Taking it altogether, however, his French is better than that of the French peasant of to-day. The worst that can be said of it is that it is archaic by comparison. His pronunciation of *t* and *d* is marked by a nasal twang; due, possibly, to the climatic agencies that are supposed by some to be responsible for the .twang of the down-east Yankee. The educated French Canadian speaks as good French, of course, as the educated Parisian; but he uses fewer gestures.

Till the exodus made it a matter of self-interest to learn English, the *habitants* were averse to doing so. They had an idea, to which color was given by the Canadian constitution of 1841, that the Government wanted to transform them into Englishmen and Protestants. With the English-speaking Canadians in Ontario and the seaboard provinces they are united politically : but the union is an uneasy one; and they have jealously maintained their language, religion, and laws. If they are learning English now, it is not because they desire to establish more intimate relations with the English provinces, so much as because it is a help to them when they go to New England.

Arthur Buies tells of a text-book on agricultural chemistry having been condemned by the ecclesiastical censor on the ground that it contained nothing about the Virgin Mary. What he means is that in the schools everything has hitherto been subordinated to religious instruction. The rural schools, taught by nuns, Brothers, and badly paid lay-teachers, are mere nurseries for preparing the child for First Communion. The public schools are Catholic schools regulated by a council composed of the bishops and an equal number of laymen. The English minority of the Province is allowed separate schools, which are undenominational. In the Province of Ontario, the case is reversed: the Catholic minority enjoys state-aided separate schools; whilst the public schools of the non-Catholic majority are undenominational.

In 1824 the Seminary of Quebec reported that one-fourth of the rural population could read ; whilst one-tenth could " write their names, some badly enough." Some years afterward, when the British Government began to encourage primary education,—which the clergy had so sadly neglected,—an act had to be passed empowering school trustees to sign their names with a cross. According to the last census 15 per cent of the population is unable to read, and 18 per cent unable to write. There is a growing demand that less time should be devoted to catechism and more to English and the three R's. " New England," says a prominent school reformer, " is the future home of a large proportion of our people : at present we go there without any knowledge of English, and are handicapped. Let us teach that language properly to every boy and girl, so that they shall not be aliens out-and-out when they cross the frontier." Others advocate the removal of the schools from clerical control; but that, I suspect, is a long way off.

New-England influence is largely responsible for what Ultramontanes call the " New-England spirit,"—hostility to the exorbitant pretensions of the Ultramontane clergy, and particularly to their interference in elections. The early bishops not only harangued the people on religious topics and such stock subjects as card-playing, dancing after sundown, Sabbath-breaking, loudness in dress, usury, fortune-telling, resorting to magic and abracadabras, etc., but dictated to and advised them in all affairs of importance. What with the paternal edicts of the civil, and the *mandements* of the spiritual, arm, the colonists were regulated " down to the end of their nails."

The Ultramontanes, who made their appearance forty years ago, took it for granted that the people were as amenable to clerical rule in the nineteenth century as they had been in the seventeenth ; that in the interval they had not grown in intellectual stature. In defining the prerogatives of the Church they went farther than the first bishops —ecclesiastics of the Gallican type—had cared or dared to go. The Church, they said, is, from her divine origin, superior to the state, and paramount in all matters falling under the head of faith and morals,— that is to say, within a sphere to which nobody but herself has a right to set limits. It follows that she is entitled, nay, bound, to interfere in politics whenever, in her judgment, faith and morals are at stake,—in other words, whenever she pleases.

The Dominion Election Act contains a clause, copied from the English statutes, voiding parliamentary elections at which undue spiritual influence has been exercised. It is " undue influence " when the priest threatens to withhold the sacraments from a voter and his family if they vote the Liberal ticket, or when from the pulpit or altar he consigns the Liberal party to hell-fire. When they were called to account for these practices the Ultramontanes replied that Parliament had exceeded its powers in restraining the clergy from acting as they saw fit at elections; that it was neither more nor less than putting the state above the Church. In a judgment read by Cardinal Taschereau's brother, the Supreme Court of Canada made short work of that defence. An attempt to form a Centre or Catholic party in Parliament, with the bishops directing its policy, was defeated by the opposition of the Liberals, headed by Mr. Laurier, now Premier of the Dominion. At the recent general election, at which the Manitoba school question was the issue, the bishops published a joint *mandement* in favor of the reëstablishment of the separate schools, but did not declare openly against Mr. Laurier, who had just voted against a bill, introduced by Sir Charles Tupper, over-riding the legislation of Manitoba and restoring the schools by Federal enactment. The older clergy, however, " made it hot " for Mr. Laurier in the rural districts. The younger clergy were friendly, as friendly as they could be under the circumstances; and, thanks to their quiet sympathy and to the New-England spirit amongst the electors,—who, besides, desired to see a French Canadian at the head of affairs,—Mr. Laurier carried the Province by two to one. French-Canadian newspapers published in New England were circulated as Liberal literature; and New-England French Canadians, some of American birth, took the stump for Liberal candidates. " New England," cries a despairing Ultramontane pulpit orator, " has precipitated a revolution, has filled the land with all the plagues condemned by the Syllabus." However that may be, New England must henceforth be reckoned with in Canadian politics. For obvious reasons its influence will be greater than that of Irish Americans in the affairs of Ireland.

The Church in Quebec is empowered by law to collect tithes and *fabrique* assessments. The tithe is every twenty-sixth bushel of the cereal crops, deliverable cleaned, threshed, and winnowed, at the *presbytère* or manse on or before Easter. Of late, tithes have been collected from hay, and a " supplementary " or cash tithe from the inhabitants of

towns and villages. The *fabrique* assessment is a *pro-rata* tax levied
on farms for the construction and repair of churches and *presbytères*.
When the priest gets a majority of the Catholic freeholders in his
parish to petition for a new church the bishop appoints commissioners
to assess the rate and do the work. Neither tithes nor *fabrique* taxes
are paid by Protestants. The tithe is not a heavy charge, and under
the voluntary system the people would probably pay as much ; but the
fabrique tax becomes a grinding impost when the bishop creates new
parishes by subdividing old ones and insists on replacing wooden
churches with fine stone edifices.

The exemption of ecclesiastical property from taxation is also a serious matter in a poor community where the Church and the religious
Orders, of which there are about sixty, possess so much. In some
parishes the value of the exempt property exceeds that of the taxable.
The depression of agriculture is giving rise to an agitation for the
abolition of *fabrique* taxes and exemptions, and for the secularization of the clerical estates,—reforms demanded in vain by the Liberals
fifty years ago. " Hell," writes Father Lacasse on behalf of the clergy,
" awaits those who refuse to bear these divinely ordained burdens."
" Our friends in New England," the reformers answer, " are not called
upon to pay them, yet God blesses them above us. How do you account for that ? "

The influence of New England is seen in other things. The clergy
still keep an eye on the newspapers, and ban and boycott them when
they go too far; but I do not think they would now venture to ban a
literary society and refuse Christian burial to one of its members, as
they did with Guibord five-and-twenty years ago. Everyone, even to
the *curé*, is beginning to have his doubts about the miracles reported
at Beaupré. No doubt Saint Anne did work miracles there in the
early days; but it is different now. To do them justice, the priests in
charge of the shrine are reducing the strain on one's powers of belief
as honest inability to believe increases. Formerly, cures of cancer,
paralysis, and blindness were of everyday occurrence. Now, the recovery of lost money and friends, the cure of hysteria in girls, and the
conversion of Protestant husbands by Catholic wives are about the
only wonders one hears of; and the official reporter goes out of his
way to allow that, after all, natural causes may have been operative.
It cannot be said, however, that the fading of the robust faith of the
habitant is accompanied by greater worldly happiness.

Nor is contact with New England improving the manners of this *peuple de gentilshommes.* Along the frontier they are less polite than they used to be and more self-opinionated; but without doubt they have gained more than they have lost. They make good American citizens; for they have many excellent qualities. They are quick at learning, frugal, industrious, and, from having been thrown on their own resources, are capable of turning their hands to anything and of doing it pretty well. Those who picture the *habitant* as a mere troglodyte like the French peasant of Zola do him rank injustice.

As for the political changes which the exodus is likely to bring about, the general opinion of French Canadians who think about the matter at all is that some day it must lead to the union of Canada with the United States. The exodus from English-speaking Canada is proportionately just as great. But Quebec is not bound to England by any sentimental ties; and the force of attraction exerted by the United States meets with much less resistance there than in the other provinces. Long after the British flag had superseded the French flag on the rock of Quebec, the people on the south shore used to look across the river and mutter, "Nous reverrons pourtant nos bonnes gens." That dream has gone, though a warm affection for France remains.

Except the want of free access to the American market, the *habitant* has nothing to complain of under British rule: all the same he is British only in name. On public holidays, when the Union Jack is flying in the English provinces, he hoists the Tricolor, and lately has taken to placing the Stars and Stripes just below it. He is opposed to the Imperial Federation idea, and at the recent election voted against Mr. Chamberlain's imperial zollverein project because he regarded it as a step toward closer union with England and the Old World. Sensible Englishmen can hardly believe that he could be coaxed into fighting England's battles abroad,—perhaps against his mother country,—still less into taking up arms against his relatives in New England, because England had fallen foul of the United States in Venezuela. It may be well, however, to repeat that political union with the United States is seldom discussed among French Canadians. The race is now astride the boundary line; and the forces of nature are making for its reunion under one flag: but nature takes her time about such matters.

Edwd. Farrer.

FRANCE AS A FIELD FOR AMERICAN STUDENTS.

THERE is no centre of learning more richly supplied than Paris with schools and faculties for advanced instruction in nearly every department of learning and research; and there is no country more ready than France to open the doors of its educational institutions to foreign students. That intellectual sympathy of France with America which dates from the residence of Franklin in Paris has never died out, and is now cherished by leading Frenchmen to an extent which insures a warm welcome to the visiting American. Yet, while our students have been flocking to Germany by thousands, comparatively few have availed themselves of the advantages for pursuing liberal studies which France has to offer them. The subject has been recently discussed by eminent educators both in France and this country; and there is reason to believe that in the reorganization of the University of France, which is now going on, the desirability of making that and similar institutions attractive to the foreign student will not be lost sight of.

Why American students have in the past preferred Germany to France may be seen by a glance at the higher educational system of that country. The German university is a well-understood and well-defined organization, of which the workings, so far as they concern the student, are familiar to all interested in them. In the student's progress there is a well-defined point at which he may seek admission to the university, and an equally well-defined goal for which he is to strive. One who has gained the degree of Bachelor of Arts at any of our better American colleges, is more than qualified to enter upon the course; and, by good work, he may fairly expect to obtain his degree within three years. His necessary studies during that time are easily ascertained and mapped out; he terminates his course by an examination; and demonstrates his fitness to become an active citizen in the republic of letters by writing an original thesis on his chosen subject. This production is expected to show merit on the part of the author as an original investigator, while, at the same time, the requirements are not beyond the powers of a young man of fair talent, application, and industry. When all the requirements are satisfied, the degree of Doctor of Philosophy, or Doctor of Medicine, as the case may be, is the official certificate of his success; and its significance is everywhere known and recognized.

Social life at a German university is extremely attractive; and the occasional presence of young gentlemen who attend more for the society of their fellow-students than for purposes of learning, adds to its charm without necessarily distracting the serious student. All the arrangements have, by long trial and experience, been so adjusted as to strike the happiest mean between conditions too easy to imply merit and too difficult to be hopefully encountered.

So different are the conditions in France, that it is scarcely possible to say whether any such system does or does not exist there. The facilities for study are unrivalled. There are faculties of science, letters, law, and medicine, whose reputation is as wide as the world. A combination of these faculties in one city is frequently called a university. These faculties are far from including in their scope all that France has to offer to a foreign student. The latter has so wide a choice of schools, teachers, and laboratories that he may find it hard to select from so rich an assortment. But, notwithstanding this wealth of choice, it is difficult for the foreign visitor or student to recognize any such well-defined system as that seen in a German university. It is a curious fact that while the great movement which introduced the modern régime into France organized and unified all other departments of its public activity, including the system of elementary and secondary education, it seems, so far, to have done little toward moulding the ancient foundations of learning into a unified whole. Still more indefinite is the academic degree for which the student has to strive. It is true that the *Baccalauréat* is a general degree, of which the conditions are readily understood. But, being the most elementary degree, bestowed at the close of the secondary course in the Lycée, it is not one for which a foreigner need strive. After the Frenchman who has taken his *Baccalauréat* has completed a three-year course at an advanced institution he may come forth as a *Licencié*, an *Agrégé*, an *Ancien Élève*, an *Élève breveté*, an *Archiviste paléographe*, and may, quite possibly, secure one of several other equally indefinite designations. Ultimately he may become a Doctor of Science, or Doctor of Letters, on conditions which I shall hereafter mention. It is now contemplated to provide for a general University Doctorate corresponding to that of Philosophy in Germany and the United States; but, in the past, no such degree has been attainable.

21

The question of the advantages which France offers to the American student has recently excited so much interest, and the present writer has been so frequently asked for information on the subject, that he proposes, in the present article, to make a brief statement thereupon. He can have little to say about the purely professional schools; not only for the very good reason that he knows little about them, but because their crowded condition is now rendering it necessary to impose restrictions on admission to them. Of these schools the most renowned has been that of medicine. During the last few years there has been such an unprecedented influx of foreign students to this school, that restrictive measures became absolutely necessary. These measures were rendered the more urgent from the fact that large numbers of the visitors settled in France and competed with the already underpaid native physicians. It is therefore not to be expected that foreign students will find it so easy to gain admission to this school in the future as it has been in the past; indeed it is quite likely that they may find it impossible.

While the same is not strictly true of the schools of art, yet their celebrity also attracts foreign students in such numbers that some restrictive measures can scarcely fail to be necessary in the near future.

Leaving out of consideration these professional schools, and also such institutions as the École Polytechnique and École Normale Supérieure, —which are intended exclusively for French aspirants to the public service,—the visiting student still has a wide choice from the best that the French capital can afford. The special schools which may attract him are too varied and numerous to be even mentioned. I shall therefore confine myself to the three great foundations of liberal education.

First among these, we have the ancient and renowned University of Paris—more familiarly known as the Sorbonne. The latter is no longer the debating ground for the great questions of theology, it having been invaded and conquered by the faculties of science and letters. The building erected by Richelieu has, during the past ten years, been gradually replaced by another, which, when completed, will be the most magnificent temple ever erected to the cause of education. The cost of this structure has already gone far into the millions; and millions more will doubtless be expended before it is complete. The courses are divided into two sets; viz., those open to all comers, and those which require an enrolment or *inscription*. It should please the visitor to know that the former include instruction by the full professors; so that the student cannot, under any circumstances, find difficulty in hearing the greatest men of France,—unless indeed the mere number of those seeking the privilege should exceed the available accommodations. However this may be in the department of letters, there is not much danger of its occurring in that of exact science. A visit paid by the writer to the lecture-room of the leading professor of mathematics showed the presence of less than a score of auditors, a few of whom were women.

- The Sorbonne is by no means satisfied with simply allowing its students to listen to courses of lectures. It therefore provides, on a large scale, a system of *conférences* or *cours fermés*, which are designed to drill the student in special problems and questions, as well as for explaining and developing in detail those subjects which the professor cannot fully dwell upon in his regular course. The instruction here is given mostly by assistant professors; but it must not be inferred from this title that they are tyros in science. In the department of mathematics, the teachers at the Sorbonne include men who, in addition to holding a very high rank among the mathematicians of the world, have displayed that force and elegance in treating their subject which has long been a feature of French science, and who have prepared textbooks unequalled for clearness and precision. Heretofore, admission to these courses has been mostly confined to holders of the French *Baccalauréat;* but there is no regulation absolutely requiring this qualification. If any American student who has taken his Bachelor's degree wishes to enroll himself at the Sorbonne as a student, he will experience no difficulty except that arising from the increasing numbers who flock thither for instruction. At a *conférence* at which the writer was present, the number attending was so great that any individual must have felt himself somewhat at a disadvantage.

Next in age and dignity to the Sorbonne comes the Collége de France, situated in its immediate neighborhood. This institution dates from the time of Francis I, who was led to found it in consequence of the failure of the University to give that attention to Oriental subjects, and especially Greek and Hebrew, which he thought they fairly demanded. Thus, from the beginning, Oriental and general philology has been one of the specialties of the institution. The Collége occupies a field almost as wide as that of the Sorbonne; covering, in fact, special subjects which the latter scarcely touches. The range at the student's choice extends from the discourses of Levasseur on the economic conditions of various countries, and the advanced mathematics of Jordan, in one direction, to the investigations of the leading physiologists and anatomists of France in another.   Here, as at the Sorbonne, the instruction is free to all; being limited only by the numbers who seek admission to the more popular courses.

The third great foundation is the École Pratique des Hautes Études. This school is, so far as the writer knows, a quite unique organization. It is of recent origin; dating from the second Empire.   The object in view was to utilize those facilities afforded by the Capital for instruction and research which had, until that time, been neglected.   Its organization may be said to be almost unhampered by conditions.   Its work is divided into five branches, each directed by an administrative commission of five members.   Any person eminent in any branch of knowledge, and desiring to teach young men how to study and investigate, may become a member of the faculty.   Any youth desiring to learn and investigate may enroll himself in the school without money and without price, on the single condition that he is able to avail himself of the advantages offered him.   The institution has no local habitation.   Wherever in Paris there is a laboratory at the command of a professor, there may teacher and students assemble: wherever there is a room, there may the professor be heard.   Much of the instruction is given at the Sorbonne; and probably more will be given when the latter is completed: but the greater part of it is scattered over the innumerable scientific institutions of the Capital.   The primary object is to make the student an investigator by the actual practice of investigation, under the direction of his professor.

Neither this school nor the Collége de France confers degrees. From the very nature of their constitution they do not offer a well-defined curriculum having a beginning and an end.   The conferring of academic degrees is the especial function of the University.   Here the only degrees for which the American student is likely to be an aspirant are the Licentiate and the Doctorate.   The regulations governing these honors differ so much from those with which we are familiar in this country and in Germany, that some explanation is necessary.

The student is supposed to enter the University after taking his *Baccalauréat;* as he does in Germany after completing his course at the Gymnasium, or in this country after having become a Bachelor of Arts. But the system of combining the secondary and higher education is more symmetrical and logical in both France and Germany than it is in England and America.   In the former countries a sharp line is drawn between the general liberal training at the Lycée and the

Gymnasium—which may be supposed to terminate about the age of eighteen—and the subsequent work at the University. The completion of the former, in France at least, is marked by the Bachelor's degree. The corresponding sharp line in our own country is found only between the high school and the college. But our scholars do not leave the high school with the degree of Bachelor; on the contrary, they have a four-year course at college before receiving it. Moreover, the advanced or university courses, in our leading educational institutions, have been partially grafted upon and combined with the college courses. Thus it happens that what at Harvard and elsewhere are regarded as courses preparatory to the Bachelor's degree become, in France and Germany, studies preparatory to the Licentiate, or the Doctorate. The result of this is that in France the Licentiate may be won by courses little more advanced in the special subjects chosen by the student than those which have been taken by the Bachelor of Arts leaving Harvard or Johns Hopkins.

The Doctor's degree in science or letters is also awarded on terms radically different from those of the German or American university. Residence at the University is not obligatory after the Licentiate has been taken. No examination is required, except such as may be implied in the defence of a thesis. The latter is wholly different from the thesis of the German or American student, as regards the amount of research and maturity of work expected of it. Instead of being the first essay of the beginner in original investigation, it is expected to show the mature hand of a master. Instead of being a thin pamphlet, it is either a goodly volume, or a memoir of such a character that it would be accepted by a learned society for its transactions. It is therefore said, and doubtless with justice, that the Doctor's degree is much more difficult of attainment at the Sorbonne than in Germany.

The proposed new University Doctorate may materially change these conditions; but the problem of adapting it to the French system is not without difficulty. How it will be grappled with will doubtless appear when all the facilities of the new Sorbonne are at the command of the student.

The question whether our students should at once transfer their preference in respect of higher education from Germany to France, is one not easy to answer. The fact is that no American student need now go abroad to complete his education, unless in very exceptional cases. The development of our own universities during the past twenty years has been such that he can find as good instruction at home as abroad. The purpose of a residence abroad is not to acquire an education unattainable at home, but to afford the student that breadth of culture which is gained only by residence in a country different from his own, and by intercourse with the masters of learning in other lands. These ends, it appears to me, can be as well gained by the student in France as in any other country; and he will receive a warm welcome when it is once known that he appreciates it. An attempt has been made to form special organizations for his benefit which, though they may not be wholly successful, are none the less worthy of appreciation,—especially as evincing the feeling entertained by Frenchmen for our own country.

If it be true that the Frenchman does not possess the art of making a foreign visitor feel at home, it is because he aims at so high a standard of hospitality that it cannot be extended to all the world, nor kept up as a daily practice. This, it may be expected, he will remedy when he finds that the foreign visitor expects nothing of the kind, but desires only a friendly welcome, and intercourse without ceremony or display.

SIMON NEWCOMB.

THE EMPEROR WILLIAM II.

WHEN the Columbus quadricentennial was celebrated in Chicago, the Emperor William was the only monarch who took notice of that memorable event. His telegram to the President ran as follows: "The German Emperor sends you, through the German Minister, his sincere congratulations on the occasion of the four hundredth anniversary of the discovery of America, and couples with the same his hearty good wishes for the further prosperity of the great country of which you are the head."

The Emperor's good-will toward the mighty republic beyond the ocean had been of long standing, as he himself said to the American Ambassador in Berlin, Mr. Phelps, on the occasion of his presenting his credentials in September, 1889. His words were:—

"From my youth up I have had a great admiration for the great and rising community which you are here called on to represent; and the study of its history in peace and war has always been of the greatest interest to me. Among the many high qualities which your countrymen possess, it is their spirit of enterprise, their love of order, and their talent for invention which draw the attention of the whole world to them. Germans find themselves all the more attracted by the people of the United States, in that they are closely connected with the North Americans by the many ties which go side by side with community of blood. The ruling sentiment of the two peoples is that of kinship and proved friendship; and the future can only add to the cordiality of our relations."

This address to Mr. Phelps and the telegram above quoted are characteristic of William II. However one may judge him, he, of all living monarchs, excites the most attention and the most lively interest. He is the typical modern ruler, the child of his age. With great and lofty aims in view, he does his best to fall in with the demands of the day. That he constantly re-excites this interest and attention is due in the first place to his strongly marked personality. "Personality is the greatest good fortune that can befall the sons of men," says Goethe somewhere; and this good fortune has fallen to the lot of Germany's present ruler. The Emperor William feels himself strong in himself; he has a strong will and a strong hand; he possesses the consciousness

of wishing to do right and of being able to do so, and is convinced
that he is able worthily to fill the high place to which Providence
has called him. His sense of duty is unshakable; he gives a strict
account of his doings to himself; and if at times, in the overflowing
consciousness of youth and strength, he enters upon a wrong course, as
soon as he sees that the majority of his people is not in accord with
him, he retraces his steps and takes the right one. For he is quick to
perceive this fact; and however strong the influence of the moment is
within him, and however strong the impulse which at times urges him
to give rapid effect to his feelings, yet he never forgets his responsibility. He realizes at the right moment that millions of eyes are bent
on him, now in high hope, now in anxiety, and now again in warning.

With this grave and resolute nature he combines another—deeply
religious, sensitive, and romantic. The "Kingship by the grace of
God" is no empty phrase to him. He is steeped to the last fibre of his
being in the consciousness of the responsibility of his position; and
nothing could induce him to believe this to be the result of an
"accident of birth." The will of the Almighty has called him to it;
and a sense of this gives him, in an increased degree, the power to act
with confidence and to avoid all hesitation and indecision.

The fear which was felt at first, that he would prove to be strictly
orthodox and throw himself into the arms of the orthodox party, has
not, to the great relief of the best men among his people, been realized.
He has too high a respect for religion to attach himself to any party
on such grounds; and any attempts—of which there were not a few—
to thus gain him over, were rudely repulsed, and only did harm to
those who made them. His careful solicitude for ecclesiastical buildings in Berlin has often made people—chiefly in the provinces—shake
their heads over him; but those people did not know that in Berlin
there has been for many years a great deficiency of such buildings,
and that the churches have been constantly overcrowded.

The sincere piety of the Emperor shows the spiritual side of his
nature: it is closely bound up with the belief in his destiny, and forms
a contrast with his, in other respects, practical views of life. What
the Orientals call "fate" is to him a dispensation of Providence, and a
sign of the pleasure of God.

This unshakable confidence in the authority reposed in him by a
Higher Power gives the Emperor his astonishing elasticity: it enables
him to easily overcome disappointments, and fills him with ever-fresh
exultation in the execution of a difficult task. He has certainly had

disappointments enough; and the golden burden of the crown must often have lain heavy on his head.

Let us try to realize the circumstances under which he came to the throne, and the reception his personality and his method of government met with. There is no doubt that as the successor of William I and Frederick III he was regarded with confidence; but this feeling partook more or less of a historical nature. Personally but little was known about him, except that he had had an excellent civil and military education, and that he was heart and soul a soldier. He had scarcely ever taken part in public business; and, at the few state occasions on which he had appeared, he showed himself distant, retiring, and, to use a Prussian phrase, "buttoned up in his uniform." He had never made any disguise of his admiration for Prince Bismarck; having often visited the Chancellor unofficially of an evening, and listened for hours attentively to his talk and maxims. What the Prince thought of the then heir to the throne, and his probable course of action when he should succeed to it, was contained in the prophetic dictum, "He will one day be his own chancellor."

People who had come in contact with the Crown Prince at court and had had opportunities of observing him closely agreed with this judgment, and spoke highly of his zeal and industry in applying himself to and carrying out the varied tasks set him. Especial stress was laid on a criticism of the Prince which appeared in a pamphlet entitled "Court and Society in Berlin." This pamphlet, written by Count Paul Vasili (a M. de Moudion, *alias* Foucault), was published in 1884, and was immediately suppressed in Germany. It was consequently read all the more eagerly by the higher classes. It proved so correct in its more important points, that I quote it here at length:—

"Prince William is just four-and-twenty, so that it is hard to say how he will turn out. He is undoubtedly a young man with a future, and has wit, intelligence, and pluck. He is the cleverest of the royal princes, and is courageous, enterprising, ambitious, hot-headed but warm-hearted, most sympathetic; he has 'go,' fire, and mobility in character and mind, readiness in intercourse, and this to such an extent that one might almost fancy he was not a German. He is enthusiastically fond of the army, and is in turn much beloved by it. In spite of his youth, he has known how to make himself popular with all classes of society. He is well taught, has read much, forms plans for the prosperity of his country, and has remarkable understanding for everything connected with policy. He will certainly be a man of mark, and probably a great monarch. Prussia will perhaps find in him another Frederick the Great, but without that ruler's scepticism; besides which he possesses a sprightliness of character that will soften down the touches of harshness which will belong to him as a true Hohenzollern. He will be above all a personal monarch, and will not allow himself to be led;

he will have a sound and temperate judgment, a quick decision, a firm will, and energetic action. If he comes to the throne, he will carry on the work of his grandfather, and will certainly undo that of his father, whatever it may be. The enemies of Germany will find in him an adversary to be feared ; and he may well prove the Henry IV of his country."

Such was the judgment of a Frenchman who hated Germany, and which it is doubly interesting to recall now. It was destined, at least in all material points, to be more quickly proved correct than anyone expected. After being heir to the throne for little more than three months, the Prince succeeded to it as William II. He found a new day come, and herculean tasks suddenly set before him. A whole age was buried in the grave with William I; a new era in the development of Prussia and Germany had begun ; the most important questions awaited decision ; unexpected desires were proclaimed ; hopes that had never before been suspected looked for realization ; a mighty shock seemed to pass through the nation, which felt that many things had become unstable which before had been held to be firm as a rock.

The last period of the rule of William I had been a quiet and secure one. At times there were dull growls of discontent from the industrial quarters of Berlin and the industrial towns in the provinces ; but these were as distant thunder, and the person and throne of the venerable patriarch among the rulers of the world were undisturbed by them. The consciousness of security, of possessing a charm against all evils, so long as the gray-haired emperor ruled, was universal.

Then came the great reaction, when the Emperor Frederick too had bowed his weary head in eternal slumber. A young and, as was generally believed, a wholly inexperienced ruler had ascended the throne ; in a thousand places sedition seethed and bubbled ; the person of the Emperor became the sport of conflicting opinions ; every utterance of his was repeated, mostly in a garbled form ; parties crowded about him right and left, endeavoring to gain him over to their private interests, and to share in his authority ; new counsellors were to be forced on him ; there was no end to the intrigues ; and, overtopping all in importance and weight, the social question raised its threatening head, and with resonant voice demanded satisfaction of its claims.

True, the iron chancellor, Prince Bismarck, stood at the young monarch's side ; but, in addition to the fact that he was often in weak health, and retired into private life at Friedrichsruh or Varzin, it soon became clear, to those who were able to judge, that the two could not long go on governing together. It was felt that it could not be long before the fiery, restless, resolute Emperor found the influence of the Chancellor—who was 75 years old—an intolerable burden, and would shake himself free from it. That this would happen so quickly and in such an unexpected way as it did, no one could have foreseen; nor that the breach would be so complete, and that social reforms would be made the pretext for it.

" Above all, I shall (in the spirit of my grandfather) continue to aim at making imperial legislation tend to the further protection of the working-classes ; a protection which the principles of Christian morality bid us give, as far as may be, to the poor and needy in the struggle for life. I hope that in this way it will be possible to counteract, to a great degree, unsound social principles; and I am convinced that in my efforts on behalf of our domestic prosperity I shall have the unanimous support of all true partisans of the Crown and of the Federated Governments without distinction of party."

By such words did the Emperor, at the first opening of the Reichstag, in June, 1888, make it known that the protection of the poor and oppressed was to be one of his chief cares as a ruler, and that he too was a representative of empire based on social principles.

Under William I the Artisans' Savings Law had been enacted, securing millions of Germans against poverty during sickness, accident, and in old age. This was a measure of vast importance; and it excited the admiration of other states, particularly on account of the rapidity with which it had been passed. That it laid many burdens on the industrial and mechanical classes and caused them many new difficulties was unavoidable; and Prince Bismarck wished for a pause in social legislation. But this did not agree with the intentions of the Emperor. He wished to extend the protection of the working-classes still further; and the great strike of miners in the Rhine country and in Westphalia, in the spring of 1889, furnished him with a pretext for interfering actively in the affairs of those classes. The Emperor also acted as mediator. At an audience given to the mine-owners he said :—

"I desire to recommend to all concerned to keep as far as possible in touch with the workmen. It is quite natural that everyone should try to get as much of the means of life as possible. The workmen read the newspapers and know what proportion their pay bears to the profits of the companies that employ them. It is not to be wondered at that they should wish to have a certain share in those profits."

From that time the Emperor never allowed the question of provision for artisans to rest. He was constantly mentioning it in the Staatsrath ; he expressed in detail his views as to a day of rest on

Sunday, and as to fixed hours of labor; he discussed the protection of women and children; and since, if Germany legislated alone on the matter, its industries might suffer heavy loss, he proposed an agreement between the principal industrial states, and invited an international conference on the subject at Berlin.   Before it could meet, however, Prince Bismarck resigned and retired in dudgeon to Friedrichsruh.

Undaunted the Emperor pursued the path he had entered on. The Sunday day of rest was introduced; the Government workshops became models as regards provision for the workmen; the hours of labor for women and children were reduced; in connection with several of the royal mines and railways committees of workmen were formed; and on May 7, 1891, the sweeping laws for the protection of artisans were adopted by the Diet. The Emperor had good reason for saying, when inspecting the Krupp factories at Essen, "German workmen! You know that our House has always cared for the working-classes. I have shown the world the way in which I mean to go; and I say again to-day that I shall continue in that way."

If the Emperor showed that the lot of those of his subjects who had to earn their living by manual labor was a matter of especial interest to him, yet he also left no room for doubt that he was determined to repress with iron severity all attempts at disorder.   His firm and manly behavior contributed much to the reassuring of the public mind in Germany; for, during the early portion of his reign, the bugbear of democracy had caused much alarm. If people had before believed that in many cases—not only abroad but in Germany—the social question could be solved only by "blood and iron," and that a civil war was inevitable within a short time, they now came to think quite differently, and to judge social-democratic affairs much more dispassionately, because they looked at them less from the political than from the social and economical point of view; in this way trying to bring about a peaceful solution.

That, in spite of all such efforts and the care of the Government for the working-classes,—which is greater than in any other country whatever,—socialism is steadily on the increase in Germany, and that at the last elections the number of Deputies representing the Social Democrats increased from 36 to 44, is not a matter of astonishment to those acquainted with the facts.   Discontent is general, not only in Germany but elsewhere; and it finds free vent on German soil in universal suffrage.   However, of the 1,323,000 votes cast in its favor at the last election, scarcely a twentieth part can be considered as given by Social Democrats who are such from conviction, and who would be ready, if necessary, to stand by their principles in action.

The other parties, especially that of the greater *bourgeoisie*, are not a little to blame for this enormous increase in Social Democracy. That class is still sunk in a deep political slumber, and even to-day is accurately portrayed in the caricature of " German Michael," with his nightcap pulled down over his ears, indifferent to all about him. If this *bourgeoisie*, which forms the sound nucleus of the German people, would rouse itself, and endeavor to support a safe national policy such as the Emperor would approve, the state of parties in Germany would be much improved, and the Government would at least know on whom it could depend. It really seems as if there must be storms from without or within before these millions of citizens, who can talk so wisely over their beer, and criticize so keenly, can be brought to realize that they would be doing a patriotic act in forming a powerful party which should not be at the mercy of any special principles. Ah those special objects of all kinds!—How they worried the Emperor, in spite of the fact that he had declared plainly enough, in a speech which attracted much attention, that no class could claim to be favored at the expense of others, and that it was the business of the Sovereign to weigh the interests of all classes against each other, and to see that the general interest of the whole country was not endangered! That is the only interest which the Emperor always has in view. It is his guide in choosing men to fill responsible posts in the government, and enables him to avoid the charge of selecting his advisers purely from personal considerations.

That mistakes in selection sometimes occur is natural enough; but if the Emperor sees that the men he has chosen are serving interests other than those which he has in view, or are at variance with the aims of the majority of his people, he dismisses them ruthlessly. " The Emperor has a man ready to take the place of every one of us," a Prussian minister once declared; and the remark was eminently true as characteristic of the Emperor's way of governing. He does not wish to be influenced in his decisions by elements which it is impossible for him always to control. He has quite broken with the famous dictum, " Le roi règne, mais il ne gouverne pas." Perhaps he is the first ruler to govern personally and yet uphold the principles of the constitution; thus welding together the old and new methods of government. There may be risks about such a course; but it has its advantages, especially where a firm and self-reliant character is con-

cerned. If William II were not such a man, he would have long since
lost heart, and adopted the much more convenient, safe, and unexcit-
ing method of governing through chancellors and ministers, which
seems inseparable from monarchies with traditions, and which may
end by endangering their apparently firmly based prosperity.

But fears about the future are not compatible with such qualities
as the Emperor possesses ; and, besides, he has a much too soldierlike
nature to be afraid of anything,—god-fearing, resolute, and daring as he
is.   The motto that he wrote under his own portrait which he presented
to a clergyman of merit, " He who trusts only in God and stands firm,
has not built on the sand," came from his very soul.   William II is a
soldier through and through ; and the first proclamation that he issued
after ascending the throne was addressed to the army, which, to him,
is the incarnation of the flower of his people.   It ran, " We belong to
each other, the army and I ; we were made for each other; and will
hold together unfailingly, if God so please, whether he sends us peace
or war."   He is not a soldier by tradition, as his father was, but of his
own choice and conviction, like his grandfather.   From an early age
he trained himself in all kinds of sport; was a skilled fencer and a
bold rider, heading his squadron of hussars, and engaging in many a
ride which was not appropriate to an heir to a throne.   To him soldiers
are a privileged people ; and it is not his fault if at times men are still
improperly treated in the German army.   When an officer was dismissed for such conduct, the Emperor wrote on the order of dismissal,
" I should never have thought that I had such a brutal officer in
my army."   While yet a prince, and colonel of the Hussar Regiment
of the Guard at Potsdam, he forbade his officers to indulge in play.
As some of these gentlemen disregarded the prohibition, the Prince
tried to get his grandfather to punish them severely ; and, finding that
the latter would not accede to his request, he proffered his resignation as colonel.   This showed that the Prince was concerned with the
moral welfare of the army; and as Emperor he has concerned himself
with it still more, energetically suppressing excessive luxury and
gambling among the officers.

At the same time he endeavored to increase materially the prepar-
edness of the German army for war, and succeeded most thoroughly in
doing so.   For, under the long rule of William I, the army had not, in
times of peace, degenerated; but, out of consideration for its aged chief,
it had abstained from many innovations which had gradually become
matters of necessity.   Moreover, the aged monarch was very loath to

part with his generals, though they might be too old for serious work, and unfit to lead the troops into action.

Here then there was much to do; and it was done. Not only was the army increased in proportion to the increase in the population, but it was remodelled in many respects, especially as regards the age of the officers.

The Emperor expects a great deal of his army and its leaders, and often they seem to have reached the limits of human capacity; but he himself sets them the example, urging them on, and himself never tiring. What he gets through during the manœuvres excites the admiration of everybody. You should see him on his charger, galloping over the scene of operations at a pace which his suite can hardly maintain, following the movements of the troops with a keen eye, and often, by a brief word of command, altering their direction. He concerns himself at such times about the smallest detail; keeps his eye on every company which is within sight; and often goes himself to see whether his orders have been carried out to the minutest particulars. Frequently he changes the position of the outposts at the last moment, and at times visits them quite unexpectedly by night, to see that they are in order. While the manœuvres are going on he never knows what physical weariness is; often leaving his quarters at three or four o'clock in the morning, and not returning to them till six or seven in the evening. The intervening time is passed mainly on horseback. A good and sure rider, he turns up with his staff, as a rule, quite unexpectedly, in different places; takes over the command; and is always concerned in the first place for the men, their personal comfort being plainly his especial care.

His criticisms are calm and to the point. However generous he may be, he can find fault very sharply. Many an officer of high rank has doubtless felt a qualm as he has heard the signal sounding over the field to summon him to the Emperor's criticism of his operations. In case of a glaring mistake the Emperor is remorseless; and on one occasion he even sent a prince—nearly akin to him—and his regiment straight back to their garrison. On these occasions the independence of judgment and rapidity of decision of the Emperor are conspicuous. "As far as my experience goes, to my mind, that ought to have been done in such and such a way," he says; and then follows, in brief terms, a clear exposition of the right way to do it. Though one or the other of the higher officers in question may not formerly have quite agreed with the tactical instruction so given, opinions have changed greatly in the last few years, and one now hears distinguished leaders combining to recognize the Emperor's tactical capacity and military powers of observation.

Of course this fondness for things military, which showed itself plainly even when he was a prince, gave rise to the most improbable reports when he came to the throne. He was spoken of as a "Soldier Emperor"; and there was no lack of warlike prophecies. But he has shown himself the most pacific of monarchs, and is always proclaiming his love of peace. "I should consider the man as a maniac or a criminal who urged the two peoples on to make war against each other," he declared to Jules Simon, when he attended the Workmen's Congress at Berlin. He knows how to appreciate the power which his army puts into his hands; but he knows, too, what it costs at times, if such power is misused. Though resolved to maintain his own and the Empire's honor to the last drop of his blood, and to avenge any insult in exemplary fashion, he will avoid anything that might lead to a conflict,—true to the words that he uttered at Bremen in April, 1890: "The highest duty of the ruler is to concern himself with the maintenance of peace."

People have often asked themselves which of his ancestors the Emperor most reminds them of; and various comparisons have been instituted, now in his favor, and again to his discredit. But none of the princes who have preceded him on the throne can be fitly compared to him; for he is the child of a new age, and in thorough sympathy with the aspirations of a united Germany, which none of his predecessors, except his father, has been. His is a personality apart, which will not fit into any existing historical frame. He has, however, certain points of resemblance with almost all the Hohenzollern princes who have made themselves remarkable in history. He shares with the Great Elector his love for personal administration, and the conscientiousness that leads him to see to everything himself; with Frederick I his fondness for the externals of sovereignty; with Frederick William I his love for soldiering and the chase; with Frederick the Great his musical and poetical occupations; with Frederick William III his absence of affectation and simplicity in domestic life; with Frederick William IV his fondness for oratorical effort and love of art; and, lastly, with William I his straightforwardness and devotion to such friends as he has once found true.

This many-sidedness, which has been no less prominent of later years, would be alarming, and might be justly characterized as an overstraining of all the powers, were it not the fact that the Emperor always finds relaxation and recovers his elasticity in his domestic circle. Here he is near to us as a man ; here he appears in a different character from either of those we have been describing. Grave, conscientious, and constantly mindful of his high position and great responsibility as a ruler, in his home he is kind and affable ; full of all the feelings of a father and spouse; often giving free vent to his good humor. He has a great deal of sprightliness and joviality in his temperament, and, as a " born Berliner,"—for, as is well known, not above a third of the inhabitants of "Athens on the Spree" are such, the rest being immigrants,—he uses on occasion the true Berlin patter for fun.

With all his gift of rapid receptivity, and his capacity for going deeply into a subject and quickly getting a general idea of it, the Emperor is not easily induced to give up an opinion he has once formed. Persuasion is of no use in such a case: he must be convinced by solid argument. He is not open to attempts to influence him ; and the removal from Berlin of several very high personages, who might fairly have counted on his friendship, is ascribed simply to the fact that the Emperor wished to avoid the slightest suspicion of being influenced by them. In spite of the separation, however, he remained on terms of personal good-will toward them.

It is owing to his frank and resolute character that he always throws himself heart and soul into a cause; and where he has not already done so, his interest in it is very readily excited. There is no "routine-bred indifference" about him, such as grows into a habit with so many other princes. This comes out plainly in his public utterances. Whether he is opening the Diet in state, judging pictures at an art exhibition, proposing a toast on a festive occasion, engaging in a long conversation with a princely guest, or presenting to his consort in a few gracious words someone that he has invited to table,—whatever he says always produces the impression of real personal interest.

He is on the very best of terms with his wife. Once, at Schleswig, the home of the Empress, he spoke of her in loud, hearty tones as the pearl, more costly than any other gift, which that province had offered him. On another occasion he playfully declared to one of the friends of his youth that in his wife's dictionary three words beginning with a K were her favorites, " Kirche," " Kinder," " Küche " ("church," "children," " cooking "); adding, that he thought much more of a woman who, like his wife, could prepare a tasty dish than of ladies who interfered in politics and affected to be clever, but would never know

22

anything about keeping house decently. These and many other speeches which have become known are the best proofs how highly the Emperor prizes German domestic life and its affections; and one hears often enough from people about the court that he is never more contented and happy than when with his family.

The imperial household is in the main simply conducted, and presents a sharp contrast to the pomp and display of the court on state occasions. The tone is cosy and homelike; and in the family circle the strict prescriptions of etiquette are disregarded. All members of the family, even distant relatives, use the familiar "thou" in speaking to each other; and their intercourse is as easy and unconstrained as that of the most thoroughly *bourgeois* household.

If the Emperor, when his spouse is away, talks about her to others, he calls her "my wife," or "the Empress"; while she generally speaks of him as "the Emperor," though to his face she often calls him "Willy." The children are addressed by their imperial parents by all sorts of pet names; though at times they also use nicknames, which refer to one or other of their little pranks. When she is away from them, the Empress always speaks of them as "my children"; but the Emperor, though the youngest is a princess, always says "my boys"; and the words have a special heartiness about them.

The children cling to their parents with touching love and devotion; and the latter, in their turn, when away from home, constantly think of the little ones, and bring back all kinds of presents as surprises for them. Once, when the Emperor won a thaler at a shooting competition of one of the Guard regiments, he took it with a smile of pleasure, remarking, "I will buy something for my boys with it; it will make them so happy!"

Not an evening passes without the Empress going to the children's bedsides, and praying with them, and kissing them good-night. On one occasion the three elder princes, who slept together in a separate room, begged so hard that she would come in again when she returned from the theatre that she consented, thinking that they would be asleep long before then. When, several hours later, the Empress went cautiously into their room again, the heads of the three lads looked out gayly from among the pillows. "Why, children!" cried she in astonishment, "not asleep yet? How have you managed that?" "Oh, mamma," said they, hardly able to speak for chuckling, "we tied a thread round our legs, and when one of us fell asleep, the others pulled at it, and then he was wide awake again at once!"

What a deep and touching expression of his devoted love for his gentle and beautiful mamma did one of the princes find when he was undergoing religious instruction! When one day they came to a passage about all men being sinners, Prince Eitel Friedrich looked down at first thoughtfully, and then cried resolutely, "No, no, that is not true, for our mamma is not a sinner!"

The day begins early for the imperial pair. The Emperor rises before seven o'clock, takes a cold bath, at once puts on uniform, and breakfasts with his consort. Even when he has to get up much earlier, either for a review or to go shooting, he always has her company. Directly after breakfast, or sometimes during the meal, the children come in to say good-morning, which does not take long, especially with the elder ones, as their studies begin soon. Then the Emperor goes to his study, arranges the distribution of the day with his adjutants, receives the report of the court marshal, and takes a ride about nine— generally accompanied by his wife—in the direction of the Zoölogical Gardens. This is followed by a long walk; for the imperial Castle at Berlin has no grounds whatever about it. When he gets back to the Castle, there is writing to be done, there are reports and receptions to attend to, which fully occupy the forenoon and are continued in the afternoon.

About two o'clock, when no pressing engagements arise to prevent it, the imperial pair lunch in the dining-hall; the young princes being frequently present at this meal, and occasionally a guest specially invited by the Emperor. The two *flügel-adjutanten* or equerries and the ladies-in-waiting are in attendance.

Like Frederick the Great, William II likes good company at table; so there are always several guests at the six o'clock dinner,—as at the supper that follows at nine,—who are welcomed by him with a hearty shake of the hand. The meal generally consists of but few courses; but, however small the company, the table is always laid with costly plate and the choicest flowers. Of the latter the Emperor is particularly fond. It is at these small gatherings, after which cigars and Munich beer are handed round, that he shows himself most unconstrained. Almost every department of public life is freely handled on these occasions; and the Emperor encourages his guests, who are often scholars and artists, to speak freely. It frequently happens at such times that opinions differ to an extent unbefitting such a place; but the Emperor always knows how to interpose in a conciliatory way, or to put an end to the war of words by a sharp speech.

These little evening parties often last till eleven or twelve o'clock. If the Emperor is in a particularly good humor, he conducts his guests, as soon as the meal is over, to an old vaulted chamber in the basement. Here the old brown wainscoting and the seats around the walls, over which are hung plaques of Dutch china and bronze, as well as the old marble fireplace,—dating from the time of the Electors,—in which great logs crackle in winter, have a most cosy effect, and invite to confidential chat. The Emperor, it may be remarked, partakes freely of the food on the table,—especially certain favorite dishes,—but is very sparing in the use of wine and beer; though he presses these on his guests, and is an attentive and kind host.

In spite of the excessive quantity of daily work which he has to do, the Emperor finds time in which to devote himself to his family. He often pays a visit to his wife in the brief interval between two reports or receptions, to talk over things with her; for, however absolute he may be in other ways, he likes to hear and take into consideration the opinion of his consort on all but political and military questions. They are happy hours and full of refreshment which the imperial pair pass together between dinner and supper; for then the children are with them, and loud sounds of jubilation often issue from their apartments.

The bearing of the Empress is always full of gentleness and simplicity; and she is a striking instance of the truth of the saying, that that woman is the best who is least talked about. Innumerable evidences of warm love for her neighbor and of self-sacrificing charity are never heard of by the public; but, though enjoyed in secret, they are none the less a means of happiness to her. On one evening in every week she calls her ladies-in-waiting about her, and under her guidance and with her help they do work for poor families; while the extensive support given by the court to those in need is the outcome of personal inquiries of the Empress. She wishes to spread happiness around her, because she is happy herself; and the saying of a high official who has been brought much into contact with the imperial pair, that theirs is one of the happiest families in Germany, has foundation in fact.

The Emperor has much and most responsible work to do, and the hours—more frequently minutes only—of which he has the free disposal, are numbered. I am fully justified in saying that he is only secure from interruption when he is on the high seas, and the messengers, who at other times follow him everywhere with closely-packed despatch-cases, are unable to find him out. He can get through his day's task completely only by dint of long practice, by the most careful collaboration of the various officials, and by such a careful distribution of his time as leaves not a minute out of account.

The day generally begins with the examination of the correspondence received; the letters usually amounting to several hundreds. Many of these are petitions and are at once laid aside to be further dealt with by the civil staff. Where he recognizes the writing or the arms on a letter, the Emperor himself opens it, and either passes it on with a brief remark in writing to his private secretaries, or, more rarely, reserves it to be answered by himself. The series of reports is generally opened by that of the court marshal, who makes his in the Emperor's study. It generally takes up a good deal of time; for it deals with the conduct of the Emperor's household, the granting of audiences, the taking over of Protectorates, the giving permission for charitable lotteries, and the arrangement of journeys and visits.

But other matters are submitted to him by the marshal; for the Emperor likes to decide personally everything that concerns him and his court. Consequently plans for intended alterations in the palaces, for laying out new gardens, sketches and models prepared by artists for presents and prizes to be given by the Emperor, are laid before him. In addition, his attention is drawn to jubilees, special festivities, and occasions when he will have to return thanks; while the more pressing petitions are placed before him. After his short forenoon drive, and after lunch, the reports and receptions are resumed, the various ministers and heads of departments attend, audiences are given, various great personages are received, and officers and others make their reports. In the intervals between these duties the Emperor looks through important papers,—and he thinks a good many things important.

A great deal of time, especially in the winter months, is absorbed owing to the necessity, attaching to the Emperor's position, of his being personally present on great occasions. At such times even urgent business is laid aside for days together; and, not infrequently, when the acclamations of the people have died away, the electric lamps on the Emperor's writing-table burn late into the night. Not only that; but by his bedside are placed paper and pencil for him to make notes with.

It is manifest that with so much business to transact, there can be but little time left for reading. The Emperor, however, manages to keep himself well posted in the most important military works that appear at home and abroad. He also has brought to him every day a portfolio full of cuttings from the principal political organs of Berlin and the great provincial towns.

As regards belles-lettres, he prefers historical novels; though he does not neglect the more important works published in foreign countries. He also keeps a careful watch on the progress of art, both at home and abroad. For the Emperor is highly gifted as regards artistic qualities, and loves to be brought into contact with the great lights of art, and to encourage them in every way. All scientific questions, inventions, and discoveries awake the liveliest interest in his mind; and what he likes best is to have such matters explained to him by the savants in person, so as to get as deep an insight as possible into them. As soon as the news began to spread of Professor Roentgen's discovery of the X-rays, he sent a telegraphic invitation to the Professor, and listened for hours to his demonstrations with the closest attention. When a well-known Berlin savant, Professor Werder, who had been personally attached to the Emperor, died, the latter ordered a monument to be put over his grave, with the inscription, "Amico Imperator.".

That, when all his powers are thus taxed to the uttermost, the Emperor at times finds himself in urgent need of relaxation, is a matter of course; and even the cruises, for which he was so blamed in the early days of his rule, are frequently the result of political aims. "In my youth I was never allowed to take long journeys," he said once in public, "because it was my grandfather's wish that I should always be at his side; but I consider it necessary for a ruler to inform himself personally about everything, and to form his opinions at first hand, to be personally acquainted with his neighbors, to establish friendly relations with them, and to maintain such. These are the aims with which I undertake my travels." The Emperor is always turning the prow of his stately yacht, the "Hohenzollern," northward, as the splendid scenery of Norway and the simplicity of its inhabitants have a strong attraction for him; and he always returns home thoroughly re-invigorated.

The picture that William II presents is that of a prince quite by himself; but it is an engaging and attractive picture none the less. Of one thing we may be quite sure; viz., that, should a time of danger ever arise for the German Empire during his reign, that empire will have at its head a man in the best sense of the word,—a man who knows what he wants; resolute and German to the core; fit to cope with troublous times, and to steer the ship of state with a sure hand. And the German nation will obey him with full confidence and trust.

PAUL LINDENBERG.

THE AUTOCRAT OF CONGRESS.

ARMED with a plenitude of power beside which the authority of the President of the United States seems mean and insignificant, the Speaker of the House of Representatives is to-day the autocrat of Congress. He is the absolute arbiter of the destinies of all legislation, the court of last resort from whose decision there is no appeal. In the hands of designing or unscrupulous men the control now vested in the office of Speaker could easily menace the Republic with gravest danger. Even as it is, these functions have reached that all-compelling degree which demands something more than mere casual attention.

Occasion did not always necessitate this criticism. There was a time, not so very long since, when, instead of being their czar-like ruler, the Speaker of the House was rightfully the servant of the men who elevated him to his high position. It is true that in those days the absence of tyrannical prerogative was accompanied by deadlocks in the House, when hours and even weeks were lost through the employment of filibustering tactics. Against this wanton waste of time there was a very general protest; especially as the power to delay and finally to prevent action was exercised not alone against measures involving vital principles of government, but also in opposition to petty partisan schemes which rose to no higher plane than the distribution of spoils. That the inability of the Speaker to prevent the operation of obstructive tactics was provocative of evil is not to be denied; and the clamor of an impatient people against the continuance of such a practice was not surprising. Still, on the other hand, filibustering had its uses. It obtained for the minority—which was sometimes very close to a majority—some equitable rights which the drastic exercise of majority power otherwise denied.

But the question of filibustering was peremptorily decided in the negative by the Speaker of the House under peculiar circumstances. The Fifty-first Congress, at the time of its organization, contained a very narrow majority of Republicans. It became necessary to increase this majority to an extent which would insure the easier and more certain despatch of business;—a tariff bill and a so-called force bill, for instance, being demanded;—and Democrats holding certificates of election were ousted and Republican contestants seated with questionable celerity. The Democratic minority, angered at a proceeding so greatly at variance with legislative honesty and fairness, rebelled. They resorted to every parliamentary means to save their colleagues from speedy slaughter. To meet this emergency the Speaker of the House became a law unto himself. He conducted the daily business under that elastic code known as general parliamentary law, until he could secure the necessary majority to adopt new rules framed for the exigencies of the occasion. He counted a quorum instead of relying upon the record of personal responses; he became the judge of other men's purposes and intentions by deciding in his own mind whether certain motions were dilatory in their nature and then declining to entertain them; he refused to recognize members of the opposing party while according every privilege to those who were of his own political ideas; he became, in fact as well as in name, a parliamentary czar.

In the excitement of those stormy times party lines were closely drawn; and the Speaker was sustained in his action by the Republican Members of the House. No other course was open. A few there were, it is true, who anticipated with prophetic foresight the logical conclusion of a practical dictatorship. These few were promptly dragooned into the ranks; and their weak voices were unheard or unnoticed in the chorus of praise which ascended from loyal party followers. In due time a code of rules intended to curb and muzzle the turbulent and troublesome minority was framed. It departed from the precedents of the past, and lodged in the Speaker an extent of power almost beyond conception.

One of the most important innovations became known as the "special order." Under this scheme the programme of business in the House became vested in the Committee on Rules, which determined the measure to be taken up, the length of time to be allotted to debate, and the hour at which the vote should be taken. It is true that this "special order" was subject to the approval of the House; but party discipline could always be and has always been successfully relied upon to uphold the Committee. There are five Members in the Committee on Rules: three of the majority party, including the Speaker, and two of the minority. While this committee had in the past exercised more or less supervision of affairs, it became, under the new dispensation, the supreme head. Its members charted the route to be followed through the legislative sea. Their disposition to accord a hearing to a measure had first to be secured before that proposition, however meritorious, could receive consideration in the House.

Ordinarily the lodgment of a directing power in the hands of five men—albeit 5 is a very small proportion of 356—might be excusable and wise; but, as a matter of fact, the practical operation of the present system reduces this quintette to a single individual—the Speaker of the House. In the first place, the two Members representing the minority are simply figure-heads. Their votes are as nothing in the balance against the majority; and frequently they are not even consulted. The original five, thus decreased to three, are still further reduced by an easy process to one. The two Members who are of the Speaker's political persuasion are selected by him with the full understanding that they will be the creatures of his will. Such an agreement may not be expressly stipulated in the bond; but its practical operation in that direction is certainly observable in the experience of the past few years. Neither of these two Members would ever break from his party and his chief to side with the hostile organization. If he did, he would be instantly deposed. Consequently, the pivot finally centres in the Speaker himself. Without his gracious sanction, no measure can come before the House. With him upon the side of any proposition, half the battle is gained; with him arrayed against it, the House is denied the opportunity of considering it, much less of voting upon it.

These are not exaggerated words. The Congress which has just closed afforded two striking examples of what could be done and what could not be done, according to the pleasure of the Speaker. The first instance was the bill to refund the debt of the Union and Central Pacific railroads. Here was a proposition which the Speaker favored. He had spent some time upon the Pacific coast during the Congressional recess, and was undoubtedly impressed by the earnestness with which certain parties interested in those roads sought Congressional action. Besides, he had had occasion to familiarize himself with the public feeling of that section of the country. Without analyzing the causes that swayed his mind, however, the fact remains that he assented to the assignment of several days for debate upon the refunding bill; even arranging that a Sunday should intervene between the close of the discussion and the taking of the vote. It so happened that the measure was overwhelmingly defeated; which all the more emphasizes by contrast the other case to which I desire to call attention.

The measure just alluded to was forced into the legislative arena with all the weight of the Speaker's influence thrown in its favor; and yet events demonstrated that it was unacceptable to a large majority of the Members of the House, irrespective of party. On the other hand, consideration for the Nicaragua Canal Bill was implored of the Speaker in a formal written appeal, to which about three hundred Members signed their names. The importance of this legislation needs no emphasis by me. Eight-tenths of the members of Congress were ready and anxious to debate and then act upon some proposition which should insure the building of a waterway to link the Atlantic with the Pacific, connecting the undeveloped resources of the Far West with the manufacturing cities of the Eastern coast, and shortening the route to Hawaii, Japan, China, and Australia by thousands of miles. In the Committee on Commerce were the signatures of 80,000 persons attached to petitions praying Congressional action; while only eighty-seven individuals were registered in opposition. Numberless boards of trade and chambers of commerce also filed their endorsement of the project. In the face of such overwhelming preponderance of sentiment, one would think that Congress would hardly have dared to hesitate. Congress as a body would not; but Congress as dominated by a single individual ignored the popular demand because, forsooth, that individual was adamantine in his antagonism to the proposed legislation. He was undoubtedly actuated by patriotic motives, believing that no private enterprise of such gigantic proportions should be endorsed by the Government. Still, it would seem as if this were a decision which rested with the representatives of the people. And let it be suggested, merely for the sake of illustrating the moral, that the same influences which operated favorably for the transcontinental lines might have been exercised in hostility to their formidable rival. Happily, such criticism does not and, in fact, could not obtain against the present occupant of the Speaker's chair. But the very fact that serious contingencies may arise under the present system emphasizes its evils and only too plainly indicates the danger which is threatened by the continued exercise of this one-man power.

It will naturally be asked why a Member does not appeal directly to the House in behalf of an important national measure; especially when, as in the case of the Nicaragua Canal Bill, he would be assured beforehand of the support of a majority of his colleagues. The answer exemplifies again the dominance of the Speaker. Not a Member of the House can secure the promise of recognition by the Speaker until he has acquainted the latter with the proposition which he intends to bring to the notice of the House. Without recognition he rises in vain.

Consequently, every Member becomes subordinated to the caprice of the occupant of the Speaker's chair. No matter how important in point of aggregated wealth, commercial enterprise, or population may be the district which the Member represents; chosen though he be as a tribune of the people on an equality with the man who happens to be temporarily elevated to the custody of the gavel, he dwindles to a nonentity, save only as the Speaker suffers him occasionally to shake off the parliamentary chains which bind him. I have known more instances than one in which a Congressman has been relegated to private life because he failed in the matter of legislation vitally concerning his constituents. He would not have felt the force of this fatal discontent had the question at 'issue been considered and then defeated: his critics upbraided him and held him responsible because it had never even been brought to the attention of the House. Yet the fault did not lie with him. He was not delinquent: he was the victim of a system which made him dependent upon the Speaker's pleasure. It is no wonder that a man who is thus all-controlling is dined and wined and fêted and initiated into the enjoyments of the highest and most exclusive social life in Washington. Any man susceptible to these influences might be—I do not say he is or would be—disposed to give friendly regard to those Members who were in a position to offer him such advantages. At any rate, the opportunity for discrimination thus temptingly afforded should be removed.

But, although I have shown how the Speaker dominates the one committee which schedules legislation, and how he arbitrarily exercises the right of recognition, I have yet to mention what is, after all, the basis of the Speaker's autocratic power in shaping the destiny of proposed laws. The appointment of the committees of the House— those minor machines which sift out the wheat from the chaff in thousands of bills—is absolutely and solely in the hands of the Speaker. As soon as he is chosen for his high office he begins the work of framing these committees. He can, if he be so disposed, reward the friends who have given him their cordial support in the contest for the Speakership and revenge himself upon those who had the bad judgment or the temerity to oppose him. It may seem harsh to suggest that public position has been prostituted to the gratification of personal ends; but that even Speakers are in their passions like unto the commonest of human clay has been unfortunately proved more than once.

In the assignment of Members to commanding places the Speaker attracts to himself a personal support which intrenches him all the more strongly in his position. He does not rely upon this, however, for influencing legislation, but, like a good architect, sees that the foundation of his structure is well laid. In the appointment of the committees this one man shapes the policy of the Congress over which he is to preside. Is he against the free coinage of silver? He can and does select men whom he can depend upon to report adversely upon a bill designed to secure that end; or, if the House is discovered to be friendly, the measure can be pigeon-holed. Is he inimical to a Federal uniform bankruptcy law? The Committee on Judiciary, when appointed, can be relied upon in its kindred antagonism. Is he for any legislation favorable to railroads? The committee, forthwith, is composed of a majority of men committed to his view. Are public buildings to be constructed? Are river and harbor improvements to be generously or niggardly dealt with? Is a general scheme for a revision of the finances of the country to be framed or ignored? In these and in a hundred other cases the desires of the Speaker are reflected in the personnel of the committees he appoints. Under these circumstances, the question is not what will the House do, but what are the purposes of the Speaker. If disposed to a jingo policy, he can place upon his Committee on Foreign Affairs enough men of ardent temperament, whose bump of belligerency is larger than that of judgment, to insure the report of soul-stirring but injudicious resolutions. If, on the other hand, he be controlled by conservative influences, it is impossible for the House to find any opportunity to express its sentiments upon a question swaying the public mind. Witness the fact, for instance, that not one of the Cuban resolutions introduced in the last House was ever reported back from the Committee on Foreign Affairs.

Certainly it needs no further argument or citation of fact to prove that the Speaker is, indeed, the autocrat of Congress. He frames the committees to suit his ideas; he decides what measures shall be heard; he recognizes or ignores any Member. Is the lodgment in him of such tremendous power a wise, prudent, or desirable thing? The question demands thoughtful consideration. Some there are—mostly recipients of favors from the Speaker's hands and secure always of his friendly coöperation—who will assert that, because his sovereignty has thus far been exercised more frequently for the country's good than to its injury, there is no occasion for its curtailment. With this more or less selfish view I cannot agree. While it may operate occasionally for good, such power presents untold opportunities for evil. I doubt the wisdom of its continuance.

Members of Congress are already becoming restive under the bonds which they have unwittingly forged for themselves. They find that the Representative of the flourishing manufacturing district, of the farming community, of the commercial centre, is reduced to a mere cipher in the transaction of public business, and his legislative functions are usurped. His usefulness to his people at home is not only impaired, but is actually rendered *nil*, unless he manages to ingratiate himself with the Speaker. Chairmen of committees, when questioned regarding prospective legislation, are compelled shamefacedly to confess that it is the Speaker who is to be consulted. What is the result? If the individual member is outside the charmed circle of favored friends, his constituents clamor in vain while he chafes, silent and powerless, in his seat: if the bill which the chairman of committee is supposed to have in charge finds not favor in the Speaker's eye, it remains coffined upon a calendar already burdened with legislative corpses.

Now, then, as to the remedy. It is conceded, of course, that in a body of 356 Members some rules more or less arbitrary are necessary to insure the orderly conduct of business. Equally apparent is it, also, that the House cannot begin to act upon the multitude of measures which are introduced. Neither are the rules which obtain in the Senate applicable to the House. In the former body, any Senator arising and addressing the chair must be recognized; and no preliminary private announcement of his purpose is demanded. He can move to proceed to the consideration of any bill or resolution on the calendar, important or unimportant, and the question, not being debatable, must at once be determined by a vote; its disposition being dependent solely on the will of a majority of the Senate. It is true that a "steering committee," composed of nine Senators of the majority party, is empowered to arrange the order of business in regard to paramount measures, and that their schedule almost universally receives the assent of their colleagues; but the fact still remains that the programme is always subject to overthrow if it is not in accord with the views of a majority. In the House, I admit, such latitude as this would be impossible; but there is a happy medium between unrestricted freedom and autocratic control.

The lines along which these reforms could be instituted suggest themselves without difficulty. First of all, the absolute power of naming the committees should be divorced from the Speaker, and intrusted to a committee named at the caucuses of the two leading parties in the House. If it be successfully contended that this arrangement, although working admirably in the Senate, would not operate satisfactorily in an unwieldy body like the House, then it would at least be wise to place the Speaker in a position where he must regard the respectful demands of his colleagues. When, for example, he is presented, as he was recently, with the appeal of more than a majority of Members to grant consideration to the Nicaragua Canal Bill and to the public-building bills upon the calendar, he should be required to yield to that combined request. Great as he is, he is not greater than all the men who placed him in his position. If needs be, the rule might be so framed as to compel his obedience only to a majority of the Members of his own party; thus relieving him from the possibility of being held subject to the wiles or whims of his political opponents. Under such a rule the measures desired by the House could be brought up for consideration; the length of the debate being arbitrarily fixed, as now, by the Committee on Rules. At the conclusion of the discussion the vote could be taken. If the bill should be beaten, the Speaker would be vindicated in his opposition. If it should pass, the responsibility would be with the House and with each individual Member thereof, who is answerable to his constituents. At any rate, the Members would have been allowed the privilege of recording their position, —a favor or a right which they do not now enjoy.

To some such solution of the problem, no valid objection can be raised. It would not block the wheels of Congress with matters of small concern, because the consent of a majority could not be obtained save for the consideration of supreme questions. It would, of course, decrease the prerogatives and influence of the Speaker. No longer would his room at the Capitol be crowded with suppliant Members, or his private residence be haunted by men whose projects are to be promoted or destroyed by his decision. But this is "a consummation devoutly to be wished." Even the Supreme Court of the United States—the highest judicial tribunal in the land—attempts no settlement of a case except by a majority of the court. To make the Chief Justice the final arbiter of every legal dispute would be as little sensible as to continue the investiture in the Speaker of the parliamentary power which he now enjoys. Something must be done, unless the House of Representatives is to dwindle to an aggregation of mere puppets—the useless, idle servants of a great people. Something must be done; otherwise the Speaker of the House will become not only the autocrat of Congress, but the autocrat of the whole nation.

HENRY LITCHFIELD WEST.

FALLACIES CONCERNING PRAYER.

THE fact revealed by the spectroscope, that the physical elements of the earth exist also in the stars, supports the faith that a moral nature like our own inhabits the universe. That the moral nature which is above the world is a supplicable nature, equally with the moral nature embodied in man, is a thoroughly reasonable assumption. Prayer, therefore, is grounded in reason, and needs only a rational development in thought and in expression.

Prof. Joseph Henry has observed that the whole progress of the physical sciences has been a series of interrogations of the Author of nature, in which every intelligent question has received an intelligible answer. This is the point of view in which one may fully accept the saying, " Laborare est orare." Science and Religion offer practically the same prayer—" Show me Thy way, O God." The specific difference is in the characteristic interest of each. Science, with its prayer of the intellect, is interested in the progress of knowledge. Religion, with its prayer of the heart, is interested in the progress of moral sympathy with righteousness.

But when one begins to argue, from the universal instinct of mankind, that prayer is a proper function of the life which, as the Stoics held, should be according to nature, one is often withstood by a reference to savages. " See what sort of deities men naturally pray to, and what sort of prayers men naturally offer!" That men thought to be scientific consider this a scientific mode of reasoning is a curious phenomenon. The truly natural is the raw rather than the ripe, in men, if not in grapes. It is as preposterous to go for light on the subject of prayer to such a fact as ancient devil-worship, as to turn to the embryo for a gauge of the genius of Shakespeare.

But whether in the savage who regards his deity as the physical progenitor of his tribe, or in the philosopher who thinks of God as the self-existent Universal Life which is the origin of all being and the source of all change, prayer assumes community of nature between man and God as constituting a basis of Divine sympathy with the world in its stress and strain. And so Cardinal Manning's theory of prayer, that it is a means of realizing man's relation to God, is the most natural one. In this relation, the higher being must be not only the support and refuge of the lower, but also the norm and law. And so, just as natural appetite is necessary to prompt our attention to natural wants, an instinctive craving for God's help is requisite to promote remembrance of our duty to Him. It is this craving which gives the first impulse to prayer,—chiefly to the petitionary form of it, against which the current objections to prayer are mainly urged. While limiting attention to this, it must be noted that this is not the only, or only effective, form of prayer, any more than asking favors is the only form of communion among friends. Indeed, it is not unlikely that in the higher ranges of spiritual development the petitionary element in prayer will be found to grow less and less.

For many ages men have been trying by blundering experiment to realize their relation to God as the Author and Ruler of physical nature, but with partial success. Small wonder if less success has followed similar effort in the moral realm. None, indeed, confess failures in prayer more than those who are most given to it. Such failures prayerful men commonly impute only to their own ignorance and blundering. It is quite probable that the majority of all who pray have not learned to pray rationally any more than to live rationally; but that there is a rational prayer is as credible as that there is a rational life.

The problem of prayer, continually baffling, continually inviting, is not the only problem of the kind before the world. Science has problems of its own equally tantalizing. But this is a problem of the moral nature, which, as embodied in the world, essays to commune helpfully with the kindred moral nature that is above the world. On such a problem, as Prof. Bowne remarks in his "Principles of Ethics," a generation that is still in an embryonic stage of morality will be more reasonable in suspecting its scepticism as raw than in relying on its insight as ripe.

Already, however, the problem has been cleared of some fallacies by the leaders of religious thought. Such fallacies are: (1) the conception that prayer to God is comparable with prayer to the ruler of a state, who takes a petition into consideration, and grants or denies it as he judges best; (2) the notion that prayer aims to bring in an interfering power to alter miraculously the physical order of things; (3) the idea, akin to this, that prayer for moral betterment, as for the forgiveness of sins, can break the connection of cause and effect, so as to avert the natural consequences of any breach of physical or moral law. Some, with whom we go a mile in this direction, would have us go twain, and draw from the rejection of these fallacies equally fallacious conclusions. It is with these conclusions that I am now concerned.

As to the first, we assume the reality of a Divine purpose as sufficiently indicated in the evolution of nature and of man, and that this purpose cannot be contingent or indeterminate. It follows, of course, that a prayer which crosses that purpose is, so far as its object is concerned, a futile effort; but it does not follow that the prayer which falls in with that purpose is superfluous. Such a notion is a relic of the old thought of God as external to the world, and of the will of God as static rather than dynamic, aboriginally complete rather than eternally unfolding. It is out of date now, when the theist conceives of all the forces of the universe, in nature or in man, as Divine, and thinks of the Divine will as the movement of " an increasing purpose " through all the complex interplay of these forces, whether free or unfree.

The Divine purpose, whatever view we take of it, is realized through various agencies. The prayer which is in line with it serves to focus our will in that line, and to engage us more actively in pursuing it. For instance, the thrice-repeated prayer of Jesus in Gethsemane, " Thy will be done,"—so commonly misunderstood as expressing resignation to the inevitable,—was simple self-devotement to the thing that was to be done. It nerved Him to surrender His life at a crisis when He might easily have escaped. The beneficent consequences which that self-devotement has produced in the religious development of mankind are evidence, not only of a Divine purpose realizing itself through His free act, but also of the efficacy of prayer that is in line with a Divine purpose.

To pray daily that we may act with conscientious uprightness and kindness in daily affairs will be conceded to be conducive thereto. Many allege, however, that it is only a reflex effect upon ourselves which ensues. But this is not a full account of it. A reflected force does something. Of course, the primary effect of the prayer for uprightness is a reflex effect upon the man who prays; but it does not end there : something more ensues. The reflex effect in him passes directly outward into an objective effect produced by the uprightness which the prayer has promoted. This effect is extended to other men, and to what they do. It influences the course of human affairs in ever-widening circles. Consequently the reflex effect of prayer upon the prayerful becomes a determining power in the world for the promotion

23

of Divine ends. Thus, far from being superfluous is the prayer which accords with the Divine purpose.

As to the second point, there is indeed no interference through prayer with the natural order of things; but it is fallacious to conclude from this, that whatever there is in our prayers of petition for physical or spiritual benefit must be eliminated. Taking up first the physical, let us see if any interference with the ordinary laws of causation is necessarily involved in prayer for the healing of the sick.

Extravagant assertions of the power of prayer for healing have brought it into some discredit. But it is as wide of the mark to say that prayer has no power of that sort, as to say that it has all power. Unqualified, indeed, are St. James's words: "The prayer of faith shall save the sick, and the Lord shall raise him up." But of course he did not forget that all must die. That prayer will have a curative effect to a certain extent, is the only meaning fairly imputable to him. Every physician will say the same, because he knows that auto-suggestion and expectant attention have a certain curative effect. When a bread pill produces the soporific effect of a morphine pill upon the patient who takes it as morphine, what we recognize is a psychological cause of sleep substituted for a physiological cause. The bread pill is necessary to bring the psychological cause into action.

Here we see what it is that prayer for the healing of the sick may legitimately undertake to effect; viz., no breach at all in the order of natural causation, but simply the substitution of a psychological for a physiological cause of cure. When the case is one to which a psychological cause is adequate, the cure will follow. Of course the condition of its effectiveness is, that the patient must fully believe in the healing power of prayer. At least, the prayer tends to call into activity the psychical powers of auto-suggestion and expectant attention. These are, indeed, equally effective, whether generated through prayer or otherwise; but I am now considering the power. If an undevout mind regards prayer in this case as mere incantation, a reverent mind is nearer the truth in holding that "there is no power but of God": whether in the psychical body or the political, "the powers that be are ordained of God."

Now it matters nothing for a valid judgment here that there is a large class of persons who are altogether superior in their own view to any such therapeutic agent. But denying a therapeutic agent to be a panacea does not expunge it from the list of remedies. Psychological therapeutics, however imperfectly understood, hold as secure—though not yet so large—a place as the physiological, which not long ago were in an equally crude state. It is with this as yet undeveloped province of the healing art that prayer stands in natural affinity. If it prove inadequate, so do all remedies sometimes. Certain physiological remedies are good for those only with whose constitutions they agree; and this much at least can be said of prayer. It might avail with a believer where it would fail with an unbeliever. Faith is as far from being impotent as from being omnipotent. "Possunt quia posse videntur." There is no field of effort in which this does not hold good.

The point just made, that a physical effect results in certain cases from a psychical cause brought into action by prayer, suggests some criticism of the assertion that it is irrational to pray for rain. This is usually put forward with such airy and even supercilious confidence that one who holds no brief for either side, but is simply concerned for close reasoning, may be justified in a search for weak points. To maintain a universal negative, one must either have universal knowledge, or be able to show an absolute impossibility. Let us see then what is actually known about this.

We know that our wills are among the causes which affect the order of nature within certain limits. By clearing forests we change a climate. By scientific manipulation of physical elements we produce new varieties of plants and animals. It is scientifically held possible to produce rain at times and places where atmospheric conditions are favorable to certain modes of operation. How much now must one know to warrant him in saying that he knows, rather than supposes, it irrational to pray for rain, in a climate that is not rainless? He must know: either (a) that there are no invisible intelligences superior to us; or (b) that, if there be, they are not sympathetically related to us; or (c) that, if they be so related to us, they have no such power as ours to effect changes in physical order according to physical law; or (d) that, if they have, they are not susceptible, like us, to any telepathic influence, such as the wills of a multitude of kindred beings united in fervent prayer might conjecturally exert; or (e), if they be susceptible, that they are positively inhibited, by some limitation of an unknowable kind, from responsive action; or (f), if this be not the case, that failure to bring them helpfully into action is not due to an imperfect development of psychical power in us, but to a natural impossibility.

Until we have adequate knowledge in all these particulars, it is certainly premature to dogmatize, either pro or con. Suspense of judgment is certainly a rational attitude for anyone who bethinks him-

self that there may be more things in heaven and earth than his philosophy has dreamed of.   The rationality of prayer for rain is wholly a
question of probability.   If indemonstrable, it is also irrefutable.   In
estimating the worth of the probability, it must be said that none of the
open points above stated is either arbitrarily taken or involves incredi-
bility.   At this point, it may be worth noting that the poets for the
most part—certainly all the great poets—have firmly held to the objective efficacy of prayer as a power within the natural order of things.

> " At any rate,
> That there are beings above us, I believe ;
> And when we lift up holy hands of prayer,
> I will not say they will not give us aid."

Some readers will probably arch their eyebrows here, and ask if
we are not steering toward the Roman Catholic doctrine of the invoca-
tion of saints.   By no means.   That doctrine localizes God; setting
him afar, where He has to be approached by intermediaries.   We follow rather the thought of Virgil, "Jovis omnia plena."   We simply
refuse to localize God, the Universal Life, energizing through all the
powers of the unseen environment, with which we come into conscious
correspondence through prayer.

Third,—The widespread illusion, that prayer for moral betterment
may operate as a cut-off of the evil consequences of an evil life, is a
dangerous fallacy ; though many religious teachers have countenanced
it.   But no less fallacious is the illusion, fostered by some who seem to
be scientific, that the prayer, " Create in me a clean heart, O God," involves an appeal for miraculous interference.   We are told that praying
for a changed character and for a change of weather equally attempt
the disturbance of natural causation, since character and weather are
alike produced by natural causes.   Under the term " natural " we are,
of course, to include all moral as well as physical causes, however dis-
similar these two orders of nature.   Is it then supposed by the objector
that the petitioner for a clean heart is making no endeavor for it, and
fancies that he shall obtain it without endeavor ?   The Scriptures themselves say interchangeably, " Create in me a clean heart," and, " Make
you a new heart."   Why, then, this phrasing of the duty to make the
heart clean into a petition to God to make it clean ?

The reason is not far to seek.   First, this petition is an expressive
confession that man apart from God is nothing ; that it is only from the
Divine inworking and indwelling that the normal issues of life come.

Next, this confession is also a pledge of our purposed concurrence with Him to whom we appeal, and a girding of the will to work with Him toward the cleanness of heart we pray for. What more can be demanded here of natural causation adequate to the desired effect on character? Taken merely as words, "Create in me a clean heart" might be construed as a plea for a miraculous work. So might "The sun rises" be construed into assent to the Ptolemaic astronomy. But, as a matter of fact, they are never so used except by the foolish or perverse, or those who from such specimens spin flimsy objections.

The homœopathic rule, *similia similibus*, is inapplicable to the cure of error. On the one hand, many prayers for moral betterment are open to the objection that they contemplate a breach of causation. Many pray for the forgiveness of sins as for a governmental amnesty, which breaks the line of causation by arresting the operation of law against past offences. On the other hand, it is equally fallacious to conclude that there is no place in the natural order of causation for the forgiveness of sins, or for the prayer for it. The question turns on what is intended by the term "forgiveness." Strictly taken, it is expressive of personal feeling. In every instance it signifies the restoration of right feelings and relations between the offender and the offended. It is often extended beyond this to mean the cancelling of certain natural consequences of the offence. But this we often feel that we must not do, even when it is in our power. The best interests of the offender himself, and the interests of others, unite in the demand that he shall abide certain consequences of his act, although restored to favor and good-will. How then can it be contended that prayer for the Divine forgiveness must involve the breach of causation which forgiveness between man and man does not require? All that one can reasonably hold the Divine forgiveness as involving is the renewal of the harmony between the individual will and the Universal will that has been broken by human waywardness.

In using our anthropomorphic religious phraseology it behoves us to guard against its illusive tendency; but use it we must—some of it at least—or remain speechless with risk of becoming thoughtless: for it is all we have. When we ask a neighbor's forgiveness, we ask him to change his mind toward us. But we do not ask God to change; at least, not if we think wisely. Our request to our neighbor implies that we feel toward him as we ought. This is all that our prayer to God can rationally imply. It is complete in its expression of the return of a wayward will to loyalty and obedience. Doubtless, through various misconceptions of God, much more is often added which is either mere verbiage or worse, and thus also in need of forgiveness. The Divine forgiveness is not to be begged for, but to be accepted; as the sunlight upon the face is to be had by turning to it. But the desire of it and the acceptance of it demand clear realization in consciousness, and therefore require expression in prayer. The true norm of such expression is not " Have mercy upon us miserable offenders ": it is in the words which Jesus puts into the mouth of the penitent prodigal,—" Father, I have sinned."

Here we have to take account of the deprecatory element in such a prayer. Some demand that deprecation shall be eliminated from prayer, as being a relic of that self-mutilation which accompanied primitive devil-worship. One may well object to certain expressions of self-abasement in prayer; as in Watts's lines,

> " Great God, how infinite art thou!
> What worthless worms are we ! "

But, on the other hand, in any clear consciousness of an unattained ideal some self-abasement is both a common and an inevitable experience. Object, as we must, to deprecation in the literal sense of the word, as an attempt to avert evil by entreaty, there is at the heart of it a consciousness which must not be extirpated. Perception of the contrast between what we are and what we ought to be inevitably produces that self-abasement, or, if another phrase is required, that sincerely felt humility of the imperfect before the Perfect, which is the condition alike of patient effort for better things and of prayer as auxiliary thereto. The objection, therefore, that prayer for the forgiveness of sins involves a breach of the laws of causation, may be valid enough against some popular notions, and some church teaching, but is of no force against the conception of it here presented.

Some consideration is now demanded of the causative relation in which the prayer for forgiveness stands to the effects of an evil life. Our past deeds are indestructible. Their consequences flow on without break or cut-off. The transgressor's future can never be the same that it would have been, had his past been free from transgression. What, then, is the utmost that can take effect *directly* in and through his prayer for forgiveness? Simply the righting of his voluntary relation to God. This is, of course, a reflex effect; but, like any other effect, it becomes in turn a cause of further effects. These, however indirect, must be counted as effects of his prayer, or of the inward change in him which is both expressed and promoted by his prayer. Without the least breach of causation, a new cause has been added to the causes at work in the past; and this new factor must somehow affect the product. Thus the prayer will be found, after all, to have a certain potency for change in the natural connection of cause and effect. A typical instance is that of St. Paul, whose past vehemence as a persecutor became, on his conversion, a spur to zeal as an apostle. Scientifically expressed, it is a clear case of the persistence of energy with convertibility of force.

It is plain here that while the evil past counts for its full effect, it counts also in another direction. So the muck-heap, which counts for poison and death while it rots above ground, counts for fertility and life when put under ground. The debt of consequences due to the past must be paid to the last farthing. But the new-strung will, the aspiration, the hope, which now face that debt, have changed the conditions of dealing with it. Prayer brings these new factors into the problem. Their efficacy in creating, as it were, a sinking-fund for that debt must be credited to the account of prayer. Moreover, such is the interaction of mind and body, that physical as well as moral betterment is often discoverable in the result.

Strange that it has not entered the minds of those who write against the reasonableness of prayer for physical or moral betterment, that there may be more tenable ideas than the old and crude notions against which they direct their polemics. What would such men of science say, if theologians should fancy it worth while to combat the defunct theories of medicine, chemistry, and physics, which line the road of scientific progress, as the bones of beasts fringe a caravan route across a desert? Theology as well as science should be allowed the right to bury its dead.

A point where controversy has generated more heat than light can now be adequately treated. Prof. Tyndall's famous test, proposed for a scientific estimate of the effectiveness of prayer, assumed that this is to be proved or disproved according as particular prayers for specific objects are or are not "answered." This is a mistake analogous to that of suspending the question of the Divine control of events upon the occurrence of miracles in Palestine or elsewhere. It requires no special cases of "answer" to evince the effectiveness of prayer: it is attested by the ethical development of mankind.

The great pioneers of moral progress, the men who have wrought most influentially for the moral enlightenment and reformation of the world, have habitually communed in prayer with the Unseen Power. On this they have depended for the replenishment of their own inner springs of action and endurance. Witness Jesus, following days of active benevolence in the city with nights of prayer on the mountain. The reflex inward effects pass out into the objective effects wrought by these great lives in the world. The changes they brought to pass in the thoughts and actions of mankind must be held as in large measure resultant from their habitual prayer. Then there is the host of martyrs of all kinds, to whose constancy in evil times it was due that desperate struggles for truth and righteousness were crowned with victory. What but the confident committal of their cause to Him who judges righteously nerved them to brave the fire and the sword? Nor can account be omitted of the multitude of obscure lives, to whose conscientious fidelity in common duties the present order and stability of society are due; who seek in religion the sanctions of morality; who daily look up to God as Father and Judge; and who in doing so find the spur to honest successful effort. This is the true line of sight in which to look for convincing attestation of the objective as well as the subjective efficacy of prayer. Like the Divine control, to which it is in fact subsidiary, it is not an occasional, but a constant, factor in the unfolding of the order of the living world.

Thus far our concern has chiefly been to clear the subject of some fallacies and pseudo-scientific prejudices. It remains now to indicate some points of a mainly constructive line of thought.

Prayer, as Coleridge insisted, is a very different thing from saying prayers. It is an activity of the whole man. Real prayer engrosses and focuses feeling and desire, thought and will, for the direction of the whole self upon its object. Here, undeniably, a real force is apparent, as much as in any movement of our will upon the external world. It is the force of an ethico-spiritual nature, not isolated, but related to nature of the same kind, both seen and unseen. To deem it futile, "a chimera buzzing in a vacuum," is to escape one difficulty by rushing into a greater,—at least for anyone who remembers that action and reaction are inseparable.

The records of the Society for Psychical Research abound in fully verified instances of communications sped from friend to friend, in a moment across hundreds of miles, in some supreme crisis which called into momentary action some previously latent energy of the spirit. Such cases suggest the yet undiscovered possibilities and limits of prayer, considered simply as a mode of psychical force moving upon an unseen psychical environment, through which, as through the physical, Divine forces are ever energizing in the interplay of action and reaction. That religious enthusiasm dwells closer to the springs of this mysterious force than our present science or philosophy, is thoroughly credible. The saying attributed to Jesus, that, if He chose, He could by prayer summon myriads of spirits to His aid, is not to be thought the idle fantasy of one unique in spiritual insight and energy. Much more reasonable is it to suppose that men in an embryonic stage of moral and spiritual development are as incapable of employing such a force intelligently as are savages of using mathematical instruments.

Viewing prayer as a real force in the complex of world-forces, Dr. F. H. Hedge has well observed that it will tend to overbear or to be overborne, according to its intensity. Many prayers, including all the merely formal, are, by defect of energy, foredoomed to failure; just as many infants die through defect of vitality. Like other forces, prayer will also be most effective in the line of least resistance. The prayer must be weak whose force is that of a mere individual interest, dissociated from, or indifferent if not antagonistic to, the general welfare of the world. That prayer is strong which blends with the great tide of aspiration and effort toward Divine ends. What John Stuart Mill observed of justice is true of prayer. An interest of personal apart from general welfare is an element of impurity in it, and therefore an element of weakness. The Lord's Prayer significantly conforms to this law of efficiency. How notably is its reference to the personal and transient subordinated to and uplifted by its interest in the universal and eternal! This is characteristic of that effectual prayer which the New Testament describes as being in the "name," that is, in the spirit, of Jesus. There is, of course, an organic relation of human needs to Divine ends which cannot always be consciously realized, even in prayer. On psychical principles it would be least realized in the automatic uprightness of the faithful life, which is, as Origen said, the practical utterance of the Lord's Prayer.

The question which some still think it worth while to ask, "Why does a loving God, who knows our needs, require us to petition for their supply?" both reveals the fundamental misconception and brings into contrast the fundamental truth in regard to the whole subject. Dr. Edward Caird has noted, as a strange survival of the pagan mode of thought among Christians, that some of them still conceive of prayer as an attempt to get God to do man's will, rather than as an aspiration

to get God's will done by men.   Jesus has expressly cautioned us not
to think that either He prays or we pray for the purpose of informing
God about our needs or inducing Him to supply them.   What end,
then, is served by petitionary prayer for the things God knows we
need, and that He wills to bestow ?   Surely no thinker is unaware that
verbal expression has much to do with both clearness of thought and
the concentration of attention and will.   It is reason enough for engaging in petitionary prayer, that the confession in words of our wants to
God enables and pledges us in a clearer consciousness to work out more
reverently and patiently the Divine conditions of their supply.

Thus it is that through prayer the individual will strives toward
unity with the Universal will.   To impute to the leaders of religious
thought to-day the crude, primitive fancy of bending the Divine will
into line with the human is unworthy of any who profess to keep
abreast of the world's advancing intelligence.   The true function of
prayer is to lift the will of man into line with the will of God.   This it
does by its effect in clarifying moral insight, deepening reverent convictions of responsibility, and dedicating self more thoroughly to
Divine ends, which can be accomplished in the world no sooner or
more fully than men devote themselves to their fulfilment.

God, or atoms !   This is the alternative which is ultimately forced
upon us by the question whether to pray or not to pray.   From intellectual perplexity there is no escape, whichever solution of the mystery
of life we elect.   To the moral certainty which the problem yields,
one of the greatest names in contemporary science has just left us his
posthumous testimony that there is "a vacuum in the soul of man
which nothing can fill but faith in God."[1]   Of this faith the vital
breath is prayer.

JAMES MORRIS WHITON.

[1] GEORGE J. ROMANES, in "Thoughts on Religion," p. 162.

WAS POE A PLAGIARIST?

VERY few people to-day, even in literary circles, know anything about Thomas Holley Chivers, M.D. And even these know very little. He was a poet of at least one book before Bryant made that brief anthology of sixty or more American poets in 1840;—mostly names that have vanished long since into the everlasting inane;—but he was not there represented. His first volume of verse appeared in 1837; though fugitive lyrics from his pen were doubtless afloat on the periodical seas long before that year. Poems over his signature were contributed as late as 1853 to "Graham's Magazine" and to the "Waverley Magazine" of Boston.

It is, however, simply repeating an indubitable fact, to say that a large part of the poetry of Chivers is mainly trash,—of no account whatever, and not above the reams of stanzas which from time immemorial have decorated as "original" the country newspaper's poet's corner. But now and then he struck a note quite above this dead and wide-pervading commonplace; and, whenever he did, the verses brought forth were apt to suggest the mechanism and flavor of Poe. He not only said at various times—especially in a series of letters which he wrote to Mr. Rufus W. Griswold, Poe's biographer, and which are now in the possession of his son [1]—that Poe had borrowed largely from him, but he put the transaction in much bolder terms. The charge of flagrant plagiarism of himself by Poe, in respect even of "The Raven" and "Annabel Lee," was not withheld, but was violently advanced by Chivers. Nor was he alone in making this charge. Some of his friends took it up and repeated it with a vehemence and an ability worthy of a most sacred cause. There is circumstance enough about this, to say nothing of its singularity, to elevate Chivers into something of a topic, —one worth considering at least for a moment.

What is known about this author is, that he published seven or eight volumes of poems between, and inclusive of, 1837 and 1858,—a

[1] Mr. W. M. GRISWOLD, of Cambridge, Massachusetts, to whom I am greatly indebted for many of these facts.

period of twenty-one years. Many of them antedate Poe's period of literary activity, and not a few have the Poe afflatus and melody so strongly inherent in them that even the non-critical reader could not mistake their related quality. In Chivers's "Lily Adair," which crowns his high-water mark of poetic achievement, the Poe manner stands out conspicuously. This refrain from it, for instance, varied in some details at the end of each stanza, illustrates what I mean:—

> " In her chariot of fire translated,
>   Like Elijah, she passed through the air,
> To the city of God golden-gated—
> The home of my Lily Adair—
> Of my star-crowned Lily Adair—
> Of my God-loved Lily Adair—
> Of my beautiful, dutiful Lily Adair."

Chivers, in this poem, and in others which resemble Poe's work, made Biblical allusion a dominant trait to an extent that Poe did not, and really attained, though not always with perfect sanity, to much of Poe's witchery and charm.

It is not my intention in this article to repeat the history and evidence which I presented and published elsewhere a year and a half ago concerning Chivers's claims against Poe. It will be sufficient for the purpose now in hand if I report, as briefly as may be, what Chivers and his friends, and those who antagonized the Chivers assumption, had to say about it forty-four years ago.

In a quite able and stalwart way Chivers himself opened the contest, under the *nom de plume* of "Fiat Justitia," in the "Waverley Magazine" of July 30, 1853. In a long article, entitled "Origin of Poe's 'Raven,'" he claims that the laudators of Poe—particularly N. P. Willis, who said of "The Raven" that it "electrified the world of imaginative readers, and has become the type of a school of poetry of its own"— "betray not only a deplorable ignorance of the current literature of the day, but the most abject poverty of mind in the knowledge of the true nature of poetry." He then quotes from his own book, "The Lost Pleiad," the following lines from the poem "To Allegra in Heaven," which was published in 1842,—a few years before "The Raven" appeared. He asserts that these lines "show the intelligent reader the true and only source from which Poe obtained his style" in that poem :—

> " Holy angels now are bending to receive thy soul ascending
>   Up to Heaven to joys unending, and to bliss which is divine ;

While thy pale cold form is fading under Death's dark wings now shading
　　Thee with gloom which is pervading this poor broken heart of mine!
And as God doth lift the spirit up to Heaven there to inherit
　　Those rewards which it doth merit, such as none have reaped before;
Thy dear father will to-morrow lay thy body with deep sorrow,
　　In the grave which is so narrow, there to rest forevermore."

In this article Chivers also says that Poe is not entitled to priority in the use of the refrain "Nevermore." It was Chivers, he says (still writing under his *nom de plume*), who originated this in a poem entitled "Lament on the Death of my Mother," published in 1837 in the Middletown, Connecticut, "Sentinel and Witness." The following extract from it is the proof he offers:—

"Not in the mighty realms of human thought,
　　Nor in the kingdom of the earth around;
Nor where the pleasures of the world are sought,
　　Nor where the sorrows of the earth are found—
Nor on the borders of the great deep sea,
Wilt thou return again from heaven to me—
　　　No, nevermore!"

The reader, I imagine, will be likely to think that Poe gave this refrain a more potent and appalling quality.

It is urged that Poe knew of Chivers's "The Lost Pleiad, and Other Poems," as he "spoke of it in the highest terms in the 'Broadway Journal' in 1845." The writer admits that "Poe was a great artist, a consummate genius; no man that ever lived having possessed a higher sense of the poetic art than he did." But he urges that this fact must not obliterate the other; viz., that he took the liberty, arrogated by genius, to borrow.

After saying that Chivers (he speaks of himself all along as another person) was the first poet to make the trochaic rhythm express an elegiac theme, and the first to use the euphonic alliteration adopted by Poe, he cites the following extract from a poem of his published before Poe's masterpiece in verse appeared:—

° "As an egg, when broken, never can be mended, but must ever
　　Be the same crushed egg forever, so shall this dark heart of mine,
Which, though broken, is still breaking, and shall nevermore cease aching,
　　For the sleep which has no waking—for the sleep which now is thine!"

To step up to "The Raven" from so grotesquely low a level, one might easily consider—even were the charge of plagiarism proved—a complete absolution of blame.

And, if this is admitted to be the fountain whence Poe got his form, an irreverent critic might say he reproduced it with unsurpassable effect and dissociated from it the atmosphere of Humpty-Dumpty.

In the "Waverley Magazine" of August 13 of the same year, "Fiat Justitia" (Chivers) is taken in hand by "H. S. C." and "J. J. P.," on behalf of Poe. The difference in altitude and genius of the two writers is emphasized by them. Poe's personal character is palliated; but the question of priority in the use of the Poe alliterative rhythm is not argued. The only reply touching this is by the first of the two writers, who shows that "Nevermore," as a refrain, is nobody's trademark, since it has been used even earlier than Chivers's employment of it. As an instance buttressing this statement, he offers the following stanzas from a very old scrap-book in which the poem of which they are a part is credited to the Cheshire, England, "Herald":—

> "Now the holy pansies bloom
> Round about thy lonely tomb;
> All thy little woes are o'er;
> We shall meet thee here no more—
> Nevermore!
>
> But the robin loves to sing
> Near thee in the early spring;
> Thee his song will cheer no more
> By our trellised cottage door
> Nevermore!"

The same writer asks if his antagonist cannot, by his form of logic, prove that Poe stole his poem of "The Bells" from the nursery rhyme of "Ding Dong Bell." A week later than this, "Fiat Justitia" re-appears in the "Waverley Magazine," together with an ally signing himself "Felix Forresti" (possibly Chivers again [1]), who, seeing him attacked by two knights of the pen, "takes up the cudgels" for Chivers. In fact, to be more truthful, all these writers—speaking metaphorically—take up pitchforks and machetes. Their Billingsgate style savors of the Arizona "Howler," and seems impossible to Boston. In this week's onslaught, however, no point of note occurs, except that the latter writer exhumes from a poem by Chivers, upon Poe, which was

---

[1] That an author could so write of himself, under masked signatures, is surprising. But the articles were substantially made up from his letters to Mr. R. W. Griswold, Poe's biographer.

published in the Georgia " Citizen " about 1850, the following lines:—

> " Like the great prophet in the desert lone,
> He stood here waiting for the golden morning ;
> From Death's dark vale I hear his distant moan
> Coming to scourge the world he was adorning—
> Scorning, in glory now, their impotence of scorning.
> And now in apotheosis divine,
> He stands enthroned upon the immortal mountains
> Of God's eternity, for evermore to shine—
> Star-crowned, all purified with oil-anointings—
> Drinking with Ulalume from out th' eternal fountains."

And the writer adds : " Until both . . . champions [of Poe] can write just such lines as these, they had better ' shut up shop.' "

But neither side " shut up shop" just then. In the issue of September 10, "Fiat Justitia" and " J. J. P." reappear. The former occupies nearly three columns with extracts from Chivers's poems to show the Poe manner, and to prove that it was in these poems Poe found it. The following sample is from "The Lost Pleiad":—

> " And though my grief is more than vain,
> Yet shall I never cease to grieve ;
> Because no more, while I shall live,
> Will I behold thy face again !
> No more while I have life or breath,
> No more till I shall turn to dust !
> But I shall see thee after death,
> And in the heavens above I trust."

The following extract is from Chivers's " Memoralia ":—

> " I shall never more see pleasure,
> Pleasure nevermore, but pain—
> Pleasure, losing that dear treasure
> Whom I loved here without measure,
> Whose sweet eyes were Heaven's own azure,
> Speaking, mild, like sunny rain ;
> I shall nevermore see pleasure
> For his coming back again ! "

Of "The Lost Pleiad " volume, " Fiat Justitia " says that a Cincinnati reviewer declared, some years ago, that " there is nothing in the wide scope of literature, where passion, pathos, and pure art are combined, more touchingly tender than this whole unsurpassed and (in our opinion) unsurpassable poem."

Another sample of Chivers's pre-Poe likeness the writer finds in a poem titled "Ellen Æyre," which was printed in a Philadelphia paper in 1836. He gives this stanza from it:—

> "Like the Lamb's wife, seen in vision,
>   Coming down from heaven above,
> Making earth like Fields Elysian,
>   Golden city of God's love—
> Pure as jasper—clear as crystal—
>   Decked with twelve gates richly rare—
> Statued with twelve angels vestal—
>   Was the form of Ellen Æyre—
> Gentle girl so debonair—
> Whitest, brightest of all cities, saintly angel, Ellen Æyre."

Very many other Poe-resembling extracts are given; but these must suffice from the verse. To show that Poe borrowed from Chivers in a prose criticism, our writer copies the following passage from an article by Chivers in the Atlanta "Luminary":—

"There is poetry in the music of the birds—in the diamond radiance of the evening star—in the sun-illumined whiteness of the fleecy clouds—in the open frankness of the radiant fields—in the soft, retiring mystery of the vales—in the cloud-sustaining grandeur of the many-folded hills—in the revolutions of the spheres—in the roll of rivers, and the run of rills."

Now look on this, from Poe's "The Poetic Principle":—

"He recognizes the ambrosia, which nourishes his soul, in the bright orbs that shine in heaven . . . in the waving of the grain-fields—in the blue distance of mountains—in the grouping of clouds . . . in the twinkling of the half-hidden brooks—in the gleaming of silver rivers—in the repose of sequestered lakes—in the star-mirroring depths of lonely wells . . . in the song of birds—in the sighing of the night-wind . . . in the fresh breath of the woods, etc."

Triumphantly the writer says, "Now . . . you will no longer wonder where Poe obtained his very delightful knowledge of the art of poetry." Not only the Chivers prose extract, but also the verse passages quoted by him were written, he affirms, "long anterior" to the parallel passages in Poe.

In the "Waverley" of September 24 following, "J. J. P." quotes Poe as saying of "The Raven," "I pretend to no originality in either the rhythm or metre." He also quotes Poe as saying of the passage by Chivers containing the egg simile: "That the lines very narrowly missed *sublimity* we will grant; that they came within a step of it we admit; but, unhappily, the step is that *one* step which, time out of mind, has intervened between the *sublime* and the *ridiculous*."

The whole controversy was continued with warmth in the "Waverley Magazine" of October 1, 1853, by "Fiat Justitia," who began it. I am told, too, that it was reopened in a later volume. As the "Magazine" office files were long ago destroyed by fire, I cannot say how the renewed controversy fared; though it probably closed with nothing fresher than new epithets coined by the combatants. Nor is anything that is particularly new added by this article. It was mainly a threshing of the old straw, which, all the way through, was supplemented by a rhythm analysis that would take too much space to follow. From the Chivers poem "To Allegra in Heaven" he adduces this theretofore unquoted line,

> "Like some snow-white cloud just under Heaven some breeze
> has torn asunder—"

which he thinks suggested Poe's two lines:—

> "And the silken sad uncertain rustling of each purple curtain"—
> . . . .
> "Much I marvelled this ungainly fowl to hear discourse so plainly."

Chivers, it seems, wrote for a variety of periodicals, among which were "Graham's Magazine" and "Peterson's"; and in the year this controversy was raging he contributed poems to the "Waverley Magazine" itself. In "Fiat Justitia's" contention, it is said that Poe was obliged to reply in the "Broadway Journal," in defence of the plagiaristic charge, to some writer using somewhere the *nom de plume* of "Outis." There was, in connection with the Chivers assumption and advocacy, a surprisingly earnest and hot assault. Only one more of these militant articles (possibly by Chivers again) shall I notice here. He, signing himself "Philo Veritas" in the "Waverley Magazine" of October 8, 1853, communicates a "Railroad Song" taken from "Graham's," which was written by Chivers, and which he terms "a truly *original* poem." He does so in part for the purpose of "exposing one of the most pitiful plagiarisms" known—the "wishy-washy thing" entitled "Railroad Lyric," that had appeared in "Putnam's Monthly" of the previous May. Here are some lines from the one hundred and thirteen composing Chivers's poem :—

> "All aboard! Yes! Tingle, tingle,
> Goes the bell as we all mingle—
> No one sitting solely single—
> As the steam begins to fizzle—

24

With a kind of sighing sizzle—
Ending in a piercing whistle—
 .   "   "   .

And the cars begin to rattle,
And the springs go tittle-tattle—
Driving off the grazing cattle,
As if Death were Hell pursuing
To his uttermost undoing,
Down the iron road to ruin—
With a clitter, clatter, clatter,
Like the Devil beating batter
Up in Hell in iron platter,
As if something was the matter;
Then it changes to a clanking,
And a clinking and a clanking,
And a clanking and a clinking—
 .   .   .   .

As if Hell for our damnation,
Had come down with desolation
 .   .   .   .

While the engine overteeming
With excruciating screaming,   .
Spits his vengeance out in steaming.
 .   .   .   .

Still repeating clitter, clatter
Clitter, clatter, clitter, clatter
As if something was the matter—
While the woodlands all are ringing,
And the birds forget their singing,
And away to Heaven go winging.
 .   .   .   .

Then returns again to clatter
Clitter, clatter, clitter, clatter
Like the Devil beating batter
Up in Hell in iron platter—
Which subsides into a clankey,
And a clinkey and a clankey
And a clankey and a clinkey
And a clinkey, clankey, clankey—
Then to witchey, witchey, witchey,
Chewey-witchey, chewey-witchey—
Chewey-witchey, witchey, witchey,
Then returns again to fizzle,
With a kind of sighing sizzle—
Ending in a piercing whistle—
And the song that I now offer
For Apollo's golden coffer—
With the friendship that I proffer—
Is for riding on a Rail."

There was one poem of Chivers's, entitled " The Little Boy Blue,"
copied in the " Waverley Magazine," which is singularly saturated
with the nomenclature and manner that Poe affected.   Here are a few
illustrative stanzas out of the thirty-seven to which it extended :—

" The little boy blue
    Was the boy that was born
In the forests of Dew
    On the Mountains of Morn.

.   .   .   .

There the pomegranate bells—
    They were made to denote
How much music now dwells
    In the nightingale's throat.

.   .   .   .

On the green banks of On,
    By the city of No,
There he taught the wild swan
    Her white bugle to blow.

.   .   .   .

Where the cherubim rode
    On four lions of gold,
There this cherub abode
    Making new what was old.

.   .   .   .

When the angels came down
    To the shepherds at night,
Near to Bethlehem Town
    Clad in garments of light,
There the little Boy Blue
    Blew aloud on his horn,
Songs as soft as the dew
    From the Mountains of Morn. \

.   .   .   .

But another bright place
    I would stop to declare,
For the Angel of the Face
    Of Jehovah was there.

.   .   .   .

Now this happy soul dwells
    Where the waters are sweet,
Near the Seven-fold Wells
    Made by Jesus's feet."

Not only are the Poe phrases here, but here, too, is the tossing,
tumultuous imagination of William Blake.   I know of no writer who,
so much as Chivers did, fell into Blake's phantasmagorial extravagance,

The upshot of this cursory consideration of the voluminous controversy—beginning before Poe died, and virulently continued for some years after his death—shows that Poe knew Chivers's work and paid attention to him in more than one reference. The literary representatives of the minor poet appear, also, to bring forward some striking examples of verse which he wrote, which was outwardly like Poe's, and which considerably antedated "The Bells," "The Raven," and "Annabel Lee," on which Poe's poetic fame rests.

What conclusion must be drawn from these facts? Each reader will be certain to make his own. No critic will doubt that to Poe belonged the wonderful magic and mastery of this species of song. If to him who says a thing best the thing belongs, no one will hesitate to decide that Poe is entitled to the bays which crown him. It is a fact that, with all the contemporary airing of the subject, it is Poe's celebrity and not Chivers's that remains. The finer instinct and touch are what the world takes account of. Chivers, except at rare intervals, did not approach near enough to the true altitude. He put no boundary between what was grotesque and what was inspired. He was too short-breathed to stay poised on the heights, and was but accidentally poetic. But we may accord him a single leaf of laurel, if no more, for what he came so near achieving in the musical lyric of "Lily Adair." Truly enough Shakespeare says:—

> "The lunatic, the lover and the poet,
> Are of imagination all compact . . ."

Their mental and spiritual territories interblend. The same frenzy is the endowment of each—as charcoal is in essence the diamond. As you differentiate and develop it you make your titular distinction and place. But it is not a small thing to have been mingled in some slight association with genius, and to have some credit you with it. In an Oriental poem the clay pipe speaks of its contentment, since it cannot be a rose, of having, by a fortunate association, attained to some of the rose's fragrance.

JOEL BENTON.

SOCIALISM IN FRANCE.

"Socialism long ago ceased to exist."—
(Gen. VON GOSSLER, Minister of War,
in the Reichstag, 12 Feb., 1897.)

HAD the Emperor William's minister really spoken truly, the history of socialism might be summed up in a short epitaph : "There were those senseless enough to believe that social justice might be enthroned among men. They proclaimed it to their contemporaries, who, on examination, saw that it was folly. Peace and pity to their memory ! There is no law but that of the strongest."

Have we reached this point ? Despite the imposing authority of a minister of the German Emperor, it does not appear to me in the least proven. "If I order you," said William II to his soldiers, "to fire on your father and your mother, you must obey me." This superior rule of government has one peculiar advantage—it reduces the organization of society to the simple expression of one arbitrary will disposing at discretion of the very life of the governed. That is the rudimentary conception of primitive societies. It is hardly a matter of pride for us, nearing the twentieth century, that one of the most powerful potentates of Europe should openly claim for himself the absolute control of his fellow-beings, which so many savage autocrats are content to exercise without venturing to formulate in terms of such offensive brutality. I am well aware that it is pure bravado, and that, should he seek to act on it, he would have trouble. This régime, indeed, implies that the human herd is so basely submissive that it will be itself the instrument of its own degradation. This is not quite true of most of the nations of Europe, though it is, as Tolstoï never tires of proclaiming, the logical end, the final point of military government.

On our old continent we see in our streets antique structures which were once forms of living thought; so we preserve institutions of the past logically out of harmony with the modern conditions that we call progress. The anachronism of the Emperor William is thus to be explained. But through the *débris* of the past the peoples are plowing their way. They have conceived the idea that men own themselves and can and should freely dispose of themselves. By this the death-blow has been given to theocracy and to the rule of one man in the long struggle of the centuries for the vindication of liberty, from the times of classic antiquity to our day.

Despite certain relapses of adverse fortune, France of the eighteenth century, and the Revolution that was the outcome of the thought of its philosophers, completed—at least in doctrine—the emancipation of the intellect. America at the same period founded a free government, the vastest field of experiment ever opened; and Jefferson, in the Declaration of Independence, proclaimed, as the purpose of man's free activity, "the pursuit of happiness." What is the pursuit of happiness in the multiplied forms taken by the spontaneous or acquired manifestations of being, if not the tendency to the full development of life? But life, to be developed, must first be assured; and the problem of living presents itself before all other questions. Governments by authority have not solved it for the mass of human beings making up the social body; nor, as yet, have the governments founded on liberty solved it. To feed the slave as a beast of burden, denying him the poor favor of shortening his sufferings in the shambles, is the primitive method of sustaining the life of society, and is progress only as compared with cannibalism. The institution still flourishes among savage peoples; and down to the middle of the nineteenth century it prospered, on the American continents, side by side with the most remarkable organization of liberty won for Christ by the Anglo-Saxon and Latin races. And at certain points on the globe, at least, the experiment was pursued of assuring human life—the primary foundation of the pursuit of happiness—by liberty alone.

We are still debating the result of this experiment. The early theorists of political economy, with the fine confidence of men of pure doctrine, asserted—and not less presumptuously their successors continue to assert—that the one solution of the social problem lies in the magic formula of universal liberty. Meanwhile theory has been followed by practice. In the several lands under the variously named forms of liberty, what have we seen? All human liberties in mutual conflict in an inexorable struggle for life, ending in the inevitable subjection of the weak to the law of the strongest. Only appearances have changed. Doubtless there was progress, since for a time human energies were liberated,—but only straightway again to fall under the yoke of antique Force, mistress of the world.

Men must live: that is the supreme law. Is not he who strives for daily bread vanquished in advance by him who, commanding the means of living, exerts himself only to secure added happiness? What becomes of liberty here, when there is wanting the prime condition of its exercise—equality? To let loose in the world all opposing liberties, assuring nothing but an equal share of space and light, would be but to promise victory to the strongest. But what must it be when social inequalities, aggravating natural inequalities, give all the weapons to one, snatching them from another? What then is this much-vaunted liberty? Is it not of necessity opposed by the resistless need of individual appropriation, and by those fetters upon the spontaneous energy of the individual supplied by the social desire, which is at least equal to the aspiration toward liberty?

And this very liberty, this liberty of defeat for some, of oppression for others,—is not this deliberately perverted by the masters of political power, by those who dominate organized society, by the strong for the strong; combining all social forces for their own profit, claiming both the liberty of reducing wages to the merest possibility of life for the wage-earners, and the protection of customs tariffs for their own dividends?

In these conditions what is economic liberty but an elegant form of social swindling which saves appearances by means of argument, but in reality is hardly more merciful to the confused mass of the disinherited than those régimes not yet arrived at the grand conception of human solidarity? To-day, as in the past, the social deficit which is revealed in hunger, nakedness, and the long train of ills, can be met only by the uncertain chance of passing pity, by the hazard of egoistic charity in search of compensation beyond the grave. Charity was, in its time, a wondrous conquest, the unfolding of a sentiment of love that becomes nobler as it is more disinterested. We are still only too far from that ideal. But already in the actual stage of human ills, charity, individual or organized, has so palpably failed, that no one can expect from it a solution of the social problem. Besides, scattering charity, left to each one's impulse, even when reinforced by aid officially distributed, does nothing but make up the insufficiency of wages; and thus it perpetuates the very economic conditions sought to be remedied.

The precursors of the revolution of 1848, recognizing the failure of individual action in resisting the oppression of the individual, saw a supreme resource in association. The principle in itself is just; but it has only shifted the problem. Association of the weak was made difficult by want of discipline and adequate culture; and, if successful, it only delivered them, vanquished in advance, into the hands of the associated strong. The idea cannot, however, be said to have been barren. Certain organizations for assistance, which on the whole have prospered, issued from this movement—trade-unions, syndicates, popular banks, coöperative societies. These at least, in view of the future, are signs of capital importance. But what has come from the concentration of the efforts of men who can contribute in any form only their capacity for labor, in comparison with the stupendous effects of the concentration of capital able to put the lives of thousands of men in the hands of one man, thus reëstablishing for the profit of a privileged class a power more formidable perhaps than ancient feudalism, the overthrow of which cost so much blood? Furthermore, these incorporated societies invite the savings of the working class—inadequate for their own emancipation—and add them to the accumulated capital employed by the masters of economic power to secure their domination. Thus the force of the subjugated helps to keep them under the yoke they have worn themselves out in trying to break.

In these conditions, what is more natural than for the mind that seeks the supreme liberating power to turn toward the higher association, decisive in its force—society represented by the organized action of the state? The idea is ancient; and, as the enemies of communism have admitted, collective property may be of remoter origin than individual appropriation itself. Even the most rudimentary civilization invokes the parallel development of two forces, individual and collective, and their expansion—by antagonism and by mutual support—in the diverse changes of human activity.

Aggregation is, in point of doctrine, the guarantee of the individual, whose welfare is the supreme end of the state. But the power given to some to secure this end has always resulted in the creation of dominant oligarchies. The social problem is to break down these and, if possible, to bring about the reign of justice on the earth. Is there anything simpler than that the total power, including all others, should be made to regulate the distribution of universal justice among all men, without distinction? The simplicity of the conception is the danger; for the individual groaning under oligarchic combinations feels but little reassurance in the thought of being delivered defenceless to the monstrous power of the irresponsible will of all. From this feeling, by a natural reaction, spring the claims of anarchy, proclaiming that the free development of the individual outranks every other need, and resulting in the ideal of the communism of liberty (*communisme libertaire*)—the harmonious outcome of the energies of liberated man.

These are the two extreme hypotheses between which, doubtless for a long time to come, will oscillate the diverse socialist conceptions, ranging from the universalized collectivism of Karl Marx and the agrarian collectivism of George to the mutualism of Proudhon, or the anarchy of Elisée Réclus and Kropotkin. There is no intention, in this article, of expounding the doctrines of the different schools of contemporary socialism. Special books on that subject abound; and the theories are at the present time presented to public opinion in all countries where progress is active.

France—ancient land of revolutions—cannot remain in inert contemplation of the universal effort toward the social emancipation of the workers. In the past she has furnished illustrious thinkers by whom the first furrows in the long uncultivated field of social reform were broadly traced. Her form of government, purely democratic in appearance, seems to-day to enable her to place the study of the new conditions of labor, among a people eager to realize justice, in the front rank of her concerns. Only it happens, when we consider closely the course of the French mind, that we find it on the one hand prompt in generalization and bold of initiative in speculation, and on the other hand obstinately wedded to conservatism and routine in daily dealing with facts. We must therefore expect to find socialism everywhere à la mode in France, and socialist opinion remarkably active, and at the same time to perceive extraordinary aversion in the governing class—in deed, not in words—toward reforms which involve the right of social intervention in the relations of capital and labor.

Nothing is so characteristic of the present régime in France as the disproportion between the hopes it suggests to the French mind and the realities with which it pays such splendid promises. The incapacity to bring about the most timid fiscal reform in a country burdened with the heaviest debt and the most incoherent system of taxation is enough to doom to disappointment in advance all hope of social reforms. Perhaps it would be unfair to throw on the government of the bourgeoisie the exclusive responsibility for this state of things. It is true that no impulse toward reform has ever come from them, and that they have shown themselves as curiously incapable of directing the country in an evolution of peaceful liberty as the ancienne noblesse. It must be admitted, however, that the country itself, while it expects that the abuses of routine, which it tolerates with no adequate protest, will bring about those ill-ordered movements of opinion that are in the traditions of France, appears quite unable to impose on the government a systematic effort toward reformatory action. This mental situation throws a certain vivid light on the present state of socialist thought and action in France.

To begin with that which is most ancient in history and also the latest comer in the social struggles of our time, Christian socialism has hardly more than a questionable and questioned existence as yet, in spite of the cautious encouragement of the author of the encyclical on the condition of the working class.

It will soon be two thousand years since Jesus of Nazareth passed through the field of corn with his disciples, and these, being hungry, gathered the ears and, rubbing them in their hands, ate the corn. This was on the Sabbath day, as the Gospels relate; and that was what shocked the Pharisees. "Behold, thy disciples do that which is not lawful to do upon the Sabbath day." And Jesus answered with the example of David, who, being hungry, went into the temple and ate of the shewbread and gave to those that were with him, which was lawful only to the priests. We note, not without some surprise, that the disapproval of the Pharisees and the response of Jesus relate only to the respect due the Sabbath, and not to the right of property, which the Christians of to-day look upon as the keystone of the arch of the social edifice. We must conclude that Jesus, who gave Himself but slight concern for the terrestrial domain, admitted, at least by implication, as a primordial law, that he who is hungry should eat. This principle, to-day universally condemned by established authorities, would lead anyone who relied on the Gospels straight to the prison door. Such is the effect of historic evolution. Pharisaism, overcome for the moment, seizes again its advantage under the disguise of new formulas. Millions and millions of Christians go on repeating the word of Christ while, in complete peace of conscience, practising the contrary doctrine. On the command, "Thou shalt not judge," rest all judicial institutions. It was a great discovery for the Catholic priests, in 1848, to find socialism in the Gospels. They had hardly got over their amazement when the *coup d'état* of Prince Louis Napoleon bade them attend to other business. They willingly obeyed; and to a layman, a soldier, M. de Mun—astonished to see the insurgents of 1871, shot down in heaps, "die with insolence,"—belongs the honor of having, in our day, planted the banner of Christian socialism on the loftiest battlement of the fortress of the Catholic Church in France. M. de Mun, who, to tell the truth, rejects the name of socialist, at first dreamed only of organizing the industrial world in syndicates of workmen and employers under the tutelage and arbitration of the Church. Later, questions of the regulation of labor absorbed all his attention. It is an open secret that he is acting under the direct inspiration of Pope Leo XIII; and it is a curious phenomenon that French Catholicism should receive from the very summit of the hierarchy the impulse toward social reform.

Socialism of the chair may be regarded as non-existent in the French Republic. The governing *bourgeoisie* have got no farther than the absolute dogmas of political economy; and that is one of the most curious symptoms of the mental condition of the Republicans in power. Still our people consent to follow, at a long distance, other civilized nations, by adopting for form's sake some of the laws for the protection of factory workers. But this is with so poor a grace that the law as to accidents to workers has been more than fifteen years before the Chambers, with no assurance that it will not take fifteen years more to pass it. I say nothing of the application of laws already enacted. It is, for the most part, singularly defective. Ask senators and deputies, and they will not absolutely deny the right of the state to regulate the conditions of labor; but they are careful not to accept the doctrine. That does not hinder them, however, from recognizing the right and duty of the state to protect their own industrial or agricultural incomes by customs duties as high as the patience of the consumer—weighed down by taxes for the benefit of the state and of individuals—will permit.

In these conditions how can we be surprised that official instruction —which, in France, is everything—is confined almost exclusively within the narrow circle of political economy. Thanks to free instruction, so painfully acquired, the modern notions of social justice are beginning to make their way. Thanks to certain liberal institutions —due to that private initiative so rare in France—professorships of opposing aims are arising face to face with each other; and our youths are beginning to understand that the determination of the laws of political economy by no means involves for us absolute submissiveness, since progress consists in opposing laws to laws for the well-being of man. Gravitation does not allow us to rise from the earth, nor to follow the course of streams against the downward current; and gravitation seems—does it not?—to be the sovereign law of the world. Nevertheless there are other laws—the reality of which is no less certain— ingeniously opposed to this supreme law, which permit us to be borne in the air and to mount the course of rivers at express speed. Why may not the laws of the distribution of wealth in a given social state be advantageously modified for the benefit of men in general by a new social state? Are we the inert slaves of political economy; or should we seek, in determining the laws of social relations, a means to overcome those who are opposed to man's full development? When this simple truth shall have penetrated the corps of instruction in the French Republic, socialism of the chair will be established in our country. As yet it is not.

As for the socialism which takes the name of "revolutionary"— and which may be called the socialism of the directed classes as opposed to the nascent socialism of the directing classes—that, on the contrary, is fully developing its thought. A part of the landed property—though less than is generally believed—is so minutely divided that there is danger in talking to the peasants of the nationalization of the soil. Right or wrong, and whether the mediocre advantages of the present system can or cannot be replaced by the still hypothetical advantages of some future system, our rustics are singularly rebellious toward anything that touches the fundamental sentiment of individual property. This is the reason why M. Jaurès himself, whose propaganda is directed to the rural as well as to the city population, has never been able to speak of the national appropriation of the soil, except with infinite precaution as to language.

The manufacturing workmen see individual property only in the most offensive form; viz. excessive concentration in the hands of one side by side with extremest deprivation for the many; and they very gladly join in a new development of social property, which appears to them to be the logical remedy for the ills they suffer. This sentiment is the foundation of the party of revolutionary collectivism, which, it would seem, may be regarded as the introduction to a régime of communism based on authority (*communisme autoritaire*).

Considering only the external facts, this party has made remarkable progress among the working class for some years past. Under the guidance and impulse of energetic chiefs, writers, speakers, and men of action, it has made itself a social and political power, and henceforth must be reckoned with. But, obeying the law of development of every organism, the party, as it has extended its area, has given rise to distinct aggregations, sometimes diverse to the point of antagonism. This is a source of strength or of weakness according to the point of view. My own judgment is that there is nothing better for the propaganda of an idea than diversity of groups. Concentration for the purpose of action suffers, of course; but, since the period for effective united action by the public powers still appears quite remote, no serious harm from this state of things is as yet shown. This united action is the mission of the national or international congresses, which are preparing for it by the maintenance between the groups of an adequate cohesion. Only this result must be obtained, as in every parliamentary assembly, by the action of the majority; and this sometimes aggravates the dissensions which it is intended to allay and to fuse in common action for the success of all. This was very noticeable at the last congress at London, where the French delegation was so deeply divided between men who aimed at political action and those who placed their trust wholly in action by syndicates or unions.

It is the wish of M. Jaurès that socialism shall take advantage of all the means of action offered by *bourgeois* society. The notion is a good one; and the first results attained certainly seem encouraging. Nevertheless when the chief strength of a party is in criticism, there is danger in assuming the responsibility for positive action in which the inevitable variety of temperaments must be reconciled; and this is especially true when a new ideal must be preserved as a source of inspiration and impulse in the mind of the masses, always simple and eager for encouragement. Doubtless this is the reason why M. Jules Guesde, that strict guardian of the dogma of Marx, has never tried to formulate the doctrine in proposals of law—to which his function as a legislator offered him seductive temptation. Unfortunately this prudence—if it be that —will be generally taken as a confession of weakness, so long as the doctrine is confined to theory and practical tests are avoided.

Whatever precautions may be taken, if one is in Parliament he must conform to the conditions of the parliamentary régime and, when occasion offers, present precise solutions for definite questions, as M. Jaurès has for the sugar question and the wheat question. This requires a good deal of effort; and it is not always appreciated by the purely militant section of the party, who regard the " parliamentarians " with contempt. The truth is that the advantage of an appeal to universal suffrage and of carrying elections is inevitably offset by the attenuation of theory required to bring together a sufficient number of votes from the various social groups differing in enlightenment and in interests. I should not venture to assert absolutely that revolutionary collectivism is diluted as it spreads; but I cannot ignore the infinite pains taken by a man like M. Millerand to make the transition easy for minds that, at the start, are frightened by the word "collectivism."

Nothing could be more instructive in this regard than the discourses at the banquet of St. Mandé in 1896. It is true that M. Millerand entrenched himself behind this defensive formula: "*In my opinion no man is a socialist who does not accept the necessary and progressive substitution of social property for capitalist property*"; and M. Guesde hastened to interpret this in the narrowest sense: "*Like us, after us, Millerand declares that socialism and collectivism are but one and the same thing.*" But now notice the commentary of M. Millerand on his own words:—

"Is not the socialist idea summed up completely in the energetic purpose to ensure for each being, in the bosom of society, the integral development of his personality? This necessarily implies two conditions, each the factor of the other: first, the individual appropriation of the things necessary to the security and defence of the individual, that is to say, property; then, liberty, which is merely a sounding and empty word if it has not property as its basis and defence."

And farther on:—

"Collectivism recognizes that the nominal development of capitalist society substitutes tyrannical monopoly by a minority for individual property, the condition and defence of liberty. It does not revolt against recognized facts: it bows to them. It does not propose to reascend the current of the centuries or to arrest the transformation of humanity. On the contrary, it bends to its laws; and, since it is a law of sociologic evolution that all means of production and exchange pass from the form of individual property to that of capitalist property, its entire contention is this: In the measure that these immense capitalist properties, which dry up and destroy small property and individual property, are formed, in that measure social property shall be substituted for capitalist property."

Such collectivism as this, it will be seen, gives a broad basis for discussion in the parliaments of the *bourgeoisie*.

But by the side of parliamentary action, action by syndicates is going on. This is an organization of leaders rather than a popular one, and is a fruitful source of energy from which both the "anti-parliamentarians" and such deputies as M. Guesde and M. Vaillant intend in certain conditions to draw all the revolutionary force that it will yield. Consciously or unconsciously, with the help of some of the leaders and in spite of others, the idea in which, on the whole, this effort is crystallizing is to be summed up in one phrase—*a general strike*. Of course I do not mean to say that all the syndicates in France have set themselves this aim. That would be obviously false. What I believe exactly is that this idea floats as a sort of logical ideal of evolution over these rudimentary organizations, and might, later, if occasion proved favorable, draw in a great majority of minds. The absurd struggle of our industrial *bourgeoisie* against the syndicates, by turning them from their natural field of action, leaves them no recourse but in revolutionary hopes. This result is equally due—to be just to all—to the lack of continuity in effort and the absence of discipline and method, which in France have prevented the great labor organizations from attaining the success of which we see examples in England and in the United States. The general strike is certainly not easy to carry out. But this idea of such a passive revolt, the potency of which would be decisive if it were really general, is calculated to tempt the spirit of theory and inflame the imagination of the industrial masses who are everywhere crashing against the *non possumus* of their masters. It is not surprising, therefore, that numbers of men—particularly those who prefer action to talk—rest their hopes on action of this sort, which, even if it led only to partial attempts, would none the less induce the gravest conflicts.

In opposition to the collectivist organizations, arises the force of the idea of anarchy. This is the natural reaction of minds which fear oppression by all for the same reason that they fear the abuse of authority by the few. On the side of anarchy is the resistless impulse toward liberty which grows with the development of the personality. Disregarding the acts of individual violence, which are generally condemned, and which, properly speaking, spring from no social theory and are the work of unbalanced minds, there may be recognized in the doctrine of liberty the indispensable counterpoise to socialism based on authority. Despite their refusal to let themselves be enlisted under the colors of any organization—or perhaps for this very reason,—the anarchists proved at the congress of London that they were a force with which in the future the socialist groups must more and more reckon. In any case they must at present be credited with certain intellectual forces in literature, art, and science superior to those that can be evoked by the other schools of social renovation.

This glance—superficial as it is—over what may be called the socialist mentality of the single country of France, suffices to permit us to appreciate at its just value the inept remark of the German dullard, " *Socialism long ago ceased to exist.*" Let us pity the man who in his innocence can utter such words; not seeing that the régime definitively doomed is that of which he is one of the last representatives. Government is made for men, not men for government,—that is the great conquest of civilization. Liberty without bread, bread without liberty,—these are diverse forms of the same servitude. The need of liberty in action, the appetite for individual appropriation, must be reconciled in proportions changing with the necessity for social action, to secure the realization of the changing ideal of justice. The conception of liberty itself varies with the mentality of the social *milieu;* and the conciliation of the individual development of each with that of others will result not from an absolute formula, but from successive compromises, springing from the general achievement of human culture.

For the moment, outside even of the humanitarian question, a problem is presented which the sabre of the fierce von Gossler seems to me to be impotent to solve. Industrial production is encumbering our warehouses with an accumulation of goods which goes on increasing from day to day, and for which every one is seeking an outlet. Now these consumers, which are being painfully hunted for at the ends of the earth, exist in the very factories from which the manufactured products issue. They are the laborious masses, lacking the very necessaries of life, who would be the first to present themselves in the market, if their full value as consumers, after their function as producers is accomplished, were left to them by better compensation for their work·and a more equitable division of the burdens of taxation.

Meanwhile production increases every day, the burdens of labor augment, and unbridled competition keeps wages at the minimum while their purchasing power diminishes. Thus the greatest outlet for industry is being closed by the extreme logical development of our industrial régime. Since the humanitarian sentiment has as yet failed to bring about a solution of the problem, the very vigor of economic fatalities, reacting from extreme abuses, must cause a better order of division to prevail. Thus, in proportion as emancipated man attains full consciousness of himself, the implacable greed of oligarchies, which deprive such an extraordinarily great number of workers of the products of their work, shall come to an end.

Doubtless we are not yet at this point. But we are already on the road to it. Lend ear, O sword-bearer of the German Emperor, to the vast murmur! You say, " *Socialism has ceased to exist* "; and Humanity with one voice answers you, " *Socialism begins.*"

G. Clémenceau.

The Forum

JUNE, 1897.

THE TRANS-MISSOURI DECISION.

" . . . the more things improve, the louder become the exclamations about their badness . . . In proportion as the evil decreases, the denunciation of it increases; and as fast as natural causes are shown to be powerful there grows up the belief that they are powerless."

HERBERT SPENCER, in " A Plea for Liberty."

" Let the country make the railroads and the railroads will make the country." GEORGE STEPHENSON.

" All we ask is that it shall be a tribunal which is impartial and that is thoroughly informed." ROBERT STEPHENSON.

" I still cling to the simple faith that even in legislation it 's a good thing, before making laws, to know what you are making laws about."

CHARLES FRANCIS ADAMS.

THE recent Trans-Missouri decision of the Supreme Court, by a majority of one, held that the Anti-Trust Act of 1890, which declared illegal " every contract, combination in the form of trust or otherwise, or conspiracy in restraint of trade or commerce among the several States, etc.," applied to a railway association contract; the language of the opinion being that

" . . . without proof of the allegation that the agreement was entered into for the purpose of restraining trade or commerce or for maintaining rates above what was reasonable . . ."

" The necessary effect of the agreement is to restrain trade or commerce, no matter what the intent was on the part of those who signed it."

Of sixteen judges who passed upon some phases of this general

Copyright, 1896, by The Forum Publishing Company.

Permission to re-publish articles is reserved.

issue, ten substantially sustained the railway's contention. That five of those sixteen were upon the Supreme Bench of course gave effect to its major opinion; but the narrow majority of that court and the large adverse number in the lower courts have justified the strong public interest and comment with which the decision has been received.

Aside from that view, the more than usually important legal questions involved in this judgment affect great issues and policies; and, so far as the railways are concerned, it will continue to be strongly questioned:—(a) Is the Anti-Trust law constitutional? (b) Did Congress intend it to apply to railways and does it so apply? (c) If it does embrace them, did the Court differentiate justly between reasonable and unreasonable restraints of trade? (d) Do railway agreements having similar purposes unreasonably restrain commerce? (e) If so, are not the things declared by the Anti-Trust law as misdemeanors, crimes which constitutionally entitle those accused to trial by jury?

However these contentions may be ultimately decided by the courts, legislative relief should and will be earnestly sought.

Section 5 of the Interstate Commerce Act of 1887 forbade the pooling of freights; and the pending judgment of the Supreme Court may forbid any other rate agreements. This will leave no recourse but individual railway action, which is always diverse and antagonistic. It is not the purpose to discuss now this estoppel of freedom of reasonable contract in a nation dedicated to liberty, nor the striking contrasts between the protection of reasonable railway rights in Europe and the lack of due legislative protection in America; but the comparison is naturally attracting American capital and that of other nations to the greater security which other and wiser countries offer. Nor is it my present intention to argue that our railways are entitled to greater protection than they have received because they represent the nation's greatest material, fiscal, and employing interests, charge the lowest rates, pay the highest wages, and receive smaller dividends than any other railways in the world, while receiving the least legislative consideration.

From the Granger cases of twenty or more years ago until now, various popular phrases have much influenced the public mind, such as: "Oppression and monopoly," "Clothed with a public interest," "Public policy," "To destroy competition," "Combinations of capital," "The rights of shippers"; and now the shibboleth is, "In restraint of trade."

When the railways have pleaded that these maxims convey mutual meanings and rights, and that transportation competition differs from

mercantile rivalry, they have been confronted with definitions by legislatures and courts interpreting those watchwords to mean that the rights
of the public to manage railway property should be enlarged while
those of its owners should be lessened, until now, regardless of all
former guises, the armies of socialism, re-inforced by the pending
decision, are advancing these old banners toward dangerous business
policies against which no changes of import tariffs or policy of finance
can restore commercial confidence. Unrest, consequently, walks everywhere.

I therefore argue the public necessity and equity for legalized
railway compacts; that they do not and will not unreasonably restrain
trade or commerce; and that their intent is an important feature of
their creation, in practice if not in law. The necessity for such associated railway action has been repeatedly endorsed by governmental
witnesses.

The Cullom Report of 1886, said :—

"A basis of fixed rates would seem to depend upon a general predetermina-
tion of the rates to be established by the carriers interested. It seems necessary,
therefore, to leave a way open by which such agreements can be made, in order
to avoid the constant friction that would otherwise be occasioned."

Pursuant thereto, the Interstate Act, at the date of the Supreme
Court decision, forbade the pooling of freights, but in Section 6 required,

"that every common carrier subject to the provisions of this act, shall print
and keep open to public inspection schedules showing the rates and fares and
charges for the transportation of passengers and property which any such common
carrier has established," and that, " no advance shall be made in the rates, fares,
and charges which have been established and published as aforesaid . . . except after ten days public notice." Also that " . . . reductions in such published rates, fares, or charges shall only be made after three (3) days public
notice."

And penalties were provided for neglect or refusal to so publish rates,
fares, and charges.

The same section further said :—

"It shall be unlawful . . . to charge, demand, collect, or receive from any
person or persons *a greater or less* compensation . . . than is specified in such
published schedule of rates, fares, and charges."

These provisions of law stood as governmental instructions directing
the manner in which the railways should individually prepare, issue,
and proclaim their freight and passenger charges. That they all published like rates was a further public advantage.

The first Interstate Commerce Commission especially considered the relation of railway associations to itself ; and, with the eminent constitutional lawyer, Hon. T. M. Cooley, at its head, that body said in its first annual report:—

"To make railroads of the greatest possible service to the country, *contract* relations will be essential, because there would need to be joint tariffs, joint running arrangements and interchange of cars. . . . some of which were obviously beyond the reach of compulsory legislation."

The same report said that: " Some regulations, in addition to those made by the law, are almost, if not altogether, indispensable. . . . An association of officers or agents is made the means of bringing about the desired unity of action."

These conclusions were based upon the proposition, apparent at the outset, that all traffic, whether large or small, passing between competitive points must be shared by two or more traders and by two or more carriers between such points.

Harmony in determining their transportation rates and relations is clearly preferable to strife: for, in whatever view considered, competition is made honorable; and the parity of rates required by the common law, by the statutory law, and by the interests of the public can be accomplished only by discussion, concession, and agreement between them. The law alone cannot achieve this result or defeat it; and the coöperation of the railways, after conferences with forwarders, has been found the only means by which this trade and transportation equality can be secured.

The practical application of the law and this status should be made clear. There are ten railway routes from Chicago to New York which may hold different views as to proper rates and classifications between these traffic centres. Before they can announce and publish equal rates they must harmonize those differences; otherwise, their charges would be different, discriminating, and chaotic, and would disturb trade as much as if the same differences existed on one route. The latter being forbidden by law, the former is at least commercially undesirable, even if legal. The same Chicago lines may also differ as to the rate relations of Chicago to Milwaukee, etc., on the north, and as to Peoria and St. Louis, on the south; and similarly those cities may differ with Chicago.

Unless, therefore, agreements are arrived at as to the proper rates at each point and the relative rates to and from adjacent cities, additional disasters to trade may, and restraint of trade will, result from such geographical dissensions, rates may become irregular and unprofitable, and some shippers and points will be preferred, to the detriment of others.

Merchants must also have foreknowledge upon which to base their trade calculations; otherwise, sales of grain, merchandise, etc., and the relations of the carrying rates to such transactions would be purely conjectural. Rates so individually made would surely prove discriminating; and petitions would promptly go to Congress to save trade from such disastrous favoritism. The railways must also predetermine what charges they will require forwarders and travellers to pay for transportation services; otherwise, not only will some shippers from the same points be put at a disadvantage with others, but the merchants of Chicago, for example, might be discriminated against by lower rates from St. Louis, which would control the eastward business of cities farther west.

Further geographical necessities arise. The relations of destinations to each other must be as clearly defined as the starting-points. Suppose, as an extreme example, that the shortest all-rail route from St. Louis to the seaboard being to Baltimore, that route fixed the export grain rates without relation to or regard for the routes or shippers from Chicago to New York or Boston, by which means the competitive grain traffic from beyond the Mississippi was controlled, great wrong would be wrought; and St. Louis and Baltimore would enjoy preferences which would ruin other merchants, cities, and districts. For this reason Section 3 of the Interstate Act declares it "unlawful for any common carrier . . . to make or give any undue or unreasonable preference or advantage " in favor of any "locality." But how can these parities be arrived at except by railway agreements?

Multiply these illustrations by the complications upon 180,000 miles of railway which, in 1895, moved 764,000,000 tons of freight and carried 544,000,000 passengers,—a large majority of each being competitive,—and the necessity for conference must be apparent.

Add the rivalries of oceans, lakes, rivers, canals, and the need to adapt railway rates to such competitions, and the mere mention of these complex conditions should show the necessity for conference, harmony, foreknowledge, and the due observance of equal and reasonable competitive rates, involving "agreements," "understandings," or "conferences."

Associations were organized, resting upon the good faith of the parties, to prevent discriminations to favored shippers and to establish not only common rates, but common classifications, rules, regulations, terminal charges, and fares in all the respects which constitute essential elements of carrying equality. They were also, of course, intended to avoid unwarranted depletions of the rates and fares to which the carriers are reasonably entitled.

Have such associations unreasonably restrained commerce ? Each of the numberless seekers after drawbacks regards a refusal to concede the preference he solicits as a restraint upon *his* trade; but in no other sense can railway associations be so regarded, because their primary purpose is to abolish such preferences and to extend all fair trade. No railway company is so ignorantly managed as to contract or strive for the restraint of business. They labor in and out of season, by fair, and sometimes by questionable, means, to enlarge commerce, to better their own conditions and those of their patrons, and to improve their relations to the public as the quickest way to financial and traffic eminence. They have sought, and should seek in equity and law, to restrain those wrongful practices which are falsely denominated " competition," which proceed from strife, concealment, and favoritism, and to correct the endeavors of unscrupulous merchants to defeat the rates, classifications, and rules adopted for the common public and railway benefit. They have sought to enlarge rather than to restrain trade by increasing the proportions of traffic carried in through cars, which, being originally taken locally from point to point, encountered transfers, delays, different local rates, bills of lading, classifications, rules, and charges. They have greatly accelerated the movement of freight and passengers, made uniform through bills of lading and way-bills, issued through tickets and baggage checks, and established common inspections to ascertain that accurate weights were charged.

They have equalized and given to local stations rates corresponding with through points. They have adjusted differences with water routes. They have sought to harmonize rather than to destroy.

Between the Mississippi River and the seaboard, and north of the Ohio River there are approximately 10,000 points between which through rates and bills of lading are given. A majority of these places being actually or commercially competitive, the various railway interests convene and determine the due rate relations of each to the other. If each railway at each competitive point exercised an individual right to make its own arrangements regardless of the others, legalized commercial chaos would result. It is due to the railroads, and not to the law, that this anarchy of rates does not now prevail.

They have therefore done more to remove trade restraints and enlarge and equalize internal and external commerce than all the other policies, laws, and agencies of the nation.

Such agreements upon railway rules and rates are therefore more essential to the public interest than are the uniform orders of the Secretary of the Treasury to the collectors of internal revenue and of customs at the different ports, or the instructions of the State Department to its consular agents.

The observance or enforcement of all law is aided, if not accomplished, by associations which coöperate with law. Witness the associations for the prevention of crime, the aid of charity, the diffusion of knowledge, etc. These reach many questions which the law cannot touch. The New York Chamber of Commerce is an influential instance.

It is more needful that railways should have associated relations than that great cities should have clearing-houses for their banks or stock exchanges, produce exchanges, and boards of trade, to establish standards of mercantile honor, quality of goods, and essential rules of purchase, sale, delivery, etc. They are as necessary in some form as that townships should be subordinate to the county, the counties to the State, and the States to the Federal Union. It is as desirable that the railways should be represented by clearly defined organizations and delegates to provide regulations, tariffs, etc.; as it is that the House of Representatives should exist to define rules for the conduct of public business, and to fix and change import, export, and internal tariffs. The import tariff is not so important as railway tariffs, being less complex and affecting fewer nations and people; yet it requires months of conference and forbearance to arrive at any desired result. Can the railways with a larger issue do less?

When the Interstate Commerce law took effect there were over thirty freight classifications in vogue, which are now substantially reduced to four governing schedules.

The value of associations has also been shown in the compilation and issue of statistics. A prominent instance has recently transpired in the contention of the New York Produce Exchange that the differential rates to ports south of New York are unduly great. Certain data were called for in that case which could not have been submitted had not the associations kept them.

There were originally more than twenty corporations between Chicago and New York in the Lake Shore and New York Central route, each possessing (and still retaining) legal powers to charge reasonable local rates and impose local regulations.   Conference and associations have unified these routes and rates more in the public interest than to the benefit of the railroads.   They have provided for the more speedy transit and greater convenience of the carriage of express matter and the mails.   They have equalized the localities on the Atlantic, and have harmonized the competitions of the Pacific-Coast points. They have endeavored to equalize routes of unequal facility by a regulated system of differential rates.   They make bills of lading issued in Hong Kong redeemable in Bremen.

Associations are the most valuable adjuncts of the Interstate Commerce Commission.   Without their aid the Commission cannot possibly solve its problems or accomplish its tasks : with their help it *may* do so. Were the public to choose wisely which to abandon, it had better dissolve the national Commission, because to wipe out all forms of voluntary railway organization—which, more than law, maintain necessary methods of trade—would be to throw the business of the country into a chaos from which the Interstate Commission itself could not evolve order. The advocates of the dismemberment of such associations know literally nothing of the great services they have rendered the public.   It is also a delusion to suppose that they limit competition.   True railway rivalries are more active under associations than without them, because they stop competition and substitute the higher rivalry of improved facilities and rebates.   As well say that the Senate stops intellectual or local rivalry because it is a body representing competitive States.

The opinion of the minority of the Supreme Court in the Trans-Missouri suit states this case clearly as follows : —

" That the interstate commerce rates, all of which are controlled by the provisions as to reasonableness, were not intended to fluctuate hourly and daily as competition might ebb and flow, results from the fact that the published rates could not either be increased or reduced except after a specified time.   It follows then that agreements as to reasonable rates and against their secret reduction conform exactly to the terms of the act."

The following cogent reasoning was added :—

" Suppose three joint lines of railroads between Chicago and New York, each made up of many roads.   How could a joint rate be agreed on by the roads composing one of these continuous lines, without an ascertainment of the rate existing on the other continuous line ?   What contract could be made with safety for transportation over one of the lines without taking into account the rate of all the others ?   There certainly could be no prevention of unjust discrimination as to the persons and places within a given territory unless the rates of all competing lines within the territory be considered and the sudden change of the published rates of all such lines be guarded against."

The minority opinion used these words, italicized as quoted:—

"In view of these facts, when the Interstate act *expressly forbids contracts and combinations between railroads for pooling, and makes no mention of other contracts*, it is clear that the continued existence of such contracts was contemplated, and they are not intended to be forbidden by the act."

Those associations existed when the Anti-Trust law of 1890 was passed and were not prohibited by it.

The opinion further says :—

"It is . . . therefore not to be denied that the agreement between carriers, the validity of which is here drawn in question, seeking to secure uniform classification and to prevent the undercutting of the published rates, even though such agreements be made with competing as well as joint lines, is in accord with the plain text of the Interstate Commerce act. . .

The judicial declaration, that carriers cannot agree among themselves for the purpose of aiding in the enforcement of the provisions of the Interstate Commerce law, will strike a blow at the beneficial results of that act, and will have a direct tendency to produce the preferences and discriminations which it was one of the main objects of the act to frustrate. The great complexity of the subject, the numerous interests concerned in it, the vast area over which it operates, present difficulties enough without . . . it being advisable to add to them by holding that a contract which is supported by the text of the law is invalid, because, although it is reasonable and just, it must be considered as in restraint of trade."

The Second Annual Report of the Interstate Commerce Commission took the ground that traffic associations were not merely permissible, but desirable. It said:—

"While the Commission is not at this time prepared to recommend general legislation toward the establishment or promotion of relations between the carriers that shall better subserve the public interest than those which are now common, it must nevertheless look forward to the possibility of something of that nature becoming at some time imperative. . . . Without legislation to favor it, little can be done beyond the formation of consulting and advisory associations."

A careful study of public comments upon the recent decision fails to show that any public or trade body has approved the application of the Anti-Trust law to railroads. It is also a marked feature of the discussion that the actual users of the railways do not demur to the rates now in force nor to the rules or regulations applying thereto which are condemned by the decision.

In contemplating the alternative which will be forced upon the railway companies if the Supreme Court decision be maintained, it is proper to say that while pooling has been commended and resorted to abroad, was recommended by the Cullom committee, and has been en-dorsed by the most eminent railway experts of this and other coun-tries, it remains forbidden here by law.   If it continue forbidden, and the railways are to be interdicted from forming traffic associations, what remains for railways and public protection, in their mutual re-lations?   If the railway companies may not meet and agree upon mutual rates, fares, rules, conditions, classifications, tickets, liabilities for persons and property, excursion rates for great public occasions, times of trains, etc., in what condition are they and the public to be left?   The resultant differences of condition would introduce more uncertainties into all commercial conditions, would lead to more pref-erences and discriminations, and constitute a greater restraint of trade than if competitive lines agreed to and published common rates, fares, and rules.   Forwarders and receivers and travellers engaged in actual contact with this problem all know that practical freedom of trade is not to be obtained by its legal restriction, and that the liberty of reasón-able contract, which has, from time immemorial, justified proper agree-ments, has secured that parity of railway conditions which is the first essential of freedom of trade, the removal of restraint, and the stoppage of favoritism.

The case may therefore be briefly stated to be, that the majority in interest of mileage, earnings, dividends, and tonnage should control and determine reasonable rates and fares.   The recent decision exactly reverses this sound principle, and gives to one and the weakest line, whether in facilities or morals, not only the power which it might formerly assert, but now the apparent legal right and duty to deter-mine its rates and therefore the rates for all other shippers and railways between the points whereat such line competes.   For no one will pay more than the lowest rates.   There is no corresponding instance of the power of a minority in any trade or commercial exchange of the world; and any legal decision under which one company may thus fix the charges for all others, introduces elements of uncertainty, speculation, and danger to which the public attention cannot be too frequently attracted, and for which a legislative remedy cannot be too persistently demanded, or speedily granted.

Judge Cooley in his address to the National Convention of State Railway Commissioners at Washington, March, 1891, said:—

". . . one of the most important things to be accomplished in the regulation of railroads is to secure steadiness of rates . . . . I mean the sort of steadiness that makes changes only in the proper direction and when it does make them does so deliberately, carefully, after consideration of all the interests involved, and after such reasonable notice to the public as well as to the railroad interests as will enable due provision to be made by others to prevent heedless loss and injury therefrom."

He also said, in an article entitled "Legal View of Pooling," January, 1887: "It will be as wise for the State to encourage and protect whatever in corporate arrangements is of beneficial tendency as it will to suppress what is mischievous."

Everything which is right is assailed by something which is wrong. The maintenance of a right, therefore, always involves the restraint of a wrong; but when, as in the Supreme Court decision, the reasonable rights of carriers are restrained and the wrongs of discrimination encouraged under the cloak of individual action, a reversal of equity and legal precedents is exhibited which merits the searching public review it is now receiving.

Charges of trade restraint against associations which do not restrain but extend traffic; allegations that they discriminate, when they are formed to stop discrimination; transportation agreements adjudged, without proofs, to be entered into to increase rates, whereas they constantly reduce them; assertions that railway organizations oppress producers, when they really extend the markets for their products; and unsupported assertions of detriment to trade which are promptly disproved by evidence of benefits,—these are some of the paradoxes of unintelligent arguments against American railways, which legislatures, trade bodies, and courts have too long heeded and which they should now analyze and dismiss.

GEO. R. BLANCHARD.

A NEW FORM OF GOVERNMENT.

A DESPOTISM in a modern republic is surely a great novelty; and yet we have had recently in several States something which closely resembles this. In defining the three chief forms of government, Montesquieu says:—

"The republican is that in which the people in a body, or only a part of the people, exercise sovereign power; the monarchic is that in which a single man governs, but according to fixed and established laws; while in the despotic one man, without law or rule, controls everything by his will and caprice."

It would be difficult to formulate a more accurate description of modern "Boss" government than this third definition supplies, as that government has been administered by Mr. Platt in New York, Mr. Quay in Pennsylvania, Mr. Gorman in Maryland, and Mr. Cox in Ohio. None of these has had any law or rule to control his conduct other than his own will and caprice. Each has obtained his power by securing control of the nominating machinery of his party, by methods which I shall examine fully later; and each has used it to concentrate in himself the chief functions of the government of the State. Mr. Platt has done this to a greater extent than any other of our bosses, past or present, and has brought the new system to such a high state of perfection that his case is worthy of full and thoughtful consideration.

The foundation of the Platt despotism was laid in the winter of 1894, when the Republican party came into control of both branches of the State Legislature. He assumed direction of the Legislature; and before the session closed it had become customary for the party leaders in the two Houses to go to New York city at the end of each week to consult with him as to the conduct of public business. In the following winter, the Governorship also came under Republican control; and then Mr. Platt openly assumed autocratic or despotic powers. He selected the officers for the two Houses of the Legislature, and dictated the arrangement of the committees. Every Saturday and Sunday the leaders of the two Houses repaired to New York city where, with trusted local Republican politicians, they met Mr. Platt in his business office, or hotel rooms, and decided upon the legislative proceedings for the following week. Appointments for office were also discussed and settled there. In scarcely an important instance did the Legislature fail to obey the orders which reached it from Mr. Platt during this session. Some of his plans were thwarted by the refusal of the Governor to give his consent to them; but these were usually cases of minor importance, and did not weaken Mr. Platt's power.

Much the same condition of things continued through the session of 1896. It was during this session that Mr. Platt took the first step in what has since become his most striking exhibition of despotic power. He had the Legislature pass a bill creating a commission to draft a charter for the proposed city of Greater New York. Under the constitutional requirement this bill was submitted to the mayors of New York and Brooklyn for approval: it was disapproved by both. In withholding their approval, the mayors gave official voice to the public sentiment of their communities; for the provisions of the bill had excited strong opposition in all intelligent quarters in the two cities. Yet when the measure was returned to Albany, it was again passed by both Houses, under orders from Mr. Platt. It was at this time that the phrase "jam it through" made its first appearance. The meaning of it was that the orders of the boss must be obeyed by his followers, in spite of all opposition or criticism. The bill, after its second passage, went to the Governor; and he made it a law with his signature. It was a personal triumph for Mr. Platt: for public sentiment was strongly against the bill; and there was nothing of real weight in its support except his orders to "jam it through." Without those orders it would not have passed either House a second time. This was a notable act of absolute despotism. There were many others to follow.

The overshadowing importance of the Presidential campaign was of incalculable value to Mr. Platt in the election of 1896. It enabled him to lay his plans free from scrutiny or even observation; and the national alarm which carried the State of New York for McKinley by 268,000 plurality swept Platt into power again more firmly than ever. It was not until it began to be said that he would be chosen to the United States Senate by the new Legislature that people realized what had happened. Discussion soon revealed the fact that the Republican majority, comprising 150 of the 200 Members in both Houses, were as irrevocably pledged to him as if they had been his personal property. It mattered not in the least that there was no popular support whatever for his candidacy. It mattered not in the least that he had no qualifications for the place. These considerations did not enter into the question at all. The Members of the Legislature had promised him that they would do his will in all matters; and his will was that they should elect him to the United States Senate. His comment on his election was: "Well, I got there." And yet the intelligence and morality of his party, as well as of the people generally, were solidly arrayed against him; and a candidate of preëminent fitness was put forward by the Republicans in opposition to him. This candidate, after a vigorous campaign had been made in his behalf, received seven votes in the Republican caucus, and not a single vote in the election itself; the entire Republican majority voting for Mr. Platt.

The Legislature which performed this act was, of course, organized as usual by Mr. Platt himself. He did the work even more openly than before; having the Members meet him in New York city, and arranging all matters there. He held his weekly conferences as usual, and gave out their results without reservation to the newspapers; thus admitting that the real work of government was carried on in his room rather than at Albany. This became strikingly apparent after Mr. Platt took his seat as United States Senator on March 4. He left Washington at the close of each week, going to New York city for the express purpose of holding his Sunday conference or governmental council with his legislative and other agents. This conference had all the authority of a cabinet council; and at its close its decisions were given to the reporters as constituting the legislative programme for the ensuing week.

The most impressive demonstration of the despotic power behind these decisions was made in connection with the proposed charter for Greater New York. This had been drawn by the commission created by the act of 1896. It had been prepared in secret, and only very inadequate opportunity had been given for public inspection of it before it was sent to the Legislature; yet, in the brief time afforded, it had been condemned in very strong terms by what I may truthfully call the organized and individual intelligence of the community. The Bar Association, through a committee which contained several of the leading lawyers of the city, subjected it to expert legal examination, and declared it to be so full of defects and confusing provisions as to be "deplorable," and to give rise, if made law, "to mischiefs far outweighing any benefits which might reasonably be expected to flow from it." The Chamber of Commerce, the Board of Trade, the Clearing House Association, the City Club, the Union League Club, the Reform Club, the Real Estate Exchange, all the reputable ex-mayors, and other

officials expressed equally strong condemnation, especially of certain
leading provisions of the instrument; and the Legislature was formally
requested to give more time to the subject by postponing the date on
which the charter should become operative. Not the slightest attention was paid at Albany to any of these requests. The Bar Association's objections were passed over in silence, as indeed were all the
protests. The charter, excepting a few trifling changes, was passed
without amendment by both Houses of the Legislature by an overwhelming vote. Only 6 of the 114 Republican Members voted against
it in the Assembly; and only 1 of the 36 Republican Members in the
Senate. There was no debate upon it in the Assembly. The men
who voted for the charter said not a word in its favor, and not a
word in explanation of their course in voting against all proposals to
amend it. In the Senate the charter's chief advocates declared frankly
their belief that it was a measure of "political suicide," since it was
certain to put the proposed enlarged city into the hands of their opponents, the Democrats; yet they all voted for it because it had been made
a party measure, that is, the despot had said it must pass. After its
first passage it was sent, for public hearings and approval, to the mayors
of the three cities affected by its provisions. The opposition developed at the hearings in New York city was very impressive—so much
so that Mayor Strong, who as an *ex-officio* member of the charter commission had signed the report which had accompanied it when it went
to the Legislature, was moved by a "strong sense of public duty" to veto
it because of "serious and fundamental defects." When the charter,
with his veto message, arrived in Albany, the two Houses passed it
again by virtually the same vote as at first, and without either reading
the Mayor's message, or more than barely mentioning his name. One
of the Members who voted for it said privately:—"If it were not for
the fact that the 'old man' wants it, I doubt if the charter would get a
dozen votes in the Legislature outside the Brooklyn and Long-Island
members."

I have gone into this charter episode somewhat in detail because it
presents the most extreme illustration of the new form of government
thus far afforded. A more complete defiance of the right of the people to a voice in the conduct of their public affairs could scarcely be
made. A system of government which they had objected to because
it flew directly in the face of all experience,—its leading provisions
embodying methods of administration which had been tried and abandoned as pernicious, and which no great city in the world employs to-

day,—was thrust upon them in contemptuous disregard of their wishes. No reason was given for this course except that Mr. Platt desired it. His "will and caprice" were supreme in the matter. The desires of three millions of people, expressed through their most truly represent- ative men and organizations, counted as nothing with the Legislature.

Before passing to a consideration of the source of this despotic power, I wish to dwell for a moment upon a very striking feature of this new form of government. Its supreme acts are almost invariably per- formed in silence. Its motto in such cases is, "Vote and don't talk." When Mr. Platt was nominated in the Republican caucus for United States Senator, not a word was said in his commendation by his ad- vocates. He was simply put in nomination; and the votes were cast for him in silence. When he was elected by the two Houses of the Legislature, the same silence was maintained. I think this was entirely without precedent in such cases. There was the same silence when the New York charter passed the Assembly, and only a partial break in it when the Senate voted on the same measure. A like phase, which is also new, is seen in the treatment which is given to hostile criticism, either of men or measures. This is simply ignored. It is not even mentioned. Formerly, when a candidate for office was shown to have a damaging record, it was thought necessary to defend him. Under the new method of government, he is "jammed" into the place in silence. Formerly when a legislative measure was attacked, and alleged defects in it were pointed out, its advocates met the objections in the best way they could. Under the new method, the measure is "jammed through" in silence. Popular will, public opinion in any form, are treated as of too little account to be even noticed. The will of the despot is supreme; and the people, in the language of the politician, are "not in it."

Upon what does this power rest? How does it come about that the Legislature regards itself as the representative of Mr. Platt rather than of the people? There is no longer any mystery about this. The power rests upon money, raised as "campaign contributions" from both individuals and corporations, but mainly from corporations. The system by which this is made to give one man control of the government was originated by Richard Croker in 1893, when he was boss of Tammany Hall. Previ- ous to his advent, campaign contributions were made to the chairmen of political committees. They were given for no specific purpose except to gain the general good-will of the organizations. When the party boss appeared and began to dominate everyone else in the party, the practice of paying the money to him followed naturally. At the same time the money became something more than a campaign contribution. The contributors, if they were corporations, had been in the habit of sending to Albany each year both special agents and money to be used in defeating hostile legislation or "strikes." Lawyers had to be retained to appear before committees and make arguments against such measures; and when this method of opposition failed to be effective, lobbyists had to be retained to employ other means. All this was very expensive. The boss, in control of both Houses of the Legislature, stepped in with the proposition that a lump sum be given to him each year, and that he, in consideration of this payment, should guarantee complete protection from hostile legislative action. Mr. Croker is believed to have laid the foundation of a very handsome fortune through this invention. In his time, all corporations ceased to send their attorneys to Albany, the business of individual lobbyists was nearly or quite ruined, and his discipline was so strict that no Member of the majority in either House would venture even to introduce a bill which was hostile to the wishes of a contributing corporation. When the Republicans supplanted the Democrats in power, Mr. Platt adopted Mr. Croker's system as his own, and extended it over the entire State.

I will cite some of the most outspoken definitions of this system which have been made in the recent past, and which, though widely published, have never been contradicted. Mr. Wheeler H. Peckham, one of the ablest and most honored members of the New York bar, declared in a public speech, in March, 1894, that the payment of money to the boss by corporations, as the "price of peace," was general; naming one corporation which he said he knew paid $50,000 yearly, and adding that he had knowledge of a second which paid a similar amount. Mr. Henry O. Havemeyer, president of the sugar trust, testified before the Senate Investigating Committee at Washington, in June, 1894, that the trust made campaign contributions each year to New York political organizations, adding: "Every individual and corporation and firm—trust, or whatever you call it—does these things." Mr. E. C. Benedict, a director in many corporations, said, in a published interview, in December last:—

"The government of this State is in the hands of three houses; and the third house does business on the principle of 'stand and deliver.' That 's the way the Legislature treats corporations. I am mentioning no names; but I will say that the present ruler is as much more expensive than the former one of a different political stripe, as an educated, high-priced man is than an ignorant and low-priced one."

26

Mr. W. D. Guthrie, a reputable and able member of the New York bar, said, in a speech in Carnegie Hall, New York, on December 23, 1896:—

" Since the days of Tweed, a new system of political corruption has come into existence. The individual legislator is now seldom directly bribed. Corporations or individuals seeking protection or valuable charter rights at the hands of the Legislature retain a recognized political boss, and pay him for the service to be rendered. This secures the desired favor. They pretend that these payments are contributions to the party; but as a matter of fact they are tributes to the fund of the boss, who turns over to the national, State, or county committee as much of the spoil as he sees fit, distributing most of it for the purpose of electing to the Legislature his own nominees. In form it is a contribution to the party: in substance and truth it is bribery and blackmail. Most of these contributions are made by corporations. The items are entered on their books under fictitious sundry accounts and hidden from public investigation."

It is admitted by Mr. Platt's friends that he raises money in this way, and takes "contributions" in return for legislative protection and other favors to come; and the only excuse made for his conduct in so doing is that he uses the money for his party and not for his personal enrichment. Just how this, if true, makes his conduct any less reprehensible, I am unable to see. Why it should be accounted a virtue to refrain from self-corruption while corrupting the politics of an entire State, is something which passes my comprehension. But these are points upon which I do not wish to dwell now. It being conceded that Mr. Platt collects contributions, let us see how he uses them to give him his power. On this point some recent testimony by his fellow-boss, Mr. Quay of Pennsylvania, is very illuminating. Mr. Quay, let me say parenthetically, is almost as despotic a boss as Mr. Platt, and is scarcely less open in his methods. He controls the Legislature of his State in nearly all important political matters, and at times, though not regularly, goes from Washington to Harrisburg and openly directs its operations. He dictates all nominations, including those for United States Senator; and his candidates are almost invariably successful. In December of last year he had a controversy with the Republican Business Men's League of Philadelphia in reference to the new Senator from Pennsylvania; and in the course of it a letter was published which showed how it came about that Mr. Quay was master of the Republican majority in the Legislature. The author of the letter was the chairman of the Republican State Committee; and it was a sample of a number which he had sent to many candidates for the Legislature a few months earlier. It ran: "By request of Senator Quay I take great pleasure in enclosing contribution to defray your campaign expenses." Each letter contained a check for $500 in the case of a Senatorial candidate, and in the case of a candidate for the lower House one for $250. That is the system in all its simplicity. The boss supplies candidates with the money necessary for them to get the nominations in the primaries and to pay their campaign expenses afterward; and he supplies it always with the understanding that he shall own the candidate after election. "I would like to vote for Mr. Choate for Senator," said a New York legislator last winter, "but I am not quite sure but that something which was said when I went to see Platt last fall binds me to vote for him." There is always "something said"; and, in addition to this obligation to the boss, there is the absolute certainty that, if the boss be not obeyed in all things, there will be no campaign contribution next time and no reëlection. The same power which has lifted the legislator into political life can drive him out of it whenever he ceases to give satisfaction.

The results of this control of the nominating machinery are wholly bad. From the nature of the case, it fills the public offices with unfit men, since no man of character will consent to enter public life under such conditions. In the great majority of instances the men selected by the boss for legislative candidates are persons who have either failed in life, or never tried to succeed. Either they have never followed a regular calling, or have tried one calling after another without success. Some of them are in debt, many of them would like to be, and all of them find themselves getting a living more easily than ever before. They feel deeply grateful to the man who has lifted them into this happy condition, and are naturally desirous of prolonging it. They know that their fitness for public office had nothing whatever to do with their selection; and they know that a demonstration of fitness would be fatal to their continuance in office. They, therefore, follow the orders of their political creator blindly and even joyfully, and in complete disregard of the people, who really had nothing to do with their promotion to office, and will have no deciding voice in their continuance in it. Their only guide to conduct is, "What does the old man want?" This is not a fictitious phrase, but one that is heard daily at Albany during a session of the Legislature. Platt is universally spoken of among his followers as the "old man"; and the fate of every party measure is decided by the knowledge of what he wants done with it.

Of course the more absolute the boss's control of the Legislature, the greater his capacity for collecting contributions from the corporations. The natural instinct of legislators who have never possessed any property is to get at people who possess a good deal and make them give up some of it. Left to themselves, a boss-nominated body of lawmakers would give themselves up mainly to "strike" legislation. The worse they are, the larger the basis upon which the boss can rest his demand for "contributions," because of the difficulty he will have in restraining so hungry and reckless a body. All this works together for good to the boss and his followers. The more he gets, the larger are their individual shares. If a corporation be backward about giving, a bill threatening its business by cutting down its profits has only to appear in the Legislature to bring it to terms. When it is considered that there are in the city of New York more than 2,000 corporations, all subject to legislative interference, and with an aggregate capital of nearly two billions of dollars, it is easy to see how a boss can raise a campaign fund of sufficient size to pay the expenses of a very large number of candidates. He need not and does not stop with legislative candidates, but extends aid to all candidates for State offices and for Congress; demanding and obtaining from each the same understanding as to conduct in office that he obtains from legislative nominees. His control of the nominating machinery makes him absolute master of State conventions; and no man can become a nominee for Governor or other State office except with his consent. Mr. Platt's power is more absolute than that of any other boss, because of the vastly greater invested wealth upon which he is able to make his levies. New York is the centre of the corporate wealth of the land; and, as a field for a despot of his type, it has no equal. Other bosses do the best they can with the resources at their command; for all of them have large cities within their domains, and all work by similar methods, laying the foundations of their power in the primaries and nominating conventions.

The bosses have, in fact, taken the control of the nominating machinery of politics away from the people. We had a striking illustration of this on a large scale in 1896. Mr. Hanna, in behalf of Mr. McKinley, went into the primaries of one State after another, and secured from them delegates to the National Republican Convention who, when chosen, were pledged to vote for Mr. McKinley as the nominee for the Presidency. There was little concealment about this proceeding. As fast as delegates were obtained in this manner the result was announced in the press. Weeks in advance of the meeting of the Convention, Mr. Hanna's assistants published lists of delegates showing a majority of the Convention in favor of Mr. McKinley. This pre-convention campaign had been conducted on the presumption that the tariff was to be the leading issue of the forthcoming Presidential campaign; and Mr. McKinley's nomination was prearranged on that basis. By the time the Convention had assembled, the tariff had been completely overshadowed by the currency issue, which had assumed momentous importance; but, although Mr. McKinley's record upon this question was far from satisfactory, and a large proportion of his party desired the nomination of some man whose candidacy would give stronger assurance of currency reform after election, it was found impossible to break the ranks of his pledged delegates. His nomination had been settled in the primaries in much the same way as the State bosses secure their Members of the Legislature. Debts were incurred, which were paid off in various ways after Mr. McKinley became President. Appointments to office were made which were explicable only on this basis; and in many instances there was little attempt to conceal the nature of the transaction. But the greatest debt of all was paid in a new tariff bill which had no other excuse for existence. The country had been carried for McKinley through a national alarm about its honor and credit, which had brought to his support, on the common platform of sound money, men of all political beliefs. He was elected on the issue of sound money and currency reform, not on that of a high tariff. Yet, as soon as he entered upon his duties, he called Congress together in extra session, and sent to it a Message which called for the enactment of a new tariff, and made no mention of currency reform. The tariff bill, which had already been prepared, was not a measure for raising revenue, but for increasing the burdens of taxation in the interest of protected manufacturers. Like the McKinley tariff of 1890, it had to be enacted to pay campaign debts,—in this instance, debts which had been incurred in depriving the people of their control of the nominating system.

It comes to the same thing in national and State applications of this new system of government; namely, that the people must pay the price of its operation. They pay in the misuse of their public offices, in the increased burdens which come from unwise and extravagant legislation and from unjust and unnecessary taxation. They will pay later, also, in the consequences which will flow from the exercise of the functions of government by men who obtain and maintain their power by means of money collected from great corporations. Not only have the people lost control of the nominating machinery, but they are no longer represented by their legislators. Most of these sit and act in the halls of legislation not as the servants of the people, but as the servants of the boss, who in turn serves the corporations. In what boss-controlled legislature of to-day can a hearing be secured for a grievance, no matter how just, against a corporation that has made a " contribu-tion " ? Could there be a more dangerous proceeding than this—a surer way in which to stimulate socialistic and populistic hatred of corpora-tions, trusts, and all forms of aggregated wealth ? In making the boss a despot, by supplying him with the force upon which his power rests, are not his contributors sowing the wind for a whirlwind the devas-tating possibilities of which no man can foresee ?

What are the remedies for this loss of the nominating machinery? The old one, that good men must go into the primaries, should be abandoned as hopeless, so far at least as the larger cities are concerned. The good men will not go, because they have learned from experience the uselessness of doing so. This fact has been too well established to be either disputed or disregarded longer. I have very little faith in laws for the reformation of primaries, for punishing illegal voting and other irregularities in them. The best and most rigorous laws will not secure good nominations from primaries controlled by men who do not desire good government. It is idle to expect that men who spend their time and energies in getting possession of the prima-ries will use them to bring forth the kind of nominations which are dis-pleasing to themselves. If they could not make them produce the nominations which please them, they would abandon them at once. They have only one restraining influence; and that is—not to make their nominations so bad that there will be no hope of success with them at the polls. It is in the power of the advocates of good govern-ment to magnify this influence in such a way as to improve greatly the character of party nominees. Let all idea of " going into the primaries " be abandoned. There is nothing sacred about the primary. It is a modern invention, unknown to the founders of our government. It has become an engine of corruption and evil, and should be either neutral-ized or destroyed.

Under the Australian ballot laws, which are in force in nearly all our States, a complete weapon against the primary is supplied in the privilege to nominate by petition. This gives small bodies of citizens in every voting district in the land the power to hold a threat over every regular party primary. If a bad nomination be made in a primary, let its character be fully revealed, and let it be opposed at once by a good nomination on petition. Very little machinery is necessary for this. The main thing is the public interest and patriotic spirit which are necessary for any action to promote good government. If we have not these, it will be useless to hope for good results from any kind of remedy. What too many of us have been looking for is the discovery of a sovereign remedy for the cure of ills which result from neglect of the duties of citizenship. We must get it into our heads that there is no such remedy. The advocates and operators of bad government work unceasingly. They cannot be prevented from accomplishing their purposes except by equal industry and perseverance on the part of their opponents. Abusing them for their unpatriotic conduct, seeking to restrain them by laws,—these will accomplish little. They will not use the power which they work and struggle to possess in such a way as to suit us, but in such a way as to suit themselves. That is what they want it for. If we want it for other purposes, we must work harder than they do, and get it away from them. We must organize, and be ready at all times to work for what we want. There should be in every voting district an enrolled list of all voters interested in good government. With this ready at hand, a nomination by petition would be a very easy matter. Organization of this most desirable kind has been made in Chicago by the Municipal Voters' League, and is now under way in New York by the Citizens' Union. The Chicago League—which investigates the records of all candidates, and publishes the facts about them—previously to the recent election, condemned twenty-eight out of thirty-four aldermen as unfit for reëlection; and all but two of these were defeated, most of them for renomination, and the rest at the polls.

Undoubtedly a great deal can be done to break down the power of the bosses by stringent corrupt-practice laws requiring sworn publicity of all receipts and expenditures by both candidates and committees. The boss-controlled Legislature of New York has shown its fear of such laws by refusing on several occasions to allow the present inadequate law in that State to be amended in such a way as to include committees as well as candidates in the requirement of sworn publication, and in refusing also to allow any other change to be made in the law which might force into daylight the uses made of corporation money. With a rigorous law compelling full publicity, and with another law making the payment of money for campaign purposes by a corporation a penal offence, a second field of usefulness would be opened to the organized advocates of honest government. They could make it their duty to secure the enforcement of these laws. The reason why the corrupt-practice laws which we have in fifteen of our States have not been more successful lies in the absence of active public sentiment in their support. It is made nobody's business to enforce them; and they are consequently violated with impunity. With an organized body of vigilant, determined citizens in every district, these laws would soon become a tremendous power for good government. A few applications of their penalties would put an end to the greater part of existing corruption. The secret ballot has driven corruption away from the polls into the primaries and nominating conventions. Corrupt-practice laws, rigorously enforced, will drive it out of this branch of our political system also; but the purification can be accomplished only by hard and persistent work.

This is the beginning and end of the whole matter. If we want honest government, honest men must combine and work to get it. They must do this not in one election, but in every election. The bosses have taken possession of our nominating system, and through it have established their despotisms, because of the neglect of the duties of citizenship by the great mass of the people. These despotisms will continue just as long as this neglect continues. Railing at them, feeling ashamed of them, getting despondent about the future of popular government because of them, will not disturb them a particle. If we are too busy, or too indifferent, or too lazy, or too unpatriotic to attend to the business of government ourselves, the bosses will attend to it for us in their own way, and be mighty glad of the opportunity. The responsibility for it and the shame of it rest not upon them, but upon us. When the burden becomes intolerable, there will be an "uprising of the people in their might and majesty"; and the bosses, together with their system, will be swept away. When this upheaval will come, no man can say; but one would think that it must be at hand. Schopenhauer, in his essay on "Government," quotes Stobæus, a Greek writer of the fifth century, as mentioning a Persian custom by which, whenever a king died, there were five days of anarchy, in order that the people might perceive the advantage of having kings and laws. It may be that an inscrutable Providence is subjecting us to a period of boss despotism in order that we may perceive the advantage of popular government and may exert ourselves sufficiently to bring about its restoration.

JOSEPH B. BISHOP.

THE FUTILITY OF THE SPELLING GRIND.—II.

THE results of my spelling-tests, representing the work of 33,000 children, published in THE FORUM for April, showed what our teachers had been able to accomplish, and, consequently, what standards in this subject we were justified in establishing. Thus far, the feasibility of establishing definite standards has been denied, on the ground that the influence of instruction is so profoundly modified by conditions inherent in the pupils that the results obtained in one classroom would not necessarily indicate what we had a right to expect in another. In the present article, however, I shall endeavor to prove, by an analysis of the factors involved, that, so far as spelling is concerned, the results are not dependent on conditions over which the teacher has no control, but that, whether satisfactory or unsatisfactory, the causes may be found on the side of instruction. When my analysis is completed, I shall present an outline of what my investigations have led me to regard as the most rational plan of treating the subject.

In presenting my data, I shall first direct attention individually to the factors brought into play by the pupils, viz., age, nationality, heredity, and environment, and show how the mysteries are dissipated when the first ray of light is thrown upon them. The elements involved in instruction will then be considered in the same manner.

If the ability to spell were influenced by age, the results, naturally, would be in favor of the older pupils. That the averages received by these were not higher than those obtained by the younger ones, however, is proved by the figures presented in Table No. 1. These figures show, on the contrary, that in the majority of instances the results were in favor of the younger pupils. This may be accounted for by the fact that the younger children in a class are frequently the brighter and the more mature, having overtaken the older pupils by reason of these characteristics. Moreover, that the best spellers are to be found, as a rule, among the brightest pupils, is shown by Table No. 2, which indicates the influence of intellect on spelling. As the task of computing the results by ages, intellect, and so on from the papers of individual children was found to be very laborious, only a portion of the papers received were so utilized.

TABLE NO. 1.

	City.	FOURTH YEAR.			FIFTH YEAR.			SIXTH YEAR.			SEVENTH YEAR.			EIGHTH YEAR.		
		Age.	No. of Pupils.	Genl. Average.	Age.	No. of Pupils.	Genl. Average.	Age.	No. of Pupils.	Genl. Average.	Age.	No. of Pupils.	Genl. Average.	Age.	No. of Pupils.	Genl. Average.
COLUMN-TEST.	1	9–11	131	72.5	9–12	107	78.	9–13	72	85.9	9–14	88	88.5	12–14	24	94.4
	"	12–15	78	67.4	13–17	69	75.9	14–17	56	84.9	15–17	38	86.6	15–18	60	93.5
	2	9–12	167	51.5	10–12	136	71.	11–13	137	77.	11–13	82	86.5	12–14	76	90.9
	"	13–16	16	55.1	13–15	57	59.9	14–17	63	74.1	14–16	105	83.1	15–19	111	86.6
	11	9–11	111	56.1	10–12	61	70.1	10–13	112	75.1	11–14	77	83.2	13–15	37	90.5
	"	12–15	104	48.1	13–16	91	63.5	14–17	74	78.3	15–18	63	84.	16–18	13	91.7
SENTENCE-TEST.	1	9–11	72	69.5	10–12	56	81.6	12–13	22	79.9	12–14	43	76.7	12–14	35	86.9
	"	12–15	39	59.1	13–15	38	78.8	14–16	10	68.3	15–17	21	77.8	15–17	52	84.9
	*7	8–10	47	68.9	10–12	56	81.4	12–13	22	79.2	12–14	43	76.6	12–14	35	87.2
	"	11–13	27	59.	13–15	38	78.9	14–16	10	68.3	15–17	21	77.8	15–17	52	84.8
	†9	9–11	55	70.2	10–12	38	75.5	11–13	38	73.1	12–14	44	86.2			
	"	12–15	51	64.7	13–15	45	76.2	14–16	55	74.7	15–17	32	86.5			

* School A.   † School B.

TABLE NO. 2.

No. of Cities.	Grade.	No. of Classes.	No. Pupils Intellect 1.	Average.	No. Pupils Intellect 2.	Average.	No. Pupils Intellect 3.	Average.	No. Pupils Intellect 4.	Average.
3	4	16	112	78.7	169	70.5	152	58.8	54	52.1
3	5	16	117	86.	239	77.7	166	71.1	59	61.6
3	6	23	164	88.7	263	84.3	182	78.	69	73.7
3	7	19	116	93.4	216	88.3	155	77.5	59	79.2
2	8	8	56	94.	99	89.3	97	87.8	20	81.5

TABLE NO. 3.

	GRADE.	No. of Cities.	No. of Classes.	No. of Pupils.	General Average.	Children of Foreign Parentage.	Average.	No. of Children hearing Foreign Language at home.	Average.	Children of Unskilled Laborers.	Average.
COLUMN-TEST.	Fourth.........	21	119	3700	53.5	1051	52.	815	52.	670	53.2
	Fifth..........	21	126	3560	64.3	1126	66.3	814	65.1	619	64.2
	Sixth..........	21	122	3594	75.6	1032	74.9	790	74.1	584	74.3
	Seventh........	21	109	3107	81.	914	81.6	621	80.9	361	79.
	Eighth	21	71	2088	84.2	608	85.3	345	85.9	204	82.
SENTENCE-TEST.	Fourth	4	27	821	64.7	155	65.2	159	64.9	129	62.5
	Fifth..........	4	29	829	76.	153	77.4	157	76.7	129	74.5
	Sixth..........	4	22	778	69.7	185	69.6	165	70.3	119	70.4
	Seventh	4	18	566	78.8	81	82.5	52	81.5	55	76.8
	Eighth.........	4	19	528	83.1	72	83.2	64	83.2	76	85.

As in the preceding article, the cities are indicated in the tables by numbers, and the individual schools by letters. The first test, it will be recalled, consisted of a column of fifty words, and the second, of sentences; fifty test-words being employed in the fourth- and fifth-, and seventy-five in the sixth-, seventh-, and eighth-year classes. The third test, spelling in compositions, will not be considered here. In Table No. 2, which shows the influence of intellect on spelling, "Intellect 1" indicates the brightest, and "Intellect 4," the dullest pupils. The difference in favor of the brightest pupils, when compared with the dullest, is very striking. The lesson to be learned from Table No. 2 is, that an unusually high or low class-average may now and then be accounted for by an exceptionally bright or dull .set of pupils. Occasionally, therefore, the teacher may be allowed to plead "dull pupils" as an excuse for poor results. While this might offer a loophole for an incompetent teacher, the danger of being misled by such a plea is not great, because, in most instances, the teacher's statement can be verified by reference to the principal. Teachers habitually cursed with dull pupils cannot be placed too soon on the retired list. If the results throughout a building should be unsatisfactory, to plead "dull pupils" would of course be ridiculous.

Next, a comparison of the results obtained by children representing the foreign element with those secured by the American element (Table No. 3) shows that the influence of nationality on spelling is nil. Indeed, the percentages, if not identical, are slightly in favor of the foreign element. These figures, computed from the papers of pupils attending schools of all varieties, are substantiated by the fact already mentioned; viz., that the results in schools attended almost entirely by children of foreigners were fully as good as those in schools where most of the pupils were from American homes. Moreover, in spelling, nationality furnishes a very broad clue to heredity. And as the excellent spelling so frequently found among the children of foreigners cannot be regarded as the perpetuation of a family trait, the influence of heredity on spelling must also be put down as immaterial.

In Table No. 3, the influence of environment is also shown; the results obtained by children of unskilled laborers, whose home surroundings are presumably unfavorable, being compared with results obtained by all classes of children examined. And here again, strange as it may seem, the percentages were practically equal; thus showing that home environment exerts, apparently, as little influence on spelling as the other factors that I have discussed.

As the facts that I have presented would indicate that the results of instruction in spelling are not materially modified by conditions over which the teacher has no control, it is evident that the causes of success and failure must be sought among the elements brought into play by the teacher. The most important of these are: First, the amount of time devoted to spelling; second, the methods of teaching the subject; third, the selection of words; and, last, the personal equation of the teacher. These points will now be individually considered.

Concerning the amount of time devoted to spelling, I need only repeat what was mentioned in my last article, namely, that an increase of time beyond a certain minimum is not rewarded by better results; or in other words, that all the time beyond this minimum is simply thrown away. This, in my opinion, was conclusively proved by the table presented in THE FORUM for April, which showed that the results obtained by forty or fifty minutes' daily instruction were not better than those obtained where not more than ten or fifteen minutes had been devoted to the subject. As the time element is the central point around which the possibility of enriching the course revolves, my researches would have been amply repaid if they had led to nothing beyond this discovery.

Those who regard as incredible my statement concerning the time element in spelling may possibly find some food for reflection in my article on "Economy of Time in Teaching," which appeared in the February number of THE FORUM. Again, conviction may be carried by the facts presented in a letter just received from Dr. Eucken, Professor of Philosophy in the University of Jena. Prof. Eucken writes as follows:

JENA, April 19, 1897.

MY DEAR DOCTOR:

I have read your articles in THE FORUM with great interest; and I am pleased that you are laboring with so much energy toward the exclusion of useless matters from the course, so that attention may be centred on the essentials. The results presented in your last article, "The Futility of the Spelling Grind," are also very interesting, and cannot fail to lead to serious reflection.

That instruction, particularly in the lower grades, is in need of simplification, we have had occasion to experience with our own children. It appeared to us that, for the little the children actually acquired in the public schools, they were obliged to spend far too much time in the schoolroom. We therefore organized a small private class (3 to 5 children) for the purpose of covering the work of the lower grades. The children received from 5 to 8 hours' instruction per week. The results were perfectly satisfactory. The requirements were met excellently, so that the children were enabled immediately to enter the next higher grade.

No doubt the number of pupils played an important part in the achievement;

but the success must certainly be largely attributed to the better methods employed in our little private school.

I therefore wish you all possible success in your endeavors. Obviously, in America, they are duly recognized and appreciated.

Very respectfully yours,

DR. J. M. RICE.   R. EUCKEN.

Next, concerning the influence of methods, a very comprehensive study was made, through personal interviews with some two hundred teachers whose pupils had taken part in my tests. These teachers were questioned, to the minutest details, in regard to the course they had pursued. As the table showing a summary of these interviews side by side with the results was found too complicated for publication, I shall be able to present only the deductions to be drawn therefrom.

In brief, these deductions may be summarized in the statement, that there is no direct relation between methods and results. In other words, the results varied as much under the same as they did under different methods of instruction.

For example, among the points that have given rise to endless discussion, is that concerning the value of oral spelling; some believing it to be vital, while others claim that it is actually detrimental. My tests showed that, while in some of the schools, where a special feature had been made of oral spelling, the results were favorable, in others they were unfavorable. And the same conditions were shown where oral spelling had been abandoned. Second, much discussion has arisen as to whether, in written spelling, the words of the lesson should be placed in columns or in sentences. But the claim of superiority in favor of sentence over column spelling was by no means corroborated, the results of the sentence method varying just as much as those of the column method.

In addition to questions on the fundamental elements, an inquiry was made concerning the details relating to these methods; such as the mode of dividing words into syllables, both in oral and written spelling, the different ways in which misspelled words were made up by the pupils, the frequency of reviews, and so on; but no direct relation between devices and results could be traced. A very careful study was made as to whether there is any foundation for the theory that when children learn to read by the phonic method they fall into the habit of spelling phonetically, and therefore become poor spellers. The analysis showed that some of the best results had been obtained where the phonic method had been employed; that, in fact, the phonic method had long formed a feature in the cities where the highest averages were made. Another theory, that the best spelling is produced in schools where the most general reading is done, also proved unfounded. Nor did the schools where most time was devoted to written language make the best showing.

In recent years, a device, known as the sight or flash method, has found its way into some of our schools. This method, in brief, is as follows: A word is written on the board by the teacher, who permits the pupils to glance at it for a moment. The word is then erased, and the pupils are called upon to reproduce it on the board from memory. In this way, one word after another is written until the lesson is completed. Some who have used this method look upon it as a panacea: others have no confidence in it whatever. Judging by my results, the claims in its favor are not warranted: on the contrary, in some of the schools where it had been faithfully tried, the results were particularly discouraging.

The facts here presented, in my opinion, will admit of only one conclusion ; viz., that the results are not determined by the methods employed, but by the ability of those who use them. In other words, the first place must be given to the personal equation of the teacher; while methods and devices play only a subordinate part.

It seems to me, therefore, that the evils now ascribed to uncontrollable circumstances should be attributed in large part to a lack on the part of the teacher of those qualifications which are essential to success. Consequently, when reasonable demands are not met within a reasonable time limit, we are justified in inferring that the fault lies with the teacher and not with the pupils. An instructive experience I once encountered will serve to illustrate this point. On leaving a classroom in which I had heard a few recitations, I complimented the teacher on the intelligence of her pupils. She replied: " You must not give me credit for that. *These children are Russians ; and one can do anything with Russians.*" It so happened that on the next day, I visited a classroom, in which the children were exceptionally dull. On this occasion the teacher remarked: " You must not blame me for their stupidity. *My pupils are Russians ; and one cannot do anything with Russians.*"

Finally, I shall call attention to an important factor, on the side of instruction, whose influence, though manifest, is not affected by the spirit of the teacher. I refer to the selection of words for the spelling course. It is only in this element that I can find an explanation of the most puzzling feature shown in the tables accompanying the preceding article, namely, that classes which received exceptionally low averages on the column-test, did just as well as others on the sentence- and composition-tests. That these poor results cannot be attributed to lack of experience in writing words in columns, is proved by the fact that, in most of the schools where they were secured, column spelling had formed a regular feature in instruction. Nor can they be accounted for by the fact, previously mentioned, that the exceptionally high percentages were not trustworthy; for the results to which I now refer were far below those obtained in some instances where the words were dictated by myself. I believe, therefore, that the lack of success on this particular test was due to the fact that it contained certain classes of words on which these pupils had not been drilled; although, with few exceptions, the words employed were very common ones.

A careful analysis showed that in most instances where the low averages on the column-test were obtained, the spelling-book had been abandoned; although where it had been set aside, the results were not always low. In many such cases, the words are selected entirely from the other school-books,—reader, geography, history, arithmetic, science, and so on,—when opportunity for using them in school work arises. Words not directly needed are liable to be neglected, however common they may be. Thus, in selecting words for the needs of the schoolroom, rather than of life, the danger arises of giving precedence to technical and unusual words, while the common ones play only a subordinate part.

It is claimed in favor of this method of selection, that it is the more natural one. In my opinion, however, no method of teaching can be more unnatural; for, when the words are thus selected, the pedagogical principle—from the easy to the difficult—is disregarded, and systematic progress abandoned. Moreover, from a practical standpoint, the method is a most wasteful one, because much of the time which should be devoted to practical spelling is spent in studying words seldom used outside the schoolroom. When the need for such words arises in life, resort may be had to the dictionary. If the dictionary must be more or less frequently employed, in spite of instruction in spelling, it is safer to run our chances with the unusual words, than with those in constant use. The danger of leading children into bad habits if we permit them to misspell words in their written work could be obviated without completely perverting instruction in spelling. It would be necessary simply to tell the pupils how to spell the uncommon

and technical words, or to place them on the board, when occasion required.   Thus, children might be led incidentally to learn how to spell
the rarer words, while the spelling period proper might be spent on
practical work.

The absurdities incident to the so-called "natural method" were
shown very clearly during one of my visits to a fifth-year class, when
the pupils, who had studied the pine, were about to write a composition on the subject.   In preparation, the spelling-lesson of the day
consisted of the following words : *Exogen, erect, cylindrical, coniferal,
irregular, indestructible, pins, resinous,* and *whorls.*   First, as for systematic progress in spelling—from the easy to the difficult—a more absurd
combination could be scarcely devised.   And second, from the practical point of view, such words as *exogen, coniferal, whorls,* are entirely
out of place—at least until perfection in common words has been
reached.   And that drill in common words was still sorely needed in
this instance, was shown by the results obtained by the pupils on some
of the simple words in my sentence-test ; the forty-four papers submitted showing errors as follows: *running* 9, *slipped* 27, *believe* 17,
changeable 30, *baking* 7, *piece* 11, *careful* 12, *waiting* 9, *getting* 9, *driving*
11, and *hopping* 17.   In the grade representing the latter half of the
fourth school-year, containing pupils soon to be promoted into the class
just spoken of, the results in forty papers on words in my column-
test showed the following errors : *bureau* and *chocolate* 39, *pigeon* 38,
biscuit, celery, vegetable 37, *February* 36, *Wednesday* 34, *dough* 31, *autumn*
27, *cabbage* 24, *bedstead, beggar, steel* 23, *tailor* 22.   Are we justified in
such cases as these in spending our time on unusual words ?

Having presented my data, it will now be in place to say a few
words concerning the course in spelling which I have been led to regard as the most rational and fruitful.   First, as to oral and written,
column and sentence spelling, I shall say only this, that the wise teacher
will acquaint herself with as many methods and devices as possible,
and change from one to the other, in order to relieve the tedium and to
meet the needs of individual children.   Before all, she will beware of
running off at a tangent with any particular method, because none yet
discovered has proved a panacea.

Second, under no circumstances should more than fifteen minutes
daily be devoted to the subject.   Whatever benefit the pupils receive
from their instruction in spelling will be obtained within this period.

Third, I would recommend that the words be carefully graded, not
only in regard to orthographical difficulties, but in accordance with the

vocabulary of the child as well. In this way, the course in spelling might become as systematic as in other subjects.

Fourth, precedence should be given to common words, while technical and unusual words should be taught incidentally. By excluding words of the latter classes, the course would be materially abridged, and the chances of producing good practical spellers proportionately increased.

Fifth, the course should be further abridged by excluding words that contain no catch, *i. e.*, words which naturally spell themselves. My researches on this point would indicate that more than half the common words belong to this category, and consequently need not be studied. The ideal ground to be covered in spelling would be represented, therefore, by a carefully graded list of the common words most liable to be misspelled. The number of words in this list, according to my estimate, would be between six and seven thousand.

When the words have been selected, the next step will lie in a systematic treatment of the difficulties. And here again the course is open to simplification, by separating the words that may be learned collectively from those which must be mastered individually.

The words that can be acquired collectively are those to which rules of spelling apply. While, in some instances, the exceptions are so numerous as to rob the rules of their value, a few of them, nevertheless, are very reliable, at least for all practical purposes. And, as these few rules govern thousands of words, it would be much less burdensome to master them than to memorize such words individually. Among these rules, two are particularly comprehensive, and should be taught, year after year, until applied automatically. They are: first, the rule referring to the doubling of the consonant, as in *run–running*; and, second, the rule concerning the dropping of the final e, as in *bake–baking*. That so many children, even in the highest grammar grade, should spell *lose* with two o's, does not necessarily throw discredit on the teacher; but that a child who has attended school four years or more should write " While runing he sliped," or " She was bakeing cake," is as unpardonable as if he were unable to add 2 and 2. And yet out of 252 pupils in the fourth school-year, whose papers were examined with reference to this point, *running* was misspelled by 94, *slipped* by 126, and *baking* by 69.

That little advantage is now taken of rules, is indicated by the fact that, broadly speaking, as many errors were made on words governed by rules, as on those to which they did not apply. The comparison

27

is shown in the following table, which is based on the sentence test:

TABLE NO. 4.

No. of Schools.	Grade.	No. of Pupils.	General Average.	Results on words under the rule.	Results on words not under rule.
3	4	252	66.4	60.9	69.
3	5	232	76.4	72.6	78.2
3	6	311	71.	73.2	70.2
3	7	191	80.9	81.9	80.6
2	8	62	86.3	91.4	85.4

In the fourth- and fifth-year classes, it will be seen that the results were in favor of words not under the rule. In the sixth-year classes, however, the scale began to turn.

The words that must be studied individually are those in which no clue is given, either by sounds or rules. The best to be done with such words, until our spelling is reformed, is to bring them to the notice of the child, and trust to chance for the results. - The simple reform of dropping the silent letter in the last syllable of such words as *beggar, driver, doctor, mantel, bundle, metal,* would enable us to strike no less than 15 per cent of the words from the described list. Again, in the long vowel sounds the difficulties are endless; the same sound being represented in so many different ways that it is a marvel to be able to master them at all. To illustrate: *blue, to, too, two, who, shoe, you, ewe; lieu, view, new (knew); no (know), sew, beau, toe, owe, oh, dough, goat.* Again, the choice between *ee* and *ea,* as in *feed, read,* is extremely puzzling. What a boon to our children it would be, to rid spelling of such peculiarities as these!

The difficulties in English spelling were most vividly demonstrated by the numerous ways in which the younger children endeavored to get at some of the words. In a fourth-year class of forty pupils, for example, the word *physician* was misspelled in forty different ways, *chandelier* in 32, *machinery* in 27, *bureau* and *chocolate* in 23, *vegetable* in 19, *furniture* in 18, *biscuit* in 17, *Wednesday* in 15, *celery* and *pigeon* in 14, *baggage* in 13, *February* and *cabbage* in 11, *dough* in 9. Some of the combinations were as follows:

For *physician: fusition, fesition, fisition, fusition, fazition, fisision, facision, fizeshon, fazishon, fusashon, physichan, phyzision, physicion, phacicion, physision, phisishon, phasichian, phisishon, vasition, vecition, fasision, fosi-*

shen, fursishon, fushistion, feshishon, phisican, fusison, fesision, phsishen, fazuishen, phosion, fusion, fysion, fazshen, fishon, phasian, phacion, fegtion, phyasishen, phsam; for *chocolate: chocalate, choclate, choclet, chocklet, chocklate, chockolit, chocklod, chokolat, chokelate, chokelat, chalkolet, chaclote, chaclate, chalket, cholet, cholate, choalate, chalcolate, choctlet, choaklate, choclelot, chouilet, cacklet;* for *bureau: buro, burow, buroe, buerow, burreau, burro, burou, buero, beauro, beaurow, beaurew, beuro, beuroe, berro, berow, berrow, biro, beiro, brewro, bewer, beroueo, broe, berrobe;* for *vegetable: vegitable, vegitabels, vegatable, vegtable, vegtible, vegtibale, vegeatabel, vegitble, vegitbul, vegatobol, vegitale, vetable, vegeable, vegubale, veguable, vegatabe, vegitalb, vegtful, vestuble;* for *furniture: furnature, furnishture, funeture, funiture, furnutor, furnisher, furnachure, furnichure, fruniture, furiture, furnerchur, ferichure, furicher, furichur, furuner, ferichrue, furercure.*

Finally, I would suggest a separate list of those puzzling small words, which, though constantly used in writing, are yet so frequently misspelled. Among these may be mentioned *to, too, there, their, hear, here, any, many, much, such, which, those, whose,* and *does.* In all such a list need not include more than 150 or 200 words. As these words cannot be too often brought to the notice of the child, the drill should be begun as early as possible, and continued throughout the entire course. Even in the highest grammar grade, a considerable number of pupils will write *dose* for *does, who's* for *whose, there* for *their, to* for *too,* etc. The sentence, "Too much food is harmful," was given to very many children East and West; and in the sixth-year classes from 40 to 75 per cent of the pupils began the sentence with "To."

Although a liberal admixture of methods and a judicious selection of words would be of material assistance, nothing can take the place of that personal power which distinguishes the successful from the unsuccessful teacher. Consequently, our efforts should be primarily directed toward supplying our schools with competent teachers. As the number required precludes the possibility of limiting the selection to those who are born for the profession, our only course lies in developing the requisite powers, as well as we can, where they are naturally weak. To this end, I believe that no means can be more effective than to prescribe a definite task, to be completed in a given time, and to make the tenure of office depend on the ability to meet the demand. If my proposition should consider the results alone, then of course it would be fraught with the danger of leading us back to the era of endless mechanical drill; but so long as the time limit is a *sine qua non,* this danger is entirely averted.

J. M. RICE.

A PROPAGATOR OF PAUPERISM: THE DISPENSARY.

AGES before the Epistle to the Corinthians declared that charity was the greatest of all the virtues, the instinct of sympathy for the weaker man guaranteed the help and protection of the stronger. It is a pity that high aims of helpfulness should be misdirected, and the laudable motives for their fulfilment misconstrued; but more is the pity that it is true. To such as may not have given special attention to the subject which forms the text of the present article, the statement that so-called medical charity, as it is bestowed in the various hospitals and dispensaries throughout the land, is very grossly abused will carry with it a lamentable significance. It is, however, an old story with the medical profession, which is mostly concerned in these dispensations, and an unwholesome truth as applied to many of the lay managers of such benefactions.

It may be broadly stated, as the result of exhaustive statistical study, that fully 50 per cent of the patients who apply for free medical aid are totally undeserving of such charity. The main reason for this is that no effectual means are taken by the managers of these institutions to correct the abuse. For the sake of donations and the ostensible good accomplished by the treatment of a large number of patients, these charities are managed on the usual business principles of proving their right to be and to prosper on the assumed basis of demand and supply.

In New York alone there are one hundred and sixteen dispensaries each one of which is vying with the other in propagating the worst form of pauperism. The public is being taught that nothing is more freely given than medical advice to any who may ask for it. The institutions in question are crowded daily by hundreds of well-to-do patients, who are encouraged to defraud the really poor and to cheat the charitably disposed doctor of his legitimate fee. All this goes on in spite of protests, and in open defiance of all the laws of ordinary decency and fair play. The managers of these so-called charities, who virtually have the matter in their own hands, while openly pretending to deplore present conditions, are covertly combating every effort at reform, on the ground of its impracticability.

The more we study the question in its various aspects the more evident is the fact that medical charity, as now offered, is very much overdone. Instead of vaunting not itself, it is puffed up beyond any resemblance to what it once gloried to be, and is now a bloated mass of rottenness that extends to the very core of laudable intentions.

It is high time that such a condition should be candidly discussed and impartially judged. It is useless to assume that no one is directly to blame; and we need not go farther than the boards of management of these institutions to fix the main onus of the wrong-doing. In times gone by, the administration of needful help to the sick poor was altogether in the hands of the physician; and it was the glory of the medical profession to claim that no really meritorious case was ever denied free assistance. Unlike any of the members of the other liberal callings, with the physician it was never a question of money, nor of any equivalent other than the satisfaction of performing a bounden duty to humanity. Advantage has been taken of the latter condition from the time the good Samaritan ordered treatment for the first notable charity patient in history; and the ever-ready doctor has thus been made the victim of every benevolent scheme, true or false. Unconsciously he has slowly and surely become the ready tool of every corporation that claims to provide for the poor. Strange as it may appear, the man who is the most essential factor in the case, and without whose voluntary offices it would be impossible to treat the sick at all, is now virtually precluded from saying anything regarding the method in which the treatment should be carried out. The managers of the dispensaries and of other charities have taken the whole matter so entirely out of his hands that he has become the abject servant rather than the rightful master. The medical attendants may do all the work; but they have virtually no voice in the government of these institutions. In other words, the managers, influenced solely by the determination to do all they can for their respective institutions, make rules to suit themselves, and compel the medical staff either to submit to them or to resign. Under such circumstances it is not difficult to see where the main responsibility for the abuses of charity, so numerous and so grave, should properly rest. It would appear that charity is monopolized in the same way as any other marketable commodity that is ruled by money. The money-changers are apparently in full possession of the temple. The millionaire philanthropists stand in the same relation to the medical profession as did the camel to the Arab when his beast asked the privilege of poking his nose into his master's tent. When the camel finally occupied it there was no room for the owner; and he was forced to vacate accordingly. Similarly it happens that the doctor is generally on the outside when any efforts at internal reforms are in order.

The least hope of any change in policy is with those dispensaries that are bountifully endowed. The leading institution of this class in New York city is located on the West Side, and, in view of its defiant abuse of all kinds of medical charity, has earned for itself the unenviable sobriquet of the "diamond dispensary." For such as know its methods it is unnecessary to ask the origin of such a designation. It has such a high reputation for the number and pecuniary ability of its patients that it would appear to be rather a credit than a disgrace to receive its outrageously misdirected charity. Such at least is the inevitable conclusions that may be based upon the large average of well-to-do people who claim daily the benefits of free medical treatment so lavishly and indiscriminately furnished to all who apply. For the sake of receiving free advice, other matters are allowed to become of secondary consideration. Many of these visitors are from out-of-town districts, and will pay several dollars for car-fare, will ask for a written diagnosis of their disease and an extra prescription, and will then complain if they are kept waiting beyond the time for their return train. The examining doctor is content to ride to the dispensary in a horse-car: the patient comes and returns in a cab. It is no longer a joke to refer to the display of diamonds or the number of women clad in seal-skins in the patients' waiting-room. Nor does it appear to be unlikely that, in the near future, conveniences will not be required for checking bicycles and distributing carriage numbers in the order of the different arrivals. In this connection, the following description by an eye-witness in the waiting-room of this dispensary may be interesting:—

"The reception-room held about two hundred at a time. Nobody was turned away. Fully 50 per cent of the applicants were well dressed, and 10 per cent of them were finely dressed. Three women wore fur coats that had not been handed down from somebody else. There was an attractive display of fine millinery; and the men, more than half of them, bore no evidences of poverty. But all obtained free treatment supposed to be given to paupers—'poor persons.' "

Although the particular institution in question may be justly considered as the head and front of the offending, similar so-called charities throughout New York city are equally guilty of like fraudulent practices. Such instances as the following carry with them their own moral:—

"During the examination of a dispensary patient a roll of bills dropped from her pocket. The doctor picked it up and remarked : 'Madam, this is a free dispensary ; and, as you are able to pay a fee for medical advice, I must decline to treat you here.' 'Well,' replied the woman, 'that money is for something else. You are paid by the city, and must prescribe for me.' On being assured that the doctor received no salary from any source, the patient became indignant, and protested that she was entitled to attention equally with the 'lady' who had preceded her and from whom she had rented a house the week before."

A still more striking case is related by another physician :—

"A wretchedly clad woman presented herself to me at the dispensary and asked for treatment. She gave a name that I afterward found was assumed. She was badly in need of attention and said she could not pay. I believed her and agreed to treat her. It was an interesting case ; and she consented to appear before the class of fifty or sixty doctors.

One day, after she had been before the class several times and treated, I was driving with my wife in Central Park. We were passed by a magnificent team and carriage,—spanking horses, nobby coachman and footman, and glittering harness. In the carriage was a lady whose features were familiar ; but I could not remember where I had seen her. That same day my charity patient presented herself, attired as usual in the poorest of clothes. I recognized her as the lady of the fine turnout. I said nothing, as I thought I would investigate. A few days later I saw the same carriage in front of a fashionable shop, and got a good view of my patient as she alighted. When she next presented herself I asked her for her real name. She gave me her assumed dispensary name. Then I told her she was deceiving me ; and she finally disclosed her identity. She was the wife of a man known all over the city as a millionaire. I sent a bill to her husband ; and it was paid without a word."

Here are additional testimonies of a similar nature :—

"A woman keeping a fashionable boarding-house in the neighborhood of Madison Avenue, New York, always visits a dispensary when she requires medical service. Were she able to moderate her bibulous propensities and pay for medical attendance out of such savings, I am sure both she and some striving doctor would be benefited. In the same house the wife of a man who receives a salary of twenty-eight hundred dollars a year has for months attended the free out-door department of a hospital in New York. From the same house also, a man with rheumatism, whose wife earns fifty dollars a week on the stage, receives free electric treatment at a dispensary."

Says a distinguished professor of New York city :—

"I recall the case of a German family to whom I gave free treatment in the dispensary for five years, and then found out by accident that the head of the family paid taxes on $100,000 worth of real estate.

Another regular dispensary patient was a woman who was afterward ascertained to be the wife of one of the wealthiest and most prominent hardware merchants in the city.

I can name a man, a resident of Fifth Avenue, who came into an estate worth millions, and who used to take his child regularly to a dispensary to get free treatment.

One day a woman came to me at the dispensary and requested free treatment. She was poorly dressed, and said she was unable to pay. I gave her a prescription. Afterward I found out that her husband had given her five dollars to pay for the very service that she obtained free."

The following assertion from a hard-worked dispensary doctor is equally significant:

"It is not a novel experience for one to meet at the theatre, or out riding on a wheel, the very patients who were too poor, forsooth, to pay a doctor, and hence availed themselves of dispensary treatment. In the clinic in which I am an assistant it is not an unusual thing for men to ask if their trouble would be aggravated by the use of a bicycle. One patient had the temerity to ask me if horseback riding was likely to prove injurious."

It is not necessary, for the sake of proving a rule, to multiply illustrations. There is not a physician in any large city who is connected, even indirectly, with dispensary work who is not willing to assert that the whole system of medical charity is most notoriously and outrageously misapplied.

The dispensary managers also admit the fact; but they shift most of the blame upon the doctors, who are always so eager to serve the poor without pay. While the medical man, for purely charitable reasons as well as for professional experience, is ever ready to treat gratuitously the really helpless sufferer, it does not necessarily follow that he should be expected to care for the well-to-do on a like basis. While there may be occasional exceptions to a general rule of full payment for an "interesting" case, it nevertheless holds good in a strictly ethical sense that no patient, no matter who, what, or where he is, or what the interest in the study of any rare or particular ailment from which he may suffer, is ever entitled to free treatment if able to pay even a nominal professional fee. Naturally, all other things being equal, the progressive medical man engrossed in the examination of unusual conditions of disease would give more thought to an interesting case than to one of ordinary occurrence. Why should the doctor not be paid and interested at the same time? If anything, the lucky patient with the rare malady should have the grim satisfaction of claiming more of the doctor's attention than is received by his less accommodating neighbor for the same money. Unfortunately for poor humanity, there are enough of such diseases among the poor, who are always entitled to the doctor's services, to give him all the satisfaction he needs, without wasting his time on those who can, but will not, pay for his work.

The profession is sufficiently in earnest in its efforts to stop the present abuses to yield any supposed advantages along such a line to the

pressing expediency of adopting absolute rules for separating the paying from the non-paying clients. There would be no difficulty in effecting a proper understanding on such a point, if the managers were willing to be consistent in other directions. They have all the power to do
and to dare, but prefer seemingly to haggle over trifles rather than to
settle great questions. In fact this has been abundantly proved of late
by the futile efforts of the Committee of Medical Societies in their conferences with various boards of dispensary managers. Evidently something more than appeals from the rank and file of the medical profession
is needed before these stubborn boards will loosen their grip or yield
their usurped positions. The time has evidently come when plain words
should be spoken to the public, especially that part of it which supports
these institutions. It is not true that poor people suffer for want of
skilled medical attendance. On the contrary, they obtain vastly more
than they have a right to expect. Charity, as applied to most of the
dispensaries, especially those in the wealthy districts, is a mere name.
Vast sums of money are wasted yearly on worthless and undeserving
persons. There would not be any danger of the really poor suffering,
if half the hospitals and two-thirds of the dispensaries were closed to-
morrow. No millionaire, anxious to fit the camel to the eye of the
needle and quiet his conscience by lending to the Lord, need worry because the dispensaries may suffer for want of necessary funds. As it
is, the thrift of one class now ministers to the improvidence of the other.
The anodyne which quiets the conscience of the giver paralyzes the soul
of the taker.

It is justly claimed that the doctors are in part to blame for initiating the very evil from the stupendous growth of which they
and the community at large are now suffering so much. It is not
difficult to associate the conditions of cause and effect in discussing
the question from the purely professional aspect. The weak point
with the physician has been his desire for increased clinical experience,
and the advancement in his business interests which such experience
may bring. Like all other good things, it has been very much overdone. Nor are his eyes yet open to the fact that he is fast drifting to
the bad, in his zeal for doing the good. It is quite true that he has not
yet fully awakened to the necessity of calling a halt in the only way that
may tend to mitigate, or possibly arrest, a rapidly growing evil. The
men at the dispensaries know that they are doing wrong in curtailing
their own incomes and those of their brethren by treating in their
clinic rooms patients who are able, and perhaps willing, to pay a

fee in their respective offices; yet they are afraid seemingly to take an active stand against the fraud. Individually they object to the unfairness of the thing; but collectively they submit to its consequences. If they could be content to limit their studies to the proper cases for treatment, and to resist resolutely the temptation to go farther, much of the existing abuse would be at once remedied. If there were concerted action in this direction, the dispensary managers would find it to their interest to come to terms. The chances of such a condition, considering the eagerness for medical appointments, the reputation of holding them, and the desire for increased experience, are too remote to be at present considered. The profession is not yet sufficiently unanimous in its own interests to make this possible. It must be still further disciplined in its destructive tendencies. The managers are profiting by this weakness, and are complacently contemplating the strange spectacle of the fabled worm that is turned upon itself in the vain effort to feed on its own vitals.

So long as one of the main objects of medical teaching is to gain clinical material at all hazards, so long will the present evils be beyond the possibility of any immediate remedy by the profession itself. In fact the dispensary in New York city which abuses medical charity the most of all is one that was founded by a millionaire with the avowed object of supplying illustrative cases, rich or poor, for the lecture-room of a neighboring medical college. Such material, it is true, is very necessary for educational purposes; but the ultimate and only benefit accrues to the medical school, whose interest it is to coax students to its doors, take fees for tuition, and overload the medical market with aspiring young men whose very subsistence is denied them by persistently taking from them, by means of these false charities, every reasonable means of legitimate support. It is the old trick of blowing hot and cold with the same breath,—improving goods, at the same time destroying their market value. With shame be it said, many of the appointments in dispensaries are secured with the understanding that certain public clinics shall be regularly supplied with patients who, as an equivalent for free treatment, are expected to appear before a medical class, submit to public examination, and be the text for a medical or surgical lecture. New York, Boston, Philadelphia, Baltimore, Cinciunati, Chicago, and other teaching centres are more than well supplied with such schools, public and private, undergraduate and post-graduate, that claim the clinical material from the hundreds of ambitious medical satellites who seem to be satisfied with the merely nominal honor of a position in a self-constituted and conveniently expansive faculty. Much as the profession may object to the general unfairness of the lay managers of the dispensaries, it can never have a reasonable basis of compromise for necessary reforms until it manifests the intention of remedying one of the main evils of the system for which it is itself certainly and directly accountable.

This mistaken eagerness for dispensary experience reacts disastrously upon the profession in many ways. Although at first it may be a question between the ins and the outs in the dispensary business, in the long run it must prove that the profession is persistently working toward its own ultimate destruction as a remunerative calling. The swindling dispensary patient receives everything, and yields virtually nothing in return. Even the rarity of his disease is an unearned increment on his part, for which he should have no privileged compensation. He simply takes charity, robs the willing doctor, and cheats the deserving poor. It would appear that the medical man of the near future must educate himself at great expense of time and money, must study in the hospitals, take post-graduate courses, and, with a necessarily independent income, be ever ready to meet and minister to the veriest pauper. He must be content to spend his time and capital in distributing samples of his skill to all comers, with the delusion that his business is increasing with the number of his patients. The younger medical men in the various dispensary-ridden cities feel the truth of this prediction more than those already established in the profession; for the physician starting in practice must depend upon such patients as are able to pay only small fees. The great majority of such clients now go to a convenient dispensary. Whenever any of these spurious charities starts in a given locality the incomes of the medical men of the neighborhood fall to the extent of one-half to two-thirds of their former amounts. In contemplation of this fact it is easy to understand why the younger men, more especially, are the persistently active and consistently determined opposers of the dispensary abuse. Certainly no one is unjust enough to deny to them the right to make an honest living by the legitimate practice of a very useful and highly honorable calling. It depends a great deal upon the mettle of these men whether or not the main issue upon which the professional aspect of this question rests will yet be brought to the front. Dr. Walter Brooks Brouner, in an able article on this subject in a recent issue of the "Medical Record," forcibly and directly presents the younger physicians' side of the argument :—

"Think of it! If a doctor attends a clinic three times a week for fifty-two weeks, treating daily on an average five patients, every one of whom could pay a moderate fee, say $1.00 (yet this is a small average), what has he done? Simply deprived the profession of $780 in one year. It does not take much of an arithmetician to estimate the net result of a year of such work. If we suppose that 25 per cent of the two million and odd visits made by patients at dispensaries had been paid in our offices instead, at the small sum of $1.00 *per capita*, $500,000 would have been placed to the credit of the profession. This means that if five hundred doctors of New York city had gotten an even share of the work, each would have had to his credit in the bank $1,000 for the year."

Not only do the dispensaries, by their lax methods of discrimination, allow incomes to be diverted from the expectant medical beginner, but these institutions openly bid for pay from every applicant. It may not be generally known that the great majority of these charities charge every patient from ten to twenty-five cents for advice and medicine. One of these, which is connected with the oldest and wealthiest hospital corporations in New York city, charges one dollar a month to all applicants, under the transparently hypocritical plea of preserving the self-respect of the swindling recipient and of making him feel that he is not the worst specimen of a pauper. The income from this source is considered sufficient to pay all the running expenses of these generous and noble benefactions. The sums thus collected by the different dispensaries vary in yearly amounts from five to fifteen thousand dollars; and yet this is quietly, covertly, and persistently done in the name of pure charity! This is not only striving to demonstrate that medical service as such is worth nothing, but that skill in compounding a prescription has no practical value; the possible original cost of the medicine being the only pecuniary factor in the consideration. The average of handsome profit is struck by the uniformly exacted standard fee, it being generally understood that many of the drugs are donations from wholesale houses, are mixed by the gallon, and economically dispensed in stock prescriptions. The ordinary manufacturer rails against the injustice of prison labor; but what about the business profit of the outside pharmacist, and the harm to the doctor's legitimate work by the fraudulent methods of these so-called charities, to which he so constantly and willingly tenders his best services?

While it must be admitted that no confessedly poor patient can be denied the privilege of free medical service, either with or without the dispensary system, the present shameful ministration to a large number of undeserving people is fraught with every form of evil to the individual recipient of false charity, and to the community at large, which so tacitly abets it. There is not only a wrong diversion of funds conscientiously contributed for a specific purpose, but there is an open bid for pauperism in its worst form.   There appears to be a subtle influence regarding medical pauperism which does not obtain in many of the other forms of alms-taking.   The man who would scorn to take a loaf of bread from his baker, a pair of shoes from his shoemaker, or a bag of coal from his coal-dealer, coaxes himself to believe that he is doing a smart thing by lying to the doctor in order to get free advice.   It would appear that his bodily weakness, affecting his resisting power against disease, extends its baleful effects to his conscience ; rendering him unable to overcome those influences which eventually tend to undermine the very foundation of his personal honor.   He first begins his career as a pauper by simply taking what he should not receive, and ends by begging for what he does not deserve.   The dispensary gives him his first lesson in the easy down-grade to indigence, idleness, and degradation.   He may scorn the tramp ; but the latter has not the additional disgrace of flying false colors.   The community which closes its eyes to the ultimate possibilities of such conditions becomes equally culpable with the offender himself.   It is as much the duty of the people to combat these pernicious tendencies as it is to remedy all other equally fraudulent practices.   To most persons the subject appears to be a very delicate one, the frank discussion of which is hemmed in by the fear of possibly hindering the presumably well-directed aims of necessary charity.   Such a view, however, is based on false premises, as can be easily proved by a calm study of glaring and incontrovertible facts.

In the various attempts that have been made to remedy the evils of the present system, numerous obstacles have presented themselves. Thus far it has been seemingly impossible to reconcile differences of opinion between the lay managers and the medical attendants regarding the relative expediency of proposed reforms.   The managers conduct the dispensary on purely business principles, while the medical and surgical attendants are actuated by a desire for professional advancement and increased clinical opportunities.   Each party shifts the responsibility for wrong-doing by blaming the other side.   There is apparently no authoritative court to which any appeal can be made. Each managerial board has absolute control of its own institution.   It has been able to say that it will do this or that thing ; and there is the end to argument.   Various schemes have been suggested for weeding out the large number of unworthy applicants ; but none of these, for obvious reasons, has gained general favor. Beyond the mere show of discrimination between deserving and undeserving patients, no practical result has followed; and the doors are as widely open as ever. The most reasonable measure proposed, and that most generally recommended, has been one providing for the systematic examination of all who plead poverty as an excuse for patronizing the institution. Notwithstanding the difficulty in getting at the truth in all cases, there is no doubt that a perfected plan of registration on such a basis would be of incalculable service. There is no reason why anyone should suffer under such a rule, as all emergency cases could be treated without question,—for the first time at least,—while non-urgent ones could safely wait until they had been investigated by a visiting committee or properly indorsed as worthy objects of charity by some responsible person accepted as such by the institution. Numerous facilities to this end are offered at nominal rates by the charity organizations of different cities. If a person should be discovered as giving a false name or address, he could be branded at once as a liar and a fraud, and be refused treatment. If it were also reported that he was able to pay, a like check could be placed on his continued visits. All this should be done before the applicant is allowed to see the doctor; as the latter has enough to occupy every minute of his valuable time in attending to his patients,—often as many as thirty in an hour. Under these circumstances it can be easily seen that the medical attendant could have no possible temptation to discriminate in favor of specially interesting cases for clinical purposes. For the want of such a preliminary examination, hundreds of undeserving cases are hurried along the line; for it often happens that the overworked prescriber is the only person who can stand between the truth and falsehood of anyone who gains entrance to the examining-room with a perfunctory ticket of admission.

The unwillingness of the dispensary authorities to adopt a uniform method of inspection, and to enforce a standard regulation for charitable relief, naturally suggests the advisability of some form of centralized governmental control of the entire system. Each State should enact suitable laws to such an end, and make it obligatory on every charitable institution to be governed by fixed statutory rules, under the penalty, on overt disobedience, of the annulment of their respective charters. It would then be possible to limit the number of dispensaries and hospitals to the actual needs of the poor in each community. This would necessarily bring such as remain to a rational working basis, and discourage the mushroom growth of the numerous private charities that are scattered in every nook and corner of our larger cities. The extent of this reduction can be estimated from the fact that but 25 per cent represents the actual deserving poor of any ordinary community. A still further improvement on the present plan would be the abolition of all institutions not strictly charitable in character. Under such a designation would come all such as received fees or similar returns from applicants. This would do away very properly with the ten-cent, twenty-five-cent, and dollar tax on the patient, who, if really poor, should pay nothing. It is not beyond reasonable hope that in the near future all these institutions may be not only directed, but supported, by the State, the same as our public hospitals, insane asylums, and other similar institutions of charity. Already an attempt is being made in the State of New York, by the enactment of a law making most of these conditions a possibility; the controlling authority being the State Board of Charities. The bill provides that "no person shall apply for free treatment in any dispensary, nor shall any person or persons or corporations conducting such dispensary give treatment or medical aid to any person unless such person shall be a poor person and unable to pay for medical treatment." It also abolishes the obnoxious dispensary fee, by providing that all poor patients shall be treated free of any charges for services or appliances; and that all persons applying for dispensary relief shall, under pain of punishment for misdemeanor, give proof of their inability to pay for services not only by personal attestation of the fact, but by certificates from either the landlord, police captain, alderman, or any reputable charity organization of the district. The latter provision is probably the most reasonable means to the desired end, as not infrequently many landlords would be only too willing to encourage a practice of which they themselves are ofttimes easy victims.

This is a movement in the right direction; and when the authority for controlling all dispensaries, great or small, public or private, is vested in a State board of charities having power to inflict penalties, correct flagrant abuses, establish clearing-houses of general information, annul charters, and act as a board of appeal on disputed questions of management, there is a reasonable promise that many, if not all, of the present abuses, lay and medical, will be eventually corrected. At least it will be exceedingly interesting to all concerned to watch the detail-working of a law calculated to remedy one of the greatest evils of our present faulty charity system.

GEO. F. SHRADY.

AMERICAN ARCHÆOLOGICAL WORK IN GREECE.

WHEN the American explorers commenced operations in Bœotia, their principal objective was Plataia. The historic celebrity of that name lent to the site itself an absorbing archæological interest.

A few words will suffice to remind the reader of the glorious but tragic history of the gallant little Bœotian town, which, alone of the other Greek cities, shared with Athens the imperishable laurels of Marathon, and which became later the scene of the great battle against the Persian invaders and of their final rout (479 B.C.). The town had been previously sacked and burned by Mardonius, the Persian commander; and the great victory having been won on its devastated territory, the allied Greeks awarded the Platæans, out of the Persian spoils, eighty talents (about $153,000) with which to rebuild their homes and erect the temple of Athena Areia. They further declared Plataia an inviolable city, and conferred on its citizens honors and special privileges; making them guardians of the tombs of the heroes who fell for the freedom of Greece, and entrusting them with the celebration of the festival of the Eleutheria, sacred to Zeus the Deliverer, which continued every fifth year, down to the time of Plutarch. The large-hearted patriotism of the Platæans, however, was as opposed to the time-serving policy of the Thebans as their origin was said to have been distinct from that of their neighbors and irreconcilable foes. The two cities stood only five miles apart; and the Thebans, sallying from their stronghold and disposing of superior forces, could easily surprise their enemies, after a march of only two hours. The Platæans, therefore, having to depend only upon the rather distant alliance of Athens, fortified their city and, later, built extensive walls. The Thebans did, as a matter of fact, attempt to carry the place by surprise at the outbreak of the Peloponnesian War (431 B.C.). But, having been repulsed with great slaughter, they returned with the Lacedæmonians and laid siege to Plataia, which was defended with unsurpassed heroism for a period of three years. When at length the garrison, having been reduced to two hundred and twenty-five men, surrendered, the Thebans razed the city to the ground.

In 387 the Lacedæmonians, being now at war with the Thebans, reinstated in their old homes the survivors of the Platæans, who had meanwhile found refuge in Athens. But the city was again taken and destroyed by the Thebans in 372, and again restored, for the third time, by Philip of Macedon, after the battle of Chæronea in 338. Five centuries later Plataia was visited by Pausanias, who refers to the temple of Hera, as well as to that of Athena Areia, which boasted of a famous statue by Phidias, and of the paintings of Polygnotos and Onatas. Of the temple of Zeus Eleutherius nothing then remained but the statue of the god and an altar. But mention is made of another temple, that of Demeter Eleusinia, and of the tomb of Leitus, the only one of the Bœotian chiefs who returned from Troy. In the fifth century of our era Plataia is referred to by Hierocles, the Neo-Platonist; and about a hundred years later Procopios (" De Ædif.," iv. 2) states that its walls were restored once more by the Emperor Justinian. After this, Plataia gradually sinks out of view. Its exposed situation must have rendered it an easy prey to the successive invaders who swept over Northern Greece. But its site has remained marked by a vast and confused mass of ruins.

Of modern travellers, Leake serves here again as our most reliable guide. The ruins stand on a fan-shaped, flat plateau—whence, most probably, the name of the ancient city—about 1,400 metres long from north to south and 1,000 metres in its greatest width. It stretches northward into the plain from off the steep and rugged slope of Mount Kithæron, which rises majestically to the south. About a mile north of the city the river Oëroë flows through the plain westward toward the Euripus; while the Asopos, which has its source in the immediate vicinity, travels westward to the Gulf of Corinth. On the plateau, the line of the outer walls—about eight feet in thickness and fortified with towers—forms an elongated triangle. Two inner walls mark off a rounded enclosure to the southwest, and a smaller triangular area to the extreme south. The latter embraces the highest point of the entire site, and, being separated from the lower rocks of Kithæron by a ravine only fifty yards wide at its narrowest part, is supposed by Leake to have been the acropolis in pre-Persian times, and to have included the entire original city. Its walls are of a more ancient construction than the rest, and are probably the only portions dating prior to the Persian war. "In almost every other part the masonry is of a less ancient kind, and the ruins of former buildings may be detected among the materials; which is no more than consistent with the troubled his-

28

tory of later Plataia and the many repairs and renewals it underwent." The temple of Zeus Eleutherius, and the adjacent tombs of the Athenians, the Lacedæmonians, and the other Greeks, were situated outside the principal gate, the foundations of which Leake traced not far from the northeastern angle of the wall. This spot he believed to be the one marked by a ruined church—apparently the same church which Dodwell (i. 279) attributes to St. Demetrius, and in which he noticed two inscriptions imbedded.

As we shall see, the results of the first and second campaigns were not brilliant. It was only thanks to Mr. Washington's persevering enthusiasm and conscientious labors that substantial results were obtained in the spring of 1891, and the situation was thus saved.

Through the exertions of Mr. Wesley Harper, Dr. Lamborn, and Mr. H. G. Marquand, a sufficient sum had been collected to warrant the undertaking of the work, which was accordingly begun on April 2, 1889, with sixty-three workmen; Dr. Waldstein assuming the direction. His object, as explained in the report, was first to find some architectural, artistic, or epigraphic clue indicating points upon which work might be concentrated. Byzantine churches are, as we have seen, rich depositories of such indications; and the extensive site of Plataia included no less than nine such ruins visible above ground. It was therefore decided to dig near several of these; and, the force of workmen having been divided into three sections, the party under Dr. Waldstein explored, during the first three days, an equal number of these structures; but with only negative results. Mr. F. B. Tarbell examined the church believed to have been sacred to St. Demetrius, and two other similar ruins; but he quitted the excavations on the second day. Mr. J. C. Rolfe, after three days' work on the church of St. Nicolas and another church to the west of the city wall, was joined by Dr. Waldstein; their efforts being now concentrated upon a three-apsed church, where Mr. Tarbell had dug on the first day. This structure yielded only a number of classic architectural fragments.

At this point the work of the first season at Plataia, which lasted only four days, was brought to a close; and it would have been reckoned as of a purely tentative character, had not the researches of Messrs. Tarbell and Rolfe resulted in the discovery of twelve inscriptions, subsequently published by them in the fifth volume of the "Papers." The most important of these is a Latin inscription which had served, in the three-apsed church, as a paving-stone, and was partly imbedded under its walls. As it lay face uppermost, about half the lettering on the right side was worn away; while, of the fifty-five lines which compose it, the first is chipped off. On examination it proved to be the first portion of the preamble of the famous Edict of Diocletian (A.D. 285) "De Pretiis Rerum Venalium," which fixed the maximum prices of commodities throughout the empire.

The text of this Edict was already known from other inscriptions; but in it important gaps existed, which were now supplied by the Platæan copy,—noteworthy also by the fact that it is the only version of the Edict in the Latin original found in Greece proper. Several fragments of the Greek translation had been previously discovered in other parts of the country; and during the excavations of the second season yet another portion of the Greek version was unearthed at Plataia,—the stele on which it is engraved having done duty as a covering-stone to a Byzantine grave. This portion contains a chapter relating to the prices of textiles; and, from squeezes of the inscription and copies sent to him, Prof. Mommsen, who had for many years devoted himself to the study of the numerous extant fragments of the Edict, edited, at the request of the American School, this latest fragment and published it in the fifth volume of the "Papers."

The second campaign at Plataia partook more of the character of topographical research than of systematic excavations. After some delay, arising from the severity of the weather, Mr. Washington began work on February 19, and later on he was joined by all the members of the School, with Dr. Waldstein at their head. The work of this season was brought to a close on March 12. The sites of Byzantine churches were again taken as starting-points; but all attempts at tracing the temples of Demeter and of Hera proved abortive; the main result of the season's exploration being confined to four more inscriptions. With regard to topography, Mr. Washington undertook to make a careful and definitive survey of the entire site, the extant accounts of which fail to give satisfactory data, or mark with accuracy the exact position and present condition of the city walls. Mr. Washington's exhaustive report, accompanied by a map and the ground-plans of six of the Byzantine churches by Mr. H. D. Hall, is inserted in the "Papers," and shows that the walls, built principally of the rough gray marble quarried out of the southern ridge of Kithæron, are assignable to five distinct periods—from the earliest polygonal to the later Roman and Byzantine styles of masonry.

Another important matter was the elucidation of certain questions connected with the battle-field of Plataia. The accounts of the battle, and the description of the Persian encampments and the successive positions of the Greeks given by Herodotus, Thucydides, Plutarch, and other ancient writers, have been the source of many doubts and disputations.   The task therefore of studying the whole question afresh was now confided to Mr. W. Irving Hunt, with the result that his "Notes on the Battle-field of Plataia" have cleared up several hitherto contested points, and have defined the famous "island" of Oëroë.

The continuance of the exploration of Plataia during a third season was due to Mr. Washington, whose devotion and intelligent enthusiasm were recompensed by a notable success.   He resumed work on April 20, 1891; devoting the first three days to a renewed search of the several spots marked by Byzantine churches, ruined walls, and hewn blocks of stone.   Each point however was successively abandoned in despair. Finally, on April 23, he moved to a place nearer the centre of the walls, where a series of sockets cut in the protruding rock was noticed, and which were supposed to have held votive offerings.   A little to the south the ground rises one and one-half to two metres above the field, forming a terrace some forty by thirty metres.   Hewn blocks were found here,—some fallen below the terrace, and others *in situ.*   The spot seemed promising; and two parallel trenches running north and south of the terrace were dug.   After half an hour's work a wall was laid bare in each trench, a few feet below the surface.   The entire force of workmen was now employed in following up the lines of this wall and in sinking additional cross-trenches to the bed-rock.   In the space of four days the foundations of a longitudinal building with cross-walls and an outer encircling wall were cleared.

These foundations are built of smoothly cut blocks of porous stone. Only one block of gray marble—of the kind in general use at Plataia —still rests on the southeastern corner; and another marble block, part of the upper course of the *crepidoma,* showing the trace of one of the steps, was found near the northeastern corner.   With the exception of a few pieces of roofing-tiles, not a single fragment of any part of the superstructure was discernible anywhere near the spot.   The foundation-walls and the two marble fragments just referred to were the only architectural remains giving any clue to the reconstruction of the building, the determination of its age, or the elucidation of its character and purpose.   But the ingenuity and resourcefulness of the trained archæologist are equal to the solution of problems of this kind.   The physiologist, in reconstructing some extinct animal out of the evidence supplied by a couple of bones, accomplishes a feat perhaps less remarkable than the reconstruction of entire edifices and whole cities by the intelligent and close reasoning of the archæologist. Therefore the careful study, by means of which Mr. Washington succeeded in determining satisfactorily the above three points, deserves some explanation, however brief. It is a typical instance of archæological investigation. I should add that a small terra-cotta statuette of a seated and veiled woman, of a very simple type, and a coin of the Emperor Licinius (A.D. 307–324) were found among the ruins, within the area of which a layer of blackened earth next the rock was also visible.

Let us now see by what process of reasoning the problem was solved. To begin with, the ground plan of the foundations shows them to be those of a peripteral Doric temple of the archaic type. Now, the more complete remains of similar temples, such as the Heræum at Olympia, serve to determine the setting back, from the edge of the extant lower course of gray marble, of the usual three steps on which the columns of Greek temples rest. This point having thus been determined, the diameter of the columns is easily arrived at, since their entire weight must fall within the breadth of the underlying foundation-wall. Consequently, by following the measurements of the extant foundations, the distance from centre to centre of the angle-columns is fixed at 13.30 metres on the ends and at 46.50 metres on the flanks of the temple. The usual proportions of intercolumnation being known from other early Doric structures, the dimensions just obtained lead to the conclusion that this temple must have been a hexastyle; i. e., it had six columns at each end and eighteen or nineteen on each flank. As to material, the fact that not a vestige of the superstructure remains, must be taken to point to the probability of its having been built of marble; for such material was used up with avidity, both by the Byzantines and the Turks, in the manufacture of lime. Preference would, of course, be given to what was within easy reach; and the site of this temple is on level and exposed ground.

With regard to its age, the style and workmanship of the masonry, the shape of the iron clamps (as indicated by the holes on the stone blocks—for the clamps themselves had disappeared), the arrangement of the cella, and the ratio of the number of end and flank columns—six to eighteen—assign the foundation-walls to the end of the sixth or the beginning of the fifth century B.C. The layer of blackened earth, referred to above, points to the fact that the building which originally stood on these foundations was destroyed by fire. And, from the historic facts known to us, it may be safely inferred that it was rebuilt, as we shall presently see, in 427 B.C. on these same foundations. When inquiring next to which divinity this temple was dedicated, we find that the range of selection is narrowed down to Hera, Athena Areia, the Eleusinian Demeter, and Artemis Eukleia, who were all honored, as we know, with noteworthy sanctuaries at Plataia. The alternative supposition, that this temple might have been sacred to some other divinity, is not tenable; since, if such were the case, so important and commanding an edifice would not have been passed over in silence by ancient writers, who refer to other shrines at Plataia less noteworthy than the above. The temple of Demeter is spoken of as lying at a distance from the city. That of Artemis is mentioned by Plutarch once ("Aristid.," xx); but, as it is ignored by Pausanias, it could not have been of much importance. As regards the temple of Athena, both Plutarch and Pausanias (but, strangely enough, not Herodotus) state that it was erected out of the share of the Persian spoils ceded to the Platæans. There is, however, no indication of its locality ; and altogether our information respecting it is vague and scanty.

Not so in the case of the Heræum. The temple of Hera is first mentioned in connection with the battle of Plataia, when the left wing of the Greek army, falling back before the Persians, took up a position in front of the sacred precincts, which, Herodotus says, lay "before the city." It is also related that the Spartan commander,—who was stationed at a certain distance, close to the temple of Demeter,— finding the sacrifices unpropitious, looked up toward the Heræum and invoked the help of the goddess. When, half a century later, the Thebans razed Plataia to the ground, they constructed near the Heræum an inn two hundred feet square for the accommodation of pilgrims to the shrine. They also erected (427 B.C.) in honor of Hera "a marble temple of a hundred feet." This was the temple which Pausanias visited, and which he describes as standing "within the city " and as remarkable for its great size and the statues it contained,—two by Praxiteles and one by Kallimachos.

The apparent contradiction between Herodotus and Pausanias, as to the locality of the temple, is easily reconcilable. The remains of the city walls indicate that the city was originally confined to the southern elevation of the plateau, and that later it extended northward to its outer and lower portion, where the temple stands. So that when Pausanias saw it, in the second century of our era, it was, as a matter of fact, within the then extended city walls; whereas, at the time of the battle of Plataia (479 B.C.), to which Herodotus refers, the site of the temple was still outside the walls and just "before the city." This also explains the retrograde movement of a portion of the Greek army on to the plateau, where they ranged themselves under the shadow of the sanctuary of the great goddess, while the Spartan commander invoked her aid, looking up from the position he held lower down in the plain.

At that time the temple itself, with the rest of the city of Plataia, must have been already laid waste by the Persians. The evidence of the layer of blackened earth on the foundations leaves no doubt that it was burnt at an early date. Now, as the masonry of the extant foundations is clearly pre-Persian, and as the statement of Thucydides is that the Thebans "erected to Hera a marble temple of a hundred feet," the natural inference is that the temple which the Platæans rebuilt after the rout of the Persians, must have been an inferior structure. Thucydides distinctly states that the later one was of marble. It was therefore pulled down by the Thebans and reërected—in honor of a divinity they also specially revered—with greater splendor, but on the same ancient foundations. The original localities of sanctuaries were scrupulously regarded by the Greeks.

The indications of the locality itself support the theory that here stood the temple of Hera. I have already alluded to the sockets sunk in the adjoining rocks for votive stelæ. Just below the terrace, on which are the foundations, and a little to the north, Mr. Washington traced the remains of an extensive building; and these are no doubt the remains of the great inn which the Thebans built near the temple. With regard to the objects found in the ruins, the small clay figure is supposed to have been a votive copy of the seated statue of Hera by Kallimachos. This figurine has a veil over the head; and Hera, the bride of Zeus, was generally represented as veiled. Finally, the coin of Licinius would testify that the temple must have been still standing in his time—about a hundred and fifty years after Pausanias.

Such briefly is the able and ingenious argument, in which hardly a link is wanting, whereby Mr. Washington establishes the identity of his discovery with the famous Heræum of the Platæans. It is an achievement that reflects great credit on the American archæologist, who moreover upheld the honor of the School by prosecuting the exploration of Plataia to a definite conclusion. Even as it is, the foundations of the Heræum itself have not been entirely cleared of earth; and in archæological explorations only the complete clearance of a site can guarantee that all that may be found has actually been secured. It is this system of absolute thoroughness which the Germans adopted with such brilliant results at Olympia. It is the only safe and truly scientific system.

But, while Mr. Washington was assiduously toiling at Plataia, other undertakings had already engaged the attention of the Directors of the School. Early in 1889 certain unauthorized excavations made in the neighborhood of Eretria and, later, a more systematic exploration of its ancient necropolis, undertaken by the Greek Archæological Society, yielded a rich harvest of vases, terra-cotta figurines, and other considerable objects. Irrespective of these finds, however, both the historical fame of the city and its extant remains above ground were sufficient to invite serious attention. Therefore, in the summer of 1890 the American School obtained permission to explore this site also.

The ancient city of Eretria was situated on a small projection of the island of Eubœa, a little to the southwest of Chalcis, at a point where the Strait of Euripus, being only four miles broad, presents the aspect of an inland sea. Lying out of the beaten track of travellers and on a spot not easy of access, Eretria was seldom visited. Dodwell (ii. 154) and, more especially, Leake are, in this instance also, the best of modern guides. Leake, who states that "Eretria by means of its desolation has preserved remains affording an interesting confirmation of the former importance of the city," refers to the commanding towers of its acropolis, its city walls, and theatre, and to numerous foundations of buildings. These remains suffered considerably since Leake's time, owing to the fact that King Otho, attracted by its classic memories, chose the site of Eretria as a settlement for the survivors of the heroic island of Psara, which had been completely devastated by the Turks. The plan of a modern town was laid out within the area of the ancient walls and, on the rising ground, a naval school was erected for the young Psariot sailors; considerable quantities of the accessible old material being utilized in this abortive revival. The swamp fevers of the marsh, which had gradually extended to within the walls, rendered the place uninhabitable, especially during the hot season; so that at the present time about four hundred people tenant for part of the year some of the one hundred and fifty modern houses, which, in their turn, are now mostly in ruins.

It was in these surroundings that the Americans entered upon the exploration of Eretria on February 1, 1891. The first season's work, which, ending on March 20, was interfered with by rigorous weather, and included only twenty-eight days, was under the superintendence of the

Annual Director of the School, Prof. Rufus Richardson, who undertook also the elucidation of inscriptions. Mr. A. Fossum, of Johns Hopkins University, and Mr. C. L. Brownson, of Yale, had charge of the excavation of the theatre; while Mr. J. Pickard, of Dartmouth College, and Mr. J. W. Gilbert, of Brown University, surveyed the walls of the city and produced an excellent topographical map of the district. Finally, Dr. Waldstein searched the extensive lines of graves outside the walls; making several interesting finds of vases and other small objects. The alleged finding of Aristotle's tomb, believed in and announced at first, but very properly withdrawn later, need not be referred to here.

Mr. Pickard's able "Topographical Study" has supplied ample details of the site and the ancient fortifications. The acropolis, at the northeastern corner, stands on an eminence 116 metres high, and forms an irregular enclosure 200 metres across. From it, two parallel walls, each about 1,200 metres in length, extend down to the harbor in irregular lines, 600 metres apart at their abutment. At intervals of about fifty-five yards they were dotted with towers 6 to 9 metres in diameter. Of these walls, the entire circuit of which is two and one-half miles, only the foundations remain. The walls and towers of the citadel however still stand, some four metres above ground; their imposing proportions, and the weather-worn surface of the huge blocks quarried from the bed-rock from which they rise, testifying to their great antiquity. A cross-wall separates the citadel from the lower city; and at this point, concealed under slight elevations of earth, are the remains of the towers which guarded the gates leading out into the Sacred Way. The course of this ancient road can be followed for miles to the east, by the multitude of graves which line it on either side. Finally, numerous remains of various other structures, marking the lines of the streets of the city, are still traceable on the steep hillsides.

Of the auditorium of the theatre, which stood lower down, close to the western wall, the entire area was found covered by a shroud of earth varying from 1 to 3 metres in depth; but the general outline of the *cavea* was easily discernible. The fact that the natural slope available higher up the hill had not been taken advantage of, as was almost invariably the case in Greek theatres, but that an artificial mound had been raised to support the rising rows of seats, suggested that the location of the theatre had been decided by the proximity of an ancient sanctuary of Dionysos. The *cavea* forms slightly more than half a circle, with a diameter, on the level of the orchestra, of 24.88

metres, which is larger than the theatre at Athens (22.50) or at Epidauros (24.50); although the entire capacity of the *cavea* in each of these theatres is much greater.   Of the thrones of the priests and officials, only fragments were discovered ; but the front rows of the seats, which were found in fairly good preservation, are so low as to suggest that cushions were placed on them, as was undoubtedly the case in the Dionysiac theatre of Athens.   The orchestra was overlaid with beaten earth only,—paving, such as is seen in Athens, having been introduced in Roman times,—and was bounded by a curb, between which and the lowest step the usual sunken drain carried off the rain-water into a subterranean aqueduct.

Independently of this, another tunnel-like passage, 13 metres in length and 2 in height, passes obliquely under the orchestra and abuts at its centre, into which it opens by a flight of steps.' Similar steps give access to it from under the proscenium.   The discovery of a feature so distinct and novel in the structural economy of a Greek theatre led, as we have seen in a previous article, to a closer investigation of a similar passage noticed at Sicyon, which, however, served there also as a drain.   In the present case, the points of the theatre joined by means of this tunnel left no doubt that its purpose was to enable persons engaged in the performance to appear suddenly on the orchestra, before the spectators, and again disappear from view.   Such apparitions would not have been compatible with the rôle of the chorus, whose movements to and from the orchestra are well defined.   The inference therefore seemed conclusive that the secret passage was destined for the use of actors who, leaving the dressing-rooms in the rear of the proscenium, had to emerge in the orchestra as if from below.

There are situations in the Greek drama which, without the intervention of some such device, had been hitherto unintelligible.   Some years prior to this discovery, Prof. Wilamowitz pointed out (" Hermes " [1886], xxi. 608) that it was necessary to conceive the existence of an *estrade* in the centre of the orchestra in order to understand aright that passage of the " Persians " (v. 619–675) of Æschylus, in which the chorus, urged by Atossa to call up the ghost of Darius, supplicate the powers of the lower world and invoke Darius to rise above the mound that covers his tomb.   Darius appears in the midst of the chorus—who stand around his grave—and again vanishes from view.   This and other passages in the Greek tragedies, such as the disappearance of Prometheus and the Oceanidæ in " Prometheus Bound," could have been represented satisfactorily only by the help of a concealed passage leading to the centre of the orchestra : the stage itself of the Greek theatre offered no other suitable appliance. In an extant fragment of Æschylus's " Sisyphos," allusion is made to such subterraneous movement of the actor. Furthermore, the "Steps of Charon," of which Pollux ("Onomasticon," iv. 132) speaks, and as to the precise meaning of which there existed considerable divergence of opinion, can be explained intelligibly only by this latest discovery at Eretria. Subsequently to this, German archæologists found similar passages in the theatres of Magnesia and Tralles, in Asia Minor ; and indications of a like structure are announced from Argos. All these evidences confirm the convincing explanation given by the American explorers of their discovery.

But the most important part of the Eretrian theatre is the stagebuilding. It is of importance on account of its elaborate design and the successive modifications it underwent, which serve as evidence of the developments in the architecture of the Greek theatre. Its remains range from the earliest polygonal masonry to work of the first century B.C. In its main dispositions it answers to the stagebuilding at Athens, with the exception of a vaulted passage running under its entire breadth on to the orchestra, to the probable use of which I shall refer presently. The plans of the theatre and its reconstruction, as drawn by Mr. Fossum, were approved and corroborated by Prof. Dörpfeld, who had visited the site. Their joint conclusions however gave rise to an animated controversy as to the economy of the Greek stage; Mr. E. A. Gardner, Director of the British School, Mr. Loring, and Miss Sellers expressing very divergent opinions. But Prof. Dörpfeld's profound study of the subject, as set forth in the exhaustive work which he published a few months ago, may, I think, be accepted as a safe guide.

The first season was now brought to a close. Twenty-eight days' work on a site of such vast possibilities could not have amounted to much more than tentative search. A second campaign was therefore undertaken in January, 1892, under Prof. W. C. Poland, then Annual Director, who, accompanied by Messrs. Brownson and Fox, continued, for a short while, the clearing of the theatre. But the work still lagged; the centre of interest having again been transferred by Dr. Waldstein to Argos. Nothing further was done during the ensuing year; but on May 3, 1894, Prof. Richardson, accompanied by Messrs. E. Capps, O. S. Hill, C. Peabody, and Prof. Phillips, resumed the exploration with as much judgment as success.

The conjecture, that the location of the theatre was determined by a preëxisting sanctuary of Dionysos in the vicinity, was now to be tested. Attracted by some hewn stones, protruding from among the bushes, some sixty feet to the southwest of the theatre, Prof. Richardson dug trenches, which, in the course of the first forenoon, revealed the platform of a building about 12.50 by 23 metres. The disposition of these foundations, which lay a couple of feet beneath the surface, indicated a temple. No vestige was found of the marble superstructure. It must have invited destruction by its exposed position, and must have disappeared in the lime-kilns which now yawn near the theatre. Some fourteen metres to the east of this platform another large foundation— the nature of which had puzzled the excavators of 1891 and had been considerably disturbed on the supposition that it was a tomb—was now completely cleared. From its form, and position in connection with the temple, it was inferred that it supported the great altar of the deity there worshipped. As it stands to the rear of the stage and directly opposite the vaulted passage which runs under it, it would appear that that passage served as an entrance for the procession of priests, officials, actors, and chorus who, after the sacrificial rites, marched in pomp from the sacred precincts on to the orchestra. "Nowhere else in Greece can one see the group of the three structures that belonged to the well-organized worship of Dionysos—temple, altar, and theatre—so well preserved as here."

On the other, the western, side of the temple, a stylobate 20 metres long and 1.20 wide was found to extend obliquely to the north, in the direction of the theatre. Close to this foundation four marble bases and some fragments of columns were discovered. It was clear they supported choragic monuments; the whole forming a kind of gallery between the sacred precincts and the theatre. The fragments of four inscriptions, subsequently unearthed, left no doubt that the monuments commemorated victories in dramatic and musical contests celebrated in the theatre. No inscription was found confirmatory of the conjecture that the site was that of the sanctuary of Dionysos; but the grouping of these monuments with the temple and the theatre forced that conclusion upon the explorers.

The one great sanctuary, however, was, as already stated, the temple of Artemis Amarysia—a title under which Artemis was worshipped also in Attica, where it survives in the name of the village of Maroussi. That temple was not only the chief shrine of the Eretrians, but, as Livy states, a pilgrimage for the inhabitants of Karystos. Prof. Richardson therefore sought to determine this most important question of Eretrian topography. Strabo says that the village of Amarynthus was seven stadia outside the walls; and he refers to the temple of the Amarynthian Artemis. The seven stadia thus vaguely mentioned have been supposed by successive archæologists to lie in every imaginable direction. Some thirty years ago the Greek authorities acquired an important inscription bearing the text of a treaty between Eretria and Histiæa, and prescribing that it should be set up at Amarynthus,—obviously in the great temple which, as was customary among the Greeks, was also the public record office. The precise spot in Eubœa where this inscription was found was never ascertained; but it is believed to have been Bathia. But Bathia is at a much greater distance than seven stadia from Eretria. A little beyond the seven stadia, however, to the east of the walls,—a direction which Prof. Richardson considered likely on other grounds,—an isolated hill known as Kotroni rises out of the plain; and as the geographer Stephanus of Byzantium writes "Amarynthus = νῆσος " (an island), Prof. Richardson concluded that this definition might refer to the isolated hill, much in the way that the " island of Oëroë " is spoken of by Herodotus (ix. 51) as lying in the battle-field of Plataia. Moreover, an old church stood on a terrace at the foot of Kotroni; and some inscribed slabs had been found there. These considerations urged Prof. Richardson, who had already visited the spot in 1891, to explore it now. But two days' work with a considerable force of workmen revealed no other Hellenic remains than a couple of sepulchral inscriptions. The great and renowned temple of Artemis, therefore, is still to be sought and found.

Meanwhile in the city itself progress was made in clearing additional portions of the theatre. Between the theatre and the naval school of King Otho some walls, which appeared above the surface, were excavated, revealing the continuous foundations of houses on either side of a street, and, in one case, a fine floor of cement and pebbles. Search trenches were dug on the plateau of the citadel, but without material result. Finally, diggings were made at the foot of the acropolis, one hundred and seventy-five metres to the east of the theatre, where a protruding block attracted Prof. Richardson's attention. A set of four " tubs " or tanks, inlaid with stucco and connected by water-conduits, was found here, backed against a wall twenty feet in length. The entire aspect of this spot—to which the humorous designation of " the city laundry " was provisionally given—and the fact that a well-preserved male statue, now in the Central Museum at Athens, was unearthed here in 1885, promised well for further search.

At this point, after a sojourn of three weeks, which furnished only fourteen working-days, the season's operations were brought to a close. For so short a campaign, the results attained were not inconsiderable. The topographical information alone entitled Prof. Richardson to write:

"In the case of such an important city, and one whose history interests us so deeply, of which no ancient writer has given us any description, this is more of an addition to our archæological information than the discovery of a whole town in Macedonia or Cappadocia."

Still, the excavation of the theatre remained, after the lapse of four years, an incomplete undertaking. Like the theatre at Thorikos, it stood in unpleasant "contrast to the theatre at Megapolis so faultlessly excavated by the British School." And this was the more noticeable, since the archæological importance of the Eretrian theatre attracted the yearly visits of Prof. Dörpfeld's touring students. "It must be done by the Americans," Mr. Capps wrote, "if they wish to be looked upon by archæologists as thoroughly competent and conscientious excavators." Prof. Richardson, therefore, commenced, on May 20, 1895, a fourth campaign of four weeks, with the result that, finally, under the intelligent superintendence of Mr. T. W. Heermance, the theatre was freed entirely of its shroud of earth.

The mysterious "city laundry" engaged the personal attention of Prof. Richardson, who, on proceeding to clear the ground, found the four "tubs" resting on the cemented floor of a large room. This was connected with several other rooms forming, around an open court, a large building one hundred and fifty feet square. Its general disposition, another row of smaller tanks,—possibly foot-baths,—and the liberal system of water-supply within it, suggested that it was a gymnasium. This conjecture was soon placed beyond doubt by the discovery of a marble base with an inscription commemorating the athletic victory of a youth, whose statue had stood on it. Two other inscriptions of greater importance were soon unearthed. The one, quite perfect and consisting of forty-nine lines, was recovered under circumstances which indicate the discrimination and care that must govern archæological research. A stone, supposed to form a step, was covered, during a heavy rainstorm, with a layer of liquid mud, which, drying rapidly under the hot sun, revealed a little moulding. This attracted the attention of Prof. Richardson, who found the stone to end in a sort of gable. On its being raised off the ground, the earth under it had taken the impression of the inscription so perfectly that it could be read almost as easily as from the stone.

In this inscription Eretria records the honors conferred on Epinikos, the son of Nikomachos, a gymnasiarch, who furnished the funds for prizes in contests and was at pains to procure oil of the finest quality for anointing the gymnasts. For these and other services it is enacted, "to the end that all may know that the state is not ungrateful, and that the public may have many emulators of his example," that "Epinikos receive a crown of olive and that the decree be cut on a marble stele which shall be set up in the gymnasium in the most conspicuous place." The "most conspicuous place" was, no doubt, the exact spot where the inscription was found. It is also recorded of Epinikos that he procured at his own expense a teacher of eloquence and, what we may designate in modern parlance, a drill-sergeant. The other inscription refers in similar terms to another donor, Mantidoros, who furnished a Homeric philologist, Dionysios, the son of Philotas, an Athenian, for the instruction of the youth who frequented the gymnasium.

In addition to these highly interesting inscriptions, which date from the middle of the second century B. C., several pieces of sculpture were found; notably a bearded head of Dionysos, of archaic type, resembling the one in the Central Museum. Also the upper part of a youthful head, belonging to a good period, and, finally, the upper two-thirds of a massive head of a man. On seeing the latter fragment the Greek Ephor at Eretria declared that it must be the missing part of a bust the lower portion of which was in the local museum. As a matter of fact, the two fragments fitted perfectly. Reunited, after centuries of separation, they may now be seen at Athens as one of the best and most characteristic portrait busts which adorn the Central Museum. Of the minor objects found, several coins are noteworthy; especially one bearing a wreathed head of Hercules and, on the reverse, a trireme upon water. It dates back probably to the pre-Persian days of Eretria's *thalassocratia*—her supremacy at sea.

The American exploration of Eretria was thus brought to a close— creditably, thanks to Prof. Richardson's labors. But the whole site is still teeming with important remains a few feet under the surface. The American archæologists had here the opportunity of achieving, by concentrated and systematic work, results analogous to those of the exploration of Olympia. But other counsels had already committed the School to the excavations at Argos. Argos and the other work accomplished by the American School up to the present time will form the subject of my next and concluding article.

J. GENNADIUS.

THE CASE OF CAPTAIN DREYFUS.

THE Frenchman who believes himself to be independent, a reformer, and given to incredulity, still preserves a faith and a superstition: a superstition in the forms of justice as they are practised in France; an absolute faith in every man who, temporarily or habitually, discharges the duties of a magistrate. The *bourgeoisie* and the people have brought about revolutions, erected barricades, poured out their blood in overturning four thrones within a century, but, nevertheless, submit without protest to the tyranny of some hundreds of men who are examining magistrates. These magistrates are answerable to themselves alone; and the law delivers into their hands without any responsibility the life, liberty, and honor of their fellow-citizens. Any man whose life may be blameless, should he be accused by the most degraded of beings, comes under their jurisdiction. At a word from them he is cut off from the rest of the world, imprisoned in a dungeon, becomes a slave, the victim of an inquisitor with unlimited powers. It is through this inquisitor that his friends are acquainted of the accusation against him, that the public press is informed, and public opinion instructed. He can obtain no lawyer to defend him until the day of trial, when he appears in court to listen to a clerk read the proposal that he be condemned to isolation, or to examination by a crafty and unscrupulous cross-questioner, the nature of whose office has destroyed in him all sense of morality.

However, occasionally on the day of trial an accused man may be allowed to defend himself; at least he may speak and find those who are willing to listen. They have tortured him; but they allow him to speak. Above the heads of his judges and beyond them he may obtain an audience and make known the truth. At any rate those who hear him have under their eyes the factors in the case. They are able to judge for themselves, to form an opinion. The prosecution and the defence are conducted in public. That is guaranteed. What becomes of that guarantee when, after a secret examination, he who should be before the eyes of all as a prisoner on trial is judged behind closed doors?

Such proceedings, however, are commonly accepted. They satisfy the great majority of citizens; and if there be a dissatisfied minority, they keep silence. Strange contradiction! Those minds which scientific cultivation and a habit of criticism have accustomed to verify every statement with the utmost care,—these are they who most readily base their opinion on statements impossible of proof. They place in men who happen to be public functionaries a confidence which they with-hold from the wisest authorities and greatest philosophers; and this confidence is bestowed all the more readily because the sentences of these men flatter their prejudices, or rather their passions. Suppose, now, that these prejudices and passions of the public are carefully played upon day by day; imagine a tribunal equally possessed, a stranger to every idea of legality, and ignorant, I will not say of the tricks of procedure, but of the laws which it is temporarily charged to administer; know that the judges composing it are of all men the least independent, that they are influenced by codes and points of honor which render them incapable of understanding even the meaning of justice! Take, now, a man belonging to a class especially exposed to general malevolence; accuse him of a crime capable of arousing the fanaticism of the mob, since it wounds not only an individual, but the class to which he belongs; put that man in close confinement; render it impossible for him to defend himself; and then, with the aid of every falsehood and calumny, let loose upon him the fiercest anger and hatred. Bring him before the tribunal of which I have just spoken; remembering that the men who compose it are those who are most particularly-injured by the crime of which the prisoner has been accused. Close the door of the court-room. Keep every voice from being heard; remember, finally, that all rights of defence have been withheld; and then, to crown all, knowing nothing of the accusation, affirm that the accused is guilty.

It may seem that I have, in jest, set forth the greatest improba-bilities. Nevertheless every condition that I have named actually ex-ists. There is a man—Capt. Dreyfus—who has been arrested, accused, judged, and condemned, without the knowledge upon what ground he was arrested; of what he was accused; how he was judged; or why he was condemned. In spite of this, public opinion has unhesitatingly pronounced him guilty, has heaped upon him its anger and execration. The instinct of self-defence has not impelled any citizen to arise and say: "No man should be arrested, judged, condemned in this way. If such proceedings are allowed it is at the expense of each man's

29

liberty. I declare that man *a priori* innocent, since I know not of
what crime he has been accused, and am ignorant of the charges presented against him, of the manner in which he has inculpated himself,
and of the defence which he has to offer. I am accustomed to use my
own judgment in all matters, and I cannot have the judgment of
another imposed on me without the possibility of testing it."

They would have answered such an objector: "You are a bad
citizen; for you do not take into account the quality of the tribunal
which has pronounced sentence. Is it not a military tribunal? And
can you believe that the seven officers composing it are capable of
being mistaken?"

That is indeed the final argument, the peremptory response in
every country largely controlled by the military; where the army remains the last and most redoubtable of fetiches; where a man, simply
because he wears a uniform, is regarded as incorruptible and infallible.
"But," you say, "if the army be an object of so much respect in
France, how was it that when Capt. Dreyfus was accused of treason
a great outcry was not raised against the accusation? Why did
not that officer find friends eager to defend him?" Because that
obsidional fever with which the nation had been burning for twenty-
seven years, and which exists in all countries bèneath the régime of an
armed peace, was excited to an incredible degree.

"That is not sufficient reason," you say, "for the horrible hatred
which has been showered upon him. What is the cause of this?"
Have I not said that Capt. Dreyfus belonged to a class of pariahs?
He was a soldier; but he was also a Jew: and it is on this account that
he has been thus prosecuted. That is why his trial is a story of
passion. On account of it his cause becomes not merely a national
affair, but one which concerns humanity. It creates an interest in one
who was the victim of prejudice, not only among his compatriots, but
among all men,—who are his brothers, since they are human beings.

Is then Capt. Dreyfus innocent? He is innocent. What proof
can I give of it? Those who care to go over his trial with me to the
end ; to follow, step by step, its developments; to keep pace with the
examination ; to expose the accusation ; to dispute the complaints and
sentence;—those will be able to answer that question for themselves.

In 1894, if we may accept the statement of one of the witnesses at
the Dreyfus trial, Commandant Henry notified the Minister of War
that certain documents and notes had been betrayed to foreign Powers.

This in itself was not an unusual occurrence; and to account for it, it is but necessary to study the process of international espionage essential to and the corollary of militarism. Why then was it considered a matter of so much importance on this occasion? Because it was known that treason was charged against an officer. How was this known? Because, according to the deposition of Commandant Henry, a reliable person had informed him of it. Who was that reliable person? No one has ever known. They have refused to give his name, to make him appear as a witness. Thus the accusation rests upon the affirmation of an unknown man whose assertions have never been submitted to proof. Following the declaration of the mysterious one, a rigid surveillance, it is said, was established at the bureau of the minister. The officers were closely followed. Nothing was discovered until the day when Col. Sandher, Chief of the Bureau of Statistics, sent to the Minister of War, Gen. Mercier, an unsigned letter—a memorandum of a packet of papers. On receipt of that letter, the handwriting of the officers was examined and compared with that of the memorandum and, no result having been obtained, the Commandant Du Paty de Clam, who, it appeared, had special graphological knowledge, was appealed to. He, after an examination, affirmed that the handwriting in the letter resembled that of Capt. Dreyfus. The memorandum was then sent successively to two experts—M. Gobert, expert to the Bank of France, and M. Bertillon, Commissary of Police, chief of the *Service de l' Identité judiciare.* M. Gobert, after studying the two handwritings, declared that the incriminating letter could have been written by a person other than the one suspected. M. Bertillon affirmed that the same person had written all the matter sent to him.

Having obtained these two contradictory reports, the Minister of War ordered the arrest of Capt. Dreyfus. Without hesitation Gen. Mercier had a man imprisoned on the testimony of an expert in handwriting.

Did the past conduct of Capt. Dreyfus warrant such action? Were any charges formulated against him, of which the expert testimony of M. Bertillon was merely a confirmation? No. Nothing in the life of Capt. Dreyfus justified even a shadow of suspicion. He was an Alsatian, belonging to a family of Alsatian *protestaires* of Mulhouse, the members of which had frequently been banished from Alsace by the German government.

He had entered the Ecole Polytechnique at the age of eighteen; he had been one of the most brilliant scholars at the École de Guerre;

and his enemies had never been able to represent him as other than an active and ambitious officer. He was not in need, but rich. He was married, the father of two children; and the accusation itself has established the fact that his life was a well-regulated one. His accusers have never been able to prove that he kept suspicious company, carried on an unusual correspondence, or led a mysterious life. Nevertheless, the statement of a man with a mania for graphology was sufficient to throw into prison one whose honesty and uprightness were unassailable.

On October 15, 1894, Capt. Dreyfus, summoned by the Minister of War, was placed under arrest by M. Cochefort, *Chef de la Sûreté,* and by Commandant Henry, attached to the bureau of information of the minister. This arrest had been preceded by a melodramatic comedy planned by Commandant Du Paty de Clam. It consisted in reading to Capt. Dreyfus a letter containing some of the sentences in the memorandum which he was accused of having written. M. Du Paty de Clam, a remarkable psychologist, thought that he observed certain expressions of uneasiness in Capt. Dreyfus; and later on it was maintained that it was this manifest evidence of guilt which had brought about the arrest.

As a matter of fact, if the arrest was made on October 15, the warrant for the arrest was dated the previous day, when the accusation must have been based solely upon the affirmation of an expert in handwriting. On his arrest, Capt. Dreyfus was taken to the prison of Cherche-Midi, and, his name having been entered on the books, a warrant was issued to search his house. The search was fruitless. Everything was examined, however, including the private correspondence of the Captain and books of household expenses; but nothing was found. He was then simply a prisoner. Commandant Du Paty de Clam was delegated by the Minister of War as officer of the judiciary of police, and charged with the conduct of the examination. For seventeen days Capt. Dreyfus was kept in close confinement, and his wife was forbidden to mention his arrest to his relatives—even those most closely related. For seventeen days he was kept ignorant of the charge against him; which is the usual custom in such cases. And what was the nature of the examination? It consisted simply in questioning Capt. Dreyfus and his wife in regard to the most varied subjects. No witness was heard. As for the inquiry, it was intrusted principally to the lowest police officials, whose reports bore such evidence of falsehood that they could not be accepted by the public prosecutor.

After seventeen days the proofs of guilt were prepared by Commandant Du Paty de Clam: they had no other basis than that of personal impressions. They were sufficient, however, as the bench was satisfied. A second examining magistrate was named and ordered to draw up the charges. This magistrate, Commandant Besson D'Ormescheville, took up the inquiry and summoned twenty-two witnesses. The testimony of the latter and the police examinations lasted two months. When finished, no result was arrived at: not a single charge could be made from them; and when Capt. Dreyfus was brought before the court-martial he was accused, as on the first day, without proofs, on the mere statement of experts in handwriting, of having written a memorandum relative to documents betrayed to a foreign Power. Why, under such circumstances, was not a verdict of "Not proven" handed down? What was it that urged on the examining officers, the staff, the minister, and the government itself? Public opinion. Who was responsible for the state of that opinion? The entire press. What was the attitude of the press? It was scandalous; and it was positively stated that all the newspapers were subject to the terrorism of the anti-Semitic journal, "La Libre Parole," sustained by clerical and anti-Jewish papers, such as "La Croix," and various jingo publications. On October 31, a notice in "La Libre Parole," mysteriously communicated, stated that an officer accused of high treason was detained at the prison of Cherche-Midi, and that this officer was a Jew. The next day the accused was "the traitor Dreyfus"; and the most bitter, most abominable campaign had begun.

No one knew the charges brought against this man; and he was pre-condemned. The most contradictory and hostile reports were published in the press. Capt. Dreyfus, it was said, had been a traitor ever since he entered the army; he was a traitor at Fontainebleau, at Mons, at Paris, at the École de Guerre, and finally at the office of the Staff, which he had entered only for treasonable purposes. The mob was delighted with the statement that the Captain had betrayed to a foreigner the names of officers sent on special missions, the secrets of mobilization, transport, and concentration of troops. He had been seen at work at Monaco, Nice, London, Brussels, Rome, Berlin, St. Petersburg, and the frontier towns. He frequented "flash" resorts, gambled everywhere, followed the races; performing, at the same time, his regular duties at the Ministry of War, and discharging the ordinary obligations, which his dissimulation demanded. It was stated that he had always been an object of suspicion; that his habits of life were loose.

Some said that he was ruined, and head over ears in debt; others that he was a millionaire, with property at Bordeaux, Bourges, and houses in Paris, bought with funds for which he could not account. It is a noteworthy fact that some of these statements were found in the secret reports of the police and recognized as false too late, extracts from them being given to well-known anti-Semitic papers by the men who were most directly concerned in the examination and who had thus influenced public opinion. At the same time in "La Croix," in "La Libre Parole," and in several other newspapers following their example, the most furious diatribes were hurled against the Jews,—the hated race to which Dreyfus belonged. The term Israelite was a synonym for traitor. Cartoons were circulated, representing on one side Judas betraying Christ, and on the other, Dreyfus receiving a bag of gold from Germany. Amusing contradiction,—had it not appeared in connection with so tragic an affair,—that the Jew without a country should be represented as an ardent German! It was stated that his brothers—those who had been driven from Alsace as *protestaires*—were officers in the Prussian army.

Every day sensational news was printed in large type. One day the traitor had accomplices, and they had been discovered; the next, he had been betraying for years the most important secrets,—he himself had avowed this with the most revolting cynicism. Public opinion was sustained at the highest pitch, blinding the least prejudiced. No defence, no appeal to the good sense and impartiality of the public, were permitted in any newspaper. Through fear of the anti-Semitic howling, the press, which boasts of its independence, kept silence.

The Jew Dreyfus was helpless against the will of the anti-Semitic mob. From the day on which the public was informed of the arrest and imprisonment of the Captain, it had predeclared the impossibility of any defence. Anti-Semitic papers and clerical publications, lying without scruple, had built up a great conspiracy. The whole body of Israelitish citizens was represented as devoted to Germany and hating France; as desirous of saving not an innocent man, but one well known to be guilty. Apocryphal stories invented in the newspaper offices were circulated deliberately and shamelessly. A fortune had been offered to the experts; it had been sought to influence the magistrates; when the magistrates entered the court-room, unconsciously a prejudice had taken possession of them, distorting their judgment; they dared not lend themselves to clemency for fear of being accused of corruption. In fact, of the case of Capt. Dreyfus was created a formidable anti-

Semitic and clerical war-machine, which was made good use of. For if the names of Triponé, Bonnet, de Schwartz, Boilot, Guillot—all condemned for treason or espionage—are passed over in silence, the name of Dreyfus is heard constantly. They intend to make of it a synonym for treason, and the symbol of a race.

Did those who knew the truth, who were aware of the innocence of the unfortunate man thus exposed to the hatred of all, do anything to allay the torrent of anger and hatred? On the contrary, they submitted to anti-Semitic terrorism, not daring to resist it; or rather, by adding to it, they took advantage of the patriotic excitement and by flattering it endeavored to restore their diminished influence and waning popularity.

It was proclaimed everywhere that Capt. Dreyfus was a traitor in behalf of Germany; and this statement was made at the time of the trial during the earliest examination by Commandant Du Paty de Clam. It is true that the unknown who had delivered that memorandum to Col. Sandher, Chief of the Bureau of Statistics, had stated that it came from the German Ambassador. Three depositions were made by M. de Munster, the German Ambassador,—to M. Casimir-Périer, President of the Republic, to M. Dupuis, President of the Council, and to M. Hanotaux, Minister of Foreign Affairs. Three times, and to each of these men, the Ambassador stated that neither this memorandum nor the documents mentioned in it had ever been at the German Embassy; and that never, directly or indirectly, had Capt. Dreyfus been in communication with the German government. Finally he offered himself as a witness before the court-martial. Dreading the violence of the attacks from the low patriotic press, the government took no further notice of these depositions than to publish through the Havas agency two ambiguous articles, which the government newspapers carefully relegated to their third page.

That was not all. The Minister of War publicly took part in the question. Forgetting—or perhaps remembering—the influence which he would have on the military judges, Gen. Mercier permitted himself to be interviewed from the earliest days of the examination. On November 28, 1894, he said to the editor of "Le Figaro," M. Leser:—

"I submitted to the President of the Council and to my colleagues the overwhelming evidence which was communicated to me; and the arrest of Capt. Dreyfus was immediately ordered. Many inexact statements have been written on this subject. It has been said that Capt. Dreyfus offered secret documents to the Italian government. That is a mistake. I cannot say more because the examination is not yet concluded. It is only necessary to repeat that the guilt of this officer is absolutely certain, and that he has had civilian accomplices."

Inspired from the same source, M. Leser added: "At the Staff Office it is known, on reliable authority, that Dreyfus has been in communication for three years with the agents of a foreign Power, which was neither the Italian government nor that of Austria-Hungary." Not a word of this was true. Gen. Mercier had in his possession only the contradictory statements of the experts. As for the "overwhelming evidence" referred to,—neither the indictment nor the documents contain a trace of it. Nor is anything found therein regarding the civilian accomplices and the pretended relations of Capt. Dreyfus with the agents of a foreign Power. Gen. Mercier knowingly uttered a falsehood; and in thus taking part against an accused man, unable to defend himself publicly, he was guilty of the most odious, unprecedented, disloyal, and cowardly action. He violated the most elementary principles of equity. He dictated, in advance, a judgment to his subordinates, too readily inclined by training to accept the statements of their superior officers. He suborned justice, rendered a defence impossible, deceived public opinion, and was instrumental in surrounding the prisoner with an atmosphere of prejudice, and in directing a current of condemnation, which could lead only to conviction.

Why did he act thus? To avoid admitting with what incredible, unjustifiable readiness he had proceeded to arrest a man on no other ground than the word of an expert; also from personal motives.

What was the position of Gen. Mercier before the campaign against Dreyfus? The case of Turpin had lowered him in the estimation of moderate patriots. For the journals of the opposition he was "l'homme au flair d'artilleur." He was attacked by "L'Intransigeant," "La Patrie," "La Presse," and "La Libre Parole." His position in the Dupuis cabinet was compromised. The Dreyfus case gave him the opportunity of reinstating himself. From the day that it was made public, official notes printed in the newspapers represented Gen. Mercier as the paragon of patriotism. It was he who, in opposition to ministers, had advocated steadfastly the arrest of the "traitor." He had been opposed on all sides. He had threatened to appeal to France, to the outraged country; and his soldierly strength of purpose and his loyalty had forced the hands of his colleagues. Subjected to attacks, supplications, and threats, he had remained obdurate. The same papers which a month before had rolled him in the dust now placed him on a pinnacle. They proclaimed that the patriots could feel secure so long as Gen. Mercier was in power; they represented him as followed by the animosity of the other ministers; and defied them to rid themselves of the patriotic general.   The rôle that he thus assumed he continued to play after the Captain was condemned.

I have pointed out the state of public opinion at the time of Capt. Dreyfus's appearance before his judges, and how they, through the pressure brought to bear upon them by the press, through fear of placing their honor under suspicion, and through the influence of their superior officers, found themselves in a most awkward situation, and one the least appropriate to the exercise of justice.   Most of the military judges had a very indefinite understanding of the case submitted to them. Some, when it came to a ballot for condemnation or acquittal, refrained from voting.   Of the others the majority voted for condemnation, not on the proofs submitted to them, for there were none, but on the affirmations of their superior officers that such proofs existed.

When, on December 19, 1894, Capt. Dreyfus appeared before the court-martial no charge rested upon him.   After four days of debate behind closed doors, it was concluded that he had no suspicious relations; that his travels to foreign countries, the riches which he could not account for, his poverty, gambling habits, and relations with women, —were all fabrications.   The commissioner of the government, Commandant Brisset, declared that he was unable to find any motive that could have actuated Capt. Dreyfus to treason.   He refuted all the lies and calumnies contained in the police reports, and recognized the perfect honesty of the accused man, and the uprightness of his life.

Of what, then, was Capt. Dreyfus accused on that day?   Of having forwarded documents to a foreign embassy.   What were the proofs brought forward?   A letter, a sort of memorandum, containing a list of the documents delivered.   That letter, repudiated by the Captain, was, it was said, in his handwriting.   Three experts substantiated this, and two denied it; and it was on this unique testimony that they condemned the man.   What did that memorandum contain?   Here are the text and the facsimile, together with facsimiles of the handwriting of Capt. Dreyfus both before the accusation and after he was condemned. These letters will enable independent and unprejudiced graphologists to form an opinion.

TEXT OF THE DOCUMENT.

"In the absence of any intimation of your desire to see me, I now send you certain information of interest.

(1) A note on the hydraulic brake of 120.   (Method of operating.)

(2) A note on *les troupes de couverture.*   (Certain changes will be made by the new plan.)

(3) A note on the changes in artillery formations.

(4) A note relating to Madagascar.

(5) The project relative to the manual of field-firing, March 14, 1894.

This last paper is very hard to procure and I can have it at my disposal but for a few days. The minister has issued to the corps a definite number; and they are responsible for them. Each officer is obliged to return his copy after the manœuvres. If, therefore, you wish me to take from it such facts as are of interest to you, and hold them at your disposal, I will obtain it, provided you do not wish me to make a copy *in extenso*, and address it to you.

I am on my way to the manœuvres."

How did this paper get into the hands of the minister? According to more or less contradictory reports, it was found among the waste papers at the German Embassy,—papers which a servant had been in the habit of selling to rag-men, who were no other than agents of the bureau of information of the Minister of War. How much importance is to be attached to this story? It is certain that this memorandum was written on a simple sheet of paper, torn into four pieces, and carefully put together,—a sheet of thin bank post paper, specially watermarked, of which no specimen was found at the house of Capt. Dreyfus. What then was the value of this paper as a basis for accusation? The recognition of the authenticity of a handwriting is not in itself sufficient to justify a serious accusation. Furthermore it should be noted that, according to the accusing reports themselves, the handwriting in the memorandum does not resemble that of Capt. Dreyfus. It is different. But M. Bertillon, the so-called expert, and prejudiced agent of the government,—whose testimony is therefore inadmissible,—concluded that he ought to form a hypothesis on the subject. He, therefore, declared that if there were differences in the handwriting they had been purposely introduced by Capt. Dreyfus.

So, apart from the testimony of these graphologists, so open to contest, and upon which it is impossible to base an accusation, without further proof than this testimony, there is no evidence that Capt. Dreyfus ever had in his hands the documents in question, or that he had the material necessary to compile the notes contained in the memorandum. Further, the contrary has been proved.

The commissioner of the government, discharging the functions of a public minister, stated that no proof could be found during the course of the trial. On one point, the knowledge of "the project relative to the manual of field-firing," the indictment said: "Capt. Dreyfus acknowledged during the first cross-examination that he had held several conversations with a superior officer of the second bureau of the army staff." The indictment lied. Capt. Dreyfus stated that he had spoken

Quand tu

je plaignais à un…
je savais que faire, je
que le seul moyen de
jamais l'ennuyer,
de cher d'occuper,
intellectuellement
mutuellement.

me demandais, avec
ais de doute, de te
exemple de le genre de
à… l'amour… a te bien

Monsieur que je conjuguement intéressants
1° en voir en le prix hydraulique
B. 120 et le manière dont sont construits
ces prix.
2° une note sur le forge… le corrections…
… modification sont apportés par
le revoir un plan…
3° une note sur une modification au…
… mations de l'intérieur;
… communauté ultérieur à Madagascar.
5° le progrès de moment de été de…
l'intérieur de congres… (16 mars 1894)

Ce dernier Document est extrêmement

A.   Text of Document attributed to Capt. Dreyfus.

B.   Authentic Handwriting of Capt. Dreyfus in 1890.

C.   Authentic Handwriting of Capt. Dreyfus in 1895 after his trial.

c.

with that officer—Commandant Jeannel—on a totally different subject. He asked to be confronted with him. The request was refused; a similar refusal being given to the request to have Commandant Jeannel produced at the trial. Why? Because Commandant Jeannel had substantiated the statement of Capt. Dreyfus,—which, however, did not prevent the false statement from being retained in the indictment. It can now be affirmed that there is not in the papers, and there was not produced at the trial, any other charge than the actual existence of the document in question.

- It is not necessary to establish the genuineness of that document. Its very nature shows it to be spurious. If a traitor actually existed, what need had he to send with his papers a useless commercial and compromising memorandum. Usually it is a spy's first care to destroy every trace of his acts. If he gives up papers, he puts them in the hands of a trusted go-between; but he never writes. How would such a memorandum, with the documents mentioned in it, ever reach its destination? By the post? What folly! Through a go-between? Who is he? And besides, in either case, where was the need of a memorandum?

Now look at the document itself! It is written by an illiterate person, by one ignorant of the common modes of expression. Capt. Dreyfus was no such person. Furthermore, it is written by someone ignorant of ordinary military terms, especially those relating to the artillery.

Let me now sum up. Capt. Dreyfus was arrested on the contradictory findings of two experts. For seventeen days he was kept in ignorance of the charges made against him. The examination was conducted in a most high-handed manner by Commandant Du Paty de Clam, and was planned by M. Besson d'Ormescheville. It had no other result than to show the absolute groundlessness of the charges made against Capt. Dreyfus, and the falsehoods of the police reports, which were exposed by witnesses and which the prosecution dared not accept.

Where did the paper on which the accusation rests come from? According to the report of M. Besson d'Ormescheville, Gen. Gonse, in delivering it at the office of Police Judiciary M. Du Paty de Clam, asserted that it had been addressed to a foreign Power; that it had come into his hands; but that, in obedience to official directions from the Minister of War, he could not say through what means he had obtained possession of it. At the trial, M. Du Paty de Clam made it clearly understood that it came from the German Embassy. Thus, the prosecution did not know how this undated, unsigned paper left the hands

of the inculpated man. The defence did not know through what channels it came from the embassy which had had possession of it. To
whom was the letter addressed? Who stole and forwarded it? No
answer has been given to either of these questions. .

During the two months' inquiry was it discovered that Capt. Dreyfus had had suspicious dealings? No. This strange document said,
however, " In the absence of any intimation that you desire to see me."
Did he see, then, this mysterious correspondent? His manner of living was carefully looked into. He was followed. All his actions were
investigated; and no compromising associations could be discovered.
His correspondence was examined. M. Du Paty de Clam forced from
Mme. Dreyfus the letters which she had received from the Captain during their engagement. This examination was of no service to the
prosecution. No fact had been discovered on which to base the charge
that Capt. Dreyfus had had any dealings with the agent of a foreign
Power *even in the service of the Staff Office.*

At the hearing, the depositions of the witnesses were of no importance. They were but personal estimations of the character of Capt.
Dreyfus. Some said that he was a braggart and a prattler; others represented him as taciturn and conceited. Was a motive given for such
an odious action? What led Capt. Dreyfus to commit an act of
treason? On that point the prosecution was silent.

Was he in need? No: he was rich. Had he passions and vices to
indulge? None. Was he avaricious? No. He spent his money
freely, and had not added to his property. Was he an invalid, a creature of impulse, capable of acting without reason? No: he was self-
possessed, a man of character, courage, and energy. What strong
motive led this fortunate man to thus risk all his happiness? None.
To this man, with no motive for an evil deed, with no accusing fact
against him, whom the examination showed to be upright, a hard worker,
leading a regular and worthy life,—to this man a mysterious paper was
shown. It was said to him: " You wrote this. Three experts declare
it, two deny it." This man, appealing to his past career, affirmed that
he had committed no such act. He asserted his innocence. The uprightness of his life was acknowledged; and yet on the contradictory
testimony of these experts in handwriting he was condemned to life-
long exile.

As a matter of fact, that alone would not have been sufficient to
condemn him. With that single charge against him the court-martial
would have acquitted him. Why then was he condemned? Because

in the Council Chamber Gen. Mercier, in defiance of the strictest rules of equity, presented to the judges, it is said, a document which rendered certain the guilt of the accused.

This document Capt. Dreyfus and his lawyer were ignorant of. It was never submitted to them. They were unable to estimate its value. They could not discuss it. What was this document? In "L'Eclair," in an article which appeared on September 15, 1896, its existence was first brought to notice, as a means of putting an end to the doubt which existed and still exists in many minds. There existed, it was said, a letter in cypher written by an attaché of the German Embassy at Paris to a colleague of the Embassy at Rome,—a letter which contained this sentence: "Truly that animal Dreyfus becomes very exacting."

How much of this is to be believed? It is in part true. It is true that a document was shown to the judges, and that it referred to a letter. "L'Eclair" was well informed; which is not remarkable since it procured the information from Gen. Mercier, who took part once more in the debates in regard to the Dreyfus case. After the false news of his escape, in September, 1896, certain papers, "Le Jour," "L'Autorité," and others, insinuated that Capt. Dreyfus had been convicted upon insufficient proofs in an unjustifiable manner, and that his guilt could not be affirmed. Then Gen. Mercier thought that he ought to take part in the discussion. He did so by inspiring the articles in "L'Eclair," and, as he lied to M. Leser, when interviewed by him at the time of the trial ("Figaro," November 28, 1894), so he now lied again. In fact the letter attributed to the German military attaché (M. de Munster repudiated it on three occasions) was written not in cypher, but in French— How probable!—and the sentence which it contained was this: "*And that rascal D., is he always so exacting?*" Further, it had been sent to the Minister of War through the Office of Foreign Affairs, not in September, a few days before the discovery of the memorandum, as Gen. Mercier stated, but eight months previously. "L'Eclair" also stated that Capt. Dreyfus was suspected immediately. Gen. Mercier told another lie. When that letter came to the bureau of information, but little importance was attached to it. They contented themselves with suspecting a concierge of the Minister of War whose name began with the letter D; but the theory was abandoned. The letter was filed, and only left the office of the Minister of War when it was needed to find a conviction against Dreyfus. Up to the present time no one has denied the existence of that letter.

Mme. Dreyfus having, through a petition to the Chamber, protested against the methods of procedure in her husband's case, and having asked for another trial, received an answer, indefinite, *confuse*, and dishonest, ignoring the grounds of her petition, and confined to affirming the horror which treason should inspire.

Thus it was established that the conviction of Capt. Dreyfus without proof of his guilt was brought about by showing to the judges a letter systematically concealed from the accused man and his lawyer. Is it permissible to condemn without allowing the means of defence? Is it not monstrous that it was made possible, outside the court-room, to influence the mind, decision, and sentence of the judges? Is it permissible for anyone to enter the council chamber and say to the magistrate: "Forget what you have heard in favor of the man whom you are to judge. We have ourselves certain documents which, for reasons of state or politics, we have concealed and ask you to keep secret. We affirm that these documents are authentic, are in actual existence. Condemn!" And on that a tribunal, with two of its members dissenting (for the alleged unanimity among the judges is a myth), pronounced sentence. No officer arose and said: "Something at variance with all equity is demanded of us. We should not allow it."

And the public had been so completely misled that it did not trouble itself about the methods by which the accused, who was pronounced the most odious of traitors, had been condemned. Even those whose patriotism was disturbed, in that the charge affected an officer, forgot the methods employed in the trial, because they were convinced, in the interests of an offended fatherland, of the necessity of chastisement by any means whatever. Had this not been so, millions of voices would have cried: "If such abuse of power and such arbitrary methods be allowed, each man's liberty is in danger. It is at the mercy of the public prosecutor; and every citizen under accusation loses the most elementary guarantees of defence!"

They will arise perhaps to-morrow, after the restrictions have been removed, and will protest in the name of Justice, saying, with me: "Capt. Dreyfus is an innocent victim of a horrible plot; he was overborne by religious hate; his conviction was obtained through illegal means; he must have another trial!" And public opinion, stronger than governments, more powerful than political interests will triumph.

May those in every country who believe that nothing is indifferent to them which affects Humanity and, higher than man, Right and Justice,—may they labor with me to hasten that day!

VINDEX.

WHEN DID JOHN CABOT DISCOVER NORTH AMERICA?

EXTENSIVE preparations are being made at Bristol, England, in Cánada, and in Newfoundland to commemorate, on the twenty-fourth of this present month, the landing of John Cabot on the coast of the North-American continent. The intention is praiseworthy; but it is well to recollect that we do not know exactly when and where he first sighted the New World. Nor do we possess means of ascertaining these two points, admittedly of paramount importance in a celebration of that character.

The alleged date of the landfall rests exclusively upon a statement brought forward, for the first time, forty-seven years after the event, and which, thus far, stands uncorroborated. It is contained in a pamphlet in Spanish, written about 1544 by one Dr. Grajales, of the Puerto de Santa Maria, concerning whom we do not know anything else. It was printed out of Spain, and was intended to accompany a map by Sebastian Cabot, apparently engraved in the Netherlands. The type which served for printing the pamphlet was also used to print two series of legends pasted on the right and left of the only copy of that map known, which is now in the National Library at Paris.

Translated, the passage relating to the date reads as follows :—

"No. 8. This land was discovered by John Cabot, a Venetian, and Sebastian Cabot, his son, in the year of the birth of our Saviour Jesus Christ fourteen hundred and ninety-four, on the twenty-fourth of June in the morning, to which they gave the name '*prima tierra vista*'; and a large island adjacent to it they named 'Sant Juan,' it having been discovered on the day of that saint."

The numeral corresponds to that given in the inscription, "De la tierra de los bacallaos ve á tabla primera, No. 3" ("Concerning the country of codfish, see the first table No. 3" [Error for 8]). This inscription is engraved in the map over the region now known as Canada, and embraces the country extending from New Brunswick to Labrador inclusive.

The year 1494 is clearly an anachronism, as the voyage was not undertaken until 1497, by virtue of letters patent granted on March 5,

1496. As to the month, this also is doubtful, for the following reasons: When John Cabot returned to England, he gave an account of his voyage, which is briefly reported in a letter written from London August 23, 1497, by Lorenzo Pasqualigo to his brothers in Venice, and by two despatches sent by Raimondo di Soncino to the Duke of Milan, August 24 and December 18, 1497.

Pasqualigo states that John Cabot "coasted three hundred leagues [of the newly discovered country]." This statement is corroborated by Soncino, who "saw the description of the country discovered by Cabot marked in a chart and on a solid globe which the latter had made." These three hundred leagues amounted actually to six hundred, as Cabot had to retrace his course when sailing homeward. Now John Cabot was already in London on August 10, 1497, which implies that he had reached Bristol about five days earlier. If we accept the alleged date of June 24 as that of his landfall in America, it leaves only forty-two days between his arrival within sight of the New World and his return to England.

We must assume that Cabot and his small crew of eighteen men, after a voyage said to have lasted more than fifty-two days (they had left England early in May, 1497), rested awhile, and devoted some time to refitting or repairing their diminutive craft (" uno piccolo naviglio e xviii persone se pose a la fortuna "), as well as to taking in wood and water, and renewing the stock of victuals, which could be done only by hunting and salting game on shore. To these necessary delays must be added the time spent in skirting to.and fro along three hundred leagues of coast. Nor should it be forgotten that, in ranging an unknown and dangerous shore, only a moderate rate of speed could have been maintained. How could all this have been accomplished in the limited time which the alleged landfall on June 24 leaves to Cabot before his return to England? If we suppose that, owing to westerly winds and the Gulf Stream, he effected the homeward voyage in one-third less time than is stated to have been required for the outward passage, that is, thirty-four days instead of fifty-two, then, as Cabot was already back in Bristol on August 5, he must have taken the necessary rest in the new land, made the indispensable repairs, effected landings, and renewed his stock of provisions, besides coasting six hundred leagues, all within eight days!

The date June 24, therefore, is highly improbable. It may have originated in connection with an imaginary island which figures in old Portuguese charts, close to the northeast coast, in about 50° lat.

In some maps, Wolfenbüttel B, for instance, the cartographer has placed it within the Gulf of St. Lawrence. That island was probably supposed by Sebastian Cabot, in 1544, to be identical with the one—also imaginary, as I propose to show—which he then borrowed from a French map, where it is inserted in the same place. Dr. Grajales, who knew of the almost constant practice in those days of naming islands after the saints on whose days they were discovered, may well have assumed the date of June 24—that of the festival of St. John the Baptist—on seeing that the island was labelled in those maps, " I. de San Juan."

As regards the landfall, the first cartographical mention of the transatlantic discoveries of the English is to be found in the planisphere executed between June and August, 1500, by Juan de la Cosa, the owner and master of Columbus's flagship during his first voyage across the Atlantic Ocean. In that celebrated chart, there is in the proximity and to the west of Cuba an unbroken coast-line, delineated like a continent, and extending northward to the extremity of the map. On the northern portion of that seaboard La Cosa has placed a continuous line of British flags. The most southern inscription in that part of the coast in the chart is, " Mar descubierta por ingleses " (" Sea discovered by the English "). The northernmost reads, " Cabo de ynglaterra " (" The Cape of England ").

On July 25, 1498, Pedro de Ayala wrote from London to Ferdinand and Isabella that he possessed the chart or *mappamundi* which Cabot had brought with him, and that he would send it to their Majesties. It is fair therefore to infer that La Cosa's delineations embody the results of Cabot's voyage. Unfortunately, owing to the absence of degrees of latitude and longitude, as well as to the style of the projection, the various positions cannot be determined ; for the cartographical data are totally inadequate to enable anyone to locate the landfall. It is even impossible to ascertain whether the *Mar descubierta por ingleses* or the *Cabo de ynglaterra* was first seen, and to what locality either of them corresponds. The two most competent scholars who ever studied the question—Humboldt and Kohl—came to different conclusions. For the former, the *Cabo de ynglaterra* is a cape near Belle Isle; for the latter, it is Cape Race.

Further, John Cabot made a second voyage to the New World, sailing from Bristol in April, 1498, from which voyage he, or his companions, must have returned before 1500. There is consequently no reason why La Cosa's map may not also include geographical information brought back by the second expedition.   This is all the more likely, as the extent of the east coast covered with English flags is greater in his map than the distance between the eastern extremity of Porto Rico and the westernmost coast of Cuba, that is, at least, nineteen degrees, or three hundred and eighty marine leagues.   How are we to distinguish between these conflicting data?

It is not until a quarter of a century after La Cosa had made his planisphere that we find a Spanish map exhibiting the northeastern region of North America, named then either " Baccalaos " (" The codfish country "), or " Tierra del Labrador " (" The land of the Laborer "), or both, and set forth as being the *locus* of the discoveries made by the English.   The Sevillian cartographers however seem to have drawn a distinction, by ascribing the *Baccalaos* to Corte Real, or the Portuguese, and the *Tierra del Labrador* to the British navigators, or the Cabots.

The services of Sebastian Cabot were engaged, in 1512, by Ferdinand of Aragon chiefly on account of his supposed knowledge of the geography of North America; he having appropriated to himself the merit of the discovery of the American continent made by his father. He filled in Spain the office of Pilot-Major from February, 1518, until October, 1547, remaining titulary of the post during his absence at La Plata.   Not only was Sebastian Cabot, by virtue of his functions, supervisor of the chair of cosmography, but he was also a member of the commission of pilots and geographers required by King Ferdinand to make a general revision of all maps.   It is evident, therefore, that the charts made in Spain, particularly by the cosmographers to his Majesty, must have represented North America according to Sebastian Cabot's notions, and doubtless borrowed from him the legends inscribed thereon.   Let us see now where the discoveries of the English were invariably located in such maps.

We still possess five specimens of Sevillian cartography, which, considering the royal ordinances of the time, and the fact that three maps are stated explicitly to be the work of Charles the Fifth's cartographers, we assume to be derived directly from the *Padron General* or standard official map.

The first and roughest of all is the map sent from Seville in 1527 by an English merchant, Robert Thorne, to Dr. Lee, the ambassador of Henry VIII in Spain.   In it, the northern extremity of the east coast bears the inscription, " Nova terra laboratorum dicta," and on its seaboard we read, " Terra hec ab Anglis primum fuit inventa."   The region thus said to have been discovered by the English extends from 50° to 65° N. lat. We then have two very elaborate manuscript planispheres, known as the "Weimar" maps. One is anonymous and dated 1527. The other, bearing date 1529, is signed by Diego Ribeiro, who was his Majesty's cosmographer and master chart-maker, as well as Sebastian Cabot's colleague in the Badajoz Junta. The first of these mentions only the *Tierra del laborador*, which is placed between 56° and 60° N. lat. This region, however, is meant for the field of English discoveries in 1497, and probably 1498, as is shown by the Weimar Ribeiro map of 1529, made on the same scale and after the same pattern, and where the inscription is followed by the additional remark, " *Esta tierra descubrieron los Ingleses* " ("This land was discovered by the English"). And what shows still more clearly the identity of these English discoveries with those accomplished by John Cabot and his companions, is the legend added in the same place by Ribeiro in the Propaganda duplicate of his great map: "Tierra del Labrador, laqual descubrieron los Ingleses de la villa de Bristol" ("The Land of the Laborer, which was discovered by the English of the town of Bristol"). Finally, we have the map called "Wolfenbüttel B," anonymous and undated, but certainly constructed in Seville before 1531. This also bears the inscription across Labrador, between 56° and 60° N. lat.: "Descubierta por los Yngleses de la vila de Bristol."

The chain of evidence is complete; and it shows that in Seville, during the first forty years of the sixteenth century, cosmographers always located the transatlantic discoveries of the English, implying those of John Cabot, at least ten degrees north of Cape Breton,—according to the scale of latitude inscribed on the Weimar maps. This fact requires to be kept in mind ; for that location is due, directly or indirectly, to Sebastian Cabot, in consequence of the official positions which he filled in Spain for so many years.

In 1544, the engraved *mappamundi* of Sebastian Cabot, already mentioned, appeared in Antwerp or in Augsburg. There do we see for the first time a different *locus* ascribed to the transatlantic discoveries of the English under the flag of Henry VII.

This map gives a geographical representation of the Gulf of St. Lawrence and its vicinity entirely unlike that which had figured previously in Spanish charts, particularly in those which were constructed by the state cosmographers of Spain at the time when Sebastian Cabot was at their head. Nor was it ever reproduced in maps emanating from Spanish chart-makers. On the extremity of a large peninsula of the northeast coast, we read, "Prima tierra vista," that is, "the first land seen,"—or the alleged landfall of Cabot.

The locality was doubtless intended to represent Cape Breton. Then, in a gulf adjoining, which is meant for the Gulf of St. Lawrence, there is a very large island, named "I. de S. Juan." This unexpected insular configuration is explained in Grajales's legend 8, which I have already cited.

In reality, there is no such island anywhere near the north coast of Cape Breton, unless it be Newfoundland. In those days, however, and for many years after 1497, Newfoundland was believed to form part of the mainland. The falsity of the statement can be easily accounted for : Sebastian Cabot's entire configuration of that locality and most of the legends and names inscribed in it have been boldly plagiarized from the Dieppe map drawn by the French cartographer, Nicolas Desliens, in 1541. This map, which is now in the Dresden Royal Library, is based upon the discoveries of Jacques Cartier.[1]

Further, in this plagiarism of Sebastian Cabot's his delineation of the pretended "Isla de S. Juan" does not even represent an existing island. What he has thus depicted, and claims to have discovered and named, is, in reality, only a cartographical distortion,—an amalgam of islets, sunken rocks, shoals, and sandbars, known as "The Magdalens." These, some French cartographer (probably Desliens himself) had conglomerated by mistake, ascribing to them the shape of a compact island of considerable dimensions ; and Cabot actually reproduces it with no other authority than the erroneous map itself.

In this way was John Cabot's discovery located in 1544 at such a great distance from the latitude where it had figured in all the Spanish maps made while Sebastian held the office of Pilot-Major, and according to models necessarily constructed from data furnished by him.

It lies with the believers in the authenticity of the landfall at Cape Breton to account for this sudden and unexpected change, and to explain why, after constantly inscribing the discovery in Labrador, Sebastian Cabot came at such a late hour to place it at least 10 degrees farther south. His admirers have hitherto neglected to answer this all-important question seriously, and with an adequate knowledge of the subject. They allege that as the Spanish government was very jealous of imparting to foreigners any information concerning its colonial enterprises and discoveries, chart-makers were prohibited—even under penalty of

---

[1] See the facsimiles in "John Cabot, the Discoverer of North America." London : B. F. Stevens, 1896, pp. 94–95.

death!—from marking on maps any geographical data of the kind. This theory I myself believed in to a degree when I commenced studying American cartography thirty-four years ago, and even subsequently. It is, nevertheless, erroneous in every respect.

In the first place, there is no evidence whatever that, notwithstanding the rights conveyed by the Bulls of Demarcation, Spain ever laid claim to the northeast coast of America. The inference is rather the other way. The famous map of Juan de la Cosa, Columbus's own pilot, and Chief Cartographer of Spain, not only sets forth that the northeastern borders of America were discovered by the English, but acknowledges tacitly the supremacy of England over the region, by dotting it entirely with British flags.

True it is that, in 1511, one Juan de Agramonte obtained from Queen Juana leave to go with two vessels "to ascertain the secret of the new land," that is, the strait which was supposed to lead to Cathay through the Baccalaos; but it was "on condition that two of his pilots should be Bretons brought direct from Brittany." This shows that Spain was not yet then in possession of the geographical knowledge requisite for such an enterprise.

The Spaniards in fact never sailed north of the Carolinas until 1524, when Estevan Gomez was sent in search of the western passage. Nor do we find them visiting that coast again until 1541, when Ares de Sea was commissioned by Charles V to see "what Jacques Cartier had discovered in the country called Canada." Further, we have the positive statement of Oviedo, then State Chronicler for the Indies, that his countrymen and himself had no knowledge of the Northern regions; and that was the reason why the model map of Chavès did not extend beyond 21° 15'. Spain, therefore, had nothing to conceal regarding the geography of the northeast coast of America.

In the second place, there is not a shadow of evidence that Spain ever concealed her transatlantic discoveries, or prohibited cartographical information concerning them. Thus do we see Christopher Columbus himself, who, more than anyone else, was interested in preventing transgressions of his privileges and of the rights of the Crown, order, without any hesitation, for the use even of a Venetian admiral, "a map of the newly discovered lands, detailed and complete." When Magellan had accomplished his famous discovery of the straits that bear his name, which one might suppose Spain would have reserved exclusively to herself, it was at once graphically described in all maps and globes, with the exact route. And what is more, the information was conveyed openly to the Archbishop of Salzburg, by Maximilianus Transylvanus, the secretary of Charles V. Several other instances of the kind could be cited.

It stands to reason that it would have been impossible to keep such information secret. Did not the numerous ships equipped in Seville, in Cadiz, and in Palos for the New World carry charts? And was it not indispensable that such maps should be as exact and complete as possible? Look at the relatively numerous specimens of Sevillian hydrography which have come down to us. Do they not set forth all and singular the geographical knowledge of the New World which the Spanish pilots and cosmographers possessed in the first half of the sixteenth century? When once in the hands of the four hundred pilots and masters who at one time were together in the employ of Castile, exclusively for the American trade, how could they escape the curiosity of the numerous merchants and adventurers who flocked into the southern ports, waiting for a favorable opportunity to cross the ocean and explore new countries?

My opponents reply by quoting the following passage from the above-mentioned letter sent in 1527 from Seville, by Robert Thorne, with a map, to Dr. Lee: "That it [the map] is not to be showed or communicated there [in England] with many of that court. For though there is nothing in it prejudiciall to the emperor, yet it may be a cause of paine to the maker, as well for that none may make these cards but certayne appointed and allowed masters." What does this prove? Only that Thorne's map had not been indorsed by the competent authorities, as the law required. But this obligation was not intended to withhold geographical information. The government acted in the interest of the fisc, and more particularly of navigation, which suffered greatly from a competition created by incompetent cartographers. And we have only to cast a glance at Thorne's map in Hakluyt to see that it is scarcely possible to imagine a poorer specimen of cartographical handiwork. The words in Thorne's letter, "though there is nothing in it [the map] prejudiciall to the emperor," the reference to the pilots, who alone are authorized to make maps, and the fact that its configurations are identical with those in all the charts of the time, without any addition whatever, show conclusively that the proviso accompanying the transmission of the map to Dr. Lee was not prompted by the motives which certain critics allege.

Again, if the Spanish government had any particular reasons for making a secret of the geography of the Baccalaos region, how is it that Sebastian Cabot, who was Pilot-Major of Spain, inscribes so fully —and as exactly as he could—in a map intended to be engraved, the configurations of Cape Breton, Newfoundland, and Labrador, and this chiefly in the interest of a rival nation? Moreover the history of Spanish jurisprudence in the sixteenth century leaves no room to doubt that had it been so great a crime to mark maritime discoveries in maps, we should find some ordinance or law on the subject. There are no traces of anything of the kind in the numerous *Recapitulaciones de Leyes* published in Spain.

I venture to suggest another explanation. It is, I think, now admitted by all who have read the authentic documents published in my latest work [1] on the subject, that Sebastian Cabot was an unmitigated charlatan, who frequently disguised the truth, and was constantly engaged in plotting and corresponding in secret with foreign rulers, all whom he betrayed in turn. He had tried several times to ingratiate himself with the English king. In 1538, he intrigued to influence Sir Thomas Wyatt, resident ambassador at the court of Spain, to recommend his services to Henry VIII, which in fact was done by Sir Philip Hoby when he returned to London. But the manœuvre succeeded only several years later.

At that time, a great change had taken place in the relative importance of the northern coast of the new continent. The seas which bordered the Baccalaos region were no longer a mere common fishing-ground frequented by the smacks of Portugal, Biscay, Normandy, and England. The successful explorations of Jacques Cartier had been followed by the planting of French colonies. The part selected was not Labrador, on which, in all the maps of the period, was inscribed the uninviting legend, "No ay en ella cosa de provecho" ("Here there is nothing of utility "). On the contrary, the French had chosen the country around the Gulf of St. Lawrence and Cape Breton, which the reports of Cartier and Roberval to Francis I represented to be a beautiful and fertile country, with rich copper-mines, fine ports, and the most navigable rivers in the world.

Under the circumstances, the cartographical statement of Sebastian Cabot, as embodied in the planisphere of 1544, may well have been a suggestion of British claims, and a bid for the favor of the King of England. To place near the entrance of the Gulf of St. Lawrence the landfall of 1497, was tantamount to declaring that region to be English dominion, as the discovery had been accomplished by a vessel sailing

---

[1] "John and Sebastian Cabot." New York: Dodd, Mead & Co., 1896.

under the British flag—"sub banneris vexillis et insigniis nostris," said Henry VII.

Nor was the hint conveyed by Sebastian at an unseasonable time; England being then at war with France, and continuing so until 1547. At all events, it is certain that, to use the language of Hakluyt, "the title which England has to that part of America which is from Florida sixty-seven degrees northward" is or was derived "from the letters granted to John Cabot and his three sons."

Convinced that the location of the landfall at Cape Breton is an after-thought of Sebastian Cabot, and devoid of all authenticity, there is nothing left but to examine the data furnished in 1497 by John Cabot himself. These are contained in the first dispatch of Soncino, which I translate:—

"After sailing from Bristol . . the ship passed Ireland more to the west; then sailed toward the north, and afterward east [Error for "west"], when, after a few days, the North Star was to the right."

This is all we possess, in the nature of positive data, to determine where, in 1497, John Cabot effected his landfall. Technically speaking, the only conclusion which geographers could infer from such scanty details was that the landfall had to be sought north of 51° 15′ N. lat., being that of the southern extremity of Ireland. Ireland, however, extends to 55° 15′ N. lat. From what point between these two parallels did John Cabot sail westward? Supposing that it was Valencia, and that the route continued due west, he would have sighted Belle Isle or its vicinity. But Cabot said positively that he altered his course when to the west of Ireland and stood to the northward. From what latitude exactly, and where he again put his ship on the western tack, are questions which no one can answer beyond stating that it was north of 51° 15′. I have surmised and said that, according to Soncino's statement, and taking into account the extremely northern latitudes in which all the Spanish maps located the British discoveries in the New World, the landfall must have been in Labrador, west of Belle Isle, between Sandwich Bay and Cape Chudley, in about 53° 30′ N. lat. But this estimate I bring forward only as a supposition.

Dr. S. E. Dawson, in an able and interesting paper published in the twelfth volume of the "Transactions" of the Royal Society of Canada has opposed this conclusion; and his arguments deserve to be attentively examined.

A remarkable circumstance related in John Cabot's verbal account of his first transatlantic voyage, was the extraordinary number of codfish which he saw in the sea laving the newly discovered regions.

I referred to Cape Chudley as a locality where cod were more plentiful than anywhere else. My opponent shows that now cod arrive there only after August 15, at which date Cabot was already back in England, and, that, consequently, Cape Chudley cannot have been his landfall. But I have never said that Cape Chudley was John Cabot's landfall. I only advanced the supposition that this cape may have been the *terminus* of Cabot's exploration of the three hundred marine leagues westward. The most therefore that can be made out of the argument is that Cabot found no cod at Cape Chudley when he reached the place.

Nor can it be inferred from the absence of cod in Southern Labrador before the twentieth of June that Cabot's landfall must be located where the fish is already to be found at that date; *i. e.*, Newfoundland, or Nova Scotia. Cabot does not say when and where exactly "that sea is covered with fishes." He may have observed the fact only *when returning* from Cape Chudley, homeward bound. Now, if, according to my hypothesis, he effected his return from Labrador to Bristol in about thirty-four days, arriving in the latter port on August 5, he might well have noticed the amazing number of codfish in Southern Labrador, or on the coast of Newfoundland, between June 20 and the first week in July, and have continued to see it for a long distance.

A more important question mooted by Dr. Dawson—and in the true scientific spirit, although with doubtful conclusions—is that of the deviation of the magnetic needle.

The patriotic critic, avowedly availing himself of the data furnished by Mr. Charles A. Scott in his valuable paper on the variation of the compass off the Bahama Islands at the time of the landfall of Columbus in 1492, has formed the following opinion :—

"If Columbus on a direct western course dropped two hundred and forty miles from Gomara, his point of departure to his landfall in the Antilles, in 1492, with a variation of one point west, it is altogether probable that John Cabot, with a variation of a point and a half [?], would have dropped, in 1497, three hundred and sixty miles to the south on his western course across the Atlantic; and, again, if John Cabot laid his course to the west by compass from latitude 53° north, the variation, so much greater [?] than that observed by Columbus, would have carried him clear of Cape Race and to the next probable landfall, Cape Breton."—(*Trans. Royal Society of Canada*, Sect. xi, 1894, p. 58.)

Such are the principal reasons alleged against the probability of the landing of Cabot on the coast of Labrador, and in favor of the opinion that it was in the vicinity of Cape Breton. The argument so far from being decisive is, on the contrary, entirely hypothetical and problematic.

The laws of the secular motion of the curves of equal variation on the surface of the globe are yet too little known to enable anyone to infer, from the variations which Columbus experienced in or about 25° N. lat., the variations which Cabot experienced in 53° N. lat. There is nothing whatever to show that the variations experienced by Cabot were not inferior to one point and a half west, or that they were not *nil*, or even eastwardly. Again : If the variations experienced by Columbus can be determined more or less approximately by inferences drawn from his own journal, we possess no such information concerning the route followed by Cabot. There is no ground, therefore, to say that if the variation experienced by Columbus was one point west, the variation experienced by Cabot must have been one point and a half; nor can such consequence be inferred from any known fact.

Even in admitting that Cabot experienced a variation of a point and a half, it is not exact to infer therefrom that if with a variation of one point Columbus dropped two hundred and forty miles in a course of about 3,150 miles, Cabot dropped proportionately in a much shorter course, that is, three hundred and sixty miles for a variation of a point and a half. The inference would still be inexact, even if Cabot's course and that of Columbus had been of precisely equal length. Any mathematician could have told Dr. Dawson that such deviations are to each other as the tangents of the angles of variation, and *not as the variations themselves*. Then the route of Columbus and that of John Cabot were traversed under circumstances wholly different. The causes of the dropping in the two courses—among which the variations of the compass are the least weighty for Cabot's route—did not exercise an influence equally important over both courses. We should not, therefore, determine from the dropping in one course the dropping experienced in the other.

Nor is it logical to take into account only the differences in the variations of the compass. The route of Columbus was entirely in latitudes where fine weather and a smooth sea prevailed. It was besides in the region of northeast trade-winds. The navigator has not then to contend against the errors of reckoning due to beating against head-winds and to changes of course and speed in bad weather. The currents, as well as the winds, were favorable to Columbus. Finally, if he did experience a variation of one point westward, it was only in the meridian of 40° W. East of that meridian the variations were much less, and possibly in a contrary direction, as he probably cut the line of no variation between 28° and 32° W. long. There was therefore, as regards the variation, a partial compensation.

If we now examine the regions necessarily traversed by Cabot, we find that he did not enjoy such advantages. He sailed constantly in the region of the brave west winds, that is, with head-winds which compelled him to tack nearly the whole time. This tacking had to be carried out in latitudes where gales and heavy seas are almost constant. The consequence of these difficulties is made apparent in the expression of Soncino, that Cabot was compelled "to wander a good deal." In such a case it is impossible to ascertain the error, or deviation between the course actually made by the navigator and that which he believed himself to have made.

Under these circumstances, it is bold to assume, as Dr. Dawson does, that Cabot's course was "west magnetic," and that the corresponding true course was this magnetic course west, corrected exactly by $1\frac{1}{2}$ points of variation northwesterly. Yet, my opponent's belief that the landfall actually was at Cape Breton rests mainly upon this supposition.

Well may we say, therefore, that with our present sources of information no one is warranted in asserting that John Cabot discovered the continent of North America on June 24, 1497, and that his landfall was Cape Breton.

HENRY HARRISSE.

THE GRIEVANCE OF THE WEST.

AN opportunity was afforded me in the last Presidential election to do some campaign work in the States of Ohio and Indiana; and, though my work was interrupted by an unfortunate circumstance, it was sufficiently extensive to bring me into direct contact with a great many farmers, merchants, and taxpayers generally, who were complaining, as was natural, of the hard times. There was, of course, the usual division of sentiment in regard to the remedy; but the sound-money advocates admitted frankly a condition of things that required more than a perfunctory consideration. The exigencies of the campaign directed all attention to the federal issues concerning the tariff and the currency; but they did not prevent frequent allusion, by many with whom I talked, to questions which had no connection with the main issues, though it was the impression of all who made complaint of the situation that the whole trouble was with the currency and the tariff.

There were two main complaints made by the farmers, besides that against trusts. They were: (1) That farm labor was as high as it had been in more prosperous times when prices for grain were higher; and (2) that the salaries of public officials ought to be reduced to correspond with the universal fall in prices.

Here was, for me, a very interesting condition demanding an attention which it did not then and does not yet receive from the people making complaint. One of the most amusing features of it was that every argument addressed to the laboring classes, to hold their allegiance to a gold standard, only confirmed the opinion of those who wanted an excuse for reducing wages and salaries. The silver advocates told the farmers that free silver would raise the prices of agricultural products and farm values; and the gold advocates admitted this, though with a qualification. On the other hand, the gold advocates showed that salaries and wages would be reduced by free silver; and the farmers, not knowing anything about the economic question on its own merits, and finding that they did not have to choose between the two parties, *but could believe both*, selected free silver as the remedy in favor of their interests. No amount of argument on the abstract questions of public confidence and honesty, or on matters remote from their immediate interests, could move them; for they saw a direct way to cure the evils of which they complained. No one ventured to suggest a local remedy for their grievances, which should be perfectly compatible with a sound currency. The politicians were the salaried officers against whom one of the complaints was directed; and, besides being too ignorant to know anything about the problem, they were too much interested in the *status quo* to offer any policy except that which would sustain public confidence in our institutions,—they to retain all their immunities, political and economic, in the result of a favorable election.

County politics almost all over the West are honeycombed with "rings" and corruption, precisely like Tammany in New York. On the other hand, the people themselves were in the densest ignorance of the real cause of unreduced wages. Consequently, whenever I was called upon to answer the farmer's argument for free silver, I turned questioner and began a series of inquiries about the county's or township's method of relief for the poor; and I invariably found a most astonishing condition of things. I found in fact a real grievance of which not a word had been said, and of whose very existence everybody seemed to be unconscious. This was a system of poor-relief, as bad as anything that existed in the worst days of charity in Europe. My argument was to the effect that the real cause of complaint was a system of taxation that ought to be abolished, and not the badness of the gold standard.

I think it will be important to point out some of the facts, and the lessons that they teach, so that the attention of the agricultural classes may be directed to home problems for reflection, instead of trying to revolutionize federal government along the lines of socialism. They require to be shown that what they are suffering from now is a form of socialism of the worst kind.

Of course, to analyze all the grievances, just and unjust, of the farmers would take me over tariff and currency problems, as well as the influence of natural economic forces, such as the law of diminishing returns, and unscientific farming. But this would be an ungrateful task; while the problem which I wish to discuss, though an old one, presents wholly new features to the majority of Western people, who accept without question their responsibility for poverty, and never study the effects of the policy that they have adopted. Hence, in the midst of currency controversies and questions of taxation, as the agricultural classes have at last become sensitive on the price of farm labor, it will be useful to point out a remedy that lies wholly within their own power, and that requires no tampering with either tariff or monetary problems for its application.

Let us look at some of the facts that came within my immediate observation and that occasioned the complaint which I have mentioned. The corn-crop of the West in 1896 was one of the largest and best ever known. It created a demand for labor. But hard times and the prospect of a very low price for the product made it impossible for farmers to pay the old prices for cutting and husking. In spite of mechanical improvements for dispensing with hand labor in cutting corn, there was a sharp demand for such labor ; but it was generally refused unless the price of past years was promised. Often I met cases where laborers, under the pressure of necessity, accepted the reduced terms ; and these were usually men who had come from a distance. In some cases the home laborers intimidated them for offering their services at reduced rates, to the extent that, for fear of injury, they abandoned their work ; and many farmers, being unable to pay the old prices, had to harvest their own corn-crop.

Now it is no wonder that, with such teaching as the average politician gave the farmers, they rushed to free silver to increase the price of their products and to diminish the purchasing power of wages. They had only to believe the free-silver claim, that prices would rise by coining silver at the ratio of 16 to 1, and the gold advocate's, that it would reduce wages. But when I asked them what system of poor-relief was in vogue, I invariably got the answer that the county commissioners, or poor-law officers, had full power to distribute, as they saw fit, food, fuel, and clothing to any man or woman who could show a need of them. Want alone, and this not always severe or pressing, was sufficient to invoke the blessing of charity ; and the applicant was helped very much after the latter half of Louis Blanc's maxim but without regard to the first half : "From every one according to his power, and to every one according to his needs."

I seized the opportunity to point out the consequences of such a policy, and to explain that it was absurd to expect a laborer to take lower wages when he could get his living by taxes on the community. Charity sustained him up to the level of the standard of living ; and he had no more need to work than a king, unless he got wages above the price of charity. This way of looking at the matter had never occurred to my farmer friends. I improved the occasion to suggest the remedy, which, while the public sentiment is receptive, ought to be pushed throughout the West for all it is worth. It is, *to abolish absolutely all outdoor relief.*

Not to say anything of the large number of individual cases of fraudulent charity which were mentioned to me, I may refer to two facts of larger interest concerning the cost of relief to whole counties. The first was the statement of a grocer in Springfield, Ohio, who told me that his share of the commissioners' orders for groceries last year for the relief of the poor was $200 ; and he was only one of a hundred grocers among whom such orders were distributed. Fuel and clothing would go to other classes of dealers ; and one can imagine what the expense would be to the community. In the next county, of which Xenia is the county-seat, the commissioners, I was told, were obliged to issue bonds to pay a deficit of $5,000, caused by poor-relief. The total cost of relief in that county was $20,336, or nearly 22 per cent of the whole expenses for county administration.

It will be interesting to consult the statistics for the whole State, and to note, on a large scale, the economic and social influences which make for discontent and unrest, and which prove at the same time extravagance in government and depreciation of values.

In 1892, the cost of outdoor relief in the State of Ohio was $453,-603 ; in 1893, $456,457 ; in 1894, $585,457. The increase during the last of these three years is very large, amounting to $129,000. But we get little idea of what this means to the State unless we can compare it with the total sums spent for charity in all forms ; noting also that competent judges speak of such charity as a growing and dangerous evil. Mr. H. C. Filler, Chairman of the Committee on County Committees in the Ohio State Conference of Charities, at its meeting in 1892, said :—

" It is not expected that I startle this intelligent audience with a new theory upon a subject as old as Mount Sinai. If I can only say something which will awaken a renewed interest in the minds and hearts of the great benevolent class whose souls seem bent on bettering the condition of the helpless, without losing sight of the unhesitating philanthropists who contributed last year from the tax duplicate the munificent sum of $1,200,000.00 to be used in accord with that heavenly injunction of succoring the poor, I will have done some good.

In order to more fully understand the growing importance of the subject, I will illustrate by a few figures. In the year ending August, 1881, Franklin County maintained a daily average number of 218 people, costing $24,700.81 ; for the same period we gave outdoor relief to 1,692, at a cost of $7,094.05, making the total pauper population, of 1,910, cost $31,794.86. The year ending August 31, 1891, we provided in the infirmary for a daily average of 309 inmates at a cost of $34,354.85, and relieved on the outside the wants, real or supposed, of 10,733, at an expense of $20,671.45, making the outlay $55,026.30 for the relief of 11,042 people—about one-tenth of the population of the capital county of this State, the increase in paupers being about 400 per cent,—far in advance of the increase in population. The small increase in the cash may be accounted for in the stubborn fight made by the directors in curtailing the amount, giving the lowest possible figure. The growth, numerically, shows where the bounty would end if unbounded privileges were given to this class. In 1881, the average number of inmates in the infirmaries of Ohio was 5,171, which cost $564,647.19. There were relieved on the outside 8,022, at an expense of $259,733.71, making for the year 13,193 reported paupers, which cost $824,380.90. In 1891, ten years after, the average number in the infirmaries was 6,393, which cost $715,960.14, and you supported, in whole or in part, on the outside 54,121, at a cost of $430,761.76, making the total number of paupers in Ohio 60,514, costing the fabulous sum of $1,146,721.90,—an increase in one decade of 47,321, at an additional expense of $322,341.00."

Such figures speak for themselves, especially when we consider the high percentage of outdoor relief and the probability that the administration of indoor relief—partly from defective management, but mainly from the indifference of the public to its organization on any but a sentimental basis—costs much more than is necessary. That it is wholly superfluous is shown by the experience of Cincinnati in the winter of 1884–1885, when the outdoor relief was cut off because the directors had stolen all the money. Nobody suffered more than usual ; and the organized charities were able to cope with all the real suffering. But the figures given appear still more instructive when compared with those for all forms of charity in the State, as shown in the following table :—

STATISTICS OF COST OF ALL CHARITIES.

Institutions.	1892.	1893.	1894.
Asylums for the Insane............	$832,680.30	$796,265.93	$865,701.65
Institution for the Feeble-minded...	112,239.31	111,436.83	135,220.56
" " " Deaf and Dumb..	80,011.49	80,431.71	88,629.05
" " " Blind...........	51,455.13	48,630.02	55,970.68
Working Home for the Blind.......	10,122.98	4,695.12	15,919.24
Soldiers' and Sailors' Orphans' Home.	150,148.97	143,668.42	144,970.27
" " " Home........	134,872.87	111,889.33	138,528.65
Boys' Industrial School.............	84,263.34	52,199.43	95,485.92
Ohio Hospital for Epileptics........	....	....	39,417.95
Girls' Industrial Home.............	34,556.99	21,343.50	36,958.80
Ohio Penitentiary	257,440.58	295,451.49	270,905.61
Workhouses, etc...................	204,081.57	264,816.91	157,113.32
County Infirmaries	772,113.17	395,801.16	848,730.54
County Children's Homes...........	234,852.70	250,390.64	242,554.01
County Jails	123,283.99	115,874.76	136,159.74
Outdoor Relief....................	481,879.23	472,207.74	585,457.10
Soldiers' Relief Commission........	395,676.83	328,961.28	318,192.38
Totals......................	$3,959,679.45	$3,491,064.27	$4,175,915.47

Unfortunately I have not the figures for 1895 and 1896, as the reports for those years are not accessible to me. But there are several features noticeable in those that I have given. In the first place, the cost of both indoor and outdoor relief for the respective years is $1,253,-992.40, $868,008.90, and $1,434,187.64. To these sums ought also to be added the cost of workhouses and houses of refuge, which are municipal, as distinct from county, infirmaries and a sort of institution intermediate between the jail and the penitentiary. The cost of charity in which there is room for much economy would, therefore, be considerably larger. But, omitting the cost of workhouses as belonging to correction rather than charity, we find that the outdoor relief represents respectively 40, 55, and 41 per cent of the whole cost of relief for poverty proper. The number of persons receiving outdoor relief during the three years was 54,663, 52,652, and 100,361, respectively. Adding those who received indoor relief, we have 67,592, 66,457, and 115,867. The large increase in 1894 was probably due to the panic of 1893.

I may briefly compare the poor-law relief of Indiana with that of Ohio. For 1893, the total cost of relief, indoor and outdoor, was $876,-127; for 1894, it was $980,058; and for 1895, it was $1,020,535—showing a constant increase. In Pennsylvania, for 1892, it was $1,255,803; for 1893, $1,918,982; and for 1894, $2,121,044. These items show not only a large increase, but also that probably the same general cost of relief prevails everywhere; and all that I desire to establish by the figures is the enormity of the cost, which ought to be diminished in the interest of economic administration, of land values, and of justice to all parties involved in the struggle for existence.

There are three important things to be enforced by these figures and the relation of poor-relief to existing economic conditions. They are: (1) The opportunity to abolish outdoor relief afforded by the present feeling of the agricultural classes in regard to wages; (2) that such a policy would afford at least a partial redress for the grievances of which farmers complain; (3) the effect of outdoor relief and over-taxation upon land values.

If the agricultural classes could be made to see the enormous injustice to themselves of protection, their grievance might easily be redressed by lower tariffs or what is known in economics as "free trade." But, since they are blind to this injustice, and are tempted to meddle with currency problems as a remedy for evils whose cause they do not know and which are serious, and, since they have come to see clearly that somehow wages and salaries have not fallen with the

31

prices of their products, it is certainly an opportune time to agitate the importance of abolishing outdoor relief. Here is an opportunity even to weaken the opposition to sound currency by showing that the trouble is with our system of taxation and socialistic poor-relief, and not with the gold standard.

I certainly found in my campaign work a very receptive mind for my view of the case. I was able to show very clearly the absurdity of expecting wages to fall when the farmer taxed himself to see that his neighbor did not have to work. No sane man is going to work if he can live on the taxes of the community, unless he gets more for his work than poor-law relief will give him. Usually this relief, coupled with the philanthropic tendencies of the community, will secure relief equal to the standard of living. Hence a man is not likely to work unless his wages give him a profit over the standard of living. He is assured of his living without labor, and hence will not accept lower wages so long as this assurance lasts. Consequently the farmer can be shown that he must either abolish this sort of relief or patiently endure the consequences. He will at the same time decrease his rate of taxation and the wages of farm labor, and add this much to the value of the land ; while he will also diminish the amount of poverty.

That outdoor relief only increases the amount of poverty, and that its abolition will injure no one, but rather benefit the community, is proved, not only by the unanimous opinion of experts, but by actual experience. Nothing proves it better than the incident already mentioned in the reference to Cincinnati. But the experience of Brooklyn, New York, is a still better illustration. I quote the statements of Mr. Alexander Johnston, Superintendent of the Asylum for the Feeble-minded at Fort Wayne, Indiana :—

" In the year 1879, the city of Brooklyn was expending annually about $125,-000 in outdoor relief. Hon. Seth Low, the reform mayor of the city, now president of Columbia College, found that there was no authority for it in law ; and it was stopped in mid-winter, suddenly. The results were amazing. Nobody died of starvation ; the number in the poorhouse was not increased. The results showed that the $125,000 annually spent in outdoor relief were wasted and worse than wasted. All the apparent difference was that there was no longer seen in front of the relief officer's door, a great string of people with baskets waiting for their rations. There was in Brooklyn at that time, and there is to this day, a society for the improvement of the condition of the poor, dispensing private charity to the amount of $25,000 to $30,000 annually. The society usually made its main collection in November, and a supplementary collection in February. That year was the first for many years that the society did *not make a supplementary collection.* There was no perceptible difference in the call for private charity. The year following, the city of Philadelphia took this lesson to heart and cut off all outdoor relief except coal; and one year later they cut that off also. The city of Philadelphia had spent annually $60,000 for coal and $80,000 for provisions. The private charitable societies went ahead and did their work. Except for a few weeks, they experienced no increase of demand."

In Chicago, during the fall of 1887, outdoor relief was cut off for several months. There was no suffering, and no increase of the poorhouse population. The author quoted above gives also the experience of Indianapolis :—

"In Indianapolis, in the year 1880, the distribution of outdoor relief amounted to between $85,000 and $90,000 among a population of 75,000,—more than a dollar a head given in official outdoor relief. At that time a man was elected township trustee, Mr. Smith King, who said to the county commissioners : 'If you will give me help in my office, I will reduce this outdoor relief enormously.' He opened his office, commenced a thorough system of record-keeping and investigation, and reduced the amount in one year to $25,000. The following year it was reduced to $17,000 ; and in the course of his four years' term he reduced it to $7,000 a year, without anybody suffering, without any injury to the worthy poor, and without any increase of the poorhouse population."

In spite of this experience, the outdoor relief of the State of Indiana for 1895 was nearly $600,000 ; and no tendency was shown by the Legislature to remedy the evil. The experience of Brookline, Massachusetts, is quite as interesting as any that has been quoted. This suburb of Boston about fifteen years ago had a population of 6,000. Its appropriation for outdoor relief was $9,000, and its poor-list, after every effort to reduce it, was 355 persons. The board of overseers resolved to put a stop to a policy which invited the immigration of paupers from other towns ; so they built an almshouse, and then refused all outdoor relief, save in certain exceptional cases. Within one year the total pauper list was reduced to fifty-three persons, and the cost of exceptional cases to $2,000 ; thus saving $7,000 to the taxpayer.

"There was no increased demand upon private charity; and there were no beggars. Old men and women, whose children had been perfectly willing that they should have outdoor relief, suddenly found devoted sons anxious to support them rather than have them go to the house ; men and women who had declared themselves too weak to work recovered their strength with marvellous rapidity ; and the laborer, all whose earnings had barely been enough to support him through the summer, now saved for the winter and saved enough to keep him in tolerable comfort."

The experiences that have been quoted ought to prove the propriety of abolishing outdoor relief. But as I am not urging this on the ground of legitimate charity, I shall not dwell upon that side of the

matter.   Here I am interested in the economic and political aspects of
the problem, and in the advantages that will accrue equally to the
classes that complain so bitterly of our monetary system, to charity
reformers, and to sound-currency advocates.

Local taxation is a problem that can be attacked now as never before ; and, by a judicious economy of salaries and poor-law relief, one
of the most important sources of discontent may be removed.   At one
stroke the States of Indiana and Ohio might easily save nearly $600,-
000 a year by cutting off outdoor relief alone.   The Clerk of the Ohio
Conference of Charities said in 1893 : " Outdoor relief, as at present
administered, *involves the minimum of true relief with the maximum of
fraud* " ; and yet no steps have been taken to remedy the evil.

Moreover, outdoor relief is not the only economy possible.   Many
of those connected with the system of indoor relief—which is admitted
on all hands to be necessary—join in the demand for economic reforms
in that system ; and I have no doubt that a judicious reorganization of
it along scientific lines would save at least 30 per cent of the amount
expended in legitimate charity—legitimate in method.   This would be a
further $250,000; and if we note that, with United States pensions and
Soldiers' Homes, there is no excuse for the enormous sum spent in relief for soldiers, we observe an opportunity of saving $315,000 more.
Adding these to the $585,000 of outdoor relief, we have the sum of
$1,150,000, which is probably without the slightest excuse for its dis-
bursement in any form of charity.   This is nearly 30 per cent of the
whole expenses for charity; while the sum for outdoor relief and the
possible economy in indoor relief, which would be $835,000, is about
60 per cent of the amount spent for the relief of pauperism alone.

The population of Ohio at this date was 3,600,000.   Counting four
to the family, which is certainly a low estimate, there would not be over
900,000 who could be taxpayers.   Poverty and other conditions would
probably reduce this number by 400,000, leaving only 500,000 persons
to pay the taxes.   This makes over $2 *per capita* which might be
saved in the taxation for poor-relief alone, not to mention the saving in
the reduction of wages and salaries, and the increase of the State's
wealth from the augmented production of her 100,000 paupers.

Some illustrations of the effect of this administrative extravagance
upon land values can be taken from the experience of the English poor-
law prior to 1834.   This law, by the indiscriminate nature of its charity
and the unlimited taxation imposed to carry it out, had created a veritable paradise for the poor.   The mere fact of want was sufficient to

secure aid; and this aid was construed as a right which could be enforced by the law. . The Report of the Poor Law Commissioners appointed in 1832 shows what the effect of this policy was upon property
and the poor alike. There is scarcely any publication in existence that
is so suggestive of the real consequences that must attend a sentimental
socialism. One might almost ransack the annals of history in vain for
so demoralizing an experiment as. that law had been. That Report
shows that nothing was done by a sentimental public to restrain the
increase of paupers, or to protect the rights of property. Taxes were
imposed to meet every case of want, and a premium placed upon idleness; while thrift and honesty had to contend, at uneven odds, against
laziness. The result was that land depreciated in value until in many
cases the poor-rates absorbed all, or nearly all, the rents, and farms
went out of cultivation.

The Report says:—

"In the parish of Cholesbury, the population of which has been almost sta-
tionary since 1801, in which, within the memory of persons now living, the rates
were only £10 11s. ($53) a year, and only one person received the relief, the sum
raised for the relief of the poor rose from £99 4s. ($496) a year in 1816 to £150 5s.
($751) in 1831; and in 1832, when it was proceeding at the rate of £367 ($1,835) a
year, suddenly ceased in consequence of the impossibility to continue its collection; the landlords having given up their rents, the farmers their tenancies, and
the clergyman his glebe and tithes. The clergyman, Mr. Jeston, states that in
October, 1832, the parish officers threw up their books, and the poor assembled
before his door while he was in bed, asking for advice and food. Partly from his
own small means, partly from the charity of neighbors, and partly by rates in aid
imposed on the neighboring parishes, they were for some time supported. In
Cholesbury, therefore, the expense of maintaining the poor has not only swallowed
up the whole value of the land, but it requires even the assistance for two years
of rates in aid from other parishes to enable the able-bodied, after the land has
been given up to them, to support themselves; and the aged and impotent must
even then remain a burden on the neighboring parishes.

In Wigston Magna, in 1832, the value of property has fallen one-half since
1820, and is not saleable even at that reduction. In Leicestershire the poor-rate
exceeds £1 ($5) an acre and is rapidly increasing; and a general opinion prevails
that the day is not distant when rent will cease altogether. In Lenham, Kent, a
farm of forty-two acres of good land, tithe-free and well situated, was thrown
up by the tenant because the poor-rate amounted to £300 ($1,500) a year. In
Cambridgeshire, land that produces thirty bushels of wheat per acre will not rent
for anything on account of the poor-rates. Downing College has a property of
5,000 acres, and cannot obtain tenants for the same reason. In Westfield, Sussex,
the annual value of the real property assessed in 1815 was £3,390 ($16,950); in
1829, it was only £1,959 ($9,795). It has undoubtedly fallen in value since the last
valuation, i. e., in the last two years; and the population has been more than
trebled in 30 years. In 1801, it was 306; in 1811, it was 707; in 1821, it was 897;

and in 1831, it was 938, and that in spite of an emigration of considerable amount, at the parish expense, in 1829. The eighteen-penny children will eat up this parish in ten years more, unless some relief be afforded."

These are sufficiently ominous examples of the effect of taxation for poor-relief upon the value of property. Things, of course, have not yet reached so bad a pass in this country; but they may very soon reach it, if the present policy continue unchecked. Similar quotations to the above could be made to show the effect upon the number of paupers created by the law, and its influence upon the rate of wages; but there is not space for this. My main object will be accomplished if the figures I have given shall awaken an intelligent concern for the extravagant taxation which our "penny wise, pound foolish" politicians impose upon property, and which is ignorantly endured by the population until they are ready for any revolutionary policy except the right one to secure relief. While they are sensitive to the economic facts which are a consequence of bad legislation, is the opportune time to urge the radical reform here suggested. The taxpayer can be easily shown the fatal influence of outdoor and other illegitimate relief, and, if organized in the right way, may hold the balance of power in elections.

The trouble, of course, with our degenerating institutions is to get rid of our lawmakers of the present kind. They are too much interested in postponing or escaping the day of judgment for themselves, to take up any reforms of a local kind. They may even endeavor to divert attention from the evils here considered by raising false issues; hence the work must fall to other hands.

While a goodly number of people are well enough convinced that our politicians are a combination of fools and knaves whom it were better to hang and quarter than to send to the Legislature for making laws, they are powerless to reform matters until the dense agricultural ignorance on problems of taxation is removed, and property-holders are made to see that no more blackmail, in the form of taxes, is imposed to pay political debts by unwise charity. It is certainly an opportune time to agitate widely this great reform, and therewith to modify, directly or indirectly, the tendency to seek relief from taxation by disturbing the currency. Is any class of the community equal to the emergency?

JAMES H. HYSLOP.

CONTEMPORARY AMERICAN ESSAYISTS.

To those who regard the literature of a country as the reflection of its social, ethical, and intellectual evolution, the recent revival of the American essay and of the interest in it is a most interesting and significant phenomenon; though the state of mind of which it is the symptom hardly requires this added element for its clear diagnosis.

The essay implies, both on the part of those who write and on the part of those who read, the pause of reflection, the backward gaze, the philosophic mind. It is a commonplace of criticism, though it has not failed of denial from those who strain at novelty, that all literatures oscillate between creative epochs of strenuous onward effort and epochs of critical assimilation. As our intellectual life becomes more intense, these periods succeed one another at shorter intervals.

In times of confident creation the attitude toward the past is not so much iconoclastic as contemptuous. The France of Racine dismisses with a smile the France of Ronsard. Shakespeare treats the work of his predecessors as clay in his potter's hand, or as treasure trove. And in a lesser degree we can recall a time when American men of letters, flushed with the effort of war, intoxicated with the wine of science, feeling, with the *Wagner* of Goethe's "Faust," that Nature was opening to us so many doors and such new vistas that surely we should at last catch her secret, turned away from the contemplative, the analytic, and the critical to the romantic and imaginative forms of literature. But during the last decade, and perhaps somewhat earlier, there has been a noteworthy subsiding of this self-confident spirit; and with this the novelist has yielded somewhat of his dominant place to the historian and the essayist.

We are passing through the same stage of literary evolution as the French; only that with them the habit of literary criticism and self-criticism makes the tendency more marked and more easily studied. Here, as there, it might seem that for the time the minds of men had overleaped themselves; as though in this strange *fin du siècle* we were pausing in our letters and art, uncertain of the onward way, and seeking, in more acute apprehension, deeper penetration, and keener analy-

sis of what has been and is, an answer to our perplexity of what shall
be.   Here, as there, originality, never absent, manifests itself too often
in a studied eccentricity, and wastes its energy in a search for the novel
and bizarre,—a search that is most futile when most successful.

Our literary age is a time of questioning, of criticism of ourselves
and of life; and this finds expression in essays and in the fact that these
essays find publishers and purchasers.   Many of these essays have indeed first seen the light in the magazines and reviews; but the existence and popularity of these journals are only other evidences of the
same state of mind.   They have contributed very much to make this
form of literary expression possible to some who might otherwise never
have attempted it; and they have influenced the mode of its development both for good and ill.   For, while there has never been a time
since the day when George William Curtis first sat in the Easy Chair,
when the essay as a criticism of life has been without noble expression
in our periodical literature, yet in these latter days there has been much
writing of this kind that fosters mental dissipation rather than nutrition;
and many, by confining their literary diet to these peptonized articles,
have lost the art of reading books that call for sustained attention.

On the other hand, it is probably to the magazine that our essays
owe their new and surely more attractive form.   If we contrast them
in this their last estate with those of the venerable quarterly "North
American" (*Quantum mutatus ab illo!*) in the palmy days of Emerson
and Lowell we shall note a radical difference both in form and substance.   This is due in part to consideration for the larger audience of
our great magazines, and in part to the changed standard of our cultured
readers, who are grown, as Chaucer would have said, "so nice of their
mete" that they will no longer accept length for fulness nor heaviness for
profundity.   It is perhaps doubtful if they ever did.   The typical critic
of Lowell's "Fable," whose very old nothings pleased very old fools,
"filled up the space nothing else was prepared for; and nobody read
what nobody cared for."   How wholly this satire has lost its point.
No form of literature to-day is read with more interest, or enjoyed
more keenly, by the fit company—which, though still few, is constantly growing—of those who can judge of such delights as our best
essayists afford.

Perhaps none among us is making such permanent contributions to
literature as Emerson or Lowell or Poe.   Yet one cannot resist a suspicion that these profit a little by distance, and that as our own writers
recede there may remain work done in this decade that, as criticism,

may rank with the very best; though perhaps since the death of Curtis none can vie with Lowell in grace and correctness of style.

But the generous foison of the magazines does not satisfy our demand for literary and critical retrospect. We wish to ruminate, to chew the cud of our favorite essays; and so they are republished in increasing numbers. Within the last ten years a well-known firm, after carrying their dainty series of American essayists to its fifteenth volume, have already published five volumes of a second collection of contemporary essayists on a larger scale; and although other publishers have not gathered books of this kind into series under a collective title, a cursory examination of the chief lists indicates that the annual output of essays in volumes in America has nearly doubled in the past decade. It is with these books alone that I propose to deal; examining the work of some of the more popular or significant essayists; fixing their place in the development of critical and literary art; and, if it may be, inducing still other kindred spirits to spend their recreative hours browsing in these pleasant pastures.

Joining the old essay to the new, handing down the tradition and the inspiration that they received, are Curtis, Higginson, and Warner, whose earliest work coincided with the prime of Emerson and Lowell, and of whom two are still writing to-day, and the third has but recently passed from us. Emerson's first essays were published in 1836; Lowell's, in 1845. The former's "Letters and Social Aims" appeared in 1876; Lowell's last volume, ten years later. The essays of Curtis began to appear in 1853; Higginson's "Outdoor Papers" were collected in 1863; and Warner's "Summer in my Garden" was published in 1870. Yet in spirit all these three belong far more to the new than to the old era. Already in Curtis the essays are shorter, more immediately practical, as befitted the occupant of the Easy Chair. The three charming little volumes that have been collected from his writings show no great acumen in literary criticism. For that the time was not ripe. But whether as orator, reformer, or *raconteur*, Curtis invariably set up and steadfastly maintained the highest standard of social and political democracy. Since he comes to us from a period of confident creation, his work is never carping or negative. It resembles that of Addison more than that of any contemporary. Both are perennial types of the mellow citizen of the world.

In Mr. Higginson's work there breathes also the moral earnestness of the 'sixties. But in him the humorist is at strife with the reformer. He delights in paradox, and occasionally lets himself be clever at the

expense of literary proportion and justice. The apparent easy familiarity of his style, the art with which he hides his art, so that his essays
suggest the conversation of a brilliant but dogmatically subjective
talker, mark a noteworthy step in the development of the contemporary essay. He is one of our greatest masters of pure, crisp, though
somewhat acrid, English; proving that in his hands our language is,
as he has himself said in a recent essay, not inferior to the French in
" weapons of precision." His own work furnishes the best antidote
to that vulgarity of style which he deplores. He at least possesses
that " drop more of nervous fluid " that he attributes to his countrymen. He is one of the most quotable of essayists; for the stimulant
acuteness of his epigrams makes them cling in the mind, as when he
tells us that " timidity, not conceit, is our national foible," or that "to
be really a cosmopolitan one must be at home even in one's own
country."

More delicately restrained, more dispassionate than either of these,
is Mr. Warner. His pungent and witty, yet wise and kindly essays
revealed to us a truly French perception of beauty of form, and a new
virtuosity in literary color. His early work was interpenetrated with
mellow sympathy for all the pure outgoings of youth. No one has
caught the American boy and girl better; no one has shown more
dramatic instinct in setting a scene or in letting a story tell itself in a
dry, clever, bantering, paradoxical tone which wins a smile that seldom
degenerates into a laugh. In 1870, this was a new note in American humor; and it still remains the most pleasing trait of that peculiar and
often meretricious product. Yet Mr. Warner's latest volume, " The
Relation of Literature to Life," shows that he is capable also of sustained nobility of thought,—as when he speaks of the supreme place
of the poet in the life of society, or protests against the fiction that
masks itself behind a pretence of " art for art," that it may " force us
to sup with unpleasant company on misery and sensuousness in tales
so utterly unpleasant that we are ready to welcome any disaster as a
relief, and then—the latest and finest touch of modern art—to leave
the whole weltering mass in a chaos without conclusion and without
possible issue." Thus Mr. Warner joins the literary critics, of whom
there will be more to say presently; but his most characteristic contribution to the revival of the essay is to be sought rather in such
volumes as " As We Were Saying," and " As We Go."

Another, and quite another, link with the past is John Burroughs,
who, like Thoreau and Whitman, of whom he has written most appre-

ciatively, has let nature form him into a man of letters. "Constant intercourse with bookish men and literary circles," he tells us, "would have dwarfed and killed my literary faculty. This perpetual rubbing of heads together, as in the literary clubs, seems to result in literary sterility." Absence of it has produced in Burroughs "a feminine idiosyncrasy" in both man and style. He is direct, sincere, genial, unaffected, genuine, a keen observer and a loving reporter of nature. But if he is always picturesque he is often careless in style, slovenly in rhetoric, and reckless in criticism of literary art. He is at his best out of doors, as for instance in "Riverby," or in "A Year in the Fields." The woods, the fields, air, and water are instinct to him with an ever-changing life and kaleidoscopic interest, rousing in us bookmen a delighted though futile desire to go and do likewise. No one to-day interprets better for us those gentler aspects of nature, "the beneficence and, good-will of the earth," and that "constant succession of little tragedies and comedies among its inhabitants" that our student eyes are too dim to see and our ears too untutored to hear. There is indeed repetition and monotony in the essays, as there is in nature. Better than to read all his volumes is it, through the slow assimilation of one, to grow responsive to the genial author's personality, so unruffled and gentle, so simple and refreshing, that his colloquialisms and even his solecisms seem only to give us a more familiar flavor of the soil.

But our interest is naturally rather with the men of to-day and to-morrow than with those of to-day and yesterday, and among these we shall find the dominant interest is in questions of literary art. Mr. Howells, for instance, after his most successful career as a novelist, preaches his somewhat militant realism by precept as well as example in "Criticism and Fiction" and in "Impressions and Experiences." Where he touches social or economic matters, as in "The Tribulations of a Cheerful Giver,"—that so roused the ire of some modern professors of the dismal science,—his tone is pessimistic and his trumpet gives a very uncertain call. The present order satisfies him as little as it does his traveller from Altruria; but he has no social nostrum. Yet if he hesitates here, it is only that he may be the more dogmatic in literature, where even those who cannot say his shibboleth recognize a power rarely equalled by his contemporaries. Mr. Howells has the great advantage that comes from a well-defined standard and a positive æsthetic creed. This phase of his work is most significant; for it challenged answer, and so contributed essentially to the gradual clarifying of critical ideas that one notices in the younger essayists.

Mr. Howells's "Criticism and Fiction" is most stimulating and suggestive; but his buoyant confidence in realism à outrance, his intolerance of all that savors of romanticism, make him a somewhat dangerous guide, except to those trained not only to read and understand, but also to weigh and consider. In this intransigent apology he declares war on all academic criticism, which seems to him to foster a petrifaction of taste and to divert men's minds from present realities to the worn-out ideals of the past. He thinks that "it is really the critic's business to classify and analyze the works of the human mind very much as the naturalist classifies the objects of his study,"—an idea that might have been suggested by Sainte-Beuve. "Then," he continues, "if the critic would confine himself to explaining how and why any specimen is irregular he would do far more for the public than he now does, though he would still be quite dispensable." But surely this is a petty and narrow view. Can it be that Mr. Howells is piqued that men still read and praise Walter Scott and Fenimore Cooper? The true critic has no shibboleth. He is neither realist nor idealist, romantic nor naturalistic. He analyzes, interprets, and enjoys literary art in all its forms, widening the appreciation of his readers by deepening their apprehension. Such criticism is less a science of classification than an art of initiation. Of course that many latter-day critics, English and American, are blind leaders, is obvious to all who can see; and what Mr. Howells says of them is in the main as true and deserved as it is keen and caustic. But we may see in France, if we will not discern the prophets in our own country, how criticism may mould a public taste that it fascinates, and maintain and upbuild a literary instinct. So long as our critics are content, as Mr. Howells would have them be, "to report, not to create, to discover principles, not to establish them," they can affect, and deserve to influence, neither an author nor his ultimate success. But recently Mr. Howells was himself made the subject of a study so fascinating and subtle that perhaps he has already seen the light, and realized that to our closing century criticism may become what Anatole France says it already is in France—the ultimate evolution of literary expression asserting for itself the place that theology has abandoned, "the last of all the literary forms, that will end by absorbing them all."

In style, Mr. Howells's essays are direct and virile; and he admires these qualities in others. There is much of the Puritan virus in his literary morals. Fiction for pleasure's sake gets short shrift from him. Our American fiction, it seems, "works from without inward," and is therefore superior to the English, which "works from within outward."

At times Mr. Howells has the seriousness of an augur, as with temples cinct he pours his libation on the altar of fiction and utters his " Procul este, profani ! " Does Mr. Howells think that because he is serious "there shall be no more cakes and ale " ?

In genial contrast to the critical dogmatism of Mr. Howells is the catholic sympathy of Mr. Brander Matthews. He is always delightful and often so helpful that one finishes his four volumes of essays with regret that a stream that flows with such apparent ease should flow so sparingly. There is something indecorous, as Mr. Matthews somewhere says, in superlative commendation of the living; and it may suffice to say that the recent reading or re-reading of more than forty volumes by American critics has left the impression that no one among us is doing more than Mr. Brander Matthews to foster systematic criticism. Perhaps this is due in large part to his intimate acquaintance with those schools of French criticism that have contributed so essentially to clarify the ideas of the public, and to develop the art of fiction and of the drama in France. This has made his point of view that of a healthy cosmopolitan, thoroughly at home among all the great modern literatures, and thus provided with the sole equipment that can fit a man to elucidate the tendencies of our own. To this broad knowledge he owes, and by it he justifies, his confident Americanism. It is with no vainglorious boast that he asserts our literary independence of England ; for his horizon reaches beyond Britain. He measures our achievement not by an English standard, but by the whole output of the century ; and, if need be, he can judge it from the perspective of ancient art also, as in his suggestive parallel between the ancient and the modern drama. It is natural, therefore, that no one among us should insist as strongly as he on the fundamental distinction of the genres, so fatal to that vague and ephemeral impressionism that has characterized a great past of our dramatic criticism, and done so much to check the development of a native dramatic school. None among us has stated so luminously as he the functions of the critic as the guide of readers, the expositor of talent, and the discoverer of genius. But his work is not only sound. It is brilliant, witty, epigrammatic, studded with pregnant phrases that contain the quintessence of an argument, or of shrewd social observation, or of genial *blague.* These last are the flowers by the way that beckon us to the ripe fruit beyond. And one feels always that there is so much more beyond that Mr. Matthews might give us from his generous store.

More delicately polished, with something of the poet's touch, is

Mr. Woodberry's single volume of "Studies in Literature and Life," which, as I think some reviewer said, "unifies the sentiment of our present age with the enduring spirit of art." And somewhat similar commendation might be given to the "Little Leaders" which Mr. William Morton Payne has selected from his contributions to "The Dial," that staunch upholder of high literary ideals in the West. This book, in the clear glow of its love of letters, is the most scholarly criticism that that section has yet given to us, and stands in striking contrast to Mr. Garland's nearly synchronous "Crumbling Idols," whose chief interest seems to be that it proves the need of just such a dose of hellebore as Mr. Payne administers so effectually.

But the number of persons who have published occasional volumes of essays is so great that it is possible to name but few among the more significant. One would not pass in silence, though it is impossible to discuss, the lucid and keen if somewhat patronizing "Stelligeri" of Mr. Barret Wendell, nor the light, chatty, mildly antiquarian volumes of Mr. Laurence Hutton,—a little superficial, perhaps, in scholarship, and with wit more kindly than keen. Significant, too, is the republication of Mr. Godkin's "Reflections and Comments," some of which, written a score of years ago, prove their perennial quality by their perfect adaptability to present conditions, and might have served as campaign documents in 1896. And then there are Mr. Woodrow Wilson, Mr. William Winter, Mr. Julian Ralph, Mr. Corson, Miss Coolidge, and many others, among whom I should delight to honor Mr. Lafcadio Hearn and Mr. Henry James, if they would still suffer themselves to be reckoned as Americans. Nor must one forget the literary essays of the late Prof. Boyesen, who, with lurking philistinism and paradoxical emphasis, but always with originality and vigor, served as *fidus Achates* to Mr. Howells in a root-and-branch crusade against what they thought to be the survivals of romanticism.

Mr. Mabie's genial thoughtfulness and Miss Repplier's thoughtful playfulness invite longer notice. Both are so original, so unique; and each in a different way is so delightful. Mr. Mabie's work seems to grow steadily in interest and depth, from the outdoor musings "Under the Trees," and the first series of reflections by his "Study Fire," through the "Short Studies in Literature" and the "Essays in Literary Inspiration," to the riper wisdom of the second series of "My Study Fire" and the "Essays on Books and Culture," and on "Nature and Culture." It is in "A Word about Humor," the concluding essay in "Literary Inspiration," that Mr. Mabie seems to me to reveal most of his own nature. Like those other humorists of whom he speaks, he gives us "not glimpses, but views of life, not detached comments, but comprehensive interpretations."

His early volumes were divided between tributes to the influences of nature and the natural outflowings of the full mind of a ripe scholar. For he was born a man of letters, instinct with subtle thoughts, delicate fancies, and elusive graces of expression. The ease of his writing is witnessed by the recurrence of ideas and even of phrases in the earlier, and to a less degree in the later, volumes. But, as Chaucer tells his little son Louis, it is better that he should say it twice than that we should forget it once. For there is perhaps none among our essayists who suggests so deep a spiritual insight into the ethical significance of the literature of the world, none who guides with such genial, sunny hopefulness toward "the noblest conception of the range and significance of life." For optimism is the foundation of humor. All humorists seem to him optimists; and because they are optimists "humor springs up like a fountain of joy in them." His literary sympathies are sane, reverent, uplifting. A vivid perception of fundamental tendencies and vital forces in literature gives a pregnant unity to the whole body of his critical writing, which however has the defects of its qualities, subordinating consistently art to ethics, and witty, winsome lightness of touch to a noble sense of the dignity and privilege of the scholarly life. To read Mr. Mabie's robust words on criticism as an educator and interpreter, is to be upborne from our work-a-day life into an atmosphere of calm brightness where no crude surfeit reigns. One feels that this atmospheree must be that of his own personality.

In interesting contrast to the limpid depth of these critical essays is the piquant brilliancy of Miss Repplier's five volumes, in which, as someone has said, "the gospel of giving pleasure to others binds all together," and is indeed almost the sole bond of union. Miss Repplier has such a refreshing belief in the joy of life that she can write even the praises of war, and is never more delightful than when she dwells fondly on the delights of leisure or proclaims her infidelity to the gospel of work. The volumes all resemble one another in their lively satire and lambent brightness. She is throughout the genial missioner of art for art. Humor to her is its own excuse for being. She will occasionally sacrifice exactness of expression to a brilliant sarcasm; but grace, cleverness, lightness, and worldly common sense are her birthright. A very broad range of quotations suggests wide and careful reading; but perhaps she has read more than she has assimilated. One is constantly, and not always willingly, diverted from her own thought to that of others, of men of every race and age; and it must be confessed that the somewhat captious description of one of her earlier volumes as " potted literature " was not altogether inept. But it is a most savory *olla podrida*, never without a dominant spice of the author's individuality, and served in a style that is the very perfection of daintiness.

There is not much trace of development in her volumes. All breathe the same gentle regret of old times, the same scepticism of the naturalistic gospel, the same playful irony, and almost the same range of reading. Throughout she pleads effectively against literary shamming; and her robust honesty of judgment finds refreshing expression in " Books that have Hindered me," while her exquisite capacity for literary enjoyment can be felt in her treatment of " English Love Songs," that " in their delicate beauty endure like fragile pieces of porcelain to prove how frail a thing can bear the weight of immortality." Very significant of Miss Repplier's qualities and of her limitations is one of the " Essays in Idleness " on " Wit and Humor," especially if we contrast it with Mr. Mabie's " Word about Humor." Hers is the easier, perhaps the pleasanter, reading; but it is the play of a butterfly fancy around the flower of which Mr. Mabie is studying the root and the seed. Hers is the flashlight of wit; his the steady, subdued, yet penetrating illumination of humor. It was said of these " Essays in Idleness " that they vexed an expectant appetite. Her last volume more nearly justifies the expectation that was aroused by the first. The cleverness is maintained: but the work has a more modern tone, more actuality; and it is pleasant to see her emerge at times from the quotations behind which she is too wont to mask her thought as behind a cloud of witnesses and give us a less interrupted enjoyment of her own mind. Probably none will ever read Miss Repplier for instruction: but she affords a charming recreation for minds of gentle nurture; and her gospel of the joyous life in letters is a beneficence in this age of excrescent naturalism.

And so, as one reviews the field of American letters, one may take heart of grace to say that our development in no way lags behind that of England, that it has in it the promise of an evolution as brilliant, as varied, and perhaps more critically sound. Above all it is independent, and so is contributing an important, perhaps an essential, part to the growth of a distinctly national literature.

BENJAMIN W. WELLS.

PAUL BOURGET.

SUAVE elegances; little barons, countesses; white-and-pink tailor-dressed blondes; swells who sport themselves with equal "sveltness" under a Palermo sun or in a London fog; dreams of deep foliage in gorgeous conservatories; soft lamps, capped by shades of supple silk; yachts, resplendent with golden ornaments, replete with luxuries of all kinds, and bright with feminine beauty of various types,—real floating strong-boxes, the property of wonderful Americans whose hearts are as rich in beautiful and delicate feelings as are their bank-accounts in redundant cyphers,—such are the personages and the surroundings Bourget loves to introduce and describe in his novels.

An intense care for *souls* seems only to have increased our author's preoccupation about *things;* and though physiology has not with him, as with the Goncourts and with Zola, encroached upon psychology, yet upholstery, dress, fashions, and "five-o'clocks" occupy a most prominent position in all his books. Thus it happens that most of Bourget's personages express their inner being more by their tastes than by their feelings; these tastes themselves being so strongly influenced by the atmosphere of frivolity surrounding them, that, freed from its pressure, their possessors might become quite different persons. We can imagine a *Noëmie Hurtrel* ("L'Irreparable"), for instance, a *Hélène Chazel* ("Un Crime d'Amour") or an *Ely de Carlsberg* ("Une Idylle tragique") entirely other than what they are, if the surplus of money and leisure which leads to their errors were taken from them—especially *Noëmie Hurtrel*, who, betrayed by a libertine, proves herself victorious over the commonly resulting deterioration of character; thus showing what elements of real individuality resided in her, could she but have freed herself from the empty frivolity of her surroundings. Bourget's heroes and heroines follow but too often the moral bent of their circumstances. This subordination of the inner personality to the outward pressure of *entourage* leads at times to strange conclusions; as in the case of *Hélène Chazel*, when she speaks admiringly to *de Querne* of her past purity: "Quand je me suis donnée à vous j'étais si pure. Je n'avais rien, rien sur ma conscience." If *Hélène Chazel*,

32

the prototype of hysterical amorous fantasy, and *de Querne*, the perfection of cold-heartedness, are true representatives of modern lovers in the France of the nineteenth century, the depopulation of that country should be looked upon as a blessing.   The posterity of such a couple could only be regarded as calamitous.   As to *Mme. de Carlsberg*, who is introduced as a romantic type of the woman *à grandes passions*, what shall the reader infer of these *grandes passions* when, before he has reached the third chapter of the book, he discovers that she is already entering with *Hautefeuille* on her third love experience?   Now, without going back to Mérimée's "Carmen," it would be a matter of difficulty to find among the fathers of romance in France one who would trust in the reader's good-will enough to beg for his interest and sympathy in favor of a lady whose *grandes passions* are as multifarious as her caprices, and who really designates as "passions" what scarcely deserve a name at once so grave and so implicitly tragic. Incoherence of character is met with in Bourget's novels not only with regard to women, but quite as commonly with his men.   *De Querne*, for example, is sketched as a *roué* and a *Lovelace;* but he suddenly becomes a Vincent de Paul, and this transformation of a *Don Juan* into a henpecked lover is no less a matter of wonderment to the reader than the curious quality of the *grandes passions* of *Mme. de Carlsberg*.

Regarded in the treble character of poet, critic, and novelist, Bourget strikes me as being truer to himself as a critic—in his studies of contemporary writers, for instance—than he is as a novelist.   His essays on contemporary psychology are truer to life and less characterized by contradictions than the psychology of some of his fictitious personages.   The emotional world is not his natural fatherland: the world of passion comes to him rather through the imagination than through the feelings.   It is in the brain-world, in the intellect proper, that he dwells more naturally.   " Beauty," he writes, " is made up of lyrism, of the splendor of what the eye can see, of the magic of dreams."   Dreams, power of evocation, lyrism,—three decided operations of the brain rather than of the feelings.   The gift of observation itself, according to him, is but the result of the atavism of confession among Roman Catholics, the outcome of the habit of self-examination, —another brain-sport, which in his eyes has led to the knowledge of others through the study of self.   This last conclusion, as to confession leading to depth of observation, appears to me dubious, inasmuch as none are assured whether the parents of Balzac, of George Sand, or of Dumas, were fast practisers of the rite.   Moreover, what would become of all the English school of romancers—Richardson, Fielding, Sterne, George Eliot—if Protestants, who do not confess, were to be bereft of the literary gifts which, according to Bourget, confession alone can confer? Whether or not the practice of self-examination, in view of such religious act, is beneficial to the romancer's mission as an observer of humanity, remains unanswered; but that the power of observation in itself is held by Bourget as the main gift of the novelist, his works sufficiently show. With Bourget the intellectual effort is held above the impulse of natural inspiration. A man of great parts, of observation; a reproducer of what he sees, a sketcher of what he reads, far more than a sensitive philosopher who, subordinating his emotional capacities to the modification of his reason, writes the history of *lived* incidents and experienced passions,—such appears to me Bourget the novelist.

Men and women the luxury and leisure of whose social position naturally lead to a life of emptiness, are those whom Bourget chooses most frequently to depict. Vainly in all his works should we seek the study of a rural individuality such as Balzac, Mme. Sand, George Eliot, have immortalized. Let us but alter in imagination the worldly circumstances of a *Suzanne Moraines* ("Mensonges"), or an *Ely de Carlsberg*, and we at once strike at the very source of their moral life. If we suppose these ladies empty at pocket and overburdened with home duties, we at once destroy the very essence of their passion-life; as this only finds its root in the outward worldly exchange of parties and meetings, which cannot exist without an abundance of money. Every incident of the heart-life of Bourget's heroes and heroines is subservient to this or that worldly circumstance, which will bring together or tear asunder the loving couples whose reunion or separation is generally dependent upon social evolution. On the other hand what has the world to say to a *Eugénie Grandet's* feelings, to an *Adam Bede's* emotions, to an *Emma Bovary's* desires? These characters are human. They bear the stamp of no period, the fashions of no epoch. They who invented them searched for their patterns among human hearts. Bourget's personages, on the contrary, are essentially factitious; they move in an atmosphere redolent of opopanax and musk. Their emotions emanate from their brains long before they are felt by their hearts.

The social *milieu* in which Bourget's men develop is, it should be mentioned to a foreign reader, the least really French that can be imagined. Long before he wrote his "Cosmopolis" our author lived in, and inspired himself from, the rich Israelitish colony resident in

Paris. Money, beauty, culture, are to be found in that society, and precisely in the order in which I mention them; viz., money, as the autocrat; beauty as the means to money; and culture as the servant of both—or more truly as the spice, the relish which comes in opportunely to testify to the omnipotence of money and to show how well-arranged dinners and ably managed receptions bring the pride of Horaces to composition in our days, as they did in the time of Augustus. From this very "goldy" society, where truffles pave the road to orders for paintings, and the smiles of love buy at a cheaper rate the homage of Academicians; from this particularly un-French society, where the only fatherland is wealth, has Bourget taken most of his types. As *Emma Bovary*, *Germinie Lacerteux*, or *Denise* ("Au Bonheur des Dames," by Zola) are unmistakably good or bad, yet nevertheless *true*, types; just as these personages are French, and necessarily French, so, on the other hand, *Suzanne Moraines*, *Hélène Chazel*, *Noëmie Hurtrel*, are cosmopolitanized Frenchwomen,—women who, though brought up and living in Paris, have been thrown so much among un-French elements as to lose the characteristics of their race.

"La Française est avant tout une femme de tête." I will not discuss here the question of the merits or demerits which this assertion involves: I simply state the fact. In following her reason the Frenchwoman comes to the same self-denial as often as she might do in following nobler feelings; but the basis of her character is reason. In the name of reason she marries; in the name of reason she hoards; in the name of reason she even lies. Now, reason being eminently opposed to mere sensual enjoyment, none can be farther from a *Eugénie Grandet* or a *Mme. Narueffe* than a *Hélène Chazel* or a *Noëmie Hurtrel.* Balzac's heroines, whether in the order of passion or in the order of virtue, always fight, and sometimes conquer. Bourget's heroines are mostly possessed of that Semitic indifference and *laisser aller* in the moral world which is a remnant of orientalism.

Enjoyment by all bodily means is the natural tendency of modern Jewish society, newly admitted to and intoxicated by the privileges of equality with those who, not a century ago, burned and hanged them; and from this society Bourget drew the concepts of most of his feminine types. Of the austere, mass-going, humbly dressed *grande dame française*, Bourget's novels· are ignorant. Cosmopolis is his world. His mission has been to initiate the French reader into cosmopolitan Paris society. Even when his ladies seem French they are not so; in their souls, or in their habits. Bourget is a subtle psychologist;

but the psychology he practises in most of his types is the psychology of a rather newly modified French personality. A foreigner, after reading his books, would fancy he had there approached real French society, and, being unable to reconcile in any way the outlines of Balzac's personages with those of Bourget,—the difference of time and period not accounting sufficiently for the gulf between them,—would naturally conclude either that these romancers cannot have painted personages of the same country, or that one of them is inexact.

Another peculiarity in Bourget, very suggestive of the modifications undergone by young *viveurs* of our time, is the way in which his heroes, *de Querne* and *du Prat*, for instance, turn, before ending in a vague humanitarianism, to a vague Tolstoïism,—in fact to that kind of idealistic anxiety which has come to novel-writers in France through Ibsen and the Northern school. Flaubert as well as Balzac, and Maupassant equally with Flaubert,—both being French to the core,—have introduced metaphysical suggestions in their human studies ; but the psychologist of modern modified Frenchmen and Frenchwomen is, more than any other—Paul Bourget. Let the foreign reader see in him the very faithful painter of a fraction of Parisian society essentially modified by Israelitish and cosmopolitan elements ; of a world which is not what the French call " la société " ; of a world where wealth plays the part of birth in the Old France and of brain-power in the rising democracy. Remembering that the pleasure-mad ladies and their empty-headed and empty-hearted lovers whom Bourget portrays are illustrations only of a very small minority of what Paris can boast in the way of un-French French people, foreigners who read " Mensonges," " Un Crime d'Amour," " Une Idylle tragique,". etc., run no risk of believing that *Suzanne Moraines* or *Hélène Chazel* are types of the ordinary French *bourgeoise* in good society. That there exist numbers of *Suzanne Moraines* among the best and choicest of social groups is not to be denied ; but to assert that venality in gallantry is as common with a certain order of the French world as in other countries would be a great error.

The world which Bourget has mostly painted is, as I have said, very un-French : it is a world of pleasure and of pleasure only. Bourget does not dwell, like Flaubert or Balzac, among all species of humanity, among provincials and Parisians, among poor and wealthy, among nobles and burghers,—no ; Bourget is the psychologist of *a* society. He very subtly, very delicately, and very powerfully paints the men and women of his country, who, by living as much as they

can out of the sphere of their own natural surroundings, by rushing to
Monte Carlo, to Cowes, to Rome, or anywhere where they may be
called by their own ennui and frivolity, become as unlike their own
native race as can be imagined.

Psychology proper is Bourget's best field of work; and, therefore,
before considering his novels, I shall first examine his studies on his
contemporaries. His " Essais de Psychologie contemporaine " are certainly among the best titles to fame of a writer whose critical faculties
are far superior to his powers of imagination.

I.

Bourget is a living antithesis to Zola. Not a personage, not a
situation in his books, but with Bourget it is radically in opposition
to what Zola would have made of it. Zola deals mostly with the uneducated classes : Bourget's first care, on the contrary, seems to be that
his heroes shall be wealthy and uncommon. Remarkable has been the
success which, from the very commencement of his career, has greeted
Bourget. No long fight with ill-fortune, but success from the appearance of his first verses, " La Vie inquiète," " Les Aveux," " Edel," etc.
Indeed all his earlier writings met with immediate appreciation. Of
the " Essais de Psychologie contemporaine," the studies of Baudelaire,
of Taine, of Renan, are the best.

In his " Baudelaire " our author starts with the destruction of all the
received theories about healthy or unhealthy literature. " There is no
such thing as health, or the contrary, in the world of the soul," writes
Bourget to the unmetaphysical observer. Our troubles, our faculties,
our virtues, our vices, our sacrifices, our volitions, are mere changeful
and variegated combinations,—normal *because* changeful. There exist
no healthy or unhealthy loves. Why should the loves of Daphnis
and Chloe be in any way healthier than the loves described by Baudelaire ? An overcrowded and meanly furnished boudoir is in no wise
more or less healthy than the trees under which Chloe meets her pas-
toral mate. In humanity health is never transferable to the psychological regions. Baudelaire appears to Bourget as *the* one who has
understood and painted the ennui of his period,—the yawnings and
gapings of the refined monster, due above all to the complications of
modern life, the over-refinement of our tears, and the sophisticated
nature of our gayeties, which have made us morally euphuists of the
inner life. " C'est de la préciosité morale." Bourget's Baudelaire is

a living and very true likeness because quite a literary one, devoid of any cantish *redites* about Baudelaire the man.

Our author's taste for wealthy society betrays itself in an aristocratical preference, which makes Renan dear to him above all others; for Renan is an enemy to the illiterate. With regard to Renan's exegetic performances, Bourget disclaims any enthusiasm. Faith to him is and must remain simple and childlike. Renan's dazzling rhetoric is too literary; meaning by that, perhaps, rather unevangelical. But then, Renan is such a writer! And style is in itself an aristocracy.

Whatever the gap between Baudelaire and Renan it is not greater than the distance between the classically critical ability of a Bourget and the powerfully creative gifts of a Flaubert. Still, Bourget's admiration for the "Norman bear" is deep and sincere; and if his natural bent necessarily leads him to the cult of cleverness rather than to that of spontaneous genius, Flaubert nevertheless receives, under Bourget's pen, a treatment in no way offensive to his worshippers. Pacing his study, Châteaubriand in hand, quoting aloud whole passages of "Atala," Flaubert should have been seen. One of his favorite paragraphs was, "Among the secular oaks the dazzling moon indiscreetly reveals to the wild old shores the mysteries of nature." "Images," writes Bourget, "with Flaubert, always preceded the outlived experience." Flaubert chiefly painted from his own intellectual conceit, rather than from remembrance. Images, and sound, *i.e.*, the sonority of a written phrase, were the inspiring principles of the author of "Salammbô." "I only know," he would say, "the worth of a phrase after I have sung it to myself." This undercurrent of lyrism in Flaubert himself accounts for the dreams and aspirations with which he has imbued *Emma Bovary's* wishes. In fact lyrism is a fundamental *leit motif* in "Mme. Bovary" and in "L'Éducation sentimentale: roman d'un jeune homme." It is in the incoherence of *Moreau* and *Emma's* lyrism contrasted with the banality and commonplaceness of their surroundings that the accuracy of these studies is seen. It is the discrepancy between the inner aspirations of *Emma Bovary* and her human possibilities which causes her to become the dupe of all those empty-headed creatures whom she mistakes for men such as she would wish them to be. The justification of these ways of his heroes and heroines is to be found in Flaubert's own words. "To escape the risk of being commonplace," he writes to the Goncourts, "men of my generation went in for suicide, comrades of mine blew their brains out, hanged themselves. These over-dramatic views

of life and death did not succeed in making me the least less selfish.
Though I could have shed tears enough over fictitious miseries to fill a
pond, I could remain as indifferent as a tree in the presence of real
sorrows and catastrophes." Save *Frederick Moreau*, who has at times
slight, very slight, touches of a *de Querne*, none of Flaubert's types at
all resembles any of Bourget's. Flaubert's personages are over-thinkers:
they die by living their thoughts. St. Anthony dies of too much
thought and love for his Christ: *Emma Bovary* dies of living her
divers dreams and her thoughts. And one of the best scenes portray-
ing this over-activity of mind is depicted in the passage quoted by
Bourget from "Madame Bovary," where the heads of husband and
wife, though meeting together on the pillow, wander so far from each
other in their imagination. *Charles Bovary* dreamed he was listening
to the breath of his child. He loved to think of her,—how she would
grow and develop. *Emma* imagined she was tearing away at the
gallop of four vigorous horses, hurrying on toward a country whence
they would never return,—her lover, and herself. The quotation is
not only humoristic, as showing the discrepancy between the grandilo-
quent dreams of *Emma* and the homely realities of her surroundings,
but it evidences the existence in Flaubert himself of that untiring
activity of mind with which he endows the personages of his invention.
Style was Flaubert's tormentor; and, though he has not said of himself
what Edmond de Goncourt said of Jules, "He died of style," still style
was his constant preoccupation. He touched and retouched, arranged,
altered, and would work whole nights hunting after perfection. "The
word and the thought," would he often repeat, "are one; the thought
is not outside the word: it is as inseparable from it as the word is inseparable from the phrase."

If Flaubert's personages think more than they act; if with them
speculation destroys action, with Bourget the reverse is often the case.
Had *Noëmie Hurtrel*, for instance, applied more of her meditative faculties to her own personal case, she would not have been driven to despair
and suicide. The same with *du Prat*. Both are victims to absence of
thought: they are mastered by events because they follow them with
the impulse of their natures.

Taine appears to Bourget only as the philosopher. Of Taine the
historian, the critic, the initiator of foreign thought in France, Bourget
makes utter neglect. The philosophical principles of Taine and Bourget
in regard to literature, however, are as contradictory as the methods of
Zola and Bourget in novel-writing. Bourget is a decided separatist,—

one who, like Descartes, entirely separates in humanity the promptings of the person and the suggestions of the soul. In the same being, according to Bourget, are two distinct impulses,—and not only distinct, but opposed,—the promptings of the spiritual being, and the promptings of the bodily being; seldom meeting toward the same conclusions. Taine's views, on the contrary, go to affirm that man is the result of a climate, of a group, of a pressure of ideas, of an atmosphere moral and real. Minutiæ is the characteristic of Bourget's philosophy and psychology; minutiæ to a defect; minutiæ about which Beyle would have certainly applied his remark, "La minutie en psychologie peut aller trop loin, lorsque, par exemple, elle transforme en hommes de simples manches à sabres!"

A "tonified" Baudelaire, a Renan freed from all anti-religious aggressiveness, a lion-like Flaubert in search of perfection, a softened, tender Beyle,[1]—such are the modifications that Bourget's delicate and subtle psychology has imposed upon the well-known writers whom he has studied. One of the excellences of these essays is their comprehensiveness. In all his models Bourget has shirked nothing. He has taken account of all contingencies; of the heart qualities and gifts as much as of the brain gifts. He writes :—

"There exist souls of election with whom the development of the mind and of the intellect is in no way detrimental to the full swing in them of the life of passion as well. In such natures, cerebral fever and creative powers are but an addition to the fermentations of natural normal life. The capacity of such natures for affection and love is increased instead of being destroyed by reason of their consciousness."

As Bourget's novel, "Le Disciple," is rather a work of pure dissective psychology than a romance of passion, it will find its natural place here, immediately after the psychological sketches, and before his other novels.

II.

The theme of "Le Disciple,"—well characterized "the diagnosis of others through the magnified study of self,"—such as it is, fastened itself upon Bourget's mind through a most tragic criminal case which happened in Algiers in the year 1889. A young man named Chambige, belonging to the French bureaucratic middle class, killed his mistress; failing afterward in his attempt to kill himself. During the

[1] Bourget's sketch of Beyle ("De Stendhal") gives quite a new and lovable aspect of the great critic.

interval of imprisonment between his arrest and his judgment, Chambige addressed most dithyrambic letters to Bourget, charging all the
contemporaneous novel-writers with having instigated his crime by the
spirit of pessimism prevalent in the modern literature of fiction.   The
verdict on Chambige was one of "irresponsibility"; and, shortly after
this true and terrible case, appeared "Le Disciple."   *Robert Greslou*,
the "disciple," is the acme and essence of the egotist.   The vaguest
movement of his own lungs is to *Greslou* a matter of the intensest significance.   He has kept a journal on his every palpitation since his
childhood.   He writes :—

> "At the age of twelve my faculties of observation were such, that one of my
> dearest wishes was to be in possession of the opinion my mother had formed of
> me.   I wished to compare what I really was with what was thought of me.   I
> waited for the occasion; and one day I listened to my mother's estimation of my-
> self in a conversation with a friend of hers.   The conclusion I drew from that day
> forward was, that between what I was and what she thought me to be there
> existed no more likeness than between my real visage and the reflection of it in a
> colored looking-glass."

Robert Greslou, an obscure professor, recriminates against the whole
world; and, knowing no limits to his aspirations, he considers himself
frustrated in all his desires simply because he fails in the satisfaction of
his ambition.   "Le Psychologie de Dieu," a book written by one *Prof.
Sixte*, who, under Bourget's pen, represents the modern pessimistic
doctrinarian, has made *Greslou* the passionate "disciple" of *Sixte*.
This book is one of pure speculation, the Professor being essentially
one of those innocent scientists after the fashion of Jean Paul Richter's
Maria Hilf—innocent but dangerous.   He plays with the most intricate cobwebs of moral life, quite unconscious of the perturbations his
conclusions—born of speculation purely—may induce if transported
from dreamland into real life.   In this book, which theorizes on
the passions generally, *Greslou* discovers elements which he resolves
upon applying in his own life,—methods, so to say, indifferent or
curious, and, speculatively speaking, in both cases harmless; whereas, ripened and working in an over-excited brain and a discontented
mind, they may become nefarious, if from the world of speculation
they are transferred to the world of action.   *Greslou* becomes tutor in
the household of the *Marquis de Jussat-Raudon*, where he promptly
decides upon playing to *Charlotte*, the daughter of his patron, the part
St. Preux played toward *Heloïse* in the work of Rousseau.   His success
is followed by both their deaths, for *Charlotte* poisons herself and *Greslou*
is shot dead by her brother.

"Le Disciple" is not only an implicit satire upon the danger of philosophers writing platonically upon passions unlived by them; but it also shows what havoc pessimistic doctrines of any kind may make among discontented souls. Love of self, carried to morbidity and crime, is the essence of "Le Disciple." Preoccupation of self, carried almost to monomania, forms the basis of *Noëmie Hurtrel.* With *Noëmie,* also, despair takes the place of remorse; but *Noëmie* was sufficiently armed by Bourget: she had brains and moral energy enough to rise by a strong effort of will above the unique and deleterious contemplation of *ego* which absorbs her very essence. False sensitiveness, taking the form of a sustained worship of "I," is the "case" of *Noëmie Hurtrel*; and such cases are common with our author. So common, indeed, that almost all his personages are moral cases;—*de Querne,* whose case is such absence of feeling that he cannot love; *Mme. de Carlsberg,* whose case is impossibility of fidelity in her affections; *Chazel,* whose case is such utter trust in those particularly who betray him that it is akin to lack of penetration. *Noëmie Hurtrel's* error of losing herself in over-meditation upon her own destiny prevents her from any useful undertaking. She leads a fruitless life, through the impossibility of tearing herself from herself.

III.

The brain, I repeat, is with Bourget the main dwelling of all the concepts of his heroes and heroines. Consequently the loves of these personages are oftener loves of the imagination than of the heart. "Un Crime d'Amour," which might as appropriately be entitled "Lack of Love," is the story of an artificial brain-love on the part of the hero, of a headlong caprice on the part of the heroine. "La Terre promise" tells of a little girl who will only know real love long after she has outlived the mild schoolgirl tale she hears at first. "Une Idylle tragique" is the story of a neurasthenic lady in search of passion through divers essays of dreamy fancies. The case of *Hélène Chazel* in "Un Crime d'Amour," as cases go, is far from being a new one: it is the hackneyed narrative of the husband's best friend alienating the wife. The only novelty in the matter is the descriptive mania of Bourget,—his dwelling upon screens, lamp-shades, bookcases, carpets, upholstery of every known kind, long after the reader is entitled to expect that the portrait of the heroes should replace the sketch of things belonging to the surrounding frame. If the errors of moral insight which abound in "Un Crime d'Amour" happened only to *Hélène* and *de Querne,* love might justify them; but *Robert Greslou, Mme. de Carlsberg, Hautefeuille,* err in the same way with regard to their own inner status. Is this then the error of the author himself? Or do the falsified views of the characters of his imagination impose their own crooked conclusions on the novelist? It is easier in such matters to estimate results than to perceive causes. The results of these strange morals are for women to betray the most trusting husbands, believing themselves angels, and for *Lovelaces* to turn to Vincents de Paul. Unexpectedly strange and curiously unsound, to say the least! A beautiful feeling of humanitarian sympathy gleams through "Un Crime d'Amour" toward the close, however, making it end more pathetically than it began. *De Querne,* speculating on the difficulties which exist for the philosopher who would rest assured that the explanation of earthly life is to be given in Paradise, and on the emptiness of man's destiny when deprived of future rewards, concludes that the solidarity of misery is in itself a sufficient cause for man to brace himself to the short-lived and dolorous effort of living. *Noëmie Hurtrel,* in "L'Irreparable," is again a variety of *de Querne,* in so far that the key of her nature is a morbid brooding over a tragic event of which she has been the victim.

An impulsive, unconscious creature is *Noëmie,*—unconscious, at least, of any effort to rise above the events which assail her; and though Bourget has at first shown her to the reader as a woman of culture and intellectual aspirations, his opinion of her species is so willingly, so purposely, a misestimating one, that he endows her with no wish to abstract herself from self-absorption either by study or by humanitarian deeds of any sort. We are informed by the author that *Noëmie Hurtrel* is one of those modern dabblers in philosophy who meddle in Schopenhauer and Kant, in the subjective and the objective; one of those who read, perhaps, rather than assimilate, and whose only wish, if they do assimilate, is to re-talk what they have absorbed. Though the woman who should cure a heartsore with an application of Plato would be very unwomanly indeed if she proceeded thus in the acute period of her trouble, yet a woman whose mind is at all developed, as Bourget insists in telling us *Noëmie Hurtrel's* was, might at least make an effort of some kind. The self-abandonment of *Noëmie* can only be accounted for by the ineffaceable trace in her heart of the injury inflicted on her at her start in life. She has been weakened gradually through the passing years by the remembrance of a slur. She would have confessed to *Lord Wadham* and poured out all her heart into his; but *Lord Wadham* has no such element as a heart in him, and *Noëmie* is thrown back upon herself, till, hypnotized by her fixed idea and unable to battle any more, she walks out of existence. "Morte pour rien" is the best epitome of the whole drama,—"died uselessly," as she had lived uselessly. More religious or more frivolous, *Noëmie* would have reconquered herself, as *Henriette Scilly* and *Ely de Carlsberg* did,—the one through the nobility of her unbending and rather childish dignity; the other through her love of the world.

Henriette Scilly, however, rises to the complete sacrifice of self by intense religious feeling. She has gone to Palermo with her mother and her future husband, *Francis Nayrac*, when, on an unlucky day, *Pauline Raffraye* projects herself on *Henriette's* horizon. This lady is accompanied by a little girl of about ten years, the daughter of *Francis Nayrac* and *Pauline* in past years. *Henriette* speaks to the child; and the guardedness of the child's answers, as well as some secret instinct, prompts *Henriette* to guess that there exists some bond between *Nayrac* and the child's mother. Meanwhile *Pauline* dies. The old and much-used system of hearing through open doors serves *Henriette*. She hears a prolonged explanation between her mother and *Nayrac*, and perceives that the discussion turns upon the adoption by *Nayrac* of the little girl. *Henriette* at once resolves upon giving up her marriage; thus sacrificing herself, and leaving the father entirely to his duties. She refuses to hear any of *Nayrac's* prayers. Occasions to express himself pessimistically about women are almost as dear to Bourget as to Dumas *fils*. Traitoresses and false women abound in his books. However this may be, *Henriette Scilly's* sacrifice is such that, though the reader is not led to believe in any possibility of relenting on her part, yet it may be inferred that as time passes she will some day think of father and child and, perhaps, alter her decision.

"La Terre promise" is a mild book. It holds in Bourget's works about the same place as the "Rêve" holds in Zola's. It is a book of courtship to the Académie, written in a widely different order of thought from "Une Idylle tragique," for instance. The evolution from a *Suzanne Moraines* to the heroine of "Notre Cœur" is rich in varieties of types. At Bourget's starting-point his heroes are mostly pleasure-seeking men and women. *Suzanne Moraines* is a modern *Manon Lescaut* without the generous heart of her prototype.

His journey to America has marked in Bourget a new era. Till then the saddest sides of the society of all great cities are exploited by our author: venality, adultery, lying, and dishonesty of every kind are his favorite themes. In *Ely de Carlsberg*, at least, we are brought face to face with a disinterested, but certainly very changeful, heart; for, in the space of a very few chapters, we see her love three different men. At the beginning of the book she has already loved *Olivier du Prat*, married the *Archduke*, and begun her liaison with *Pierre Hautefeuille*. *Ely* is a victim to her tyrannic *Archduke*,—an archduke of the modern pattern, a scientist with a laboratory and a young secretary who receives for all his work nought but ill words and hard dealings. *Ely* has met *Olivier du Prat* at Rome; and *Olivier* has since married. Now he has come to Monte Carlo, where he meets *Pierre Hautefeuille*, his former college chum. Hearing of *Hautefeuille's* success with *Mme. de Carlsberg* he grows restless, and, after various attempts at reinstating his friendship with *Pierre*, finally abandons himself to the return of his love for *Ely*, going so far as to introduce himself one night into the *Archduke's* garden. The *Archduke*, who is more despotic than jealous, discovers him, his *aide* shoots at haphazard, and *Olivier* falls dead. Henceforward *Hautefeuille* and *Mme. de Carlsberg* are forever divided by *Olivier's* death. All around *Mme. de Carlsberg* in this book are grouped most humoristic sketches,— *Fregoso*, the Genoese owner of a beautiful gallery, for instance ; *Marsh*, the American, and his niece *Flossie*. *Marsh* is a sentimental millionaire whose yacht contains a chapel dedicated to the memory of a deceased daughter of his, a girl of seventeen. Her marble statue is the object on his part of a cult, and to this holy room none are admitted save in the attitude of prayer. The amalgam in *Richard Marsh* of money, love, generous chivalry, gaudiness, and simplicity ; the diverse moods in which he alternately treats those whom he helps as a tribe of paupers, or with delicacy seeks the means of being to them a providence ;—these contradictions in his character, the natural results of a lack of the polish which education gives and which fails the self-made nabob, are most carefully depicted by Bourget; cosmopolitanism, as I have already said, being his most distinctive feature.

The women of Bourget's novels are mostly captivating conversationalists,—because Bourget himself is the talker,—but their brains never react upon their doings. All are, more or less, as empty of purpose as poor *Noëmie Hurtrel*, though all do not go to the same extremes. A reëdition of *Noëmie* is to be found in "Deuxième Amour," though this time the victim, *Claire*, executes her heart, while remaining alive. *Claire* has been married very young to a man whom she discovers to be a thief. Her horror of him combined with her love for another causes her to elope with *Gerard*. A short experience of

Gerard, however, dispels all illusions from *Claire.* This one is not a thief; but he lacks delicacy of feeling, which she finds at last in a friend of *Gerard,* whom she loves for himself, not with the wish of getting away from such a low character as her husband. This love, however, she renounces, and *Elie,* receiving the letter in which she announces that he will never see her again, states that he now knows "ce que c'est qu'un grand amour,"—that great loves are great, fruitful tortures, through which souls rise to their highest levels. Among "Profils perdus" let us mark also the Russian doctoress. "She would accept my compliments and *empressements* with her placid, masculine look; her speeches upon love, death, maternity, and all other subjects were of the coarsest materialism; and, as one listened to her, one felt her very hand was virgin of a man's kiss." In fact, a rather neurasthenic humanity in search of duality of feeling,—a humanity preoccupied with the study of its soul through the medium of its intellect, and in counting the pulsations of its brain. Such is the humanity Bourget shows us. It may well be said of our novelist that he is innocent of the creation of a single simple nature.

IV.

Whether sophisticated and complicated through the multiplicity of their contradictory feelings or through the pursuit of making apparent their inner life, Bourget's creatures are never simple. They are not simple because in them effects do not follow causes in a normal, natural way. Love, generous love, great love, is full blown in Bourget's heroines. Yet the heart, instead of following the bent of self-forgetfulness, which is the effect of real love, goes farther and farther on the road of selfishness; and the anomaly is seen throughout Bourget's books of a nature at once generous in its feelings and egotistical in its life. The men and women we read of in Bourget's novels are morally so deficient that their will never interferes to help them in the hour of need, —cold, reasoning, pleasure-seekers, snobs, creatures in whom even instinct seems a product of the brain, so factitious and unnatural are they.

As to Bourget's attempts at cynicism, they are very mild indeed. He, however, seems to believe no one ever tied together such astoundingly contradictory assertions as that, for instance, in "Cruelle Énigme," that the man who had worshipped a woman for her purity was held to her next by the lowest resources of sensuality! "The wildest physical desires may be felt simultaneously with the sincerest contempt." What is there so new in all this? Above all, what, critically speaking, is this method of proximating "physical desires" and "contempt"? Why this confusion of physiology and psychology? Most of Bourget's lovers fall to the description Renè Dorimée gives of the modern young man. "They are mostly," writes Dorimée, "poor attenuated creatures whom maternal spoiling and over-universitarian work has altogether destroyed." Zola has taken life in its whole. Maupassant has selected physiology and psychology. Bourget's principal merit is his sincerity about a certain world—a world where moral nullity is the result of over-leisure.

Bourget is in the realm of romance what Frederick Amiel is in the realm of thinkers and philosophers—a subtle, ingenious, highly gifted, but partial student of his time; rather prone, however, to what is easy and abnormal than to what is real and natural. With a wonderful dexterity of pen, a very acute, almost womanly, intuition, and a rare morbidity of grace about all his writings, it is probable that Bourget will remain more known as a critic than as a romancer.

The personages he has created will be short-lived. *De Quernes* and *Larchers* will, necessarily, be replaced by the generations of athletic men whom modern sports are developing; and as to *Mmes. Moraines*, *Chazel*, and others,—these were, after all, but refashioned *Narueffes* and *Meingens* out of Balzac's *Comédie humaine*. It may be said of Bourget, as it was of Musset, that his glass is small; but, whereas Musset filled his glass with his own soul, Bourget has filled his with souls so artificial and so factitious that they will evaporate, and of Bourget the novelist leave certainly less than of Bourget the critic.

YETTA BLAZE DE BURY.

The Forum

JULY, 1897.

THE POWERS AND THE GRÆCO-TURKISH WAR.

It is, perhaps, presumptuous for a writer in this country, who is neither diplomat nor soldier, nor yet in a position to know the secret springs of action which are influencing the Powers of Europe, to discuss the causes, the conduct, or the probable results of the recent brief war between Greece and Turkey. His judgment must be from the outside: it must be based upon documents which have seen the light, and can only guess at the hidden motives, the jealousies, the fears, the ambitions of the European governments. And yet, in our distance and in our lack of personal concern, may we not find reasons which will help us to take a calmer and broader view of the questions involved than would be possible in the case of a participant or of one vitally interested? We have the warmest sympathy for the doctrine of nationality which animates the Greek race,—a race more largely resident outside of Greece than in it. We see the advantage to civilization of the growth of constitutional government upon the edge of the despotic East, though that government may be weak and faulty. And we have a natural, a hereditary bias in favor of a people brave yet volatile, who represent to us the struggle for liberty in its early and later manifestations; whose history recalls to our minds Thermopylæ as well as Botzaris. Until the tongues of those who do know the real causes of the present situation are loosed, then, we may perhaps profitably consider some of its outward aspects, and without suspicion of leaning to the Turkish side.

At the conclusion of the Treaty of Vienna in 1815, Turkey-in-Europe was more than twice its present size. States have risen and

Copyright, 1896, by The Forum Publishing Company.

Permission to re-publish articles is reserved.

have fallen since then; but no other considerable state has sunk so low, has lost so much. That this should be true of the only non-Christian government in Europe is significant. It has not been the result of chance. What is the inference? It is this: that one of the serious problems of the century in Europe has been to get rid of Turkish sovereignty, and that this problem has gone a long way toward solution. For seventy years, step by step, various Turkish provinces have been wrested from the Porte, and, after a taste of the intermediate state of semi-sovereignty, have gained their independence. Thus the Ottoman Power in Europe has dwindled. Every man's hand was against it. Every war helped, every treaty sanctified the process; and the map of Europe since 1886 shows the result. The working out of the problem has been complicated and difficult. It has involved the decay of a strong military Power on the one hand: on the other, it has had constantly to face the jealousies of its own agents. So that whenever the process became too rapid, and threatened the aggrandizement of some particular state, then the rest called a halt. Turkey's enemies became her friends simply in their own defence.

Thus the "balance of power" principle has dominated the century. The problem was not only how to free European soil of Turkish dominion; but how to do it without a general embroilment. There was pressure tempered by fear—the fear of one another. Turkey's enemies hated her none the less when the pressure slackened; but they feared Russia more. This century-long problem has given to Europe a set of political policies, of ideals, even of phrases, too familiar to need illustration. It has also created in Europe an ever-present dread of the consequences of the Porte's overthrow,—a dark background which clouds the sense of present security. Now self-interest is the guide of national policies; and the essence of self-interest is fear.

In the course of working out the problem mentioned, the Greek kingdom was set up. It was the beneficiary of the "Concert of the Powers." In an interesting essay[1] published in 1884, the English publicist, Mr. T. J. Lawrence, derives the European Concert from the combination of states which overcame Napoleon. Tracing the growth of this policy of concord, he shows how it was jeopardized by the principle of absolutism which found expression in the Holy Alliance, yet survived, and exists as a kind of general committee to superintend the affairs of Europe. Oftentimes the Concert falls short of its duty; sometimes it exceeds it; other leagues may coexist with it or within it; war

[1] "Essays on Modern International Law." London, 1884.

between its members may suspend it. But its growth has been natural; its existence may therefore be prolonged, if not permanent; and its object is peace. Mr. Lawrence even finds in it the possible germ of a High Court of Appeal, and argues that the old doctrine of the equality of states must yield, has yielded, to the right òf superintendence lodged in the hands of the six great Powers.

We need not go to such lengths as this. We may believe that the European Concert is governed by the lower as well as by the higher motives; by selfishness, distrust, and fear, as well as by the spirit of peace and goodwill to men. Nevertheless we cannot fail to see in it the dominating influence in Europe for nearly a century. It created Belgium and settled its international status. It neutralized Switzerland and Savoy, Luxemburg, and the Suez Canal. It has opened the rivers of Europe to commerce, has abolished privateering, has granted invaluable privileges to neutral trade, has twice checked Russian encroachment upon Turkey. And Greece, in particular, has been its ward, its beneficiary. At Navarino, in 1827, the Powers carved a Greek state out of Turkey, though leaving it under Turkish suzerainty. The line ran from the Gulf of Volo to that of Arta, through the mountain range of Othrys, where the Turkish advance was recently stopped by armistice. Thessaly and Epirus were expressly excluded and left in Turkish hands, because they had not earned freedom through insurrection.

In 1832, the Concert gave Greece independence and a king, under the guarantee of Great Britain, France, and Russia.

The Concert was interrupted, or tested, in 1856. But, though Russia was checked, and Turkey's integrity guaranteed, the former lost no territory; while the latter was constrained to grant equal rights to her Christian subjects, and to confirm the privileges of Moldavia, Wallachia, and Servia. When Greece showed signs of uneasiness during that war, the Powers "protected" and occupied her.

In 1863, by the Treaty of London, Great Britain ceded her rights in the Ionian Islands to Greece, the Concert authorizing the annexation. That same year the Greeks demanded a new king; and the Powers acquiesced in their second choice, Prince George of Denmark.

Six years later, Greece again became troublesome. Her Cretan neighbors and kinsmen had been massacred by their masters in thousands; and Greece could not but try to help and save them. But a solemn "Declaration of the Allied Powers relative to the obligations of Greece toward Turkey" forbade such conduct.

The next decade was a very troubled one in Southeastern Europe.

Turkish atrocities in Bulgaria led to Russian intervention; and the Russian war profited the Danubian peoples. Greece, too, saw her opportunity, and, starting an outbreak in Thessaly, prepared to use it. With threats and with promises she was quieted. The dismemberment must not come too fast. At San Stefano Russia dictated terms to Turkey: but the other Powers had the last word; and at Berlin Russia was shorn of the fruits of her victory.

In the treaty framed by the Berlin Congress in 1878, Roumania, Bulgaria, Servia, Montenegro,—every little state except Greece,—were taken care of. Greece ardently desired Thessaly and Epirus. In the thirteenth protocol of the Berlin Congress (an ill-omened number), she was given the promise of an increase of territory, as in the interest of the peace of Europe. The frontier suggested was to run from the Salembria to Kalamos on the Ionian Sea. This would include Janina as well as Larissa. But, unfortunately, no specific annexation was decided on: Greece was merely encouraged to negotiate with Turkey directly. The Congress also declared that the Greek provinces of Turkey, with Crete, should, in accordance with the Treaty of San Stefano, receive autonomy, secured by a European guarantee; and the Powers were to offer their good offices toward this end. And so, with respect to the Greeks and to Greece, everything was left to the future. In the Treaty itself there was only this reference:—

"If the Porte and Greece shall not succeed in agreeing upon the rectification of frontier indicated in the Thirteenth Protocol of the Congress of Berlin, Germany, Austria-Hungary, France, Great Britain, Italy, and Russia reserve the right of mediation to help out the two parties in their negotiations."—ART. xxiv.

Could anything have been vaguer? Like the reforms promised by the Porte in Epirus, Thessaly, and Crete, this indefinite proviso needed pressure to be realized. Accordingly the Greeks, taking to heart the experience of the past, began to agitate, in order to obtain a hearing and their treaty rights. This plan worked. The Berlin Conference was reopened to discuss the Greek frontier; but no Greek representative was admitted. This was ominous. Montenegro, also, found it hard to get her treaty rights. Clearly more agitation was needed; so the Greeks made ready to seize Epirus and Thessaly. The Powers prevented such an impertinence, but called a fresh conference at Constantinople for the following year (1881). This failed to make good the promises of the Berlin Congress; but, after a tedious diplomatic struggle, it did award Thessaly and an insignificant portion of Epirus to Greece. Turkey had offered to cede Crete and to allow a slight rectification of frontier; but the Powers, under the lead of Great Britain, insisted upon the cession of Thessaly, with a frontier which followed the mountain-divide north of the Vale of Tempe, crossed the principal branch of the Salembria River, ran along the mountain-crest westerly, then struck and descended the Arta to its mouth in the gulf of that name. This was as much as could be wrung out of Turkey, unless as the result of a successful war waged by Greece against her.

Though accepting this line, Greece was far from being satisfied with it, and in 1886 armed, and tried to seize Epirus. Once more the Concert asserted itself, and, by a month's pacific blockade of the Greek coast, put on the straitjacket. This brings us to the threshold of present events. The narrative illustrates also—and this is my immediate object—the constant control of Greek affairs which the Concert has asserted. Greece has been created, enlarged, restrained, bullied, and rewarded according to the dictates of the moment. The Concert gave and the Concert hath taken away,—yet the name of the Concert has not been altogether blessed.

In the light of this constant intervention, to speak of the equality of Greece in the family of nations, in any other than an abstract sense, is an absurdity. Whatever the law, whatever her rights, in fact she has been a protected state under the care of a committee of the Powers, whose policy has been shifting, contradictory, the result of compromise, but with this end ever in view,—to avoid the danger of a general embroilment. This danger is not imaginary. Even a trivial outbreak, if not sternly dealt with, may bring it on. It is the alternative to the maintenance of the Concert. It means widespread destruction of credits, public and private. It means new frontiers, perhaps new states. It means the unknown. For half a century and more, it has been the nightmare of Europe. Fear of it is the key to the situation.

Let us turn now to the present complication. Once more Greece has disturbed the peace and quiet of the Concert. Animated by a strong sense of nationality and of sympathy for those of her race still under Turkish rule; smarting, too, under the failure to secure that increase of domain of which the Treaty of Berlin held out the expectation, she has put in practice once again the well-proved policy of growth by agitation. She has rights under treaty which cannot be realized; and so in truth have others. Russia has never been paid the Turkish indemnity promised at San Stefano. Crete and Epirus have never been granted autonomy or the reforms prescribed at Berlin. Without multiplying instances, it is enough to say that international law and treaty obligations have fared hardly at the hands of all parties.   When Lord Salisbury declared, therefore, that the policy of the Powers was to preserve peace by the strict observance of international obligations, we must interpret him liberally.   For *observance* perhaps he meant *avoidance.*

The trouble began in Crete.   During 1895 the humanity and moral sense of the civilized world had been shocked by one of those strange outbreaks of Turkish ferocity, which are so foreign to our ideas of economics, of religion, of law, as to be incomprehensible.   Accordingly, when, early in 1897, a similar catastrophe seemed to be impending in Crete, the Christian world, particularly in Greece, took alarm. This was the more natural, as only thirty years earlier—and since then also—frightful cruelties had been committed in this same island by the Turks, while putting down a popular rising.

By the first week in February, the fighting throughout Crete had become general.   The result is well known.   Anarchy spread.   Five thousand Christians in Canea were defeated, sought refuge upon the shipping in the harbor, and were carried to Greece.   It was announced that the Porte intended to land more troops and restore authority. Then the Greek king determined to risk his throne, and sent a fleet to Crete to deport fugitives and prevent Turkish reinforcements.   Possibly he would have risked his throne had he *not* sent it.   Col. Vassos, with an expedition of two thousand men, was also landed on the island; and the Cretans flocked to his standard.   Then the Powers interfered as in duty bound, sent ships to Crete, landed marines, tried to protect the weak of all races, and even fired upon the Christian insurgents.   Their policy was to set up an autonomous government under the suzerainty of the Porte, enforcing the withdrawal of the Greek troops, and leaving a small Turkish garrison.

To secure obedience, as an *ultimatum* they ordered the evacuation of the Greek force in six days.   The Greek reply was a refusal, couched, however, in moderate and conciliatory terms.   It pleaded for annexation rather than autonomy, argued that order could be maintained only by Greek troops, and suggested a plebiscite.

In all this, Greece was technically in the wrong.   She had not been charged with the carrying out of Cretan reforms; so that in landing Vassos in Crete she was invading the rights of Turkey, Crete's master, without legal or treaty warrant.   What the real spring of Greek action was, we cannot say.

Yet whatever intrigue may lie hidden, whatever assurances may have been given to King George, whatever political necessity thus found expression, the action was entirely in line with much that had gone before; and the general object must have been to gain territory at the expense of Turkey, by worrying the Concert. As usual, the Concert responded by pressure. The curious details of its blockade of the Cretan coast are fresh in mind. It may be remarked, however, that this pacific-blockade usage is an abomination, a contradiction in terms. While denying the existence of war, it claims the rights of war. It is pure coercion applied by the strong to the weak. If the neutral trader is subjected to it, it is certainly illegal. Had there been traffic between Crete and the United States to be affected by it, our government should have declined to submit to such an imposition.

Bottled up in Crete, Greece continued her agitation in the north, mobilizing troops, and sending them to the Thessalian frontier. Turkey did the same; yet neither party desired to seem the aggressor. The Powers threatened an extension of their blockade to Greece itself, and warned both parties in these terms: "The Powers, being firmly resolved to maintain the general peace, have decided not to permit the aggressor in any case to reap the least advantage from such aggression."

The gathering forces remained inactive until the middle of April. While the two were manœuvring for position, certain irregular troops, equipped by the Greek patriotic society, Ethnikè Hetairia, were sent over the borders into both Epirus and Macedonia, to break communications and raise the country. This was an act for which, in spite of its disclaimer, the Greek government must be held responsible, as our own would be should it permit Fenian filibusters to raid across our frontier into Canada.

This movement caused the Concert great concern; nor had it adequate means of prevention. A Greek force penetrating Macedonia might be the signal for attack upon the Turkish flank by Montenegro and Servia and Bulgaria: it threatened just what the Powers were strenuously trying to guard against,—the break-up of Turkey-in-Europe before they were ready for it. No wonder then that Turkey had their sympathy and their backing. To their relief, these irregulars were driven back; but not until they had "drawn" Turkey. War was not declared: it came unheralded. Both contestants addressed circulars to the Powers, each charging the other with responsibility for the war. The Turkish circular disclaimed the idea of conquest, and promised to make peace if Greece withdrew her army from Crete and the Thessalian frontier; while Greece based her action upon the right of self-defence, and claimed an invasion of her soil.

Of the conduct and strategy of the war, it is too soon to speak. So far as appears, both combatants have observed the rules of modern warfare. The stories of Turkish barbarities have no authority and have been contradicted. The Turkish peasant farmer has shown his endurance, patience, and splendid soldierly qualities, as often before. The impotence of the Greek fleet is a puzzle. Perhaps Capt. Mahan has led us to expect too much from fleets. They can be effective only where circumstances permit. In 1870 they played no part. Here there was no army to carry and convoy, as in Corea, no rival fleet to engage, no capital city to attack with any chance of success.

Still we expected at least the appearance of activity, descents upon the coast, bombardments of fortified places, the landing of expeditionary forces to break communications and raise the country. Of this sort of work there has been little. May not the true explanation be, that the Powers warned the Greek government that the fleet must engage in no offensive work, under penalty of a blockade or even of its destruction. Such a demand might have shocked the moral sense of France and England, but would have been consistent with the policy of the Concert. The most significant facts in the contest have been: the sympathy of the civilized world for Greece, and the support given by European governments to Turkey. The breaking out of the war brought the Powers anxiety indescribable; for Servia and Bulgaria began to mobilize and to formulate their demands. Its progress restored their equanimity and apparent control of the situation; and Servia and Bulgaria subsided.

There came a moment in May when the reins slipped in the Concert's grasp. The fighting spirit of the Turk was up. Flushed with victory, he acted as if he were at liberty to reap its fruits. He aped the pretensions of a Power. Having conquered the whole of Thessaly, he actually threatened to keep it, and to insist upon a big indemnity besides, or else to refuse an armistice. But it was only for a moment. He was reminded of the warning at the outset, that, whatever the result of the war might be, neither party could be allowed to benefit by it. The Concert was a unit in denouncing his assurance; and the Porte speedily yielded.

In that speech of Lord Salisbury's, already quoted, he said further:

"The peculiarity of this strange crisis is that the war cannot be left to work out its natural results. It is impossible that Europe should allow Christian communities to fall under the Sultan's government. But it must not be supposed, because this doctrine throws its aegis over Greece, that, therefore, she is to be free from all penalties attaching to unwise or unrighteous action."

And again, speaking of both belligerents: "in the dim future no one could know to which of the two it might become necessary to appeal for a solution of problems that must be solved."

If this is to be construed as the voice of the Concert, it lays down with sufficient clearness the settlement intended,—a money indemnity, but no substantial cession of territory. Turkey, of course, must have something to show for her victory, else there might be an inconvenient and fanatical popular outbreak. This something, if it took the shape of hard cash, would undoubtedly suit the Sultan best, and perhaps the badly paid army likewise; but, the European creditors of Greece would hardly contemplate with equanimity fixed charges ahead of their own, and specifically secured as theirs are not. So that we may look to see the war indemnity pared down to the lowest sum practicable. A rectification of frontier in the Turkish interest is hardly necessary; for the present line, strategically speaking, is favorable enough.

It is true the Powers may have a struggle to enforce such terms; for, after all, they are playing with edged tools. Like the knives which the juggler whirls up into the air and catches with either hand, a slip or a falter, with them, may mean bloodshed. Yet Turkey is the ward of the Concert, no less than Greece,—a sullen, obstinate, disagreeable ward, yielding obedience under pressure only. It is improbable, one might venture to say impossible, that Turkey should set up its own will against the united will of the Powers. And at the present moment, in spite of the presence of its victorious army upon Christian soil, Turkey is weaker than ever. Her fleet has proved itself worthless; a hint of permission from her masters would let loose upon her two, if not three, separate attacks from the Balkan peoples. Each year reduces her, not to bankruptcy,—that she does not mind,—but nearer to inability to raise any money at all; though, in truth, it appears that a bankrupt state, like a bankrupt railway, is peculiarly adapted for war. And more than all this, the Armenian atrocities have so kindled public opinion in certain quarters as to make any policy of Turkish support far more difficult. She may delude herself for a moment with the idea that she can stand alone; but the dream cannot be realized. The same mighty forces are at work. The actors in this little tragedy are but as flies upon the wheel. The problem of the century still presses for solution.

And now, if our statement of this problem in its broadest aspect be correct, the present crisis may be, and should be made to serve as, a step onward. For Crete is still on the hands of the Powers. If Turkey is, and for seventy years has been, in process of dismemberment; if it is

the policy and to the interest of Christian Europe that the Turkish sovereignty should be expelled gradually,—avoiding the dangerous aggrandizement of any one state, and avoiding a general convulsion,—
then here is an opportunity.   Crete must never go back to Turkey.   It
has suffered in the past as much as Bulgaria or Armenia from Turkish
massacre.   Reforms have been promised it, in treaty terms, which have
never been realized.   Self-government and a withdrawal of Turkish
troops are now pledged to it, under conditions to ensure order.

This and more should be given it.   Its eventual lot should be decided by its own plebiscite; so that, after a certain probation, under the
guardianship of the Powers, Crete might be annexed to Greece, if it so
willed; but so that in any event it should be free from Turkish control
forever.   Its union with Greece is natural; whether the latter is to be
regarded as an eventual heir of Turkey or not.   Greece is a maritime
state capable of maintaining the connection.   The two are alike in race,
religion, and speech.   The union could balk no lawful and proper ambitions.   Such disposition would follow the line of least resistance.

Can the gradual settlement of the Eastern problem here outlined
continue to a final issue?   Who will succeed Turkey?   These are
great questions and variously answered.   " I am the heir," declares the
Russian.   " The apple must sometime drop into my capacious lap.   I
have waited.   I can wait."   " I am the heir," cries the Slav in the Bal-
kans.   " I am young and lusty.   I look forward and not back.   Give
me the spoils, make of me and mine one solid state, and the problem is
solved."   " I am the heir," says the Greek, " the heir of the ages.   I
represent beauty and civilization and the mighty past.   My speech, my
blood, are spread wide over the Levant.   Drive out and keep out the
barbarian.   The golden age will come again."   But we recall the religious intolerance, the boundless ambition, the awful despotism of
Russia, and draw back.   The blood of Stambuloff cries out against Bulgaria, and she stands but a puppet in another's hands.   Nor has Greece
deserved that noblest word of praise, " Thou hast been faithful over a
few things: I will make thee ruler over many things."

And so the problem is ever the same: its solution approaches ever
so slowly; and statesmen bend all their energies to avert the dreaded
catastrophe.   Greece has our sympathy, our pity, our affection; but
we can see and make allowance for the generation-long struggle of
the Powers also,—a struggle which takes on every aspect, of heartless
cruelty, of generous concession, of blind fear.   And the object of it is
peace—when there is no peace.   THEODORE S. WOOLSEY.

THE RIGHTS OF FOREIGNERS IN TURKEY.

THE attention of the world has of late been so often called to the anomalous position of the Ottoman Empire in the modern family of nations, and the peculiar relations which have grown up as the sole *modus vivendi* between it and its Christian neighbors are so imperfectly understood by Americans in general, that a brief explanation of the origin and growth of these relations seems to be called for ; the more so as our own relations with the Empire have recently assumed an unusual importance and gravity.

The Sublime Porte has long maintained with the outside world the externals, at least, of international comity. It has in foreign lands its embassies, legations, consulates, and agencies. It is bound to other nations by various treaties and conventions, some of them dating from the last century. Foreign capital and enterprise have endowed it with a semblance of material civilization; and it has even been admitted into the Universal Postal Union. But this admission to a *quasi*-equality with the nations about her has been accorded to Turkey, not as a matter of right, but of favor. It is the result of a series of concessions made by the other Powers for the benefit of the foreign element, in whose hands the commerce and industries of the country chiefly rest. The great Powers have, more than once, categorically refused to concede to the Turks, *quâ* Turks, equal rights with other independent nations.

Turkey is still in many respects a mediæval power, maintaining unchanged the religious and administrative traditions of the fifteenth century. The Ottomans have never assimilated the modern and Western culture. The " Young Turk " party, which has essayed to do this, is under the imperial proscription. The Turk has always camped in Europe, not built himself a home there. The *Rayas* (native Christians)—the still surviving populations of the conquered Byzantine provinces—have never been admitted to citizenship of any sort in the Empire; they have even been systematically excluded from the army, and deprived of any semblance of equal rights with the Moslems. Turkey has, in short, wholly failed to vindicate her claim to her conquered European provinces by the benefits of an ordinarily decent and far-seeing government.

It is because of the utterly irreconcilable antagonism between the mediæval Turkish system and modern ideas that the Powers have refused to Turkey the position and rights of an equal. Not only do they interfere in both the foreign and domestic affairs of the Porte, but they have always insisted on exacting for their own citizens in Turkey rights and privileges which they would not for a moment think of granting in return to Turks in their own domains. These peculiar rights and immunities, recognized in formal treaties, and made common to all the Treaty Powers by "most favored nation" clauses, are based on what are called the "Capitulations." These charters lie at the foundation of all intercourse between Turkey and the civilized world; and their origin and significance should be clearly understood by everyone who has more than a passing interest in Oriental affairs.

The Capitulations of the Ottoman Empire are a series of grants of privilege and immunity, accorded by various sultans to those Christian nations with which they have desired to maintain commercial or political intercourse. The name is derived from the sections or *capitula* into which they are divided. They were not originally treaties; for no Moslem could, under the Sacred Law,—the *Shariyé Sharîf*,—treat with Christian Powers as equals. "Mohammedan jurisprudence," says Van Dyck, "recognizes between Mohammedan and non-Mohammedan nations but one category of relations—that of *Djehâd* or Holy War."[1] By the Sacred Law all Giaours (Christian dogs) are under the ban. Yet, although devoted to destruction, they may be spared for a season, whenever this is for the advantage of Islam. Now the Mohammedan conquerors were a people neither commercial nor seafaring by instinct. It accordingly became necessary in the Middle Ages to encourage commerce with the West by concessions to the traders of Christendom; and it was this necessity which produced the Capitulations. These were called *Ahd-Namah* or *Tamassûk;* that is, letters of privilege, sworn promises, as from a superior to an inferior. They were concessions made from a purely selfish motive,—that of supplying the new empire with the commercial advantages and industries which the warlike conquerors were themselves incapable of maintaining; and there was neither the effort nor the desire to secure reciprocal

[1] VAN DYCK'S "Report on the Capitulations of the Ottoman Empire," in Senate Documents 1880-81, vol. III. I desire to express my great indebtedness to this admirable and exhaustive Report.

privileges for Turks in foreign lands. A Turkish colony under a
Christian ruler did not enter the conqueror's mind as even a remote
possibility.

The earliest authentic Capitulations appear to have been those
granted by the sultans of various Mediterranean Arab states, in the
twelfth century, to Florence and Pisa. These antedate by nearly three
hundred years the first of the Turkish grants,—that made by Mehmet
the Conqueror to the Genoese in 1453. Genoa at that time led in the commerce of Constantinople; maintaining in that city a merchant colony
with its own municipal administration and *Podestà*. Traces of the town-
wall and a portion of the Palazzo del Podestà of the Genoese *faubourg*
are still visible in the quarter called Galata; and the Genoese watch-
tower still dominates the north side of the Golden Horn. The Vene-
tians were the chief rivals of the Genoese; and to them the Conqueror
gave a Capitulation in the following year.

The privileges thus accorded were confirmed and enlarged repeatedly by Mehmet II himself, and by subsequent sultans. In 1528 Francis I secured from Soliman I, by a Capitulation, the confirmation of
privileges previously accorded to the French and Catalans. This in
its turn was confirmed and extended by later monarchs; the most
notable of its enlargements being that secured, in 1740, by Louis XV
from Mahmûd I, by which the rights, privileges, and immunities of
the French religious establishments—churches, hospitals, missions,
schools, and monasteries—were defined and greatly augmented. It is
by the application of the "most favored nation" clause to this Capitulation that the same rights and immunities are enjoyed by all the
Treaty Powers; and it is under its protection that the beneficent work
of the American missions has been conducted for nearly seventy years.
The earliest Capitulation to the English dates from 1579 (Murâd
[Amurath] III to Elizabeth); those to Holland, Austria, Russia, and
Prussia following respectively in 1598, 1606, 1711, and 1761.

With the gradual decay of the Ottoman Power and the advance of
the Christian nations, the Sublime Porte has been compelled to confirm
and perpetuate these one-sided grants by formal treaties, in spite of the
Sacred Law. In these treaties it is the Christian Powers who refuse to
enter into relations of reciprocal equality with Turkey. They refuse
because of the unchangeable character of Islam. No jot or tittle of the
Sacred Law has been, or ever can be, abrogated. No such thing exists,
under Islam, as international law or the inherent rights of humanity.
Death is still the only rightful portion of the unbeliever in the Faith,

There is, outside of the Capitulations or of compulsion by external power, no right of legation, no immunity of ambassadors, no right to the protection of life and property, to trial by one's peers, to immunity from arrest without due process of law, to testify in court, to be represented by an advocate, to travel, to carry on business, even to live, for any one not a Moslem. This is no mere theory: it is a fact, which of late has received awful proofs in Armenia. The Law of Nations is absolutely incompatible with Mohammedan principles. What, therefore, the Capitulations granted in 1453 to the Christians, as a necessity for the advantage of the Turk, the Christians now cling to and insist upon for their own advantage, as their only protection from the arbitrary and cruel oppressions of a Power which asks to be received into the comity of civilized nations, while rejecting every principle upon which that comity is based. The Capitulations are now the price of the friendship and amity of the civilized world towards Turkey.

Since 1861 every treaty has contained an identical clause,[1] making available for each Power all rights bestowed upon any other; so that with respect to the Capitulations, all Treaty Powers stand on a level. The several Capitulations, however various in form, entitle the foreigner in Turkey to the following privileges and immunities:—

I. Permission to enter Turkish territory, to navigate Turkish waters, and to travel, alike for trade and for pilgrimage, to holy places.

II. Freedom to follow the customs of one's own country, and to perform the rites and fulfil the duties of one's own religion.

III. Exemption from all taxes or tribute except customs duties.

IV. Judgment by one's own ambassador or consul in civil or criminal suits with a fellow-countryman, and enforcement of the decision by the help of the local authorities.

V. Civil causes between natives and foreigners tried in the local courts must be heard in the presence of the consul or his dragoman.

VI. So also in case of crimes of foreigners against natives, the consul or his dragoman must be present at the trial.

(In the more recent treaties, however, the jurisdiction in such cases is with the consul, not with the local courts; and under "most favored nation" clauses this provision is insisted upon by all the Powers, our own included. It is also specified that any foreigner arrested by the

[1] "All the rights, privileges, and immunities that the Sublime Porte now grants, or may hereafter grant, to the subjects, vessels, commerce, or navigation of any other foreign Power, the enjoyment of which it shall tolerate, shall likewise be accorded, and the exercise of the enjoyment of the same shall be allowed, to the subjects, ships, commerce, and navigation of. . . ."

local authorities shall be taken to the nearest consul of his nation, if not more than nine hours distant (about 27 miles): if there be none within that distance, he may be put in the local prison, and the legation or nearest consul notified.)

VII. Inviolability of the foreigner's domicile by Ottoman officers, unless accompanied by a deputy of the ambassador or consul, and then only in cases of urgent necessity.

VIII. The right of bequest, and of the administration by the consul of the estates of intestate foreigners of his nation.

IX. Prohibition of the extension to Ottomans or *Rayas* of protection and asylum by foreign ambassadors and consuls.

All these privileges belong of right to Americans[1] in Turkey; and nearly every one of them, at one time or another, has had to be invoked in their behalf. The most precious, and at the same time, to an American mind, the most anomalous of these privileges, is that of *ex-territoriality*, involved in the fourth, fifth, and sixth paragraphs of the above list. This recognizes the foreigner as practically under the jurisdiction of the courts of his own country, and amenable to their procedure. Although subject to all local laws and police regulations, and to arrest by the local authorities, he is under the constant protection of his own government, and must be tried by the consular courts, except in certain civil actions specified in the treaties. Thus in 1879, P. Mirzan, a naturalized American citizen, was tried before our Minister, Hon. Horace Maynard, for the murder of an Ottoman subject, Dr. Dahan, in Alexandria. He was sentenced to death; but, upon the commutation of his sentence, by President Hayes, to imprisonment for life, he was sent to the United States, where he died in prison some years later.

This singular restriction of the authority of the Porte within its own dominions is not unique in international relations. It is only within the last three years that the privileges of ex-territoriality have been abrogated in Japan by recently signed treaties with other Powers: they are still exacted of the Chinese government. Their justification, indeed their reason of existence, lies in the irresponsible and untrustworthy character of the courts and legal procedure of a country as yet imperfectly civilized. When one realizes that the testimony of a Christian is invalid in the Turkish courts, unless corroborated by a Moslem; that the word of one Moslem, however notoriously dishonest

[1] By Article IV of the Treaty of 1830; by the Treaty of 1862 (though this is claimed by Turkey to have expired); and by *adet* (usage) established or admitted by numerous official acts.

he may be, outweighs legally the testimony of a dozen reputable Christians ; and that legally valid Moslem testimony is often openly for sale or hire, one. begins to understand how necessary is some such protection against denials of justice.

Second only to this provision of the Capitulations in value, as a protection against arbitrary arrest and oppression, is the inviolability of the foreigner's domicile. The right of judicial or police visitation and search is not conceded to the Turkish government, for the simple reason that it cannot be trusted to exercise such a right with discretion or justice. The foreigner's house is his castle, even more truly than the Briton's house in his own island. The Turkish policeman and the military officer alike must stop at the door or gate of the foreigner's premises and wait for permission to enter. Not even the Sultan can pass the threshold against the owner's will, except in the company of a duly appointed deputy from the embassy or nearest consulate.

Such a restriction of the police functions of the government would, of course, not be tolerated by any Power not under foreign tutelage. In the Middle Ages, when all government was arbitrary and more or less irresponsible, such provisions and limitations of authority were not uncommon. Exemption from domiciliary visitation was in those days conceded by the sultans as an inducement to foreigners to settle in the Empire. It is now insisted upon by the Powers, because the conditions which made it necessary in 1453 have not been sensibly ameliorated.

Among many instances of its operation, I may cite one as an illustration. In 1894, the Turkish officials in the province of Aleppo, having accused certain of the Armenian professors in the American college at Aintab of conspiracy and sedition, and the college authorities of aiding and abetting the conspiracy, demanded permission to search the premises. Had this been accorded without reserve, there is not the slightest doubt but that the wished-for incriminating evidence would have been forthcoming, smuggled in by the officers appointed to discover it. Mr. Riddle, our efficient Secretary of Legation, was sent by the United States Minister, Mr. Terrell, to accompany the officers in the search, in accordance with this clause of the Capitulations. The officers were not in any way interfered with by the Secretary in the performance of their duties ; but they were closely watched from beginning to end. They were obliged to confess that they could not discover the slightest shred of evidence to support their allegations.

The Capitulations are a necessity of the situation. Only by their protection is the resident foreigner enabled to live, travel, worship, and do business without fear of constant interference and oppression. As it is, his life is not free from worries. The Capitulations do not relieve him from the operation of local municipal and police regulations; and these are sufficiently oppressive and contradictory to make life burdensome. The stupidity and caprice of officials, the confusion and clash of authority, the utter lack of coördination and system in and between the different departments of the government, and the venality and corruption in every branch of the administration, both local and imperial, are inconceivable to anyone who has not experienced them personally.

A word should be said concerning the French Capitulations of 1740, as it is largely under their provisions that foreign missions and charitable institutions carry on their work. These Capitulations, extended to Great Britain by the Treaty of 1809, and made of universal application by " most favored nation " clauses since 1861, not only recognize the right of foreign communions to maintain missions, monasteries, hospitals, and schools in the Empire, but invite and encourage them to do so by granting peculiar privileges to such institutions. Among these privileges is the specific exemption from customs duties of a portion of their annual importations of materials and supplies. Foreign missions, in other words, have been welcomed by the Turkish government, as conducing to the general welfare and prosperity of the *Raya* populations, and hence of the Empire. This attitude dates from 1740, as already stated, and has been traditional with the government until very recent years. Abdul Aziz in 1864 even enacted these privileges and exemptions into the organic law of the land by a special edict or *tanzimat.* It is a wholly mistaken view which sees in the foreign missions in Turkey, of whatever communion or nationality, an enterprise forced upon Turkey against her will, seeking to overthrow the established religion and national institutions,[1] and tolerated only by the great long-suffering of a too patient government.

The Capitulations are, as we have said, a mediæval conception, remaining in force to-day simply because Turkey has not yet emerged from mediæval conditions.[2] Yet she is restive under their implied re-

[1] There are no missions to the Moslems. The existing missions, except one or two to the Jews, confine their efforts to the native Christian communities.

[2] As late as the beginning of this century, the mediæval Moslem conception of treaties, as concessions to be paid for in cash, appears in the " treaties " concluded by the United States with Algiers, Barbary, and Tunis, 1786-1805. For that of 1786 with Barbary, Abd-er-Rahman demanded $150,000 tribute. That of 1795 with Algiers cost the United States $992,000, of which a large part was trib-

34

proach; and it is not surprising that she has taken occasion, by her recent victories in Greece, to demand their abrogation with respect to that country. It is very certain that the Greeks would rather make almost any other sacrifice than yield to this condition; and it is equally certain that the Powers would never tolerate the enforcement of Turkey's demand. When in 1856, by the Treaty of Paris, the Ottoman Empire was admitted to a qualified membership in the political family of European nations, the maintenance of the Capitulations was a part of the price of the favor. Smarting under this reproach, the Ottoman plenipotentiary at the Paris Conference begged for the modification of this condition. The reply of the Congress was the famous "Protocol of 1856," couched in the following language :—

> "The plenipotentiaries recognize that the Capitulations belong to a situation to whose termination the Treaty of Peace must necessarily tend, and that the privileges stipulated in them circumscribe the authority of the Porte within regrettably narrow limits; that there is occasion for conciliatory concessions; but that it is important to proportion these to the reforms which Turkey may introduce into her administration, so as to combine these guarantees with such as result from the measures *carried into execution* by the Porte *(dont la Porte poursuit l'application)*."

Many and brilliant the reforms the Porte has placed upon paper, as admirable in substance as in their beautiful Arabic calligraphy; but when and where has the Porte ever "pursued the application" of one among them all?

The Capitulations are the charter of life, liberty, and the pursuit of happiness for the foreign resident in Turkey. The Porte can hardly expect to see them repealed or seriously modified until some other dynasty than that of Osman shall sit on the throne of the sultans, and some other race than that of the Seljûks sway the destinies of Macedonia, Thrace, the Epirus, and Asia Minor. No such fundamental reform as would justify their abrogation can be looked for under present conditions.   A. D. F. HAMLIN.

ute-money, paid biennially under the guise of a "consular present." These payments ceased in 1815 only. Our war with Tripoli was a consequence of the Bashaw's demand for a similar "present"; and up to 1802, the maintenance of treaty relations with Turkey and its vassal states had cost the United States over two million dollars in tribute and presents.

IS NON-PARTISANSHIP IN MUNICIPAL GOVERNMENT FEASIBLE?

IT sounds well and seems reasonable to urge that city government is primarily and principally a matter of business administration, and, therefore, that city elections should not be contested on party lines, but simply on local and personal issues. That I understand to be what is called non-partisanship in municipal affairs. Of what importance is it, asks the advocate of non-partisanship, whether the mayor of your city be Democrat or Republican on State or national issues? His duties are purely administrative and local: whether he believe in a high tariff or a low tariff, in a gold, a silver, or a bimetallic standard, or in paper money, in a strict construction of the Constitution or a free construction, is of no immediate importance in the discharge of the duties of his office. Fitness, honesty, and fearlessness are the essential qualifications; and fidelity to local interests, according to his conceptions and convictions, is the test by which he and his administration should be judged. Let men differ, if they will, say these reformers, over questions of State and Federal policy; only do not let their differences enter into municipal elections or administrations. Let that expression of citizenship be encouraged which, unhampered and uninfluenced by party affiliations, seeks to eliminate political considerations from local affairs, and to insure the conduct of city government upon business principles, according to business methods.

We hear much of such talk nowadays. So high an ideal, so specious a proposition, finds many a sincere supporter. Whether, as a remedy for municipal evils, it is practicable and effective, or whether it is impracticable and visionary, the discussion which it excites is helpful; and the sentiment behind it, when honest, promotes that healthy interest in public affairs which is essential to good government.

I have been asked by the Editor of THE FORUM to contribute to this discussion; and I shall be frank enough at the outset to state the conclusion to which my experience and observation have led me; namely, that anything approaching disinterested and successful non-partisanship in city government, however well intended, is, under existing conditions, almost impossible. I believe, therefore, that, for the present at least, municipal government is safer, as a rule, in the responsible hands of partisans than in the necessarily irresponsible and uncertain hands of non-partisans.

The movement for municipal non-partisanship has gained strength from two principal causes. One is the general tendency throughout the country toward a loosening of party ties. In the absence of intense issues there is an increasing number of independent voters, who cast their ballots first for the candidates and platform of one party, then for the candidates and platform of another party, as suits their convictions or their whims. This uncertain element has made elections uncertain; and victories have generally followed the course taken by the independent voters. Success has naturally magnified the importance of the Independent; and the revelation of his importance has produced the so-called professional Independent element in politics, which, conscious of possessing a probable balance of power, is not reluctant to use it; sometimes wisely, sometimes unwisely, sometimes fairly, sometimes unfairly, many times narrowly and whimsically. Behind that exercise of power is the undoubted conviction that the position of the Independent is the only logical and intelligent position in politics, when parties are evenly divided as to numbers, and not widely separated as to principles. The professional Independent element seeks aggressively to break down the lines of party: it is behind the demand for non-partisanship in municipal affairs; probably thinking, with reason, that a disposition and habit to break party ties in local elections will make easy a severance of party bonds in other elections. Independence, in their opinion, is intelligence; and intelligence in voting means a higher standard of official men and measures. The latter proposition we may admit to be indisputable, even if we regard the former assumption with scepticism, in view of certain political results not yet forgotten.

In addition to the impetus furnished to the non-partisan idea in municipal affairs by the growth of the Independent movement generally, a most important influence has been exerted by the apparent failures of some partisan governments in cities. We must confess that in some instances these have been conspicuous and humiliating. The exposure of jobbery, corruption, and extravagance—though often exaggerated in order to serve selfish interests—has rightly stirred communities with indignation, and induced citizens to join together irrespective of party for self-protection. To the extent that partisan government has accompanied such municipal evils, it has been compelled to bear their odium; and the success of the party in State and national contests has frequently been prevented by having to carry this heavy burden of administrative sins heaped up by local political adherents who, treacherous to party name and party principles, have used the party name to promote private plunder. But municipal failures have not been alone confined to local government by party. Some of the worst instances of maladministration have occurred under nominal non-partisanship; and, if we are to judge of partisan or non-partisan administrations solely by their failures, non-partisanship must be condemned as well as partisanship. Moreover, when the causes of failure of partisan municipal government are analyzed, it will be found that official plunder and knavery have succeeded chiefly when party ties have been weakening, when interest in party issues or organizations has waned, and when, by reason of such indifference, the bad men of a party are permitted to stain its good name as well as to ignore its principles. They must share the responsibility of failure and disgrace, therefore, whose indifference has encouraged or permitted such a political condition to exist.

There would be more to commend in non-partisanship in local affairs if the sentiment for it were more generally and absolutely honest. The fact is, however, that sincerity in the cause is confined to a comparative few, unable of themselves to exert much influence; so that the main support, under present conditions, must come from disaffected political factions and minorities who seek by such alliances to gain power.

A so-called citizens' movement, springing perhaps from actual and serious grievances, animated by the most unselfish interest, and intent only on the accomplishment of good, finds itself confronted with conditions as they exist, and compelled to use, in order to be successful, the very methods which non-partisanship deplores. This is the weakness of municipal non-partisanship. Representatives of Good Government clubs and other civic organizations confer, with a view to the nomination and election of a non-partisan ticket. Their actual numbers are small. Behind them is, we will say, an honest and praiseworthy sentiment, with but few votes and no disciplined or ramified organization. Watching them and encouraging them is the miscellaneous assortment of political "outs,"—organizations of disaffected elements, offshoots of the large parties, perhaps one of the large parties itself (now in the minority of course),—all chiefly animated by the desire for political success and the rewards and opportunities which come with it, willing to make loud professions of reform, and anxiously playing for position in a campaign to be opened. A succession of conferences follows; the first difficulty encountered being, as a rule, not any difference among the parleying representatives as to the principles or issues of the campaign, —for those are usually left to the original non-partisans,—but a difference as to the proportionate representation of the various political organizations on the ticket, and as to the availability of the names suggested for candidates.

Thus, at one bound, whether willing or not, those who fancy themselves developing and practising their theory of non-partisanship are plunged into the same kind of politics which they have condemned in parties. The ticket is nominated, not in convention by delegates duly chosen after public notice, but in a club corner, by self-appointed nominators. It gives thorough satisfaction to nobody; for it is a compromise of conflicting interests: the nominees are responsible to no one organization, but each considers himself the representative of the association by which he was put forward. The candidates are not usually the men the reformers want: for the ideal public officer is not always a vote-getter; and, of course, so practical a consideration as availability is not lost sight of even by these idealists. For the head of the ticket is often chosen, therefore, a neutral man, without positive qualities, and, consequently, free from antagonisms, whose actual qualifications for the office are unknown, however respectable he may be or however honest his intentions. The subordinate places on the ticket are filled with ex-office-holders out of a job, with men who have served one or another of the component elements making up the non-partisan conglomerate, or with men more or less trustworthy and capable, but not conspicuously fitted for the offices for which they are named. The German vote and the Irish vote are not forgotten in the selection of candidates. In short, the ideal non-partisanship has become a nondescript loose-jointed partisanship; nominations being determined in secret and by dicker, and elections contested by methods not perceptibly differing from those which are condemned as necessarily inseparable from party machinery.

Such non-partisan movements, when successful, usually culminate in a single victory. As might be expected from an alliance between so many diverse and uncertain elements, the results of victory are usually disappointing. Few so-called non-partisan administrations survive one experience: they die and are born again in different shapes after a lapse of time. The untried, unknown candidates sometimes exhibit excellent qualifications in office, but are more often administrative failures, if not actual disgraces. Among the officers who make up their administration, there is not the cohesiveness and harmony which usually characterize participants in partisan government; but jealousies and irresponsibility bring the administration into contempt or ridicule, and frustrate mutual coöperation for the public good. The hope of renomination and reëlection, which, in the absence of higher motives, is an incentive toward a good record, is ñot present: for it is contrary to history and human nature to expect a successful remixing of such a variety of elements; and the official incumbent, if inclined to be careless or unfaithful, ignores or perverts the duties and responsibilities of his office.

The observation and memory of recent non-partisan movements in New York and Brooklyn confirm the conviction that the picture which I have presented is neither overdrawn nor unfair. I believe that the net result of the non-partisan movement which elected Mayor Strong has been of distinct advantage, in some respects, to the people of New York; but its merits have been confined to the services of a comparatively few men who have conducted their offices with conspicuous fidelity and intelligence. As a test or demonstration of what constitutes genuine non-partisanship, it has been a failure. Genuine non-partisanship was impossible from the time that the Committee of Seventy bargained with Stecklerites, O'Brienites, State Democrats, German Reform Democrats, Platt and Anti-Platt Republicans, for a union against Tammany; for non-partisanship was the thing least desired by most of the political organizations which combined with the Committee. They saw in combination a chance for factional success: they had nothing to lose, but probably something to gain, by such a fusion. They shouted with the Seventy for non-partisanship, and joined with vehemence in the denunciation of Tammany's alleged wickedness and extravagance in its administration of city government. When the election brought a victory, there was a distribution of municipal offices. Were they filled with the conspicuously fit, irrespective of party, according to the non-partisan idea? Not at all. They were carefully parcelled out, according to the most extreme partisan methods, to those who had contributed votes to the election of the new administration, and in proportion to the number of votes contributed. With nice exactness and with fine appreciation, the new mayor rewarded one by one the associations which had combined for his election; and, in his desire to be fair in this recognition, he occasionally made the natural mistake of appointing unfit men. These objectionable appointments have been obstacles to his administration; and he seems to have had neither sympathy nor coöperation from the appointees in his effort to give the people good government. No sense of party obligation holds them; and no party is responsible for them.

Of course all this is very far from the platform of non-partisanship on which Mayor Strong was elected. The spirit is that of partisanship without the restraining influences of party attachment and responsibility. Yet no better opportunity for the promotion and illustration of non-partisanship has been afforded than that offered by the campaign and administration of Mayor Strong. Public sentiment, as expressed through the newspapers and in the pulpits, strongly favored and expected it; and the candidate's earnestness and sincerity were unquestioned. The fact that so-called non-partisan government has ignominiously failed under such favorable conditions, strengthens the conviction that, as human nature is at present constituted, and as conditions at present exist, genuine non-partisanship in local affairs is too ideal, is impossible of attainment. Much more practicable and effective is a party government, held to strict accountability by a watchful public, which knows then where to locate responsibility for misdoings, and can administer discipline with telling effect either at the primaries or in the voting-booths.

Partisanship in city government differs from non-partisanship in being a reflection of conditions as they exist—not as they ought to be. Nine-tenths of the voters, more or less, get their politics, like their religion, in the cradle. Party and church lines are closely drawn about them during life. It is only the exceptional man who breaks away from the political environment and atmosphere to which he has been used; and his separation is the result of conviction, association, or selfishness. Party divisions or organizations have always existed, and probably always will. It is not essential, of course, as the non-partisans urge, that divisions on State and national issues should extend to purely local issues. But they do thus extend; and it is the most natural thing that the same parties which, through the machinery supplied by their organization, present candidates to the people's suffrages at State and Federal elections, should, by the same process, put forward candidates for local offices, and wage these contests on party lines.

Illogical and unreasonable as division on party lines in municipal contests may be called, I do not see that, in itself, it is an evil: I do feel that it is often a powerful bulwark to the cause of order and good government. Where universal suffrage prevails, as it does in America, and no qualification of intelligence or property is imposed, it is a very fortunate thing that men are divided into parties, and that the strength of party ties is able to restrain the ignorant, the depraved, the impetuous from the advocacy of dangerous doctrines, or the support of unsafe men. In the great cities of New York and Brooklyn, where so large a proportion of the voters are of foreign birth, and where there are so many ignorant persons easily swayed by un-American influences, the restraint laid upon that element by the powerful political organizations, with their clubs and workers in every election district, has many times been the greatest protection to good government in those cities, and must still continue to be to the government of Greater New York. To encourage political independence among the ignorant and vicious, and to break down the power of political organizations which hold these in check, is to stimulate anarchy and to open the way for socialistic attacks upon property. The possible evils of partisan government had better long be endured than to incur any risk of delivering the city over to the power of such dangerous elements.

Conceding, moreover, as the advocates of non-partisanship do, that party divisions and organizations are needed and desirable in State and national politics,—although logically it would seem that, if the theory of non-partisanship were sound in local politics, it should apply equally in larger politics,—the best way to keep alive and active organizations for the success of political principles that concern State and Federal governments, is by encouraging party activity in municipal affairs. A battle for tariff reform or honest money might be lost, if party activity were reserved only for Federal elections. Municipal politics frequently appeal directly to the party organization; and, while it is true that a candidate's ideas or opinions on the tariff or money question do not affect his ability to discharge municipal duties faithfully and satisfactorily, and that for this reason division on party lines is unnecessary, nevertheless, such divisions are not only harmless, if properly directed, but absolutely essential for effective party work in the wider fields of political activity.

Behind any defence of municipal government by party, however, must stand the imperative condition that the party organization be intelligent, honest, and broad-minded. Corrupt and incapable local organizations cannot give good local government, and are a menace to party success in either State or national contests. But with clean men directing party effort, encouraging the nomination of good men for office, and insisting upon honest, faithful public service as a condition for rewards, municipal government is safe in partisan hands, and evils which have grown up under control by party need not exist.

My suggestion, therefore, to those who deplore partisanship in municipal affairs, is to think carefully before they try to break down local political organizations, lest, in doing so, they invite from unseen sources graver dangers than have yet confronted us, and evils not so easily eradicated as those which might be due to corrupt party government.

The more practical and useful effort is to build up, purify, and broaden political organizations, so that their great power may be more effectively wielded for good government, whether in the city, the State, or the nation. A constant watchful citizenship, yielding its support to the party which renders the best public service, can accomplish much more permanent good by working through an existing and well-developed organization than by spasmodic efforts in methods which both, experience and common sense indicate to be ineffective and uncertain.

ROSWELL P. FLOWER.

MAYOR STRONG'S EXPERIMENT IN NEW YORK CITY.

THE old city of New York is approaching the end of its official existence. It is a noteworthy circumstance that its last mayor should have inaugurated an experiment in the non-partisan administration of municipal affairs, as distinguished from one under the auspices and control of a political party. For several years there has been a steady growth of public opinion in favor of the separation of municipal affairs from State and national politics. This sentiment had already attained substantial proportions prior to 1894. During the first six months of that year there was an exposure of corruption in the Police Department of the city of New York which startled the people of the entire State. This exposure was the result of the "Lexow Investigation."

The situation was well stated in the platform of the Committee of Seventy:—

"The government of the city of New York, in the hands of its present administrators, is marked by corruption, inefficiency, and extravagance: its municipal departments are not conducted in the interests of the city at large, but for private gain and partisan advantage. All classes of citizens, rich and poor alike, suffer under these conditions. This misgovernment endangers the health and morality of the community, and deprives its citizens of the protection of life and property to which they are entitled."

The Committee of Seventy was appointed at a citizens' meeting held on September 6, 1894. A platform was adopted affirming the necessity for a complete divorce of municipal government from party politics; and numerous conferences were held by the Committee with representatives of various organizations opposed to Tammany Hall, for the purpose of inducing them to unite upon that platform. Two large general conferences were held, to which all the anti-Tammany organizations were invited to send delegates. At the second of these meetings the announcement was made that the Committee of Seventy had decided to present a list of candidates, headed by William L. Strong for mayor. The reception of the ticket was not, at first, such as to promise unity of action; but no efforts were spared to bring this about. These efforts finally resulted in the formal endorsement of the ticket of the Committee of Seventy by the anti-Tammany organizations; and the candidates of the Committee were all elected by very large majorities.

The election was carried upon a great wave of popular indignation. It was succeeded by a buoyant state of expectancy. Men felt that the millennium in municipal affairs had arrived. There was a reaction as the people awoke to the realization of the fact that not everything they had hoped for was to be accomplished. This went on until, at the close of 1895, there was a general, deep feeling of disappointment—and even resentment in the minds of many—at what was deemed to be the failure of Mayor Strong's administration. This has been succeeded by a better spirit of satisfaction with the good that has been accomplished.

The first municipal election for Greater New York is at hand: public interest is aroused to the gravity of the problem presented in that election. Plans are already made to secure a union of the forces opposed to the principles and practices of Tammany Hall; and an appeal will be made to all citizens to join in an effort to secure a non-partisan business administration of municipal affairs, free from the control of any political organization. The answer to that appeal will be decided by the opinion of people on the comparative importance of the failures and successes of Mayor Strong's administration. The time is ripe for estimating the net results of his work.

No fair judgment can be formed without first considering the difficulties of Mayor Strong's position at the start. While the platform of the Committee of Seventy declared in the broadest terms that "municipal government should be entirely divorced from party politics and from selfish personal ambition or gain," the actual work of the Committee was directed to the point of securing the support of political organizations for that platform and for the candidates nominated upon it. The nominations were made upon a distinct plan of apportionment of certain places on the ticket to the political organizations which endorsed the platform. This was clearly recognized by Mr. Strong, and made the basis of his acceptance of the nomination of the Committee of Seventy. I quote in full his letter addressed to Mr. Joseph Larocque, chairman:—

" DEAR SIR :

The platform adopted by the 'Committee of Seventy' meets with my entire approval; and, if a majority of the anti-Tammany organizations, including the Republicans, in the city of New York approve of my nomination for mayor, with the distinct understanding that the affairs of the government of the city of New York shall be administered in the interests of good government, and absolutely non-partisan, then I shall be very willing to accept the nomination from all these organizations, and, if elected, shall adhere to this policy during my administration of the affairs of the city of New York, as mayor, and make all appointments without regard to party lines.   ´   Respectfully yours,

W. L. STRONG."

There are two specific points upon which pledges were made in the platform and in Mr. Strong's letter of acceptance :

I. That his appointments should be non-partisan.

II. That business principles, and not politics, should be his guide in the administration of municipal affairs.

There is no authoritative definition of a non-partisan appointment. If non-partisan appointments meant the appointment to office of men who had never had any connection with any political organization in the city of New York, the Mayor would have been confronted with two alternatives: He must either have appointed non-residents, or, residents who had been so indifferent to their civic duties that they had never made any effort to direct or control public opinion upon political questions.   It will hardly be contended that the universal adoption of such a rule in appointments would have been well received or generally approved.   Its success may well be doubted.

The appointment of men who have been active in the work of any political organization will always give some appearance of partisanship to a municipal government.   This difficulty will confront any executive officer who is endeavoring to administer his office upon a non-partisan basis.   In the case of Mayor Strong the difficulty was increased by the circumstances of his nomination and election.   If he had appointed men, without any knowledge of their political connections, all his appointees might have been Republicans.   This would not have been an improbable result, because his long affiliation with the Republican party had given him a wider acquaintance among its members. But such a result would have laid him open to the most serious charge of partisanship, which no disclaimer of intention could have dispelled. If each man appointed to an office had been competent to fulfil its duties, and had devoted himself solely to the public service, the fact that he belonged to and was proposed by one of the political organizations which endorsed the ticket of the Committee of Seventy would not have constituted a violation of the spirit of the movement that elected Mayor Strong.   The Committee of Seventy itself had nominated men because they were members of those same organizations.

My view of non-partisanship is this : The officer does not administer his office under the control or for the benefit of the political organizations to which he belongs, but is guided by what he believes to be the best interests of the people at large.

It has been unfortunate for Mayor Strong, but perhaps fortunate for the cause of non-partisan municipal government, that those officers who have proved least competent and have most subordinated the public welfare to personal or political ends have been those in whose appointment the endorsement of some political organization or faction figured most largely. His mistakes are well known ; but, judged by the above test, the appointments of Mayor Strong are not open to general criticism. This is best proved by the record of his administration under the second promise.

Now, what has been accomplished by reason of the employment of business principles, in lieu of politics, in the work of the departments?

The Police Department was the centre of the storm of popular indignation that preceded Mayor Strong's election.   It has been the object of scornful criticism since, by reason of bickerings in the Board.   It shall be the first to answer the query as to the success of Mayor Strong's administration.

THE POLICE DEPARTMENT.

There is an inherent difficulty in reviewing the non-partisan administration of a department which is by law made bi-partisan.   Non-partisanship, as applied to such a department, means that its internal administration must be based upon the merit system in appointments and promotions, and upon ordinary business principles in routine matters ; to which must be added, of course, a strict system of supervision and discipline.   The success of non-partisanship and the failure of partisanship were never more clearly contrasted than in the record of this department for the last two years.   In so far as the Police Board has adhered strictly to the principles of non-partisanship, its administration has been an unqualified success : where it has departed from those principles it has been a failure.   The deadlock in the Board has assumed, at times, the proportions of a public scandal.   In no proper sense, however, can this be charged to Mayor Strong.   The possibility of such a deadlock was one of the inherent defects of the bi-partisan law ; and a mistake of judgment in the selection of the Board transformed this possibility into a living reality.   With four men of such positive and different personalities as the Commissioners, the wonder is that the deadlock occurred in two matters only during two years.   The intense hostility of the two commissioners who were the recognized leaders in this deadlock gave a prominence to the contest which the points involved did not warrant. These points were two: (1) The promotion of Acting-Inspectors McCullagh and Brooks. These officers had been serving faithfully in the grade of inspector for more than two years. They had stood at the head of two eligible lists, and were favored by three commissioners. Nothing, except the provision that the four commissioners must be unanimous, prevented their promotion. (2) The preferment by Commissioner Andrews of charges against the Chief of Police of a grave breach of discipline. Two of the commissioners refused to approve the charges and to permit any investigation.

The substantial results of the change in the character of the administration of the Department can be fully appreciated by a review of the improvement which has been accomplished in its internal affairs and its efficiency in the public service.

The new Board found the Department in a demoralized state. No material improvement in its condition had been made since the adjournment of the Lexow Committee. This investigation had been followed by an extraordinary session of the Grand Jury; and twenty-six officers, including one inspector and five captains, were under suspension on account of indictments for crime. Two hundred and sixty-eight vacancies existed in the Department; and by July 15 this number had increased to three hundred and fifty-five. It included one chief, three inspectors, eleven captains, and eleven sergeants. Important legislative changes were pending; and uncertainty and distrust pervaded the entire Department. Special powers of reorganization were denied by the Legislature; but the new Board, by its adoption of new methods of administration and enforcement of strict and impartial discipline, speedily caused the retirement of many officers.

One point upon which special stress must be laid is, that all improvement in the Department has been accomplished in spite of the absurd provisions of the particular law under which it is administered. The two worst features of the bi-partisan Act are: (1) That it divides responsibility; and (2) that it increases the difficulty of securing unity of action.

The first was the result of giving all power of detail of officers to the chief. The second was due to the limitations upon the power of a majority of the Commission. A four-headed commission is always in danger of a deadlock. There is, however, a chance that three of the members will act together. The framers of the bi-partisan bill provided against this chance with an ingenuity which could not have been surpassed. They stipulated that no promotion should be made except by the unanimous vote of the Board, unless on the written recommendation of the chief. The present chief announces that under no circumstances, save in the absence or death of a commissioner, will he make such a recommendation.

In another respect the law gives to the chief the power to control or block the promotion of new men. The original appointment of a patrolman is made by a majority of the Board. A patrolman's first advancement is to the duty of roundsman. But the promotion from patrolman to roundsman is called a "detail," and must be made by the chief. He designates the men from whose ranks all subsequent promotions must be made. From the roundsmen thus appointed the Board can make promotions to sergeancies, then to captaincies, and so on; but these promotions must be made by a unanimous vote until the office of chief is reached, when the majority once more regains its power. With the control of "details" and promotions in its own hands, the Board could have guaranteed that men should not be promoted or transferred for political reasons; but with this power taken away the Board could no longer be held responsible on that score.

The full disadvantages of the new law were not apparent at first, because the new Board had under it, in the higher positions, only acting officers; and it continued to exercise the powers the old Board had formerly possessed. During ten months of unchecked control, the Board accomplished an almost incredible amount of work for the reorganization of the Department.

Reorganization and Discipline.—From October 8, 1895, to December 31 of the same year, 206 patrolmen were appointed. In 1896, this number was increased by 958 permanent appointments and 398 appointments on probation; making a total of 1,356 for the year.

In 1894, the total promotions for the year were: Sergeants, 12; roundsmen, 16—total, 28; in 1895, chief, 1; detective-sergeants, 22; roundsmen, 40—total, 63; in 1896, deputy-chief, 1; inspector, 1; captains, 19; sergeants, 36; detective-sergeants, 6; roundsmen, 65—total, 128.

Dismissals were substituted for the light penalties which had been previously inflicted for grave breaches of discipline; and heavier penalties were imposed for all grades of offences.

In 1893, 11 officers were dismissed upon charges; in 1894, 41; in 1895, 88 (of whom 68 were dismissed by the new Board); in 1896, 81;

making a total of 149 officers dismissed by the present Board prior to January 1, 1897.

The fines imposed in 1893 amounted to $15,664.65; in 1894, $14,-871.90; in 1895, $23,139.90; in 1896, $29,768.28.

While enforcing discipline and inflicting severe penalties on the one hand, the Board, on the other hand, has publicly commended officers for gallant and meritorious service, and has largely increased the annual awards of honorable mentions, engrossed certificates, and medals of honor.

The Honest Enforcement of the Laws.—The most praiseworthy part played by the new Board was its stand for the rigid and honest enforcement of all laws. That the Excise law could not be enforced in New York had been commonly asserted. Its partial and uneven enforcement had afforded an efficient means of corrupting the officers and of blackmailing the liquor-dealers. The Board determined that the wealthy liquor-dealers, and those who possessed great political influence, should be treated precisely like the weaker ones. All places alike were closed on Sundays; yet, fewer arrests were made. In the year preceding the accession to office of the new Board, more than ten thousand persons were arrested for violation of the Sunday law: during the twelve months of the enforcement of the law, five thousand seven hundred only were arrested. This decrease is the best evidence of the extent to which arrests had been formerly made for purposes of blackmail or political intimidation.

The statistics show further that the number of arrests for more important crimes has been increased. At the same time there has been a marked diminution in the number of crimes committed where the criminal was not arrested. These results reflect all the more credit upon the force, because, for the first time in its history, it has warred upon all criminals, instead of protecting some for the purpose of catching others. When the present Board took office, all sorts of purveyors of vice were allowed to ply their trade unmolested; partly in consideration of paying blackmail to the police, and partly in consideration of giving information about criminals who belonged to the unprotected classes. This business of blackmail and protection has been entirely broken up. The force has done better work than ever before against those criminals who threatened life and property. In proportion to the population of the city, fewer crimes of violence, fewer murders and burglaries have been committed. Crime and vice are under better control in New York City

35

than ever before ; and life and property are safer. The arrests for all offences made by the detective bureau in the year ending May 1, 1895, numbered 1,384 ; in 1896, 2,527. The number of felons convicted in the year ending May 1, 1895, was 269 ; in 1896, 365. The convictions for misdemeanors in 1895 were 105 ; in 1896, 215.

Other important improvements have been accomplished by the Board. Among these may be mentioned the establishment of the police bicycle squad ; the abolition of the " Tramp " lodging-house ; the adoption of the Bertillon system of identification of criminals ; the increase of the patrol-wagon force ; the extension of the system of police matrons ; the improvement of the condition of the old station-houses and the construction of new ones.

THE DEPARTMENT OF STREET CLEANING.

The former streets are a memory to all. A few thoroughfares and some streets in the brown-stone districts were carefully cleaned ; but the others were shamefully neglected. Gutters and entrances of sewer culverts were choked with rotting garbage, pools of slimy water, and heaps of litter. In the tenement districts all these conditions were intensified. The marvellous change wrought in the past two years is conceded by the most rabid opponents of the present administration ; but such concession is always accompanied with the exulting cry of " increased expenditure."

The ash-barrel nuisance has been abolished. The barrels have been ordered off the curb-line, and are kept inside the stoop-line, as ordered by the Sanitary Code. The sidewalks are free from unsightly and malodorous encumbrances. The collection of all kinds of material is made, in most cases, twice every day. There is no delay in removal ; there is no accumulation ; there are no mounds of refuse on the sidewalks and in the streets. As the streets became clean and free from trucks, the children took possession of them ; and their elders soon followed. In the tenement-house districts, they are now one immense playground for the children, and a promenade for adults.

At present, 433 miles of paved streets are cleaned by the Department. Of these, 35½ are cleaned four or more times every day ; 50½, three times ; 283½, twice ; 63½, once a day. The total, on the basis of *one sweeping every day*, is 924 miles,—nine miles farther than the distance from New York to Chicago !

The improvement in the physical condition of the laborers of the Department is striking. Formerly they were a lot of slipshod loafers, all occupying their positions for political reasons.   Most of the drivers were recruited from a distinct class of young toughs and thugs, banded together in different parts of the city under names known to the police as the "Stable Gang," the "Barracks Gang," and the like.   Dismissals were rarely made; and a man with any political pull at all found no difficulty in securing reinstatement.   Soon, the entire force was thoroughly imbued with the conviction that the only thing required of it was street-cleaning, and that of the very hardest kind.   Under the pace thus set many men dropped out; but many more remained.   These have been transformed into decent and self-respecting laborers, who appreciate the standards by which they are judged, and ask only for a fair field and no favor.   The adoption of the white uniform made street-cleaning an occupation, not an accident of position.   The annual parade did much to complete what the uniform had begun.   It was awaited with ridicule, but received with astonishment and admiration. The men realized the impression they created.   They were proud of their positions, of their white clothes, and of themselves.   From that moment the uniform assumed a new significance to their tenement-house friends and neighbors.

The system of arbitration introduced by Commissioner Waring has done much to improve the discipline and elevate the standard of the men.

The removal of the trucks from the streets has been a signal success. Around and beneath these obstructions the streets were usually in the most filthy condition.   The truck-owners made no pretence to keep them clean.   The space beneath the trucks was a most convenient dumping-ground for the surplus filth and rubbish of the neighborhood; and any paper blown about would invariably seek its final resting-place under the protection of the wheels.   In the tenement streets the trucks were resorts for the dissolute youth of both sexes.   They were converted into gambling-dens and haunts of tough gangs.   Mothers were forced to keep their children indoors after nightfall; and even the adults preferred to remain in the stifling houses, rather than sit outside in an environment of refuse and at the risk of insult from the ribald occupants of the vehicles.

Complaints of individuals and societies alike were referred to the district superintendents, who, in many cases, were political leaders and able to distinguish a Republican from a Democratic truck.   Trucks belonging to the party in power were rarely removed.   Never had a commissioner entertained the desperate idea of suppressing the evil: it meant

political annihilation. Despite predictions of failure, however, the reform was accomplished. By the advent of the summer of 1895, the
streets were practically cleared. The crusade brought hardships to a
few individuals; but such cases were rare. The principal offenders
were the rich brewers, manufacturers, and merchants. The benefit to
the city has been acknowledged by the truckmen who were sufferers at
the time of the change. No future administration will dare to let the
trucks return. Certainly the nuisance will never be known again if
the women and children of the tenements are consulted.

The removal of sweepings and ashes in bags is a companion piece of
progress. There is a total absence of the old eyesore of piles of street-
dirt in the gutters awaiting collection by the carts. For the collection
of ashes a patent, galvanized iron can has been devised, with an adjust-
able bottom composed of two doors opening outward through which the
ashes are dropped into the bag without the clouds of dust that marked
the old system of removal in open carts. In some districts, paper and
light rubbish, such as rags, excelsior, straw, bottles, broken glass, tin
cans, and old shoes, are now collected in bags or tied up in light bundles.
The collection is made by a driver in response to a signal-card displayed
in the lower windows of the house. The bags or bundles are not un-
tied until the crematory is reached. By this method the most prolific
cause of the littering of the streets has been removed.

In the matter of the removal of snow, the present Commissioner has
completely distanced all his predecessors. Prior to January 1895, the
work of removal was done mainly by the regular force; additional laborers and carts being hired when the fall was very heavy. The street
area opened to traffic by this method was necessarily insignificant. In
the early months of 1895, the new Commissioner was forced to make the
best of the conditions as he found them. Removal was prosecuted day
and night; and 253,481 loads of snow were removed in *five weeks*, at a
cost of $173,639.20, as against 221,569 loads removed for $176,737.34,
under the various commissioners occupying office during the *five years*
beginning with 1889. In this short time more snow was removed at less
expense than in the entire five years prior to the present administration;
notwithstanding the fact that the laborers were paid $2.00 per day, while
former commissioners paid them but $1.50.

In the following autumn the Commissioner introduced the system,
now in force, of removal by contract. The work is done by the contractor in the manner and at the places indicated by the Commissioner.
The contract for removal is let in cubic yards. Department inspectors

at the loading- and dumping-places tally the loads and protect the city's interests. Snow is no longer taken from unimportant side-streets and dumped in other streets only a few blocks away. All cartmen must get their loads from the designated places, and dump them into the river before receiving the token of the city's indebtedness. The Department has thus been relieved of the care and labor incident to the hiring of carts and men, keeping their time, and making up pay-rolls. The Department laborers have been retained in their own sections upon cross-walks and gutters; and the interruptions to the regular work of the Department have been reduced to a minimum.

A comparison of the period prior to 1895, under all the commissioners as far back as the year 1881 (when the Department of Street Cleaning was taken from the control of the Police Department and became a separate branch of the city government), with that since the inauguration of the present administration on January 15, 1895, gives surprising results. The amount of snow removed in that portion of the winter of 1894–95 when the Department was under the direction of the present commissioner, and in the two complete winters, 1895–96, and 1896–97, was almost twice the entire amount removed in the thirteen and one-half winters prior to January 15, 1895. The average per winter for the present administration is 495,977 loads, against 55,-568 loads for the winters preceding. The total cost of removal, for 596,625 loads, under all former commissioners was $453,105.79, or an average cost per load of $0.759. Under the present administration, for 1,233,412 loads, it has been $882,980.88,—an average cost per load of $0.716. This is more than four cents lower than the average for all the previous administrations. The low price of $0.636 for the winter just passed will undoubtedly be diminished in the winter of 1897–98.

A comparison of the mileage of streets cleaned shows that under former administrations 22.80 miles only were cleaned; while now 144.42 miles are cleaned after every snowstorm. The latter mileage includes all the city's important thoroughfares and the worst of its tenement streets. The congested tenement district east of the Bowery and south of Houston Street was never touched formerly: now it is practically cleared after every storm.

A most important feature of the snow work under Mayor Strong's administration has been the agreement entered into with the street railways for the removal of snow from curb to curb over certain portions of their lines, in lieu of the removal between the tracks over their entire lines. Formerly the snow was swept to one side, which made its

removal more difficult, and traffic almost impossible. Now the railways clear *from curb to curb* over eleven miles of street in each storm,
—a saving to the city, for the past winter alone, of $35,598.53.

The ordinances relating to the Department have been enforced.
The equipment of the mechanical bureau and the repair shop has been
improved. The shops, stables, crematories, dumps, steel pockets, boats,
and barges have been renovated or reconstructed. Experiments have
been conducted for the successful solution of the problem of the final
disposition of garbage ; and valuable progress has been made.

THE HEALTH DEPARTMENT.

The work of the Health Department has been extended, both by
legislative enactment of new duties and by increased administrative activity. Strict measures to prevent the sale of watered, impure, or adul-
terated milk have been adopted by the Board. The sale of milk,
cream, or condensed milk in the city of New York without a permit
from the Board of Health, has been forbidden. Measures have been
inaugurated for the systematic examination of all the milch cows within
the city limits by the "tuberculin test." The sanitary supervision
of tuberculosis by the Health Department has resulted in a marked decrease in the death-rate from that disease. The act regulating the employment of women and children in mercantile establishments imposed
upon the Health Department new duties in reference to the inspection
of such places of business, and the certification of the educational and
physical qualifications of the children employed in them.

The most important new function of the Board has been the execution of the new tenement-house law. Mayor Strong approved the new
law ; and the machinery for its enforcement was set in motion promptly.
Some of the worst evils of life in the tenements have thereby been abolished. The hazard of midnight fires has been met through the banish-
ment of dangerous trades from tenement houses. The cruller bakeries
were the worst of these. The owners have been forced to give up the
crullers, or to make their bakeries fireproof. Paint and oil stores, feed
stores, and all other depots of inflammable wares in tenement houses
have been put under the control of the Fire Department and the Department of Buildings.

No tenement has been built in New York in the past two years that
has not had one-fourth of the lot upon which it stands left open to the
light and air. The dark bedroom is gone for good. Every room must
have a window opening on the outer air. Dark hallways must be lighted.

The worst of the old rookeries are gone.   Sixteen rear tenements of the most vicious type were seized, and the tenants ordered out.   Other buildings were condemned in quick succession ; the death registry serving as guide for the sanitary officials.   The landlords resorted to the courts, but were beaten.   Ninety-four tenements have been seized, of which twenty-two have been destroyed, ten have been remodelled under the direction of the Department, and the rest stand vacant.

⎯ Within the present year the Board has established a system of medical inspection of school children.   It has appointed a chief medical school inspector, with a staff of 150 inspectors ; every school being visited each day.   All ailing children are examined ; and those found to be suffering from contagious or infectious disease are sent home.

THE PUBLIC SCHOOLS.

No more difficult problem confronted Mayor Strong than the reformation of the public schools.   They were founded upon an antiquated system, and were entangled in an endless network of red tape and legal forms.   A growing section of the city would outstrip its demands before the simplest improvements in school facilities could be procured. For nearly two years the work of the Department was handicapped by the struggle to get rid of the ward trustees.   With the success of that movement, and the reorganization of the Board in sympathy with the new law, the real progress began.

At the opening of the present year, ten new school buildings were in course of construction, to furnish accommodation for 13,978 pupils. Contracts for three additional buildings had been awarded by the Board of Education, and were before the Board of Estimate and Apportionment for approval.   These will furnish accommodation for 5,104 children.   Plans had also been approved for ten other buildings.   In all, the twenty-three schools will furnish accommodation for 31,378.   During the year 1896, the city acquired ten sites for new buildings as well as seventeen sites for additions, and improvement in light, ventilation, and sanitation.   Twenty-eight other sites were in process of acquisition by condemnation proceedings.   The Board of Education had also approved thirteen sites which they had not yet submitted to the Corporation Counsel for action.

Within the past two years, the Legislature has authorized the issue of bonds by the city to the amount of $15,000,000 for the acquisition of school sites and erection of buildings.   It has authorized a further issue of $2,500,000 for the establishment of high schools.   The legal pro-

cedure in condemnation of property for school purposes has been sim-
plified and shortened. These plans and funds will enable the city to
remove the reproach, that tens of thousands of its children are in the
streets for lack of school facilities.

THE DEPARTMENT OF PUBLIC WORKS.

For the first time in its history, the revenue collected last year from
water rents was more than enough to reimburse the city for the entire
outlay of the Department of Public Works. The increase in the cash
collections of 1896 over 1895 was $187,204.48, and over 1894, $347,-
786.56. The storage capacity of the Croton Water-shed has been increased from 17,579,000,000 gallons in 1894 to nearly 39,000,000,000
gallons in 1896. During the past year, twenty miles of water-mains
have been constructed ; and work is now in progress in Fifth Avenue
on a water-main capable of carrying 50,000;000 gallons of water daily
from the Central Park reservoir to the lower part of the city.

Asphalt pavements have been substituted for worn-out granite pavements as far as the appropriations permitted. More than twenty miles
of asphalt pavement were laid during 1896. The "Collis Bicycle
Strips" have brought comfort and safety to every wheelman. Old
lamps have been replaced by new and ornamental ones, bearing on the
glass the names of streets and the numbers of the corner houses. The
Boulevard has been beautified with grass-plots and Welsbach lights.

For many years the charge for vault-space under the sidewalks, in
front of buildings, was seventy-five cents per square foot. The present
Commissioner has established the charge at $2.00 per square foot.

THE DOCK DEPARTMENT.

The Commissioners of the Dock Department have laid the foundations of an extension of the dock facilities of New York Harbor which
will considerably increase the commerce of the port. Their plan for
the improvement of the water-front between Charles Street and West
Twenty-third Street creates 4.82 miles of new wharfage room, exclusive
of 1,960 feet for ferry purposes. It is the only large scheme of water-
front improvement which has not been more or less fragmentary ; and
it is the first one worthy of the city. Agreements to lease the proposed
new piers between Charles and Gansevoort streets will give rentals
yielding an annual revenue of over 5 per cent interest on the total expenditures. This improvement will not be a burden to the taxpayer:

on the contrary, it will produce a net revenue in addition to its great commercial advantages.

Want of space prevents a detailed reference to the work of the other departments, of all of which it may be said that they have acquitted themselves with credit, as well as with honor to the city government.

FINANCES.

The one charge of failure that may be pressed plausibly against the administration of Mayor Strong is the increase in the expenditures of the city government. For several years prior to his administration, there had been a steady annual increase in the public debt. This increase was mainly for expenditures on improvements of a permanent character, such as the purchase of lands for public parks and docks, the erection of school buildings, police- and fire-stations, armories, museums, hospitals, asylums, bridges over the Harlem River, the repairing of streets and avenues, increasing the water-supply, and similar changes rendered necessary by the growth of the city. This regular annual increase in the public debt has been accelerated during Mayor Strong's administration for the simple reason that the construction of all such permanent improvements has been accelerated. Those already planned have been finished or pressed forward toward completion. New works have been projected, and in many cases executed, with a promptness formerly unknown in New York.

The financial success of a municipal administration must be measured by the same standards that would be applied to any large business enterprise, or to the execution of a great charitable bequest. It should not be determined by the actual expenditures themselves, but by an intelligent comparison of *the results achieved by the expenditures,* whether greater or less than in a former year. Judging by such a comparison, the people of the city of New York may be well satisfied with Mayor Strong as trustee of the city's funds. They have paid more because they have received more—both in quantity and quality—than in former years.

The experiment of non-partisan municipal government has been a success. The lesson is plain : Try it again.

FRANK D. PAVEY.

THE McKINLEY ADMINISTRATION AND PROSPERITY.

THE present heavy depression of industry is certainly a far cry from the cheerful bustle of prosperity which the general public expected as a consequence of Mr. McKinley's election. Indeed so universal was the belief in recovery, in case of Republican success, that last November was regarded as the turning-point of all industrial suffering. The feeling of confidence immediately after the election caused a great rise in the prices of securities,—only to be followed, within a month or two, by a steady and disheartening decline. Since then industry has moved with leaden feet. Why should it not go swiftly on? Why have all expectations been so cruelly disappointed?

The conditions of to-day, however, cannot be disassociated from those of yesterday. The modern business organism does not work normally immediately after a great shock,—any more than the human system after a violent railway collision. And during the panic in the summer of 1896 our business had such a shock as left it in a shattered condition. No one can forget the desperate tension of trade and credit during that period; indeed it is not yet gone. Nevertheless, it may not be sufficiently realized that a painful, perhaps a prolonged, process of invalidism must be endured before conditions can again become normal.

Before the election some evidently felt: "Stop the cause of the panic, and business will instantly right itself." The fear of a disastrous fall from the existing gold standard to one of silver (one-half as valuable) had—in proportion to the belief in the success of the Silver candidates—made prices and contracts uncertain, confused all estimates as to the future, stopped buying, and paralyzed industry. "Remove this fear," it was felt, "and all will be well again. Elect Mr. McKinley and the Sound-money candidates in November, and industry will resume its activity." But herein was a fatal omission,— the failure to understand fully what had already taken place. If a burglar shoots me, and several times sends bullets crashing through my body, am I just as active and healthy as formerly, the moment he stops shooting—the moment he stops the cause of my wounds? Evi-

dently not: the damage has already been done ; and while the cessation of shooting may save me from additional injury, it will not cure
the wounds inflicted.   Removing the burglar does not cure my hurt:
painful surgical operations, time, and slow physical recuperation are
necessary to complete recovery.   Similarly, the passing of Mr. Bryan
and the removal of the fear of the silver standard—perhaps after all
only temporarily—could not of themselves cure the country of the
injuries and losses inflicted during the panic of 1896 ; to say nothing
of the results traceable to 1893.

To regard the election of an Executive for the nation as decisive for
the adoption of a good or bad currency, would be natural only on the
assumption that the mass of the people do not think.   It is almost
pathetic to see a great, lusty country like ours still hugging the political delusion that a campaign for an Executive Officer settles the policy
of the Legislative branch of our government.   No matter what the
views of a President, he cannot carry them out until they have become enacted into the law of the land.   A President can do scarcely
anything in the enactment of the legislative platform of his party,
—except in so far as he can influence legislation by the distribution of executive patronage,—unless Congress first enacts laws, which
he is then sworn to execute, whether they suit his own views or
not.   So far as bad industrial conditions depend upon remedial legislation, very little responsibility rests upon the President, but very
much upon his party : little rests upon the Executive, but very much
upon Members of the House and Senate.   And yet, in the Presidential campaigns, the managers of the show, by great attractions,
adroitly draw off our attention to the choice of an Executive,—of course
because the managers have the Executive spoils to distribute,—while
Members of Congress and State legislators who choose Senators, the
real arbiters of industrial remedies, slip into office almost unnoticed.   It
is a most extraordinary case of perverted emphasis.   The mass of voters
are in dire need of corrective legislation on the currency ; and yet they
are hoodwinked by manipulating politicians who wish Executive appointments, and who succeed in making their matter the main issue.
It is time for us to concentrate our chief attention upon the men who
make our laws, rather than upon the men who execute them.

This simple fact must explain why the election of Mr. McKinley,
in and by itself, has produced so little effect in the restoration of prosperity.   In itself his election, as a remedial action, was nothing.   The
great vote given to the platform on which he stood was, of course, a

declaration of tremendous force in favor of maintaining the existing gold standard as against a depreciated silver standard; but no change in existing conditions can result until these views are cast into the definite law of the land.   Moreover, only so far as this voting took effect in the choice of our national legislators did it in any effectual way improve the chances for prosperity.   And as regards this matter, it should be noted that the shrewd, penetrating men of affairs, whose pecuniary interests are at stake in industry, know all this well enough.

This is why the situation in the winter after the election was one of cautious expectancy.   The winter session of Congress did nothing whatever to change the conditions under which industry had been dragging along since 1893, and under which it had suffered a great cataclysm in 1896.   Nothing was settled: everything was a matter of guesswork.   Existing conditions contained the same possibilities for the future as those that had developed into ruinous events in the past: the unstable conditions of the currency, the legal regulations of bonds and gold reserves, were such that an agitation for the silver standard on a formidable scale in 1896 was capable of producing wide-spread and phenomenal ruin to industry.   This result was branded into our consciousness by enormous losses and by months of desperate anxiety and strain.   If this could take place in 1896, then—conditions remaining unchanged—why could not similar disaster come in 1898, or in 1900?

The panic of last year, by its failures and liquidations, produced a breakdown in the reciprocal relations of producers and buyers.   When a high building has been blown down, we know it cannot instantly be rebuilt in its original form: on the contrary, each brick and sill must be slowly and laboriously relaid.   So, in the case of industry after a panic, the seller (if he survive) must slowly rediscover the buyer who has means to buy with and a desire to buy.   For this reciprocal re-adjustment both time and skill are demanded.   Not until some branch of production (perhaps agriculture) gains new purchasing power, does the growing demand, increasing concurrently with production, spread in ever-widening circles to many occupations,—until, finally, all available capital and labor find employment in new adjustments.   Nothing, of course, should be allowed to intercept this return to health and prosperity.   Potential disaster would lessen the confidence of commercial enterprise, even if industry were in a normal and healthy state: much more would it create disturbance, if industry were already reduced by as much suffering as it could safely bear.   It is as if the patient, not yet recovered from the burglar's shots, should find his old enemy still lurking about the curtains of his bed, looking for a chance to inflict a new wound. We see, then, a debilitated and sensitive business organism again threatened by the possibilities of currency dangers before it has recovered from the injuries of the past. The magnitude of Mr. Bryan's vote is a shadow even now lying over the world of trade.

We are now in a position to review the events since Mr. McKinley's election which have delayed the expected prosperity. Apart from the fact that failures and liquidations reaching back as far as 1893 have made the situation difficult, we are met by the one great cause of industrial inaction; viz., uncertainty as to the future. Never, for any length of time, since the passage of the Bland-Allison Bill in 1878, has industry been given quiet and certainty as to the standard upon which all operations are based: this fatal instability brought on the ruinous panic of 1893, and added to it that of 1896. The fear as to what the standard might be has existed, and is still present, in every investor's, in every employer's mind. Keeping this in view, have the events subsequent to Mr. McKinley's election tended to diminish or to increase the uncertainty as to the standard on which business is necessarily transacted?

The maintenance of the existing gold standard—which was the central issue of the last campaign—cannot be permanently secured so long as our monetary legislation remains as it is. Under the great embarrassments due to our existing laws, it was with great difficulty that even so courageous an Executive as Mr. Cleveland kept intact the gold reserve. Our present abundant supply of gold is due merely to the happy incidents of our international trade. During the recent years of depression, our people have been working hard, and spending little; consequently our exports have increased and our imports have diminished. In 1896, our excess of exports once reached the hitherto unparalleled sum of $325,000,000. This placed foreigners in debt to us; so that we not only did not need to export our own products of gold, but, in addition, it was sent to us in millions. (We have gold enough and to spare, but no industry sufficient to absorb it.) For this reason, both the banks and the Treasury have easily increased their gold holdings; the latter to the amount of $155,000,000. But there is no permanency in this. Recent events show this very clearly. The likelihood of the passage of higher tariff duties by Congress has caused heavy imports of goods in the last few months. And these very imports have offset credits due us against our former heavy exports;

thereby making gold exports possible, and already weakening our gold reserve in the Treasury by perhaps $10,000,000. A serious reversal of our international trade would at once put our gold reserve, and consequently our standard of payments, in jeopardy.

For these and other reasons, our men of affairs cannot feel certain as to the future of our standard. Our foreign trade is big with possibilities of disturbance. And some internal conditions, moreover, are not so promising as to give much confidence. So long as our laws are what they now are, it is to be remembered that the Silver agitation can accomplish its ends by creating in the mind of the public a distrust in the power of the Administration to maintain gold payments; for the disappearance of the gold reserve would bring us to silver payments quite as effectually as positive legislation in favor of free coinage of silver. If any reaction against the Republican party should take place at an early date, which would give the Silver party a majority in the House,—and that is not an impossible contingency,— it would create a situation full of peril to the existing standard. Such possibilities as these show what uncertainties surround our long-suffering industries in their unequal struggle for existence. The coming of a new President has not removed these uncertainties.

Although the President cannot be held responsible for legislative enactments,—since it is Congress that must be held accountable for legislation—yet the President, together with his party, has many ways of aiding a good or a bad policy. As we well know, producers all over our land hoped that the election of last November would finally dispose of the Silver agitation which had shaken confidence in our standard, and thus put an end to the insistent questioning of the very basis of commerce and production. Certainly it was the duty of an intelligent Executive to do all in his power to bring this agitation to a close. Instead of that we have some evidences of the superior strategy of the Silver managers. Even before Mr. McKinley's inauguration, a Silver Senator was sent abroad as an unofficial agent "to see what could be done for silver,"—as if it were not about time that long-suffering industry should have something done to protect it against the Silver combination that would destroy the existing standard, bring on panics (as in 1893 and 1896), cause losses of untold millions; in fact, do anything, no matter what the cost to the country at large, provided its members could utilize this Government as a tool to support their special, selfish interests.

Then, when Mr. McKinley, after assuming office, sent three commissioners to Europe in the interests of silver, and selected at least two members who represented to the public the policy of free coinage of silver,—the very policy against which the whole campaign of 1896 was waged,—it was a shock to confidence not easily borne in silence. In effect, this mission, so far as it was serious, and not mere politics, served only to keep up the old dangerous agitation regarding our standard. And it did worse than this. Once more, Silver partisans were given the use of government money to spread abroad in Europe— where we are constantly seeking capital to exploit the newer portions of our land—views which came from the defeated element in the recent elections. No wonder Europe is sensitive as to American financial methods. Moreover, this partisan body will be given the use of the government printing office to distribute their views broadcast over the country, and to keep adroitly the Silver issue before the public. Could anything be worse for business? Instead of strengthening the results of the November election, so far as it lay in the power of the Executive, this action, dignified with a nation's authority, has more or less counteracted its moral advantages.[1] And in so far it has not worked to remove the shadow of uncertainty hanging over our industries.

There is undoubtedly more in this coquetting with the Silver combination than appears on the surface. Indeed the secret history of the Silver agitation, its bargains, its strategy, would by itself form an interesting story. It is common property to many persons in Washington and elsewhere. In fact, a Silver Senator some years ago cynically admitted the existence of a compact between legislators representing certain manufacturing interests and the Silver agents, by which reciprocal aid was given by votes. There is certainly nothing *a priori* exceptional in this. And even more definite evidence can be cited. The Sherman Act of July 14, 1890, which nearly brought us to the silver standard, and did bring us to the panic of 1893, was the consideration granted by the Republican party to the Silver men in return for the passage of the Tariff Act of that year.[2]

[1] It is not to the point to say that international bimetallism was a part of the St. Louis platform. The essential point in it was the maintenance of the " existing gold standard " ; and a plank which included the admission that the existing standard was injurious, and that silver must be taken up for the reason that existing conditions were working damage, completely antagonized the principal issue, on which the election was afterwards unmistakably won. The struggle by which " gold " was inserted into the platform would be meaningless on any other interpretation.

[2] *Vide* the speech of Senator Teller in the Senate, April 29, 1896 : " He [Sher-

This bargaining, which has other ramifications, split upon the rock of commercial events,—an obstacle beyond the control even of shifty politicians.   The burden of the Sherman Act being more than a weakened currency system could bear, it gave way : one might barter away a sound currency for a mess of pottage, but the inevitable results to trade and commerce could not be stayed.   The business interests, indignant at the Silver legislation which had brought on the panic of 1893, rose in anger and assisted President Cleveland to induce Congress to repeal the purchase clause of the Sherman Act.   This, however, took away from one of the two parties to the compact the reward for its votes.   And this explains the manœuvring between the Western Silver Senators and the Republican party up to the very close of the St. Louis Convention of 1896.   Would the Republican leaders renew the old compact?   The situation had its evident difficulties. After the havoc wrought by Silver legislation in 1893, the Republicans could not defy public opinion and satisfy the demands of the Silver party.   If they would not, then how could they expect to have the Silver votes for their Tariff legislation?   -

These elements went to make up a most interesting condition of affairs at St. Louis.   Just at this time came the loud voice of public opinion—quite unexpected by the politicians—which, with unmistakable force, demanded and obtained the declaration for the maintenance of "the existing gold standard," even at the sacrifice of the Silver Republicans.   It was this courageous party action which won success for its ticket.   But, after the dramatic public performance at St. Louis, one is led to consider how strictly this represents the present relation between the Republican leaders and the Silver Senators.   The Tariff Bill cannot be passed without an understanding with the Silver group.   If so, what is the *quid pro quo?*   The present open bargaining in the Senate is depressing and discouraging enough.   The friends of industrial prosperity may well keep a sharp lookout to see "what is being done for silver" at this juncture.   It may be a part of the superior strategy of the Silver group to allow the tariff legislators to go to extremes; confident in the alienation thereby of many Sound-money advocates and the consequent division of the forces they must meet in coming campaigns.

But what furtherance of monetary reform for the relief of business is to come out of such a situation?   The prospect is certainly not very

man] believed, first, that it would secure the passage of a tariff bill," and other passages.

bright. Hence, no cautious man will invest a million, or even a hundred, dollars, in any permanent operation of industry so long as doubt exists as to whether he will get back money of the same kind that he puts in. Therefore, business waits.

To some minds, however, the present depression seems more or less related to the passage of higher protective duties; and there is no little truth in this. Not only the currency, but the tariff, has a present influence on industry in so far as it works for certainty or distrust. While it is apparent that higher taxation *per se* cannot secure prosperity, a certain large measure of prosperity is possible even with heavy taxation, provided that it is accompanied by some certainty as to the future.

A tariff bill was expected from the McKinley administration by most well-informed men, if only to provide a larger income to meet existing deficits; but it was generally assumed that it would be a moderate measure. Indeed, in the days immediately following the election, in a flush of grateful appreciation for the help of Sound-money Democrats, Republican newspapers freely suggested a tariff with such reasonable duties that these new allies might have no reason for ever leaving the Republican fold. And, during the campaign, the statement in the St. Louis platform to the effect that the party was not pledged to any particular "schedules" was explained to mean that no such extreme duties as those in the McKinley bill (which might be suggested by the nomination of Mr. McKinley himself) were intended. The necessity of the special session of Congress was based on the imperative need of additional revenues to overcome the deficit, and not ostensibly on the need for greater protection. Moreover, it was urged, that if the gold reserve were to be kept intact, or a surplus provided with which to retire greenbacks, more income was demanded. It need not be said that these aims do not seem to have guided the framers of tariff legislation up to the present time. A moderate bill, so adjusted as to provide sufficient revenues, followed by a speedy adjournment of Congress would, no doubt, have given the country—even though suspicious of the monetary situation—great encouragement to undertake important enterprises.

Instead of this what was the country given? A tariff of exaggerations, a tariff of scandals, a tariff of barbarisms, a tariff which antagonized both Republicans and Democrats, and whose extreme provisions have been so thoroughly advertised throughout the length and breadth of the land that counter-agitation for a reform of customs duties is seen

36

to be quite inevitably a part of the future, even before the bill is enacted.   Instead of an Act likely to be acquiesced in, and under which
the industries affected could count upon some reasonable certainty for
a few years ahead, the exasperation at the methods of our national
legislators is so intense, so contemptuous, that permanency of tariff
legislation is "an iridescent dream."   It is believed that this legislation
is being framed neither in accordance with protective principles *per se*,
nor for purposes of revenue, but by a process of bargaining for selfish
gain which will not bear the light.   The system by which the special
interests are themselves not merely permitted, but invited, to fix the
customs duties levied on their products may be compared to disputants
sitting in court and passing judgment upon their own cases.   Such a
system contains in itself the elements of its own destruction.

That the tariff situation has not conduced to establish confidence
in investors and producers as to the future, is too apparent everywhere
to need mention here.   It has already created material for an explosive reaction, and thereby removed certainty far into the future.   As
if the uncertainty of frequent changes in the tariff were not enough,
we see the committees of the Senate in the power of the Silver Senators.   It may not be a pleasant thing to say, but never before—at
least in this generation—has there been such widespread loss of confidence in the honor and integrity of our public servants in Congress.
One almost hesitates to put into words the frequent admissions of
thoughtful men that national legislation is to-day bargained for, if not
actually bought and sold.   So far has suspicion gone, that it is even
bruited about, as matter of common report, that while the President
himself may not have made election promises, yet his agents have engaged for him, in the form of a tariff bill, to allow numerous interests to
recoup themselves from the country for advances made to secure the
nomination and election of their candidate.   The audacity, the unblushing
"grab," displayed in Washington gives color to such reports; else why
should such legislation be given its strange preëminence over monetary
reform ?   And why should the President have allowed himself to open
the special session of Congress with a Message in which there was not
one word in regard to monetary legislation—the main question of the
campaign?   Why is it seemingly admitted in Washington that it is
Utopian to talk of a bill retiring greenbacks?

It is evident that the wrong conditions are deeper than mere party
platforms.   It is not a matter to be remedied by turning from one
party to another.   In 1894, the country scornfully rejected the Demo-

crats, largely because the favors granted to special interests in the Senate, in the modification of the Wilson Bill, disgusted the voters. It was believed that the Democrats had not virtue enough to withstand the temptations which such bills create.   And yet there is now a strong belief that, in similar circumstances, a Republican is no more to be trusted than a Democratic Senator.   When one sees how much basis there is for this distrust, one does not feel surprised at much of the blind hatred of political corruption expressed by some honest supporters of Mr. Bryan.   If we faced the matter squarely, we should find much to justify the existence of Bryanism.

In this state of the public mind, even if the Tariff Bill be enacted, we shall not, by any means, see the fetters removed from our hampered industries.   Tariff agitation will leave protected industries no lengthened period of certainty ; and the popular disgust may show itself in a political reaction at the polls which will still further excite doubt as to the future of our standard.   And, if we bear in mind, in addition to these grave obstacles to prosperity, the surprising and sweeping decision of the Supreme Court in the Trans-Missouri Traffic Association, by which ordinary agreements in trade are made illegal, and the vast capital engaged in railway transportation made timid and uncertain as to the future, we may well wonder that we are no worse off.   Is there any difficulty in understanding why an industrial system, already weakened by two panics, looks to the future with timidity ; why production is limited, and labor out of employment; why purchases are small?   J. LAURENCE LAUGHLIN.

WHY SPAIN HAS FAILED IN CUBA.

ON October 28, 1492, Columbus, touching upon the shores of Cuba, wrote in his log-book, " Of all lands this is the most beautiful ever beheld by human eyes." The government of Spain has been keeping that diary ever since. The second entry related the slaughter of the peaceful Indians by the " white men descended from Heaven." Succeeding pages for four centuries tell a continuous tale of injustice, oppression, bloodshed, official corruption, and strange and ferocious hatred of offspring by the mother country. Those who now guide the pen of Spanish record are writing the last familiar chapter. Cuban chroniclers will soon begin where Columbus left off, by adding to his log-book entry, " And the land shall be as free as it is beautiful, and independent forever."

To make this entry and enjoy the manifold blessings of liberty, a handful of ragged and poorly armed revolutionists, scattered over the country, are successfully opposing a well-equipped army more than twice as large as the United States army in the Mexican war, and exceeding by 119,000 men the government forces engaged in all our Indian wars since the Declaration of Independence. Why this great force has been unable in two years and five months to exterminate the last band of patriots, is a puzzle to military men and a mystery to the world. The solution is not afforded by the defensible character of the country, and the advantage possessed by the insurgents through their familiarity with its swamps, mountain passes, and natural strongholds. This knowledge, as well as their dash, bravery, and heroic endurance of hardships, has undoubtedly been of great service to the rebels; but it has not made them invincible. All these elements in favor of the insurgents are more than neutralized by their ignorance of the art of war, in which the thousands upon thousands of regular troops, led by the foremost generals of Spain, are supposed to be highly skilled.

It was not a difficult military problem that was presented to this invading host. Spain was in possession of every important city, of all the lines of communication and supply, and had in well-distributed garrisons, at the outbreak of the insurrection on February 24, 1895, an army of 20,320 men. There were also nearly 60,000 volunteers or militia, ready to be called out to quell civil disturbances. There were only a few hundred Cubans in revolt by the end of March, when re-inforcements from Spain were demanded, and an additional force of 7,000 troops was landed. Captain-General Isasi was recalled, and General Campos, with more troops, took command on April 10. The revolution, born in the mountainous province of Santiago de Cuba, was spreading slowly westward. Dissatisfaction at Madrid caused Campos's recall on January 17, 1896; and, on February 10, General Valeriño Weyler y Nicolau, Marquis of Tenerife, took command. Captain-General Weyler was "clothed with legal omnipotence." He took the field in person. He asked for—and Spain, on the verge of bankruptcy, in her patriotism and her confidence in her chosen commander, supplied—more than 200,000 men to put down what was still, so far as the number of insurrectionists in arms was concerned, a small local uprising.

The spectacle of Spain pouring out her gold and her children's blood to preserve her national territory, was sublime: the use to which this great sacrifice has been put is a crime against a confiding people whose faith has been dishonored. General Weyler should have subdued the rebellion within ninety days. No unprejudiced military authority who has studied the two forces, and made due allowance for the advantages possessed by those who fight upon their native soil, will dissent from this proposition. There are Spanish generals in Cuba who admit its truth. There are others who have returned, disgusted, to Spain because their suggestions of plans to end the war were not allowed to be disclosed at the Palace.

A four months' stay in Cuba, beginning in January and ending with April of this year, much of which time was passed in observing the forces in the field, has resulted in the conviction, on my part, that it has not been the purpose of General Weyler to end the rebellion. Conversations with Spanish officers, from generals to corporals, showed that the same motives that were evidently actuating the commander in allowing the war to drag along were prompting a large proportion of the staff and line in carrying out the policy of their superior. The recital of a few experiences, the description of actual conditions, an explanation of methods employed, and an account of the poor result achieved where success was possible, will prove this indictment. If it be admitted that General Weyler has the slightest military ability, the situation in Cuba to-day will convict him.

The two eastern provinces, Santiago de Cuba and Puerto Principe, are already "Cuba Libre." There the new government is discharging all its functions almost without annoyance. In the other four provinces, the rebels are practically the rulers outside the large cities. For more than two years, with a maximum strength of scarcely 30,000 indifferently armed guerilla soldiers, the insurgents have, on a narrow island, successfully waged war against 235,000 well-armed troops, assisted by militia, supported by a navy, and maintained by constant supplies.

· It is no reflection upon the valor of the insurgents to say that it has been made comparatively easy for them to keep up the strife. General Weyler began his campaign by building small forts all over the island. This was a novel plan for the commander of an invading army to adopt. It put the Spanish forces at the start in the position of seeming to seek their own safety, awaiting attack, instead of pursuing and conquering the enemy. The number of these forts, erected and in process of building, is astonishing. They are placed within short distances of one another along every railroad; they are found in great numbers even in the meanest villages; and they stretch like links of a chain from one side of the island to the other, where the two famous but useless and expensive trochas have been constructed.

These forts are garrisoned with an average of eight men. As the defenders never leave them, it is estimated that at least 150,000 of Weyler's force of 235,000 are thus prevented from taking active part in the campaign. The balance of the army not doing clerical or staff duty is divided into columns, which march to little purpose from one of the fortified towns to another. They never camp at night in the open field, for they have no tents and no commissariat. They are obliged at nightfall—even when hotly pursuing the enemy—to seek some village, where they bivouac within or around the walls of the fortifications, or go to a "sugar central"—also protected by forts—to rest themselves under the eaves of the larger buildings. More often these columns return at night to the point from which they started in the morning. It is necessary for them to change their base of supply, if they wish to make progress through the country; and they do not do this until they have scoured the vicinity in all directions, in their daily marches.

On these marches the huts of the *pacíficos* are burned; and the peaceful folk who are not killed are forced to go to the nearest fortified town and there remain. Crops are destroyed; and nothing is left that can possibly give aid or succor to the insurgents. Occasionally a band of rebels will be met and attacked. Both sides fight with bravery; but neither shows good judgment nor tactical skill.   The Cubans charge on horseback with little attempt at formation or method.   The Spanish infantry throws itself into a hollow square to meet the onslaught.   This is the only formation that the regulars in the field seem to understand. If the Cubans break the square, they cut through it; but, strange to say, seldom return to engage the column.   If the Spanish soldiers repulse the rebels, they fire a few volleys and allow them to ride off unpursued. Neither side follows up an advantage in such encounters, but seems content with the result of engagements that are soon over.   A well-planned, long-sustained battle is unknown in Cuba.   The Cubans, if taken by surprise, scatter immediately.   The Spaniards have been ambushed so often that they are very loath to follow.   Unless in greatly superior numbers, they avoid trying issues with detachments of rebels they may chance to meet.   In the uplands and mountains the Cuban bands are fairly secure from assault.   They dash into the open country, pounce upon a column, kill a few soldiers, and get away with small loss.   The Spaniards fear to pursue, lest they be led into a narrow pass and shot to pieces,—a fate which many a valorous column has met.

The inefficiency of the Spanish officers is demonstrated by their failure to make these tactics of the Cubans dangerous and costly.   The plowboy soldier from Spain is a brave fellow.   He is undrilled, poorly fed, badly clothed, and neglected; but he is ever ready to go after the rebels and engage them in their strongholds.   General Weyler's method of campaigning, and the lack of military experience or knowledge on the part of the subordinate officers, hold the troops back and allow the rebel chiefs, with less men and even less skill, to continue successfully their peculiar method of warfare.   In the field, the Spanish invader acts more frequently on the defensive than on the aggressive.

For over a year General Maximo Gomez, the commander-in-chief of the Army of Liberation, has moved with impunity from point to point, in a small stretch of country in the vicinity of Sancti Spiritus, in the mountainous northeast corner of Santa Clara Province.   This extraordinary man has well been termed "The Old Fox."   While he does not possess the military talent of General Calixto Garcia, who has practically wrested the provinces of Santiago de Cuba and Puerto Principe from Spanish rule, it is doubtful if, as a master of guerilla tactics, General Gomez has an equal.   His march from one end of the island to the other, on the breaking out of the revolution,—when the people in the greater part of the country through which he passed had not yet risen in rebellion, and strong Spanish forces were active in every province,—evidenced his ability as a bush fighter and raider. He has made his fame secure, by directing, from headquarters, the movements of his widely separated forces, which, in spite of the operations of 20,000 troops kept in the vicinity, have never been forced from a section of country scarcely one hundred miles square—and that section in the very centre of the island.

General Gomez never has more than 300 or 400 men with him. His favorite camp is near Arroyo Blanco, on a high plateau, difficult to approach and covered with dense thicket. He posts his outer pickets at least three miles away, in the directions from which the enemy may come. The Spaniards, whenever possible, march by road; and, with these highways well guarded, Gomez sleeps secure. He knows that his pickets will be informed by some Cuban long before the Spanish column leaves or passes the nearest village to attack him. A shot from the farthest sentry causes little or no excitement in Gomez's camp. The report throws the Spanish column into fears of attack or ambush; and it moves forward very slowly and carefully. Two pickets at such a time have been known to hold 2,000 men at bay for a whole day. If the column presses on, and General Gomez hears a shot from a sentinel near by, he will rise leisurely from his hammock and give orders to prepare to move camp. He has had so many experiences of this kind that not until he hears the volley-shooting of the oncoming Spaniards will he call for his horse, give the word to march, and disappear, followed by his entire force, into the tropical underbrush, which closes like a curtain behind them, leaving the Spaniards to discover a deserted camp, without the slightest trace of the path taken by its recent occupants.

Sometimes Gomez will move only a mile or two. The Spaniards do not usually give chase. If they do, Gomez takes a keen delight in leading them in a circle. If he can throw them off by nightfall, he goes to sleep in his camp of the morning happier than if he had won a battle. The Spaniards learn nothing through such experiences. Gomez varies the game occasionally by marching directly toward the rear of the foe, and there, reinforced by other insurgent bands of the neighborhood, falling upon the column and punishing it severely. While his immediate force is only a handful, the General can call to his aid, in a short time, nearly 6,000 men. The Cubans are divided into small bands, under experienced chiefs, and are hidden away in camps similar to the one described. When they are attacked, they escape by the same tactics. They are not often disturbed: for the country is hostile to the Spaniards; and they can rarely find a Cuban who will disclose the whereabouts of the native forces.

There is little or no pretence of drilling the Cuban soldiers. If they learn by trumpet signal when to break camp, to attack, to retreat, and to scatter, they think they know enough for all practical purposes of war. They are courageous, but nervous, under fire, and rarely wait for orders to attack. The knowledge that they are going into skirmish, and the sight of the enemy make them so excited that they would not hear the commands of their similarly agitated officers if any were given. Americans who have joined the insurgent ranks with the belief that they could teach the Cubans how to fight by military rule, and drill their raw forces into sturdy disciplined troops, have been wofully disappointed. Such attempts soon cease. The Cuban soldier refuses to learn the most ordinary tactics. He believes he is a better fighter than any foreigner; that he alone understands how to struggle with the Spaniard; and that, as a horseman, it is impossible for anyone to improve him. He dislikes marching on foot; and there is no infantry in the Cuban army worthy of the name. The Cubans feel more courageous on horseback, and prefer to do all their fighting in the saddle. They will frequently attack the Spanish forts astride their wonderful little ponies, and ride up to the very loopholes in the face of volley upon volley.

If the horse escapes slaughter, its chances of being ridden to death are increased. Its master has no mercy upon it, no knowledge of how to care for the faithful animal, and no inclination to save its strength by dismounting and easing saddle-girths and packstraps when leisurely making ascents. Not even in this particular will the Cuban take advice. He also resents reflections upon his marksmanship, which is far from good. The Spaniard is no better shot. Neither side does any target practising,—the Cuban, because he cannot afford to waste his ammunition; and the Spaniard, because his officer does not take the trouble to instruct him. The Spaniards rarely raise their rifles to their shoulders. Whole battalions deliver successive volleys with every man holding the butt under his arm. This enables him to steady the weapon more easily while he works the magazine; but the bullets invariably seek the sky. After one "battle" in which there was rapid firing for twenty minutes by evenly matched forces, it was found that no one was killed or injured. A chemist of a neighboring sugar estate, who weighed one of the bullets and did a little figuring, declared that more than half a ton of lead had been shot into the mountain peaks.

The deadly weapon of the war is the Cuban machete. It is the tool and arm of the native from boyhood. In peace it is a scythe and grub-hook, and serves every purpose for which a knife can be used. It then varies in form and size. In war it is a long, narrow, razor-like blade, blunt at the point, but sharpened on both edges and hilted like a sword. It becomes a cleaver—an extended double-edged battleaxe—which in accustomed hands severs the head from the body with one stroke, or, striking on the shoulder, splits the trunk in twain. The Spaniards have a wholesome dread of the fearful weapon. It has won more fights for the Cubans than all the rifles landed by filibustering expeditions. General Gomez gives the order "Al machete!" whenever possible. It is a brave column that will stand its ground to receive the charge of hundreds of yelling Cubans, rushing toward it on frantic ponies, flashing their deadly blades in air.

Considerable dynamite has found its way into the insurgent lines; but its use is little understood. Now and then trains have been blown up; but, on the whole, the damage done with this explosive has been small. The Cuban operators never think of exploding bombs in round-houses, and destroying the motive power of a road at one stroke. They blow up hand-cars, now and then an engine, and occasionally a culvert, all which are quickly repaired: they leave long bridges, the destruction of which would cripple the railroad. There would be no more danger attending attempts to blow up the bridges than is incurred in demolishing other kinds of railroad property. All are equally well guarded. The size of the bridges seems to fill the Cubans with an overpowering sense of the magnitude of the operation; and they will turn their backs upon it, to risk their lives in doing something which, even if successful, is of no value.

The troops of Spain are but little better drilled than those of Cuba. The privates are splendid raw material for soldiers. They are small, wiry men, or rather boys,—for nearly all are beardless,—and they have excellent teeth, fine limbs, and the most buoyant nature under trying circumstances. With all their hardships in a land which they are attempting unwillingly to keep enslaved, the conscripts are good-natured and often light-hearted, and inclined to joke and sing in hours of ease. They are wonderful marchers. It is common for a column of these youngsters, after a cup of coffee and a bite of bread at daylight, to put twenty-five hot miles behind them before their breakfast at eleven o'clock. It is not extraordinary for the same column to repeat the operation by returning on the same day. They never complain, and always respond quickly and willingly to every demand made upon their endurance by their officers. They do it for Spain and Spain alone.

The wasted patriotism of these ignorant, stout-hearted, abused soldier lads is pitiable. Their officers seem to have nothing in common with them. They take no care of them, and come in contact with them as little as possible. Acts of cruelty are frequent. The soldiers have no respect for the ability of their superiors; and their superiors regard them as human cattle. The ordinary interest of an officer in the welfare of his men is entirely lacking. The privates were hastily drafted in Spain, formed into battalions, and rushed across the ocean to Cuba. It was the largest military force ever transported by sea, and it was gathered in a manner that reflects credit upon the home government; but no attention has been paid to moulding this material into soldiers. An experience of several weeks with various columns in the field did not show that the troops were drilled or instructed in the use of their arms. They were given the Mauzer magazine rifle,—a superb weapon; but they have not been taught how to care for it nor how to use it effectively. An examination of several hundreds of these fine rifles, after two months' service, showed them to be in foul condition and more or less out of order. The sights of many of the guns were gone. The men explained that they had long since knocked them off because they tore their clothes. The other accoutrements were often seen tied up with string, wire, and rope.

The officers make no attempt to have the men look neat and orderly. Their uniforms of blue and white drill are invariably filthy; and their stockingless feet are enclosed in *alpargatas* (straw shoes), which are serviceable in dry weather, but which become heavy and go to pieces when the ground is swampy or the rains begin. The slouchy figures are topped by roughly made and dirty straw hats. There is nothing soldierly about the troops or their fortifications. Arm the Italian laborer—so common a sight in New York on his way to work—with a rifle instead of a bag of bread, and you have, in appearance, a sample of the Spanish troops. Their bravery and desire to fight, so as to end the war and go home, are unquestionable: their lament is that their officers will not lead them against the insurgents. This is the kind of soldier General Weyler keeps inactive in his numberless forts, to become homesick and forlorn, and to die slowly of insufficient food or the deadly diseases of the climate.

The greater part of the skirmishing by the Spanish is done by the mounted guerillas,—a nondescript organization composed of renegade

Cubans, former bandits, and negroes forced to serve or be killed. Each company is supposed to be under a regular army officer; but many are commanded by "reformed" brigand chiefs, who control their movements just as they directed their bands of outlaws before the war. Many of the outrages against life and property which have shocked all civilized nations are committed by these troops. The responsibility for their acts, as well as for the cruel deeds of the regulars, rests upon General Weyler. He attempts to throw it off by pleading that when the atrocities are committed no army officer is in command. There are enough idle Spanish officers of the regular army in Cuba to command five times as many men as there are in the ranks of both armies.

The hotels, cafés, and parks of every city and town on the island are constantly filled with officers smoking, dining, and idling their time away. They are temperate only in drinking. On entering any great centre of population, one is struck by the great number of these "café generals." Over one hundred have been counted in a stroll in the Parque Central in Havana. At that time the neighboring cafés were filled with officers; and they abounded in the clubs and theatres. What can be seen in the capital is observable wherever there is a settlement on the island. Last April there were in Cuba 47 Spanish generals: the field and company officers numbered nearly 11,000. An estimate, made from the best figures obtainable in Havana at the time, showed that there were nearly 30,000 officers, privates, and military attachés doing special duty, and thus prevented from taking any part in active operations. Many of the generals supposed to be in the field were stationed in the larger cities, which were made the centres of the military departments. They frequently ruled the zone as would a conqueror exacting tribute from the people. It was to them that the sugar-planters, tobacco-plantation owners, and cattle-ranch proprietors had to come to ask for soldiers to protect their property. If the soldiers were supplied without a monetary consideration, which was not often, a threat to withdraw them for alleged military manœuvres soon followed.

On an American sugar-estate, supplied with troops to save the ripened cane from being burned by the insurgents, the writer had absolute proof that thousands of dollars were paid to the Spanish general commanding the district, in order that the troops might remain. Colonels and captains were also beneficiaries. At breakfast one morning, the manager of the estate jokingly asked the colonel of a passing column if the war was not turning out too profitable to be speedily closed. The colonel replied in an assumed tone of injury : " You make a crop every year : we do not get a chance to make one in ten years.   This is our harvest.   You ought to be charitable and let us alone."

The large property-owners in Cuba, including, it must be confessed, the American proprietors, have, by their "charity" to the foes of freedom, lengthened this harvest and made it profitable.   They have always paid tribute to Spanish civil officials to escape their full taxes and the effect of laws which would otherwise have been made vexatious.   They have invested considerable capital in this way ; and they do not care to lose its benefits.   They say that if the Cuban should obtain control of the government, he would be more avaricious in his demands than the Spaniard, and less apt to accord the benefits and the immunity paid for. The landed proprietors therefore prefer the existing order of things.

This is the explanation of the puzzling attitude of freeborn Americans, who represented to President Cleveland and Secretary Olney that they were thoroughly contented with Spanish dominion, and asserted that, in their judgment, the establishment of a Cuban Republic would be the worst possible outcome of the war.   When expostulated with by the writer, after their frank admission of the reason why they favored the Spanish side, many of the proprietors of these great estates defended themselves by saying that the Cuban is not fit to govern himself, and that the vast amount of foreign capital invested in the island should not be endangered by an experimental change of government.   The civil woes of the Cuban were acknowledged, and the personal outrages inflicted upon him admitted ; but his cry for liberty and a chance to show himself capable of self-government was drowned by the pleadings of dollars and cents.

In one province, the *commandante militar*, when ordered by General Weyler to purchase several hundred horses in the neighborhood, and to pay for them with due-bills on Spain, informed the horse-owners that they need not give up their valuable animals for a worthless $50 draft, but that they could arrange the matter with his secretary.   One of the horse-owners paid at the rate of $100 for every horse he was asked to furnish, and was told that horses good enough for the service would be bought in New Orleans or Mexico to make up his quota. The secretary of this *commandante* was said, by a bank clerk who keeps his account, to have deposited $40,000 within three months.   The amount of the account of the *commandante* was not learned.

Every steamer that goes eastward along the north or south coast is loaded with troops.   They pass other steamers going westward similarly laden. There is no military necessity for such transportation of forces. In moving from one town to another, if the point of departure is on a railroad connecting with the coast, a march overland of a few miles only is thereby avoided. The troops are taken on a train to a steamer, carried hundreds of miles to a second port, there transported across the island to another steamer, brought down the coast, placed on a train, and moved to the objective town. This is a very common practice. It can only be surmised that an understanding as to commissions exists between the steamboat and railroad companies and the military authorities. It is clearly evident that the money of Spain is lavishly spent in needless transportation.

It would be charitable, in view of its possible advantages, to look at the fort-building as a mere extravagance. The soldiers do the work; but there is much expensive material bought, and contractors have to oversee the building. These forts may be needed at some points to protect property; but they would not be deemed indispensable by a general commanding a great invading army who meant to pursue the enemy and annihilate it. The vast number that has been built has cost Spain an enormous sum. If it has been honestly expended, it has nevertheless been wasted. During the time thus taken to guard against attack, General Weyler has given the insurgent army opportunity to recruit and become well seasoned. He has given the people time to think and to act.

The outbreak which, like a small fire, could have been easily extinguished at the start, has spread, and now blazes in every part of the island. The insurrection has become a revolution. The movement was thought at first to be a negro uprising; and few of the white Cubans were in sympathy with it. To-day the whole native population, amounting to 1,300,000, is actively or secretly trying to throw off the Spanish yoke. The Spanish forces have grown discouraged; and all the officers who are not profiting by the war are disgusted by the failure of the royal army.

General Weyler puts no heart into rank or file by taking the field; for neither has confidence in his ability as a military man. His aimless wanderings in the neighborhood of Santa Clara and Sancti Spiritus during the dry season just passed have not improved the estimation in which he is held by his troops. He has able generals, yet he refuses to listen to their advice, and pursues his own policy. This, it is clear, does not contemplate a determined attempt to encircle Maximo Gomez, close in upon him, capture him, and push on to Puerto Principe and Santiago de Cuba to wrest these provinces from Calixto Garcia. The other insurgent bands roaming in the western country might safely be left to the troops that could be spared to conduct similar operations against them. A campaign of this nature would end the war. It would likewise end "the harvest." The officers and soldiers would go back to Spain on a peace footing and less pay. The chances of promotion made easy by brilliant reports of battles never fought would disappear. A promotion carries with it not only honor, but a decoration, which increases the stipend of the wearer in active and retired service.

The Cuban is fighting from higher motives. There are former bandits and foreign adventurers in their army; but the great bulk is made up of educated, patriotic white Cubans, who are struggling for civil rights and the independence of their country. The proportion of negroes to whites in the army is about four to ten.

While not over 10 per cent of the white Cubans have joined the insurgent ranks, they are all against Spain. The 90 per cent who have not gone out to fight are daily risking deportation, or "life-imprisonment in perpetual chains," to help their brothers in the "long grass." The impossibility of securing arms keeps the apparently peaceful Cuban out of the active conflict. It has been truthfully said that if guns should rain from heaven not one would touch the ground.

Helped by the corruption of the Spanish, the Cuban insurgents have been able to establish and maintain the capital of their republic at Cubitas. This is a small village on the top of a mountain only twenty-five miles from the city of Puerto Principe. It would be difficult to carry it by storm; but if General Weyler had laid siege on his arrival it would have fallen before this. Where a Cuban can go, a Spaniard ought to be able to follow. There are large and small detachments of insurgent troops whose duty it is to protect the government officials and enable them to discharge their duties. Every department is in working order; laws are made and executed by authority, taxes collected, marriages performed, schools maintained, newspapers published, and a postal service kept in operation.

The power of the Cuban Republic extends over considerable territory. It has firm possession of the two eastern provinces, except in the cities; and its ability to exercise civil functions is gradually extending toward Havana. A government order from Cubitas is easily delivered to the forces in the enemy's country. This is possible on account of the peculiar instructions given by General Weyler to his soldiers protecting the trochas, the railroads, and fortified towns. He directs them to go into their forts when attacked, and not to surrender under any circumstances. The Cubans have no desire to capture these forts, because such victories would be costly and of no profit. They could not hold a fort after they had captured it. They are entirely satisfied to have the Spaniards stay within the fortification while they are moving about the country.

When a Cuban band desires to pass a fort, it sends two or three men to open fire on it. The garrison shuts itself up and pours a hot fire from the loopholes. In the meantime the band passes by at a safe distance. Towns and villages and even cities are entered in the same manner. Being thus able to loot shops and supply-depots, and having plenty of vegetables in their truck-patches on the mountains, the rebels cannot be starved into subjection any more rapidly than they can be conquered by arms under the present policy of the Spanish commander, which is more like that of a pirate ashore than it is of a loyal general engaged in suppressing the foes of his sovereign.

Possessing only a third of the island, with 300,000 loyal Spanish residents remaining in the four uncontrolled provinces, the Cuban Republic has not yet achieved its independence. Its progress in war, and the improving condition of its civil government, clearly entitle it, under the requirements of international law, to look to all liberty-loving nations for recognition of its belligerent rights. Until such action is taken by the United States, the Spaniard will continue to regard the Cuban as a reptile, and treat him as such. Prisoners of war will be shot, as they always have been; the hospitals of sick and wounded insurgents will continue to be raided, their inmates slaughtered in their hammocks; and the whole rural population will be kept in the fortified towns by order of General Weyler, for the avowed purpose of "killing off the insurgent breed by starvation, in order that fresh colonists may come from Spain to make the island loyal" to its unnatural mother.

If recognized as belligerents, the Cubans, without further aid, can win their independence. If these well-earned rights are not accorded, the sickening struggle will go on until the subject of it is destroyed. In the end, the ruins will be lost to Spain. Her army has settled upon the country like hungry wolves upon a wounded fawn. Her sovereignty, like a tree doomed to fall, is toppling, not from the machete-blows upon its trunk, but from the germs of corruption that are rotting away its roots.   THOMAS GOLD ALVORD, JR.

JOHANNES BRAHMS.

It is quite impossible for an American to appreciate the importance which, in Europe, attaches to newspaper criticism. I do not doubt but that during the recent war between Greece and Turkey the readers of the Vienna "Neue Freie Presse" turned first to the *feuilleton* to look for Hanslick's critique of the last concert or opera before they scanned the despatches from Athens or Constantinople. It is entirely within bounds to say that it was Hanslick's antagonism to Wagner and his friendly attitude toward Brahms that threw musical Germany into two hostile camps. Hanslick caused Wagner many bitter hours; and it is said—humorously, of course—that, when little Siegfried Wagner had the tantrums, Frau Cosima could immediately frighten him into good behavior by calling out: "Hab' Acht! Der Hanslick kommt." ("Take care! Here's Hanslick.")

I doubt if Brahms personally sympathized with Hanslick's attitude. Certainly he himself went his own way quietly enough. He is known to have been a close student of Wagner's scores. He valued highly several Wagner autographs which had come into his possession; and, from friends of his, we learn that on several occasions he defended Wagner against hostile criticism. Wagner, naturally enough, was exasperated by the attacks made upon him and his art under cover of Brahms's name; and his hostility to Brahms was undisguised. He sneeringly dubbed him a "musical Messiah," and said, sarcastically, that Brahms was a composer "whose importance lay in his not wishing to create any striking effects." He also spoke of certain composers "whose resemblance to Beethoven was limited to their appropriating Beethoven's ideas,"—a reference to the superficial resemblance between the theme of the last movement of Brahms's "First Symphony" and that of the last movement of Beethoven's "Ninth."

Yet these great contemporaries had no point of rivalry in common: they were devoted to wholly different phases of musical composition; and, had not Wagner's opponents chosen Brahms as a bulwark from behind which to attack and harass Wagner, I cannot conceive how their art interests could ever have clashed. Wagner was devoted wholly to

37

the stage, and was the successful creator of an entirely new form of musico-dramatic composition. Brahms not only never attempted to compose an opera, but did not care for opera as an art-form. He rarely visited the theatre, and more rarely sat through an entire operatic performance. Not infrequently, after the first act, he would remark to his companion, " You know I understand nothing about the theatre," and would then rise, and leave. So far as he can be said to have had any preference at all among modern operas, his favorite was Bizet's " Carmen,"—by no means an unfortunate choice. As a man, he had an aversion to marriage; as a composer, to opera; and he classed them together. " Toward marriage," he once said, " my position is the same as toward opera. If I had already composed an opera and, for all I care, seen it fail, I should certainly compose another. But I cannot make up my mind to a first opera or a first marriage." There is a fine sense of artistic self-esteem in that " for all I care, seen it fail." No creator in any field of art can be great, if he works with a view to popularity. He may enjoy the glamour of temporary success; but his success ends where that of a real genius begins.

Now that both Wagner and Brahms have passed away, it is to be hoped that the differences between Wagnerians and Brahmsians, which should never have existed, will be wiped out. Fortunately Cosima Wagner, with womanly tact, has herself held out the olive branch in a letter to Hans Richter, written shortly after Brahms's death, which, while it shows the exclusiveness of the inner Bayreuth cult, is at the same time a tribute to Brahms as a musician and a man. Mme. Wagner's letter at least creates an armistice which may prove to be the beginning of a permanent peace,—a concert of musical Europe,—and seems to me, therefore, of great importance. As it has not been widely circulated in English, I give it here :—

" BAYREUTH, April 7, 1897.

MY DEAR, HIGHLY VALUED FRIEND :

The gentlemen of the *Gesellschaft der Musikfreunde* have shown me and my children the honor of notifying us of the passing away of Johannes Brahms. I know of no one better qualified than the faithful friend of our house to transmit the acknowledgment of our thanks for this distinguished attention.

My withdrawal, many years since, from all concert-life has left me wholly unfamiliar with the compositions of the deceased. With the single exception of a piece of chamber-music, none of his works, which have attracted so much attention and won such distinction, has come to my hearing. Personally, also, I had only a passing meeting with him, in the director's box at Vienna, where he had the courtesy to have himself presented to me.

At the same time I have not remained ignorant of his chivalrous spirit and attitude toward our art; nor of the fact that his enlightenment was too great for him to have misapprehended what was, perhaps, foreign to him. His character was too noble for him to have nurtured hostility. And this is surely enough to have awakened my genuine sympathy. I beg of you to convey it.

COSIMA WAGNER."

May the effect of this letter be as happy as its phraseology !

Brahms was sixty-four years old when he died. Forty-four years before he had been launched on his career by no less a celebrity than Schumann. Yet he is by no means fully appreciated even now. The trouble with Brahms, so far as concerns public appreciation, is that he never, so to speak, led up to himself. The public expect a composer to be " early," " middle," and " late." His " early," or more or less imitative, period prepares them for the assertion of his distinctive individuality after he has outgrown the influence of his predecessors. His contemporary fame usually rests upon this " middle " period. When he ventures beyond that point, he is accused of excessive subjectivity or morbidness and of violating the principles of true art; which, in fact, he does, by creating new and truer principles. And so a composer's " late " period usually remains a sealed book to all but a few choice spirits until many years after his death. I doubt if we, even in this late year of grace, fully appreciate the " Ninth Symphony," or the last sonatas and quartettes. Brahms declined to be " early," or even " middle." He began " late "; his first works being as Brahmsian as any he ever wrote. The public had to grow up to him from the very beginning—and the public hates to grow.

Poets, novelists, and painters often come of artistically barren ancestry. Nearly all the great composers, on the other hand, have sprung from musical stock. It seems necessary for a family to be in a state of musical fermentation for at least a generation before a great composer can rise to its surface. It is not surprising, therefore, to find that Brahms's father played double-bass in the Hamburg Stadt-theater, and was proficient on other instruments.

Brahms was born in Hamburg in 1833. At fourteen he made his *début* there as a pianist; so that his genius for music must have asserted itself at the proverbial early age. The year 1853 was one of the most significant in his career. It was in that year that Schumann published, in the " Neue Zeitschrift für Musik," his now famous article, " Neue Bahnen," in which he pointed to a composer only twenty years old, not one of whose compositions had as yet been published, as the legitimate successor of Beethoven. The following is an extract from that article :—

"Many new and remarkable geniuses have made their appearance. . . . I thought to follow with interest the pathways of these elect. There would, there must, after such promise, suddenly appear one who should utter the highest ideal expression of the times, who should claim the mastership by no gradual development, but burst upon us fully equipped, as Minerva sprang from the head of Jupiter. And he has come, this chosen youth over whose cradle the Graces and Heroes seem to have kept watch. His name is—Johannes Brahms."

An anecdote, delightfully Brahmsian, both true and charming, tells how Brahms was brought to Schumann's notice. Remenyi, the violinist, was making a concert-tour, and Brahms was accompanying him in a double sense—on the tour and on the piano. At Göttingen they found the pitch of the piano rather low. Beethoven's "Kreutzer Sonata" for violin and piano was on the programme. Without the notes before him, Brahms, without any ado, played the piano part in a key half a tone higher than the original. This remarkable, certainly unusual, feat was witnessed by Joachim, who persuaded the young musician to abandon the tour, and gave him a letter to Schumann, whom Brahms forthwith visited, and to whom he showed a number of his manuscript compositions. The result was " Neue Bahnen."

Such a tribute might have ruined many a young genius; but, as I have already noted, the public did not allow Brahms to become spoiled. When I read "Neue Bahnen" for the first time—more than twenty years after its appearance—Brahms's works were practically unknown in America. The "Hungarian Dances"—on the title-page of which he has placed, with characteristic modesty, "Arranged by Johannes Brahms," though they are as much his as the "Hungarian Rhapsodies" and "Fantasia" are Liszt's—were his first compositions to attract attention in this country. They became very popular; yet, when later his "First Symphony" was played here for the first time, doubts as to the accuracy of Schumann's prophecy were expressed, and it was questioned if von Bülow had not exaggerated the merits of the Symphony when he spoke of it as "the Tenth." Even now, his works—when their depth and beauty are considered—are making their way but slowly. With the appreciation of Brahms, it is much as with the appreciation of Browning. The latter's admirers are numerous and most ardent; but he can hardly be called a popular poet. Similarly Brahms's admirers are numerous and ardent;—indeed there is no need of a select Brahmsian cult as there once was with Browning; —but he is not yet a popular composer. The similarity between Brahms and Browning is not limited to this one external. Both achieve dramatic intensity through a terseness of expression which at times seems harsh; both are original; and the works of both are resonant with that deep baritone *timbre* which is most characteristic of manhood. Fortunately too, like Browning, Brahms was not diverted from his ideals by any desire to cater to popular taste. He worked quietly on, indifferent to the fate of his work with the public. He found, as other geniuses have found, his greatest reward in the joy of creating. When Cherubini was complaining on his deathbed of the popular indifference to his music, someone remarked, "But, Maestro, think of posthumous fame!" Whereupon Cherubini quietly said, "My friend, at a time like this, poor jokes are out of place." But, after all, there is enough satisfaction to atone for contemporary indifference in the feeling that in the years to come one will be appreciated, not forgotten.

The work which first established Brahms's reputation in Germany was his "German Requiem" (*Op.* 47), first given in its entirety in the Cathedral at Bremen in April, 1868. Brahms had had some experience in conducting vocal societies, through which he had acquired facility in handling choral masses; and he had already composed a number of secular and sacred choruses—among them a "Funeral Hymn" which seems in a measure to prelude the "Requiem."

This latter is undoubtedly the most important choral work of modern times. It is a German requiem in so far that Brahms, both in form and spirit, made a radical departure from the requiem of the Latin Church, selecting and arranging the text from the German Bible, and choosing such verses as made it a song of hope rather than of grief; and as the text, though taken from different portions of the Bible, is pervaded by a certain unity of spirit, so this unity is preserved in the music. It is in seven divisions, all of which seem, however, to have sprung from the single idea of hope in a divine future; the impression of unity being enhanced by a repetition, toward the finale of the work, of the principal theme of the first chorus. Besides such technical triumphs as the pedal-point fugue in D in the third chorus, and the climacteric double fugue at the end of the sixth, the work abounds in many tender and benign passages, of which, perhaps, the most exquisite is that message of peace, "Yea, I will comfort you," for solo soprano and chorus, in the fifth division.

This requiem is Brahmsian to the core. It is faultless as regards form; but, while conservative in this respect, it is, musically, modern of the modern. Even the fugues belong to the nineteenth century. They are, perhaps, the only fugues composed since the passing away of the great contrapuntists that do not wear *perruques*. It is the great distinction of Brahms to have shown that thoroughly modern music can be composed within established forms. Brahms is the successor of no classical composer. He has been a conservator of classical form, especially in his symphonies, sonatas, and works of chamber-music; but in the music which he has created within these forms he has shown himself the most original and most modern composer, except Wagner, of the last half of this century. I do not wish my attitude toward Wagner to be misunderstood. I consider him the greatest of all composers. Yet I cannot fail to recognize the depth and beauty of Brahms's genius, and the importance of the service he has rendered to music. But for him, the music-drama might have become a juggernaut.

The "German Requiem" marks one extreme of Brahms's work for chorus; the charming "Liebeslieder," in waltz-form, the other. I mention these also for another reason. For many years Hanslick was an intimate friend of Brahms, and his prophet among critics. Yet, with fine, artistic tact, Brahms not once, during their intercourse, referred to Hanslick's numerous enthusiastic criticisms of his music. But, upon opening the "Liebeslieder," Hanslick found that they were dedicated to him.

In his symphonies and works of chamber-music, Brahms again shows his complete mastery of form,—that mastery which controls instead of being controlled,—and does not hesitate to make innovations where these grow out of artistic necessities and are in keeping with the eternal verities of art. For instance, in his piano quintette, unexcelled by any work of its class, he developed the first movement to the extent of introducing a third theme in addition to the two sanctioned by the traditional form. The last movement of his "Fourth Symphony" is a wholly new departure in symphonic writing—so new that it has proved somewhat of a *crux* even to Brahmsians. It is, however, nothing more than an eight-bar theme with variations,—a revival of the old *passacaglia*. The variations bear the Brahms stamp. Each is characteristic and individual, yet is obviously related æsthetically to the original theme.

The original minuet division of the symphony—later on the *scherzo*—has been changed by Brahms into a kind of *intermezzo*,—a word I do not use here in its technical sense. These *intermezzi* are among the most charming things he has composed. They form points of rest between the longer divisions of his symphonies. While not yielding to these in amazing technical construction, they appeal more readily to the emotions, and, therefore, have been almost immediately appreciated. If

I remember rightly, when Brahms's "First Symphony" had its initial hearing in New York, the first movement, with its strenuous yet sombre passion, and the second movement, with its lovely theme elusively evading the tonal cadence,—which is at last reached through a series of unexpected and beautiful modulations,—were understood by comparatively few. But the *allegretto* was encored. The *allegretto* of the "Third Symphony" is a musical pearl; and the *andante moderato* of the "Fourth" has the sad beauty of an elegy. Brahms's dramatic concentration is apparent in many passages in these symphonies; witness, in the introduction to the "First," the superb climax reached through a series of chromatic progressions encompassed within only four bars. Brahms is not a *virtuoso* in instrumentation,—or rather his thoughts have not that external brilliancy that lends itself to virtuosity of instrumentation. He lays more stress on the what than on the how. Yet there are some lovely bits; such as the horn solo introducing the *coda* in the first movement of the "Second Symphony," and the *coda* itself, which is full of sensuous charm.

Brahms's songs seem to be more generally appreciated than his other works. They, too, made their way slowly at first; but now Brahms's *Lieder* are included in the *repertoire* of almost every concert singer of eminence, and are heard with growing frequency even in America, where Brahms has been far more neglected than in Germany and England. There are also a number of amateurs in New York (and I presume there are such in other cities) with whom the singing of Brahms amounts almost to a cult. It is a fact that, with Brahms, familiarity breeds, instead of contempt, something even more than admiration—a deep and abiding love almost amounting to worship.

Brahms has composed nearly one hundred and sixty songs. His last published work was a group of "Ernste Lieder" ("Serious Songs"), —a title which, as his death followed so soon after their publication, had a solemnly prophetic significance.

Brahms's fame could rest securely upon his songs. Still working within established forms, he has again poured thoroughly original and, above all, thoroughly modern music into them. His are the most modern songs—more modern even than those of Schumann or Franz. Schubert, Schumann, Franz, and Brahms are the four great figures in the development of the *Lied*.

Schubert was primarily a melodist; and, although a number of his songs, like "Auf dem Wasser zu Singen," "Die Junge Nonne," "Hark, Hark, the Lark !" and, most notably, "Der Erlkönig," have realistically

descriptive accompaniments, they and the vocal melody are not inter-
woven or interknit, but rather stand out one from the other: so that
his songs, as a whole, are most famous for their melodious beauty.
Schubert was not at all exacting in his choice of words.   Anything in
the way of verse seemed to satisfy him; and it has been said that, if
poetry had given out, he could have set sign-boards to music.   Schumann and Franz, on the other hand, were most careful in the choice of
subjects for their songs.   With them, a song was not a thing to be tossed
off in the inspiration of the moment: it was something to be not only
musically composed, but also *intellectually thought out.*   Voice and accompaniment become, with them, more interdependent; prelude and
postlude, more significant; and the piano part is emotionally expressive
rather than realistically descriptive.   With Franz, the detailed working
out of his material is carried almost to the extreme of subjectivity.   He
himself disclaimed dramatic intentions.   Fortunately this disclaimer
was only another instance of genius being mistaken in itself, as anyone
who has heard Lehmann sing "Im Herbst" must realize.   Quite
unconsciously, Schumann and Franz, when writing their *Lieder*, were, .
in fact, composing little music-dramas with one *Leitmotif* instead of
twenty.

Brahms is as careful as either Schumann or Franz in selecting the
poetic material for his songs; but in setting a poem to music he seeks
to penetrate into the very heart of the poet, and to interpret the emotional significance of the poem as a whole.   This emotional trend of
the words he embodies in his vocal melody.   A Brahms song is not a
realistic expression of every passing mood reflected in the poet's lines.
It is the musical expression of the thought or feeling out of which the
poem grew, and so includes those minor moods as it develops with unerring certainty toward its climax.   Thus again we have an illustration of
Brahms's power of concentration.   The inter-relation between the vocal
melody and the accompaniment is absolute.   The latter rarely carries
the melody, but is closely interknit with it harmonically; so that voice
and accompaniment glide, flow, or rush on together in one great stream
of music.   Brahms is truly Bachian in his compact leading of parts.
For complete grasp of subject and terseness of expression, note the
brief, constantly recurring phrase in the depths of the accompaniment
to his very first song, "O Versenk."   In his "Wiegenlied" (*Op.* 49,
No. 4) the technical workmanship is so delicate that it actually produces the effect of greater simplicity upon the hearer.   It is an exquisite
cradle song.   Brahms never thrusts his mastership of technique upon

the listener. He regards it as an artistic means to an artistic end. Thus the emotional appeal of that beautiful song, "Wir wandelten, wir zwei zusammen," is so direct and immediate that we do not realize, until we analyze it, that it begins in canon form.

There is one great characteristic of Brahms which no student of his songs can fail to appreciate. His climaxes are musical, in the strictest, purest sense. Take, for instance: "Wie bist Du Meine Königin "— perhaps the most frequently sung of his *Lieder.* The climax is reached on the very last word of the poem—the exclamation "Wonevoll!" It is thrice repeated. Brahms produces, on the third repetition, a climax neither loud nor strenuous, but so deep, so moving, that the singer seems to be offering up his own heart; and this emotional wrench is due not to a massing of chords, not to an uprushing of runs, but to a simple prolongation of a phrase by one bar, and a superb descending sweep of the voice.

For the piano Brahms has composed two concertos, several sets of variations, and shorter pieces, among them the series from *Op.* 116–119, which preceded the "Serious Songs" (*Op.* 120), his last work. Modern piano music usually echoes Chopin and Liszt. Only one composer has been gifted with genius enough to enable him to work independently of those two great masters. The exception is Brahms. The "Intermezzo in E flat minor" (*Op.* 118, No. 6) is, to me, the most profound expression of the tragic that we have in piano music; but you will listen in vain for a note of Chopin or Liszt in it.

Brahms led a quiet life, devoted, in the largest sense of the word, to his art. Until overtaken by the disease which proved fatal, he enjoyed rugged health. It was said of him that he "made foot-tours like a student, and slept like a child." He appears also to have been a child of nature in social intercourse; which gave rise to the anecdote of his parting remark at a musical soirée in Vienna: "I beg the company's pardon if I have neglected to offend anybody this evening."

In conclusion, if I were asked to sum up in a single sentence Brahms's service to art, I should say that it consisted in his having created, within established forms, music wholly original, thoroughly modern, and profoundly beautiful. GUSTAV KOBBÉ.

A RADICAL DEFECT IN OUR CIVIL SERVICE LAW.

THE Civil Service of the United States Government had its origin in 1789, when the heads of the executive departments were empowered to make appointments to office. The first regulation regarding the power of appointment was made in 1853, when a law was enacted which provided for a partial classification of the Service, as well as for examinations to test the qualification of applicants for office in the departments at Washington. By the Act of 1871, the President was authorized to prescribe such rules for admission to the Civil Service as would best promote its efficiency. In none of these Acts, however, was the power of removal limited.

At the time of the first classification there were only 722 clerks in the departments; while the total number of employees was about 33,000. The Service increased so rapidly, however, that in 1867 it numbered 60,000; in 1877, 85,000; in 1881, 124,000; and in 1883, 131,800. This remarkable growth of a service which might be used for partisan ends has been characterized in recent years as an increasing menace to a republican form of government; and it was the recognition of this circumstance that inspired the reform movement which resulted in the Civil Service Act of 1883. As this Act has never been amended, it is the only statutory expression of the reform movement, and the only law which stands in the way of the spoilsman. While it places a slight restriction upon the power of removal,—prohibiting, as it does, the dismissal of an employee for giving or refusing to give a political contribution, or, for reasons political or religious,—nevertheless, like the Acts of 1853 and 1871, its primary object was to regulate the power of appointment. Under its provisions the fitness of every applicant for admission to the classified Service must be ascertained by an examination; the names of those who pass being entered upon a list of eligibles in the order of merit. Upon a vacancy occurring the first three names must be presented to the appointing officer by the local Civil Service Board, which certifies them; and one of the three must be selected. The names may remain on the list of eligibles for one year, and may be certified for appointment three times. If, by the end of this period, the applicant has not secured an appointment, he is dropped from the list. Whether the advocates and framers of this law, whose object was to purify politics by the destruction of official patronage, really believed that this plan would be more efficacious than one which would regulate both appointments and removals, does not appear. As the law has now been in operation for thirteen years, it may not be out of place to inquire whether it has entirely succeeded in abolishing political patronage, or whether an amendment is essential in order that the purposes of the reform movement may be accomplished.

Civil Service reform is frequently discussed in too general a manner; the main point involved not being sufficiently emphasized. A merit system of appointment having been established by law, it would appear to follow, as a logical sequence, that removals should not be made without cause. And there is a popular impression that a provision of this nature does exist—that persons in the classified service of the Government cannot be dismissed without good reason. That this view is erroneous, however, becomes clear when we consider that the Act only regulates entrance to the Service; there being no legal obstruction to removals. Consequently, although the percentage of removals is smaller than formerly, no employee, however efficient, can feel assured that he will not be one of the comparatively few to be dismissed.

While it is true that something has been done by the Act of 1883 to prevent political assessments, it is no less true that the selection of a list of eligibles—its primary aim—has become the means of enhancing the power of the spoilsman as well as of the reformer. As the power of the spoilsman to influence his supporters depends upon the value of his patronage, a fruitful soil is left for him so long as some offices remain for distribution. At present, the total number of employees is 178,717. Of these, 91,635 (including 72,371 postmasters) are unclassified and unaffected by the provisions of the Civil Service Act; 2,842 are exempt from examination; and the remainder, 84,240, are in the classified Service, admission to which can be obtained only after examination. Ninety-four thousand offices are absolutely at the disposal of the victors; and, of the 84,000 classified employees, there is not one that may not be removed at any moment without cause, if the head of his department thinks fit. While the list of eligibles debars many active and valuable political workers from obtaining positions in the classified Service, because it requires qualifications which they cannot attain, those who can qualify themselves by passing the necessary examination may be said to have an excellent point of vantage.   And it is, perhaps, for this reason that so many men in active political life are willing to give their approval to Acts for the regulation of the Civil Service, particularly so long as the power of removal shall remain unimpaired.

That, indeed, many active reformers do not regard it necessary to apply to removals the same searching investigation and supervision that now govern appointments, is shown by the following resolution, which was adopted at the annual meeting of the National Civil Service Reform League held at Philadelphia on December 11, 1896 :—

"The League fully recognizes the importance of preserving to responsible superior officers the power of removal of their subordinates, whenever in their judgment this power should be exercised in the public interest ; but the League deems it no less important that the officer exercising this power should do it with full and trustworthy information as to the facts, and that reasonable safeguards should be afforded to employees against the loss of a livelihood for personal or political reasons."

The safeguards concerning removals to which this resolution refers are not provisions of law, but simply administrative orders issued voluntarily by the heads of executive departments; thus showing that reformers as well as spoilsmen seem to be content to have the law halt at the list of eligibles.   That in fact, however, this list has proved inadequate to destroy political influence, is indicated by the following extract from the "Tenth Annual Report" of the Civil Service Commission :—

"Although the present United States Civil Service law deals with dismissals only in a narrowly limited number of cases ; yet, by the control it exercises over entrance to the Service, it has greatly reduced the risk of dismissal for political or personal reasons. Nevertheless, dismissals for these reasons do undoubtedly obtain in many instances. Upon every change of Administration, both in the departments at Washington and still more in the local offices throughout the country, instances occur where men are turned out either for political reasons or for other reasons wholly unconnected with the good of the Service or misconduct on the part of the officer removed. In some offices and bureaus, the number of removals of this kind forms a serious scandal. The Commission firmly believes that the cause for removal should always be stated in writing, that the accused should be given an opportunity to be heard in his own defence, and that, wherever the accused demands it, the cause of the removal should be published in full. We think the Commission should have the power to investigate and report upon all removals."

On page 17 of its "Eleventh Annual Report," the Civil Service Commission, referring to removals, says:—

"The Commission could much more effectively deal with these cases if it had the power to investigate all cases of dismissal, and to administer oaths. These powers ought to be conferred upon it."

On page 19, we find:—

"It has been often claimed, with some show of reason, that any interference with the arbitrary power of removal, even to the extent of requiring reasons to be stated, and giving the accused a hearing, would weaken the discipline and impair the efficiency of the Service. The Commission has never believed this to be true, but the contrary ; and it is convinced that its belief will find a complete justification in the Postal Service, under the order of the Postmaster-General. . . . And the Commission is fully convinced that, to some extent, religious and political considerations will influence dismissals until there is a requirement of law and rule that not only shall the reasons for dismissal be made a matter of record and be made known to the person to be dismissed, but that he also be given an opportunity to be heard in his own defence."

The Senate Committee on Foreign Relations of the Fifty-third Congress reports on the Consular System as follows :—

"Fitness of the candidate, permanency of tenure during good behavior, an impartial method of selection, and promotion as a reward for efficiency, are the principles on which a useful Consular Service can alone be based, with an expectation of the best results."

In view of the facts here presented, it appears to the employees that, in order to accomplish the purposes of the reform, the Act of 1883 must be amended in very material particulars. They are of the opinion (1) that, in order to prevent political assessments, a statute should be enacted which would render it unlawful for employees of the Government to make contributions for political purposes ; (2) that tenure of office during good behavior is absolutely essential ; and that, consequently, removals should be subject to the same supervision as appointments. —

There are two principal reasons assigned for opposing legislation which would establish tenure of office during good behavior. The first is, that the proper discipline of the Service requires that the arbitrary power of removal should be lodged somewhere. The employees believe that this position is untenable. They do not advocate any tenure of office more permanent than that which would depend upon merit or fitness. Under that tenure the certainty of removal for neglect or insubordination would furnish all the discipline that is necessary. The second objection raises the dread spectre of an office-holding class. It has been charged that the employees desire to create such a body, and that they are organizing to accomplish this end. The only possible class of this nature in the United States could be a number of citizens who would hold office continuously during good behavior. Again, there are persons who predict the gradual evolution of an office-holding class of citizens in whom some vested right to office would develop and in time even become hereditary; but it is difficult to believe that anyone seriously imagines that, even by provisions of law, an appointment to a clerkship could develop into a grant of a vested right. If there are persons who really entertain such fears, an investigation of the Service would show how unfounded they are.

Organizations of the employees have been formed in order that they may be more fitly represented. Through their committees, they have petitioned Congress to consider the propriety of making some provision for their retirement, when they shall have become disabled; such provision to be made at their expense and to be under governmental control. They have also pointed out the necessity of providing by law for a tenure of office during good behavior. More than this they have not sought, nor do they desire. Many persons have no true conception of the magnitude of the Service, and do not recognize the significance of the fact that officials who pass upon questions of revenues and disbursements involving many millions annually may be peremptorily removed by the head of a department without the legal necessity of assigning any specific cause. If the independence which results from the certainty of tenure of office be essential for the judge, the great interests involved in the discharge of the duties imposed by law upon executive officers and their subordinates seem to demand a similar independence, or at least a tenure of office not dependent upon the fortunes of political warfare.

DUNCAN VEAZEY.

SUGAR BOUNTIES AND THEIR INFLUENCE.

A SUBJECT now attracting widespread attention in our country is that of the bounties paid by foreign countries on exports of sugar. The discussions upon this question have emphasized the fact that the nature and magnitude of these bounties are but little understood by our people; and, as Congress has under consideration a revision of the Tariff, in which the import taxes on sugar form one of the principal items, a brief explanation of the issue at the present time may not be inopportune.

The bounties paid to sugar producers are of two classes: direct and indirect. The former is illustrated by the McKinley law of 1890, which provides for a premium to be paid on all sugar made from domestic sources. The indirect bounty—also designed to promote domestic production—provides for a drawback on taxes paid, for a partial remission of taxes, or for a direct premium on the amount of sugar exported. This bounty is burdened with a feature which has proved most troublesome. I refer to the provision for a direct tax, computed on the basis of the legal yield of sugar from beets, fixed at a given percentage. Under this system any excess of production over the legal yield escapes taxation, wholly or in part.

It is impossible within a short space to discuss the question of bounties in all its bearings. I shall, therefore, consider only the premiums or bounties paid by the German and French governments on exported sugars.

The German law now in force became effective on May 29, 1896. This law, in so far as it relates to premiums on exported sugar, is as follows :—

" Section 77. When sugar in quantities of at least 500 kilograms is exported, or deposited in public or private warehouses under official control (bonded warehouses), and not intended for domestic consumption, it is entitled to the following direct premiums :

(a) Raw sugar of at least 90 per cent purity, and refined sugar under 98 per cent purity, 2.50 marks per 100 kilograms (0.269 cent per pound).

(b) Loaf sugar and all sugars in pure white blocks or cubes of at least 99.5 per cent purity, 3.55 marks per 100 kilograms (0.383 cent per pound).

(c) For all other sugars of at least 98 per cent purity, 3.00 marks per 100 kilograms (0.324 cent per pound).

Section 79. The Bundesrath is authorized to lower or abolish the above premiums when other countries paying bounties on exported beet sugars lower or abolish them.

Section 80. The tariff on imported sugars of all kinds, solid and liquid, is 40 marks per 100 kilograms (4.32 cents per pound)."

The French law now in force bears date of April 7, 1897, and was promulgated in the "Journal Officiel" of April 8, 1897. Its provisions relating to direct bounties on exported sugars are these:—

"(a) Unrefined sugars, granular or in small crystals, of at least 98 per cent polarization for beet sugars, and 97 per cent for colonial cane sugars, the polarization being made before the deduction of loss during refining, receive a bounty of 5 francs per 100 kilograms (0.35 cent per pound) of pure sugar contained therein. When, however, sugars of this category are so pure that they polarize not less than 99.75 per cent, they are entitled at their full weight to the rate of bounty enjoyed by exported unrefined sugars.

(b) Raw sugars polarizing from 65 to 98 per cent for beet sugars and from 65 to 97 per cent for colonial cane sugars receive for each 100 kilograms of pure sugar contained therein, 3 francs 50 centimes (0.31 cent per pound).

(c) Rock crystal sugars (candied sugars) are entitled to a bounty of 4 francs 50 centimes (0.39 cent per pound) per 100 kilograms of pure sugar.

(d) Refined sugars in loaves or blocks, perfectly white, hard, and dry, 4 francs 50 centimes per 100 kilograms (0.39 cent per pound).

(e) Powdered sugars, for each 100 kilograms of pure sugar therein, 4 francs 50 centimes (0.39 cent per pound).

(f) Refined sugars in grains or crystals polarizing at least 98 per cent, 4 francs per 100 kilograms (0.35 cent per pound). When the sugars of this last category polarize 99.75, they will be considered as pure refined sugars and will be entitled to a bounty at their full weight without any deduction whatever."

It is important to note in connection with these laws, especially the French, that indirect bounties on export sugar are secured by a duplex system of taxation—a tax on the domestic industry, and one on importations. In all the sugar-producing countries of Europe the domestic sugar industry is highly taxed. In each of these, however, the duties levied on importations are invariably higher than the tax on domestic production. The object of this is to secure the consumption of domestic sugars, and practically to exclude those of foreign origin. The wisdom of such a fiscal policy cannot be discussed here. A glance at the rate of consumption, however, in the principal European countries will show how the high taxes on sugar, both internal and at the frontier, tend to restrict its consumption to a minimum.

The annual *per capita* consumption of sugar in Germany is about

27 pounds; in France, 31 pounds; in Russia, 11 pounds; in Austria, 20 pounds; in England, 86 pounds; and in the United States, 63 pounds. In other words, the rate of consumption per head is almost inversely proportional to the rate of taxation.

It is difficult to compute exactly the magnitude of the indirect bounties which accrue to the exporter by reason of this system of taxation. In France the rate of domestic taxation is based on the supposition that the yield of pure sugar is 7.75 per cent of the weight of the beets. Whatever is produced in excess of this amount escapes all or a part of the internal tax, and in this way receives an indirect bounty. The amount of this indirect bounty, therefore, varies with the yield of sugar per ton. For instance, if the yield of refined sugar be 11 per cent, the indirect premium is 8 francs 18 centimes per 100 kilograms (0.72 cent per pound); if 10 per cent, 6 francs 75 centimes per 100 kilograms; if 9 per cent, 4 francs 17 centimes per 100 kilograms (0.36 cent per pound). If, however, the manufacturer waive all claim to premiums over the legal yield, he is guaranteed a fixed premium of 4 francs 15 centimes per 100 kilograms (0.36 cent per pound) on all the refined sugar produced. It is fair to assume that the annual amount of premium on all production in excess of the legal yield will be about the mean between the above-mentioned extremes; i. e., 6 francs 75 centimes per 100 kilograms (0.59 cent per pound) on refined sugar.

In order that a government may be enabled to pay either a direct or an indirect bounty, the funds must necessarily be obtained by a tax on the sugar consumed. All fiscal legislation which provides for direct or indirect bounties must, therefore, be based on a tax on the domestic consumption; and the tax must be proportionate to the magnitude of such consumption. It is evident that the funds available for this indirect bounty depend upon the ratio between the total production and consumption. In France the selling price of sugar for domestic consumption is determined by the duty on imports. If the manufacturer could dispose of his total product for home consumption, the amount of profit would be equal to the difference between the internal tax and the tariff on foreign sugars. Now, if to this profit we add that accruing from the excess of the actual over the legal yield (7.75 per cent of pure sugar), we shall see that the manufacturer has two great sources of revenue; viz., (1) the difference between the internal and the tariff taxes; and (2) the rebate in internal tax arising from the excess of yield; this rebate alone being regarded as the true bounty. The total amount of sugar yielded in excess of that fixed

38

by law varies with the richness of the beet in saccharine matter, and the efficiency of the process of manufacture; consequently only an approximate estimate of the profits obtained in this way can be made.

The excess of production over consumption must either be carried as stock on hand or exported. The immediate purpose of the direct premium is to force this surplus into the export trade by offering it to other sugar-producing nations at less than cost price, or at least at a price lower than that of rival dealers. The consumer in the country whence the sugar is exported not only pays the freight, but also makes a contribution to the family expenses of the purchaser. Fortunately, in the United States, taxes are not yet levied for the support of private families in other countries.

During the past twelve years France has produced 7,985,093 tons of sugar, on which an indirect premium of 653,022,000 francs ($126,-033,246) was received,—a mean annual premium of 54,418,000 francs ($10,502,771). During the same period Germany produced 14,810,-333 tons, on which an indirect premium of 263,444,000 francs was paid ($50,844,692),—an annual premium of 21,954,000 francs ($4,237,058). The quantities mentioned above are expressed in metric tons, equivalent to 2204.6 pounds each. In Austria the maximum of the indirect premium is fixed by law. From 1888 to 1896 the annual rate was 5,000,000 florins ($2,023,000). Last year the maximum amount of premiums allowed by the Austrian government was 9,000,000 florins ($3,641,000), and for this year the same sum is given.

The effect of the premium on exports of sugar is twofold. In the first place, it stimulates domestic production in the country in which the premium is paid, by securing a larger market for the sugar produced. The high taxes in Continental countries restrict the home consumption, and, unless an outlet be found, the limit of the industry is soon reached. By reason of the high premium received, exporters are enabled to undersell in the markets of the world those whose sugars are grown without the stimulus of a direct or indirect bounty. In the second place, the effect of the premiums on exported sugar is to cheapen its cost to the consumers in non-producing countries, whereby the consumption in those countries is increased. The effect of the bounties is seen chiefly in England, which, in proportion to its population, is the largest sugar-consuming country in the world. England levies no import duty on sugar; consequently, the price of sugars in the London market is not subject solely to the law of supply and demand, but is cheapened in direct proportion to the amount of premiums paid by Continental countries. The result has been one of which, upon the whole, the English people have had no reason to complain. But, on the other hand, the English sugar-refiners and the British sugar-producing colonies have been practically ruined by the Continental system of bounties. Indeed, so great has been the distress produced thereby that, on various occasions, Parliament has seen fit to investigate the subject; and Parliamentary committees have not only debated upon it in London, but one such committee has recently visited all the principal colonial centres of sugar production.

In this country the effect of the Continental bounties is beginning to be seriously felt; and the situation has lately been rendered more acute by reason of the difficulties in Cuba, which island in the past has been our natural source of supply. The war has reduced the Cuban production, in round numbers, from 1,000,000 to 100,000 tons; and, by reason of the great plethora of sugar in Continental Europe, caused by the application of the bounty system, almost the whole of this deficit has been drawn from beet-sugar-producing countries. It is safe to say that, at the present rate of consumption, our annual importation of beet sugar amounts to 800,000 tons,—an increase of 700,000 tons in three years.

In formulating the revenue bill now before Congress the European bounty system must be considered. The principal difficulty involved in this bill lies in harmonizing conflicting interests of the producer and the refiner. By retaining the obsolete system of valuing sugars according to the Dutch standard of color, however, this difficulty is only increased. One hundred years ago, when the Dutch colonies produced cane sugar in a uniform manner by the same process of manufacture, the character of the sugar was rather definitely determined by its color. But modern systems of manufacture have rendered such tests absolutely worthless. The retention of this standard in our customs duties is the "open sesame" to favoritism and every conceivable fraud.

Another complication arises from a desire on the part of our sugar-refiners to levy at least a large portion of the duty according to the value of the sugar imported. The effect of such a system of valuation may be readily demonstrated by taking as an example the French sugars, on which the export premium is about one cent a pound; the actual price of the sugar being diminished by that amount. This means that the total amount of duty received by us on this sugar would be at least 40 per cent below the amount collected, if the bounty paid by

France were abolished. By reason of the great difficulty in fixing the amount of duty on sugar produced under such a complicated fiscal system as that which now obtains in France, an attempt to levy a countervailing duty equal in amount to the export premiums would not be an adequate security. Such an attempt would be followed by endless litigation; and meanwhile the revenues would suffer. An excess of duty equal to any direct bounty could easily be determined; but the amount of indirect premium would still vary from year to year with the changing conditions in the country where the sugar was produced. Even in the case of Austria, with its fixed maximum premium, it would be difficult to adjust a countervailing duty, unless the quantity of sugar exported annually were always the same. If all systems of bounty on export were abolished, and the anachronistic Dutch standard of color put aside, it would be possible to levy and collect a perfectly fair *ad valorem* import duty.

In the present state of our finances the collection of a duty on imported sugars is necessary; and all classes of political economists, whether protectionists or free-traders, can agree upon this point. It is now the duty of the people of this country to demand (1) the abrogation of the obsolete, unscientific, and erroneous Dutch standard color-test; and (2) that, pending the abolition of all premiums on exports, the duties on all imports be levied specifically, and upon their sugar content alone. The polariscope affords a speedy and accurate measure of the value of every cargo of sugar, and, when used under proper scientific safeguards, secures a perfectly honest and fair valuation, which everybody can comprehend, and which does absolute justice to all.

The problem of foreign sugar bounties should not be difficult to solve. The nature and amount of these bounties, in the two principal sugar-producing countries of Europe, have been pointed out. We have in the United States a growing sugar industry, especially in beets. There is no reason why this industry should not expand rapidly until a large part, if not all, of the sugar consumed in the United States, is of domestic origin. At present, a little less than one-sixth of the whole amount consumed is made at home. The experience of European countries points out the course we ought to pursue in regard to this great agricultural industry. The import duty on sugar should be just sufficient to raise the needed amount of revenue and to secure a moderate protection for our planters. We should never follow the erroneous policy of attempting to raise revenue by directly taxing production, and at the same time levying an equally high duty on imports;

for such a procedure would only diminish the consumption of sugar, by reason of its rapid advance in price. It is quite certain that the actual cost price of making sugar hereafter will rarely rise above three cents a pound; and the cost of the refined article to the consumer should never go beyond five cents a pound. This difference would leave a sufficient margin for the legitimate profits of transporters, refiners, and grocers.

The refining interests of our country already command such expert technical skill, such methods and machinery, as to enable them to take care of their own business without any favors from Congress. Legitimate profits in refining sugar can be easily secured without the unreliable discrimination in color made possible by the Dutch standard, and without the aid of any differential duty on refined sugar, or any complicated method of levying duties on imported sugars.

Unless the other sugar-producing countries of the world take some restrictive action, it is hard to say where the policy which is now controlling European producers will lead them. Instead of diminishing, we see the premiums on exports increasing. France has met the direct bounty offered by Germany, and is prepared to go further. Other sugar-producing countries in Europe are clamoring for the same degree of support furnished by Germany and France. Unless an end is put to this merry war, it may go on until sugar can be delivered in London at simply the cost of transportation, or at a still lower figure.

It is not my purpose to discuss here the disastrous effects which such a course will eventually produce among the Continental nations of Europe. It is sufficient to consider it in relation to our own policy, in order to ascertain how it will affect our interests. It is certain that the laws now governing the sugar industry in Europe, unless met by proper countervailing duties, will check and eventually destroy that department of our agricultural industry which is so eagerly turning its attention to the production of sugar. Our legislators need, therefore, regard only the open facts, and, rejecting all other influences, consider those alone which aim at the raising of revenue and the legitimate protection of our agricultural interests. In this way they will eventually be able to establish a fiscal policy which will be perfectly just to all parties concerned.   H. W. WILEY.

THE EVOLUTION OF THE EDUCATIONAL IDEAL.—I.

THE evolution of the educational ideal has a twofold interest: a theoretical and a practical one. (1) A theoretical interest, as regards our conception of history; for the spirit of the times, the general conformation and tendency of any given period, nowhere become so clearly discernible as in the prevailing ideal of education. (2) A practical interest; for, by following the historical development of the educational ideal, we become enabled to form an idea of the future. After all, the primary aim of all political, social, and intellectual endeavors is to furnish a standard for individual conduct. In this article I shall sketch the various changes in the educational ideal within the pale of our civilization to the present time, and in my next, point out the tendencies of the present, and their bearing on the future.

Among the modern nations of Europe three types of the educational ideal have become conspicuous; viz., (1) the Clerical, (2) the Courtly, (3) the Civic.

The Clerical-religious ideal dominates the Middle Ages, and retains a preponderant influence to the middle of the seventeenth century. The Courtly, or, as it may be termed, the Courtly-French, ideal—the ideal of polite society—becomes prominent in the seventeenth, and rules the eighteenth, century. The Civic has been in the ascendant since the middle of the eighteenth, and dominates the nineteenth, century.

(1) In the Middle Ages the church is the supreme form of intellectual life. Science and art are in her service: every form of education emanates from her. All schools are clerical organizations: the clergy are the teachers; and the scholars also, as a rule, belong to the clerical profession. The various branches of instruction comprise the clerical arts: reading, writing, the language and the science of the church, church-music, church-service, and ritualistic exercises. The laity, also, may be said to be under the influence of this educational ideal. The type of human perfection is patterned after the idea of Christian purity, and finds its perfect expression in the saint. Renunciation of the

world, and the contemplation of the eternal life are the fundamental principles that shape men's thoughts and sentiments. Such, in brief, is the type which serves as the model of all education. It is probable that the purely human desires and aspirations then, as now, exercised their sway; but the ideal itself assumed that supernatural and ascetic form which mediæval Christianity had inherited from the Christianity of the Greeks and Romans.

With the advent of the twelfth century, which left so deep an imprint upon mediæval history, the modern races of Europe, which had at first rather superficially adopted the dogma of the church and the legacy of the ancients, begin to show signs of independent activity. Worldly culture, worldly literature, and science are introduced. Among the chivalrous society of the courts a new ideal of education takes shape,—the educational ideal of the new nobility, trained to arms and the service of the state. Consequently this ideal is characterized by military skill, knightly courtesy, bravery, fidelity, and a high sense of justice, which considers the protection of the weak and the oppressed as its foremost duty. At the beginning of the thirteenth century there arise in France and Italy the first universities—organizations of a free and spontaneous growth, dedicated to instruction in the sciences. Attracted by the study of the secular sciences, especially of the law, scholars from every country of Europe flock to the cities of Northern Italy, and gather about eminent instructors. Paris adopts a new philosophy and theology, the so-called Scholastic, which, at that time, was as attractive and intoxicating as any all-embracing speculative system that had ever existed. The aim of this philosophy was a rational interpretation of Holy Scripture, which it endeavored to bring into accordance with human understanding. Nevertheless, the authority of the church remains unquestioned. The universities enjoy her favor and her patronage. Teachers and scholars—more particularly on this side of the Alps—are drawn from the ranks of the clergy; indeed, the majority of them belong to the monastic order. The culture of the nobility also is inseparable from the influence of the church.

Two great intellectual movements, the Renaissance and the Reformation, usher in the modern era. Both exercise a far-reaching influence upon the educational ideal.

The Renaissance, in its very essence, furnishes a marked contrast to the mediæval ideal of life. It is the reaction of the optimistic, secular spirit of life against the supernatural, ascetic ideal of the church. The youthful spirit of the modern races discovers that the philosophy and literature of the Greeks and Romans are much better adapted to its present needs than the supernatural doctrines and morality of òrthodox Christianity.   It is, therefore, with passionate zeal that the modern European races proceed to abolish the ideas and symbols of ancient Christianity and to substitute therefor the forms and symbols of the newly discovered antique world, which they endeavor to apply in literature, language, science, and the arts, and to incorporate in social customs.

The educational ideal which corresponds to this revolution is the development of the individual, with all his natural instincts and gifts,— the development of the subjective and personal life.   Thought is no longer fettered by church dogmatism.   Narrow social conditions are removed, and give place to the spirit of personal liberty.   The individual places his independent judgment against truths bearing the stamp of authority; his personal sentiments and ideas against currently accepted customs.   At a later period this spirit of liberty frequently degenerates into unbridled scepticism and libertinism.   The desire to carry out their individual will, regardless of consequences, frequently leads strong natures into monstrous profligacy.   At the courts of the Italian tyrants—masterfully portrayed in Burckhardt's "History of the Renaissance"—we meet with this type, which has found a somewhat belated admirer in Fr. Nietzsche.

In the third decade of the sixteenth century, the Renaissance, in its triumphal progress through all the countries of Europe, encountered a movement of different origin and of different tendencies,—that movement which emanated from Wittenberg,—the Reformation.   The spirit of Luther and his ideal of life were far removed from those of the Renaissance and its followers.   Luther was in every sense a man of the people; while the leading spirits of the Renaissance were distinguished by an aristocratic demeanor and worldly views.   Nevertheless, both movements for a short time mutually augmented each other, as counter currents occasionally produce a tidal wave.   Above all things they mutually served to overthrow the Scholastic system of philosophy and theology.   These movements, however, soon parted company and pursued separate paths.   Renaissance and humanism—art, science, and culture—flourish only in times of peace: they demand liberty for the upper classes and order for the people.   The Reformation, on the other hand, with its doctrines of a universal priesthood and universal perfection, proceeded to overthrow the dominion of the church, the priestly caste, and, with it, monastic sanctity.   Appalled, however, by the revolutionary uprising of the masses in the Peasants' War, the Reformers established territorial churches under the dominion of secular rulers. The consequence was that the school system, which had ever been connected with the church, was also, like the church, transferred to the care of the state. To sum up the results of this movement, it may be said that the Reformation neither abolished, nor intended to abolish, the old ecclesiastical ideal of education. On the contrary, it rescued this ideal, for the time being, from the acute worldliness of the Renaissance. Furthermore, the Reformation, by breaking down the universal church and transferring her power to the secular authorities, became the principal agent in bringing about that severance of education from the ecclesiastical life which was finally consummated in the seventeenth and eighteenth centuries.

As to the first statement, there can be no doubt that the Reformation reëstablished those theological and religious interests which during the sixteenth century had been subordinated to the sciences and the aristocratic culture of the upper classes. Erasmus complains that wherever the Lutheran faith takes hold, the fine arts perish. The Reformation was doubtless hostile to a rationalizing, independent spirit of criticism, such as lived in Erasmus. Luther hated Erasmus; and, when the Protestant court theologians proved that they were frequently more zealous and narrow-minded in demanding subjection to their creed than the supporters of the ancient church themselves, they might well cite Luther as their example. Neither to hesitate nor to vacillate in upholding the true doctrine,—such was the motto of these men.

Among the results of the Reformation may be counted the reaction brought about within the Catholic Church itself. Even Rome severed its association with the Renaissance and with liberalizing rationalism, and once more became conscious of the secret of its power; namely, the government and discipline of its subjects. The Order of Jesuits was established, and soon became the right hand of the church. This Order, both as regards the complete submerging of the individual in the universal, and the subjection of the natural impulses—more particularly of the intellectual—to authority, was more successful than any institution before it. And it was to this Order that, at the end of the sixteenth century, in all Catholic countries, the entire system of education was entrusted.

Taking a general survey of the system of instruction as it existed at the end of this revolutionary century, we may say that the ecclesiastical ideal of education, menaced at the beginning of the century by the advancing Renaissance, with its rationalizing tendencies, was essentially restored in Protestant, as well as Catholic, districts. Everywhere the schools are distinguished by their clerical character. In Catholic countries the teachers' seminaries are Jesuitical institutions: in Protestant countries, also, the conditions are very nearly the same. The schools are generally domiciled in old convents (as in Pforta, Meissen, Maulbronn, etc.). These old convents, now deserted by the monks and converted into schools, have merely changed their inmates; otherwise the conditions are practically the same. Even many of the old ritualistic practices are observed. The conception of the school is identical with the old ecclesiastical "scholæ seminaria ecclesiæ." The whole system of instruction is based on this principle; viz., a thorough grounding in the true doctrine. It is justly the boast of the Reformers that they were the first thoroughly to introduce religious instruction. The study of the ancient languages, the most important branch of instruction, is likewise conducted in the service of the church. Greek is taught as the language of the New Testament; and Latin is the vehicle by means of which the scientific and philosophical training indispensable to the theological profession is supplied. Johannes Sturm, the celebrated rector of the Strasburg school, summed up the educational ideal of the sixteenth century in the following typical formula: "Sapiens atque eloquens pietas." *Pietas* is the substance—the true creed: scientific culture and a logical linguistic schooling are the two attributes indispensable to the scholar, whether he be in the service of the church or of the state.

What has been said of the schools applies also to the universities. They stand in the service of the church, whether Catholic or Protestant: the curriculum merely depends upon the creed. This applies more particularly to the theological and philosophical faculties. A pedagogical philosophy sanctioned by the church has absolute sway, —in Wittenberg and Helmstedt, as well as at Rome and Ingolstadt. Thus we see that the public school, so greatly furthered by the Reformation, is once more completely under the dominion of the church.

(2) In the course of the seventeenth century a new educational ideal,—the Courtly-French,—begins to supersede that of the church. In other words, the ideal of the Renaissance once more begins to assert itself among the upper classes.

This circumstance is due to a change in the social order. The aristocracy, with the reigning dynasties at its head, once more becomes the ruling class. This change is due to the decline of the church into a civil institution. Catholicism has not recovered from the heavy blow which it received in the sixteenth century. Despite its mighty efforts, it has not regained its former eminent position. In Protestant countries the church has lost her independence entirely; while in Catholic countries the state may be said to be the ruling power. Nor have the citizens been able to maintain the position which they occupied toward the close of the Middle Ages. The cities—more particularly those of Germany—can no longer boast of the high rank by which they were distinguished in the sixteenth century (Nuremberg, Augsburg, Cologne, and Lübeck, for example). The monarchical state, as well as the nobility,—which constitutes a class indispensable to the rulers,—has obtained an ascendency over the cities. The elevation of worthy citizens, scholars, officials, and—at a somewhat later period—poets and money-lenders to the ranks of the nobility is an indication of the prevailing social standard. A man does not attain to social position until he leaves the ranks of the common people, and, by virtue of a title bestowed upon him, enters the order of the nobility.

These changes, political and social, are followed by others of an intellectual nature. The general tendency of the educational movement may be briefly characterized as secularization of education and of the intellectual life. This tendency manifests itself in every department. In that of science, theology and metaphysics are forced farther and farther into the background by mathematics, physics, and the political and social sciences. Since the days of Descartes, Hobbes, and Newton, the reputation of the exact sciences is steadily and rapidly rising. At the same time the emancipation of scientific inquiry from the thráldom of authority and tradition is consummated. Rationalism —the belief in reason—asserts itself, and, in the age of Enlightenment, obtains absolute dominion. The era of the great philosophical systems has come. Descartes and Locke, Leibnitz and Kant, now direct the ideas of mankind, as did once the great theologians.

We observe the same secularization in the fields of art and literature. The royal courts supersede the church as patrons of the arts. The architect of the seventeenth and eighteenth centuries builds castles instead of churches and town-halls. The artist, who formerly adorned the altars with pictures of the Passion and of the Saints, now furnishes portraits of the nobility, or devotes himself to the representation of pagan gods and goddesses, with and without apparel. The chase, the battle, marine scenes, and landscapes,—all are legitimate subjects for his brush. In the same manner, music and poetry are called into the service of the royal theatres and opera-houses.

All these changes are clearly discernible in the new ideal of education, whose brilliant advent takes place in the second half of the seventeenth century. Its general character is well expressed by the term, "galant-homme." The "sapiens atque eloquens pietas" is superseded by the culture of the perfect cavalier. He has all the , qualities which are demanded of a useful and agreeable member of the court. He possesses courtesy and perfect manners,—*conduite*, and *savoir vivre*,—all the arts and accomplishments; he rides and fences, dances and vaults, plays ball and the lute; he is master of French, and sometimes also of Italian. His equipment is completed by a course in the modern sciences, such as mathematics and physics (with fortification and pyrotechnics); hydraulics and mechanical engineering; geography, statistics, heraldry, history of the state, and jurisprudence. Whoever possesses all these requirements ·is a finished gentleman, eligible alike to courtly, military, and civil service.

Germany, which could boast of a greater number of courts than any other country, now creates a new order of colleges, the so-called *Ritterakademien*, to meet the requirements of the new· education. These academies, as a rule, were established at some centre of royalty (Cassel, Wolfenbüttel, Hildburghausen, etc.), and generally stood in close relation to the court itself, in order that the sons of the native princes and the nobility generally might have the benefit of an education better adapted to their needs than that of the old monastic institutions.

The universities also follow the current of the times. The study of law advances rapidly at the expense of theology, and, at the first modern universities, Halle and Göttingen, attains a positive supremacy. It furnishes the nobility with the training requisite for their political position. The costume of the court displaces the clerical garb. Distinguished professors are elevated to the ranks of the nobility, or receive titles. The student imitates the cavalier: the sword and the duel qualify him for the upper ranks. A circumstance of still greater importance is the emancipation of collegiate education, and the establishment of the principle of educational liberty. It is the boast of the University of Halle that it was the first to acquire the *libertas philosophandi*. Here modern philosophy first supersedes the Aristotelian. Christian Wolf was the first who succeeded in reducing modern thought to a complete and regular pedagogical system. The other sciences, more particularly theology, soon followed this example. Rationalistic dogmatism and historical criticism likewise first gained a footing in the University of Halle.

The schools also join the general movement. The *Gelehrtenschulen* (Latin Schools) begin to take up the study of the German and French languages, the elements of mathematics and physics, as well as history and geography. In the common schools, also, the clerical spirit is compelled to give way to the secular. To furnish the state with useful subjects is now the aim. A thorough schooling is beginning to be regarded as a matter of great economical importance; consequently, all means are employed to develop the efficiency of the pupil in every direction.

(3) About the middle of the eighteenth century the Courtly-French ideal of education begins to wane: a new educational ideal rises in the firmament, and attains the meridian toward the close of that century. This revolution is again due to changes in the social order. Democracy is advancing; the prestige of the nobility is declining. The modern state dissolves its union with the feudal territorial system, and creates an extensive official system, in which merit and efficiency are stronger credentials than nobility of birth. In the social and intellectual spheres, also, democracy is in the ascendant. The cities have gradually recovered from the devastation of the Thirty Years' War, and arrived at a moderate degree of prosperity. Above all, it is in the departments of science and literature that the masses once more come to the front. Klopstock, Gellert, Lessing, Herder, Winckelmann, Kant, Fichte, Goethe, and Schiller,—all spring from the lower and middle ranks of life: they represent the ideas of the people, and introduce them into literature. The popular drama and the novel appear. The masses, as it were, once more become conscious of their power. It is a noteworthy fact that this movement is coincident with the decline of French, and the rise of English, prestige. Among the nations of Europe, England was the land of the commons; France, the land of the court and the nobility. From the third decade of the eighteenth century forward, English thought is carried into France; Voltaire and Montesquieu being its most important propagators. At a somewhat later period, Germany, through its new popular literature, joins the movement. Shakespeare becomes celebrated; French classicism is overthrown; Locke, Shaftesbury, and Hume are read and translated. And with the English, the Greek classics—allies of the popular

spirit in its struggle against the Courtly-French ideal—come to the front. From the very outset, democracy and the new humanistic spirit are coöperative powers.

The educational ideal of this new epoch may be briefly expressed by the term, "humanistic education." Herder is the first great preacher of this new movement, the aim of which is the development of man, with all his native faculties. The ideal of the new education is a human being whose faculties enable him to form a clear and definite conception of the actual world; who, by virtue of his will, is able to recognize and follow his individual bent; whose imagination and finer emotions are trained to the perception of the beautiful and the heroic. This is a man in the full sense of the word : this is true humanistic culture.

The new educational ideal is determined by the view of life of the new humanism,—a view based upon the contemplation of the Greeks, with their perfect realization of the human idea and their admirable representation of the human type. In Greece, Nature carried out her intentions as regards human development with absolute completeness; and this is true not merely of the development of the human form, as typified in the antique sculptures, but also as regards the cultivation of the human mind; a fact to which the poetry and philosophy of the Greeks bear testimony. The demands of this second, the Protestant-Hellenic-democratic, Renaissance may be summed up in the motto, "Educate thyself according to Greek standards !" Here we have Greek humanity instead of French gallantry; a free and humane conception of human affairs instead of a courtly, conventional one; a liberal education instead of conventional training.

The educational institution which the nineteenth century has established to meet the demands of this ideal, is the humanistic gymnasium (the Latin High School of Germany). Its object is the development of all the faculties in every possible direction. To this end, a study of the ancient languages is regarded as of the utmost importance; for, by cultivating the Greek and Roman languages and literatures, we acquire skill in all mental operations. The grammar assists us greatly in formulating our ideas ; the classical poets awaken our sense of the æsthetic, and cultivate a taste for beauty and simplicity; the study of the historical and philosophical writers broadens our horizon, fills us with noble sentiments, and furnishes a historical basis for the proper conception of the present. The study of mathematics ranks next in importance, and also furnishes an excellent training to the faculties. The new era despises the utilitarian and encyclopedic attainments so highly valued by the previous epoch. True human culture, and not utility, is its aim. It is characteristic of ignoble souls to appreciate only what is absolutely utilitarian, and to overlook entirely the importance of a free, beautiful, and perfect culture of the inner life.

The new education is distinctively democratic. It is founded upon the idea of scholarship as preserved in the old institutions of learning, —upon *humaniora* and not upon *gallantiora*, as Herder so aptly expresses it. The institution in which the new education is disseminated is also democratic. The gymnasium has a pronounced tendency toward social equality. In other words, the gymnasium, by reason of its extended course and its final examination for the university, has once more compelled the aristocracy to attend the common schools. The sons of the nobility, who during the sixteenth century had everywhere attended the Latin schools, were during the two following centuries entrusted to the care of private tutors, or were sent to the *Ritterakademien* in order to receive a preparatory training for the university course. These academies have entirely disappeared during the present century; and we now know them only by name. W. von Humboldt, the founder of the Prussian gymnasium, so desired it. He says: "I cannot see the advantages of a separate education for the nobility." The system of private instruction (*Hofmeistertum*) has also entirely disappeared. We now find the sons of the nobility, even the princes of the reigning houses, in the gymnasium. The curriculum has been so greatly augmented that private instructors are no longer able to supply an equivalent education.

In addition to the above, may be mentioned the examination for the university (*Abiturientenexamen*), which is also a democratic institution. None may be admitted to the university who has not complied with the requirements of the state examination. The meaning of this is, that only an *élite*, an intellectual aristocracy, may enter the university and thereby gain admission to the various professions under governmental control. In this way an end was put to that system of patronage which, regardless of individual endowment or scientific training, secured to the sons of the nobility the highest offices in the state. It is, therefore, not astonishing that the old privileged classes were inclined to regard the gymnasium with disfavor.

In the universities, also, the anti-aristocratic tendency manifests itself. Both professors and students are representatives of national and liberal ideas. I mention only the institution of the *Burschenschaft* (one of the two great Orders of student societies in Germany), and its determined opposition to exclusiveness. It is not astonishing that the universities were feared and hated by all the Austrian and Prussian politicians of the Restoration epoch, whose sphere of influence and personal interests, so closely identified with the small principalities and petty courts, the national state now threatened to disturb.

The same educational ideal was carried by Pestalozzi and his disciples into the common schools, with the difference that the classical languages were not taught in these. In every other respect the goal was the same: Systematic education instead of mechanical memorization; independent mental activity instead of a mere mechanical recitation. The development of all the faculties of man,—particularly of independent judgment,—in contrast to a mere training for the church or a narrow social circle, is now the aim; and, in order that it may be realized, exercises in observation and logical reasoning are given. "Man as a moral being is the sole object; and it is criminal to employ him as a means to serve selfish aims." Such was the doctrine of the time, as formulated by Kant.   FRIEDRICH PAULSEN.

HAVE AMERICANS ANY SOCIAL STANDARDS?

In speaking of society, I do not mean the gayly fashionable set, the froth that floats on the topmost wave in every community, but the social world as distinct from the business, political, or intellectual world. Society in this broad sense means the interchange of courtesies, the giving and receiving of hospitality. With all its imperfections, it is, as Howells says, the nearest approach to the ideal life of anything we have. We should not rail at it even when we see it complicated by expensive entertainments or brutalized by strivings after precedence.

Is it possible in a republican country to have any social standards? The conditions seem to forbid it. In Europe the first thing that one notices—in countries except those under despotic governments with their nihilistic reactions—is the repose that pervades the social fabric. People are born to certain conditions; they never expect to attain any others; and, except in the case of volcanic genius, they are satisfied. Their mode of life has been settled for them by the traditions of centuries. Some of the unlovely features of republican society are thus unknown. There is no putting on of style, no striving to keep up appearances, no envy of the prosperous neighbor, no reading of books of etiquette. A fixed classification prevents all this.

To an American the foreign political order, the division into ranks, seems stifling. In the words of that typical Yankee, *Sam Lawson,* " It is a good deal like a pile of sheepskins; only the top one lies light." But in the social world the effect is somewhat different. The very essence of good breeding is serenity. Princes could not have their manners, were it not for their assured position. The classes are loyal, each to its own members. Nature may be crucified sometimes, because of these artificial divisions; but the social world has at least the appearance of stability, which is essential to its finest development.

In a republican country all these conditions are changed. The very essence of republicanism, as commonly understood, is that you are as good as your neighbor. As no community has yet reached that industrial condition which insures an equal division of money, this doctrine means, in the expressive vernacular, that everybody has got to hustle.

39

With people up to-day and down to-morrow, society is as unstable as the sea. The competition of American life has never been more happily illustrated than in the words of a very native American poet:—

> " You see that rooster on the fence ;
>   Just hear him crow !
> His satisfaction is immense,
> His self-possession is intense,
> His lusty lungs give evidence
>   That this is so.
>
> Another rooster sees him there
>   And hears him crow.
> With flapping wings he cleaves the air ;
> The fence top is too small to share,
> And so they fight and scratch and tear,
>   And down they go."

Constant motion is a good thing in many ways; it prevents stagnation and freezing: but when applied to the social world, we see, as it were, uneasy particles in a boiling pot ; and the scum rises. Quiet and repose and time are necessary for each component to find its proper place; and then the cream comes to the top.

Despite the popular opinion, and notwithstanding the increase of enormous individual fortunes, I believe that this country is constantly growing more democratic. The changes in social standards show this. During the first half of this century the two most marked factors in national life were the New-England and the Southern influences. The Middle West was passing through the pioneer stage ; the Far West was practically non-existent, though the horizon of California was beginning to show a golden edge. New York had not then attained its present financial importance ; and, though distinctive by reason of its Dutch element, it was far from being dominant. The New-England and the Southern populations were largely of English descent and tradition. At that time there had been no great infusions of foreign blood ; and though certain sections were modified by the French Huguenots, the Germans, the Scotch, the Irish, and the Louisianian French, the prevailing tone was English.

The society developed in these two sections was markedly unlike, owing to the difference in climate and the substratum of negro population in the South. The New Englanders had habits of thrift and frugality ; they grew rich slowly ; they did their own work, except when their establishments were large enough to keep hired help, not "servants," they waited on themselves; they showed a keen intellectual hunger, which made their region the literary and educational centre of the country; they were in bonds to the Puritan Sabbath; they talked of God and the future life; but they matched their ninepences.

The Southerners led the life of fox-hunting English squires. They had the Anglo-Saxon love of the open air; and the climate determined that their industries should be agricultural: hence they built their picturesque mansions on the plantations, not in their small and widely separated cities. The institution of slavery enabled them to exercise an unbounded hospitality, unknown and impossible in the North. In a way they followed English traditions more closely than their New-England compeers. The aristocratic church in the South was the Anglican. When estates were not large enough to provide for all the sons, the younger ones were sent into the army or navy. The bright ones with a gift for oratory went into politics by way of the law.

The social life developed under these conditions had a charm—if one could forget the dark incongruity beneath, always threatening— that no other part of our country has ever afforded. Southern housekeeping was shiftless in Northern eyes; but there was rare good cooking in some of those old kitchens, and free-hearted hospitality and constant merry-making in the dining- and drawing-rooms. The men had leisure; and there was no disproportion of the sexes, which gives so dreary an effect to many a New-England ballroom. Courtship and early marriage were the order of the day; and every girl had dozens of suitors.

Notwithstanding the awful moral deterioration, the ill wrought by slavery on the masters, some lovely traits of character were developed by the Southern life,—especially among the women. The South never had a literature till after everything else had been submerged. Even since the War the section has not been fully exploited; though the Southern States can perhaps claim at the present time a larger number of authors of excellent short stories than any other portion of the country. The old-time chivalry and generosity; the charm of manner; the upholding of ancient traditions; the cherishing of honest, if mistaken, ideals; the dignity and patience under losses;—all these qualities, set in the beautiful country life, with the tragedy of slavery either present or past, afford an unsurpassed field for literature. With all his absurdities, where is there a more lovable character than Hopkinson Smith's *Col. Carter of Cartersville?* Thomas Nelson Page, Ruth McEnery Stuart, Grace King, Richard Malcolm Johnston, and occasionally Constance Fenimore Woolson, though of New-Hampshire birth, and Mrs.

Burton Harrison, not to mention scores of others, have shown us different phases of Southern life; and the most promising of our novelists
writes from Kentucky.

In the days of which I am speaking, before telegraphs and railways
had welded every portion of the country together, the North and the
South were antagonistic, as communities of different tastes, not well
acquainted, must be. The common meeting-grounds of these opposing
forces were: first, Washington; second, the watering-places, so-called,—
summer resorts with hotels,—to which fashionable people then flocked;
and third, to some extent, the Northern schools and colleges. In each
of these places the South was socially dominant.

It was natural that the seat of government should fall under Southern influence. Before the War nine of the fifteen presidents, including
every one who had served two terms, belonged either by birth or by
residence to the South. The Southerners took an excessive interest in
politics, not only from lack of other occupations, but in order to
preserve their peculiar institution; and the capital itself, from its location, favored Southern customs.

From every point of view Washington is undoubtedly a much finer
city now than it was forty years ago; but there was a certain elegance
about it in the *ante bellum* days, which makes it possible for us to understand how horror-stricken the leaders of the old régime were when the
Lincolns and their backwoods followers appeared. The turmoil of war
brought the rabble to the front. All was confusion and chaos; old
traditions were uprooted; crude and uncouth manners were found in
high places; people with wrought-silver wine-coasters, brocades imported from England in the days of the Georges, and furniture and
china contemporary with the French kings, felt that the era of shoddy
had indeed set in.

In the other places, the summer resorts and the schools, the Southerners were not usually in the majority before the War; but they
easily held social sway. In those days the Southerners who travelled
all had money, which they spent freely. They were used to a multiplicity of servants; and they carried their servants with them—something almost unheard of in the North. The slave-owners had personal
charm, usually personal beauty; and their long habit of entertaining
made them adepts in the art of pleasing. Their hot blood and imperious tempers only gave them an additional fascination; and the
ever-felt presence of their peculiar institution lent to their lives the
romance which belongs to all mediæval survivals. However much

the cold, pale-blooded, rational Northerners may have disapproved of certain phases of character and modes of life of their brilliant congeners of the cotton States, they regarded them with interest, and looked upon them socially with awe.

The War wrecked the South.   Stripped of their money and negroes, their beautiful homes desolate, nothing left but stacks of blackened bricks overlooking deserted fields, the flower of their manhood dead, and the means of livelihood of all taken away, the Southerners learned the lessons of adversity.   Pomp and vainglory, worldly circumstance and social precedence,—all were swept away.   Nothing was left but the virtues which flourished in spite of slavery, and the new blessings which spring up from a burned land.   The South can never again be what it was, and—the Southerners are as glad of it as we.

The War was chief among the agencies which brought about the social changes of the last half-century; but other means, hardly less far-reaching, have been the development of the West, with its enormous natural resources, the progress of mechanical invention, the facilities for transportation and communication which have drawn all parts of our immense territory into intimate relations with each other, the movement of the population from the country to the cities, and, growing out of all these allied causes, the opportunity to make great fortunes quickly. All these elements are part of the romance of a new country developing under democratic conditions; but every one of them tends to disturb the social balance.   The result is that the average American is helpless in the matter of social judgments.   Middle-aged people, usually of the female sex,—for women manage society in this country,—are in a state of timid anxiety about what they shall eat, how they shall act, what they shall wear, whom they shall associate with, and where they shall go in the summer.   Everything is so different now from the way in which they were brought up.

Of course we are not all parvenus in this country.   There are some judicious minds and dignified and well-balanced characters who work out these problems for themselves; taking pride in continuing the habits of their ancestors, and making such necessary adjustments to modern conditions as time inevitably compels.   Such people do not consult books of etiquette to know when, where, how, and upon whom to leave their visiting-cards; they are not continually casting furtive glances at their neighbors' domestic arrangements to see if they themselves are keeping up with the procession; nor do they obtain their social information from the Sunday papers.   The matters that belong

to our social life are not trivial;—always remembering that I mean
society in the broad sense.   How we live shows what we are living
for.   The way a person spends his leisure, and the companions he
chooses, give a much juster indication of his character than the habits
and associates of his working-hours.

Foreigners are always puzzled by our lack of social standards.   Our
country is so vast and complex that they never see it whole.   They
are always trying to find out who sets the pace for American life;
and they can discover no order of precedence, no rank in occupation, no dominant city.   We have been gradually working into this
state of affairs.   We were not democratic when the Declaration of
Independence was signed, nor when Washington took the oath as
President.

The early settlers brought the habits of their native country with
them.   There were marked differences in station among the dwellers
along the Atlantic seaboard during the eighteenth century.   Official
position had a rank then which it has almost entirely lost.   The colonial governors were magnates indeed.   They wore scarlet broadcloth,
powdered wigs, dress swords, and travelled in coaches with outriders.
The smallest official title had dignity.   There was a time in the first
decade of this century when to be in the East-India trade was
to be a king.   That was the period during which were built the
beautiful three-story mansions, with their carved mantel-pieces and
balustrades, at Portsmouth, Salem, Newport, and the other coast towns.
The towns which have grown rapidly and made big cities of themselves, like Boston, have lost the fine old houses; but they keep some
of the traditions.

The clergy had a social power, now almost vanished.   The colonists
were determined to do away with one form of oppression by having no
established church; and then in New England they caused the minister
to be settled by the town, and persecuted and exiled all the independent
thinkers.   Mrs. Stowe says in " Old Town Folks " that *Parson Lothrop's*
wife married him because after the Revolution there were no titles in
this country, and a minister corresponded most nearly in rank to the
lords and bishops she had left at home.   She was always called " *Lady* "
Lothrop; many women receiving this courtesy title in her day.

In the last century, the students of Harvard College were catalogued
according to the rank of their parents.   John Adams, afterward President, did not come very high in the list; and there are people now
living who can remember hearing very old ladies speak of him as " that

cobbler's son." At this period there was a custom known as "dignify-ing the meeting-house," which meant the assigning of the pews accord-ing to the rank of the occupants.

We have changed all that. The President wears the same kind of clothes as the dry-goods clerk; and his carriage is inconspicuous. Few political offices command great social respect; for the men who fill them represent all degrees, both positive and negative, of civilization, education, and morals. Mr. Bryce tells of the mirth that was excited at Wellesley College when a visiting foreigner innocently inquired, "I suppose your students come from the best families in this country, —daughters of Congressmen and the like?" In some of the large cities, to be an alderman is tantamount to being socially branded.

In other countries, the army and the navy rank next to the court. In America, the officers are so few in number and so scattered that they hardly count as a social factor. The average millionaire probably re-gards them as did *Horace Chase*, in Miss Woolson's novel of that name, when he offered his brother-in-law a business position with the remark, "That ought to be a pretty good salary for a naval man."

Culture will always command respect among its devotees; and a college president is still held in some esteem, even by his own under-graduates. Even where the faculty consists only of "Mrs. Johnson and myself," the professors have some prestige. In certain cities, nota-bly Boston, literary people and others of intellectual habits are actually considered to belong in the best society; and in Baltimore a position at Johns Hopkins entitles one to a place in the social directory.

There is no socially dominant city in this country. Foreigners nat-urally look to the national capital for something resembling their own courts; but they do not find it. The population of Washington is essentially a floating one,—office-holders, department clerks, and tour-ists, with a colored substratum. Some life positions, such as a justice-ship in the Supreme Court, give a certain dignity; but the politicians —most of them—are "drest in a little brief authority." Like the throngs at the Columbian Exposition, they come from everywhere and goodness knows where. They are truly a representative crowd. Rarely from the large cities, they bring the atmosphere of the plains, the mountains, and the woods along with the training acquired in the mine, the field, the factory, the office, and the court-room. They do not pretend to be the best the country affords; but they are samples of their sections, which is what we ought to desire in a government by the people.

Washington is gloriously American. Not even the numbers of

wealthy idlers who make it their winter home, enormously increasing the scale of living, can destroy its democratic character.   Every dweller within the city may be in society, if he so choose.   Neither color, race, occupation, nor previous or present condition of servitude debars any citizen from paying his respects to all the officials at their public receptions, from the President down to the last attaché of a bureau.   Stories have been told of the wife of a secretary of state,—at the time when those officers returned calls in person,—finding one of her recent guests toiling at the washboard.   Other enterprising visitors of a little different social scale are said to pay for breakfast only at their boarding-places, because they can pick up the rest of their refreshments during their daily round of calls.

Many people have the idea that the size of a city determines its social importance, and that New York sets the standard of living for the rest of the country.   It is amusing to hear certain Americans use the word "provincial."   In a recent biography of an eminent American man of letters, the writer, himself a Bostonian, took particular pains to deplore the fact that his subject's fine humor and social ability were limited by being confined to such a little out-of-the-way town as Boston.   Where do the despisers of the provincial consider the world's capital to be?   Is it London, Paris, Pekin, or—San Francisco?   Civilization has travelled round the circle.   Perhaps we may seek it at the Equator or the North Pole?   As Col. Higginson says, a cosmopolitan is one who is at home even in his own country.   Whoever thinks that fine society or noted people are limited to big cities has forgotten that Athens, Florence, Weimar, and Concord, Massachusetts, were not large towns.   The influences emanating from these places are perhaps as enduring as those that have come from Babylon, Rome, or Chicago. The village of Stratford-on-Avon was good enough for Shakespeare to be born in.

In America especially, one who knows the country well knows that all its good things are widely distributed; otherwise, we could not have a republic.   One who is seeking the really choice and distinctive flavor of American society can find it in some of the refined New-England villages, with their high standards and quiet ways and not narrow outlook on the world—a place like Northampton, Massachusetts, years ago; or he may go to some of the old seaport towns, with their aristocratic traditions, where the same families have lived for more than two hundred years on lands deeded to them by the Indians; or he may look for it in the college communities, with their atmosphere of learning,

their venerable buildings,—"scholar factories," in Lowell's phrase,—
and the fresh young life that beats about them, drawn from every portion of the country; or he may visit the State capitals, rarely the largest
cities in their respective States, and find miniature Washingtons, with
a more substantial population and perhaps a political history that will
better bear investigation. If he would hear of gayety, he is fortunate
if he have friends in a certain South-Carolinian city, where an annual ball
has been given by the same circle of people and their descendants for
over a century, of which no public mention has ever been made; nor
have the names of the guests ever got into the newspapers. What is
New York, with her most fashionable balls, compared to this?

To those minds, whether American or foreign, who regard New
York as socially preëminent, the city stands simply for the largest collection of great fortunes in this country. George William Curtis characterized its summer annex, modern Newport, as the place where the
people were engaged in seeing who could throw the largest amount of
money farthest out into the sea. New York is no mushroom city; yet
few people—least of all, New-Yorkers themselves—ever think of its
history. Perhaps with good reason, for the old landmarks and the
long-resident families are feeble to withstand the great waves of wealth
rolling in upon them.

The fact that New York has become the publishing centre of the
country has helped its aggrandizement more than anything else. The
great publishing firms, whether of books or magazines, and the great
newspaper establishments are located there. Society stories, both
the fictitious ones of literature and the real ones of the reporters, have
their scenes laid along a narrow area extending from Washington
Square to the northern limit of Central Park. Accounts of private
balls are telegraphed across the water as if they were matters of national
importance.

I have no quarrel with the newspapers: they do their work much
more thoroughly and admirably than the old-fashioned sewing-circle,
tavern bar-room, or corner grocery. If they would only go a little
deeper and show the real nature of the people and the "functions"
they describe, the rural mind would perceive that all men are brothers,
and that there is no occasion for envy or malice. As it is, the newspaper notoriety given to the affairs of the rich, while it satisfies the
craving for romance in the minds of the toilers, undoubtedly contributes in no small degree to the discontent prevailing among certain portions of our people. Years ago, before the rise of so many wealthy

cities had made the social entertainments at Washington appear less splendid, there were so many complaints, even shrieks, against the corruption and extravagance at the national capital that Gail Hamilton felt it incumbent upon herself to write an article on "The Display of Washington Society Considered as the Origin of the Evil in the Universe." Her satire was effective, or else time has remedied the matter; for the ministers now pray for New York.

It seems strange that intelligent people do not know that the quickest way to extinguish flaunting wealth is not to notice it. Of course well-bred men and women have no interest in the social affairs of people with whom they are unacquainted; but the circulation of the New-York press reports shows that the concerns of Fifth Avenue must find readers among all classes, from Julian Ralph's acquaintances of the Battery and the Bowery to Owen Wister's cowboys—to say nothing of the thousands of well-to-do people in the smaller cities and towns, who might be supposed to have some social life of their own.

But we need not worry about New York's pretended or alleged social dominance, so long as there is Chicago. We do not know what other worlds may have to show; but Chicago is the most remarkable thing on this planet. Is there a prize of any sort going? Chicago comes along with easy swing and grasps it. Though certain invidious minds may point out that Chicago has as yet shown no overweening desire for culture, she is certainly not behind New York in this respect; and there is no doubt, as Charles Dudley Warner says, that when Chicago once takes hold of culture, she will make it hum. Chicago is the only city in the country with room enough—the only city with her suburbs inside. It has already been prophesied that Chicago is the natural newspaper centre of the country; and where the newspapers are biggest, there lies the heart of things.

It is entirely possible that within the next century Chicago may draw the national capital unto herself. A situation that was appropriate enough for the original Thirteen States is out of date now with an empire west of the Mississippi. Probably the only things that Chicago cannot grasp are Bunker Hill and Plymouth Rock; for Massachusetts institutions are wonderfully tenacious. And yet, such are the changes wrought by mechanical invention, who can say but in time even Chicago may have rivals.

If America can have no social standards because it has no order of precedence, no rank in occupation, no dominant city, it necessarily follows that, unless restrained by culture, the Republic must set inordinate value on externals, the showy, the obvious, the success of the hour. It is for this reason that the great fortunes which have accumulated with surprising rapidity in recent years have wrought such havoc in our social life. It requires a very well seasoned mind and character to withstand the sudden onslaught of wealth. Our economic and industrial conditions are such that money seems to have a tendency to gather itself into heaps; breeding corruption for the owners, while the surrounding area suffers from leanness.

The millionaires themselves often are not to blame for their fortunes: they are the product of the times. One of the most touching pictures of recent years is that shown in Mr. Warner's "A Little Journey in the World." The heroine, *Margaret*, a lovely girl, brought up in the high standards of an old, refined New-England town, makes a love-match with a New-York speculator who, later, achieves dazzling success. Her powerlessness to prevent the wrong she feels he is doing, the gradual hardening of her nature under worldly influences till she is finally buried under an avalanche of gold, are faithfully described.

The opportunity for rapid financial advancement in America, almost of necessity, ruptures family ties and sunders old associations. In foreign countries, where rank is acknowledged, the members of a house have a certain clanship; the allegiance and claims even of remote cousins being recognized. In America the president of a great railroad or an ambassador to one of the European Powers may have nieces who are village dressmakers. A plutocrat living in a house finer than some foreign palaces perhaps occasionally visits a sister whose days are spent on a remote farm where the evening relaxation is milking the cows. Two daughters of the same parents, born and reared alike, may marry: one, a man who becomes a leader in the stock exchange, the other, a street-car conductor. There are professors in our leading colleges, where culture is almost a disease, whose fathers are humble hand-workers. Anyone who thinks that the foregoing instances are exceptional does not know American society. It is but just to say that American good-nature does much toward bridging the chasms which republican opportunities make in worldly circumstances; and that in most cases it is the fault of the poor as often as the misfortune of the rich that old ties are broken.

The circumstances of earning money and the circumstances of spending it are wide apart. Unless one is a miser or a spendthrift, he will not live in the days of his riches as he does in the days of his poverty. People who are not troubled about their past, who have no scruples about ignoring the hand that fed them or the house that sheltered them, can jump from overalls to dress-coats without much trouble. These are they who chatter most glibly about society conventions, who bring home from Europe a brand-new set of clothes, manners, and phrases. I confess that I sympathize with the tough-grained old American stock that fights for its birthright, even to the extent of wearing shirt-sleeves as a house negligée, and only surrenders inch by inch the ways of its fathers.

I can think of two cases in point. An aged and wealthy judge, learned not only in law, but in literature, resolved to spend some part of his well-earned leisure in European travel. His tour was made miserable by the courses of a Continental dinner. Like his contemporaries at home, he had been brought up to think that nothing looked so well on the table as something to eat. "They won't give me my meat and potato together," growled the old judge; and he actually wasted time in arguing with the waiters and lodging complaints with the hotel authorities. An American railway magnate, wishing to attend a theatre in London, was told that no gentleman could be admitted there unless he wore what Mark Twain calls a "steel-pen coat." This dignified patriot declined to surrender his early habits. He was accustomed to wear the finest of broadcloth, but his "meeting" clothes were his best; and any place where his Sunday suit could not go would not be graced by his presence.

The present generation, which has seen the evening dinner and the dress-coat introduced into our large cities, probably finds nothing in these recitals but food for mirth; but it seems otherwise to me. Both these men were graduates of a fresh-water college, somewhat noted for the number of its distinguished alumni. They had been brought up on New-England farms, and had seen their mothers do their own washing. They had eaten pork and parsnips in the spring and boiled beef and cabbage in the fall, set on in one huge platter. Those things were associated with the influences that shaped their career, with the glorious privileges of the Republic. It was probably some dim feeling of this sort, and not a foolish hostility to established usage, that made them stand on their American customs. Manners, to their minds, had some connection with principles.

The very essence of snobbery is to disown one's antecedents, to kick down the props by which one has risen. I would rather see the other extreme,—sturdy citizens who, when they are among the Romans, do as the Bostonians do. I do not mourn over people of means who are in no haste to introduce the evening dinner into their respective towns. Of course, if we look at the matter historically, we know that not all the nation has always dined at noon. Washington used to give state dinners at four o'clock; and the afternoon dinner at two or three o'clock was the highest fashion in Boston until after the Rebellion. It is another sign of the democracy of the times that in cities the principal meal now comes after working-hours. Nothing is so well calculated to make divisions in society, to separate the business men from the people of leisure, as dinner midway in the afternoon. Except for the cooks, the evening dinner is convenient for the veriest toiler.

The dress-coat, viewed in the eye of reason, is no shirt of Nessus. It is no more expensive than a garment of some other cut; it remains in style for years, except for those who wish to follow every curve of the fashion; and its use does not mark nearly so great a social depart- ure as did the change from knee-breeches and silk stockings to plain trousers. And yet I have a sort of fellow-feeling for those descendants of the Pilgrims who vigorously rebel against this sort of attire, who will put it on when only absolutely compelled. It is associated in their minds with late hours, expensive entertainments, and all sorts of elabo- rate ceremonial, which, to use the language of one of the heroines of "Sentimental Tommy," "are words with which we have no concern."

We have survived many social changes. We are not now taught to eat with our knives; though any well-bred old lady will tell you that that was the custom fifty years ago. In these days even some of our Italian laborers have forks; and yet we are more, not less, democratic than in the early half of our century. It is possible—in some places —to get as appetizing a meal on the Pacific as on the Atlantic coast: yet the great West retains the exuberance of youth; and, except when it copies the manners of the rich and great with a vengeance, it still looks down upon the effete aristocracy of Europe. Everybody in the country rides a bicycle, and everybody belongs to a club,—those two great levellers of these latter days.

If we, as republicans, have no social standards, it is because we have abjured those which are associated with some of the forms of mediæval oppression, and have not yet arrived at a degree of culture and dignity which enables us to establish standards of our own. But as a democracy, if it be permanent, must be ever working toward that state of ideal justice which will distribute the really good things of life impartially among all its members, we may hope that the time will come when America shall have social standards because everybody will be in society.   FRANCES M. ABBOTT.

WILLIAM WORDSWORTH.

THERE is no danger, in our day, of provoking the wrath or the ridicule of the literary critic by a just estimate of the influence of Wordsworth's poetry. He has been weighed in the balances; and the verdict of posterity is: "Not wanting." The poet's disciples will not, therefore, allow any unfair criticism to go unchallenged. I wish simply to point out *how* the great poet has made this world seem more beautiful to me than it was before I studied his works.

Many readers have thought Wordsworth to be dull and heavy, and that these defects are unpardonable in a poet. It is true that his poetry is not uniformly great and attractive, and that much of what he wrote is tame. No writer could yield so much wheat and not have some chaff with it. No poet could write a long poem like "The Excursion" or "The Prelude," and be brilliant in every line. Even Homer sometimes nods. Shakespeare does not always reach the same heights; and I venture to say that Byron, who sneered so often at Wordsworth, flies very low in more than one of his poems. Many of those who do not consider Wordsworth profitable reading belong to a class that is "incapable of a feeling of poetry"; and, without the power to appreciate a poet, it is not easy to derive any pleasure or help from him.

Wordsworth is a priest and worshipper of Nature. If we recollect that the poet's life was a life of contemplation, it would be strange if his readers did not derive the calm pleasure which brief sketches and beautiful pictures of a rural landscape yield. He writes often of the Force of Nature as if that were the only living soul of the world; of "a motion and a spirit that impels all thinking things." In the " Lines Composed a Few Miles above Tintern Abbey " we find the germs of pantheism; and we are in doubt as to his theology :—

> " And I have felt
> A presence that disturbs me with the joy
> Of elevated thoughts; a sense sublime
> Of something far more deeply interfused,
> Whose dwelling is the light of setting suns,
> And the round ocean, and the living air,
> And the blue sky, and in the mind of man :

> A motion and a spirit, that impels
> All thinking things, all objects of all thought,
> And rolls through all things."

In these lines he is looking "into the life of things"; and then "the light of setting suns, and the round ocean, and the living air, and the blue sky, and the mind of man" become the abode of "a motion and a spirit." But, however vague this force appears to the reader, when he turns to the "Ecclesiastical Sonnets," he will perceive a greater force, another than that of nature, a living personal soul,—thus proving that the poet was not a pantheist:—

> "To kneeling worshippers no earthly floor
> Gives holier invitation than the deck
> Of a storm-shattered vessel saved from wreck
> (When all that man could do avail'd no more)
> By Him who raised the tempest and restrains;
> Happy the crew who this have felt, and pour
> Forth for His mercy, as the Church ordains,
> Solemn thanksgiving. Nor will *they* implore
> In vain who, for a rightful cause, give breath
> To words the Church prescribes, aiding the lip
> For the heart's sake, ere ship with hostile ship
> Encounters, armed for work of pain and death.
> Suppliants! the God to whom your cause ye trust
> Will listen, and ye know that He is just."

John Ruskin calls Wordsworth the "keenest-eyed" of all modern poets. He who loves landscape-painting loves Wordsworth, and he who has read "The Prelude" and "The Excursion" has probably felt the divine power of a chaste imagination, the all-absorbing penetration of a well-balanced mind:—

> "So fair, so sweet, withal so sensitive,
> Would that the little flowers were born to live,
> Conscious of half the pleasure which they give;
>
> That to this mountain daisy's self were known
> The beauty of its star-shaped shadow, thrown
> On the smooth surface of this naked stone!"

This is "foreground painting. There is no mistake about it. Daisy and shadow and stone-texture and all."

The great poets are very fond of the early hours of the day—in poetry. The dawn charms the fancy. Wordsworth has described the *consecrating* effects of the early morn:—

> "What soul was his, when, from the naked top
> Of some bold headland, he beheld the sun

> Rise up, and bathe the world in light ! He look'd—
> Ocean and Earth, the solid frame of Earth
> And Ocean's liquid mass, beneath him lay
> In gladness and deep joy.—The clouds were touch'd,
> And in their silent faces did he read
> Unutterable love : Sound needed none,
> Nor any voice of joy ; his spirit drank
> The spectacle ; sensation, soul, and form
> All melted into him ; They swallowed up
> His animal being ; In them did he live,
> And by them did he live ; They were his life.
> In such access of mind, in such high hour
> Of visitation from the Living God.
> Thought was not ; in enjoyment it expired ;
> No thanks he breathed, he proffered no request :
> Rapt into still communion that transcends
> The imperfect offices of prayer and praise,
> His mind was a thanksgiving to the Power
> That made him ; it was blessedness and love ! "

When the world is yet asleep and not a solitary warbler disturbs the slumbers of the grove, and the sun comes rolling over the distant hills with the hopes and disappointments of a new day hidden beneath his fiery vesture, these words of the poet suggest to the thoughtful man the sacredness of life, and the worth of a " still communion " that transcends prayer and praise.

I will now quote the beautiful lines on the daffodils which the poet saw when with his sister on the Lake of Ullswater, to illustrate the truth that he who has felt Nature in her loveliness has gained something that will ever be a pleasant remembrance. The man whose genius makes the humblest life happier by recollections of the green meadow, and of the stream that murmurs the secrets of the mountains in our ears, is our friend. The margin of the lake was fringed for a long distance with daffodils :—

> " Continuous as the stars that shine
> And twinkle on the milky way,
> They stretched in never-ending line
> Along the margin of a bay :
> Ten thousand saw I at a glance,
> Tossing their heads in sprightly dance.
>
> The waves beside them danced,—but they
> Outdid the sparkling wave in glee :
> A poet could not but be gay,
> In such a jocund company :
> I gazed—and gazed—but little thought
> What wealth the show to me had brought :

> For oft, when on my couch I lie
> In vacant or in pensive mood,
> They flash upon that inward eye
> Which is the bliss of solitude;
> And then my heart with pleasure fills,
> And dances with the daffodils."

In these verses there is a "subtle perception," and an "exquisite delicacy."

But Wordsworth is not only the poet of Nature, but of Humanity. Mr. Symington says that, "first to last," he was the friend of the humbler orders of society.

> "With a fine eye for the beauty of the material world, he also fixed his imagination on the elementary feelings which are the same in all classes, and drew out the beauty that lies in what is truly natural in human life. . . . So intensely was he interested in the public questions of the day, which he had carefully studied in their important bearings, that he would sometimes walk several miles along a country road at two o'clock in the morning in order to meet the carrier bringing his newspaper from Keswick!"

He lived during the stormy times of the French Revolution, went over to France and sympathized heartily with the people, and was compelled to flee the country for his life. But he had seen enough there to confirm him in his determination to champion the cause of the oppressed. The struggle of his fellow-men for their liberties made him acquainted with the sadness of their lot; and from that time he found a new field for his poetic efforts. In "The Prelude" and "The Excursion" are found suggestive thoughts on the subject of man. Up to this time the poet had lived apart from men; and, in order to be a poet of Humanity, it was important that he should know the needs, the struggles, and the aspirations of the "lowly train." His stay in France afforded him this opportunity. He became fond of the great thoughts of a universal mankind, and of the brotherhood of the race. He had no sympathy with those institutions that repressed the growth of man. He saw in God the source of the rights of men to equality and liberty. He would tolerate no despot over men's bodies and souls. "He felt intensely the enthusiasm of the time. He became a human poet: he felt every pulse of the movement in his own heart."

To illustrate the thought which was his consuming passion at this time, I quote his description of an old man, sorrow-stricken, roused from that sorrow by the fall of the Bastile:—

> "From that abstraction I was roused,—and how?
> Even as a thoughtful shepherd by a flash

40

Of lightning startled in a gloomy cave
Of these wild hills. For, lo ! the dread Bastile,
With all the chambers in its horrid towers,
Fell to the ground :—by violence overthrown
Of indignation ; and with shouts that drowned
The crash it made in falling ! From the wreck
A golden palace rose, or seemed to rise,
The appointed seat of equitable law
And mild paternal sway. The potent shock
I felt : the transformation I perceived,
As marvellously seized as in that moment
When, from the blind mist issuing, I beheld
Glory—beyond all glory ever seen,
Confusion infinite of heaven and earth,
Dazzling the soul. Meanwhile, prophetic harps
In every grove were ringing, ' War shall cease ;
Did ye not hear that conquest is abjured ?
Bring garlands, bring forth choicest flowers, to deck
The tree of Liberty.' "

This is a quotation from " The Excursion "—the poem that was
laughed at by many of the poet's contemporaries, and lashed in the reviews ; of which Jeffrey said : " This will never do " ; and which Byron
tried to annihilate. But, referring to the latter poet, Southey once
said : " He crush ' The Excursion ' ! He might as well attempt to
crush Mount Skiddaw ! "

Two poems, " The Brothers " and " Michael," were written, as
Wordsworth recorded in his letter to Fox, " with a view to show that
men who do not wear fine clothes can feel deeply." He says :—

" I have attempted to draw a picture of the domestic affections, as I know
they exist among a class of men who are now almost confined to the North of
England. They are small, independent proprietors of land, men of respectable
education, who daily labor on their own little properties. . . . Their little tract
of land serves as a kind of permanent rallying point for their domestic feelings.
It is a fountain fitted to the nature of social man, from which supplies of affection, as pure as his heart was intended for, are daily drawn."

It is his power of interpreting the elementary feelings common to
all mortals that has made Wordsworth the poet of humanity ; and he
is destined to live as a poet because he is natural, pure, and true to his
ideal of nature and humanity,—an ideal based upon a sympathetic
knowledge of the visible outward world and of man.

We find no artificiality in Wordsworth, nor any of the city gardens
of Pope in the Poet of Windermere. To him the country is not
" dull." The meteoric flashes of Byron are singularly absent from his

sonnets; but this deficiency (?) is supplied by thoughts simple and true, flowing deep and musical as the Severn, and hushing "half the *babbling* Wye." It is true that in the flights of his genius he never laid his hand upon the ocean's mane; but he did see, as no one else did,— not even his sister who was in the boat with him,—"the dancing daffo-dils." Perhaps he could not soliloquize in the same majestic strain as "The Prisoner of Chillon"; but he *could* and *did* trample on tyranny as effectively as Byron,—only in a different way.

Wordsworth is, moreover, a philosophic poet. He sings of the hu-man soul and of immortality, and has made that realm "from whose bourne no traveller returns" radiant to the imagination. One of the greatest odes in all literature is the one he wrote, entitled, "Intima-tions of Immortality from the Recollections of Early Childhood." These Intimations are based largely upon Plato's doctrine of Reminiscence, modified by Christianity. Plato believed in the eternal existence of ideas; in other words, he thought that knowledge and love and truth and justice are real existences, and *seen* in heaven. The gods draw life and power from their contemplation. The soul of each man, before it lives on this earth, has lived with the gods, and with them has looked upon the vision of absolute truth,—upon the divine landscape of ab-stract ideas which make up Eternal Being. Thus preëxistence and reminiscence are, in Plato, connected with the doctrine of Immortality. The child is thus nearer to God and to the vision of Glory than man. "It is fresh from the hands of God." Coming in childhood immedi-ately from God, all the world seems to the poet "apparelled in celestial light, the glory and the brightness of a dream." This definite idea of his view of immortality helps us to appreciate better these beautiful thoughts:—

> " Our birth is but a sleep, and a forgetting ::
> The Soul that rises with us, our life's Star,
>   Hath had elsewhere its setting,
>   And cometh from afar :
>   Not in entire forgetfulness,
>   And not in utter nakedness,
> But trailing clouds of glory do we come
>   From God, who is our home :
> Heaven lies about us in our infancy !
> Shades of the prison-house begin to close
>   Upon the growing Boy,
> But He beholds the light, and whence it flows
>   He sees it in his joy ;
> The Youth, who daily farther from the East

> Must travel, still is Nature's Priest,
> And by the vision splendid
> Is on his way attended ;
> At length the Man perceives it die away,
> And fade into the light of common day."

The little poem, " We are Seven," although far removed from the
Ode in the order of quality, is suggestive of immortality. It expresses
the poet's view of the life hereafter ; and even the sceptic who has read
this poem, as he stands by the open grave of his child and, through his
tears and the mist of the valley, tries to feel his way toward the other
shore, must hope that there is a better world. Tennyson staggers one
when the lips of Lazarus and of the Evangelist return no answer to
Mary's query : " Where wert thou, brother, those four days ? " Wordsworth inspires us, when the little girl, with artless simplicity, says :—

> " Two of us in the churchyard lie,
> My sister and my brother ;
> And, in the churchyard cottage, I
> Dwell near them with my mother."

A faithful study, then, of this great poet will make the student a
better man. He has had a wholesome influence on modern English
literature. Tennyson admired him, and was much influenced by him.
The " Edinburgh Review " and its editor have, by the verdict of posterity, been hushed into eternal silence concerning his merits as a poet.

There is an account of an interesting occasion in the Oxford theatre
when Wordsworth came forward to receive his honorary degree :—

" Scarcely had his name been pronounced, than from three thousand voices
at once there broke forth a burst of applause, echoed and taken up again and
again when it seemed about to die away, and that thrice repeated. There were
young eyes there filled with an emotion of which they had no need to be ashamed ;
there were hearts beating with the proud feeling of triumph that at last the world
had recognized the merit of the man they had so long loved, and acknowledged
as their teacher ; and yet when that noise was protracted, there came a reaction
in their feelings, and they began to perceive, that *that* was not, after all, the true
reward and recompense for all that Wordsworth had done for England ; it seemed
as if all that noise was vulgarizing the poet. Two young men went home together,
part of the way in silence, and one only gave expression to the feelings of the
other when he uttered those well-known, trite, and often-quoted lines—lines full
of deepest truth :—

> ' The self-approving hour whole world outweighs
> Of stupid starers and of loud huzzas :
> And more true joy Marcellus exiled feels
> Than Cæsar with a senate at his heels.' "

A. P. PEABODY.

VICTORIAN GREATER BRITAIN AND ITS FUTURE.

"From before him had already passed away two generations of intelligent men . . . and he was ruling among the third."

THESE words, used by Homer of Nestor, "the sweet speaker of the Pylians," may now, with the proper change of pronouns and tenses, be applied to Queen Victoria. From her throne she has seen two generations of men pass away; and to-day she is ruling among the third. She has reigned sixty years—longer than almost any sovereign known to history. In these sixty years great changes have come over the civilized world, and over Great Britain in particular.

Victoria came to the throne under peculiar and, on the whole, auspicious circumstances,—circumstances that made for peace, within and without. In 1837, the perturbations consequent upon the French Revolution had almost calmed down; and the nations of Europe, "sadder and wiser" for their long turmoil, were eager for peace and rest. So, likewise, the internal agitations connected with the Reform Bill (1832), and the abolition of slavery in British colonies (1833) had mainly died out; and the British people, thus launched on a new career of liberalism,—due in some degree to the French Revolution,—began to look out for new fields of constructive energy. As the representative of this rejuvenescence, a young virgin queen seemed to come with peculiar fitness. After ten years of government by a mad king, ten by a wicked one, and seven by a foolish one, the nation hailed her as an angel of promise, and set vigorously to work to realize that promise. In this they were greatly aided both by the larger ideas to which the recent disturbances had given currency, and also by a number of inventions and practical measures due to the new spirit of reflection and the new familiarity with nature born in the late struggle for liberty. While the new ideas, giving a fresh and kindlier meaning to civilization, swept away many unjust and obstructive class distinctions and religious disabilities, made provision for the poor, removed the shackles from industry, and extended the benefits of education,[1] the new inven-

[1] In 1827, the abolition of "Benefit of Clergy"; in 1828, repeal of the Corpora-

tions and practicalities supplied the fresh energy and hopefulness thus engendered with means and opportunities for their amplest development.[1] The result was an outburst of productive and commercial enterprise, and an extension of the field of commerce such as had never before been witnessed. The British were soon the first industrial and trading people of the world. And this, though partly due to the circumstances already mentioned, was also partly the outcome of their native character and propensities. Three things especially contributed to it: (1) their delight in travel, adventure, and individual initiative, coupled with a strong and somewhat narrow love for their native land; (2) their fondness for family comfort and generous living of a sort demanding the possession of ample means; (3) their desire to find positions for younger sons, unable to secure lucrative employment at home, and yet unwilling entirely to expatriate themselves. These are, obviously, the personal conditions for business enterprise.

It has been mainly through the efforts of British merchants' to extend their markets that the British nation in the last sixty years has come to extend its territory. Markets those merchants were determined to have everywhere. Among peoples ready for them they at once established them: peoples not ready they undertook to make ready or else to replace. But it is impossible to create new tastes among a people without obtaining considerable control over them; and this again is impossible without a certain amount of territorial jurisdiction. Recognizing this, and anxious to foster mercantile enterprise, —the source of her greatest wealth,—the nation has not been slow to acquire this jurisdiction in whatever way has seemed most feasible. It is important to bear this in mind. Whereas, in former times, extensions of territory were due either to conquest or discovery, or both, those acquired by Great Britain in the reign of Queen Victoria have come principally through the exigencies of commerce. This fact largely determines the nature of their relations to the mother country, and whether they are calculated to be a source of strength or of weakness to her. Within certain limits, varying according to times and circumstances, accessions of territory—provided they are contiguous and inhab-

tion and Test Acts; in 1829, Catholic Emancipation; in 1833, the first Factory Act, and the opening up of the East India trade; in 1834, the new Poor Law, and grant to National Schools; in 1836, Act for the Commutation of Tithes, etc., etc.

[1] In 1807, the first steamboat; in 1814, the first locomotive; in 1815, gaslighting in London; in 1825, the first railway, and the first iron ship; in 1829, the first lucifer matches; in 1835, introduction of the telegraph; in 1840, penny postage, etc., etc.

ited by people not differing too widely in ideals or grade of culture—are a source of strength to a nation : when these two conditions are not realized, they are apt to be a source of weakness in times of difficulty. We shall have to revert to this, when we come to consider the future outlook for Great Britain.

When Victoria came to the throne, the foreign possessions of the British were the following; viz., in America: Newfoundland, Nova Scotia, Prince Edward Island, New Brunswick, Upper and Lower Canada, British Honduras, British Guiana, Bermuda, the Bahamas, Jamaica, Trinidad, Barbadoes, Barbuda, Antigua, St. Vincent, St. Lucia, Tobago, Grenada, Montserrat, Nevis, St. Kitts, Dominica, Anguilla, the Virgin Islands, the Falkland Islands; in Europe : Gibraltar, Malta and Gozo, Heligoland, the Ionian Islands; in Asia: Ceylon, India (exclusive of Sindh, the Punjaub, and Nepal), Pegu, Penang, Province Wellesley, Singapore, Malacca, Aracan, Tenasserim, Tasmania, Australia ; in Africa: Gambia, Sierra Leone, Cape Colony, Mauritius, St. Helena, Ascension. The relations of these to the mother country were not in all cases the same. Some of them were self-governing states, some crown colonies, some merely protectorates; while over large tracts British authority was merely nominal, as in Australia and British America.

In the last sixty years the number and extent of British dependencies have enormously increased. Only two have been surrendered ; the Ionian Islands to Greece in 1864, and Heligoland to Germany in 1890. Since the promulgation in 1823 of the Monroe Doctrine no European nation has acquired fresh territory in America. Since that date, therefore, all British extensions have been in the Old World, in Asia (including Australasia), and in Africa. In Asia, Sindh, the Punjaub, Oudh, Beluchistan, and some minor provinces have been added to the Indian possessions; Burma, New Zealand, New Guinea, Fiji (with some smaller islands), Hongkong, Labuan, British Borneo, Aden, Perim, Kamaran, the Bahrein Islands, and Cyprus have been acquired. In Africa, the acquisitions have been the Gold Coast, Lagos, Yoruba, Niger Territories, British Central Africa, Caffraria, Basutoland, Natal, Zululand, Amatongaland, Bechuanaland, Ibea, Zanzibar, Somali Coast, Socotra, Tristan da Cunha, and lastly, Egypt. Besides all these, Great Britain claims suzerainty over the Transvaal Republic, and is gradually encroaching upon an extensive territory to the north and west of that (British South Africa). Again, these dependencies stand to the mother country in the same variety of relations as the older ones. Meanwhile, many of the latter have changed their relations to her and to each other. New colonies have been planted in old territories; *e. g.*, Manitoba and British Columbia, in land that was formerly held by the Hudson Bay Company. Old colonies have been broken up into parts, and each erected into a distinct dependency; as in the case of Victoria and Queensland, portions of what was once New South Wales. Dependencies once distinct have been united; *e. g.*, the Canadian provinces into the Dominion of Canada; the Indian presidencies, once governed by the East India Company, into the Empire of India; and so on. On the whole, there has been a tendency toward consolidation.

In reading over the above list of foreign possessions, long as it is, one gets but the vaguest notion of the extension of British power that has taken place in the last sixty years. It is only when we come to translate its items into square miles, population, commerce, and revenue that its full significance becomes apparent. Here, of course, the figures can be only approximate. In 1837, the foreign possessions of Great Britain covered an area of about four million square miles,—considerably more than the area of the United States, including Alaska. To-day they cover three times that number,—an area nearly equal to that of the Russian and Chinese empires together. In 1837, the population of these possessions amounted to about one hundred and ten millions: to-day it amounts to very nearly three times that number. In 1837, their commerce was worth about two hundred and fifty millions of dollars (£50,000,000): to-day it is worth ten times as much. In 1837, their revenue was about a hundred millions of dollars: to-day it is seven times as much. In other words, in Queen Victoria's reign, the foreign possessions of Great Britain, and their population, have trebled[1]; while their commerce has increased tenfold, and their revenue sevenfold. Surely it may be said that no nation known to history can show such a record of growth in a single reign, or in sixty years. Even the Romans in a thousand years did not acquire an empire one-sixth as large as that of Queen Victoria.

Such is the past. We must now turn to the future and ask what outlook it presents, what is likely to be the result for Great Britain and for the world of this unparalleled growth in territory, population, and wealth, and what policy the British must pursue in order that their power and prosperity may continue.

[1] The population of the entire British Empire is at present little short of 400,-000,000 : in other words, Queen Victoria rules over more than a fourth of the entire human race.

It is obvious enough that, if political and social strength depended upon extent of territory, material wealth, and number of population, Great Britain would be by far the mightiest nation on the face of the earth. Indeed, until recently, she thought, spoke, and acted as if she were so; and the world, on the whole, took her at her own estimate. In the last few years, however, a change of feeling has come about; and in this Great Britain herself shares. It is now generally acknowledged that Russia is the determining Power in the Old World, and that, in influence, Germany stands next to her. That Great Britain recognizes this, especially with regard to Russia, she shows in two ways : (1) by courting the favor of the United States and of France; (2) by allowing Russia to exercise power which but a few years ago she would have jealously resisted as plainly prejudicial to British interests. Obtrusive examples of such unresisted power are the recent dealings of Russia with China and Japan, and with Turkey and Greece. These have been distinctly detrimental to Great Britain; and yet she has not felt strong enough to prevent them. Indeed it seems, at the present moment, as if, with all her wealth and territory, she were about to sink into the position of a second-rate Power, compelled to shape her policy in accordance with the good pleasure of her more powerful rivals. This is certainly a poor presage; and, if it were to be realized, not only Great Britain, but all the world would be the loser. As political and moral forces, Russia and Germany, with their coarse despotism, do not compare with her. Under the circumstances, it seems pertinent to inquire what are the influences which, by depriving her of her former prestige and authority, have damped her courage and paralyzed her hands ; and then briefly to consider whether these can be removed or counteracted in such a way that she may be able to recover her lost ground, and act again as a counterpoise to the retrograde tendencies of her rivals.

These influences, it is plain enough, are many and varied; but the chief of them may be classed, for convenience' sake, under four heads: (1) personal, (2) social, (3) economic, (4) political.

(1) There is no denying that the personal characteristics of the British, and especially of the English, are a serious drawback to them. Go where you will, in the Old World or the New, you will rarely hear a good word for them. They are unsympathetic, unsociable, and overbearing : such is their reputation ; and, unfortunately, it is, in the main, deserved. That deep human culture of intelligence, heart, and will, that true gentleness or gentlemanliness, which makes its possessor a benediction and a joy, inspiring sympathy, confidence, and

goodwill, are almost unknown among Englishmen.   Their really great
virtues of frankness and justice are untempered by amenity and generosity.   As a writer in the " Revue des Deux Mondes " once said, in
an article on " British Rule in India," " Les Anglais sont justes mais
pas bons."   The consequence is that they are universally unpopular;
and every other people is ready to chuckle when they are checkmated
or humbled.   They have no friends : no one—not even this nation,
whose people may be said to be of their own flesh and blood—wishes
to make common cause with them, so deep is the dislike and distrust
of them.   If the British Empire were to be crushed to-morrow, all the
world, with the exception of the few perspicacious persons who can see
a wholesome kernel under a rude, cantankerous husk, would rejoice.
Meanwhile, it would not be sorry to see circumstances arise that might
bring about this event.

(2) That the social condition of Great Britain is a source of weakness to her, in several respects, is very evident.   This must always be
the case with a nation that, like her, has no social ideal to draw into a
common channel the energies of all her citizens.   In a characteristic
enough way, she hesitates and falters between two ideals—the mediæval
aristocratic and the modern democratic,—loyal to neither.   While Russia
is frankly aristocratic and opposed to democracy, and Germany is rapidly becoming so, both thus assuming a definite direction and aim, Great
Britain is wasting her opportunities and strength in trying to follow
two courses at once.   To-day her government is tory and aristocratic : to-
morrow it may be liberal and democratic.   To-day she is playing into
the hands of Russian and German despotism : to-morrow she may be
courting the coöperation of democratic France or the still more democratic United States.   The truth is, she is internally divided against
herself.   The old privileged classes, in their fastidious exclusiveness
and their blindness to the meaning of history, are fearful of democracy,
and would rather go back to the fleshpots of class-fostering despotism
than press forward to the promised land of universal humanity and
moral worth ; while, on the other hand, the unprivileged, privilege-op-
pressed masses, impelled by need and blind craving for their part in
human enjoyment, are willing to face the desert, with all its desolation,
being more than half assured that they will find milk and honey on the
other side.   Thus, while the personal character of the English leaves
them naked without, their want of an all-inspiring, all-directing social
ideal makes them weak and vacillating within.

(3) Though Great Britain is the richest country in the world, her

wealth is derived from sources that render it precarious and, in many respects, a cause of weakness to her. Wealth, to be really a source of strength, must be secure, and its springs easily defended. When this is not the case, it exhausts the energies of a nation, leaving few or none to expend for higher ends. Now, the springs of Great Britain's wealth lie mainly in her dependencies and her commerce. Her home productions form a mere vanishing fraction of the whole. But dependencies scattered over the whole face of the earth, some of them inhabited by disaffected races, and others within easy reach of foes or jealous rivals, are hard to defend; while foreign commerce is rendered insecure, or may even be checked, by war. In this respect Great Britain is at an enormous disadvantage, as compared with countries like Russia or the United States, whose sources of wealth, being mainly within themselves, in a continuous territory, subject to direct jurisdiction, can be defended with comparative ease, and are not likely to be jeopardized by foreign war. Thus, since Britain's wealth is specially dependent upon a state of peace, she, more than any other nation, is interested in avoiding war.

This, in itself, is, of course, a most desirable condition of things, contributing largely to the welfare of all the world; nevertheless it may be carried too far, both for the best interests of humanity and for her own honor and authority. If, by shunning war for fear of endangering the sources of her wealth, she allows her less beneficent rivals to carry out their own purposes, and to drive her into a corner where she is compelled, not only to leave them unmolested, but even, in obedience to their dictation, to aid and abet them, she at once becomes unfaithful to the cause of human civilization, and lays herself open to the dishonoring charges of selfishness and pusillanimity. That she has of late years been doing this, and with such a result, must be evident to everyone who has followed her course and marked her attitude with reference to recent events in the East. There, contrary to her own wish and better judgment, she has not only permitted Russia to deprive Japan of the legitimate fruits of her victory over China, and to gain in the latter country a foothold and an earnest of ascendency, which cannot but be detrimental to British interests, but she has stood by, with only a wordy palaver of meaningless, unsupported protests, while Turkey, under the ægis of Russia, has committed atrocities upon her Christian subjects such as would have disgraced the most barbarous of nations in the darkest of the dark ages. Nay, she has even gone further, and actually lent her aid in carrying out the policy of Russia and Germany—her two most envious rivals, and the two greatest foes of human liberty—in coercing Crete, humiliating and paralyzing Greece, and thereby crushing out all movement toward freedom and democracy in the East. And her reward has been, that she has not only earned the contempt of the despotic nations whose instrument of dirty work she has allowed herself to be, but that she is rapidly losing her prestige all the world over. The " three Emperors," after having compromised her, by forcing her to be, for a time, their accomplice, will settle the Eastern Question—to-day the most vital of all political and social questions—to suit themselves; leaving her to mutter, yelp, or bawl, to her heart's content, her helpless protests, of which, under her present government, she is so fond. She herself foresees this result, and in some degree recognizes that she has brought it upon herself, but knows not which way to turn in order to avert it. Such is the sad plight into which her economic relations have brought her.

(4) Closely connected with these are her political relations. Resting, with undisguised satisfaction, upon old laurels, and giving herself up, in fancied security, to the pursuit of wealth and what wealth brings, she has forgotten that political strength, on which, in the last resort, all other blessings depend, has for its prime conditions: (1) a territory of such nature and extent as to be at once the chief source of wealth and capable of easy defence; (2) a homogeneous people with common aims and ideals, all contributing, with patriotic enthusiasm, to the national defence, none being burdensome, disaffected, or rebellious. Accordingly, for several generations, and, especially, as we have seen, during the reign of Queen Victoria, Great Britain has scattered her people and her energies over the whole earth, without ever pausing to consider how this affected her national strength. She has thus come into possession of an empire which, while appealing forcibly to the sense of bulk, has neither of the more essential conditions of political solidity. It is neither compact, continuous, nor easily defensible; and its chief resources are unavailable without a commerce which war might readily disturb or cut off. Its inhabitants, instead of being homogeneous, harmonious, and animated by a common patriotic ideal, belong to every race under the sun, from the most cultivated to the most savage; so that anything like harmony of feeling, or community of interests and aims, is out of the question. The means of defence, instead of maintaining a constant arithmetical ratio to the extent of territory to be defended, exhibit something like a constantly diminishing geometrical one. The inhabitants of the added possessions, instead of increasing these means,

are continually drawing upon them for protection, and, in some cases, to a very considerable extent even for repression.

The weakness thus caused to the British Empire, by the whole-sale addition of non-self-defending territories, has been increased during Victoria's reign by circumstances that can be readily understood. For a generation after the close of the Napoleonic wars, all the chief nations of Europe, with the exception of Great Britain, were so exhausted and shattered that they could do little or nothing more than collect themselves, and try to settle down into some sort of quiet, regular existence of the old pattern. Britain alone, whose soil had not been desecrated by Napoleon's soldiers, was strong and enterprising. Feeling, in the flush of victory, as if all the world were hers for the winning, she started on a career of industry, commerce, and conquest, in which, for the time, she had no occasion to fear either equal or rival. Thus she became producer and purveyor for the whole world; thus she acquired untold wealth and unlimited territory; thus her voice became paramount in the councils of the nations.

But, in the last fifty years, things have been assuming a different aspect. The Continental nations, recovering from their exhaustion, have begun to look about them, and to see with surprise that she aims at the possession of every foot of land she can by any means acquire and hold, and thus threatens to leave them no place for enterprise or expansion. The result has been envy and rivalry on their part, with a determination to check, if possible, her further advance. Russia has put in a claim for Asia; Germany, France, and Italy, for Africa. Thus far, indeed, their efforts have not been crowned with any very gratifying success; but their purpose and determination are fixed and evident. There is a distinct movement among the Continental Powers to isolate Great Britain, and to act together in opposition to her. In the concert of Europe, she is a minority of one. Even the United States, for the sake of whose friendship she recently showed herself disposed to abate certain of her pretensions, has shown no readiness to make common cause with her. Thus to-day, with immense interests at stake and an immense territory to defend, Great Britain stands alone, without a friend in the world. The other Powers of Europe snub and ridicule her; and she dare not seek redress in war, as she would have done forty, or even twenty, years ago. In 1878, single-handed, she compelled Russia to cancel the treaty of San Stefano; to-day she cannot prevent the same nation from making treaties, far more prejudicial to British interests, with China and Turkey. She may protest; but she will not act.

Looking back upon what has been said of the various relations—internal and external—of Great Britain, as they have shaped themselves during the last sixty years, one cannot avoid the conclusion that, with all the enormous increase of territory and wealth which has fallen to her in that period, the close of Victoria's reign will find her in a position of great difficulty, and with a very gloomy outlook for the future. Isolated and alienated from the rest of the world, and unable to cope with its combined opposition, she bids fair to be stripped of many of her possessions, and, like Spain, once the mistress of so many lands, to sink into the position of a second-rate Power, with none so poor to do her reverence.

Though this is a consummation devoutly wished by most other nations and by the world in general, hardly any greater calamity could befall the world and the cause of human civilization. For, with all her faults and errors, all her superciliousness and rapacity, she is to-day the chief bulwark of freedom and civilization in Europe; the champion of liberty of thought, speech, action, and intercourse; the representative of healthy, vigorous, clean human life. Annihilate her influence in Europe, and the despotic empires which are gathering and combining their forces to undo the progress of five hundred years, to crush all popular movements and restore the political and spiritual claims of the dark ages, would soon have full sway over the Old World. One must be blind indeed who fails to see that the efforts of these Powers to isolate Great Britain, while making court to France and Italy, have for their end, not merely the subversion of a powerful rival, but the suppression of all that she represents. The overthrow of Great Britain means the triumph of despotism, with all the oppression, cruelty, and barbarism which Russia even now practises or connives at. Well may Russia flaunt her affinity with Turkey! Surely *this* is a consummation not devoutly to be wished by any friend of humanity, but to be averted by every possible means.

The most hopeful fact about the present gloomy outlook for Great Britain is, that it is mainly due to causes lying within herself—causes therefore, which it is in her power to remove. If her people are unpopular, it is because she has not trained and instructed them in the simple humanities of social life; if she is aimless, irresolute, and lacking in purpose and direction,—being divided against herself—it is because she palters with mediævalisms in Church, State, and Society, and does not loyally and frankly assume the dignity that belongs to her, as the champion of modernness, democracy, and freedom. If she permits her fondness for wealth to scatter her energies over the whole earth, and to bind up her hands from defending the oppressed strugglers for liberty that appeal to her, it is because, standing for no distinct moral or social ideal, she entrusts the guidance of her affairs to men of retrograde, undemocratic tendencies, narrow views, and petty class interests. If the defenceless condition of her scattered empire compels her to seek peace at all cost, and to sacrifice her dignity and authority by doing scullion-work for her brutal rivals, it is because, in thoughtless security, she has given her powers to increasing her wealth and acreage, and has neglected the conditions of political strength.

If, then, she is to escape the doom prepared for her by her foes and those of liberty, it is evident that, setting aside all false vanity, and acknowledging—to herself, at least—her past errors, she must vigorously set herself to do four things: (1) to give her people a new education, including a training in gentlemanliness and thoughtfulness, an education guided by an ideal of universal freedom and culture; (2) to adopt a thorough democratic policy, putting herself at the head of the democratic movement in Europe, abolishing, on the one hand, all unjust privilege and all childish titles, and, on the other, taking a determined stand against socialism, that materialistic dry-rot of democracy; (3) to adopt strong and comprehensive measures for the defence of such dependencies as are calculated to add to her strength, and to part with those that are otherwise [1]; (4) to consolidate her remaining empire by transforming it into a federation of sovereign states, each of which, being duly represented in Parliament, shall contribute its share to the national defence and to all national enterprises; at the same time abandoning her policy of selfish isolation, by entering into cordial relations with all the Powers whose faces are set in the same direction as hers. Thus, strong and respected within and without, and animated and directed by a definite and noble ideal, she might hope to lead the hosts of freedom to victory over the hordes of despotism, in that great, decisive battle of Armageddon, which, sooner or later, must be fought between them, before Freedom and Peace can set up their universal kingdom upon earth.

To those who believe in the mission of Great Britain, and would be sorry to see her weakened or dishonored, it is encouraging to feel that some of the tasks here enumerated have already been recognized and entered upon by her. The education of children, which, formerly, was let out to teachers as the washing of clothes was to washerwomen,

---

[1] Russia showed great wisdom in parting with Alaska and getting paid for it !

is now regarded as a matter demanding the careful attention of parents; while there is a considerable movement, headed by some very able and far-seeing men, to consolidate the empire, by drawing the dependencies into closer union with the mother country, and imparting to them a deeper interest in her welfare, by conferring upon them new privileges and responsibilities. At the time of writing this article it is reported that the Queen's "diamond jubilee," at which the governors of all the dependencies are expected to be present, and at which she will receive new titles, expressive of new relations to certain portions of the empire, will be taken advantage of, as an opportunity for discussing, and perhaps initiating, some such scheme. Let us hope that the report is true; and let us, as a nation, give her our cordial support in every effort she may make to further the cause of freedom, and to resist the growing forces of despotism!

THOMAS DAVIDSON.

The Forum

AUGUST, 1897.

A PLEA FOR THE ARMY.

In the present article, it is my purpose to discuss the following three questions; viz., (1) Is there a want of public spirit on the part of the American people? (2) Are our people unwilling to make the sacrifices necessary to secure the national safety? (3) How can we best prepare for days of national peril?

(1) As far as public spirit is concerned, there is certainly no dearth in our country. In one way or another, public spirit crops out in every Presidential Message. It is shown in the liberality of Congress toward improvements of rivers and harbors, in the construction of post-offices, in the enlargement of postal advantages, in the matter of pensions to veteran soldiers and sailors. It is evinced in superb monuments erected in honor of successful and distinguished leaders. At the mention of the names of our heroes, patriotic fervor thrills every assembly, regardless of political affinities; the "star-spangled banner," seen or sung, brings tearful joy to the eyes of the aged, love and confidence to manhood, fresh enthusiasm to childhood and youth.

In regard to the many vital problems in whose solution our people are deeply interested, such as the currency, the finances, the relations of capital and labor, and so on, there are differences of opinion frequently leading to serious contentions, and sometimes, though rarely, to riots. Yet I venture the assertion that, in spite of these contentions, nine-tenths of the people who enter into them are at heart thoroughly loyal to the flag and all that it represents. Even ignorant immigrants —those who are not vicious—love the sight of the flag. We had To-

Copyright, 1896, by The Forum Publishing Company.
Permission to republish articles is reserved.

ries and Copperheads in war: now their offspring are ashamed of their record. We have some pessimists in peace: but they are not danger-ous; for, however much they may flatter themselves, they are in a woful minority. In a word, American patriotism was never healthier, never more widespread—North and South—than now.

(2) In answer to the second question, we may confidently say that our people are always ready and willing to make sacrifices for the na-tional safety. They can be relied on to lay their property and their lives on the altar of sacrifice, and to sustain Congress and the Presi-dent in any crisis which may arise, if the necessity for such sacrifice be made clear to them.

(3) When we come to the third question—how best to prepare for days of national peril—we meet with a difficulty emanating from our most conscientious citizens, who, through misconception, are promul-gating doctrines most inimical to our safety. I refer to that form of public opinion which springs from the teachers of our children and youth, and which may, in time, by narrow and harmful precepts, rob the courts of the posse comitatus, the city of its police, the State of its conservative guard, and the country of its proper national defence.

To my mind, the teaching which discredits and dishonors the posse comitatus, the police, the national guard, the army, and the navy is clearly wrong. Where law, order, and national honor cannot be en-forced, there will be lawlessness, disorder, and national disgrace, whose end is national death.

It is not wise to tell our children that public defence by arms is always intrinsically wrong. It is not right to tell them that the world has so advanced in peace-sentiment that cities and States are now safe without guards, that absolute reliance can be placed upon peaceful diplomacy for the settlement of all conflicts likely to arise. Washing-ton, who feared God and endeavored to be governed by the teachings of Holy Writ, said: "If we desire peace, one of the most powerful instruments in our prosperity, it must be known [*i. e.*, among nations] that we are at all times ready for war."

General Sherman, with his large experience and sincere heart, said: "I cannot help plead to my countrymen, at every opportunity, to cher-ish all that is manly and noble in the military profession, because peace is enervating, and no man is wise enough to foretell when soldiers may be in demand again."

What we need is preparation by organization and discipline. With modern arms, ordnance, and ammunition, and with modern means of locomotion and communication, war comes with suddenness. The small cloud of rumor, the gathering multitudes, are followed, quicker than thought, by lightning-flashes and the roar of artillery. The war between Prussia and Austria in 1866 began and ended within two short months; and what an object lesson it presented! Prussia defeated Austria in a six weeks' campaign. Prussia was prepared for war: Austria was not.

The same· lesson is found in all other modern wars. Major G. S. Wilson, in the " Journal of the Military Science Institute," says:

" At the end of a seven months' war France was abject at the feet of Germany, despoiled of her provinces, and compelled to pay her conqueror the cost of her own humiliation. Germany was prepared for war: France was not. . . . The hordes of Chinese were as chaff before the wind in the face of Japan's organized and disciplined army."

The struggle between Turkey and Greece is no exception. Turkey was prepared for war: Greece was not. Plucky little kingdom of Greece—how American hearts yearned for her success! But poor organization, no preparation, no proper discipline or drill, and naturally no practical generalship, produced their inevitable results. God Himself did not interpose in behalf of the Greeks and miraculously deliver them, though the Great Powers stung them to action by their unjust measures. He suffered them to learn anew the old lesson; namely, that safety is found in abundant preparation and unceasing vigilance. The average American of a century ago was, in many respects, better prepared for active service than the average citizen of to-day. Everywhere was the rifle over the fireplace; the household accustomed to alarms; and the householder ready to meet Indians, or to run to his company's rendezvous in order to make head against forays from across the border. To-day he has no rifle, and seldom hears the discharge of a firearm.

It is the railway and steamship transportation over against long marches, sailing vessels, and river *bateaux*—the old method of conveying fighting men and supplies—which has practically cut off all time for proper preparation in modern warfare. As was recently demonstrated in Greece, the best of men will not immediately be good soldiers, even if collected into armed battalions. Experience is essential to overcome the natural apprehensions which a recruit always has at the approach of danger. The veteran may not be braver; but his knowledge has prepared him for what is coming, so that all unnecessary alarms are excluded. A writer in the "Service Gazette" on what war means remarks as follows :—

"War-trained troops, men who have looked upon slaughter and death upon the gigantic scale of the modern struggle, no longer exist; and the peace-trained conscript has no knowledge to correct his fear. The machinery of battle has progressed till the possibilities of our modern weapons are appalling. Torpedoes, monster guns, high explosives, the swift arbitrament of the ram at sea; on land, quick-firing guns using the deadly shrapnel, are almost untried implements. . . . The future battle will be a severer trial to the nerves than any past encounter."

Hence we feel the need of experience. The recently added terrors, he thinks, have made men's fears dominant and harder to control, in spite of force of habit and a sense of duty. I find in this country no evidence of decay of natural courage; yet I do know that organization and discipline are essential to an effective army, and that time and experience are necessary to establish a reasonable degree of discipline. This is doubly true since the seeming dangers as well as the actual perils have so evidently increased. Again, commanders, from the lower to the higher grades, must become acquainted with their men as well as with their duties. In comradeship, in mutual confidence, in common knowledge, the cementing process ever increases with time and experience.

There are some potent evils to be corrected. During our great struggle in the Civil War the soldier's uniform was an honor, and reward was given for gallant conduct. But, the danger being passed, our people, little by little, have fallen back into the old ways of doing and thinking. Citizens in common life encourage desertions from the army. They decry the regular service itself as if it were an enslavement; forgetting that, with us, all enlisted men are bona-fide volunteers. In peace it is not always the most patriotic and faithful officer—one who clings to his regiment or corps—that obtains most recognition and honor. The habit of seeking preferment through outside influences is indeed quite general, and is too often successful. If those who most frequently shirk duty obtain the rewards, the effect is doubly injurious to the military arm: it demoralizes and weakens the force, and adds to its unpopularity among the people. It is this evil, and the false notion that the army on a peace footing is idle, which give rise to the constant opposition to its increase, and, in some quarters, to its existence.

I shall not dilate upon the work of the army in time of so-called peace. I simply desire to say that if there were no other duty throughout our wide domain than the care of the army forts, posts, and public property, the task would not be inconsiderable. And when I mention that, in addition, it is called upon to drill and discipline the forces of artillery, infantry, and cavalry; to carry on the various army schools;

to take care of all the United States armories, arsenals, and depots; to perform the lighthouse duty of our enormous coasts; to carry through the river and harbor improvements; to keep in touch with the State troops, also doing staff duty with the governors; and that hundreds of officers are detailed to inspect the national guard, and to teach at our military schools, our colleges and universities, I give but a meagre outline of the work devolving upon our little army.

There is one important matter for which the army will be held responsible; viz., its part in the seacoast defence. Sites have been carefully selected about New York and other cities and along our eastern and western seaboards. There are a few heavy guns of modern construction to be raised, loaded, properly aimed, fired, and lowered; there is carefully adjusted machinery to be rightly worked and managed. Who shall intelligently meet these requirements? Who shall be ready to instruct new men, when all the guns are mounted and all the machinery is put in? The mortar batteries, a few already finished, are excellent. With satisfaction one finds squares of water-front surveyed and platted for miles out. One is led to imagine shells projected into the air and falling perhaps four at a time upon the deck of a venturesome cruiser that may invade a square. But who is there to learn all the complications involved in mortar preparation and rapid mortar firing? And who is there to teach these things to the fresh volunteer artilleryman after war has come and cities are threatened by a foreign navy? We have, in embryo, torpedo arrangements, projected shore-batteries, and theoretic floating ordnance of great power; but, when ready for use, where are the skilled artillerymen to handle them? To answer these questions is to confess a great national folly.

I like the old proverb, "Whatever is worth doing at all is worth doing well." If you make seacoast defences and furnish them with modern appliances, then man them with enough trained artillerymen to take care of the material and use it effectively. A bona-fide American is apt to be boastful. The uneducated, unread man, or one of limited experience, judges imperfectly another's trade: the less he knows of it, the easier it appears to him to be able to master its requirements. Similarly men who know the least about military affairs think they could easily wear a uniform, return salutes, go through the parade and drills, and stand guard; that they could skilfully organize, feed, clothe, train, and dispose a force to receive an attack or to make one upon an organized, well-equipped foe. Could such people once see under the hail of bullets a good speech-making officer with but little military experience, on the one hand, and, on the other, a man like Sumner, Hancock, or Sheridan,—one who by his leadership and example could almost annihilate fear, and fill every soldier under him with courage,—they would acknowledge the difference. Professional knowledge and experience are required for the development of military character and skill.

Some years ago a report which I made, advocating an increase of our regular force, was denounced by certain leaders of working-men's organizations. They claimed that I wanted to exploit militarism and maintain an Old-World establishment; that I was an enemy to organized labor and hostile to the best interests of the working-man. Those leaders misunderstood me. What I favor is only a reasonable nucleus of an army,—an educated staff, commissioned and non-commissioned, together with a number of trained soldiers sufficient to handle our guns and to be a rallying-point in case of national peril or of sudden foreign war. A large, dominating military force, proud and overbearing, I should abominate; but to maintain enough police for city and country would be only common sense. My heart goes with all working-men in every lawful effort they make to better their condition. As I understand it, they themselves do not advocate riots, lynchings, mob-rule, or any other criminal proceeding: they condemn the Anarchists, who are enemies to law and social order; and they deprecate all combinations whose purpose is to break up and destroy our government.

Without the slightest disposition to raise the military above the civil functionary, it does appear to me that an average of about one thousand trained men for each State and Territory would not be too many for the purposes I have indicated; and this number would scarcely suffice unless we should continue to develop and cherish more and more the State national guard, as well as to encourage military education in our larger institutions of learning. In view of the fact that our relations with Spain have been and still are strained, it is from sheer necessity that such measures are advocated; and it is a mistake to say, as one of our prominent newspaper correspondents puts it, that "military men desiring promotion are strongly urging the recognition of Cuban independence or belligerent rights." Take, for example, the opinion of an army officer prominent in the Engineer Corps:—

"What then, are our real needs in the way of coast defence? . . . Upon the whole extent of the Atlantic, Gulf, and Pacific coasts there are about thirty ports which demand local protection for their cities, now exposed to occupation or destruction, and of these about a dozen are so important as centres of commercial wealth that the entire country has much at stake in their security. Nine out of this number are also important as containing naval stations and depots of supply, without which our new battleships would be unable to keep the sea or perform any service in war; for it must not be forgotten that naval bases are as indispensable in these days of steam as are bases of supplies for armies in the field. In fact, this statement hardly puts the matter strongly enough; for our new ships would be exposed to capture and used against us, should they attempt to operate on their natural element, the ocean, without ports of refuge in which to find security when overmatched. Besides these thirty ports now urgently demanding protection there are about seventy others whose local importance would justify inexpensive earthworks."

Another officer, speaking of these seacoast defences, says:—

"It is estimated that, when completed, these defences would require from seventy to eighty thousand men to man them in the time of war. . . . Such eminent soldiers as Sherman and Sheridan and a host of others have time and again called attention to the dangers that threaten this country from a neglect of the army, and asked for such reasonable addition of soldiers as, in their judgment, would at least partially remedy the evil. Now, the significance of all this is simply that when an intelligent man of affairs is led by his duties to fully investigate the subject, the dangers of continued neglect of the military necessities of the country become apparent."

My association with military men has been quite extensive; and I believe the sentiment is universal among them, that our statesmen and political leaders should carefully look before they leap. Before they risk a national conflict let them glance at the present stage of preparation. Their military men want no promotion at the expense of national disaster.

Upon the causes of irritation between Spain and the United States I need not elaborate. They have resulted from press agitation; from American indignation at Spanish mismanagement in Cuban affairs; from the presence of hosts of Cuban sympathizers in our commercial cities; from commercial losses in Cuba; and from the treatment of our citizens there. We are told that our Executive proposes a qualified interference in the internal affairs of Cuba,—a territory which the Spanish government claims as part of its kingdom as much as Castile. The better treatment which we demand for our citizens in the disturbed districts of Cuba, Spain can hardly extend to her own,—to those not in revolt. Spain's *amour propre* is wounded.

Our most aggressive writers and public speakers contend that they have no fear of war with Spain, because we are so much bigger and stronger, and because of Spain's apparent exhaustion. In the end we should conquer, without doubt. But I beg rash thinkers to consider the primary dangers. They are plain enough to all foreign navies that are watching us; viz., our extensive coast and our coast trade; the exposed shipping, cities, and villages; the ability of Spain to issue the inevitable letters-of-marque to all sorts of vessels ploughing the ocean. Our navy, good as it is, cannot be everywhere at the same time. Spain on her coasts has small return to offer in the way of reprisal; so that the first great danger and loss would necessarily fall to our side. Perhaps the fright would be worse for our people than the actual losses. Let not the causers and makers of war, however, be too confident!

The Spanish troops now under arms are as follows:

In Cuba:

From before the present war.......	25,000	
National Guard.....................	60,000	
Sent since March 1, 1895............	187,282	
		272,282
In Porto Rico...................................		6,000
In the Philippine Islands...........................		36,760

In Spain:

Infantry...........................	64,190	
Cavalry...........................	14,346	
Artillery...........................	11,774	
Engineers..........................	5,294	
General Service Corps........	2,400	
Civil Guard......................	14,786	
		112,790
Total.............................		427,832

In the event of a sudden war with Spain, to meet the land side, we have 28,238 regulars—officers and men. More than half of this army would be needed in the fortifications and posts now occupied. These, in time, would be replaced by volunteers; but the process would necessarily be slow. The total number of the national guard in the United States now organized is 112,879, of which only a fraction, according to past experience, would be available outside their own States. Of course the immediate resort would be to a large force of volunteers.

It is claimed in our favor that Spain is bankrupt. But her debt, like that of Turkey, might itself beget assistance. Even if her debt should be repudiated, the people, being in earnest, might willingly make the necessary sacrifices, like our Southern confederacy of 1864. It will hardly do to trust to Spain's weakness or bankruptcy. Neither nations nor men ever surrender their vital interests to others unless compelled by force.

Surely if, for any cause, we warred with Spain, she would quickly secure allies. Monarchical establishments, however favorably disposed toward *quasi* free institutions, have a common sympathy, and are naturally jealous of us. If we enter the lists for European wars, we must expect a very widespread opposition.

A statement of England's forces is suggestive. The British army numbers: at home, 106,000 men; in the Colonies, 33,644; in India, 78,043; in Egypt, 4,407; making an aggregate of 222,094. If Great Britain has to raise yearly, as she does, more recruits than we have men in our whole army, it is, undoubtedly, because she needs them. The British army does nothing to limit or restrict the individual freedom of the citizen—except in the service itself as we do. Certainly we might risk a small force, say one-fourth as many, which would give us a reasonable nucleus without begetting even a tendency among us either to militarism or to endanger our civil liberty.

The unanimity with which Congress sustained the President in his Venezuelan Message showed how impulsively patriotic were our people. Congress exemplified the readiness of the latter for sacrifices in a cause in which they believe. It should be noted, however, that the cost of that one Message, manifested by the contraction of values in such investments as railway stocks, bonds, etc., was about equal to the cost of the entire Civil War. Temporary losses, indeed, they were; but they appeared real enough at the time. No such sudden depression would have been likely to occur if our seaboard had been properly fortified and manned, our regular army sufficiently large, and our national guard organized, armed, and equipped for such an emergency. An English military writer at the time remarked :—

"However defective our army organization may be, it is difficult to conceive that we [English] could not have 200,000 men on the Canadian frontier long before the United States could train and equip 50,000. . . . The general position of the United States and Great Britain at war would be strikingly analogous to that of China and Japan. Japan was ready; and China had made no real preparations. England *is* ready; and the United States are in no way ready."

We may yet be taught, by those who are hostile to our vital interests, to be always thoroughly prepared for defence and independence.

Upon the subject of organization, not much need be said. Secretary Lamont asked Congress for two more regiments of artillery, and for a change of organization, so that we might adopt the modern form rather than *remain alone with China*. It is evident that his requests should have been granted. Senator Proctor, while Secretary of War, formed the infantry regiments into two battalions of four companies each. This, in spite of the original ten-company formation, gave small battalions, adequate to the control of firing-line in extended order; but for effective work the regiments should preferably be larger and have the three-battalion formation.

Our small regular army being a part of our national defence, ought to be the best possible, and adequate to the work to which it is constantly put in peace and in war. In Chicago, in 1894, two thousand regulars—all that were available—were collected; and these had to be brought great distances. That they succeeded in preventing their own destruction when arrayed in the face of thousands of disaffected and violent men, was due to the coolness and courage of the officers and enlisted soldiers. When Captain Hall, in command of one troop of cavalry, rode alone in front of an angry mob of at least five thousand men and women, and begged them to listen to reason, the case seemed desperate. He told them plainly that he would have to fire if they did not go back. His nerve and self-command instantly awed them, and caused them to retire without a shot. It is not right to risk so much or to expose brave and true men to destruction, where an adequate force can be so easily provided. The larger command is the best guarantee of the peace we all love,—a peace obtained, if possible, without bloodshed.

A desire for some sort of promotion is not unreasonable; and it is essential to the continued efficiency of an army. A reasonable increase, say of one soldier to each thousand of our population, would be ample. The primary and subsequent promotions could then follow.. One senior lieutenant of artillery in our army has been a lieutenant for thirty years. The senior captain of cavalry has remained a captain since 1874. He was an officer of volunteers for ten years before he became a regular, and an enlisted man prior to that. Many second lieutenants of cavalry have served longer in the army than Sheridan, Schofield, or myself had served when we became major-generals in the field.

There are many hopeful features nowadays in the line of discipline and drill. We need simply bear in mind the 800,000 railroad men who are subjected not only to order, discipline, and obedience, prompt and unquestioned, but, in many instances, to every sort of exposure and hardship as well. The schools of the United States are remarkable for the exact obedience and movement on the part of the pupils under the slightest intimations from their superintendents and teachers. There are in these institutions probably 5,000,000 boys, who, for at least ten years of their young lives, are accustomed to take part in what General Sherman called "all that is manly and noble in the military profession." Again, the athletic exercises in Young Men's Associations, normal schools, academies, colleges, and universities are under chosen leadership; both the body and the mind of the participants being subjected to exercises corresponding to those demanded of the cadets at Annapolis and West Point. These statements indicate the ease with which 2,000,000 volunteers, whose hearts are in the cause, might be marshalled, trained, armed, and equipped for the defence of the land.

Since I entered the army in 1850, I have noted a constant improvement in that body. The average enlisted man now is not more loyal to the flag, but he is more intelligent than formerly. The introduction of athletics has given him more suppleness of action; and his movements appear freer. Of late his education has been well provided for; while discipline, which is vastly more needed in a republic than in a monarchy, has not been relaxed. The environment of officers and soldiers, as a rule, has improved their social advantages: they have come from frontiers to the neighborhood of centres of population. The enlistment is for three years only; and during that time the young men in our garrisons are simply at school: hence there can be no excuse for looseness of morals. At present, officers are proud of the intelligence and uprightness of their men. More immorality is brought into the army than is generated there. The recruiting officers reject fully as many applicants as they accept; and, if possible, they keep out a drunkard, a deserter, a debauchee, or a criminal. They are even more careful than is the civilian who hires a cook, an hostler, or a messenger. Naturally, as we wish it to be, the army is a conservative body; and, in the hands of the President, a preserver of order. In times of rebellion; in hours of mob-law and riot; in brief, during all dangers to the Republic from within or without, its history is a most flattering one.

When there was doubt as to the result of the Presidential election in the case of Tilden and Hayes, intense excitement prevailing and revolution appearing imminent, Grant's despatch, so coolly written in Philadelphia, not only exalted him, and honors his memory, but it showed us that ultimate reliance may be placed in the army when our Government is in extreme internal peril. An extract from this despatch will remind us of the event :—

" PHILADELPHIA, Nov. 10, [1876]

GENERAL W. T. SHERMAN,
        Washington, D. C.

Instruct General Augur in Louisiana and General Ruger in Florida to be vigilant with the forces at their command to preserve peace and good order, and to see that the proper and legal boards of canvassers are unmolested in the performance of their duties. Should there be any grounds of suspicion of fraudulent count on either side, it should be reported and denounced at once. No man worthy of the office of President should be willing to hold it if counted in or placed there by fraud. Either party can afford to be disappointed in the result. The country cannot afford to have the result tainted by the suspicion of illegal or false returns. . . . Send all the troops to General Augur he may deem necessary to insure entire quiet and a peaceful count of the ballots actually cast. . . .

U. S. GRANT."

In my humble judgment, therefore, we cannot do better for the country than to honor and improve our regular army, and to make it what it ought to be,—in form a model, and in size not too large, but large enough to meet the requirements.

OLIVER O. HOWARD.

THE GROWTH OF RELIGIOUS TOLERANCE IN THE UNITED STATES.

In the last century a stone-mason belonging to the Presbyterian Church of Scotland was tried and, I believe, excommunicated for helping to build an Episcopal church. The charge against him was based upon precepts in the Old Testament prohibiting the erection of altars to pagan deities in the high places of Israel. It is not more than a hundred years since, in this country, Alexander Campbell, the founder of the denomination popularly called, from his name, " Campbellites," having been caught in a furious storm in Pennsylvania, was refused shelter by a devout Presbyterian woman because he was a Baptist. Her conscience compelled her to resist the hospitable inclinations of her womanly heart; for did not St. John say, "If there come any unto you, and bring not this doctrine, receive him not into your house, neither bid him God speed"? A prominent Methodist clergyman of this country told me recently an analogous experience occurring only thirty-nine years ago. He was asked by the deacon of a Congregational church to deliver an address in the church on a Sunday afternoon—not at the hour of regular service—on the subject of temperance. The minister objected because the young man was an Arminian. "I agree with him on the subject of temperance," said he, "and if the meeting is held in the hall I shall go to hear him; but if we can invite an Arminian to speak in our pulpit on temperance on Sunday afternoon, what is to prevent our inviting him to preach in our pulpit on Sunday morning? And if he should preach his Arminianism, what would become of the doctrines of our holy religion?" The lecture was delivered in the town hall instead of in the church; and the Calvinistic minister went to the town hall to hear what he would not allow uttered in his pulpit. It is certain that no one of these incidents could occur in this year of grace 1897: it is difficult for us to understand how they could have occurred fifty or a hundred years ago.

What change has taken place? And why? What has caused it? And in what direction does it point?

In one aspect of the case, it would appear that denominationalism has increased in the last three-quarters of a century; in another aspect, that it has greatly decreased. The first foreign missionary organization in this country was undenominational. The purpose of the founders of the American Board of Commissioners for Foreign Missions was to make a society so broad that all evangelical Christians could unite in preaching the Gospel to the heathen. Now, every denomination has its own missionary organization. The first Christian publication society was undenominational. It still exists, but is weakened by the fact that every denomination has its own publication society. Denominational machinery has been multiplied. The tendency has been toward sectarian organization in Christian work. But, with this tendency, has been another to make the work itself more Christian and less sectarian. Methodists, Baptists, Congregationalists, Presbyterians, do their work by denominational agencies; but the work is undenominational. No longer do Arminians and Calvinists bombard each other from their respective pulpits. A sectarian sermon is rare, even in a Roman Catholic or a High-Church Episcopal pulpit; and a sermon levelled against another sect is still more rare. The churches are separated; but the doctrine is one. The reader can easily satisfy himself of the truth of this observation. Let him take up a Monday morning's paper and read the reports of the previous Sunday's sermons, and then endeavor, without any acquaintance with the preachers, to determine to what denominations they respectively belong. Or, if he have acquaintance with the preachers, let him analyze the sermons, and endeavor to designate to himself the features in any sermon which are characteristically Presbyterian, or Congregational, or Baptist, or Unitarian. Except in the utterances of a few polemical divines,—relics of a past age,—he will find it difficult so to do. Ministers preach in denominational pulpits; but they proclaim one and the same Christian message.

Nor is it because either school has converted the other. The Episcopalian is still a Churchman, and the Congregationalist an Independent; the Arminian still believes in free-will, and the Calvinist in Divine sovereignty. Nothing is settled. But the interest in these questions is gone. They are not, as they used to be, the themes of conversation in the social circle, nor the subject of sermons by popular preachers, nor even the topics of debate in ecclesiastical assemblies and clerical gatherings. Now and then someone is put on trial for doubting or denying some doctrine expressed or implied in the standards of the church. But generally this is not really because of his doubts or his denials of a theological formulary, but for some other reason. Heresy is the charge; but the real ground of offence is something quite different. Or, if some survivor of an ancient epoch prefers a charge of heresy against Dr. Charles Cuthbert Hall in Brooklyn, or Dr. John Watson in Liverpool, the accuser is unsupported and the charge promptly tabled. What has taken place is not the settlement of old controversies, nor an increase of the spirit of toleration for error. Indeed that spirit is of doubtful value. He who loves the truth cannot well be tolerant of error. He who respects himself will hardly be content to be tolerated by a self-constituted judge of his opinions: he who respects his neighbor will hardly be content to tolerate him as a preacher of falsehood. Intolerance of error is the negative pole of enthusiasm for truth; and, in general, the intensity of the one is in the direct ratio of the intensity of the other. The mistake of the Scotch Presbyterian, of the Pennsylvania Presbyterian, and of the New-England Calvinist was not that each was intolerant of vital error, but that the first identified Episcopacy with paganism, the second regarded Campbellism as anti-Christ, and the third considered Arminianism as oppugnant to the doctrines of our holy religion.

Two changes have taken place in the life of the church, both of them for the better, though doubtless accompanied, as all such changes are, by some adverse circumstances. First, the public interest has been transferred from theological to ethical problems,—that is, from problems in the philosophy of religion to problems in practical conduct. Second, we have grown more catholic, that is, more large-minded; have come, or are coming, to see the difference between truths and the truth, and to perceive that none of us possesses *the* truth, and that our neighbor possesses some fragment of truth which we ourselves have failed to possess. In other words, we are coming to recognize the fact that each one of us knows but in part and prophesies in part, and that only by putting these various parts together can anyone secure the whole. This will perhaps appear more clearly if we attempt briefly to trace the historic process and the causes which have coöperated in it.

The Unitarian revolt against Puritanism, which characterized the beginning of the present century, was not merely nor mainly an endeavor to substitute one dogmatism for another. It was in part a protest against a too mathematical and scholastic doctrine of the Trinity, —a protest which, it seems to some of us, rejected, with scholastic formularies, some valuable and vital truth. It was an affirmation of the inherent dignity and worth of man, and a repudiation of the dogma of "total depravity"; in repudiating which dogma, it also seems to us, the Unitarians have sometimes ignored or belittled, if they have not denied, the organic sinfulness of man as a racial fact. But, more than either, it was a protest against the measurement of life and character by theological standards, and the substitution therefor of standards purely ethical. His repudiation of dogma as a measurement of character, rather than his repudiation of any particular dogmas, was the distinguishing characteristic of William Ellery Channing's contribution to the religious life and thought of New England. His followers may sometimes have attempted to substitute a new dogma in the place of the dogmas which they discarded; they may sometimes have failed to see that no ethical laws are effective which are not vitalized by a spiritual life; that no spiritual life is possible apart from God; and that no fellowship with God is possible without some recognized manifestation of Him to the soul. But these must be regarded rather as the incidents, if not the vagaries, of the Unitarian reaction; certainly not as constituting its permanent contribution to the religious life of the church. That contribution consisted partly in its simplification of religious truth, partly in its correcter estimate of man, partly in its more rational interpretation of the Bible, but most of all in the emphasis which it placed on such fundamental declarations as, "Ye shall know them by their fruits," and "Every one that loveth is born of God." I cannot think that the Unitarian system of theology, so far as it can be said to be a system, will survive; but its insistence on a simplicity of faith and on a substitution of ethico-spiritual for dogmatic tests of character has made itself felt in every Christian church. And this substitution of a vital for an intellectual test is gradually, but surely, taking place in all denominations.

This revolution in public sentiment has been greatly expedited by contemporaneous events. Intensity of interest is rarely felt by any individual, and never by any community, in two different themes simultaneously. At the time when people began to grow weary of scholastic theology, and when the Unitarian divines began to insist upon other themes as more real and vital, moral reformers, non-theological and non-ecclesiastical, appeared upon the scene to urge such themes upon the public attention. The great Washingtonian movement swept over the country; first Dr. Lyman Beecher, then Mr. Hawkins, then Mr. Gough, furnished a new theme of public interest; men and women continued to go decorously to theological churches; but their interest was transferred from theology to temperance. This was straightway followed by the great anti-slavery agitation. Preachers who continued to serve out

to their churches dilutions of Jonathan Edwards on original sin or the
freedom of the will preached to listless congregations, whom it would
be untruthful to call auditors: the preachers who filled the churches
with eager listeners were the gradually increasing number who spoke
of the rights of the enslaved and the duties of the North.   Preachers
of righteousness appeared also outside the churches; and the lecture-
platform and the public convention gave to the people what, in too many
places, the ministry, not awake to the changed conditions, failed to give,
—instruction in the application of the Golden Rule to the problems of
the hour.   When the Civil War broke out the one question, how to
preserve the nation, took precedence of all other questions.   It was
impossible to interest fathers and mothers in curious scientific hypotheses
concerning the adjustment of Divine decrees to human freedom when
the congregation were eagerly waiting for news from Fort Donelson or
Vicksburg, Gettysburg or the Wilderness.   The problems of speculative theology, once driven out of the public mind by the more vital
problems of human liberty and national existence, never could go back
again into their old place, and never will.   For the close of the War and
the enfranchisement of the slaves were followed by other ethical problems, which, if not so exciting, were not less complicated and difficult.
The relation of the religious to secular education in the public schools,
the reform of politics, the purification of our great cities, the various
aspects of the labor question, the duty of the American citizen toward
the incoming foreign population, both in town and country,—these and
kindred questions demand the attention of the citizen.   And the citizen in turn has demanded from his religious teachers some elucidation
of principles which will help him to solve these problems righteously
and rationally.

   It is perhaps questionable whether we are much more tolerant of
each other's opinions on such questions as these than we were a century ago : whatever arouses our interest and excites our zeal also stimulates our passions and our prejudices.   But the old questions no longer
concern us.   The minister who desires to interest his congregation must
speak to them on questions in which they are interested; and these
are not the old-time questions in speculative theology.   He may still
preach theology, that is, a science of religion ; but it must be a science
which can be applied in the reconstruction of society on a Christian
foundation.   The minister of to-day who rants politics is no better
than the minister of the olden time who ranted revivalism : he may
not even be so useful a member of society.   But the follies and vices
42

of pulpit exaggeration serve to illustrate, as well as its better phases, the nature of the times and of the public demands upon the pulpit.

With this transfer of public interest from theological to ethical and spiritual problems has gone a radical change in the nature of the theological problems which interest thoughtful men and women. Darwin's "Origin of Species" was published in 1859. Almost instantly evolution, which had previously been a theory interesting cloistered students only, became a problem interesting the public and discussed in the periodicals, the journals, and the social clubs. The theological disputants of the eighteenth century all accepted, as a final authority, the words of the Bible. Not so the theological disputants of the nineteenth century. If evolution is true, the world was not made in the manner described in the first chapter of Genesis; nor man in the manner described in the second chapter; nor did sin come into the world in the manner described in the third chapter; nor was the so-called Mosaic Code, moral and ceremonial, all given by divine authority on the Mount at one time and through one man. Spiritual authority is in process of transference from the Bible to the reason and the conscience of men, as it had before, for Protestants, been transferred from the church to the Book.

If, in a company of twenty divines of to-day, a theological discussion be started, the theme will be connected with the adjustment of evolutionary theories to traditional theology: one portion of the disputants will stand by traditional theology, surrendering reluctantly, if at all, the traditional positions; the other portion will frankly throw over the old traditionalism and will be found reconstructing their ethical philosophy, their theological system, and their Biblical criticism on an evolutionary foundation. Arminians and Calvinists, Episcopalians and Independents, Baptists and Pedo-Baptists, will be found in each section. In other words, while the old dogmatic lines remain to divide the denominations, the real lines, which divide men in their vital theological sympathies, are wholly undenominational. Men who subscribe to the same theological creed are theological opponents : men who are in opposing theological camps are in reality theological allies. There is very little opportunity for denominational intolerance when the Episcopal Prof. Batten, the Presbyterian Dr. van Dyke, the Congregational Prof. Curtiss, and the Baptist Prof. Rhees combine in one book, expounding the application of the principles of the New Criticism to the Bible, and become a common target for Episcopal, Presbyterian, Congregational, and Baptist critics.

One other element in our national life has also contributed largely —possibly more largely than all other causes combined—to make the age theologically tolerant; namely, our public-school system.   It is impossible for us to estimate what has been and is the effect of this system in teaching the American people that character and life are more than dogma, and that no church has a monopoly of that religion which promotes virtue.   When a Roman-Catholic boy has been captain of a High-School nine or eleven, and has depended for school victories, which were much dearer to him than prizes or scholarships, upon the fidelity to duty of a Protestant companion, it is impossible for him to believe that his Protestant playfellow is doomed to eternal torment because he has not been confirmed in the Catholic communion; and it is equally impossible for the Protestant to regard his captain as a child of the Scarlet Woman and a citizen of the modern Babylon.   These boys, in learning to respect each other, learn to respect each other's religion,— or at least to realize that the defects in each other's creeds are not such defects as are fatal to honorable character.   They come to see that there is some truth in all creeds, and some virtue in all communions.   The process is the more efficacious because it is both gradual and unconscious, and because its result is not so much toleration for each other's vices and errors as respect for each other's virtue and intelligence.

Thus, while we are growing more indifferent about speculative theories and more interested in ethico-spiritual principles, we are also growing, not so much more tolerant, as more catholic.   Each one of us is learning that he does not "know it all."   We are beginning to perceive that truth is infinite and the individual mind finite; and we are less satisfied with our own partialism and less dissatisfied with the partial view of our neighbor.   We are beginning to distrust the negations in our own creeds and to wonder if there is not some truth in our, neighbor's affirmations.   The Arminian believes more than he used to do in Divine sovereignty, and the Calvinist more in human freedom; the Baptist more in the family as the unit of all social organization, and the Pedo-Baptist more in the right of the individual to choose his own form of faith for himself; the Catholic believes more in the authority of the individual conscience as the final court of appeal, and the Independent more in the Church of Christ as the corrector of the idiosyncrasies of the individual.   If, in this process toward a more catholic faith, we sometimes fail to discriminate between the spiritual life and its dogmatic expression, and in our growing indifference to the second sometimes grow careless concerning the first, this must be attributed to that infirmity of the human mind which habitually makes its growth unsymmetrical. And while we may well deprecate the tendency of theological unconcern to develop into spiritual indifferentism, while we may well be on our guard against it ourselves, and try to put others on guard against it, we may certainly see that the close of the nineteenth century is far in advance of the beginning, in the juster comparative estimate which it puts on speculative thought and practical life, in the more cautious estimate which each one puts upon his own opinions, and in the greater readiness of each to give respectful consideration to the opinions of his neighbor.

LYMAN ABBOTT.

EMERSON'S "THE AMERICAN SCHOLAR"
SIXTY YEARS AFTER.

THE fourth decade of this fast-flying century was a great decade. It was the time of beginnings : it was a period of newness. The westward movement of population was slowly pressing its way between the mountains and the great river and passing beyond. Mighty anticipations of mighty powers were filling the hearts and minds of men. In the middle year of the decade, Morse set up his telegraphic apparatus in his room in the University of the City of New York. Visions of wealth were filling the public eye. Values in certain lands reached a figure which they have never since reached. Reforms were in the air. Apostles of newness abounded. The Fifth Monarchy was indeed to be reëstablished. It was the age of the transcendentalists, *Redeunt Saturnia regna :* it was the age of antislavery, of temperance, of non-resistance, and "come-outism." Everybody had a mission ; and, as Lowell says, his mission was spelled with a capital M. It was, too, the age of the foundation of new colleges. In 1837 the University of Michigan began a life which for sixty years has progressed in ever-enlarging relationship. In the same year Mary Lyon founded Mt. Holyoke,—a school which at that time meant more for the education of women than any college since founded meant at the time of its beginning. Oberlin, Marietta, the University of the State of Missouri, De Pauw, Wabash, and Illinois had their beginning in this same great period.

But, be it said, in the year 1837, on the last day of August, Ralph Waldo Emerson spoke at Cambridge what for sixty years has been known as his Phi Beta Kappa address. Its subject was "The American Scholar." It was the first of the great addresses which the great man made. In his published works it stands next the essay on "Nature," which was his first noteworthy volume. It was a great address. Oliver Wendell Holmes calls it our "Intellectual Declaration of Independence" : we might denominate it our Declaration of Intellectual Independence. Mr. Lowell, in his essay on Thoreau, written in 1865, says :—

"His [Emerson's] oration before the Phi Beta Kappa Society at Cambridge, some thirty years ago, was an event without any former parallel in our literary annals, a scene to be always treasured in the memory for its picturesqueness and its inspiration. What crowded and breathless aisles, what windows clustering with eager heads, what enthusiasm of approval, what grim silence of foregone dissent! It was our Yankee version of a lecture by Abelard, our Harvard parallel to the last public appearances of Schelling." [1]

For two generations this oration has been the intellectual bread for college and other folk. Like so many other first addresses and works, it seems to be a microcosm of the whole message which the great author subsequently thought or spoke. He who would be moved by the best of the early Emerson must stoop and drink of this early and steadily flowing spring.

What are the influences which form the scholar? —that is the first question which Emerson asks. They are, is the answer, nature, books, and action. What are the duties of the scholar? They are, it may be answered, all comprehended in self-trust. Allied with this duty, or as applications of it, are the duties of trust in humanity, and in American humanity in particular. Such is the simple address, which, as Mr. Lowell says, "was an event without any former parallel in our literary annals." But the whole discourse, it is apparent, was given with such sweetness of manner, such deftness of phrase, such delicacy of allusion, with so broad a sweep of knowledge and such suggestiveness, with a flash-light power of illustration, and all with so clear a revelation of fundamental principles of being, that the oration made the man illustrious, and his message like the rising of a new sun.

It is important perhaps to study this oration in the light of the sixty years which have passed since it was spoken.

The nature which Emerson notes as one of the formative influences of the scholar is quite unlike the nature which the scholar of the present hour studies. To Emerson nature is a condition lying open to the inner eye and to the outer, splendid and infinite. Nature is the reflection of the scholar in the sky, earth, air. Its beauty is the beauty of his own mind. Its laws are the laws of his own mind. Nature thus becomes to him the measure of his attainments. So much of nature as he is ignorant of, so much of his own mind does he not yet possess. And, in fine, the ancient precept, "Know thyself!" and the modern precept, "Study nature!" become at last one maxim. But, to the scholar of to-day, nature has ceased to be simply a condition, and has become a material for his study. In the year before that in which Emerson was

[1] Prose Works, Vol. I., 366-7.

speaking, Charles Darwin had returned from his voyage in the "Beagle" round the globe, and was being moved with those suggestions which were soon to revolutionize the world's thought. Agassiz was giving his days and nights, his money and the money of his friends, to his great work on fossil fishes. To the naturalist, even at that time, nature was ceasing to be a condition, and was beginning to be a great laboratory : not so much, too, was she becoming a place for study as an object to be studied. Since that time nature has become split up into many departments for our observation. We have no longer scientists; but we have chemists, and of several sorts ; we have biologists, and of several types,—physiologists, morphologists, botanists; we have physicists, and of several sorts. Like the ancient Osiris, nature has been hewn into a thousand parts. But even with this division we have come to see the unity of nature. The doctrine of the origin of life, existing in manifold forms, the doctrine of the conservation of energy, are doctrines of a day that has dawned since 1837. To Emerson, nature was a comforting and inspiring condition : to us, nature has become a material existing in diverse forms, one in substance, sufficient for the observation and experimenting of the children of men for the endless cycles. This element in nature of forming material for observation and study is represented in the training which a foreigner, who came to these shores ten years after the Phi Beta Kappa address was spoken, gave to young naturalists. Every teacher knows that description of Agassiz throwing away text and text-books and putting the student down alone at the table with a fish before him, and telling him day after day to look at his fish. Nature is the material itself : its flowers are no longer for beauty, but for analysis; its stars are no longer for inspiration, but for observation; its fish and fowl are no longer for admiration, but food for knowledge and material for classification.

The second influence touching the scholar, says Emerson, is books. Books represent those forces of the past which pour themselves most vitally into the present. What are books for? Books, says Emerson, "are for nothing but to inspire." Books still are one of the few great motive forces. Books still inspire. Books that are the "life-blood of a master spirit," books that are vital, books that are born of life and in turn create life,—such books, breathing, give breath to flagging men; they are reservoirs of vital forces, whence flow streams of life into thousands of men without losing their own supply. Such books are as constant as the stars, fragrant as the flowers, ample as life, and as deathless as humanity. But a change in the use of books has taken place, not unlike the change which has occurred in the conception of nature. The book, like nature, has become material for the scholar's use. These records of the past are stuff for the clear understanding and exhibition of truth. It is not without significance that the shield of our oldest college consists of a wide, open book with " Veritas " written across its pages.

Every age makes its own books, as every bird makes its own nest each season. Every age takes the books of the past ages and makes them over for its own use: every age sings its own poetry, tells its own stories, writes its own history. Dryden sings not for the critical, interrogative, doubting nineteenth century, but for the light-hearted, pleasure-loving, gay, sparkling Restoration. Tennyson sings not for the courtiers of Charles II, but for the large-hearted, large-brained, sober-minded men of the sixty years of the great Queen's great reign. Fielding does not write for our age, nor Hawthorne for the age of Fielding. Hume's History belongs to the eighteenth century; summing up two mighty tendencies toward individualism and naturalism. Macaulay's volumes belong to the middle of the nineteenth century, when the great Whig movement had greatest power and was in fullest sway. Green's vigorous and compact volumes belong to the last quarter of the century, when not movement, but life, is the chief concern of man. But each of these—poet, story-teller, or historian—uses all the past, bringing into his own work whatever treasures he can gather out of the storehouse of the limitless yesterday.

When one asks the question, What have American scholars done in these sixty years through the recreating for this generation of the materials of the past? the answer is not a ground for boastfulness. In the single field of classical philology, Germany has gone as far beyond us as we have gone beyond our forefathers. The cloistered nooks of Oxford and Cambridge have also given us results in which the world rejoices. As we in America call over the list of those who have cultivated the field of classical study, we name Gildersleeve, Goodwin, Seymour, Hale, Allen, Wright, Warren, and White; but each of them would say, that not a few German scholars have gone beyond any one of their own number.

The last of the three great forces which the great Phi Beta Kappa orator names as influencing the scholar is action. Action with the scholar is subordinate; but it is essential. Without it he is not yet a man, without it thoughts can never ripen into truth. He who puts forth his total strength in fit action has the richest return of wisdom.

If it were only for a vocabulary the scholar should be covetous of action. Life is our dictionary. Life lies behind us as the quarry whence we get tiles and copestones for the masonry of to-day. The final value of action, like that of books, and better than books, is that it is a resource. Such are some of the words by which Emerson suggests the value of action in forming the scholar.

The importance of action to the scholar has, since these words were spoken, received illustration more forcible than could have seemed possible in 1837. It is significant that the largest university in the world, the University of Berlin, was founded when Germany lay in humiliation at the feet of the ruthless Napoleon. It is also significant that the first rector of this same university, the great Fichte, wrote his deathless work on the destiny of man when Germany seemed to have no destiny, except to be bound to the chariot of a Corsican adventurer. It is also still more significant that the most important act passed for the higher education in America, after the Ordinance of 1787, was the Morrill Act of 1862, giving millions of acres of land for the endowment of the higher education in certain States of the Union, passed at a time when there was doubt whether there was to be any Union. Full of meaning is it that we call a battle an action, as if a battle were the fullest, most vital form of action. The poem which I presume most would agree is the greatest poem written in this Western Hemisphere was written and read to commemorate the college boys who fell in the greatest of all civil wars :—

> " Many loved Truth, and lavished life's best oil
> Amid the dust of books to find her,
> Content at last, for guerdon of their toil,
> With the cast mantle she hath left behind her.
> Many in sad faith sought for her,
> Many with crossed hands sighed for her ;
> But these, our brothers, fought for her,
> At life's dear peril wrought for her,
> So loved her that they died for her,
> Tasting the raptured fleetness
> Of her divine completeness . . ." [1]

The man who heard someone calling, " Sumter is fired on, Fort Sumter is fired on," and replied, " What do I care, I must finish my Greek lesson," was neither scholar nor patriot, neither Greek nor American. He lacked the element of humanity, he lacked the supreme factor of

[1] JAMES RUSSELL LOWELL'S " Ode recited at the Harvard Commemoration, July 21, 1865."

life, he lacked the capacity to do,—element, factor, capacity which belong to scholarship.

The great war did much for the American people. It is possible
that the lapse of time may prove that the freedom of the negro is not
the greatest of all the great war's sociological benefits. Rather do we
not already see and feel that the supreme contest was a clarifying of
the intellect, a quickening of the conscience, an arousing of the will, a
stirring of the heart, whence have come the splendid material advance
and the noble intellectual movement of the last generation of this wonderful century? Emerson was right, not only for sixty years, but
for sixty times sixty years, when he said that action helps to make the
scholar.

It is worthy of note that Emerson does not refer to another influence that moves the scholar; though to this force he does refer in an
address given at Dartmouth College the following year. It needs only
to be mentioned to be recognized as the greatest power in the life of the
scholar as it is in the life of all men,—the power of personality. Personality, to which nature is cold matter; personality, to which the book
is only a weakened copy; personality, of which action is simply an
application,—personality is undoubtedly the greatest power in the
scholar's life. Take down the names of great men, of scholars, of
men great in any department, and read them over one by one, and
you will find that personality is the power greater in the constituting
of these great men than nature, than books, than action. It was one
college teacher who trained Emerson, Lowell, C. F. Adams, Hedge,
A. P. Peabody, Felton, Hillard, Winthrop, Holmes, Sumner, Motley,
Phillips, Bowen, Lovering, Torrey, Dana, Thoreau, Hale, Thomas
Hill, Child, Fitzedward Hall, Lane, Higginson, and Norton. It was
not method only, although method had its value; it was not
atmosphere, although atmosphere had its value; it was not nature
alone, although nature had its worth; but it was the character, personality, life of Edward Tyrrel Channing which helped to make
American literature.

I sometimes think, that in our quest for a man to sit in our chairs
of instruction and to convey knowledge, we are prone to think more of
the chair of instruction than of the man who sits in it and who gives
the instruction. We inquire with care into the academic biography of
the academic candidate; but do we inquire with sufficient care into the
vital, formative, ethical, manly, and man-making power of the soul
which teaches and inspires? The college was made to make men,—

to make men through scholarship and personal association. Let us therefore have scholars; but let us also have each scholar a man; let us have both a man who is a scholar and a scholar who is a man; let us have a scholar who was a man before he became a scholar and who is a man after he becomes a scholar.

Emerson does not forget to tell us what is the duty of the scholar. The great thinker is ethical. This duty, like the formative power, is threefold. This duty is also a unit. The one word describing this duty and these duties is "trust." This trust has three applications: to the man himself, to universal man, and to the American man. The duties therefore are: self-trust, trust in humanity, and trust in American humanity.

Sixty years have brought no change in the duty of self-trust on the part of the American scholar. The duty is not less obligatory than it was in 1837; nor have the forces that tend to weaken the scholar's trust in himself at all weakened. The increasing splendor of material treasure, the shining mark of material aims, the larger affluence of wealth, the heightened pride of place, have rather made the duty of self-trust the more imperative as they have made it the more difficult to obey. Not the idols of the markets nor the idols of the forum are to tear the American scholar from his supreme belief in the power of thought or in the dominance of culture. His voice may be still and small; but it will be heard when the storms and whirlwinds of public passion have ceased. He is to have the confidence of Garrison, crying: "I will be as harsh as truth and as uncompromising as justice; I will not equivocate; I will not excuse; I will not retreat a single inch; and I will be heard." Not in a boastfulness which betokens weakness, nor in violence which may indicate unsoundness, but in sheer simple, quiet self-trust; knowing he is right, and then proceeding forthwith the right to do, is the scholar to live his life and to do his work in the "great Task-master's eye." The scholar is to have the self-trust of Milton, but he is to have more than Milton's gentleness; he is to have the self-trust of Cardinal Newman, but he is to have more than Newman's spirit of investigation; he is to have the self-trust of Carlyle, but he is to have it free from egoistic rules and impositions. He is to hold himself to his principles, assured that the greatness of thought and of feeling, of scholarship and of knowledge, is like unto the mountains, to which he can ever lift up his eyes and be at peace.

The scholar is also to trust men. He is to be a democrat. Not to trust men is intellectual and ethical suicide. Not to trust men is to burn down the house in which the scholar lives.   The scholar is to look on humanity as his child, as his brother.   Mistaken in intellectual vision, false in premises of reasoning, wrong in method, preferring the ugly to the graceful, the cheap to the worthy, the ephemeral to the eternal, man may be; but the scholar is to know that such errors, sins, or crimes are not the errors, sins, and crimes of an alien, but of one who is of the same blood as himself.   He is, therefore, to seek to correct the offender's vision, to refine his tastes, to turn his will toward righteousness, to expel his preference of sin and to quicken his life. Man is at times and in spots selfish; but trust him.   Man is at times and in spots evil; but trust him.   Man is at times and in spots fallen; but trust him.   His fall is the fall of an angel; his evil is the evil of a saint; his foolishness—if foolishness it be—is the foolishness of delirium, which, passing away, leaves the man in his right mind.   Let the scholar trust humanity !

The American scholar is also bound by the special obligation of trusting his own brother of the same name as his own.   The American man has done much for the American scholar.   No more impressive evidence can be found of the value of the service that the American man has rendered the American scholar than is offered in the scores of colleges founded in the new commonwealths.   From the college on the bank of the Kennebec to the college at the Golden Gate, colleges present proof that to the good-will of the American citizen do they owe their being.   At times one is inclined to indulge himself in a mood of complaint; for the entire value of all our colleges, including build-ings and endowment,—the result of more than two and one-half centu-ries of gathering,—is hardly in excess of certain private fortunes.   Yet, at a time like the present, let us rather sing our song of gratitude to the benefactor of the American college than mournfully chant our Greek chorus of complaint over human selfishness.   Surely the American man has done more for the American scholar than the men of other races have done for their agencies of the higher learning.   The English-man desires to found or to perpetuate a family: he seldom gives to those indigent and ivy-covered creations of elegant leisure on the banks of the Cam and of the Isis.   The German looks to the government to endow Strasburg and Berlin.   The American democrat desires to equip his college out of his own private chest.   Millions and tens of millions of dollars are pouring into the treasuries of our colleges from private and personal beneficence.   More is now given in a single year to Am-erican colleges than had been given to all American colleges in the two hundred years between the founding of Harvard and the day of Emerson's address. Such a record the world has never made. Trust the American man to endow American scholarship!

Sixty years ago Emerson said, "We have listened too long to the courtly muses of Europe." The remark was at once true and false when it was made: the remark is now at once truer and falser than when it was made. In 1837 Everett and Bancroft and Ticknor and Longfellow had listened to the courtly muses; but they had not listened too long. Men, too, born abroad, whose work was to be in no small degree in America, as Francis Lieber, Louis Agassiz, Guyot, Charles Beck and Charles Theodore Follen, had also listened to the courtly muses; but they had not listened too long. Within the years soon to follow 1837, Lane and Child and Goodwin of Harvard and Gildersleeve, together with Gould, the astronomer, and Whitney, were to listen to the same courtly muses; but they were not to listen too long. In the last forty years hundreds upon hundreds of Americans have listened to the same strains; but no one of us dares to say that the period of listening was too long. For the truth is, that scholarship cannot be made too rich, nor the training in and for scholarly pursuits too noble. It is moreover a fact, that scholarship knows no territorial boundaries: learning is not provincial. We cannot send too many young men to Europe, provided Europe can make them better scholars than we ourselves can make them.

We are obliged to confess that the great scholars of the world are the scholars of Europe. When one calls over the names of great scholars of the last sixty years one does not find many American names. Take the great chemists of the last sixty years and whom will you name? Liebig, Dumas, Laurent and Gerhardt, Wurtz, Williamson, Hofman, Kekule, Pasteur, Bunsen, Mendeleef, Stas, and Ostwald. So also when one asks for the names of the great biologists of the last sixty years one names: von Baer, Max Schultze, Agassiz, Darwin, Huxley, de Bary, Dohrn,—of which only one is American, and he by adoption.

It is in physics that the last sixty years manifest as noble a service as in any realm of scholarship. Joseph Henry greatly resembles Faraday both in the methods and in the quality of his work. Henry's discoveries in electro-magnetism were valuable additions to those of Faraday. To him is also due much of the honor connected with the development of the telegraph. American science owes to him also a large debt for his executive work in the establishment of the Smithsonian Institution. The present Director of the Smithsonian Institution, Prof. A. P. Langley, is probably the first living authority on radiant heat, and especially the heat of the sun. The most brilliant of American physicists is Prof. Rowland; and his career since his undergraduate days, when he discovered a new method of magnetic measurement, has been one of increasing worth. But while no one of these three men would claim to be so great an experimenter as Michael Faraday, nor so great a genius as James Clerk Maxwell, nor so eminent as Lord Kelvin, nor so conspicuous in several scientific fields as von Helmholtz, yet they deserve to rank with the great physicists of the middle period of the century.

In a list of the great philosophers of the last sixty years Schopenhauer, Lotze, and Spencer should be included; not a few would add Comte; and a few, Hamilton. American books on philosophy are usually well written; but in general they lack depth and comprehensiveness. The great men in logic of this period are either Englishmen or Germans; although one should perhaps mention the work of Charles Peirce. When one thinks of the great ethical scholars of our time, the names that first occur to one are those of Englishmen,—Spencer, Green, Sidgwick, Stephen, and Martineau. In psychology, however, while one thinks of Wundt, Külpe, Maudsley, Galton, Ward, Carpenter, Ribot, and many French specialists, yet one does not forget James, Ladd, Hall, and several other Americans.

Let us not be ashamed if we have not the scholarship of Berlin and Bonn, of Leipsic and Munich. Let us not be ashamed if we have not the rich culture of Oxford and Cambridge: let us frankly confess that we have not. Let us confess to ourselves that the Germans far excel us in scholarship. Frank confession of this sort is a prerequisite to making ourselves great scholars.

For, above all else, America has the future. If we have in two hundred and fifty years, or in sixty, made few great scholars, we may believe that in the new century we may make many great scholars. The spirit of scholarship is moving on the vast and yeasty deep of knowledge and reflection. Great results we may be able to achieve in brief time.

One of the most significant features of the Greek civilization is the swiftness of its rise. A period hardly longer than lies between the entrance of the "Mayflower" into Plymouth Bay and the landing of the Atlantic Cable on its shore divides the morning of Greek civilization from its noon. In a period hardly longer than has been the life of our oldest college, Æschylus, Euripides, and Sophocles sang their great anthems of human destiny, Plato thought, Aristotle reasoned, Praxiteles and Phidias made the rock beautiful and vocal. In that brief time came into Greece, and through Greece into humanity, a beauty and a strength which are at once the glory and the despair of men. In the coming century let us hope that American civilization may rise with a swiftness akin to that which Greek life found after the Persian wars; let us trust that American civilization may rise with a beauty like that which flowered forth into Greek architecture and sculpture; let us be able to believe that it may rise with a might and majesty worthy too of the Western conqueror of the Greek; but let us pray that American civilization may rise with a permanence of beauty, of might, and of majesty which neither Greek nor Roman life knew.

CHARLES F. THWING.

THE EVOLUTION OF THE EDUCATIONAL IDEAL.—II.

In the preceding article, the evolution of the educational ideal was discussed from a historical standpoint. In this paper, I shall direct attention to the present and future aspects of the subject.

Upon the whole, it may be said that education is at present still under the influence of the civic-humanistic ideal. Nevertheless, there are tendencies discernible which foreshadow the end of its dominion. There are evidences of an internal disturbance such as that which preceded the Reformation and the French Revolution. The belief in the old ideals is shaken : new conceptions of the dignity and culture of man are beginning to gain ground.

In the present century two tendencies become conspicuous : tendencies which may be classified as the popular and the realistic.

The popular tendency is distinguished by two prominent characteristics—the national and the democratic : education is to emanate from the national life itself; and all classes of the people are to enjoy the benefits of the intellectual life of the whole nation.

(1) The national characteristic is found in all countries of Europe : everywhere the tendency to the nationalization of education is manifest. This circumstance is undoubtedly due, in a very high degree, to the nationalization of the state itself. The most remarkable characteristic of the political life of the nineteenth century is undoubtedly the formation of great national states. The example afforded by the political unification of the states of Germany and Italy has aroused the national instincts of other nations, and influenced the policy of their political leaders. The political dynasties of the eighteenth century, with their marked indifference to the nationality of the subject, have been supplanted by the modern states, which so jealously guard the national idea.

This change in the political life has influenced education in two directions. The idea of instilling national views and national culture into the minds of the pupils everywhere pervades the common schools. For this reason, instruction in history and the mother-tongue are considered of vital importance. A hundred years ago the religious element was predominant in Germany: to-day the national element is considered of equal importance.   But the common schools have a still greater task to perform'; namely, the assimilation of the foreign elements residing within the country,—an idea which was unknown at the beginning of the century.   The little state of Denmark took the initiative in this respect, in endeavoring, through the schools, to make Danish territory of the Duchy of Schleswig.   Although unsuccessful, the 'example of Denmark has been followed upon a very extensive scale.   At present Germany is endeavoring to Teutonize its Poles, Danes, and Frenchmen by means of the school; Hungary and Russia are endeavoring to Magyarize and Russify their Germans, Poles, and Roumanians.   It cannot be said that these efforts have so far been successful; indeed, it must be admitted that they have been baneful to education and culture where, as in the East, they have aimed at the extermination of the superior races.   I fear they have been so everywhere.

It is undeniable that a broad and truly humane culture is best propagated upon native soil, where the mother-tongue is spoken.   At present much time is spent in attempts to impart a slight knowledge of the foreign tongue to unwilling pupils, who rapidly forget it.   Were it not better to rely upon the persuasive power of self-interest and a superior culture?   Furthermore, may it not be said that the contrast of nationalities in one and the same state is frequently advantageous as a means of mutual improvement?   Such is the case in Switzerland and the United States; while Alsace was a serious loss to France, not merely in a political, but also in an intellectual sense, owing to the benefits which the foreign nationality contributed to the French life.

Nationalization also exerts its influence in the gymnasium.   In every country of Europe, national education is gradually forcing classical education into the background.   Here also we have a proof of the growing sentiment in favor of national worth and dignity.   The modern races no longer permit their own nationality to be subordinated to that of classical antiquity.   Men of learning, more particularly those who act as teachers and leaders of the people, are expected to be closely identified with the nation itself.

For a long period this was not the case.   During many centuries the exclusiveness of scholarly culture was a matter of pride.   The humanistic poet of the sixteenth century regarded his native language—the language of the peasant—with contempt.   The foreign language gave him a sense of exclusiveness and dignity.   Even in the schools
43

he instilled into the minds of his pupils, with the elements of Latin, a contempt of the common people and their language. The rod was the punishment for speaking in the mother-tongue. In the same manner was the Courtly-French culture anti-national and unpopular. The foreign tongue gave to "polite society" a sense of superiority, as it occasionally does to-day. The civic-humanistic education became incensed at the foreign bearing of "polite society"; it desired to be national and independent of French influence. This is not an unimportant moment in the new humanistic movement. The influence of the antique is placed against that of the French. To learn from the Greeks, the schoolmasters of the whole world, is not so humiliating to the national consciousness as to recognize the superiority of a neighboring nation.

In other respects, however, the humanistic gymnasium has not tended to diminish the distance between the exclusiveness of the scholar and the national life. The old Latin schools taught Latin as the language of the scholar, a rather superficial possession : the new gymnasium advocates classical education as a means of bringing about a transformation of the inner life,—a human Renaissance by means of Greek culture. Consequently, those who are not Greeks are but partially human. This estrangement of the scholar from the people was again a source of pride and exclusiveness. Many felt that a person unfamiliar with Latin and Greek was not an equal and was scarcely worthy of serious consideration. Since about the middle of the present century, a reaction against this scholarly exclusiveness has made itself felt. We find a proof of this in the wave of indignation against compulsory Latin which swept over the country in 1848. This reaction has become much stronger within the past generation. The victory which the reactionary movement achieved in neighboring countries is now also assured in Germany. The curriculum for 1892 shows a departure from the old method. Instruction in the dead languages has been greatly abridged ; writing in Latin has been entirely abandoned ; even the elementary instruction in this language is not begun until the pupil has attained a more mature age (about the twelfth year). On the other hand, instruction in German is strongly emphasized ; indeed, the student whose knowledge of this language is unsatisfactory is not entitled to his degree. Furthermore, pupils of schools in which Latin is not taught (the so-called *Oberrealschulen*) are now permitted to enter the university. Thus we see that the rule of classicism is broken.

I shall devote merely a few words to the similar movement which is now noticeable in the fields of art and literature. Its most striking feature is a departure from the classicist idealism, which, together with the new humanistic móvement, established its rule at the beginning of the century. Everywhere we notice the endeavor to pursue independent paths. Realism in literature is a strong protest against conventional classicism. The same is true of the new symbolism, whose dramas emphasize an idea, whose fairy-tales involve a philosophical truth, etc. The tendency of our time, like that of the seventh decade of the eighteenth century, is to create new forms and to give expression to new ideas. Architecture employs all styles, ancient and modern, in order to give an appropriate architectural expression to the sentiment of the.times. In painting, the elements of light and color are considered of greater importance than drawing. Even in sculpture, color has been introduced; a proceeding which fifty years ago would have been considered sacrilege. The discovery has since been made, however, that, as regards tinted statuary, the Greeks themselves must have been barbarians.

(2) I have mentioned the democratic tendency as a second feature of the popular movement. I use the term "democratic" to designate the tendency to allow every individual to take an active interest in the national life. This is a very conspicuous characteristic of the educational ideal of the nineteenth century. The pressure exerted by the lower classes has been met half-way, and has resulted in enormously augmenting their power.

This improvement in the condition of the masses has been brought about by the reorganization of the common school. The enlightening ideas of Pestalozzi have served to change the reading, writing, and memory schools into a popular educational institution. The Teachers' Seminaries (Normal Schools), a large number of which were founded toward the close of the last century, are to the masses what the universities are to the upper classes: they equip their teachers with a fund of scientific culture and pedagogical training. In this way, the common schools, besides giving instruction in the three R's, are enabled to supply their pupils with a general knowledge of history and physics, which may serve as a basis for future development. Germany was the first country to entrust the general education of the people to the care of the state. The great victories of Prussia proved conclusively that the augmentation of national power was due largely to her broad system of education. The well-known saying, that the victory of Sadowa was won by the Prussian schoolmaster, though somewhat one-sided, is partially true. It is an undeniable fact that the superiority of the German army was due principally to the general culture of all its members; for even the subaltern officers were graduates from the common schools. In like manner, the extraordinary economical advance of Germany during the past generation, which now begins to exert its influence upon the neighboring countries, may be traced to her universal system of education. At the same time the development of city life—a necessary consequence of the greatly improved economical conditions—has facilitated attendance at the schools and promoted the desire for improved educational methods.

This entire movement resulted in giving the masses a far greater interest, both political and intellectual, in public life. There can be no doubt that the masses which, toward the close of the eighteenth century, were still characterized by dull passivity, have now awakened to a lively interest in public affairs. They read and think: they have not merely an extensive daily press, but a complete scientific literature as well. Works on social and natural science, philosophy, and history, which are written for the masses and reflect their views, are bought and read to an extraordinary extent: even in the remotest workshop these books may be found. Whatever the intrinsic value of these writings may be, the very fact of their existence is a proof of the greatly increased intellectual activity of the masses.

There can be no doubt of the mutual relation between the political and the intellectual improvement of the masses. Equipped with the privilege of universal suffrage, which, perhaps, was not originally given to them for this purpose, the masses are already beginning to exercise a considerable influence upon public life; an influence, however, which is not at all commensurate with their aspirations. Whether they are qualified as yet to exercise the right of suffrage, which they acquired rather suddenly, is somewhat doubtful. Above all, they still lack a proper appreciation of the solidarity of national interests. For the time being, class differences have forced the sentiment of national unity into the background. I refer here more particularly to the socialistic agitation. It may be assumed, however, that a stronger pressure from without would rapidly sweep all the international oratory (or demagogism) out of Germany, and establish a spirit of unity among the people. The self-preservation of the nation, the security of its vital interests, and the maintenance of its political power are the first conditions necessary to the prosperity of the lower classes. A decline of political power, which would soon be followed by an economical deterioration, would at once recoil upon the laboring population. On the other hand, it would be well to realize more clearly than is often the case that the prosperity of the masses is the indispensable condition of national greatness. The commercial and military serviceability of the people naturally proceeds from their material, moral, and intellectual welfare; while oppression of the masses would be synonymous with a deterioration and decline of the entire nation. To substantiate this, it is necessary to consider only the probable effect of oppression upon the education of the growing generation : an impoverished and downtrodden proletariat cannot produce offspring physically and morally healthy. Whenever the social question is discussed this should not be forgotten. Indeed, the question may be briefly formulated as follows : Amid the altered conditions of life and production, how can we make it possible for the masses to rear a strong and useful progeny ?

Upon the whole it may be said that the impulse from below has been answered from above, and that the upper classes have lent a willing hand. At the beginning of the century the leading circles, more particularly those of Germany, manifested a desire to disseminate culture among the people. I would especially recall to mind the spontaneous and passionate interest with which reformatory measures—those of Pestalozzi, for example—were everywhere received. Crowned heads, statesmen, and scholars all displayed extraordinary zeal in encouraging and stimulating the movement. It was this spirit which gave birth to the common schools of Germany. Later on, a certain conservatism set in. The old nobility occasionally manifested a disposition to adopt the maxim which von Rochow, a pedagogical reformer of the eighteenth century, who was himself a Brandenberg nobleman, professes to have frequently heard expressed by men of his class : "The peasant must remain in ignorance; otherwise he cannot be held in subjection." In recent years similar opinions have occasionally been uttered by the *parvenue bourgeoisie* in reference to the culture of the industrial classes. However, this narrow-minded policy has not succeeded in checking the efforts of the statesmen and intellectual leaders to raise the standard of culture among the lower classes. Schools and societies for the advancement of higher culture are also working in the same direction. Even the churches have everywhere begun to participate in the movement by means of societies, lectures, the press, etc.

Noteworthy also are the efforts recently made by the universities to come into touch with the educational needs of the people. In the Scandinavian countries the so-called " Peasants' High Schools " have been established since about the middle of the present century, to propagate culture among the middle and lower strata of the peasantry; and the results attained have been very favorable. In countries where the English language is spoken, the universities (since 1870) have endeavored to make education accessible to those who desire self-improvement, but are prevented by reason of their daily vocations from taking a regular scientific course. In Germany also the universities are about to follow this example; and I do not believe that the bugaboo of "superficial education," which is occasionally raised in the newspapers by the representatives of "thoroughness," will intimidate them from carrying out their design. As matters stand, I consider it of far greater importance to bring about a mutual understanding between the educated and the uneducated classes than to protect the latter from the effects of a superficial education. Wherever the desire for knowledge exists, it is sure to seek sources of information; and the universities may certainly entertain the hope of supplying sources fully as good as those which are supplied to the masses from other quarters. Together with the lectures of which I have spoken, the public libraries may be mentioned. As regards the latter, however, the English-speaking nations, for several decades, have made a considerable advance.

I have mentioned the realistic tendency as the second general feature of the educational movement of our century. It is obvious that this tendency also stands in close relation to the general current of the times. In discussing this feature, I shall first dwell upon realism in politics, and then direct attention to the same phenomenon in the sciences.

Politics, toward the close of the last century, had an ideal tendency. The French Revolution, in its origin, was a purely idealistic movement: philosophical ideas, ideas of natural rights, were to be verified, and then communicated to all mankind for their salvation. To a still greater degree did the German race live in the realm of ideas; dreams of a universal republic, a human Arcadia, an everlasting reign of peace occupied the minds of its sages and poets. Napoleon I was the first great practical statesman who awakened the German nation—rudely enough, it is true—out of the realm of dreams. Not by word, but by deed, he inculcated the lesson, that a people, in order to preserve their independence, must unite for their defence. He pointed out to the German people the necessity and the signification of the state, the symbol of which is power. That the German nation well understood the lesson, was demonstrated by the uprising of 1813. The enthusiastic youth of that period suffered in the cause of German power and unity. They recognized the necessity of these ideals, although their realization was far distant; until at last Bismarck, the second great practical statesman of the century, appeared, and, with the weapons of practical politics, blood and iron, reared the structure of the Empire.

The spirit of mind engendered by these events exercises its sway over many circles. The desire for power is the maxim of the time. Political questions, whether of a foreign or domestic nature, are questions of power, not of doctrine. Some go still further and declare that every question relating to public affairs is to be regarded from this point of view: that of our social life, the labor question, for example, is "one of power, which some day will be fought out upon our streets." Even questions relating to the church are now treated in this sense; as, for example, in Rome, where practical statecraft has ever had its seat from the days of Romulus to those of Leo XIII. Even the politically constituted Protestant churches, with their parties, electoral primaries, terrorism, etc., are to-day dominated by the same idea.

The scientific movement of the nineteenth century, in many respects, runs parallel to that just mentioned. The words of Bacon, "Knowledge is power," were never so highly valued as at the present day. At the beginning of the century, the aim of science was to afford an insight into the mystery of the world and of life. Faust's magical endeavors and the speculative philosophy indicate the goal. Physical science rules to-day; and her aim is not contemplation of the world, but the mastery of the physical forces. The interests which these tendencies denote are embodied in medicine and technical science.

All this affects education and the spirit of the youthful generation. The changes in the general constitution of our educational system since the end of the eighteenth century may be briefly summed up as follows: (1) Beside the old humanistic school-system, a realistic one has sprung up: polytechnical institutes and industrial schools of every description have found room beside the Latin schools. (2) Despite strenuous opposition, a realistic course has gained admission into the old schools, and now occupies a place beside the old linguistic and humanistic course; as, for example, in the gymnasium, where mathematics and physics have advanced at the expense of the classics. In the common schools, also, religious instruction has been compelled to yield more and more room to scientific subjects.

Doubtless the spirit of our youth is in accordance with the general movement: it is centred in action and power. What has become of the æsthetic, sentimental spirit with which the youth of one hundred years ago read the works of Homer or the dramas of Goethe and Schiller, which had just then appeared? Where is the passionate enthusiasm and wonder with which the audiences of that time received the revelations of Fichte and Schelling? The young people of our day take an interest in North-Pole expeditions, travels in Africa, bicycles, aquatic sports, and the like. To obtain recognition in the outer world, is the enthusiastic endeavor of the younger generation: strength, bravery, and dominion are its ideals. And our schools promote this aim. Gymnastic exercises, which everywhere constitute an important element of education, direct the attention to bodily health and vigor and to the art of self-defence. Here, also, the desire for power is stimulated; while games and sports, which always require bodily strength, are greatly encouraged. Indeed, the sports of our pupils occasionally transcend the proper limit, and threaten to interfere with their intellectual interests. I wish also to refer here briefly to the movement which has been set on foot to develop the manual dexterity of our pupils. This movement, emanating from the North, has rapidly found friends and patrons in other countries.

At this point, as at many others, the popular and the realistic tendencies are in touch. Naturally the great masses rarely come in contact with a spiritual culture of mind; therefore, all bodily exercises, all physical efforts at work or play lessen the disparity between the upper and the lower ranks of society, establish a better understanding between them, and frequently lead to common activity. I should consider it fortunate if the course devoted to manual training should reëstablish the ancient prestige of hand-work, and eventually gain for it a higher appreciation among the upper classes. On the other hand, it would be a valuable acquisition to the national life if the gymnastic exercises and sports of our youth could once more be enjoyed in common by the people at large. In this way our laboring classes, who, even at work, are rarely brought into close relation, would once more become enabled to congregate for the purpose of mutual enjoyment on workdays as well as on holidays.

In conclusion, I shall touch upon a third tendency which has lately become somewhat conspicuous. It may be termed the individualistic tendency.

This tendency differs in some respects from those already mentioned. The popular and the realistic tendencies may be regarded as the predominant influences of the period: the individualistic movement is a reaction against a partial result of these influences; viz., the extension and increase of state control in the regulation of the life of the individual. This latter tendency is particularly evident in our educational system. The school system is, in an ever greater degree, becoming subject to state management. State inspection and control of the schools are really a development of the nineteenth century. Prior to that, education was entrusted to the family, the church, or the city. The effect of the present system has been to define education more clearly and strictly to systematize it. The examinations have become more and more exacting and stringent as regards details. If we compare, for example, the present plan of instruction for the Prussian high schools with the plans previously drawn, we shall find that the curriculum is remarkably explicit, even as regards the selection of the authors to be read in each class.

The regulation of the studies, however, is not confined to externals. The teacher must not merely follow a precise method, but he is also required to direct the views and sentiments of his pupils. Instruction in religion, history, and German is imparted with the ulterior aim of giving a definite direction to thought and sentiment. According to the Prussian curriculum of 1892, instruction in history must give the pupil an idea of the serious consequences which follow sudden and violent changes in the social order. The counterpart to this is found in France—for example, in the "Instruction Civique," by Paul Bert, a former Minister of Instruction. In this work the French Revolution is styled "the sunrise of humanity on earth, the first great and glorious revolution in the destiny of mankind, which has emancipated the masses and raised them from poverty to affluence"; while monarchy and priesthood are characterized as the hereditary foes of the people. The tendency of both these methods is virtually the same; namely, to instil certain opinions and sentiments into the youthful mind.

This is certainly not a new tendency. It is but natural that the older generation should endeavor to inculcate its own view of right. The influence of the state, however, in this regard is new. Formerly the home and the church were powerful agents in moulding the views of the growing generation. To-day the bureaucracy exercises the *selectus opinionum*, and dictates those ideas and sentiments which have met with its sanction and approval. It is from this point of view that we must study the so-called individualistic tendency: it is the reaction against the correctness enforced by the state.

This tendency is a well-defined characteristic of recent literature. Everywhere we hear the indignant protest against "conventional correctness" and the fetters which it imposes on personal life and thought. In Germany, Paul de Lagarde and Friedrich Nietzsche have been the most pronounced opponents of this "conventional correctness." Lagarde's "Deutsche Schriften" are one continuous protest against the slavery which church, state, school, and general education alike impose on the individual; and Nietzsche, also, is a standing contradiction to all that "obtains," to all-that is generally recognized as "correct." From the "Untimely Observations" to the "Dusk of the Idols," he unceasingly inveighs against the faint-hearted herds of educated fogeys, who, in consequence of their long-continued and very correct schooling, have lost all the strength and moral courage requisite to personal independence,—who dare not express or even entertain an idea which is not sanctioned by the authorities, the schools, or the newspapers. In contradistinction to this altogether too numerous class, he places the individual, who, strong and courageous within himself, attacks the citadel of "correctness," and remodels the traditional standards of value and morals; in short, the absolute revolutionist. In all this we recognize that spirit of contradiction which is opposed to all that is generally accepted as "correct."

Nietzsche is perhaps the strongest exponent of this literary-philosophical-anarchistic spirit,—a spirit which is not confined to Germany, but pervades all the countries of Europe. Everywhere we find the spirit of revolt against the old truths and ideals. Tolstoï—the Russian Rousseau of the nineteenth century—preaches a kind of sentimental anarchism. The state, with its compulsory service, its wars, and its official bodies, with their laws and regulations; the church, with a conventional belief which has nothing in common with the Gospel; the sciences, which have long since lost all faith in themselves; a society which torments itself and imagines itself to be happy,—all these conditions oppress the individual and debar him from recognizing natural truths. From the North comes Ibsen preaching the same word. He declares that the individual is strongest alone, and that the world is full of conventional falsehoods from which the veil should be torn. Kjelland, the Dane, sings the same tune. Confined from infancy within a network of narrowing ideas, man becomes tame, small, and distorted. To begin with, Latin grammar and composition at once deprive him of the power of natural speech, the Catechism deprives him of the courage to think independently; so that, by the time his confirmation comes, his tongue unhesitatingly utters what his heart does not understand.   Finally, the state examination approaches, and he passes the narrow portals of "perfect correctness," to become an official of the state. And now, as a member of polite society, he thinks and says nothing but what is deemed proper and respectable.   Whoever wishes to be a unit, and to indulge in the luxury of expressing independent ideas, is at once excommunicated: society ostracizes him and expunges his utterances.   Thus the principle of the "survival of the fittest" is gradually altered into the survival of the weakest and the most "correct."

These are the men who have caught the public ear to-day, whose books are widely read and translated into all languages, and whose plays are everywhere performed.   In all, we find the love of the uncommon, the longing for something new and original.   Yet this love is frequently succeeded by the scorn and hatred which they cherish for all that bears the official or "officious" stamp of the state and society.   At the same time it is questionable whether the ability of these men to recognize the reality of things and to create new ideals is not surpassed by their power of invective.   I incline to the belief that the latter is the case, and that their invective frequently culminates in abuse.   Nevertheless, it is a noteworthy fact that the public lends a favorable ear to these writers: there must be something in the spirit of their productions which attracts it.   I am of the opinion that this spirit of revolt is the result of the excessive tension produced by our conventional "correctness."

These ideas are further emphasized in the political and social discontent of the masses.   Lassalle belongs to those who despise the educated rabble whose education consists in the complete absence of independent thought, who know something about everything and who have cut-and-dried opinions on every subject so long as they take their partisan newspaper regularly.   This scornful tone is a conspicuous feature of the whole socialistic literature.   And now, opposed to this, we find a real or feigned belief in every species of authority, which is occasionally intensified into a veritable fanaticism of "correctness."   Where this extreme prevails all independence of thought is mercilessly condemned.   "Whoever differs from ourselves, who are conventionally correct, on political, social, ecclesiastical, or other questions; whoever does not acquiesce in all that we do or say, is in league with the enemy and is a traitor.   It were best to turn him out into the marketplace and stone him at once."   This is the cry which is daily sounded by the newspapers of the "correct" class.

I hasten to my conclusion. Let us place ourselves apart from the tumult which rages on both sides, and, closing our ears, question ourselves whether a new educational ideal may be evolved from this strife of contending factions, and what the general character of this ideal would be. If we assume that the three features which I have mentioned may be combined, we should have a popular-realistic-individualistic ideal of education. Popular, not exclusive or aristocratic in the narrower sense of the word ; national, not foreign or international, but rather the result of an evolution from the national life itself ; realistic, characterized by strength and action and not by mere thought and æsthetic sentiment ; individualistic, i. e., aiming at the development of the individual and not at the establishment of dull uniformity ; not democratic, therefore, if this word imply a general reduction to a dead level, but rather aristocratic, in the sense of an individual, not a class, aristocracy.

It would be presumptuous at the present day to state what the concrete form of such an educational ideal would be. I wish to say, however, that the society corresponding to the above ideal would be that of an aristocracy of mind. Is this the type toward which we are leaning? Is the aristocracy of birth and wealth to be supplanted by the aristocracy of personal worth and merit? This has been the philosopher's dream, from the day of Plato's "Republic" to the present hour. It is the tendency of nature. It would be the aristocracy of nature to have every individual stand independently upon his own personal merit and not upon the achievements of his father; while the influence of heredity, in the sense of the transmission of personal characteristics, would certainly not be diminished. Such is the aristocracy to which historical development seems to point. Both church and state have made considerable advances toward the realization of this idea of a personal élite, by bestowing position and influence according to the degree of personal talent and efficiency, without regard to birth and possession.

Will the future follow this path? Will a time come when the prosecution of this idea, once the idea of the liberal democracy, will be vigorously resumed? Will the tendency toward conventional correctness, apathy, and idleness be eventually overcome, in order that the ideal of personal liberty may be carried to a higher degree of perfection than has been possible during the nineteenth century? It is impossible to foretell. The future is the land of belief and not of visible reality. Still, it must be admitted that ideas have been a power in history; for, by gaining an influence upon the imagination, the phantasy, and the will, they gradually become converted into facts. As the ideal of education it will remain: each according to his natural endowment. This is as true of the individual as of the community at large. It is a misfortune for the individual and a serious loss to the community, when the methods of education and their practical application to actual life are at variance. If the educational standard is inferior to the natural capacity of the individual, a feeling of ungratified desire and humiliation is engendered. If, on the other hand, the educational demands transcend the native ability of the individual, we find, as a result, superficiality of culture, over-education, false education, or whatever that prevalent disease of our time may be termed, which afflicts so many human beings, who, destined by nature to fill a subordinate position, are continually tormented by their excess of culture.

Thus we have returned to that educational ideal which filled the soul of the youthful Wilhelm von Humboldt, and which John Stuart Mill so warmly advocates in his essay on "Liberty": Vigor and originality, not equality, nor that uniformity which disregards the demands of nature; for this produces weakness and false culture. Let us extend to every individual the liberty of developing his talents according to the demands of his nature, in order that he may reach the summit of his capacity. But let us not forget that, in the words of Kant, "we are here discussing an *idea* to which experience furnishes no parallel." Enough for us if this idea give a direction to our will. Life itself will certainly modify it.

FRIEDRICH PAULSEN.

THE MUNICIPAL GOVERNMENT OF BERLIN.

BERLIN is situated on the sandy plains that form the valley of the Spree, which winds its sluggish course through the city and makes connection with the fertile valleys of the Elbe and the Oder; thus joining the commerce of Eastern Europe with the North Sea and the Baltic. The river Spree, outside the city, spreads into a shallow stream, frequently widening into broad lakes; but within the city it is reduced to the proportions of a large canal, and is confined by walls of solid masonry. With it are connected several canals, which facilitate the transportation of heavy freight, and indeed serve as a means of traffic between different points within the city; thus relieving the local streets and railway traffic. Regular local freight-boats ply on the Spree from station to station for the transfer of freight. This extensive system of inland water traffic—greater than that of the Rhine—has been potent in building up a great commercial city.

But more powerful in city-building than a convenient waterway are the influences of war and politics. The fact that the Hohenzollerns chose Berlin as their home has been influential in making it one of the great cities of Europe. Its fortunes have followed the ascending star of this illustrious family. When the small town of Berlin-Köln fell into the hands of this thrifty family it began to improve. Under the impetus given it by Frederick the Great it took rank, in 1786, with the capitals of Europe. As the centre of the Prussian monarchy its opportunities for growth were enhanced; and since the close of the Franco-Prussian war, as the capital of the new empire, its advancement has been marvellous. At the beginning of this century the population of Berlin was 172,000; in 1870, it numbered 800,000; while at present it is nearly 2,000,000. From 1870 to 1890 it grew more rapidly than New York, kept pace with Chicago, and made twice as much progress as Philadelphia. With this rapid growth of population many problems of municipal government have arisen, which have been met and solved so wisely as to challenge admiration at almost every point. While, in attempting to solve the problems of city government in the United States, it may not be wise to think of imitating the government of

Berlin, the methods of administration in every department there yield most valuable lessons.

The long military discipline that made Prussia an independent state and, later, gave it the most perfect system of administration in Europe has had its effect on city government. The force of that excellent method of administration has become the inheritance of the modern municipal system. Government is a serious matter in Berlin; and the Germans bring to bear upon it all their great powers of organization and execution. The power of concentrated action, the thoroughness of social institutions, the seriousness with which all governmental acts are regarded, the scientific method of managing public works, the patient and exhaustive treatment of every subject in hand,—all have contributed to the perfection of the great German capital. While the Germans were very slow in taking up the problem of municipal government, the qualities just enumerated have enabled them, in very many respects, to take front rank.

The municipal government of Berlin, and in fact of all other Prussian cities, is founded on the general law of 1808, established through the influence of the reformers Stein and Hardenberg, which gave the municipalities enlarged powers of local government. Since then the constitution has been changed, notably in 1877–1884; and the old laws have been completed, revised, and adapted to the new conditions. The local government has always remained intact, and has been much stimulated by these reforms; but the powers of the Imperial government still extend to the municipality.

At present the central organization of the government of Berlin consists of a city council, composed of one hundred and twenty-six members elected by the qualified voters of the city. There is a property qualification for voters based on the class system. This excludes from the privileges of voting about 15 per cent of those who would otherwise be qualified. Those who are eligible to vote are divided into three classes according to the amount of property owned, which is determined by the amount of taxes paid. Each class represents one-third of the aggregate amount of taxes paid. The city is divided into electoral districts; and each class in each district elects a member of the council. The first class comprises a few wealthy voters; the second, a large number of well-to-do people; and the third is composed of a much larger group consisting of small property-holders and laboringmen. This system favors property rights, and places the balance of power in the hands of the wealthy. While this method seems to

Americans—who have been accustomed to look upon the elective franchise with greater liberality—to be arbitrary and unjust, it is not without merit. It recognizes at once that the city is a business corporation,
and gives those members having the greater business interest, and who
pay the larger proportion for the support of the government, the greater
power in choosing representatives. While in other instances this excess of power might prove dangerous, in Berlin its use is enlightened
and directed in the best interests of the people.

The city council becomes almost a perpetual body. Its members
are elected for six years; one-third being chosen every two years. Men
are reëlected repeatedly for good service; and many spend a large part
of their active lives as members of the council. This gives a permanence to its acts and a stability to its government, which could not
exist with a rapidly changing membership. The council chooses its
Ober-bürgermeister and *Bürgermeister*, who, in many respects, correspond
with the mayor and deputy-mayor of American cities. The council
may go outside its own membership, and indeed outside its own city,
to choose these officers. But the choice is always subject to the approval of the Emperor,—a reservation that does not seem to have
been exercised with arbitrary power.

The especial working-force of the council consists of thirty magistrates, chosen from the membership of the council by its own vote,
subject to the approval of the Governor of the Province of Branden-
burg, in which the city of Berlin is situated. These magistrates do
not sit as members of the council, but in a separate chamber. The
council and magistrates are not, however, in the relation of a lower
and an upper house; for all the standing committees are chosen from
the council at large, including both magistrates and non-magistrates.
The magistrates pass all laws for the government of the city. The
council, in its sittings, acts as a deliberative body, and may present
matters for the consideration of the body of magistrates; but it may
not pass laws. Fifteen of the thirty magistrates are paid officials, experts in their particular lines, who are chosen on account of their fitness to carry on administrative work. They spend all their time in
the service of the city, for which they receive salaries ranging from
$1,750 to $3,750 per annum. These members fill important positions
on the various standing committees; the most important being those
on buildings, streets and roadways, sanitation, hospitals and drainage,
lighting, cleaning, water-supply, parks, markets, common schools, care
of the poor, police, and finances. These committees do the great work

of city government, each furnishing a report of its specific department. It will thus be seen that the public functions of the city are great: the expenditures are consequently large. The corporation expends annually more than $20,000,000 for the government; which is not excessive, when it is considered that part of the revenue is derived from the proceeds of public works, such as water, gas, slaughter-houses, and markets. The successful conduct of so large a corporation requires much business ability. Everything is so closely accounted for, and the records are so fully published, that a rate-payer may obtain at any time a true statement of the business condition of the municipality.

The police regulations of Berlin are under the supervision of the royal power. The chief of police (*Ober-präsident*) is a royal officer, who has control of the entire system. The main body or ordinary policemen are supported by funds derived from state taxes. They have the charge of enforcing all municipal laws and rates, the management of all licences, the overseeing of street traffic and travel, the abatement of nuisances, and the bringing to justice of all offenders against the common weal. In addition to the regular police there are night watchmen, who are paid by the city, and are employed especially for the care of property. The system is carefully organized; and every precaution is taken to insure protection to property and person.

In Berlin every person is expected to keep his place; and he usually does so. If out of place, he is not long in finding it out through official notification. On entering the city,—even for a short residence,—persons must make a declaration of age, nationality, place of birth, residence, domicile, and occupation, and must state expressly the purpose for which they have come to the city. On leaving, they must also make a declaration as to whither they are going and for what purpose. Even guests at the hotels make out on arrival a similar statement, which is delivered to the police. This makes it possible to locate any resident in the city within a few minutes.

A great many people complain of German officialism, which is obnoxious to their sense of freedom. Indeed there is a saying that it is considered a misdemeanor to laugh in Berlin. Certainly there is a reverence among German officers for even the letter of the law which is frequently carried to an annoying extent. Yet careful inquiry shows that this arises more from a desire to perform a duty conscientiously than from mere snobbishness. In no other country is the devotion to duty so evident as among the serious, law-adoring Prussians. While affairs move slowly, they move surely; and it can be depended upon

44

that everything needful will be done, and that no mistakes will be made. Every department of the city government exhibits thoroughness and honesty. Men in office are public servants,—which in Germany means that they are to serve the public and not especially themselves and their friends. If lofty ideals of justice and of the majesty of law and order, devotion to duty, and a reverence for the letter of the law lead to a little over-officialism, it should be readily excused.

The methods of communication in Berlin are excellent. The postal system is exceedingly prompt and accurate. In addition to the regular service, there is a subordinate system for carrying small parcels and heavy mail at a cheaper rate. For this purpose separate boxes for depositing packages are established at convenient distances. A convenient device for the transmission of letters is the pneumatic tube, by means of which letters are sent rapidly from one station to another. These, together with the public telephone and telegraph, make the means of city communication complete.

The facilities of travel in Berlin are fairly good. Cabs are still much in evidence, there being about 8,000 registered in the city. The system is excellent, the rates moderate. A very good horse-car system is still in use, electricity having been only partially introduced. The horse-car company performs its work under a city charter with many limitations. It is held to strict accountability in everything. To prevent accidents, the car-lines have regular halting-places or stations at which passengers take the cars. These stations are usually at a short distance from cross-streets. Each car is allowed to carry only a limited number of passengers,—just so many as can comfortably sit within, or stand on the platform. Each car bears a plain inscription designating the number of seats and standing-places; and when the car is full the conductor is not allowed to take on more. This prevents overcrowding, and forces the company to provide an ample supply of cars.

The elevated railroad is built across the city, curving to stations in the most important localities. This connects with a circuit or belt-road which joins the most important suburban towns to the city. These roads are well built and exceedingly well managed. They do an enormous business; the ordinary fare being the same as the horse-car fare; viz., two and one-half cents.

One is impressed with the thoroughness of all public constructions, whether erected by the city directly or by the companies obtaining a franchise. In the construction of street railway-tracks, a solid foundation is made, upon which is laid cement six or seven inches deep, made perfectly smooth at the surface. Upon this are laid heavy rails seven inches high, which are connected by iron bands securely bolted, thus making the road one continuous piece of iron. About the rails is laid more cement, which is brought nearly to the top. Finally, a layer of asphalt brings the surface of the road exactly even with the top of the rails so that a carriage may cross without any jar. As the top of the rail is double, the wheels of the train run in a groove; and this, with the firm foundation, enables the cars to travel without jolting or noise.

The maintenance of streets is carried on with the same thoroughness. The streets of Berlin are well-constructed and kept in perfect repair. As much care is exercised in the construction of a street as by a carpenter in making a table, or a watchmaker in making a watch. The result is that, with a good foundation and perfect construction, the road lasts a long time. Nearly all the streets are of first-class asphalt. A large proportion of the remainder are of granite blocks about eight inches square. These are laid on a solid, smooth foundation; sand is driven into the crevices, and, finally, melted asphalt is poured in, cementing the whole together in an impervious layer.

The repairing and cleaning of streets are carefully provided for. The smallest seam in the asphalt or the slightest unevenness in the granite pavement is immediately repaired. Nearly all the repairs on the principal streets are carried on at night. Pieces of pavement that would be called good in New York are taken up and new pieces are laid. This is true economy; for it prevents the street from reaching a state of decay. The streets are cleaned by day and by night. Everywhere in the daytime are to be seen the uniformed army of street-cleaners. The sweepings are placed in openings at the sides of the streets, and are carted away at night. After eleven o'clock, sweeping-machines are used on some of the principal streets. The asphalt is sometimes flooded and swept with rubber brooms until it is as clean as a kitchen-floor after scrubbing-day.

The sanitation of Berlin is complete. Rigid rules are enforced with reference to garbage and sewage. Large quantities of disinfectants and deodorizers are used by the city, and furnished to private individuals free of charge. A perfect system of sewerage is maintained, which conduces greatly to the public health. From the different parts of the city the water from closets, baths, and kitchens, as well as the surface-water of the streets, is conducted through a system of sewers to central stations along the Spree, situated at the lowest elevation of the city. Here the sewage is collected in large central reservoirs. From these reservoirs it is forced by means of large pumps through great iron tubes into the country. It then passes into central stand-towers and is thence distributed, through a system of irrigation pipes and ditches, upon the land. Thus the sewage of the city becomes the fertilizer of the land, which produces fruits and vegetables for city consumption. The soil upon which the sewage is thrown is a sandy loam, quite pervious to water. Hence when the sewage is deposited, the soil acts as a filter, retaining all the solid particles and allowing the water to pass off in a comparatively pure state. A system of underground tiling is used to collect the water and return it again by small streams into the Spree. The use of antiseptics and disinfectants, and the contact of the sewage with air, sunlight, and soil remove all unhealthful conditions from the sewage-farms. The people who live on them are unusually healthy; and the hospitals of Berlin have established convalescent homes upon the farms. The peasants drink the water after filtration without any evil effects.

Before the adoption of the present system of canalization, the people of Berlin lived in much discomfort, being subject to the ravages of all sorts of contagious and miasmatic diseases. The city had rapidly grown without furnishing the means of comfort, or even common decency, to the people. But since 1875 the health of the city has improved at a ratio almost constant with the increase of the sewer system. The total death-rate has declined from 30.9 to 18.47 per thousand. The death-rate by typhus fever has been reduced from 7.7 to 0.69 per thousand.

Were Victor Hugo now living he could not complain of Berlin, as he did of Paris, that the sea is impoverishing the land by drawing off its fertilizers; for drainage in the former city yields a revenue. The city sewer system transports annually from 60,000,000 to 70,000,000 cubic metres of sewage for distribution over the broad acres lying seven to fifteen miles from the city. The area of the fields irrigated is more than 20,000 acres; or greater than the present area of the city, which is twenty-five miles. The total cost of the drainage system is about $25,000,000; and it is estimated that it will take $5,000,000 more to complete it. Yet, owing to the enormous yield of the irrigated land, it will soon return a revenue on first cost, and pay for the investment besides. As many as five crops of hay are cut in a single year; and several crops of vegetables are obtained each season.

The sewage-fields are divided into three classes: first, the most fertile fields, which are let out to market-gardeners, who supply fruits and vegetables to the city; second, the less fertile fields, suitable for raising vegetables and grains, and partly rented to peasant farmers and partly exploited by the city; third, the poorer lands used for grazing purposes and for hay. These are kept wholly under the management of the corporation, and are rapidly becoming more valuable through fertilization, cultivation, and general improvements.

One of the excellent features of the sanitary system of Berlin is the establishment of public lavatories at the corners of parks and at the intersection of thoroughfares. They are a great public convenience, and indeed are indispensable to the health and comfort of the people of any modern European city. These well-built and scrupulously kept institutions are managed by women. The accommodations are of two classes, first and second, for which are paid two and one-half and one and one-fourth cents respectively. In the first-class apartments soap, towels, comb, and brush are furnished. Perhaps this custom of providing lavatories has arisen on account of the conditions of the densely populated cities of the Old World, where different ideas of modesty and cleanliness from those in our own country prevail. At any rate, if the provisions for cleanliness and comfort are of such avail in Berlin and other European cities, they should also be of value in American cities. Small as it may appear, there is no feature of the sanitary government of Berlin that adds more to its health and comfort than this one.

The water-supply of the city is ample and pure. In 1873, the municipality, obtaining control of the water-supply, began to build a new system. Elaborate plants were established for taking the water from the broad, shallow lakes of the Spree and the Havel. The water is conveyed to the filtration-fields, where it is made pure by sand filtration. The process of filtration is mechanical, chemical, and bacteriological; so that all noxious elements are extracted from it. After this it passes into reservoirs and is thence distributed to the consumers in the city. The water-supply of a city is said to be a measure of its civilization. Certainly Berlin has been amply rewarded for its immense outlay in furnishing an abundant supply of pure water, which has contributed in every way to the health and comfort of the entire city. At present the plant is able to furnish 40,000,000 cubic metres per annum. The enterprise has proved a paying investment; for the income from private consumers covers all expenses of operation, interest, and first cost, and pays into the sinking-fund more than $600,000 per annum. The city has little trouble in collecting rents, as the water is sold to consumers by meter. Nearly all the people of Berlin live in tenement flats. When a meter is placed in a house but one charge is made and that to the owner of the house.   This saves much trouble and waste, as the landlords look after the tenants.

The city is supplied with light partly by public and partly by private enterprise.   The first gas company was established in 1827. In 1847, the city began to build its own plant and to compete with the private company.   The result of this competition was a reduction in the price of gas of 50 per cent.   The growing city furnished abundant room for the prosperity of both systems and they exist to-day in friendly rivalry.   This is quite remarkable; as it has been held by some economic philosophers that a public institution cannot successfully compete with a private one.   To private consumers gas is one dollar per thousand cubic feet.   In 1893, the city plant, after meeting all expenses, turned a net revenue of $1,250,000 into the public treasury.

In 1893, the city granted a franchise to an electric-light company; and some of the principal streets, squares, and public buildings are now lighted by electricity.   It is interesting to note, in this-connection, with what care the city guards the rights of the people in granting franchises. In the first place, the company must pay into the city treasury 10 per cent of the gross receipts.   It must furnish two central avenues with light at a nominal cost.   Its territory of operation is clearly defined; and it is compelled to put down main wires within a short time, specified in the contract.   The city may extend its street-lighting at any time at nominal rates charged by the company.   The books of the company are always open to the inspection of the public officials.   The company is bound by strict rules relative to the tearing up of streets and the laying of wires, and is limited to certain fixed charges to customers, which cannot be changed without the consent of the city council.   And finally, the city requires a deposit for security of $42,500, and requires the company to keep a renewal fund equal to 20 per cent of the invested capital.   This fund is in the form of Berlin municipal bonds, and must be kept on deposit with the city magistrates.   In addition to all this, the city reserves the right to purchase the entire plant at any time at a fair valuation, as provided in the contract.

Another interesting manner in which the city manages its contracts is shown in the street-railway franchise.   The city directs all new additions, and causes the company to pay a bonus for each separate franchise.   The company must also pay annually into the city treasury a percentage on its gross income : this rate increases with the development of business.   The minimum rate was fixed at 4 per cent; but the company is now paying nearly 8, which yields an annual payment of more than $250,000.   The company is bound by strict regulations respecting the cleaning and repairing of the streets over which its tracks are laid.   What is most remarkable is, that in 1911 the entire plant passes into the possession of the city free of expense.   It seems almost incredible that companies can flourish under such restrictions; but they appear to do so.   The manner in which the city manages franchises and contracts gives evidence of financial, legal, and business ability, which contrasts strikingly with the manner in which some of our American cities have in the past allowed companies to write their own franchises.

Among the excellent features of Berlin government are the public markets and slaughter-houses.   The suffering of the people on account of diseased meat caused the city to build a central cattle-market and slaughter-house, and to connect them with a thorough system of meat inspection.   The entire establishment covers about twenty-seven acres. The whole area is laid in cement; and the chief building is constructed of brick and stone.   Every precaution to ensure cleanliness is taken. The cattle brought to the market are fed and carefully provided for. The slaughter-house is conducted by the city; and all meats used in the city, whether of domestic or foreign origin, must be brought here for microscopical inspection.   Expert microscopists are employed. Everything is carried on with characteristic thoroughness, and so arranged that there is no delay in getting the meat on the market. All butchers and dealers are greatly pleased with the entire arrangement, and have no desire to revert to the former chaotic state of affairs.   The business pays the city 4 per cent on the first cost.   Meat is not the only food inspected by the government.   Indeed nearly everything, from beer to bread, that is manufactured in Berlin must bear the inspector's stamp before it is pronounced genuine.   But the stamp once affixed, there is no question as to the quality of the article.

It is difficult to mention all the good qualities of Berlin government.   The public squares and parks are greatly enjoyed by the people.   The Thiergarten is a large, densely wooded park in which the Berliners take especial delight.   In the summer season, its drives are filled with carriages, its walks occupied by pedestrians, its riding-roads much used by horsemen, and its immense play-grounds thronged with children and nurses.   And not a leaf or flower suffers from the multitudes that wander amid its beautiful foliage.   In this garden the benches are free; but in the smaller squares the chairs cannot be used until a five-pfennig piece is dropped in the slot: the chair then unlocks and can be occupied as long as desired.

The public hospitals are worthy of note. They are at present prepared to accommodate 3,000 patients. Some of the more modern are fully equipped with all recent appliances and conveniences, and are perfect in sanitation and ventilation. Eminent men, such as Virchow, Koch, and Martin, who have accomplished so much for the science of medicine, have brought the Berlin hospitals into prominent notice; but a more detailed statement cannot be given here. Mention should however be made of the excellent feature of establishing convalescent homes for patients. It was found that when patients were discharged they were too weak to earn a living, and consequently drifted into pauperism or relapsed into disease. Hence homes were established where they could work, according to their strength, until fully recovered.

In the care of the poor Berlin excels. There are few idlers in the city; and there is little poverty in sight. Formerly the poor lived in the basements of buildings; but these residences, where below the drainage-pipes, have been abandoned as unwholesome. The people are now housed in tolerable comfort. There are more than a thousand different institutions in Berlin for the care of the poor. Part of these are private and part public enterprises; but nearly all are conducted with a view to lessen pauperism,—not to increase it. One of the most interesting of all institutions is the labor colony, where men out of employment are furnished shelter and labor until they obtain permanent work.

The supervision of the erection of public and private buildings in Berlin prevents loose and shabby work and insures safe and sanitary construction. A standing law prevents the construction of buildings over five stories high, or four with the ground-floor. This gives a monotonous appearance to the streets, but insures uniformity. Rigorous laws relating to sewer connection and drainage are enforced; and a constant inspection of water-supply and drainage is exercised by the officials. Public buildings are constructed with the utmost care and thoroughness. The new Reichstag building and the City Hall are excellent representations of modern architecture.

Upon the whole it may be said that the business of the city is conducted with economy and profit. Whatever is necessary to be done is carried out regardless of expense; but there is no waste: nothing is done in the dark. Every detail of public works is planned, and every item of expense is estimated before the work begins. The plans, once adopted, are followed out with scientific exactness. Enquiring into the causes of Berlin's success, it will be found that the theory which American municipal reformers have been urging, that a city is a business corporation and should be conducted on business and not on political principles, is everywhere in evidence. The city insists that business men shall be placed on the council, and that specialists and experts shall be in charge of the various departments. It is considered a post of honor to be elected to the city council; and prominent lawyers, eminent statesmen, and business men are numbered among its membership. Those who fail to serve after election are fined. It is interesting to observe with what zeal the members, paid and unpaid alike, pursue the work of public administration, and with what energy private citizens coöperate in city affairs. Recognizing two kinds of institutions, those that yield revenue and those that yield no revenue, such as schools and hospitals, the officials insist that the former shall pay an income and that the latter shall be conducted with economy.

Another cause of the success of Berlin is its power of administration. In Berlin, when things are planned and ordered they are done; slowly perhaps, but surely and without delay. With a perfect system of administration like that of Berlin, a city may do anything it chooses for the welfare of the people and make an eminent success of it. The amount of service which the city has undertaken is well represented in the following paragraph from Dr. Shaw:

"The German city holds itself responsible for the education of all, for the provision of amusement, and the means of recreation; for the adaptation of the training of the young to the necessities of gaining a livelihood; for the health of families; for the moral interests of all; for the civilizing of the people; for the promotion of individual thrift; for protection against various misfortunes; for the development of advantages and opportunities in order to promote the industrial and commercial well-being of the community; and incidentally for the supply of the common services and introduction of conveniences. All this Berlin does, and does it in such a way as to earn for it the name of the best-governed city in the world."

Some think it too much governed; but, so long as the well-being of all the people is sought and maintained, so long as thrift, economy, and a perfect system of administration are maintained, how can there be too much government? Can people do too much for themselves, if everything is excellently done?

FRANK W. BLACKMAR.

THE FUTURE OF THE RED MAN.

OFTEN in the stillness of the night, when all nature seems asleep about me, there comes a gentle rapping at the door of my heart. I open it; and a voice inquires, "Pokagon, what of your people? What will their future be?" My answer is: "Mortal man has not the power to draw aside the veil of unborn time to tell the future of his race. That gift belongs to the Divine alone. But it is given to him to closely judge the future by the present and the past." Hence, in order to approximate the future of our race, we must consider our natural capabilities and our environments, as connected with the dominant race which outnumbers us—three hundred to one—in this land of our fathers.

First, then, let us carefully consider if Mis-ko-au-ne-ne-og' (the red man) possesses, or is devoid of, loyalty, sympathy, benevolence, and gratitude,—those 'heaven-born virtues requisite for Christian character and civilization. But, in doing so, let us constantly bear in mind that the character of our people has always been published to the world by the dominant race, and that human nature is now the same as when Solomon declared that "He that is first in his own cause seemeth just; but his neighbor cometh and searcheth him." In our case we have ever stood as dumb to the charges brought against us as did the Divine Master before His false accusers; hence all charges alleged against us in history should be cautiously considered, with Christian charity. There have been, and still are, too many writers who, although they have never seen an Indian in their lives, have published tragical stories of their treachery and cruelty. Mothers, for generations past, have frightened their children into obedience with that dreaded scarecrow, "Look out, or the Injuns will get you!"; creating in the infant mind a false prejudice against our race, which has given birth to that base slander, "There is no good Injun but a dead one." It is therefore no wonder that we are hated by some worse than Satan hates the salvation of human souls.

Let us glance backward to the year 1492. Columbus and his officers and crew are spending their first Christmas on the border-islands of the New World. It is not a merry, but a sad, Christmas to them. They stand crowded on the deck of the tiny ship "Niña." Four weeks since, Pinson, with the "Pinta" and her crew, deserted the squadron; and last night the flagship, "Santa Maria," that had safely borne the Admiral across an unknown sea to a strange land, was driven before the gale and stranded near the shore of Hispaniola. Deserted by her crew ·and left to the mercy of the breakers, she lies prostrate on the perilous sands, shivering and screaming in the wind like a wounded creature of life responsive to every wave that smites her.

It is early morning. Columbus sends Diego de Arna and Pedro Guthene to the great Chief of the Island, telling him of their sad disaster, and requesting that he come and help to save their goods from being swept into the sea. The Chief listens with all attention to the sad news; his heart is touched; he answers with-his tears; and orders his people to go at once, with their canoes well manned, and help to save the stranger's goods. He also sends one of his servants to the Admiral with a message of sincere regrets for his misfortunes, offering all the aid in his power. Columbus receives the servant on shipboard; and, while he listens with gratitude to the cheering message delivered in signs and broken words, he rejoices to see coming to his relief along the shore a hundred boats, manned by a thousand men, mostly naked, bearing down upon the wrecked "Santa Maria," and swarming about her like bees around their hive. The goods disappear from the ship as by magic, are rowed ashore, and safely secured. Not one native takes advantage of the disaster for his own profit. Spanish history declares that in no part of the civilized world could Columbus have received warmer or more cordial hospitality.

Touched by such tender treatment, Columbus, writing to the King and Queen of Spain, pays this beautiful tribute to the native Carib race:—

"They are a loving, uncovetous people, so docile in all things that I swear to your Majesties there is not in all the world a better race, or more delightful country. They love their neighbors as themselves; their talk is ever sweet and gentle, accompanied with smiles; and though they be naked, yet their manners are decorous and praiseworthy."

Peter Martyr, a reliable historian, has left on record the following:—

"It is certain the land among these people is as common as sun and water, and that 'mine and thine,' the seed of all misery, have no place with them. They are content with so little that in so large a country they have rather a superfluity than a scarceness, so that they seem to live in the golden world, without toil, living in open gardens not intrenched or defended with walls. They deal justly one with another without books, without laws, without judges. They take him for an evil and mischievous man who taketh pleasure in doing hurt to another ; and although they delight not in superfluities, yet they make provision for the increase of such roots whereof they make bread, content with such simple diet wherewith health is preserved and disease avoided."—(PETER MARTYR, Decade 1, Book 3.)

Does not this quotation most emphatically show that the red men of the New World did originally possess every virtue necessary for Christian civilization and enlightenment?

The question is often asked, What became of the numerous Caribs of those islands? They seemed to have vanished like leaves in autumn ; for within a few years we find them supplanted by foreign slaves. The noble Bishop Las Casas tells us, in pity, " With mine own eyes, I saw kingdoms as full of people as hives are of bees ; and now, where are they?" Almost all, he says, have perished by the sword and under the lash of cruel Spanish taskmasters, in the greedy thirst for gold.

Certain it is that in those days, which tried the souls of the Carib race, some fled from the lust and lash of their oppressors by sea to the coast of Florida, and reported to the natives there that Wau-be-au'-ne-ne-og' (white men), who fought with Awsh-kon-tay' Au-ne-me-kee' (thunder and lightning), who were cruel, vindictive, and without love, except a thirsty greed for gold, had come from the other side of Kons-ke-tchi-saw-me' (the ocean) and made slaves of Mis-ko-au-ne-ne-og' (the red man) of the islands, which was reported from tribe to tribe across the continent.

Scarcely a quarter-century passes since the enslavement of the Carib race, and Ponce de Leon, a Spanish adventurer, is landing from his squadron a large number of persons to colonize the coast of Florida. A few years previously, while in pursuit of the fountain of youth, he had been here for the first time, on the day of the "Feast of Flowers." Then, he was kindly received and welcomed by the sons of the forest. Now, as then, the air is perfumed with the odor of fruits and flowers ; and all on shore appears pleasing and inviting. The Spaniards land, and slowly climb the terrace that bounds the sea. Here they pause, planting side by side the Spanish standard and the cross. But hark! War-whoops are heard close by. And there they come,—long lines of savages from the surrounding woods, who, with slings and darts, with clubs and stones, fall upon the dreaded Spaniards. The onslaught is terrible. Many are killed ; and Ponce de Leon is mortally wounded. He now begins to realize that among the savage hosts are Caribs who have escaped from slavery and death. He well knows the bitter story of their wrong, and that this bloody chastisement is but the returning boomerang of Spanish cruelty. They flee from the avengers of blood to the ships. The report they give of the savage attack, on their return to Spain, is so terrible that years pass before another attempt is made to colonize the land of fruits and flowers.

I deem it unnecessary to explain why these peaceful natives so soon became so warlike and vindictive. Suffice it to say : " Enslave a good man and, like the wasp which stings the hand that holds it fast, he will make use of all the means which nature has placed in his power to regain his liberty." During the first century of American history, many adventurers from different European countries sailed along the eastern coast of North America,—all reporting the natives peaceable and kind when not misused.

There was a tradition among our fathers that, before the colonization of North America, an armed band of Wau-be-au'-ne-ne-og' (white men), gorgeously clad, came on the war-path from the East, reaching the Dakotas, which then extended south as far as the mouth of the Arkansas River; that they were vindictive and cruel, destroying the natives wherever they went with Awsh-kon-tay' Au-ne-me-kee' (thunder and lightning). They were looking for gold, their Man-i-to (god), and, not finding him, went down Mi-che-se-pe (the great river) and were seen no more. Those cruel adventurers, who came among us by sea and land, must have awakened hatred and revenge in the hearts of our fathers, which may have been transmitted to their children.

It should be borne in mind that several European Powers colonized this continent about the same period, among whom the English and French took the lead. Settlements were mostly made along the Atlantic coast, which was then occupied by the Algonquin family,[1] to which my tribe—the Pottawattamies—belong: they seem to have had a common origin and common language. For a time the two races lived in peace. The French in Canada seemed naturally to assimilate with our people, many of whom received the Catholic faith. In course of time there were many marriages between the two races; and we began to look upon the great King of France as our invincible sovereign: for we were taught that he was king of all kings except the King of Wau-

---

[1] It is estimated that at the beginning of the seventeenth century the Algonquins numbered at least 250,000. Their survivors number probably not more than 30,000. Originally they occupied nearly all that portion of Canada and the United States lying west of the Mississippi River. They suffered more from advancing civilization than all the other tribes.

kwing' (heaven). Their priests were devoted to their work; visiting all the tribes of the south and west, followed by French traders, planting the cross, the lilies, and the shield side by side. The tribes firmly believed that the land belonged to their great king who loved them and would, if necessary, fight their battles for them. With the exception of William Penn,[1] who settled Pennsylvania, the English who colonized the United States did not seem to have the tact of the French in their dealings with us. They were less liberal with presents, and apparently less united in their religious belief. They were not so successful as the French in obtaining native converts; although some good ministers, like Roger Williams, did much to unite the races in brotherhood, and thereby delayed the final struggle.

Inroads were being continually made into Taw-naw-ke-win' (our native land); and in seeking new homes we found ourselves invading the hunting-grounds of other tribes. The warlike Iroquois of New York would not even allow the eastern tribes to pass through their country,—as a result, our forefathers seemed compelled to make a stand against the advance of the incoming race. In doing so, our villages were laid waste with fire, our people slaughtered and burned by white warriors who seemed without number for multitude. Our fathers finally gave up the contest. Some, to avoid the Iroquois, went West through Canada. Others went West through Pennsylvania, meeting in Indiana, Michigan, and Wisconsin, then known as Indian Territory, where we found French priests and traders, who gave us a hearty welcome, assuring us that we should remain safe with them. In course of time the English, finding the French traders posted along the western frontier, gave them to understand that the land they occupied belonged to the English, as well as the right to buy fur from the natives. Hence the so-called French and Indian War was inaugurated, in the course of which many outrages were committed on the frontiers,—*all of them being charged to the Indians.* During this war a manifold tin box of curious make was found in a large village called Wa-gaw-naw-kee-zee', which lay along Lake Michigan, between Little Traverse Bay and the Straits of Mackinaw. The unsuspecting Indians opened it, and in the innermost box found a mouldy substance. Soon after, the smallpox—a disease unknown to our fathers—broke out among them; and O-daw-yo-e-waw' Da-dodse-ses' (their medicine men) all

---

[1] It is said that the treaty made by William Penn with the Indians was the only treaty never sworn to and never broken, and that during seventy years not a war-whoop was sounded in Pennsylvania.

died. In fact every one taking the disease died. Lodge after lodge was filled with unburied dead. The great village was entirely depopulated. Our fathers thought the disease was sent among them by the English because the Indians had helped the French during that war. I have passed over the ancient site of this village. Its bounds are clearly marked by second-growth forests, which now cover it. It is fifteen miles long and from one to two miles wide.

Almost on the heels of this war, after France had ceded her rights to the English, came the Revolutionary war. Our people had just begun to learn that they owed allegiance to the British, who had conquered our invincible French King. They had seen the Bourbon flag taken down from the western forts, and replaced by the red cross of St. George; and they were compelled to shout, "Long live the King,—King George who rules from the Arctic Ocean to the Gulf of Mexico."

We now began selling furs to our new masters; receiving in exchange dry-goods and Awsh-kon-tay' Ne-besh (fire-water), when we were called upon again to take the war-path, to aid our new king in subduing his rebellious colonies. We could not serve two masters at the same time; hence remained loyal to our new king, while the Iroquois of New York and Canada were divided. And so it was that all the dirty, cruel work of war between the revolutionists and the mother country was laid at the door of our people, whose mouths were dumb to defend or justify themselves in respect of the outrages charged against them. These outrages were generally planned, and frequently executed, by white men, as was, in after years, the Mountain Meadow Massacre, of Mormon notoriety, for which also we were persecuted and suffered untold disgrace.

I always think of my people in those days as the dog kept by the schoolmaster to be whipped whenever a child disobeyed. During the war of 1812 we were again incited through English influence to take the war-path. Proctor, the English general of the Northwest, said to our heroic Tecumseh, "Assemble all your warriors together, join forces with us, and we will drive the Americans beyond the Ohio River, and Michigan shall be yours forever." Such a promise, from so high an authority, awakened all the native energies of our being to regain our liberty and homes, for which we had been contending against overpowering forces.

The Ottawas and Chippeways of the north, the Pottawattamies and Miamies of the south, and other tribes gathered themselves together to make the last desperate effort to regain the promised land. In this war our cause was far more sacred to us than was the Americans' to them. They had drawn the sword in defence of *one* of their rights; we, for *all of ours;* for our very existence, for our native land, and for the graves of our fathers, most sacred to our race.

The last engagement in which the confederated Algonquin tribes fought the Americans was at the battle of the Thames in Canada, on October 5, 1813, where we and the English were defeated by General Harrison, and General Tecumseh,[1] our brave leader, was killed.

After this battle our fathers became fully convinced that the small remnant of their tribes must either accept extermination, or such terms as their enemy saw fit to give. So they sued for peace; and the American warriors, uplifted by victory, and our Algonquin fathers, bowed down by defeat, stood around the grave of the hatchet—buried forever—and smoked the pipe of peace together.

At one time I felt that our race was doomed to extermination. There was an awful unrest among the western tribes who had been pushed by the cruel march of civilization into desert places, where subsistence was impossible. Starvation drove many to steal cattle from adjacent ranches; and when some of our people were killed by the cowboys, their friends were determined to take the war-path. I never failed on such occasions to declare most emphatically, " You might as well march your warriors into the jaws of an active volcano, expecting to shut off its fire and smoke, as to attempt to beat back the westward trend of civilization. You must teach your sons everywhere that the war-path will lead them but to the grave."

[1] At the time of this battle, Tecumseh was a brigadier-general in the English army, with Proctor. I have seen in United States histories pictures of Tecumseh, tomahawk in hand about to strike a soldier named Johnson, who claimed that he shot the dreaded chief with his pistol. But I have repeatedly heard old Indian warriors say : " After the British infantry gave way, they came to an open or clear spot in the woods, and here Tecumseh ordered his men to halt and fight the Americans once more. Just then the open space was swept by American musketry ; and Tecumseh fell, saying, ' Me-daw-yo-em' o-kawd' (My leg is shot off). Hand me two loaded guns. I will have the last shot. Maw-tchawn' we-wib' (Be quick and go).' These were the last words of Tecumseh." Our fathers believed that neither the Americans nor the Indians knew who fired the fatal shot.

My father, Leopold Pokagon, had been a Pottawattamie chief thirteen years before this battle, and so remained until his death, twenty-seven years after. Most of his band were sent West in 1837. He and some five hundred of his people, having embraced Christianity, were permitted to remain in Michigan. In 1866, they numbered three hundred and fifty : nearly all were of pure Indian blood. At the present time, they number two hundred and seventy-one : nearly one-half are of mixed blood.

Having briefly reviewed some of our past history, the fact must be admitted that, when the white men first visited our shores, we were kind and confiding; standing before them like a block of marble before the sculptor, ready to be shaped into noble manhood. Instead of this, we were oftener hacked to pieces and destroyed. We further find in our brief review that the contending Powers of the Old World, striving for the mastery in the New, took advantage of our trustful, confiding natures, placing savage weapons of warfare in our hands to aid us in butchering one another.

It is useless to deny the charge, that at times we have been goaded to vindictive and cruel acts. Some of my own tribe, however, were soldiers in the Northern army during the civil war. Some of them were taken, and held prisoners in the rebel prisons, and the cruelty which, according to the tales they tell, was witnessed there was never outdone in border warfare with the scalping-knife and tomahawk. And yet I believe that, had the Northern people been placed in the South under like circumstances, their prisoners of war would have been treated with similar cruelty. It was the result of a *desperate* effort to save an expiring cause. I believe there is no reasonable person, well grounded in United States history, who will not admit that there were ten times as many who perished miserably in Southern prisons as have been killed by our people since the discovery of America. I recall these facts not to censure, but to show that *cruelty and revenge are the offspring of war, not of race,* and that nature has placed no impassable gulf between us and civilization.

It is claimed that the United States have paid out five hundred million dollars in trying to subdue the red man by military force. But now—thank Heaven!—through the influence of good men and women who have thrown the search-light of the golden rule into the great heart of the nation, her policy is changed. Where hundreds of thousands of dollars were paid out annually to fight him, like sums are now being paid yearly to educate him in citizenship and self-support; that his children may not grow up a race of savages to be again fought and again cared for at the expense of the nation. I rejoice in the policy now being pursued. If not perfect, it is certainly on the right trail to success.

While a guest at Chicago, during the World's Fair, I spent much time at the United States Indian School. There I met many delegations from different governmental schools. I was particularly interested in the delegation from Albuquerque, New Mexico, composed
45

of Navajos, Pinas-Mojaves, Pueblos, and others. · With pride I examined the articles which they had made, their clean, well-kept writing-books, and listened to their sweet vocal and instrumental music. I then and there said, in my heart: "Thanks to the Great Spirit, I do believe the remnant of our race will yet live and learn to compete with the dominant race; proving themselves worthy of the highest offices in the gift of a free people."

The Indian school at Carlisle, Pennsylvania, has done wonders in showing what can be effected for the education of our children. The test there made is a reliable one, inasmuch as that school is made up of pupils from more than sixty different tribes, from all parts of the United States. I was highly gratified a few months ago to learn that the foot-ball team from that school was able to defeat the champion Wisconsin team at Chicago, receiving many compliments from the immense crowd for their tact and self-control as well as for their physical development, —showing conclusively that our race is not, as some claim, becoming enfeebled and running out.

While I most heartily indorse the present policy of the Government in dealing with our people, I must admit—to be true to my own convictions—that I am worried over the ration system, under which so many of our people are being fed on the reservations. I greatly fear it may eventually vagabondize many of them beyond redemption. It permits the gathering of lazy, immoral white men of the worst stamp, who spend their time in idleness and in corrupting Indian morality. I do hope the Government will provide something for them to do for their own good, although it should pay her little or nothing. Again: I fear for the outcome of the Indian nations. ˙ Our people in their native state were not avaricious. They were on a common level; and, like the osprey that divides her last fish with her young, so they acted toward each other. But I find, to my sorrow, that, when you associate them with squaw men, and place them in power, they develop the wolfish greed of civilization, disregarding the rights of their less fortunate brothers. I must admit that it staggers my native brain to understand what reason, equity, or justice there is in allowing independent powers to exist within the bounds of this Republic. If the "Monroe doctrine," which has been so much petted of late years, should be enforced anywhere, it would certainly be in the line of good statesmanship to carry it out, at least in principle, at home.

Lastly, Pokagon must admit that he feels very deeply the ravages made among his people by the "intoxicating cup." Were it an open enemy outside our lines, we might meet it with success.   But alas! it is a traitor within our camp, cunning as Wa-goosh (the fox).   It embraces and kisses but to poison like the snake—without the warning rattle.   Before I associated with white men, I had supposed that they were not such slaves to that soulless tyrant as the red· man.   But I have · learned that the cruel curse enslaves alike the white man in his palace and the red man in his hut; alike the chieftain--and the king; the savage and the sage.   I am indeed puzzled to understand how it is that the white race, whose works seem almost divine, should not be able to destroy this great devil-fish, which their own hands have fashioned and launched upon the sea of human life; whose tentacles reach out into the halls of legislature and courts of law, into colleges and churches,—doing everywhere its wicked work.

As to the future of our race, it seems to me almost certain that· in time· it will lose its identity by amalgamation with the dominant race. No matter how distasteful it may seem to us, we are compelled to consider it as a probable result.   Sensitive white people can console themselves, however, with the fact, that there are to-day in the United States thousands of men and women of high social standing whose forefathers on one side were full-blooded so-called savages; and yet the society in · which they move, and in many cases they themselves, are ignorant of the fact.   All white people are not ashamed of Indian blood; in·fact, a few are proud of it. ·

At the World's Fair on Chicago Day, after ringing the new Liberty Bell, and speaking in behalf of my people, I presented Mayor Harrison, according to the programme of the day, with a duplicate of the treaty by which my father, a Pottawattamie chief, in 1833, conveyed Chicago—embracing the fair-grounds and surrounding country—to.the United States for about three cents per acre.   In·accepting the treaty, the venerable Mayor said: "Grateful to the spirit of the past, I am happy to receive this gift from the hand· of one who is able to bestow it. Chicago is proving that it recognizes the benefits conferred through this treaty.   I receive this from an Indian all the more gratefully because in my own veins courses the blood of an Indian.   Before ˜the days of Pokagon, I had my origin in the blood that ran through Pocahontas.   I stand to-day as a living witness that the Indian is worth something in this world." [1]

[1] Certain it is that the families of Harrison, Rolings, Rogers, and many others tinctured with the Indian blood of Pocahontas are superior in health to, and·fully as strong intellectually and morally as, those families from the same branch of

I have made diligent inquiries of the headmen of different tribes as to what estimate they place on the half-breeds among them. Their general reply has been, "They are certainly an improvement on the pale face, but not on the red man." Which no doubt is the case; for it is a lamentable fact that criminals, outlaws, and vagabonds are generally the first who seek homes among us, bringing with them nearly all the vices and diseases, and but few of the virtues, of civilization. Yet, notwithstanding such an unfortunate mixture, we find some grand characters who have been able to rise high above the sins of parentage. I have further found, by close observation, that those tinctured with our blood are far less subject to nervous diseases; but whether at the expense of intellectual force or otherwise, I am not so certain. Be that as it may, we cannot safely ignore the fact, that it is the physical development of the people of a nation that gives it strength and stability; that physical decay brings loss of executive ability, and has proved the overthrow of ancient kingdoms. I do not wish it to be understood that I advocate or desire the amalgamation of our people with the white race. But I speak of it as an event that is almost certain; and we had much better rock with the boat that oars us on than fight against the inevitable. I am frequently asked, "Pokagon, do you believe that the white man and the red man were originally of one blood?" My reply has been: "I do not know. But from the present outlook, they surely will be."

The index-finger of the past and present is pointing to the future, showing most conclusively that by the middle of the next century all Indian reservations and tribal relations will have passed away. Then our people will begin to scatter; and the result will be a general mixing up of the races. Through intermarriage the blood of our people, like the waters that flow into the great ocean, will be forever lost in the dominant race; and generations yet unborn will read in history of the red men of the forest, and inquire, "Where are they?"

SIMON POKAGON.

pure white blood. John Randolph of Roanoke, a near descendant of this Indian woman, and strongly marked with our race lines, was several times Congressman from Virginia, once United States Senator, and minister to Russia. In his time his speeches were more read than any others. His masterly arguments were the pride of his party and the terror of his opponents.

STATESMANSHIP IN ENGLAND AND IN THE UNITED STATES.

A YOUNGSTER who sat next to Coleridge at dinner said: "What do you think of Dr. Channing, Mr. Coleridge?" "Before I enter upon that question," said Coleridge, settling himself into his seat as if for the night, "I must put you in possession of my views *in extenso* on the religion, progress, present condition, future likelihood, and absolute essence of the Unitarian controversy, and establish the conclusions I have, on the whole, come to upon the great question of what may be termed the philosophy of religious difference."

I am to say something about the conditions of statesmanship in England and in the United States. Before entering upon that question I ought, I suppose, if there were time and space, to state my views of the English Constitution, of the American Constitutions,—State and national,—of the relations of the national and federal elements to each other in our form of government, of town-meetings, of the effect that nearly three hundred years on this continent have had on the Englishmen who have come over here, of the effect on our national character of the large admixture of Celtic, Scandinavian, and other races, of the influence of slaveholding in our Southern States, of the distinction between written and unwritten constitutions, of the law of primogeniture, of commercial, manufacturing, and agricultural employment, of the isolation caused by the oceans which separate us from Europe and Asia, of England's neighborhood to other great Powers, of the effect on national character of governing other nations and races, as compared with having a good deal more to do than a people can well do in an attempt to govern itself, together with many other equally important matters too numerous to mention. But the years of a man's life are threescore and ten. And if I were to try to deal adequately with this subject, and by reason of strength should have fourscore years, the years of any person who should read this essay through would be labor and sorrow.

It is possible here to touch upon a few points only. One great change has taken place and is going on both in England and in this country. It comes from the growth of empire. It began in England more than seventy years ago. It has come upon us by reason of our rapid growth in population and in wealth since the War, and by reason of the large number of matters which the more liberal construction of constitutional powers prevailing since slavery was overthrown has required us to deal with. It is nearly impossible now for a statesman who is in power in either country to be the leader of its advanced thought. His whole time and strength must be taken up in dealing with the routine duties of his office. This is true of the President; it is true of the heads of departments; it is true of the leaders of the dominant party in both Houses of Congress; certainly of the members of the Finance Committee of the Senate and of the Ways and Means of the House; of the Committees on Appropriations in either branch; of the members of the great Law Committees. The American statesman of to-day, who is to provide supplies to carry on the routine of our vast Administration, and so regulate economies that the supply may be equal to the demand; to determine the burden and the benefit in every detail of a tariff or a tax as it affects thousands of industries; to understand every part of the complicated mechanism of our government; and who goes to bed every night wearied and worn out with labors and anxieties to which the manager of the largest and most complicated private concern is a stranger, has little room in his life for new schemes, new principles, or new thoughts. The country owes more than it knows to the men of both parties who have, of late years, so conscientiously and faithfully performed the great labor of keeping the machinery of government in operation. But they have performed this honorable service at great cost to themselves. They have been compelled to forsake the paths of a lofty statesmanship, even when they were most fitted for them.

Were Webster, or Clay, or Calhoun alive to-day, his career as a Senator must be, from necessity, of a different character from what it was. His leadership and guidance of the public thought would be exercised by writing or speech elsewhere than in the Senate Chamber. If Benton were living now he would be known only as an insufferable bore. The public business cannot bear the interruption of the great debates of former days. The public is impatient even of discussions which are absolutely necessary. Let some of our modern critics read Benton's story, in his "Thirty Years in the Senate," of the methods by which the desires of the majority were baffled, after the great Whig victory of 1840, and by which a minority overcame the imperious leadership of Henry Clay, and they will cease to contrast unfavorably the legislative methods of to-day with those of our predecessors.

There is one fundamental difference between the conditions in England and in this country. England is still governed by a class of gentry. In one sense the English government is a free and a popular government. But her great political parties are two aristocracies, responsible to the people, and competing for the confidence of the people; yet all the time one or the other keeps the government in its own hands. The English governing classes may be likened to the members of the trained professions,—law, medicine, divinity. Every family is free to choose its own; but the choice is made from the men who are trained to the business. Occasionally there is an interloper in the pulpit, or in the doctor's office, and sometimes, though very rarely, at the bar; but, in the main, you take your professional man from the trained class.

So it has a subduing and restraining effect on political strifes in England, that they are between members of an aristocracy still. holding its place against the masses of the people. The two parties are constantly looking out for their common interests. They never fight to break a bone. Her Majesty's Government has a great respect after all for Her Majesty's Opposition; and neither faction of the gods in England will ever repeat Jupiter's experiment of calling in the giants to put down its antagonists.

We are the only people with any considerable experience of a government of the country by large masses of men. France has been a republic since 1871 only. Most of her political struggles since that date have been struggles to maintain a dynasty. Her political issues have been few in number. England's great suffrage extension was in 1884 and 1885; and still her party contests have been in the main the strifes of aristocratic leaders for power, and not between doctrines or measures determined by the opinion of great numbers of voters.

The English are a deferential people. The Englishman boasts himself of his political equality. But, in the main, John Bull loves a lord, and likes to be governed by a gentleman. This power of the governing class is preserved by the English policy of giving no pay to the Members of the House of Commons; so that nobody but a man of wealth can afford to hold a seat. It is also preserved by England's policy of giving great pay to the holders of her chief executive offices, which as a rule can be reached only through distinction in Parliament. So, while it is rare in England that a poor man can enter the high places of public service, no man who has reached them needs to abandon them from the necessity of getting his living.

The power of the governing classes there is, of course, still preserved by the law of primogeniture. Mr. Webster, in his Plymouth oration, pointed out that the equal division of real property among all the children was the true basis of a popular government; that without it republican government could not exist; and that where that system prevailed a republican government must very soon be established.

I am not able to judge whether the charge of some late English writers be true, that their landed aristocracy is changing into a plutocracy. I think, however, these statements have been much exaggerated. A like charge is frequently made as to this country; but I believe it, also, to be much exaggerated, and that the influence of wealth is, on the whole, diminishing here.

It will be hard to maintain that there is any great difference between Englishmen and Americans by reason of race. The first settlers of this country were Englishmen. Notwithstanding the great admixture of other races,—an admixture chiefly of those Northern races of which England herself was composed,—we are, in all essentials of national character, Englishmen still. Their emigrants who come here lose their distinctive character in a generation; or, if they come in childhood, their nationality cannot be detected after they grow up. It would be difficult for either country to establish the claim to an intellectual superiority over the other. The difference between us is the difference in institutions and local conditions.

The working of the American Constitution is distinguished from that of Great Britain by three influences,—periodicity, locality, and confederacy.

We choose our Chief Magistrate every four years, and the Members of one House of Congress every two years. One-third of the Senators go out of office every two years. The term of office of an individual Senator is six years. The Senate is controlled by a majority of the States. A majority of the people cannot change the policy of the country unless a majority of the States also consent. A Senator must be a citizen of the State from which he is chosen. Thus no change in the popular opinion can compel a change of policy during the four years of the President's term, nor can it compel a change of policy in a body where great and small States meet as equals, unless a majority of the States agree to the change. But the purpose and desire of the numerical majority of the American people may be baffled for twenty years by the local interests and feeling of a majority of the States, and those, perhaps, the smallest in population. This is a conservative principle more powerful than monarch or House of Lords. It is a slow and deliberate process,—it takes a great while,—for this mighty being to change its mind. This country is a compound of nation and confederacy. But in practice the influence of locality is much greater than even obedience to the Constitution demands. I am inclined to think that the operation of this single principle has more to do in distinguishing the public life of America from that of Great Britain than all our written Constitutions, State or national, would have without it.

In spite of the increase of the national authority since the War, many of our conditions are still those which belong to a confederacy. A man does not easily pass from one State to another. There is one instance where the same man—James Shields—represented, at different times, three States in the Senate of the United States; and there is another in our early history—Rufus King, who was Senator from Massachusetts and afterward from New York. But it is most unlikely that these instances will be repeated.

Even before the adoption of the Constitution, many of our States were essentially aggregations of separate towns or municipalities. Very early it was enacted in Massachusetts that the Representative must be an inhabitant of the town from which he was chosen. The consequence of this example has been most far-reaching. Throughout our Constitution, and in all our political habits we deal with separate localities on the principle of an entire equality. The Senators and Representatives in Congress must be citizens of the States they represent. With very few exceptions indeed, Representatives in Congress are taken from the districts where they dwell. The same thing is true of State legislatures. In the choice of Judges of the higher and lower courts, national and State, they are expected to represent fairly the different States and localities. The same thing is true in the formation of the Cabinet, and the selection of nearly one hundred and fifty thousand executive officers.

This necessity for considering locality in the selection of persons for high national offices embarrasses the American people at every step. No man, with rare exception, can have any considerable opportunity for public service, although he may be in accord with an overwhelming majority of his countrymen, unless he also happen to be in accord with the locality in which he dwells. When Mr. Webster was Secretary of State, Mr. Choate was the undisputed head of the American bar, unless Mr. Webster himself were to be excepted. It might easily have happened that, at the same time, the man of all others in the coun-

try fitted for Secretary of the Treasury would also have dwelt in Boston ; or the fittest persons for these three offices might have been found
living together in New York City ; yet it would never have done to make
Choate Attorney-General, or Abbott Lawrence Secretary of the Treasury,
while Webster was in the Department of State. I suppose it would
scarcely cause a remark if the three most important men in the English
Cabinet dwelt next door to each other in London, or had adjoining estates in the country. In England an able public man can be elected to
the House of Commons from any part of the three kingdoms. If he
be valuable to his party, he is entirely independent of the influence of
any one constituency. He can be kept in service for his whole life if
his party need him. This renders an able man who is valuable to his
party entirely independent of the influence of the local constituency.
Thus every able Englishman is sure of continued public service. The
careers of Daniel Webster, Henry Clay, and Charles Sumner would
have been impossible, had they happened to dwell in cities or districts
opposed to them in opinion. New York is the greatest city in the
United States. William M. Evarts was for many years the foremost
living advocate. Yet his national service, so far as it was dependent
on a seat in either House of Congress, lasted but six years. Take the
list of the great lawyers of the United States to-day. See how many
of them, who, if they were Englishmen, would be assured of a permanent place in public life, are almost wholly debarred from an opportunity of political usefulness by the accident of residence.

This gives a power to local prejudices in this country from which
England is almost wholly free. Except the Irish question,—where a difference of race and of religion, centuries of oppression, and, till lately,
a difference of language, have combined with insular position to nour-
ish and keep alive local hatreds,—there is nothing like sectional strife in
the empire of Great Britain. On the other hand, our demagogues still
appeal to the sectional hatred of South against North, or of West
against East. One would think there must be a clause in the Constitutions of some Western and Southern States to the effect that no man
should be eligible to office until he had made in public at least one
bitter attack on the East, and that no man should be continued in
office except on the condition of repeating it at least twice a year.
This is specially true of some communities which, less than a generation
ago, were waste places, and where nearly all their dwellers are natives
of the section they revile. The settler from the East sometimes hastens
eagerly to acquire the necessary qualification.

This condition of things tempts able men, who have a natural and honorable ambition for political office, constantly to watch and yield to the varying moods of special constituencies. In this way men become great political followers, but not great political leaders. This diminishes the permanent power of political parties; but it tends to deprive men of the civic courage which makes them the guides and lights of their age, and likewise deprives such leaders of the power to accomplish their purposes. It would be ungrateful to say what has just been said, without excepting the noble and generous people of Massachusetts from the comprehensiveness of this statement. It has been the beauty and comfort of her public service that she has permitted those whom she has called to it the largest freedom in acting according to their own conscience and their own judgment. She will overlook almost anything in a public man except the violation of his own conscience for the sake of pleasing her.

There is not a man in this country to-day who is secure of an opportunity for official service extending more than six years ahead, except a judge. There are probably not ten men out of the Senate of the United States who have a reasonable expectation of a term even as long.

In England, also, the country can be appealed to at any moment, a new House of Commons chosen, and a new executive brought into power if the old one cease to represent the country on an important measure. In fact, this happens in England on an average about once in four years,—a period corresponding with the interval between our Presidential elections. But it might happen every six months.

This enables England to take up and settle public questions one at a time. First, there is a struggle in the House of Commons. Then there is an appeal to the people. It is rare in England that a question is reopened after it has once been decided by the constituencies. A defeat in the House of Commons overthrows an administration, or the people must be appealed to for a new vote of confidence. The vote of the nation in one election almost always settles the question.

On the other hand, a defeat in either House of Congress, or in both Houses of Congress, even on very important measures, does not overthrow an administration; and the defeat of a party in a national election does not settle a great question. Indeed, we are always disputing what was the significance of a particular vote, and which one of a dozen or twenty matters that were debated on the hustings controlled the popular verdict.

Our constitutional arrangements and the great size of our territory make impracticable here an appeal to the people on single measures, which the ease of a general election makes simple in England.

Every Congress comes to an end, leaving many important measures undisposed of. The effect of this is, that there is a struggle between the leaders of the same party for the opportunity to bring their questions before the body to which they belong. There is no responsible leadership in the Senate, and no responsible leadership in the House, but that of the Speaker, who in theory is absolutely impartial, and in practice almost absolutely despotic. The result is that there is a struggle between the different leading committees for a chance to bring up their measures. Toward the close of the session this contest is specially apparent. A Member who has carefully prepared some important measure with which he is identified in public estimation feels that the success or failure of his political career depends upon his getting an opportunity to bring it to a vote. Statesmen of the same party are often engaged in angry altercations with each other, and in the House are apt to express bitterly their discontent with the Speaker. Many Administration measures fail in every Congress, the defeat of any one of which would have wrecked an English administration.

I think party discipline is much less powerful in the United States than in England. This comes largely from our division of powers into executive, legislative, and judicial. Our committee arrangements, also, in both Houses of Congress, interfere sadly with responsible leadership. And, as I have said, the constant sense of responsibility to local constituencies makes it hard for public men to consult either the highest national good or even the prevailing national desire and opinion. How many measures carefully framed by men to whom the responsibility for them has been assigned are upset by members of the same party with the men who frame them and are responsible for them! How difficult we find it to make a tariff! The Committee of Ways and Means report it: it is all torn to pieces in the House, unless, as in the most recent instance, the House is not trusted to hear it read, and it is passed blindfold under a suspension of the rules. When it comes to the other branch, the patched-up measure is mutilated by the committee of the Senate, and torn to pieces again by the Senate itself.

As I have said, there is not a man in the country to-day who is secure of an opportunity for official service lasting more than six years ahead, excepting a judge. There are probably not ten men out of the Senate of the United States who have a reasonable expectation of a term even so long. Now this insecurity and brevity in the term of public service make the American statesman impatient and in a hurry to accomplish his public purposes. If he be ambitious, he must hasten to make his mark. ·If he have at heart some great measure for the public good, he must accomplish it while he has the power. He must make hay while the sun shines. He must work while it is day; for the night cometh wherein no man can work. This hurry is in strange contrast with the quiet and deliberate security of the Englishman. It puts us at a great disadvantage in legislation and administration.

This disadvantage is especially manifest in our diplomacy. The American Secretary of State is eager to sign his name to a treaty, and the American Ambassador or Minister, to get the credit of some accomplishment for his country's advantage before the curtain shall fall on him. If he begin a negotiation and do not get through with it, if the negotiation be not a failure, he himself, at any rate, is a failure. How this delivers us into the hands of the quiet, secure, patient, steady Englishman, who knows that if the thing be not done this year, it will be done in some future year, and expects to be there himself to do it.

This want of security in public office, this hurry to make a mark, make the American statesman ambitious to effect some reform, or find and create some issue that does not arise naturally of itself. So political parties, or restless and energetic men who are elected to Congress or State Legislatures, are constantly seeking some new line in which they can take a lead before they are retired. Plenty of examples could be given. The scheme for biennial elections in Massachusetts always seemed to me to have no foundation in any real popular desire, but only in the desire to secure an issue. Now the Englishman who, if he be fit for it, is assured of his place in the country's service, is in no hurry. The American must act, or some other actor will take his place. The Englishman can wait. England can wait. England is in no hurry. She can watch always her opportunity to take advantage of the impatience of her antagonists. This great chess-player, since she became the first Power in Europe, after the fall of Napoleon in 1818, has made few false moves. Other countries scold at her, and revile her, and charge her with perfidy. But she bides her time. She keeps her eye steadfastly upon her object. In the main, I think the charge of duplicity against her is without foundation. If she get the advantage of her antagonists, it is their own fault and not hers.

Our State governments and municipal institutions have a great value in training men for national service, to which nothing in England corresponds. The law governing parliamentary procedure must be unknown to many intelligent men who enter the House of Commons, and probably is never acquired by many persons who have a considerable service there. But our State legislatures and municipal governments make most intelligent American citizens familiar with it.

Both countries have a free press. In both countries the newspaper attacks with unrestrained severity the public and private character of public men with whom it differs in opinion ; but the English statesman does not have turned upon his private life the search-light in whose glare the American statesman must spend his. This is, I suppose, partly because in the vast solitude of London, an espionage is impossible which is easy in Washington. I suppose, too, there is less austerity in English public opinion.

I think the conductors of English newspapers stand by their country better than ours. English people would not tolerate in their own press the stream of scurrility and falsehood which is constantly poured out on our country by some American journalists. The American people are reproached with having a bitter dislike of the mother-country. I do not think the reproach is well founded. But if it be, is it strange, when we see what descriptions of the public life in America find their way into great English journals, and seem to be acceptable to their readers, and what representatives of the American press are selected for public honors? The course of some great English newspapers toward the United States is a perpetual insult. We know that they do not represent what is best in English opinion, any more than they fitly describe what is best in American public life. But I think we are entitled to some credit from our English brethren that our international good-will has survived in spite of the London " Times " and the " Saturday Review."

The English people have an indifference to logical consistency and symmetry in their public policies. In this they differ from the French and from us. The Englishman hates a doctrinaire. So the English Constitution is a quilt of patchwork. They seem to like to have the next thing they do differ both in manner and in principle from the last. The arrangement for Irish representation in the House of Lords and in the Commons is totally unlike the arrangement for the Scotch. The curious arrangement of counties palatine, the different fashions of procedure in Lords and Commons, give the English ceremonial a quaint grotesqueness of which the American would be extremely impatient.

The Englishman is willing to let theoretical questions remain forever unsettled, whereas the American would insist on having them out. The Yankee says "I want to know what my rights are." Let any claim be made of a right under the Constitution, and let it be disputed, and somebody will insist on having it settled. In one of the English colleges,—I think King's College at Cambridge,—there is an old claim that when the judges come to hold the assizes they are entitled to occupy during their stay the house of the Head of the College. This claim is disputed by the Head of the College. When the judges approach the town, the Head of the College goes out to meet them, and says that they would be happy to have Her Majesty's Judges make their stay in the house belonging to the College while the assizes last. To which the judges reply that "they are coming." When the threshold of the dwelling is reached, the Head of the College bows and prays the judge to enter and make himself at home; and the judge bows and requests the Head of the College to enter and make himself at home, each assuming the tone of a host to a guest. And so they go in together and occupy the house. And for more than four hundred years the question, whether the judge or the Head of the College has the right to the house at the assize season, has remained unsettled. Imagine such a question remaining open for six weeks anywhere in this country !

I do not think that the Englishman likes to be flattered. He likes better to grumble and to have people complain to him about somebody or something. He seldom brags. He considers the greatness of England an assured fact, to be taken for granted, like the force of gravitation or the importance of the sun to the solar system. I hope the time is coming when we shall feel our greatness among the nations so well assured that our public men will stop talking about it. But the people now expect a good deal of boasting from our orators. Even our chaplains in their prayers inform the Lord of the greatness of this country and of the magnificence and the glory of the American people.

Our restraint under a written Constitution, and under a Supreme Court which can declare any State or national legislation unconstitutional, is hardly greater practically than the restraint upon the Englishman of his regard for precedent. Omitting questions which arise by reason of the Constitutional distribution of power between the States and the nation, it is very unlikely that anything would be done in England by act of Parliament which is not permitted under our Constitutional restraints; and these are chiefly prohibitions of violations of common right.

The want of certainty of the statesman's hold upon power, of which I have spoken, and the lack of inherited wealth, deprive us of the advantage of a class of men trained for statesmanship from youth. The questions with which the public man in this country has to deal require long and exclusive study to master them. Such study is impossible if he have at the same time to get his own living. He must, therefore, be a man of inherited wealth, or must be taken from some other calling to which he has devoted himself long enough to have laid by a competency sufficient for his support, and suitable provision for his family. So we have rarely here men like those so numerous in England, who are trained to public affairs from their youth. Wordsworth's

> "Blessed statesman he, whose mind's unselfish will
> Leaves him at ease among grand thoughts,"

may perhaps still be found in considerable numbers in England; but in this country his high thinking must go with very plain living indeed, if he have to live on his salary. We have here what England lacks, —the training for larger service of the town meeting, the city council, and the exercise of State legislative and administrative offices. We have, too, the interest in public affairs which belongs to a republic, where every man feels a responsibility and expects to understand what is going on. The Yankee baby seems to draw in a knowledge of Parliamentary law with his infant breath, and, before he can walk, is ready to rise in his cradle and raise a point of order upon his nurse. So, able and well-educated men, although their lives may have been devoted to private affairs, come to the public service, even late in life, with an intelligent interest, an extent of information, and an aptness for their work which I think are lacking in the ordinary Englishman.

But, on the other hand, what an opportunity England has to educate the children of her favored classes in her colonial service! What an opportunity in her diplomatic service! What an opportunity in her vast navy, and her trained army, always ready for war! Ours is a government by the average citizen. England is a government by the aristocracy. While this may seem to give England some special advantage in immediate results, it yet remains to be seen whether it will give her an advantage in the end. Roger Sherman used to say that he looked for the strength of the Constitution of the United States in the end not chiefly to the Senate or the Judiciary, or to any Bill of Rights, but to the fact that the interest of the men who were to administer the government would always be the same with that of the people to be governed.

England, doubtless, governs well. She obtained her great Indian empire by unjustifiable means; but she rules it better and better from generation to generation. There are no better examples of a great governing race than the men she has sent out to India during the last fifty years,—the Lawrences, the Stephens, and their companions. "The sahibs don't like us;" said an Indian philosopher, "but they are absolutely just, and they do not fear the face of man." While England has trained this race of gentlemen to govern well her three hundred and fifty millions of subjects, the United States have not governed Alaska nor their two hundred and fifty thousand Indian dependants even decently.

Whatever changes for the better or worse have happened in either country, it is still true that while the English statesman is devoted to the glory and greatness of England, and while he desires to extend her empire, and while he desires to maintain her honor unstained, the great object and purpose of all his statesmanship is that he shall be able to hand down his broad acres, his ancestral dwelling, and his stately trees from eldest son to eldest son for generations to come, though a thousand paupers starve in their hovels, and though every fifth person in the kingdom must, some time in his life, receive aid from the state. On the other hand, the great object of American statesmanship has been, is, and is to be, to keep up wages, and to educate a whole people who shall dwell in happy and comfortable homes and not in huts or hovels.

The people of both countries are enlightened, honest, patriotic, and free. They are able to command, and in the main do command, in each generation, the kind of public service which the needs of the generation require. If the lofty and stimulant leadership of the elder Pitt, if the parliamentary skill and resolute courage of the younger Pitt, if the independence and economic wisdom of Cobden and Bright, or the military genius of Wellington, be not found in the counsels of England to-day, it is because England does not need them to-day. When she needs them, they will be forthcoming. If the constructive statesmanship of the framers of the Constitution, the comprehensive wisdom of Madison, the profound insight and dominant intelligence of Hamilton, the majestic eloquence of Webster, the chivalrous leadership of Clay, the uncompromising devotion to humanity of Sumner, the patient circumspection of Lincoln, are not now to be found in the counsels of our Republic, it is because the present day demands another kind of service for the Republic. When these things are needed, they

46

will appear.   The men of letters, the political philosophers, from the time of the satires of Churchill, from the time when Wordsworth proclaimed England to be "a fen of stagnant waters," and demanded the recall of Wellington from the head of the English armies and his disgrace in the eyes of Europe, have denounced the public life of their time, as their successors do to-day.   What is wanted in this country now is the honest, faithful, industrious, and intelligent management of its business affairs, both in State and nation.   And this the generation abundantly supplies.   GEORGE F. HOAR.

THE PROPOSED ANNEXATION OF HAWAII.

On May 16 of this year the President transmitted to the Senate a proposed treaty with the so-called Republic of Hawaii, by which it is designed to merge that nation into the United States. The Executive and the Secretary of State at the same time enumerated the grounds which they deemed sufficient to warrant annexation. I shall endeavor to show that none of the arguments made in advocacy of the outlined programme is sound, that Hawaiian annexation is detrimental to the interests of the United States, and that if such a policy might at any time be desirable, its accomplishment now and under circumstances at present prevailing must be alike impolitic and dishonorable.

The President apparently relies upon the declaration that annexation is "the necessary and fitting sequel to the chain of events which, from a very early period of our history, has controlled the intercourse and prescribed the association of the United States and the Hawaiian Islands." Unfortunately for this contention, the recitals made by the Executive show merely friendly and commercial intercourse and the adoption of a uniform policy favoring Hawaiian autonomy. True, the popular suggestion which refers to the dominancy of American interests in "that neighboring territory" is noted by the President. It is now, however, actively urged that the presence in the Islands of a few Americans necessarily requires our intervention and permanent occupancy.

The Secretary of State bases his recommendation upon the authority granted by the Hawaiian Constitution of 1894. He opposes commercial union because of the dangers of the "vicissitudes of public sentiment in the two countries." He evidently wishes to strike the iron while it is hot, and seeks to make a perpetual compact because of the uncertainty of popular desire. He does not care to risk a reversal of present policies. "Let us grab it while we may," epitomizes this statesmanship. The Secretary assumes that there must be annexation or a commercial union or a protectorate. He forgets the propriety of following precedents by attending to our domestic concerns. He does not recollect that our official notice of non-interference by other Powers has always proved effective. Possibly the Administration hopes to hasten, by mid-Pacific conquest, the advent of that prosperity so confidently and vainly promised. While the President may not have felt bound fully to sustain his theories, nevertheless suggestions intended to excite sympathy have been made elsewhere from day to day. We have been told that our Pacific Coast will not be safe until we are masters of the Hawaiian Islands. It is "proper form" to allude to these South-Sea folk as "our kinsmen," to call attention to their "proximity," and to refer, as does President McKinley, to "that neighboring territory." "Neighboring," as thus used, is defined to mean "situated near by, being in the vicinity, adjacent." It is important to remember that the soil we propose to absorb—this "neighboring territory"—is more than two thousand miles from the nearest point of the present United States. Our "neighbors" are not near enough to disturb our rest. There is no garden-wall interchange of views.

But we are dogmatically told that we must have the Islands for purposes of protection; that our country cannot be safe without them. I deny the accuracy of this contention. We can make a better contest without than with Hawaii. If we accomplish annexation for defensive objects we should fortify our new domain. We must build a navy capable of sustaining it. I am unable to give figures as to the cost of proper fortifications. That the expenditure must be immense, no one will dispute. In the event of war there could be no help within call to aid the distressed islanders. A week would be consumed in transporting our navy—if we possess a navy. Our coasts are not now fortified, notwithstanding years of effort. Even New York and San Francisco are insufficiently guarded. As for our navy, Admiral Walker, before the Senate Committee on Coast Defences, described the situation, when he said, that if the English should engage us they would probably capture or destroy our navy, and that, by putting all our vessels behind Sandy Hook, we could make something of a fight for that place, but that nothing would prevent the foe from raiding the whole coast. While we are very slowly increasing our naval strength, our leading European competitors are acting with more alacrity. Our disparity as regards at least England and France is hourly becoming more and more evident.

If we must go into the foreign acquisition business we should, for quite a period, spend not less than one hundred million dollars per year for naval purposes, and almost an equal sum for coast defences. We are not prepared to commit ourselves to such idiocy.   There are some who think that we can prepare for war within twenty-four hours. Much time must be consumed in building even one war vessel; and a 12-inch gun cannot be easily turned out in less than eighteen months. It will take General Flagler three years from the beginning of his work to complete the 16-inch cannon which is being manufactured, and which will, I trust, prove to be the most powerful engine of destruction ever devised.

If, unhappily, we. shall engage in foreign contention, where will the enemy strike?   Manifestly where he can inflict the severest injury.   He will not assail the Muir Glacier, nor will he direct his armies or navies against the leper settlement of Molokai.   Boston, New York, San Francisco, and other seaports will be decidedly interested in the event of a conflict with a great naval Power.   If San Francisco were attacked after annexation, would our batteries at Honolulu be effective?   Would our battle-ships stationed there aid us?   But it is urged that England, in case of trouble, may seize Honolulu, and that the Japanese may do so.   England clearly will not operate against us from Honolulu.   She has a veritable Gibraltar at Esquimault on the Washington boundary.   Why should she divert and divide her strength by permitting her guns and ships to rust two thousand miles from her enemy, especially when she is splendidly equipped at a point within sight of the smoke of our civilization?   For more than forty `years England has denied any hostility to Hawaii.

"How about Japan?" I am asked.   Japan surely does not intend to attack us.   She, as well as Great Britain, explicitly disclaims any such purpose.   I have no fear of difficulty there.   Considerations too numerous to mention make such an occurrence highly improbable. But if it shall be otherwise and Japan shall take Hawaii, she will not thereby be enabled to assail the United States.   To reach Honolulu from Japan requires a voyage of over thirty-six hundred miles, and the Islands are not on the American-Oriental sailing route.   The capture of Hawaii would be a foolish enterprise for any antagonist of the United States.   It is palpable that we could not hold the Hawaiian Islands, if the enemy found it desirable to possess them (an unlikely hypothesis), without vast outlay and without weakening our home defences.   If we constructed impregnable forts there and mounted thereon hundreds of modern cannon, we should be left alone in our grandeur without any enemy to defeat, or anything particularly valuable to protect.   Our Honolulu armies would be as lonely as was Robinson Crusoe.   If we are to defend ourselves, we must do so at home.   Why should we seek the South Pacific in order to secure our coasts?

I have heard that the possession of the Hawaiian Islands means the control of the North Pacific.   I admit that the nation possessing this group may dominate the North Pacific; but such dominancy will not in any manner depend upon the occupancy of these spots in the ocean. The subjection of the North Pacific depends upon the naval prowess of contending nations.   The most valiant army stationed in Hawaii, and possessing the best equipment and unlimited supplies, cannot rule the North Pacific without an unrivalled naval force.   Take the case of England, now the leading sea Power.   Does that Empire need the Hawaiian Islands, located near the twentieth degree of north latitude, when she is the possessor of a magnificent fortification at Esquimault, situated close to the fiftieth degree of north latitude?   That defence is far more effective as a controlling element, so far as the North Pacific is concerned, than would be any construction at Honolulu.   The enthusiastic advocates of annexation forget that the North Pacific must yield to ships of war, and that a nation possessed of all the islands in the South Pacific would not, because of such possession, command the seas there or elsewhere.

It is averred that we shall need the Islands when we construct the Nicaragua Canal.   We are advised that we cannot otherwise properly defend that work.   The suggestions already made dispose of this pretence.   If we make and own the Canal we must fortify its approaches. The western terminus would not be better protected by guns mounted at Hawaii than by those which guard the Golden Gate.   Our battleships can be dispatched from California to Nicaragua more speedily than from Honolulu.   Nor would the presence of an enemy at the latter point imperil the Canal.   A foe can reach our shores without touching at Honolulu; and, as I have said, if we arrange matters so as to make it uncomfortable there for an enemy, he will take another course and thus steer clear of us.   The important naval Powers have numerous possessions in and on the Pacific.

But it is urged that we must have a coaling-station, and that, therefore, annexation is desirable.   Pearl Harbor is ours: if we desire to fortify it, to dredge it, to make it useful, we may do so; and a coaling-station will thus be provided without annexation.   Such a station would be unnecessary in times of peace; and in the event of war coal should be procurable upon the usual lines of commerce.   If we are to have a coaling-station in the mid-Pacific, why not fix it in the Aleutian group? No vessel engaged in Asiatic-American commerce plies anywhere near our South-Sea neighbors.

If those of our countrymen who are belligerently inclined really intend to stir up a fight with England, why not provide for the protection of an eligible Aleutian island, and from thence prey upon the enemy's commerce? Our trade is quite safe in any event. We are without ships; and, under prevailing legislation, we are likely, I regret to say, to continue deficient in that direction. I have no apprehension of difficulty with England, nor, indeed, with any nation. Our business relations with the formidable Powers are too close to permit war. The disasters which would be visited upon England in the event of a struggle with the United States are palpable. She could not inflict injury upon any of the property of the United States without involving herself in financial losses beyond estimation. Japan is busy developing her manufactures and her newly acquired domain. She is acting judiciously, and is likely to preserve her temper, notwithstanding the atrocious discriminations of the Dingley Bill. The effort to make our people believe that Japan proposes to seize Hawaii comes from the cute promoters of annexation.

It is said that annexation should be favored because Americans have paramount interests in Hawaii. This argument was made with reference to the Transvaal by the enterprising gentlemen who tried to run over the Krüger government. They have had an opportunity to reflect upon the impropriety of attempting to manage affairs without their jurisdiction. I am confident that the missionaries who settled in Hawaii did so disinterestedly. It is not likely that it was their purpose to sweep their converts from power and convert their property *lucri causa*. It would be unjust to attribute to them the commercial immorality which subsequently eventuated. No settler in any country is justified in subverting the government by whose favor he entered, merely because such subversion will add to his profit. Such is one of the excuses under which despots have confiscated and assassinated. It suggests the claims of arrogant wealth when trampling upon impoverished merit. It is the argument of might against right, of barbarism against civilization. Our brethren who went to the Hawaiian Islands embarked in ventures under a government which did not derive its authority from them nor exist by their consent. Matters have so changed that the native Hawaiian who put his property into the business which followed the coming of the progressive foreigner came out with the experience, and the energetic visitor got the wealth. The ex-Queen acted in a manner to excite the disapproval of American residents. She was thereupon captured; and, as the outcome of American valor, the Islands were subdued and the so-called Republic established. It endures in defiance of the will of the governed; and the very intelligent and positive American-Hawaiian citizens, numbering less than two thousand males, who established the prevailing oligarchy, have tendered to the United States a country which they hold by conquest, and whose inhabitants, native to the soil, and universally educated in the rudiments, are not to be consulted as to a compact which means the obliteration of nationality.

Several powerful nations of modern times, ruled upon the monarchic plan, have seized territory for commercial reasons and because of sympathy with resident subjects. But we cannot justify' ourselves upon any such ground. No such departure from our traditions and theories can be for a moment legitimately tolerated. The rôle of the despot is unsuited to the American.

It is argued that our commerce with Hawaii is so important that we cannot afford to risk outside interference. That we have valuable trade there is plain. It is also clear that large profits have been made by parties who have taken advantage of the relations of the Islands to the United States. Mr. Spalding, who has been in Hawaii since 1867, and is a leading sugar-producer, remarked, before the Senate Committee, as follows:—

" What we want is to make something out of the country; make expenses out of the country. It is not a commercial, agricultural, manufacturing, or mineral producing country; it has no resources, no available resources; never has had. All this prosperity has come from this reciprocity treaty with the United States."

The same gentleman also testified that he would not have remained in the Islands had it not been for reciprocity; that prior to that all plantation owners had failed.

Mr. Alexander has certified that rice can be profitably produced in Hawaii, and that the orange and banana flourish. I have the authority of an ardent annexationist that this statement is rather overdrawn; but Minister Stevens, in his letter of November 20, 1892, tells Secretary Foster that "sugar-raising on these islands *can be continued only by the cheapest possible labor—that of the Japanese, the Chinese, and Indian coolies,*"—a cheerful outlook for the American white laborer. Mr. Stevens writes to Secretary Foster that oranges, lemons, pineapples, and grapes can and will be successfully grown in the event of annexation.   How a change of government can add to the productive capacity of the soil, may be somewhat difficult to explain.

The above, I think,. supports the conclusion that annexation is not necessary for the preservation of our trade.   Common business sense dictates that a properly framed treaty—not the jug-handle affair now in force, which every disinterested person admits should be changed, but a really reciprocal engagement—will bring all desirable Hawaiian commerce to the United States.   The Hawaiian Islands will deal with us because their interests make such a course necessary.   Imperative .considerations will continue this status.   The man has not yet been heard from who can show that annexation will bring to the United States any advantage which will not be enjoyed as the result of our often declared policy, everywhere conceded, inhibiting foreign inter- ference, and of the making of a sensible and equitable treaty.   The citrus-fruit producers of the United States and those engaged in beet- sugar production have no cause to rejoice at the cheap-labor competition which must follow annexation.   This, however, is a minor matter.

. There are other vital objections to the validity of the proposed cession of the Hawaiian Islands to this government " of the people and by the people."   Our policy is and always has been opposed to such in- ·vestments.   Washington spoke of the advantages of our "detached and distant situation," and said, " 'T is our true policy to steer clear of permanent alliances with any portion of the foreign world."   Mr. Jef- ferson, who favored the annexation of Cuba, said in a letter written to President Madison, April 27, 1809 :—

" It will be objected to our receiving Cuba that no limit can then be drawn to our future acquisitions.   Cuba can be defended by us without a navy ; and *this de- velops the principle which ought to limit our views.   Nothing should ever be ac- cepted which would require a navy to defend it.*"

Secretary Frelinghuysen, in a note to Mr. Langston, dated June 20, 1883, says :—

"The policy of this Government, as declared on many occasions in the past, has tended toward *avoidance of possessions disconnected from the main continent.* Had the tendency of the United States been to extend territorial domain beyond seas opportunities have not been wanting to effect such a purpose, whether on the coast of Africa, in the West Indies, or *in the South Pacific.*"

He also wrote to the same minister :—

" A conviction that a fixed policy, dating back to the origin of our constitu- tional Government, was considered to make it inexpedient to attempt territorial aggrandizement which would require maintenance by a naval force in excess of any yet provided for our national uses, has led this Government to decline territorial acquisitions. *Even as simple coaling-stations, such territorial acquisitions would involve responsibility beyond their utility.* The United States has never deemed it needful to their national life to maintain impregnable fortresses along the world's highways of commerce."

Secretary Sherman, whose participancy in the present scheme has not failed to excite surprise, concludes his " Recollections " with the following remarks :—

" The events of the future are beyond the vision of mankind ; but I hope that our people will be content with internal growth, and avoid the complications of foreign acquisitions. Our family of States is already large enough to create embarrassment in the Senate ; and a republic should not hold dependent provinces or possessions. Every new acquisition will create embarrassments. Canada and Mexico as independent republics will be more valuable to the United States than if carved into additional States. The Union already embraces discordant elements enough without adding others. If my life is prolonged I will do all I can to add to the strength and prosperity of the United States, but nothing to extend its limits or to add new dangers by acquisition of foreign territory."

President McKinley, in his Inaugural Address, warned us against the temptation of territorial aggression.

Heretofore we have followed the rules thus laid down. Our extension of territory has been on the mainland, and, with the exception of Alaska, the added property has been contiguous. We entered into a tripartite agreement with England and Germany whereby we aid in maintaining a miserable counterfeit of regal greatness in authority at Samoa. This compact beween the leading republic of the world and two empires to force a barbarian ruler upon a protesting race was and is absurd enough. (Mr. Cleveland, to his credit, attempted to relieve us of this folly ; but the legislative " spirit of conquest " rendered his efforts futile.)

If we annex Hawaii, the next move will involve Samoa,—distant four thousand miles. I am aware that Secretary Marcy encouraged the annexation idea ; but his ambitious views did not convince the American people and were regarded as visionary. Nor did he have before him the domestic problems which at this hour challenge the supreme consideration of the ablest American patriot.

Is the character of the inhabitants of Hawaii such as to induce us to sigh for their society and personality ? The following table shows the various nationalities represented on the Islands ; the figures are from the last census :—

Nationality.	Males.	Females.	Total.
Hawaiians..	16,399	14,620	31,019
Part Hawaiians.................................	4,249	4,236	8,485
Americans......................................	1,975	1,111	3,086
British..........	1,406	844	2,250
Germans..	866	566	1,432
French...	56	45	101
Norwegian.....................................	216	162	378
Portuguese.....................................	8,202	6,989	15,191
Japanese.......................................	19,212	5,195	24,407
Chinese..	19,167	2,449	21,616
South Sea Islanders............................	321	134	455
Other Nationalities............................	448	152	600
Total..................................	72,517	36,503	109,020

President McKinley's Inaugural contains this suggestion :—

"A grave peril to the Republic would be a citizenship too ignorant to understand or too vicious to appreciate the great value and beneficence of our institutions and laws ; and against all who come here to make war upon them our gates must be promptly and tightly closed."

There is ample evidence that the native Hawaiians are possessed of educational qualifications covering at least the primary branches ; but these attainments are not demonstrative of their ability to discharge the duties of American citizenship, although they are sufficient to elevate them far above the degradation which they suffer at the hands of those who ignore their just demands. The mental discipline to which the native Hawaiian has been for many years subjected certainly entitles him to a hearing when his civil rights are threatened. It does not, however, follow by any means that this right of consideration means the possession of the mental and moral faculties essential to the properly equipped American citizen. While I believe the evidence tends to show the incompetency of the native Hawaiian to meet the requirements of our citizenship, it is nevertheless clear that he is not a savage or a slave ; and the land of his birth should not be disposed of without his concurrence. Captain Dutton, of the United States Ordnance Department, delivered a lecture under the auspices of the Smithsonian Institution in 1884, wherein he said :—

"The economic condition of the Hawaiian is probably superior at the present time to that of any other tropical people in the world ; and, on the whole, I think it quite safe to say that it is but very little surpassed, if at all, by that of the work-ing-classes of America. He has even more to eat and better food, plenty of beef, pork, and fish, and could have an abundance of flour if he desired it, but he pre-fers his taro. He owns his property in fee, he makes laws and executes them, he reads and writes, he has but one wife; he tills the soil and tends flocks; some-times he accumulates wealth, and sometimes he does not; he makes his will in due form, dies and receives a Christian burial; in no land in the world is property more secure."

Mr. Spalding informs us that a republic would not be a good form of government for the people of Hawaii. He told the Senate Com-mittee that the natives "are like a good many in the United States—better governed than governing," and testified as follows:—

"I have already said that a republican form of government would not be suit-able for that people. That is an independent form of government. You might, for instance, if the Hawaiian Islands were a part of the State of California, do very well. I think they would send two or three or four Representatives to the State Capitol who would be equally respectable with the Representatives sent from the present counties in California."

The general tenor of the testimony taken by the Senate Committee is, that, notwithstanding the ability of the natives to read and write, they could not maintain a republic. But I repeat, this state of affairs does not authorize the United States, nor any other Power, to ignore the de-sires of these islanders as to the form of their government. They were contented and prosperous before the oligarchy. The incompetency of the Japanese and Chinese population, consisting of about forty-six thousand souls, will not be controverted. We have stringent laws ex-cluding Chinese from the United States, and after much trouble we succeeded in negotiating a treaty virtually ratifying the Geary law; and our policy of exclusion has been enforced with comparative suc-cess. Our people, especially those who toil, are opposed to the intro-duction of servile Asiatic labor. I am aware that the treaty under consideration provides that "No Chinese, by reason of anything herein contained, shall be allowed to enter the United States from the Ha-waiian Islands." The result of this peculiar provision is problematical. The State Department repudiates the obligation of Hawaii to Japan. If this view is correct, may it not be that the Chinese residents of Ha-waii after annexation, being within the United States, will enjoy rights now participated in by their brethren in the various States? At all events, the fact remains that Hawaiian annexation means an addition to the population of the United States of more than twenty-one thousand Chinese and more than twenty-four thousand Japanese.   It is true that Japan has lately advanced astonishingly; but her laborers (of the class employed in Hawaii) are distasteful to us.   We do not care to compete with them.

Bitter hostility must arise from this incorporation of about one-quarter as many Chinamen as are now within the United States.   Do we need such a racial contribution?   Will this new contact improve us?   Will the introduction of these incongruities add to our honor or to our strength?   We are daily seeking to perfect our immigration laws and to raise the standard of citizenship.   The annexation proposition involves a wholesale infusion of deleterious constituents and agencies. The United States contain many who are not thoroughly advised concerning the responsibilities of democracy.   Have we not enough to command our attention here at home?   We are busy.   Fiscal problems, questions of a basic character, compel our attention.   Are we prepared to instil into the scattered tribes of the ocean the philosophy of free government?   Can we educate all men in the tenets of true republicanism?   The highest type of manhood is requisite to the permanency of republics.   Despotisms may for a time get along without general diffusion of knowledge; but a republic depends upon the ability, integrity, and liberty-loving disposition of the masses.   A minority only of the human family is fitted for self-rule.   Hawaiian annexation would not stimulate our intelligence, patriotism, or power.   Nor is it any answer to these observations to affirm that the destruction of a non-assimilative race will relieve us from peril.   Such an argument is the defence of the conqueror.   This powerful republic should not stifle the protests of those who are "to the manor born."   We stand in the presence of internal dangers grave enough to warn us of the impropriety of seeking new perils.   Elements of discord exist in the United States. Conflicting interests come to the surface daily.   The American people are divided at this moment as to leading financial problems.   There is more than one experiment on trial.   While I am confident of our ability to meet all exigencies, I do not believe it wise to seek new embarrassments.

There are many Americans who, while holding that annexation is desirable, are unwilling to coöperate in a movement which means the annihilation of a nation without that nation's consent.   The proposed treaty mentions the Republic of Hawaii.   This is a misnomer.   A member of the Hawaiian *de facto* judiciary has lately been quoted as stating that the government of which he is a part is really an oligarchy.   This is the truth. Mr. Stevens, through whose promotion of the revolution the alleged Hawaiian Republic was established, delivered a lecture, reported in the " Boston Journal " of November 23, 1893, in which he declared that the annexation issue ought not to be decided by popular vote because the result would be antagonistic to American interests. In other words, the theory is that the natives, who understand the situation thoroughly, but who are not sufficiently aggressive to make good citizens of the United States, ought not to be permitted to vote, because the result of such an election would mean the overthrow of usurpation. Never did a despot more confidently express the nefarious ground upon which he relied. No more impudent claim has been made in connection with this subject than that which is submitted by those who avow that the higher civilization which they represent involves the right to seize and govern, to bargain and sell.

It must be understood that I do not discuss the question of technical authority. I concede, for the sake of argument, that the provisions of the Hawaiian Constitution authorize annexation, and that our title derived therefrom would be legally good. I likewise readily assent to the doctrine that, for purposes of diplomacy, a government *de facto* must be recognized as a government *de jure.* But when we are asked to join in the obliteration of a government, it is our duty to consider the propriety of the cession, and not only to look at the question of physical ability, but likewise to ascertain the preferences of those whose political status is so vitally involved. A republic springing from universal desire should not accept a deed of empire without reference to justice. I have observed statements to the effect that the fact that the present régime had been maintained for some years is conclusive of the power to negotiate the pending treaty. As I have said, this is in a sense true. The President and Secretary of State appear to rely upon this proposition. But when it appears that the authority of the would-be grantors is based alone upon the support received from armed men, and that those whom it is designed to bring within our jurisdiction do not wish to come, I am prepared to ignore the pretences of the *de facto* government, so far as the attempt to destroy nationality is concerned, although I do not hesitate to join in recognizing it for the purposes of governmental intercourse.

If the natives are at all capable of comprehending their situation, they should be consulted : if they are utterly incompetent we should not bring them in. I will not discuss the means employed to accomplish the overthrow of the ex-Queen, nor the participancy in that *coup* of the forces of the United States. Suffice it to say that no one has claimed that the native Hawaiians, numbering about forty thousand souls, ever agreed to the governmental change or had anything to do with the adoption of the present constitution. As a condition precedent to a vote under the Hawaiian act providing for a constitutional convention, the elector was compelled to swear that he would bear full allegiance to the provisional government, and would oppose any attempt to reëstablish a monarchy. Upon complying with this requisite he became qualified to vote. The election was, therefore, confined to the narrow precincts within which those who conducted the provisional government moved. The natives who took no stock in that government were shut out; and the small but powerful oligarchy managed the election to suit the occasion. This programme has been followed ever since. A constitution is supposed to be the very basis of the government.

When a people elect delegates to a convention called for the purpose of framing an organic law, it is expected that the nature and form of government will be thoroughly discussed and solved; but the patriots who now propose to give Hawaii to the United States so prescribed the qualifications of the electors who chose delegates to the constitutional convention that all opposition was removed, and no one not in sympathy with the prevailing usurpation was allowed to be heard. The alleged Hawaiian Republic is a bogus republic. It does not exist pursuant to the will of the governed, but notwithstanding such will.

The people of the Hawaiian Islands are worthy of consideration. True they belong to an inferior race. They are not equal competitors in the world-wide field of modern aggressiveness. Had they possessed the nerve, the snap, the bravery of the Anglo-Saxon, this proposed treaty would never have been formulated. I have called attention to the circumstance that witnesses conversant with the Hawaiian character declare that while the natives would not make ideal Americans, yet they possess some educational advantages. Even before the revolution it was a very rare thing to find a native who could not read and write his mother-tongue. The editor of the Honolulu "Evening Bulletin" is authority for the statement that six out of seven native Hawaiians were on school registers last year. Rev. Oliver P. Emerson testified before the Senate Committee that he believed it would be difficult to find a single native Hawaiian over twelve years of age unable to read or write. Assuming that the natives are not adequate to the task of the highest American citizenship, is it just to deprive them of nationality without their suggestion or coöperation and against their desires? They were offered the privileges of voters at the price of servility. If I advocated annexation, I would still require the submission of the question to the real citizens of the Islands, including the native race. I cannot appreciate the attitude of the patriotic American who believes in liberty, who is prepared to defend the rights of the people, but who insists upon approving the action of a few who, exercising authority in defiance of the majority, propose, without honest title, to alienate a nation.

I have said that we must, so far as diplomacy goes, recognize those actually governing; but this does not mean that we can always properly accept title from a *de facto* ruler. We should go to the root of the claim. The moral side of the matter must not be ignored. I do not concede the integrity of the title offered. I am confident that the people whose rights are affected are antagonistic to the project. It is against our policy and interest to interfere in the affairs of remote islanders. The proposed acquisition is not necessary for our protection, nor important to our trade. Judicious treaty arrangements will secure all possible mercantile advantages. There is no danger of foreign interference in the presence of our avowed insistence upon Hawaiian autonomy; our rights in that regard being universally admitted.

STEPHEN M. WHITE.

POLITICAL ASPECTS OF THE PLAGUE IN BOMBAY.

In this article I shall endeavor to show that the bubonic plague was not an intractable disease; that its rapid spread was due largely to indifference on the part of the municipal authorities in Bombay; and, finally, that the institution of radical measures by Government sufficed at once to check the epidemic, and, within a reasonable period, to bring it to a close.

The bubonic plague appeared in Bombay toward the end of August, 1896. Incredible as it may seem, the disease raged for a month before any official notice was taken of it. As early as the first week of September the Municipal Health Officer was informed of the existence of the malady. According to his own statement, however, he had already known of it for some time. By September 3, certain physicians, who were members of the Municipal Corporation, were treating the disease as true bubonic plague.

The first cases appeared in Mandvie Ward, an abhorrently filthy district in the heart of the city, having 37,000 inhabitants, chiefly natives of the lower classes. The population in and about this ward is said to be the densest in the world. In some localities there are 760 people to the acre. Of the total population of the city, which is nearly a million, the greater part is crowded into an area of four square miles.

Despite the fact that, before September was half over, the native population had become thoroughly frightened, and an exodus from Mandvie had already begun, the Health Officer still officially ignored the whole matter. Not yet had the Municipal Commissioner taken a step to prevent the spread of the disease; nor had the press spoken. The presence of the plague was known to many; yet silence was the rule.

When three weeks of September were past, and between two and three hundred people had died of the pestilence, the subject was casually mentioned at an ordinary meeting of the Standing Committee of the Corporation (September 23). Not even then was the matter broached by the Health Officer. A private physician first called attention to it, and on the spot named the disease by its true name.

"The malady," he said, "is the bubonic plague. . . . I think it is caused by the putrid emanation from the putrefying and decomposing matter in the sewers, which are choked and can only be called cesspools." Remarks were made by several other physicians, who corroborated what had been said and stated that the Health Officer had been informed of all the facts three weeks before.

The Health Officer still sat silent; but when he had been particularly requested to say something in regard to the plague he uttered this oracular remark: "In regard to the occurrences of cases of a peculiar type of fever referred to, it may be mentioned that the type is of a suspicious character."

The apathy of the Health Officer, however, was not shared by the whole Committee. One of the physicians at this very meeting went so far as to demand that plague-patients should be isolated. But this was going too far. The Committee contented themselves with saying that something ought to be done about the plague. The Health Officer refused to admit that the disease was plague at all. For a whole month longer he admitted no "deaths from plague" into the tables of vital statistics. At the end of that time he consented to register deaths from "bubonic fever"; but the word "plague" remained officially tabooed.

The reason for this concealment was tersely stated in the Municipal Corporation: Bombay was a trading city; and knowledge of the plague would hurt trade. For this, among other more personal reasons, the Commissioner and his subordinates concealed the truth. For this reason also the chairman of the Chamber of Commerce, a month after the pest appeared, declared that there was no such thing as plague in town; naïvely adding that, as Colombo had already quarantined against Bombay, anyone might see how inimical to the welfare of the city were revelations so untimely.

The Health Officer's only step to meet the "peculiar type of fever" was to remove the accumulated filth of years. For the city, to a great extent built on land made of refuse, had never been properly cleaned; and the streets, alleys, and sewers were all overloaded with the foulest matter. For twelve years complaints had been rife in regard to the danger of allowing sullage and night-soil to collect in the alley-ways and choke up the drains: for ten years the health of the city had been steadily declining.

The Municipality spent a good deal of valuable time in discussing the cause of the plague, and could come to no definite conclusion. On the whole they were inclined to the opinion that filth was innocuous, and that the plague was due to rats. Thus the Police Officer—who had a great deal more to say about sanitation than had the Health Officer—said at the next meeting (September 30) of the Standing Committee; that rats disseminated the plague, which was brought from Hong Kong or Bagdad in sugar, raw silk, or dates. The Health Officer was working hard and doing all he could to clean the city. What more could be expected of him? Why should people talk about the Health Officer's neglect of duty?

The Municipal Commissioner, who is the chief executive of the city, is empowered, under Section 434 of the Municipal Act, to "take such special measures as he shall deem necessary to prevent the outbreak of such disease [dangerous or infectious] or the spread thereof." A Government Committee, appointed the last day of September to inquire into the plague, recommended explicitly that the Commissioner should apply for more power; although the wording of the Act, even as it stands, might easily be interpreted to confer power enough to meet every sanitary emergency.

But the Commissioner, like the Health Officer, viewed the situation very calmly. On the very day that the Standing Committee were discussing whether filth had anything to do with the plague he gave it as his opinion that there was "no cause for very serious alarm." On receiving this advice Government, loath to interfere in municipal matters, retired, and left the control of the plague in the hands of the city authorities.

This report of the condition of affairs in Bombay, made by the executive to Government, was analogous to the sadly optimistic report of the Viceroy in regard to the famine. But Government was bound to abide by the official statement made to it. The result in both cases was disastrous. In regard to Bombay, Government contented itself with proposing, on October 5, that the sanitary staff of the Municipality should be increased. Meantime the Commissioner became frightened, for the plague had now been spreading for more than a month, and there was every indication that the Health Officer's method of meeting it was without avail. A week after he had telegraphed that there was cause for alarm he drew up a Notification (October 6), the terms of which were interpreted to mean that the segregation of plague-patients would be made compulsory.

This Notification of October 6 immediately became a bone of contention. It was six months to a day before the most recalcitrant natives were brought to see that English authority could enforce segregation.

But this was under the pressure of a stronger hand than that of the Municipal Commissioner.

On September 30 the executive had applied for an extra grant of 100,000 rupees (about $33,000) for sanitary purposes. The grant was made at once; but about a third of it was spent in making manholes, and the remainder was sunk in the long-neglected work of cleaning the city and in purchasing antiquated disinfectants. Most of the appropriation was gone in three weeks (October 19). A thousand tons of silt had been dug up out of the drains. Though disinfected it still " emitted sickening smells "; and in many instances it stood for days heaped up in offensive mounds about the city. The heat was intense. Scarcely any rain had fallen in September; and in October the country was already suffering from famine-drought. The Health Officer's one thought was to remove silt and clean alley-ways. As to the segregation of plague-patients, he not only took no interest, but he expressed it as his deliberate opinion that it was " impracticable, out of the question." He had neither men nor means to enforce such a measure. The most done to prevent the spread of plague was to catch plague-patients as they ran around the city and disinfect them. But the arrest of such persons was always regarded as a happy accident. No system was employed; and thus from infected districts the fleeing natives shortly spread the plague over districts not before contaminated. The erection of a plague-hospital had been suggested; but the Commissioner did not think this necessary. There was but one hospital for infectious diseases of all kinds, and to this were sent such plague-patients as could be induced to go. But to most of the natives the idea of going to the hospital was abhorrent. They did all they could to escape detection, and preferred to die alone in the street rather than be cared for by aliens.

The publication of the Notification instantly arrayed Western sanitary science against Oriental prejudice. But the Health Officer's published statement, that segregation was " out of the question," played directly into the hands of the natives, who immediately protested against any form of enforced segregation, not only because in their opinion it was merely an English fad, but particularly on the ground that the sacred privacy of the Hindu or Mahomedan home was thereby invaded. The judgment of a committee of physicians (who had been especially appointed to report and advise), to the effect that segregation was a necessity, here went for naught. Few natives have yet learned that there is nothing holy which is opposed to the public weal.

It must not be supposed that this prejudice against the hospital and segregation was confined to the lower classes. Two-thirds of the Municipality are. Indians, Hindus, Mahomedans, and Parsees,—the most intelligent native citizens of Bombay. There was scarcely one of them that did not oppose segregation.

Another religious phase of the opposition to segregation, or indeed to the application of any sanitary regulations, was the *Kismet* theory of the Mahomedans, which has its parallel in the faith of the Hindus. According to this theory, it is impious to try to escape from the fate prepared by God. Moreover, it is useless; and hence precautions are vain. The practical result of this theory is to make the natives disregard all laws of health. Disease and death are gifts of God. No importance is attached to the sanitary condition of houses or towns.

No sooner was the Notification of October 6 signed, and a few patients had been forcibly removed to the Arthur Road Hospital for Infectious Diseases, than the health of the town unfortunately began to improve. The Municipal Commissioner at once concluded that the plague was not going to amount to much after all; his fears vanished; segregation was enforced more and more negligently as the clamor of resistance rose and the plague declined. But the malady had quietly spread itself over a wide area. Before the middle of October plague was firmly fastened on Mandvie Ward, the Fort, Kolaba, and Kamatipur, —the most thickly settled quarters of the city. In almost every instance where it appeared in a new ward the outbreak could be traced directly to contagion from a patient who had escaped from an infected locality.

The population now began to be sensibly diminished, not so much on account of death as of flight. There was only a makeshift inspection at the railway stations. Thousands of the lower classes fled during the last weeks of September from fear of the plague, and many thousands more during October from fear of the hospital. Needless to say, they carried the plague with them into the Mofussil (country districts).

At the end of the second week of October the announcement was made that the plague had been brought under control. Perhaps it had. But on October 14 the English officers of the Municipality who, according to their own declarations, already had their hand upon the throat of the foe, released their hold and let the beast go free at the bidding of the native population.

There is probably not to be found in the annals of civilization so fatuous an utterance as the Memorandum of October 14 to the Health Officer, subsequently confirmed by the Act of October 30. On the former date, because of protestations on the part of tenants in Mandvie Ward who objected to compulsory isolation, "it was decided by the Municipal Commissioner in consultation with the Health Officer," that the terms of the Notification ostensibly compelling segregation "should not be stringently put into force," as its provisions wounded the religious feelings of the community. In the first week of November formal instructions were issued to all the executive officers of the Municipality not to execute "stringently" the Notification of October 6.

That happened which might have been foreseen. The native officers, who had been forced to do a duty repugnant to themselves as well as to the patients whom they had coerced into obedience, interpreted these words to mean that they were to segregate nobody. There was, indeed, no case where, in the judgment of a family, proper segregation could not be effected at home. To send such patients to the hospital would be to enforce the law "stringently." Therefore only waifs went to the hospital. So ended the farce of segregation. Instantly the death-rate increased. The last week of October had shown the effect of segregation quietly discountenanced; but the mortality of the ensuing weeks showed the effect of its formal discontinuance. There was an ostentatious report of "marked improvement" recorded on October 24, before the order for segregation had been really rescinded. Thereafter, there was a steady increase in deaths from plague.

On the night of October 16 some miscreant had maltreated with tar the great statue of the Queen-Empress, which stands at the south end of the Esplanade. The effect of this act may be compared with that of the mutilation of the Hermes at Athens. Not only was there intense indignation on the part of the Anglo-Indians, but on the part of the natives of all classes there was a new terror added to life in Bombay. For the Queen-Empress is a divinity; her statue is a sort of idol; to desecrate it is to commit sacrilege. To add to the excitement, prophecies were circulated to the effect that the Sirkar (Imperial Government) would take signal vengeance on the people of Bombay by means of a general massacre of the inhabitants on the great feast of Divali, which occurs at the beginning of November. It was also believed that patients sent to the hospital were murdered to avenge the Queen; that disinfectants were poisons; that the blood of patients was drawn to weld together the foundations of new government buildings; and that every officer who inquired about plague-cases was a spy, who sought to compass the death of a new victim.

The people grew mad with terror. As Divali approached ,they fled in ever-increasing numbers. In the city itself riots became frequent. Mobs attacked the hospital, angrily shouting that they would slay the doctors as the doctors would slay them.

After October 20, deaths from plague were admitted (under the caption of "fever") into the weekly mortality lists. From the beginning it was evident that the number of deaths was understated. Curiously enough the Health Officer himself on a previous occasion had formally stated that "the evidence of Municipal Officers" was not worthy of acceptance. His own evidence was now found to be of the same character. In many cases single physicians testified to knowing of more deaths from plague during one week in their own limited practice than were included for the same period in the record of the Health Officer, which should have been taken from the reports of all the physicians in the city. An official acknowledgment that the municipal reports were not trustworthy was made by the Commissioner and the Police Officer on December 30. It seems unnecessary to take other testimony.

According to the most careful computation, the plague mortality, which was about 174 for the week ending November 10, rose to 242 in the next week; to 314 the week after (November 24); and to 315 in the week ending December 1. The week following, the plague-deaths numbered 591, and the total mortality rose to 1,051, the greatest ever known in the city. In another month, i. e., by December 29, the plague mortality was 1,484, and the total mortality 1,853 for the week.

The fear of death now began to prevail against religious prejudice. The more enlightened natives, as the death-rate advanced week by week, counselled a substitution for official segregation, and advised voluntary segregation, race by race, caste by caste, in hospitals erected by private subscription. But the advice came too late. Before some of these hospitals could be built the plague was nearly ended. Nor was it easy at any time to get the natives to enter their own private hospitals. Even voluntary segregation frightened them.

What was absolutely requisite was a house-to-house inspection of the city, and strict isolation of plague-patients. But what was done was to clean out drains and whitewash rooms where patients had died.

The Municipality appointed a few subordinates in the Health Department, and gave the hospital some new assistants. Most of the native physicians had run away from the city by December. The members of the Municipality also fled; notably the loquacious leaders of the people, who had been most influential in opposing sanitary regulations.

During the reign of terror which obtained in the city from November to January, Government had done nothing to show that it concerned itself with the state of affairs in Bombay.   In Bombay itself the Anglo-Indians blamed the natives for not submitting to sanitary rules, the natives blamed the Anglo-Indians for suggesting segregation; and in the latter circle the Health Officer blamed the Commissioner for neglect of duty, while other Anglo-Indians blamed the Health Officer for similar dereliction.   The Municipality was divided against itself. In all this conflict the means taken to stay the plague were inadequate; the officials were apathetic or doggedly content to toil on in a manner long shown to be unavailing.   The prospect was that nothing effective would ever be done within the limits of the city.

That something must be done, seems to have struck the attention of Government very suddenly.   As late as January 8, the Governor, Lord Sandhurst, expressed the opinion that the means hitherto adopted was all that was needful to secure a gradual cessation of the plague.   This was the politely expressed view of Surgeon-General Cleghorn also, who was sent from Calcutta to give his opinion.   But Dr. Cleghorn's formal advice was that the healthy people in an infected district should be "hutted," i. e., sent to segregation camps..   A report, embodying this suggestion was sent to the Municipality.   The report created a shibboleth: "The healthy to the huts, the sick to the hospital!"   The Municipality received the advice with its usual indifference.

But the Speech from the Throne on January 19, though it said little in respect of the plague, said just what was needful: "Take the most stringent measures."   It was high time.   The plague was now spread over the whole province of Bombay.   It was no longer a local matter.   To subdue it was an "imperial necessity," to quote Lord Sandhurst's apology for interference.

The Governor now interfered directly in the matter.   The very next day he appointed a special Plague Officer to inspect the city and "advise" the Commissioner.   Then an Assistant Health Officer, twenty medical officers, and others deemed requisite were appointed.   Not content with this, the Governor, early in February, had a special Epidemic Disease Act passed, and published a Notification authorizing, and in fact directing, the Municipal Commissioner to demolish buildings unfit for human habitation, to destroy infected articles, to require abatement of overcrowding, and to do other things necessitated by the exigency of the occasion.   The care of the city was now taken by Government officers.   Segregation camps were built; and a regular inspection of houses was begun.   The Governor's right hand in carrying out these reforms was Genl. Gatacre. The mortality of the city for the week ending February 9 was 1,911, the plague-mortality, 1,371, which, considering the greatly decreased population (for the natives were still fleeing by the thousands every day) was higher than for the last week of December. There was in fact no indication that the virulence of the plague was abating when the Government took control of the city.

While the Municipality did nothing but protest against the " wanton waste of money " involved in the carrying out of sanitary rules, the Government subdued the plague. On March 5 the Gatacre Committee was appointed : this took the sanitation of the city completely out of the hands of the Municipality. The Committee was expressly stated to be " subordinate only to Government." The Health Officer was not put on the Committee at all. The Municipal Commissioner was put on only to consent to what Government demanded. The Municipal Corporation were curtly directed " to carry into effect without delay any measures which may be ordered by the Committee." In other words the Corporation were reduced to a political cypher.

Under this sting municipal lassitude vanished. The seventy-two members of the Corporation became furious, and declared that they would not be suppressed. After this explosion they sank back into their customary attitude of careless indolence ; and, thereafter, as regards the plague, the Municipality drops out of sight.

Times were changed now in Bombay. The natives were told that the sick would be compelled to go to the hospital. Four hospitals were open to plague-patients. Hospital-huts were erected in various quarters. There were soon in the city forty-one hospitals and six hundred segregation huts. The hospital staff was strengthened. Nurses from England were cabled for. Women inspectors and physicians were appointed to examine native women ; medical certificates were insisted on ; restrictions were put upon returning inhabitants liable to bring the plague back with them ; an army of men was sent out to inspect and cleanse the city ; an extra staff of nearly a thousand men was created in the Health Department; one of four thousand in the engineering department; the idle military were put to work ; concealed cases of plague were artfully detected ; the Corporation were told that if they did not at once settle the question of the disposal of refuse (they had been dawdling over the matter for six months) it would be settled for them ; the shanties of disease and death were burned down by the hundred ; last, the great intramural graveyard of the Mahomedans was closed. This, however, is but a partial list of the many things neglected hitherto, and now accomplished only by the intervention of Government. The latter's care extended in all directions. The Municipality gave no compensation to the poor wretch whose infected goods were burned: the Government ordered compensation to be paid. The Municipality did nothing to soften the horror of the "cart of death," as the natives called the hospital-van: the Government not only improved the hospital building, which had been a disgrace to civilization, but even had rubber tires put upon the wheels of the van,—thus again softening the rigor of the law.

The mettle of their new rein-holder was soon tested by the Sunni Mahomedans, the most obstructive among the natives. When segregation was first suggested in October, the Sunni leaders opposed it; and in the Municipality their representatives were insolent enough to say that any such order would be resisted. That order was now given. The Sunnis could not believe it was intended to be taken seriously. They thought that one or two petitions and a threat or two would end the matter now as it had been ended six months before. They sent petition after petition, each more impudent than the last. They threatened resistance. But instead of yielding, the Governor said " *You must obey* "; and they obeyed. For the first time since December the plague mortality now stood in three figures instead of four. In the week ending March 2 the deaths due to plague were 938 (the week before, they had been 1,108); three weeks later they were 600; by April 20 they were 310; by May 15 they were 100 for the week. The stream of outgoing natives had continued almost undiminished till February. Then there was a back-eddy; and soon the tide turned. By the end of March the outgoing and returning inhabitants nearly balanced each other; but thereafter the latter were in excess. By April confidence was restored; and at the end of that month the plague was no longer of epidemic character anywhere in the Presidency. Oddly enough the daily death-rate began to diminish from the very day of the Notification, February 10, which inaugurated the energetic policy of Government. But informally the governmental policy had already been introduced. Whatever credit be given to Dr. Haffkine's services in aiding the Government to suppress the plague, the chief praise must rest with the Government itself. Nor was the weather an important factor. In fact it was warmer in October than in February.

To one well acquainted with Indian affairs the bare record of these events is full of significance; but for those who do not understand the political situation in India a word of explanation may be necessary.

The Anglo-Indian press is full of complaints against the apathy of the natives, their inability to meet any crisis, their do-nothing policy as contrasted with their loquacity. On the other hand, the native press complains still more bitterly of Anglo-Indian lack of sympathy and of intelligent comprehension of native character. Again, the municipalities are extremely jealous of governmental control. Nothing distressed the Bombayans—even those who were ashamed of their own City Fathers—so much as to see these Fathers put on the shelf by Government. Finally, the Anglo-Indians, especially those who have spent their lives in India, are continually harping on the Mutiny of 1857. Very few of them really understand the political background of the Mutiny. They are prone to believe that the natives are still in a state of sub-sedition and that the slightest disturbance may result in a volcanic eruption of native forces. The history of the plague is an object-lesson in respect of all these points.

As to the apathy of the natives as contrasted with the energy of the Anglo-Indians, every reader must have noticed that the most conspicuous example of personified apathy was the Municipal Commissioner, who is an Englishman. This officer was ably seconded in his do-nothing policy by the chairman of the Chamber of Commerce, by the Police Officer, and by the Engineering Officer, all of whom are English. The English Health Officer, though his labor was ill-directed, cannot be included with these; but from a wider point of view his attitude is also significant. For while the Anglo-Indian press blamed the " native apathy " of the Municipality it appeared to be forgotten that a third of the Municipal Corporation are not native, but English. Now a minority of a third is strong enough to make itself felt in word if not in action. But at no meeting of the Corporation, from September to March, was any stand taken by English energy to oppose native apathy. I am far from denying the existence of this fault among the natives; but to cite it as characteristically national is manifestly unjust. Moreover, it must be remembered that, while English apathy had no excuse save fear, half of the native's objection to doing anything was simply religious feeling and sympathy for his fellow-countrymen, who shared that feeling in respect of segregation.

Not less exaggerated, however, is the native complaint in regard to Anglo-Indian " lack of sympathy." So far as sentiment is concerned, the plaint is justified, though to make it so often betrays a lack of manliness which may explain the other lack. The Englishman is not in sympathy with the Indian; but, so far as kind acts go, there was never a conquering race in the world which treated its conquered subjects so generously and so thoughtfully.   It was the Municipality's own officers that offended most against the delicacy of the Hindus and Mahomedans in the matter of personal inspection.   The Municipality as a body did not even suggest those alleviations of distress which, on taking control of the city, Lord Sandhurst immediately introduced.   Not to the Corporation, with its two-thirds majority of natives, but to the " unsympathetic " Englishman were due the women inspectors, physicians, and nurses, so requisite to allay the discomposure of those native women who by the laws of their society and religion are not permitted to be seen by other men than their husbands.

The relation of town and presidency in India can hardly be a matter of much interest to the general reader; and this point may be dismissed with the remark, that what is needed there, as is shown by the action of the municipalities, is more centralization of power, and more control as well as more interest in municipal affairs on the part of the general Government.   As the Governor ousted the local authorities, the same scenes took place in other towns besides Bombay.   At Karachi, a terrible sub-centre of plague, the municipal officers felt so outraged at the Government's interference that they all resigned.   With so small a proportion of the population instructed in Western thought it is obviously necessary that Government should not only have control of the local centres, but should exercise it frequently enough to get the natives accustomed to it.   This is particularly true in regard to such matters as sanitation.   Filthy as was Bombay when the plague broke out, the condition of Calcutta, at the present moment, from a sanitary point of view, is much worse.   The Lieutenant-Governor took the liberty of saying so last winter.   The Municipality answered him with a storm of abuse.   The natives are quite content with insanitation.   It is evident that Government should take such matters out of native control till the Indians are educated up to the point where they can take care of themselves.

But these are minor points.   The great political lesson of the plague is taught by the result of Government's unbending attitude toward the prejudices of the Sunni Mahomedans.   There can be no doubt but that the plague would have been suppressed in October had the same attitude been adopted by the Municipal Commissioner.   But the real reason why the Commissioner did not carry out the plan of segregation was that he was alarmed at the determined opposition of the natives.   When their representatives, especially those of the Mahomedans, insisted that the populace would resist segregation *vi et armis* the Commissioner yielded the point; and the whole wretched business of the winter followed. But, in speaking to the same natives on the same subject, Lord Sandhurst said: "Let there be no talk of resistance; for, as a great steamer cuts through the water, so surely will Government cut through every obstacle." And what happened? A few riots took place in the city and suburbs (on March 8 and 21, April 6 and 7), but there was no real resistance. A show of force dissipated the malcontents. In all that effervescence of seditious talk there was not one solid particle of danger. The supposed volcano turned out to be a harmless geyser. But the metaphor is too strong. Let me say rather that the fanatical violence of which the Municipality had dared to boast proved to be but a nettle in a strong hand.

In point of fact the India of '97 is not the India of '57. Then there was silence and murder: now there is bluster and obedience. The chief seditious talk is uttered by that most harmless of natives, the Bengali Babu. In the last forty years a new generation of Mahomedans has come upon the stage. In 1857 the Mussulman still felt himself superior to the Hindu, and able to attempt a *coup d' état.* He has now no political influence: the intelligent Hindu has outstripped the Mussulman. The former is rich and holds office: the latter is poor and has no political standing. But the Hindu will never revolt: he is too much afraid of his own countrymen, and is very glad to stand under the Sirkar's umbrella.   E. WASHBURN HOPKINS.

THE FARM COLONIES OF THE SALVATION ARMY.

THE Salvation-Army method of dealing with the question of the Unemployed is, in brief, to place Waste Labor on Waste Land by means of Waste Capital; thus combining this Trinity of Waste, the separation of which means the destruction of each, the coöperation of which means the prosperity of all.

In every nation in which our world-wide work has been carried on we have found ourselves confronted with the sombre phantom of direst poverty. Its proportions have varied ; but its ghastly characteristics have been everywhere much the same.

Our business has carried us directly to this veritable " Hell Gate " of society. How to perforate the rock and honeycomb its mass with such moral dynamite as shall enable us some day, at the touch of a button, to shatter the vast obstruction to the harbor of peace and prosperity, has been our daily study and our nightly dream. However visionary the prospect may appear to others, to us it is a very tangible reality. There is but a step from the experimental accomplishments of the past to the unlimited possibilities of the future,—from the acorn to the oak, from the seedling to the tree, from the tiny rivulet to the boundless ocean.

Are we too optimistic ? Have we not a right to be so ? Would not the very stones cry out against us if we were anything else ? Stretching before us lies the vast panorama of six brief years' accomplishment. Wealth, learning, influence,—those great factors in modern achievement,—are conspicuous by their absence from our ranks. The magic wand of the millionaire has conjured for us no showers of gold. No halls of science have adorned our horizon ; no political stars have illumined our firmament ; and yet, springing " of the people," existing " for the people," and, therefore, supported " by the people," there has flashed forth from the apparent nothingness of a creative Providence, a meteor which has lightened the intense darkness of modern poverty by the benign rays of nascent hope, love, peace, and prosperity.

Within the brief space of six years there have sprung into existence, mushroomlike, some four hundred institutions, dotted like lighthouses along the dreary wreck-bestrewn shores of pauperdom, each supplied with such life-saving apparatus as enables them collectively to drag *daily* from the, alas! myriads of sinking souls, no fewer than ten thousand at a time. Think of it, oh ye who are tempted to gaze with hopelessness into those seething, storm-tossed waters, or to fold your hands in the helplessness of despair, or even to view with a measure of self-complacency the often self-inflicted woes of miserable humanity!

The financial outlay for the maintenance of this "Bridge of Sighs," —may we not rather call it a Bridge of Hope?—over which there pass daily twice ten thousand weary feet and weeping eyes, ten thousand aching hearts and storm-wrecked lives—is close upon one million dollars a year. For, though the cost of agency is practically eliminated, owing to the fact that rescuers and rescued share the same fare and shelter, nevertheless, heavy rents, and often taxes, have to be paid, and large sums laid out for equipment and food, in addition to the outlay sometimes required for improved sanitation.

How then are we able to raise so large a sum? Here comes in one of the most important features of our work; namely, its self-supporting character. The bulk of the money, and this in ever-increasing ratio, *is contributed by the Submerged themselves.* This is surely one of the most hopeful features of the situation. To those who disbelieve in the salvability of the masses of our poor,—*their willingness to work out their own regeneration,*—it may be a surprise to learn that at least three-fourths of this large sum is contributed by the Submerged.

In places where the work has been longest established, the proportion is still greater. In the city of London, for instance, we sheltered last year a daily average of more than five thousand people at a cost of $493,000. Of this amount, those whom we helped contributed no less than $470,000, leaving only the small margin of $23,000 for the charitable public to find. The entire cost of supervision was less than 5 per cent; while the above expenses included rents, rates, taxes, furniture, fittings, material, food, and all other outlays.

Our social operations in the United States have made remarkable progress during the past twelve months; our institutions having increased from about fifteen to over seventy, and their accommodations from five hundred to more than two thousand. The minimum cost of supporting criminals and paupers in public institutions is about $2.00 a week for food alone, besides all the expenses of buildings and supervision. In some jails the contract rate for feeding prisoners is 35 cents a day, exclusive of all other expenses. Now, in the Salvation Army we are able to reduce the entire expenses to an average of about 25 cents a day for food, clothing, rental, and supervision, including the least self-supporting of our institutions—such as Children's Homes, and Homes for Fallen Women and Ex-criminals.

To those who are interested in philanthropic enterprises, these facts will have special value and significance. As a rule, to get a quarter down a poor man's throat usually requires an outlay of at least 75 cents in expenses of organization, inquiry, and supervision. For ourselves, estimating the actual cash outlay in assisting 2,000 people throughout the year, at an average of from 20 to 25 cents each per day, the total for the year will be from $150,000 to say $180,000. But even at this low estimate of expenditure, I calculate that the maximum outlay from our charitable funds has been only about one-fourth of the above amount; the balance being contributed in cash or labor by the people whom we have helped.

It will be readily seen, then, that here is an agency and a plan which will make a dollar go to the utmost limit of its purchasing and saving power. Nor is it a mere untried theory, which may be liable to a thousand breakdowns, when put to the test of actual experience. It is indeed a system which has gradually, I might almost say automatically, grown out of practice.

And this leads me to call attention to another singular fact. While the underlying principles involved in our Social Colonies are the very embodiment of simplicity, the machinery itself is of a complex character. It embraces the following main departments:

I. The City Colony.

II. The Farm Colony near the city.

III. The Distant Settlement.

The first of these, the City Colony, includes quite a number of institutions. The different strata of geology find their counterpart among the poor. To the inexperienced eye, the masses of the working-class population of our great cities constitute one vast conglomeration of misery, vice, and crime. On nearer inspection, however, they are found to be classified as distinctly as those who occupy the higher rungs of the social ladder. The honest poor cling tightly to the last remnant of respectability, and will resent any attempt to make them mingle with the vicious and the criminal. Hence, for the latter, separate institutions are an absolute necessity. At the time of writing, our City Colonies in the United States include:

20 Shelters for men, with accommodation for 2,086.

3 Shelters for women, with accommodation for 250.

8 Rescue Homes for Fallen Women, with accommodation for 200.

2 Prison-Gate Homes for Ex-criminals, with accommodation for 30.

1 Farm Colony.

3 Children's Homes for Waifs and Strays, accommodating 90.

15 Slum Posts under the supervision of 45 officers.

2 Hospitals and Clinics.

5 Labor Bureaus.

5 Salvage Brigades for the collection of waste.

8 Wood Yards for temporary employment.

1 Enquiry Bureau for finding lost friends.

2 Poor Man's Lawyers.

3 Miscellaneous.

—

78 Institutions, accommodating 2,656 persons.

The above departments are under the charge of about 150 of our most devoted and skilful officers. Their average cost to us, including board, lodging, and other personal expenses, does not exceed $5 a week, though in their worldly callings they would, as a rule, be receiving from $10 to $20; and in some cases they have resigned lucrative positions to join us. Generally the Social Officer receives merely a grant of from $1 to $2 a week for clothing and personal expenses; accepting for food and lodging the same simple fare and shelter that are given to the persons helped. Thus, at a stroke, the cost of supervision is reduced to a minimum by the splendid devotion and self-sacrifice of our officers.

Not only is this the case, but in each department there is trained a band of men and women, who become experts in that particular branch of work. Regulations are drawn up for their guidance, which represent the outcome of actual experience, and which prevent the recurrence of mistakes that may have taken place in the earlier and more experimental stages. A careful system of reporting and inter-communication, together with regular visitation by our most able officers, enables each department to keep in touch with the newest developments in this art of sociology.

It is said that a Chinaman's plan for making a cabbage grow is to walk round it six times every day! It has been this personal attention to the minutest detail of our social cabbage which has been perhaps the principal secret of its rapid growth. Each Social Officer walks round his own particular cabbage many times every day, removes the slugs

48

from each individual leaf, fertilizes and waters the roots with assiduous care, and reckons that he has succeeded only in proportion to the actual results he is able to produce.   The devotion, patience, and self-sacrifice of these men and women are equalled only by the daring and the tact with which they handle the masses among whom they labor, and who recognize them as their acknowledged leaders.

Night after night the girl-captain of the slums will gather an audience of two or three hundred toughs, to whom the magnetism of our Army meetings will be an untiring attraction.   The greatest punishment is a sentence of exclusion from those meetings for a week in case of serious misbehavior.   Numbers of the worst characters are converted, and, in turn, testify to the wonderful change which has taken place in their lives.

Take again the Rescue Homes.   Through the eighty such which are scattered throughout the world, there passed last year more than 4,000 fallen women, of whom nearly 80 per cent were restored to lives of virtue.

The uniformity of plan, the universality of application, and the unity of action which characterize all these various Homes, Shelters, and other institutions throughout the world, contribute greatly to their success.

But it is particularly in regard to the Farm Colony and more distant Settlements that I had intended to write on this occasion.   While we look upon our City Colony as an essential feature in our scheme of social regeneration, we believe that the ultimate and only rational cure for the congestion of our great cities is to remove the surplus population to the land.

This is our great quarrel with the pauper policy and criminology of most civilized countries at the present day.   Instead of the surplus being removed, it is accumulated in reservoirs of ever-increasing magnitude, where, without any natural outlet, the waters stagnate; breeding corruption, disease, and death.   Those same waters judiciously distributed over the arid surface of the sparsely populated soil of our vast agricultural areas would produce a rich harvest, not of millionaires, but of thrifty, honest, self-supporting husbandmen,—a yeomanry who would be our nation's pride and strength.   The divorce of the small landed proprietor from the soil is the root-cause of the depressed state of agriculture; and, until the balance of population can be restored from the city to the country, permanent prosperity on a national basis seems to me well-nigh an impossibility.

During a recent visit to our Farm near Seattle, I was conversing with a shrewd German farmer who owned a small tract of land near ours. We had just been eating some of his potatoes,—"Beauty of Heaven" was the name that he had given them, and certainly they seemed quite fit for an angelic table,—and I was questioning him as to his farm, his family, and his success. He had been there eight years, he told me,—years of terrible financial depression in the neighboring cities of Seattle and Tacoma. "I see very little money," he remarked. "It does not matter to me whether the Gold or Silver party win the day. All the banks in Seattle may break to-morrow, but it does not affect me. I have abundance of food for myself and family; and there is enough over to pay for clothing and schooling. What more do I require?" He was not depending on the hired labor of others. His "Beauty of Heaven" potatoes tasted all the sweeter for having been planted with his own hands. His children were growing up to manhood around him. Of land there was enough and to spare. His simple wants were all supplied. To adopt his own language, what more did he require?

What that one individual had accomplished for himself by dint of his personal energy and resourcefulness, the Salvation Army is seeking to do for for thousands who have not been gifted by nature with the same opportunities, nor the same skill. The surplus population of our cities neither can nor will conduct their own exodus to the land of peace and plenty, which might and ought to be theirs. But, placed under suitable leadership, that is, with leaders who understand their habits and have no axes of their own to grind, they are capable of supplying the hiatus which separates us from national prosperity,—an ever-broadening hiatus, and one which, alas! I venture to predict, will go on broadening until this particular missing link has been supplied.

I know what is so commonly said in regard to the depressed state of agriculture, and the impossibility of making it pay, even with the help of modern improvements and appliances. But I am not pleading for large farms or fortunes. Frankly speaking, I am glad the time has come when the large ranch has almost ceased to be an attraction to capital, inasmuch as it will afford an opportunity for the working-man to get at the soil, to become his own farmer, his own laborer, his own producer, and his own consumer.

Let it not be supposed, however, that because the large ranch, in which the small farmer has become eliminated from the soil, fails to pay interest on its borrowed capital, or to afford the prospect of quickly making a vast fortune, the yeoman owner of a small block of land cannot gain from it a subsistence. India and France afford a positive contradiction to this supposition, even if we were unable to find others nearer home. By dint of persistent toil, without even the aid of fertilizers, the Indian peasant will extract from one or two acres of impoverished soil a living for his family, albeit at least half the gross produce has to be handed to the proprietor in payment of rent and taxes, or to the money-lender for exorbitant interest. And yet his instruments are the most primitive ; while every innovation is eyed with suspicion as a possible breach of caste and time-honored tradition.

It is upon the above facts that we base our Colonial plans. We plead with capital, if only in its own interests, to afford the working-man a fair chance of getting at the land. We do not ask for *charity*, or *alms*. We desire nothing better than that the whole effort should be placed on a purely commercial basis, under the personal superintendence of business men of approved probity, discretion, and energy.

During my recent visit to San Francisco I was invited to address the Chamber of Commerce upon the question ; the President himself taking the chair. As a result it was resolved that a committee of fifteen leading citizens be appointed to coöperate with the Salvation Army in our plans. Briefly the scheme was as follows : A sum of not less than $25,000 was to be raised for preliminary expenses, either by donations or as a loan on favorable terms : A tract of two or three thousand acres of land was to be bonded, and divided into small allotments of not more than five to ten acres. Cottages were to be erected, the land fenced and partly prepared, and, according to the discretion of the management, poultry and other stock supplied. Upon these allotments carefully selected Colonists were to be settled, and a weekly rent charged which would be sufficient to pay off capital and interest by easy instalments. For instance, supposing the value of a five-acre lot to be

Land, at $40 per acre..........................$200
Cottage.. 150
Improvements and Stock....................... 150
—
Total......................................$500

a weekly rental of $1 would amount to 10 per cent on the above. Of this, say 5 per cent would be for interest, and 5 per cent for repayments of capital, with liberty to pay off the balance at any earlier time, or by larger instalments. In this way the $25,000 would enable fifty families to be settled on 250 acres, divided up into five-acre blocks, the value of the land being estimated at $40 an acre.   If, however, the land were not paid for in advance, but only on the instalment principle, about eighty families could be settled on four hundred acres.   Allowing an average of four persons to each family, more than three hundred souls could thus be provided for.   The $25,000 thus invested would be drawing an annual income of $2,500, of which $1,250 would be paid as interest, if the money had been borrowed ; while the balance would either pay off the capital or be re-invested.   If the entire sum were raised in donations, the 10-per-cent income would serve to settle additional families; while the original sum would be turned over several times.

It may be asked, how should we insure the payment of the weekly rent?   The answer is: Partly by the employment of the Colonists on the settlement at a fixed scale of wages, and partly by placing the Colony in such proximity to the large ranches, which abound in California, that the members of the family could be able to earn perhaps more than sufficient for this purpose.   In other cases Colonists would be selected who had some temporary employment in the city, possibly of an uncertain character.   That large class who, living perpetually on the borders of the maelstrom of destitution, carry on a precarious and painful existence would be encouraged in this way to supplement their scanty income and to prepare for the evil day of commercial panic.   The wife and children would live upon the farm, where the husband would spend his week-ends and his holidays, till at last he would be able to snip the last cord that tied him to the town.   Large numbers of the semi-destitute artisan classes would be willing thus to try their wings and feel their feet who otherwise would not dare to launch out upon this new mode of existence.

It may be asked why the Salvation Army should particularly interest itself in this kind of work, and whether for the purpose it would not be better to dispense with the element of religion?   Doubtless there would be nothing to prevent the above plan from being successfully carried out by other organizations, whether of a secular or religious character.   I venture to think however, that the Salvation Army supplies a peculiarly suitable agency of which it would be well for capital to avail itself.   To carry out an exodus of an extensive character—there are three million people in our large cities requiring to be handled—will demand an agency which, in my opinion, must combine the following qualifications :—

1. *Cheapness.*   Otherwise the scheme will be swamped in the expense of supervision.

2. *Honesty.*   Otherwise the selfish greed of the agents will appropriate to a handful of individuals the benefits which are intended for the
mass.

3. *Skill.*   For a good fool is almost as certain, unintentionally, to
lead an excellent enterprise into the ditch of failure as a clever rascal
will, to suit his own purposes.

4. *Numbers.*   Since the successful oversight and manipulation of
large masses of men have been always found to depend on organized
supervision.

5. *Self-sacrifice.*   An agency which is thinking only of its own salaries and emoluments cannot inspire others with the spirit of cheerful
unselfishness so essential to the success of such an enterprise.

6. *Ability to inspire confidence in those whom it seeks to lead.*   This is
perhaps the most important of all.   The Salvation Army needs no introduction to the working-man.   The uniform of its officer is his or her
passport to every heart and home, to the lowest dives and saloons, to
the cottage and the attic.   To create this confidence has been the work
of years.   Its value it would be difficult to overestimate.   These classes
have so often been exploited in the interests of mere speculators that
they view with suspicion even the most tempting offers, and prefer the
evils which they know to the uncertainties and failures at which they
can only guess.

Especially is this the case with the married working-man, who would
furnish the most solid and reliable Colonist.   Family ties of affection
cause the worthiest of these to step warily in the direction of any new
paths, of the safety of which he is not absolutely sure.

But where the necessary shepherding is supplied, and the pledges
of good faith exist, it will be found comparatively easy to supply in
large numbers selected and suitable Colonists—those who are most
likely to insure the success of the scheme.   We have at the time of
writing 730 posts, under the charge of 2,300 of our American officers.
These would form suitable centres or agencies for the careful selection
of large bodies of recruits, who could be trained, equipped, and sent to
the Settlements in larger or smaller numbers as required.

The selection and training of the Colonists, I regard as one of the
most essential features of our scheme.   For this purpose, in addition
to the sifting process to which the individuals are or can be subjected
in our City Colonies, we are organizing :

a. Working-men's lectures on agricultural subjects, whereby simple
instruction can be given ;

b. Vacant lot farms, for the utilization of vacant lots in large cities, on the plan so successfully inaugurated by Governor Pingree, of Detroit;

c. Small farms in the neighborhood of cities, where a further system of rough-and-ready preparation can be gone through.

No Colonist whose character had not been thoroughly tested would be sent to any distant Settlement; thus breakdowns would be reduced to a minimum.

It may be asked, how far is land available for the purpose of these settlements? My reply is, that on this score there is absolutely no difficulty. Vast tracts of fertile soil have been already placed at our disposal, on the most liberal terms. In addition, some influential gentlemen interested in irrigation projects for arid America are pressing upon our attention the grand possibilities that exist in those vast regions. The success which has attended similar efforts under my own observation in India compels me to regard with great hopefulness these proposals; and I trust that in the not distant future, with the coöperation of these gentlemen, some successful colonies may be established by us in these districts.

At least I may promise that, so far as land, climate, water, and Colonists are concerned, no difficulty whatever need be anticipated. The one essential that is at present lacking, owing to the existing distrust in all forms of agricultural enterprise, is *capital.* That this will ultimately flow in sufficient quantities in the required direction, I think there can be no reasonable doubt; especially if a network of village banks, based on the Raiffeisen system be introduced, thus affording both the credit and the security which in the case of small agricultural holdings would be absent in the ordinary city bank.

What I would suggest is: First—that a central national council of influential gentlemen, similar to the one recently constituted in San Francisco, but with a national scope, be appointed, to coöperate with the Salvation Army in its schemes. Second—that in communication with this council there be sub-committees formed in each State, county, or city, where suitable openings may exist. Third—that leading philanthropists, capitalists, and landowners should be invited to coöperate with these central or branch councils. Further, I would propose that a definite plan of campaign be inaugurated, secretaries and treasurers appointed, funds raised, and a systematic effort made to grapple with our great pauper problem upon the principles above laid down, and on a scale worthy of the vast needs of the suffering poor.

I venture to say that if this be done, a colossal work can be quickly inaugurated, and placed on a self-sustaining and self-propagating basis. Nay, I would affirm that to do it on a large scale,—a scale worthy of the emergency and of our national honor,—will be found easier than to conduct here and there mere hole-and-corner experiments, which by their very timidity invite failure. The momentum of numbers would help to carry the enterprise over the bar of its initial difficulties. The social regeneration of the masses by the wholesale process will be found, I believe, to be easier than by the usual retail methods. It will also be more economical, and will furnish to the world an imposing object-lesson in "pauperology," if I may be permitted to coin the expression. It will thus be possible, if I mistake not, to prove to the most Malthusian mind that, after all, God is not mistaken in allowing the existence of so many human beings, that Mother Earth is still big enough and fertile enough to provide food and work for many times over her existing family, and that the worst form of folly and extravagance is that which treats as waste and superfluous matter the glorious crowning-piece of creation which bears the impress and the image of its Master Mind.

Time was when a man was thought to be worth more than a sheep : now he is valued at less than a Californian ground-squirrel ; inasmuch as we can neither poison him, eat him, nor sell his skin ! This cannot be good economy, philosophy, statesmanship, or Christianity. Something must be wrong somewhere. I trust I have been able to make it sufficiently plain what that something is and wherein consists the remedy.

The statesman or philanthropist who will write his name on the grateful memories of posterity will be the one who proves, that even for this world,—to say nothing of the next,—it is more profitable to plant a human being in the soil than to grow a potato or a beet ; that a flesh-and-blood dollar is worth more than either a gold or silver one ; that the machinery of willing hands and thinking brains and tender hearts is worth more than the most wonderful discoveries of science ; that the measure of a nation's prosperity is the happiness of its poor ; and that the removal of pauperism is the true measure of the success of its Christian statesmanship.

FREDERICK DE L. BOOTH TUCKER.

INDEX.